Adventure Guide to the

Chesapeake Bay

Barbara Radcliffe Rogers & Stillman Rogers

HUNTER

HUNTER PUBLISHING, INC.
130 Campus Drive
Edison, NJ 08818-7816
☎ 732-225-1900 / 800-255-0343 / fax 732-417-1744
www.hunterpublishing.com
E-mail hunterp@bellsouth.net

IN CANADA:
Ulysses Travel Publications
4176 Saint-Denis, Montréal, Québec
Canada H2W 2M5
☎ 514-843-9882 ext. 2232 / fax 514-843-9448

IN THE UNITED KINGDOM:
Windsor Books International
The Boundary, Wheatley Road, Garsington
Oxford, OX44 9EJ England
☎ 01865-361122 / fax 01865-361133

ISBN 1-55650-889-1
© 2001 Barbara Radcliffe Rogers & Stillman Rogers

This guide focuses on recreational activities. As all such activities contain elements of risk, the publisher, author, affiliated individuals and companies disclaim any responsibility for any injury, harm, or illness that may occur to anyone through, or by use of, the information in this book. Every effort was made to insure the accuracy of information in this book, but the publisher and author do not assume, and hereby disclaim, any liability for loss or damage caused by errors, omissions, misleading information or potential travel problems caused by this guide, even if such errors or omissions result from negligence, accident or any other cause.

Cover: Shoreline at Horsehead Wetland Center, Grasonville, MD
Back Cover: Log House at Spruce Forest Artisans Village
All photographs © 2001 Barbara Radcliffe Rogers & Stillman Rogers
Maps by Lissa K. Dailey, © 2001 Hunter Publishing, Inc.
Illustrations by Joe Kohl
Indexing by Nancy Wolff

4 3 2 1

CONTENTS

MAPS

DEDICATION

For Marylanders Charles and Shirley Radcliffe, with love.

A WORD OF THANKS

Half the fun of writing a travel guide is in the people you meet or join while traveling. Each one adds some special bit of advice, shares some place they love, or makes us look differently at what we already know. So many people helped us write this book, that we cannot possibly name them all, but here's the short version of the long list.

We especially appreciate the hospitality and advice from both sides of our family, spread throughout Eastern Maryland. Charles and Shirley in Annapolis, Suzanne and Jeff in Stevensville, Carol in Baltimore, Tom and Dierdre in Westminster, Jay in Severna Park and Washington all lent a helping hand, and if you enjoy the restaurants and attractions we suggest in their hometowns, thank them for leading us to them.

Nancy Wolff's candid comments on restaurants led us to some great meals – and likely saved us from not so great ones. Lee Ann Chearney introduced us to the best places to eat in her hometown of Oxford and the area around it. To both of them, we are most grateful.

Barbara is also grateful to Randy Kraft and Mike Deckelbaum for their expert paddling and good company on the Potomac, to Heidi Kolk for her unfailing good humor along the towpath, to Kirsten Hansen for skillful knee repair (not to mention her box lunches) and to Kate Mulligan for her thorough knowledge of the towpath and its towns.

Several people helped us with the not-so-simple mechanics and logistics of putting together the final trips. These travels are always of necessity done in a hurry just before the manuscript is turned in, to be sure that everything is as it was when we last saw it. Primary among these miracle-workers are Ann Mannix and Connie Yingling, without whom this book would be far less complete and up-to-date than it is. Others who who shared in this work include Barbara Beverungen, Tina Brown, Mayor Asa Cain, Jean Goodman, Julie Horner, Bethany Lantham, Patty Manown Mash, Diane Miller, Shelly Miller, Terry Nyquist, Margie Pein, Beth Rhoades, Herman Schieke, Estelle Seward, Barbara Stewart, Harriett Stout, Sandy Turner, Nancy Hinds, Larry Noto, and Anedra Wiseman.

Each, of course, added his or her own favorite places and adventures to the list, so that instead of getting shorter, it became longer and longer. And with each addition, the book became better and better. We thank them all.

Meanwhile, patiently waiting for the rapidly growing manuscript was our editor and friend, Lissa Dailey, to whom we owe perhaps the heartiest thanks of all. Not just for being a world-class editor (a vital position on any book), but for remaining good humored in the face of delays and last-minute additions and changes. The world needs more people like her, who see each new surprise as a challenge instead of a disaster.

And on the home front, our thanks to Dee Radcliffe, Julie and Lura Rogers, Dixie and Aram Gurian, and Frank and Maria Sibley, who always keep things running smoothly while we travel.

ABOUT THE AUTHORS

The Rogerses have lived throughout this area, primarily in Washington, Suitland, Arlington and Annapolis, and traveled into every corner reached by the Chesapeake and its tributaries. They have climbed to the highest point in Maryland (which is almost in West Virginia), hiked Appalachian and Catoctin trails, kayaked the tidal creeks of the Eastern Shore and southern Maryland, sailed in the Potomac and Chesapeake, walked and biked the C&O towpath, canoed the Potomac from its upper reaches, ridden the wooded trails on horseback, sunned on beaches from Assateague to Rehobeth, flown kites along the Anacostia embankment and taken their morning run along the trails of Rock Creek Park. Their adventures are reflected in this book.

The authors at Hoye Crest, the highest point in Maryland.

Introduction

Overview

Perhaps we should begin simply by telling why we like the Chesapeake region so much and why – apart from having lived there for so long – we chose it as a subject. First, we like water. We like to play in and on it, especially in our kayaks and under sail. We like the food that swims in it and crawls along its bottom, and we like the way chefs are treating it now, instead of simply dropping it into hot fat.

We like the shorelines: the long waves of golden marsh grasses growing even more golden in the late afternoon sun, the nearly endless stretches of white sand that border the Atlantic, the fossil-studded cliffs of Southern Maryland, the leafy banks of the upper Potomac overhung with maples. We like the birds that gather near water, the darting kingfishers, the soaring bald eagles, the white clouds of snow geese, and the other birds that migrate or winter along the Atlantic flyway.

But life, and adventure, is not all water, and when we turn our backs on the Chesapeake Bay and head west, we find the topography dearest to our hearts. We find mountains. Not soaring peaks, but friendly mountains, steep enough to climb and to create waterfalls that drop in shimmering white spray over cliffs and rocky gorges. And between the Bay and the mountains, we find a rolling, gracious landscape of prosperous farms, studded here and there with friendly, historic cities.

Maryland, which claims most of the bay's shoreline, is like a miniature American history book. Its first European settlers came in the early 1600s, like those of Plymouth. And like those who stepped off the *Mayflower*, passengers on the *Ark* and the *Dove* were met by Native Americans who had hunted, fished and farmed the lands around the bay for centuries.

The colony Lord Baltimore established grew and thrived, and buildings from that colony are still used as homes, offices and as places of worship and commerce today. As you walk through the streets of Annapolis, the architecture all around you looks much as it did in the days when Maryland's four signers of the Declaration of Independence walked there.

When Maryland was no longer a colony, but a state, a piece of land on the Potomac, with good access to the Chesapeake, was chosen for the new nation's capital. The Chesapeake area continued to be an integral part of America's history, and today has major sites reflecting all eras of that history: Native American, Colonial, Federal, the westward expansion, Industrial Revolution, and the development of powered flight and the aerospace age. In nearly any part of the lands surrounding the Chesapeake you can tour a Colonial home or church and visit a space-age site in the same day.

In our search for adventures to share between the Chesapeake and Maryland's western mountains, we have defined adventure broadly. To us, an adventure is anything you do that requires some effort, involvement, or initiative on your part. Included are learning experiences for all ages and interests, whether it's a chance to learn spinning at Charles Carroll of Carrollton's Annapolis home or sailing in Havre de Grace.

Along with the sports of fishing, paddling, walking, cycling, skiing and riding, we explore the many other ways people enjoy this region outdoors. You will learn where to find a rare stand of fringed gentians and an entire riverbank of trillium. You will read of gardens both historical and fanciful, of easy-to-reach places where you are almost certain to see bald eagles, of beaches where you can literally fill your pockets with fossilized sharks' teeth, of wild horses that cavort on the dunes, of spooky cypress swamps so deep that the sun rarely penetrates.

Surprisingly, many of the wild places are quite close to – even in – the cities. And even on the paved streets we find adventures, places that will pique your curiosity, rare and outstanding examples of architecture and art, holdovers from bygone eras, and the rich ethnic heritage of Baltimore's neighborhoods. With this book in hand, you can ride historic trolleys and trains, tour an underground catacomb of burial crypts, see inside a submarine and a Liberty Ship, talk to the restorers who are rebuilding the *Enola Gay*, pray at the shrine of America's first canonized saint, read the original verses of the *Star Spangled Banner* in Francis Scott Key's handwriting and learn firsthand about the decoding of Enigma. Then go sailing in the afternoon.

Adventure is all about the little surprises of travel, about the things you don't see or do every day. It's coming upon an illegal whiskey still beside a mountain brook, watching deer graze in the evening, paddling through cypress knees, finding a rare remnant of Arctic tundra plants, riding a Tennessee Walking Horse along the towpath of a canal, eating blue crabs at Pope's Creek, riding to Tangier Island with the morning mail, promenading the boardwalk at Ocean City.

It's all about tastes – Chincoteague oysters still redolent of sea, sweet berries from a Westminster farm, creamy cheese from a Mennonite dairy, the smokey tang of Baltimore pit beef. And about smells – wisteria in a Colonial garden, campfire smoke on Cactoctin Mountain, fresh-plowed earth of a Carroll County farm, the salty morning breeze blowing across dune grasses, bread baking in a beehive oven built while George Washington was President.

We think you will like Maryland and the Chesapeake Bay if you have never met them before. And if you already live there, we hope we can take you to some places you've never seen.

Introduction

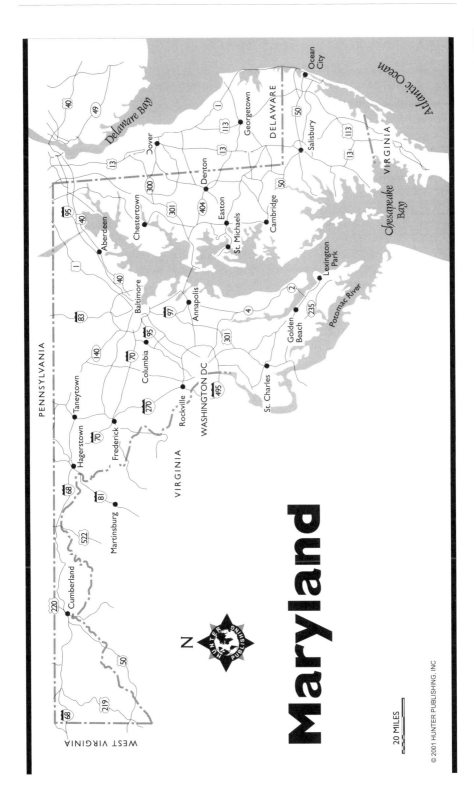

© 2001 HUNTER PUBLISHING, INC

■ History & Geography

 The region around the Chesapeake Bay is geographically and historically right in the middle of things. Its central location was a major reason for the selection of a spot on the Potomac's banks for the nation's Capital.

During the Civil War, it was literally in the middle of the fray, in the unique position of being a slave state but siding with the Union. Troops moved through and battles were fought in the corridor west of the bay, as the Confederate Army tried repeatedly to take Washington by surrounding it.

Top-grade anthracite from the coal mines near Cumberland was carried in barges along the C&O Canal to be loaded onto trains in Williamsport, then to ships in Baltimore Harbor, which carried it to fuel the first mills of the Industrial Revolution along New England rivers. Soon Baltimore itself was an industrial center as well as the transportation hub that had given it earlier prominence.

The agricultural produce of the fertile farmlands to the west and on the Eastern Shore, along with the bounty of the watermen's daily catch in the bay were processed in Baltimore's Canton neighborhood. The canneries were designed to shift from land to sea products with the changing seasons.

Geography played another role in the development of Maryland and the Chesapeake Bay. Not only was it in the middle of the East Coast, but the bay was large and well protected, cutting deep into the land, making Baltimore the coast's westernmost port. It made a natural place for the railroads to begin and end their commerce with the expanding west. Railheads could move goods directly to a major harbor for shipment all over the world.

Today history and geography combine to make the region a perfect blend for travelers. Within easy distance are some of the Atlantic's finest beaches, two lively cities, the Appalachian Trail, and an unrivaled concentration of historic sites and pre-Revolutionary buildings. Add to that the stunning collection of museums and governmental sites in Washington, DC, and you have more than enough to fill even a long vacation.

■ How To Use This Book

The Chesapeake Bay divides Maryland – and the entire region – in half. Only one bridge, the **Bay Bridge** at Annapolis, connects its two shores. And yet, as it divides them geographically, the bay ties those two shores together in a bond only those who live around a great body of water can fully understand.

County Boundaries vs. Geographic Boundaries

We have observed over decades of travel that the political divisions of states, provinces and countries usually have very little to do with the way travelers think of them. The beaches of one county look just the same as those they adjoin in the next; the western slopes of a valley are easiest visited on the same day as those facing them, even though the river may be a state line.

But tourism districts, and their brochures, information centers, B&B associations and directories, usually follow political boundaries, not geographical ones. In Maryland this is especially true, since each county has its own separate tourism department, which produces much of the written material you will find on your travels there. So to make your lives easier on the road, we have tried, wherever feasible, to divide this book according to **county lines**. However, sometimes that just didn't make sense, so we have followed logical natural boundaries. Cecil County is a case in point. Nature already carved it in half, separating its two sections with the Elk River. We just recognized that job was already done.

You will find that county identification is very important in Maryland. Natives will tell you they are from Calvert County, or from Garrett County, instead of saying the name of their town or their geographical region. These county lines are marked clearly in yellow on the state highway map, so you will have no trouble telling where the dividing lines fall.

In each case, we have described the carving job in the chapter introduction, and have included the tourism contacts for all counties included in that chapter, even when it's only a small section.

Regions Covered In This Guide

Although we describe the divisions in each chapter, it may be handy to have a quick overview of the regions covered. We begin with a region that many native Marylanders have never visited – **Garrett County**. The state's long narrow waistline makes up a region we have called **Western Canal Country**, and covers Allegany County and northern Washington County, including the city of Hagerstown. **North Central Maryland** covers southern Washington County and all of Frederick and Carroll counties, nipping over the Potomac River to add Harpers Ferry, West Virginia.

North of Baltimore continues eastward to the northern waters of the Chesapeake Bay, with Harford and Baltimore counties and the northern part of Cecil. **Baltimore** has a chapter of its own. **North of Washington** includes Montgomery and Howard counties, plus that part of Prince George's close to the Beltway corridor.

Annapolis & Anne Arundel County covers all of Anne Arundel County. The District of Columbia has a separate chapter entitled **Washington, DC**. **Southern Maryland** – which the counties themselves have grouped together for many co-operative tourism initiatives – includes Charles, St.

Mary's and Calvert counties, plus the southern part of Prince George's County.

On the other side of the Chesapeake Bay, **Upper Eastern Shore** covers the southern part of Cecil County, the northern part of Caroline County and all of Queen Anne's County, all in Maryland. **Central Eastern Shore** includes Talbot and Dorchester, as well as southern Caroline counties. **Lower Eastern Shore** is everything up to the Virginia border: Wicomico, Worcester and Somerset counties. **Virginia's Eastern Shore** reaches to the southern tip of the Delmarva Peninsula.

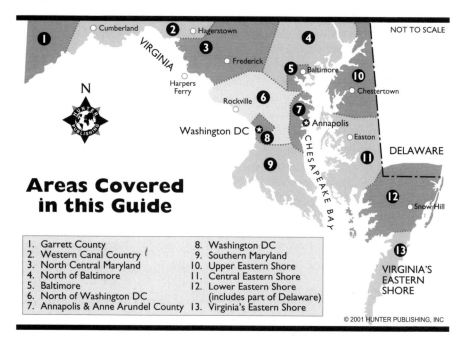

Areas Covered in this Guide

1. Garrett County
2. Western Canal Country
3. North Central Maryland
4. North of Baltimore
5. Baltimore
6. North of Washington DC
7. Annapolis & Anne Arundel County
8. Washington DC
9. Southern Maryland
10. Upper Eastern Shore
11. Central Eastern Shore
12. Lower Eastern Shore (includes part of Delaware)
13. Virginia's Eastern Shore

© 2001 HUNTER PUBLISHING, INC

Information Sources

Maryland Department of Tourism, 217 East Redwood St., Baltimore 21202; ☎ 410-767-3400, www.mdidfun.org.

Virginia Tourism, 901 East Byrd St., Richmond, VA 23219; ☎ 804-786-4484 or 800-932-5827.

Delaware Tourism Office, 99 Kings Hwy., Dover, DE 19901; ☎ 302-739-4271 or 800-441-8846.

Downtown Washington Visitors Bureau, 1300 Pennsylvania Ave., NW; ☎ 202-638-3222, www.dcchamber.org or www.washington.org

RECOMMENDED READING: *Away for the Weekend: Mid-Atlantic*, *by Eleanor Berman, published by Three Rivers Press (Clarkson Potter).*

Adventures

Adventure travel no longer means life-threatening. Life-enriching is a more accurate description. You'll find adventures of all kinds here, none of them life-threatening unless you undertake them recklessly. We give our readers credit for recognizing as dangerous such places as the top of a cliff, the brink of a waterfall, the surf in high seas, and the water during high winds.

We hope this book will encourage you to try a sport or activity you've never done before. It needn't be challenging the Youghiogheny (saying it is challenge enough) or paddling about in the ocean like an Inuit. It might be watching bald eagles fish beneath Coniwingo Dam. Or it might be seeing Misty's relatives at Chincoteague. It could be sailing on a historic skipjack out of Dogwood Harbor or flying in a World War II plane at Easton.

■ On Foot

For many people, the most rewarding way to travel is on foot. Those who enjoy watching birds or looking for woodland flowers can follow trails through all sorts of environments, from densely wooded mountains to miles of sandy seashore and around lakes and ponds or beside mountain streams. Some of the trails are wide multi-purpose paths shared with cyclists, others rough and hard to find.

TIPS FOR HIKING & WALKING SAFETY

■ Carry appropriate clothing and equipment for the time of year, remembering that both mountain and coastal weather is unpredictable and can change drastically within a few hours. Always be prepared for rain. Wear boots on rough trails or for long hikes and climbs.

■ Plan a route and stick to it. Always tell someone your planned route and the approximate time you expect to return. If you do not have traveling companions on the trail with you, check in at the park headquarters, campground office or tell your hosts at a hotel or inn.

■ Carry plenty of water and enough food for the time you expect to be on the trail, plus a little extra in case of an unexpected delay. Don't drink water from streams, even in remote places.

■ Listen to a weather report for the time you expect to be on the trail. Check trail conditions locally, especially if there has been heavy rain recently.

■ Read and obey trail warnings before you begin. During dry spells, woods may be closed to hikers as a forest fire prevention measure. It is your responsibility to check locally during times of drought.

■ Be aware of the environment and your impact on it. Stay on trails, especially in steep areas where erosion is likely, to avoid damaging trailside plants. Carry litter out with you.

■ Insects are a fact of life in the woods and on wild beaches, especially in the early summer, in wet or low places, and after rainy weather. Wear light-colored clothing and use a repellent.

■ Maryland has an abundance of rural areas that are popular places for hunting and many Marylanders enjoy both bird and game hunting. When hiking, make sure when the hunting season is in the area that you intend to walk. Some areas will be closed to hiking on specific days of the week to allow for hunting while others may be open even though hunting is in progress. If you are hiking during hunting season, it is a small and wise precaution to wear hunter orange clothing, such as a hat and/or vest for your own safety. Share the woods with courtesy. Many of the areas you hike are bought and maintained with the license fees hunters pay.

■ On Wheels

 The process of turning selected Maryland rail corridors into multi-use trails has been in progress for some years, and still continues. Several areas have such trails, which can be used by hikers, cyclists, skiers, horseback riders, and – in some areas – by snowmobilers. Their level, smooth surface makes them accessible to those in wheelchairs and others unable to travel on rough woodland trails.

These trails have, we think, the greatest appeal to cyclists, providing a traffic-free route with a dependable surface. If anything, they are often *too* straight, and therefore less interesting than winding country roads, but they often pass directly through towns, so cyclists have good access to services, including accommodations close to the trail. Local outfitters have quickly seen the potential for adventure travelers and bicycle rentals are becoming more common. Bike shuttles, so that you don't have to repeat the same route back, are still uncommon here, however.

The towpath of the **C&O Canal** is the ultimate multi-use trail, wide, well-surfaced, well-kept and passing a steady succession of interesting historical and architectural sites. You will find route descriptions for it in several chapters of this guide: Washington, North of Washington, North Central Maryland, and Western Canal Country.

BIKE SAFETY

Bicyclists in Maryland have the same rights and responsibilities as motor-driven vehicles. Be sure to observe all traffic signs and signals and all rules of the road. The wearing of **helmets** is mandatory for all bicyclists age 16 and under throughout the state. In Howard County, the age is 17, and in Montgomery, it's 18. In the town of Sykesville, in Carroll County, everyone must wear a helmet.

The state highway department maintains a phone information service for bicyclists: ☎ *800-252-8776. Leave your name, address and phone number for a return call. For maps, including the* **Maryland Bicycle Map**, *write to: Bicycle and Pedestrian Coordinator, Maryland State Highway Administration, 707 North Calvert St., Baltimore, MD 21202.*

Battle Creek Cypress Swamp, Prince Frederick.

■ On Water

 You'll never run out of water to play in and on here. It's not limited to that wide swath of blue that divides the Delmarva from the mainland. Other rivers – the **Potomac**, the **Patapsco**, the **Patuxent**, the **Chester**, the **Sassafras**, the **Nanticoke**, the **Pocomoke** and two different **Wicomicos** – as well as countless tidal creeks, enter the Bay and its tributaries, forming a coastline so ragged and indented that you could never explore every foot of it in a lifetime. In addition to those tidal estuaries are the many mountain streams that tumble and cascade, swollen with melting snow in the spring, and the lakes and ponds that dot the landscape. Whatever your water sport – except for exploring coral reefs – you'll find it here.

Boating

Maryland law requires anyone born after July 1, 1972 to have a **Certificate of Boating Safety Education** in order to operate a personal watercraft (such as a Jet Ski) or other registered vessel in Maryland waters. This includes boats under power, other than wind or muscle. Certification requires about eight hours of class instruction and successful completion of a test. Courses are given frequently, usually on successive Saturday mornings, by various parks and organizations. Anyone from out of state who wants to participate in the course, or take an equivalency test to obtain a Maryland safety certificate, should contact the Maryland Department of Natural Resources, Outdoor Education Division, 69 Prince George St., Annapolis, MD 21401; ☎ 410-974-2040. A certificate is *not* required if:

- A vessel is operated for commercial purposes.

- A person 16 years of age or older is a resident of another state, visiting Maryland for 60 days or less, in a vessel numbered in another state.

- A person is visiting Maryland for 90 days or less in a vessel from a foreign country.

- A person is operating a vesel on a body of water located on private property.

A boating safety education certificate issued by another state is valid in Maryland as long as it meets the criteria of the National Association of State Boating Law Administrators. Visit www.dnr.state.md.us/boating/regulations/bser.html for more information.

Kayaking

If you go to an outfitter for your first kayak excursion, you may be given the choice of a single or a double kayak. A strong paddler – someone with good upper body strength and coordination – will probably prefer a single kayak, and rightly so. But so should the weak paddler, if the purpose is to learn kayaking. If you're just going out for a one-shot ride, take the easier double, if you like. But if you want to learn, you're better off in your own kayak, where you can get the feel of it, learn to use the rudder, and not constantly have to follow someone else's stroke rhythm. (This was written by the weakest paddler on our team, who would never get into a double kayak unless she had one arm in a sling.) If you're a learning paddler and on the sea when a strong wind blows up, your guide/instructor should have a **tow line**, and will simply attach it to your kayak and tow you out of the wind, while you rest. If you are planning to paddle in exposed waters, ask your instructor about this. You'll feel better knowing there's a tow line available, even if you don't need it.

CANOE & KAYAK SAFETY

Although the challenges of paddling in the warmer waters of the Chesapeake don't compare to those of places where icebergs are sharing the sea, whenever you are on water in a small craft, there are a few prudent precautions you should take. The following makes a good mental checklist for any canoe or kayak trip.

■ Watch the weather. Check the forecast ahead of time and remember that meteorology in coastal regions and islands – even very large ones – is an unreliable science. The weather can, and will, change almost instantly. It can be as simple as a change in wind direction. No matter what the forecast, be prepared for bad weather, and sudden wind shifts, which can turn a friendly lake into a raging sea.

■ Plan ahead, and carefully, considering all the details. How will you get to your put-in? Where will you take out and how will you transport your canoe or car between the two?

■ Learn about the river or watershed system from a local who knows and who has canoed it recently. Better yet, take one along. A knowledgeable guide is not only good company, but can make your trip safer and more enjoyable.

■ Carry a healthy respect for the river, and scout ahead if you are in doubt of what's around the next bend. Know what the water levels are, and what hidden hazards may lurk at different levels. Know what water level makes the river canoeable; some are passable only at high water, others are deadly then. Again, local knowledge can tell you.

■ Always wear a personal flotation device (PFD). Having one isn't enough: it needs to be on you, and properly secured.

■ Be realistic about your own abilities, expertise and strength, and don't plan a trip that exceeds them.

■ Let someone know where you are going and when, so they can get help if you fail to return when expected.

Fishing

Everyone over 16 years old must have a **fishing license** when fishing any stream or pond. Streams and bodies of water may be designated as trout waters. These are areas stocked throughout the year and during stocking may be closed to fishing. Catch limit is five trout per day in designated areas and two fish per day in non-designated areas.

Fishing licenses are available in sporting goods stores, park headquarters and most general stores near fishing waters. Prices vary according the length of time, but are quite reasonable for non-residents.

Anyone planning to fish should obtain the *Freshwater Sportfishing Guide* from the **Maryland Freshwater Fisheries Service**, ☎ 410-260-8320, 800-688-FINS (3467), www.dnr.state.md.us. The same office publishes a handy annual booklet, *Tide Tables and Fishing Tips*, with line illustrations of the various game fish and suggestions for how and when to find them and what bait to use. It also lists the designated free fishing areas throughout the tidewater regions.

■ On Snow

Okay, so most people don't come to Maryland for a ski trip. But those who live there know that the trails of Garrett County's state parks and forests are both beautiful and often snowcovered. Many are shared by skiers and snowmobilers, each of whom needs to be aware and sensitive to the other's sport. Although technically skiers may have the right of way, they are expected to step off the trail when they hear a machine approaching. If you think this is unfair, remember that most of the trails are maintained by snowmobile clubs, so that little courtesy isn't out of place. Besides, if you let them speed past, the noise of their machine will be out of earshot sooner, and each of you can enjoy the snow-covered woods in your own way.

Cultural & Eco-Travel Experiences

The entire region, both in the cities and the rural areas, has a thriving cultural and arts climate. Baltimore, Washington, Annapolis and Hagerstown have especially busy performing arts calendars, and some of the nation's finest art museums are in these cities.

Local festivals include traditional Appalachian mountain music and crafts, ethnic traditions and a busy round of food and entertainment events that celebrate everything from blue crabs to red maple leaves. Wherever there is a festival, there will be food and music, at the barest minimum.

The proximity of the bay makes this entire region ideal for gardening, with long growing seasons and fairly dependable rainfall. Some simply magnificent gardens are here – the National Arboretum, Hampton and Ladew come first to mind – as well as smaller or less showy ones at historic homes and sites. Look in the cities, too, for places such as Dumbarton Oaks in Washington, the City Conservatory and Cylburn Arboretum in Baltimore, and the gardens of the Paca House in Annapolis.

Log house at Spruce Forest Artisan Village, Garrett County.

Also in this section of each chapter you will find information on crafts and on antiques, as well as farms and farmers' markets. Wineries are classed with farms, but farm museums are under *Sightseeing*.

Sightseeing

Historic sites, homes and restorations are everywhere, from the rustic log cabins of the early inland settlers to the grand plantation homes and elegant town houses of the east. After all, American history was made all around you here. Forts date from as early as the French and Indian Wars, and include famous Fort McHenry, which inspired the *Star Spangled Banner* during the War of 1812. Nearly every town of any size has its historical museum, and we like to take time to poke about in these community attics. Some are beautifully restored period homes, such as the Hammond-Harwood House in Annapolis, while others give glimpses of how families lived: the log home of Alta Schrock's family at Spruce Forest Artisan Village is an outstanding one.

Where to Stay

You knew it would be here somewhere, that disclaimer that says "don't blame us." Places and prices will change, so will ownership, and – sadly – so will chefs. If you find that a place has changed notably, drop us a note. If you find a great place where the hosts know all the hiking trails and bike routes, share it with readers of the next edition. You can write to us in care of the publisher, whose address is on the back of the title page.

We have tried to include a good variety of lodging and dining styles, although we ourselves prefer small inns and B&Bs in local family homes. For camping, you will notice that our preference runs toward quiet campgrounds with well-spaced campsites, preferably with tree cover, and without adjacent amusement parks.

To give you some idea of the prices to expect (and it is sometimes, in this changing world, only a rough idea) we have used a code of dollar signs. And because price codes are by their nature general, sometimes we have given the actual figures. We do this, of course, at our peril, knowing that prices will change immediately on the date of publication.

ACCOMMODATIONS PRICE KEY
Rates are per room, per night, double occupancy.
$ . . . . Under $50
$$ . . . . $50 to $100
$$$ . . . . $101 to $175
$$$$ . . . . $176 and up

For lodging, which includes a room for two people for one night, often (always if we've designated "B&B") with breakfast. When the price includes dinner (known as MAP, or Modified American Plan), we've said so. When we give two ranges ($-$$, for example), it can mean either that some rooms are in one range and some in another, or it can mean that the prevailing price is very close to the edge of a price range. It can also mean that rooms are cheaper on weeknights or in low season. So if a B&B has one small room that is $45 on a weeknight in March and another glorious room with a jacuzzi that is $180 on July 4, the range would be $-$$$. Which, of course tells you nothing at all. When this happens, we use real numbers, as we also do if rooms in a B&B are priced so close to the demarcation point that the codes are misleading. If rooms are all between $100 and $110, they fall in the $$$ class, leading readers to wonder if that meant $100-$110 or $170-$175.

Most adventure travelers already know to be careful with fire but, especially in the scattered undeveloped campsites of the western Maryland state forests, every spark is a potential disaster to you, the miles of forest around you, and all the creatures that call it home. This is not a place for cigarettes. Confine your campfires to existing fire rings and be sure the ground around them is completely cleared of grass, pine needles, leaves and anything else that could possibly burn. Be sure you have the required permits and that fires are allowed in the area. Keep the fire small, large enough only for essential cooking. Douse or bury your fire **completely** *before going to sleep.*

Where to Eat

We like good food, and will drive (or walk) miles out of our way to find it. We particularly enjoy well-prepared fresh seafood. We grew up with the best, and applaud the recent trends toward treating it with respect, instead of simply coating it in crumbs and tossing it in a deep fryer.

AUTHOR TIP

Because we like a bargain just as much as the next person, we have purchased a book called **Entertainment Baltimore**, *which entitles us to discounts, usually the full price of one entrée, at selected restaurants throughout the area. We saved more than its $29.95 cost after using it only twice in two of our favorite Annapolis restaurants. To order one, or to get more information,* ☎ *800-374-4464.*

While we like chefs who create innovative and unique dishes, we don't applaud the trend of putting together any weird combination just to be different, and we are happy to see that chefs in Baltimore, where you might expect such citified silliness, have not succumbed. So when we describe a menu as "innovative" or "creative" we don't mean trendy. We mean that a thoughtful chef has experimented successfully.

We think that local chefs anywhere do their best job with local ingredients and we look for restaurants which take advantage of fresh seasonal farm produce and the native seafoods.

For dining, the price represents the cost of most of the dinner entrées on the regular and daily special menu. When one or two dishes are much more expensive than the rest of the menu, we have disregarded these. When a restaurant serves a whole meal, including appetizer and dessert, under a single price, we have tried to explain this. If we missed this detail, you'll be happily surprised.

DINING PRICE KEY
The price key indicates the cost of *most* dinner entrées on a restaurant's regular and daily special menu.
$ . . . . Most under $10
$$ . . . . $10 to $20
$$$ . . . . Over $30

Garrett County

Rolling mountains drop into deep valleys cut by creeks, creating some surprisingly steep roads in this westernmost county. Although many eastern Marylanders have never seen this part of their state, it is well known to fishermen, hikers and especially to white-water enthusiasts, who travel from all over the

IN THIS CHAPTER

- Grantsville
- Oakland
- McHenry
- Swanton

continent to test their mettle on the Youghiogheny River, known almost universally as "the Yough" (pronounced "Yock"). This leafy area, with its mountains, lakes and rivers, is beautiful at any time of year, but at its most glorious in the fall, when maples and other hardwoods turn the landscapes into a sea of orange, red and yellow.

Geography & History

The Eastern Continental Divide lies west of Cumberland, formed by the long ridge of Meadow Mountain in the north and the aptly named Backbone Mountain in the south. Waters falling on their eastern slopes flow into the Potomac and thence to the Chesapeake Bay. On the west they flow via the Youghiogheny River and eventually the Mississippi, into the Gulf of Mexico. I-68 crosses the divide east of Grantsville.

A large section of eastern Garrett County is covered by state-owned parks and forests (the county as a whole has more than 80,000 acres of public

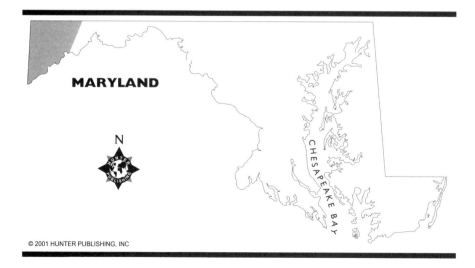

MARYLAND

N

lands). New Germany and Big Run State Parks and Savage River State Forest lie in fragmented pieces throughout a large area, so it seems as though you are constantly entering bits of it, all the way from the Allegheny County line near Frostburg to US 219 in the western part of the county. Savage River State Forest alone encompasses 52,812 acres and is the largest unit of the Parks and Forest system.

These parks protect the lands around one of the nation's finest fishing streams, the Savage River, which winds its way down through the steeply rolling eastern lands of Garrett County. A lively river through most of its course, its final section erupts into rapids where Olympic whitewater athletes test their skills.

The entire area where the parks lie – and much of the rest of the county – is filled with scenic roads that rise to ridges where views stretch over meadows and cleared farmlands. Beyond them, layer after layer of wooded hillsides extend to distant blue ridges. In the fall, spectacular is too mild a word for the colors in these vistas.

Garrett County's center is dominated by Deep Creek Lake, formed by a power company dam. Because it is artificial, it has different shore-line rules, and the entire shore is open to public access, even where the land is privately owned.

Getting Here & Getting Around

 The roads in Garrett County are well marked, even those through the vast tracts of parkland. The best map is the one in the excellent magazine-format *Garrett County Vacation Guide*, which is in a large enough scale to name roads and landmarks not on the state highway map.

Although it looks as though **US 50**, through West Virginia, would be a better route for returning east after exploring Garrett County, it is not. US 50 is winding and hilly – as are the Maryland alternatives – but it is filled with heavily laden coal trucks that slow your pace to that of a tired snail.

In the area around Deep Creek, Garrett Transit operates **Deep Creek Lake Shuttle**, which links over 20 sites around the lake, allowing you to get from one end or place to another without a car. The shuttle completes the loop in about an hour and the rate is a mere $1 per day, with unlimited rides. It stops at most of the campgrounds, markets, hotels and at the state park and Discovery Center. This is a really good deal. Call **Garrett Transit**, ☎ 301-334-9431 for the schedule. Sunday-Thursday it runs between 10 am and 10 pm, and Friday-Saturday until 1 am, with the last loop beginning at 9 pm and midnight respectively. The schedule is also printed in *The Lake Front Magazine*, a free privately printed handout magazine available at the Visitor Center (☎ 301-387-7124).

Information Sources

Garrett County's **Chamber of Commerce** is golden. Their magazine-style guide has a good map and details on little-known places. Call for a copy ahead of time or pick one up at the first visitor center you pass. Contact the chamber at 15 Visitors Center Drive, McHenry, MD 21541, ☎ 301-245-4400, or visit them on-line at www.garrettchamber.com, www.deepcreeklake.org; e-mail info@garrettchamber.com, info@deepcreeklake.org.

The **Garrett County Visitors Center** on US 219, north of Deep Creek Lake, is well stocked with brochures on local attractions and the staff is particularly helpful with details. It is open Sunday through Thursday, 9 am-5 pm; Friday and Saturday until 6 pm; ☎ 301-387-4FUN.

A state **Welcome Center** is located on I-68, east of Exit 4.

Adventures

■ Parks

New Germany and Big Run state parks and Savage River State Forest are all managed out of one park headquarters in New Germany. Ranger Joe Stevens and other staff members there are well versed in the various sports you can enjoy throughout the parks, and enthusiastic about describing them. Stop here for maps and for information and directions, as well as to register for campsites. **Savage River State Forest** is the largest facility in the state system and it is intended to protect a large watershed, of which 2,700 acres have been designated as Big Savage Wildland. Activities include hiking, biking, canoeing, fishing, riding, snowmobiling and camping. The headquarters is at **New Germany State Park**, which is smaller and is completely surrounded by Savage River State Forest. It is best used for picnicking, boating and day-use around 13-acre New Germany Lake, formed by the impoundment of Poplar Lick Creek. From I-68 at Exit 22 take Chestnut Ridge Rd. (unnumbered) south, staying to the left at a Y intersection along Lake Meadows, about 2.5 miles. At the intersection with New Germany Rd. go left about 1.5 miles; the entrance will be on the left. **Big Run State Park** is farther on down the same road. Continue down New Germany Rd. about 3.75 miles to Big Run Rd. on the left. This is a beautiful narrow road down through the ravine of Big Run stream, a distance of about 4.5 miles to the park on the shores of Savage River Reservoir.

To get to the Savage River Headquarters, take the unnumbered Chestnut Ridge Rd. south from I-68 at Exit 22, marked New Germany, and about three miles farther take a left onto New Germany Rd. The headquarters is well-marked on your right. Write to Savage River State Forest, 349 Headquarters Lane, Grantsville, MD 21536, ☎ 301-895-5759.

AUTHOR TIP

To make a short scenic tour of the area by car, continue on past the park headquarters for about 3.75 miles and turn left onto Big Run Rd. This leads down to the river and Savage River Rd. Turn left here, past BJ's store and along the river. Instead of crossing the river when the road turns right at a fork, go left onto Westernport Rd., which melds into Twin Churches Rd. to the left. This leads to New Germany Rd., which you take to the right and back to I-68 at Exit 24.

Joe Stevens, the local ranger, told us that many people who use the park today are later generations of members of the Civilian Conservation Corps (CCC), who built the park facilities and cleared the trails in the 1930s.

BJ's Store, on Savage River Rd. (☎ 301-777-0001), about a half-mile from Big Run Rd., is the unofficial headquarters for all things sporting in the area, with equipment, bait, tackle, licenses, provisions, propane fuel, firewood, and friendly, helpful advice. (See page 33 for information about canoe rentals.) Between BJ's and the knowledgeable park rangers at the New Germany headquarters, you're in good hands. You can also register at BJ's for campsites in the state forest. The store is open from May 15 through January, Monday and Tuesday, 9 am-6 pm; Wednesday and Thursday, 10 am-6 pm; Friday and Saturday, 9 am-7 pm; Sunday, 9 am-3 pm.

In the center of the county is **Deep Creek Lake State Park**, smaller than most of the others, but heavily used. Day-use fee is $2 for its well-kept facilities, which include a sandy beach, marina, fishing pier, Discovery Center and bike paths, boating and a playground. The park is on the east side of Deep Creek Lake off Route 22. From Route 219 about 2.5 miles south of the Deep Creek Bridge, take Route 22 at Thayerville. It goes over the Glendale Bridge and State Park Rd. is about a mile farther on the left. 898 State Park Rd., Swanton, MD 21561, ☎ 301-387-5563, fax 301-387-4462, www. dnr.state.md.us/publiclands/western/deepcreeklake.html.

Swallow Falls State Park and the adjoining **Herrington Manor State Park** encompass a large tract of forest and wetland, and two waterfalls. Swallow Falls has a nice picnic area with grills and a stone pavilion built by the CCC. The park brochure includes a trail map, useful for hikers, bik-

Garrett County

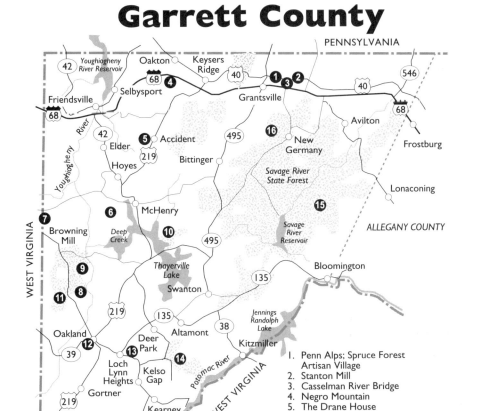

PENNSYLVANIA

WEST VIRGINIA

ALLEGANY COUNTY

Youghiogheny River Reservoir • Oakton • Keysers Ridge • Selbysport • Friendsville • Grantsville • Aviton • Frostburg • Accident • Elder • Hoyes • Bittinger • New Germany • Savage River State Forest • Lonaconing • McHenry • Browning Mill • Deep Creek • Savage River Reservoir • Thayerville Lake • Swanton • Bloomington • Oakland • Deer Park • Altamont • Jennings Randolph Lake • Kitzmiller • Loch Lynn Heights • Kelso Gap • Gortner • Kearney • Table Rock • Potomac River • WEST VIRGINIA

N

© 2001 HUNTER PUBLISHING, INC

1. Penn Alps; Spruce Forest Artisan Village
2. Stanton Mill
3. Casselman River Bridge
4. Negro Mountain
5. The Drane House
6. Wisp Ski Area
7. Cranesville Subarctic Swamp
8. Mt. Nebo Wildlife Management Area
9. Swallow Falls State Park
10. Deep Creek Lake State Park; Deep Creek Lake Discovery Center
11. Herrington Manor State Park
12. Garrett County Historical Museum; St. Matthew's Church
13. Broadford Recreation Area
14. Potomac State Forest
15. Big Run State Park
16. New Germany State Park

ers and cross-country skiers and campers. Its most popular destination is Swallow Falls, to which you should add the walk along the river past dramatic rock formations (see *On Foot*, below). Herrington Manor faces a lake, with boating and fishing as well as a swimming beach and picnic area. It offers small rustic cabins. Both parks may be contacted c/o Herrington Manor State Park, 222 Herrington Lane, Oakland, MD 21550, ☎ 301-334-9180. From Route 219 two miles past Deep Creek, turn right onto Mayhew Inn Rd. and follow it 4.5 miles. At the stop sign, turn left on Oakland Sang Rd. to Swallow Falls Rd., the first on the right. Take it and pass Swallow Falls Park and continue 4.5 miles farther to Herrington Manor State Park.

Broadford Lake, east of Oakland off Route 135, is a town-owned day-use recreation area with swimming, boating, fishing and picnicking facilities. This is an artificial lake created from the damming of Broad Ford Run. Admission is $3 per car, 9 am to sundown daily from April 15 to October 15. Take Route 135 east from Oakland; the entrance road will be on the left.

The sports center near Deep Creek Lake is **High Mountain Sports**, on US 219 opposite the lake. There you will find not only equipment for a wide range of sports, but also information from its highly knowledgeable owner, Steve Green. Route 219, ☎ 301-387-4199.

Potomac/Garrett State Forests share a headquarters, and you should go there for the best and latest information for either location. These forests contain miles of off-road trails, hiking trails, primitive camping sites, fishing and birding. Garrett Forest was the very first state forest, born back in 1906 when John W. Garrett donated 2,000 acres of wilderness to the state, starting the state's forest conservation program. It contains what is believed to be the oldest grove of trees in the state. This part of Garrett forms the bulk of the land between and around Swallow Falls and Herrington Manor state parks. Potomac State Forest is southeast of Oakland (Routes 135 and 560), and Garrett State Forest lies west and northwest, close to the West Virginia border (Herrington Manor Road, Oakland-Sang Run Road). To get to forest headquarters from Route 560, take Bethlehem Road east 3.75 miles, then go left onto Potomac Camp Road about 1.25 miles.

Behind the park headquarters there is a **Bow Range** available from mid-April through mid-November. You must bring your own equipment. Only practice tips can be used and only one shot per target per individual. Targets must be shot in numerical order and from the established peg. Registration is by honor system and is $5 per person per round. Registration envelopes are near the bulletin board.

■ On Foot

Hiking

There are many miles of hiking trails in Garrett County's vast state forest and park system, which covers a tremendous percentage of the available land. Some of these trails are better marked than others and most of them, because of the terrain, involve fording of streams or wet areas.

In the more remote areas, such as Margroff Plantation, Negro Mountain, Piney Mountain, Mt. Nebo and similar sites, side roads and trails can confuse and get you lost. Always stop at the pertinent headquarters for maps (its also a good idea to get a topo map) and the latest trail information. While there make sure they know where you are going. Tell someone back home when to expect you and where you are going as well. Watch the weather too, since rain can make trails treacherous, especially Poplar Lick, Big Run and Monroe Run trails, which closely follow the stream beds (in some cases crossing as many as 18 times) through steep ravines. In remote areas, be sure to carry food and water for emergencies.

Miles of trails attract hikers to the parklands of **Savage River State Forest** and its adjacent parks. A map of these is available at the New Germany State Park headquarters, the administrative center for the forest and the two state parks nearby. For directions and general information, see *Parks* above.

A pleasant day hike begins at the headquarters, going 6.4 miles along a ridge to the overlook above Monroe Run Hollow. The Monroe Run overlook parking area is at the trailhead, 6.5 miles south of Park headquarters on New Germany Rd., so if you have a second car, you can leave it there instead of hiking back. Serious hikers will like the hike on **Monroe Run Trail**, which has 17 (count them) creek crossings. We think its a nicer hike if you do it from the top to the bottom; the distance seems to be at least double the other way. Do this when you can leave a car at the bottom, then drive to the top and hike down. Big Run State Park, at the bottom, has camping, which you should arrange at the Savage River State Forest office. They also have trail maps there.

The Monroe Run Trail is famous for its stinging nettles. You will recognize this plant immediately if you brush one with a hand or leg.

The **Big Savage Hiking Trail** goes from St. John's Rock, close to I-68 in the north, to the whitewater campground on the Savage River in the south, approximately 17 miles. Although the trail does have six road crossings, none of those is a good place to leave a car. The trail roughly parallels the eastern border of Garrett County and passes through some of the wildest land in the state following the ridge of Big Savage Mountain, the northern extension of Backbone Mountain. The Potomac Appalachian Mountain Club calls it the "best hike in Maryland." The last end of this trail is loose rocks and steep switchbacks, as you drop about 1,000 feet in altitude rather quickly. Trail signs have been hard to follow and, although improving, its still best to have a map. Always hike this one into the river, downhill. To get to the north end get off I-68 at Exit 29 and take Beall School Rd. south 1.25 miles. Turn sharp left for another half-mile to the trailhead. On the south end take Route 135 to Bloomington near the Allegany County border. You can also take Route 36 south from Frostburg to Route 135, then go west on Route 135. Just east of Bloomington on the north side of the Savage River take Savage River Rd. west. There is a large circular "Scenic Tour Number 6" sign at the lot.

Poplar Lick Dry Trail drops from the New Germany Rd. trailhead, 3.5 miles south of park headquarters, to Savage River Rd., a hike of about 4.5 miles. The end point is upstream about four miles from BJ's store. We mean "drops," so unless you are looking for a real workout, do it downhill and have a shuttle. Get the maps at Savage River State Forest headquarters. Camping is available at Big Run State Park, downstream from BJ's.

Savage River State Forest has more trails in the western tracts of its vast territory. These lie east of Route 219. The section east of the town of Accident off Route 219, called **Margroff Plantation**, has a system of trails and woods roads. To access the trails, turn east at the main intersection in downtown Accident and follow the Accident-Bittinger Rd. about a mile to unimproved Fratz Rd. on the left. Keep to the right. These are undeveloped areas and there are no facilities, so you should be properly equipped. This is all high forested mountain top with two peaks and a saddle. Before hiking here, get trail maps and current trail information at the main Savage River State Forest headquarters in New Germany State Park.

Farther north, off Route 219, **Negro Mountain Trail System** is another set of trails that offer challenge. Again, these have no facilities so be properly equipped. From Exit 14 of I-68 go south on Route 219 about two miles and take Rabbit Hollow Rd. on the left. It will take you over hill and down dale until it intersects with a road shown variously on several maps as Bowman Mill Rd., Bowman Hill Rd. and Dung Hill Rd. (yes, there is a place called the Dunghill, farther on east of Amish Rd.). Go left, on whatever it is called this month, and in about two miles there will be a parking area on the left. If you get to Amish Rd. you have gone too far. Again, trail maps and current information should first be obtained at the main Savage River State Forest headquarters in New Germany State Park.

RECOMMENDED READING: *Finding your way around in the woods without a good guide is difficult at best and dangerous as well. Look for* **Hikes in Western Maryland**, *published by the Potomac Appalachian Trail Club, 118 Park Street, Vienna, VA 22180, generally available in bookstores and outfitters. It has specific guides to 10 of the areas in this county.* **Hiking, Cycling and Canoeing in Maryland**, *by Bryan Mac-Kay, Johns Hopkins Press, also has three of them. It, too, can be bought in bookstores.*

Tagalong Adventures specializes in guided tours that are perfect for families. These hikes usually have themes, such as local history, or might be blindfolded night hikes to make walkers more aware of the sounds and smells and feel of their natural surroundings. Led by a former park ranger who knows and loves the area and its environment, these are an excellent introduction for both children and adults. For more information on their trips, ☎ 301-245-4084.

Although bogs are usually a feature of more northern climes, a rare pocket of subarctic vegetation has remained at the Maryland-West Virginia border. **Cranesville Swamp** (bogs, swamps and marshes are often misnamed, their names having grown out of local usage long before people made scientific distinctions between them) is an interesting and easy flat walk, although the trail markers are quite confusing. The very nicely done trail map on the sign was designed to show trails as they will be, and building has lagged behind expectations.

The circular trail leads off to the right, along the edge of a wooded area, then skirts the far side of it before reaching the bog. Signs identify most of the plants, which include mosses, berries, alder and grasses in the open, and evergreen ground covers such as arbutus and tea berry in the shaded woods. The trees here are planted, their wide rows forming a corridor to a power line crossing and light forest reclaimed from an old field. The boardwalk leads across the bog, where all the typical bog species grow. Fall is the prettiest time in a bog, with the leaves of so many of the plants turning red and bronze. Cranberry leaves are so red they obscure the fruit. At the far end trees have begun to grow – tamarack and hemlock are the first. The trail continues around the far side of the bog, rejoins the entrance trail and connects to an old lane that leads back to the road just short of the parking lot.

For a shorter in-and-out route to the bog, walk back up the road you drove in on and follow the lane to the right, under the power lines. Even if you have walked dozens of northern bogs, as we have (we are especially fond of bogs), you will find this one interesting for its location so far out of range. There are many plants here that you may never have seen before.

To reach the bog from Deep Creek Lake, take Mayhew Inn Rd. west from US 219, south of the lake. At the stop sign on Sang Run Rd., go left, then right, following signs to Swallow Falls State Park. After you enter the park, go right on the next paved road, which is Cranesville Rd. It is about five miles to Cranesville, where in a clearing you will have to look hard for a small, low sign marking a lane to the left, just before a small white church. Follow the gravel road uphill, and follow the fork to the right, down into a dip. After a curve to the right you will come to the parking area and a Nature Conservancy sign.

Just north of Oakland, the **Mt. Nebo Wildlife Management Area** has a rare thing for Maryland, a red spruce bog which has been dated at approximately 18,000 years old. From Route 219 south of I-68, take Mt. Nebo Rd. to the right. There are four parking areas along both sides of the road. The area is bounded on the west side by the Oakland Sang Rd. Songbirds, grouse and turkeys proliferate here and an annual fall water impoundment attracts migrating waterfowl. Rough trails and old roads give access to this essentially wild area; ☎ 301-334-4255.

Do not go hiking or biking at Mt. Nebo Wildlife Management Area during hunting season.

Potomac/Garrett State Forests have a lot of hiking opportunities in their combined 20,000 acres. One part of Garrett State Forest links Swallow Falls and Herrington Manor state parks, practically enclosing them. North of that set of parks is another tract of Garrett that includes Piney Mountain, where there are more hiking and camping possibilities. To get there, take Cranesville Rd. north to Cranesville, then go east on Sang Run Rd. The road into the park is on the right (south) side of the road.

A far more adventurous hike takes you along the **Lost Land Trail** in the **Potomac State Forest**, on the southern edge of the county. Several creek crossings include some by adventurous means, such as swinging bridges or more precarious logs felled across the river. Begin this 3.5-mile trail at the park office, leaving a second car at the bottom or enquiring about a possible shuttle back. The trail is narrow, rocky and wet, but you will see trillium all over the ground at the bottom in mid-May, mushrooms among the rocks in the summer. Although it crosses Lostland Run at least twice, the trail generally lies between the Run and Lostland Run Rd. There is a picnic area at the bottom along the Potomac River. From top to bottom the descent is about 600 feet.

In a different section of Potomac State Forest, the most southerly tract, is a pleasant hike along snowmobile trails. This is the **Potomac River/ Wallman Rd. Loop**. The slope of the trail is gradual for the most part and it passes through forests and along a dirt road close to the North Branch of the Potomac River. This is a good family hike and there is a small primitive camping area at the beginning with self-registration. To get to this section of the State Forest, take Route 135 from Oakland to Route 560. Go south on Route 560 (at Kelso Gap it passes over the ridge of Backbone Mountain) to White Church-Steyer Rd., which you take to the left (east). It will make a couple of right-angle turns and you will come to Audley Riley Rd. at another sharp turn. Take it a short way to a Y intersection and go right onto Wallman Rd. The camping area and parking is about a half-mile down this road.

Backbone Mountain, the highest point in Maryland at 3,360 feet, is almost in West Virginia. In fact, the access trail begins over the border, and is reached from US 219 in West Virginia. It is privately owned, and the trail crosses private land, but it's no secret in Garrett County. The entrance and trail are well-marked. About 2.5 miles after you cross the state line, you will see a gated driveway on the left, leading uphill. The spot is marked by a small sign high on a tree, and usually by a spraying of red paint on the guardrail. Follow the driveway uphill to a cleared area, continuing upward to the left. This becomes a woods road, marked periodically with stone cairns and red blazes, until you reach a trail, also well marked, to the left. It continues to climb through the woods, past a rocky knoll, and finally to the summit of Backbone Mountain. Here is a state marker, a box with a sign-in book and certificates that you have been there. A thoughtful touch is a sturdy platform, where you can place your camera to make a timed shot of yourself under the sign. Allow about 45 minutes for the climb, 25 minutes back. The site is cared for and promoted by an enthusiastic group of volunteers, but we heard rumors from the state tourism officials that the landowner may not continue to allow access to the trail. As we write, the site is still open and well-marked, without any no-trespassing signs, but check locally.

AUTHOR TIP *Don't confuse this Backbone Mountain trail trail with another Backbone Mountain trail that is in a piece of Potomac State Forest east of Route 135 between Swanton and Bloomington. Backbone Mountain is a long ridge, with the Maryland high point on the south end.*

The short, and not particularly challenging, trail at **Swallow Falls State Park** passes through beautiful woods before opening onto the stream and Muddy Creek Falls. The walk takes about seven minutes. Turn around then and follow the trail along the side of the stream down through its canyon with rock cliffs and tall overhanging trees. Muddy Creek joins the

Youghiogheny River and the walk continues through a steep-sided canyon. The rock formations along the upstream side are fascinating, with small cavelets and rock faces that sometimes extend out over the trail. In the stream you will pass Lower Swallow Falls and then Upper Swallow Falls, both very attractive. Look for the flowerpot rock, a freestanding pillar of stone left after the river wore away the surrounding stone. It's called Swallow Rock for the many cliff swallows that once lived here and gave the falls their name.

A side trail leads a bit farther to Tolliver Falls. The trail passes through a virgin forest of hemlock and white pine of immense size, some of them more than 300 years old. You can combine this hike with a picnic in the pavilion; kids will enjoy the neighboring playground. A food concession is open during the regular season.

There are other trails here as well. One is a foot trail from Swallow Falls State Park through beautiful hardwood forests to **Herrington Manor State Park**, about 5.5 miles away. At Swallow Falls State Park, access this from the back of the Youth Group camping area. From Herrington Manor it begins at the northeast corner of the parking area. In winter this is a favorite cross country trail. The trail is shared with bikes so watch out for them. See *Parks*, above, for directions.

At Herrington Manor State Park another trail leaves from the far side of the lake, running northerly through the woods to Cranesville Rd. It's about five miles, and while you could double back or walk the road back to the car, a shuttle or bike would work out better. **Herrington State Park** itself has a nice series of trails through the woods on the south side of the lake. These are shorter and not particularly difficult, making them good for family outings with small children. The Red trail is 1.6 miles, Blue 2.4 miles, Yellow one mile and green .9 mile. These trails all link up to form a series of interconnected loops through beautiful hardwood forests. They start near the concession stand along the lake. Get maps for both at the Herrington Manor headquarters.

 AUTHOR TIP

At state park offices you can get, for 50¢, a map of off-road multi-use trails in Garrett County. The map is drawn against topo map sections and shows allowed uses. It also contains the addresses of all the state park headquarters and their phone numbers.

Walking Tours

Oakland's *Walking Guide to Downtown* that leads you on a trip through this neat small town with a wonderful sense of community. Highlights include their Renaissance Revival-style County Courthouse, the 1884 Queen Anne-style B&O railroad depot and the new farmers' market where local farmers – Amish, Mennonites and others – sell their produce and crafts. The walking tour guide is published by the Greater Oakland Business Association, ☎ 301-533-4470, www.oaklandmd.com.

■ On Wheels

Mountain biking is popular in the area, with an active club working to build and extend trails. Most of these are intermediate double-track trails, with a few easy and a few advanced. Very few trails are off-limits to cyclists. The loop around the lake is 10 miles long, but don't try it on weekends, when traffic is heavy. New trails are in progress near the town of Accident, in that portion of the Savage River State Forest.

The trail from **Herrington Manor State Park** to Swallow Falls State park – the same one used by cross-country skiers in the winter – is about five miles one-way, past beaver dams and over bridges through gently rolling terrain.

For a workout on a bike, follow the trails through Deep Creek Lake State Park. In late October, when the leaves are off, you can see for miles from the top. And you'll have the park to yourself.

KID-FRIENDLY

*For biking with kids, try the **Oakland Youghiogheny Glades Park**. It has a one-mile paved path with loops and bridges. You can access this trail from Liberty St.*

Near Deep Creek, contact **High Mountain Sports**. When owner Steve Green became frustrated over the lack of a good bike trail map, he made one himself, which he sells for $3. High Mountain is a Trek mountain bike dealer and rents equipment, too. The store is open daily, 9-5, on Route 219, Deep Creek Lake, ☎ 301-387-4199, a half-mile south of the Route 219 bridge. Bike package rates are also available; call for details. Rental rates are $25 for a full day, $18 for a half-day; a two-hour lesson is $12.

■ On Water

Boating

There are boat ramps at **Big Run State Park**, **Bloomington Lake**, **Broadford Lake**, **Deep Creek Lake State Park**, **Herrington Manor State Park**, **New Germany State Park** and at **Youghiogheny Reservoir**. The only one of these with a pier is **Deep Creek**.

Deep Creek Lake State Park has the major summer sports lake in this area. Formed as an electric generation dam decades ago, the lake is now a key part of the area's economic life and provides plenty of opportunity for boating of all kinds. There are many boat rental companies servicing the area. The state park is just about in the middle of the eastern shore, so from there you can head out in any direction. See *Parks*, page 20, for more information.

BOAT RENTALS AT DEEP CREEK LAKE

Echo Marina rents a wide variety of boats for use on the lake. They range from a 14-foot fishing boat at $11 an hour ($40 a day) to a 115 hp ski boat for $36 an hour ($168 a day) to a 140 hp boat for $42 an hour ($210 a day). They have other options as well, so check with them at 19638 Garrett Highway, Oakland, MD 21550, ☎ 301-387-5855. They also have water ski rentals. Security deposit ($100 in *cash*) is required at time of pick-up for all inboard/outboard motor boats. Rates do not include gas.

Also in the rental business is **Bill's Marine Service, Inc.** which has everything from 9.9 hp fishing boats to 190 hp powerboats. Choices include pontoon boats for leisurely tours of the lake. A 115 hp ski boat costs $36 an hour ($121 for up to eight hours), while a 50 hp pontoon boat will run about $31.50 an hour ($145 up to eight hours). Fishing boats are $11 an hour (eight hours for $40).

Deep Creek Lake Enterprises Boat Rentals rents only by the eight-hour period. A 24-foot pontoon boat rents for $125; a six-seater ski boat, $200; paddleboats are available for $10 per hour or $25 per day. They are open daily, 8:30-5, from Memorial Day to Labor Day. 2039 Deep Creek Drive, PO Box 902, McHenry 21541, ☎ 301-387-9130.

Crystal Waters, Inc. offers powerboat rentals up to 90 hp starting at $16 for 40-50 hp to $42 an hour for 85-90 hp. Pontoon boats start at $20 an hour for one with six hp and go up to $30 per hour for a 28-foot, 12 hp pontoon boat. Pedal boats are $6/hr and a 25 hp fishing boat costs $11 per hour or $50 a day. They also rent canoes ($6 an hour, $25 per day) and water-skiing equipment. PO Box 70, McHenry, MD 21541 ☎ 301-387-5515.

Also with competitive rates is **Quality Marine, Inc** which has 24-foot pontoon boats at $60 for two hours ($125/day) and ski equipment. They are across from the Post Office in McHenry, PO Box 37, McHenry, 21541, ☎ 301-387-5677.

Deep Creek Outfitters has a large selection of boats for rent, with a 50-foot runabout at $20 an hour or $95 a day. Powerboats for water-skiing begin at $26 an hour. Pontoon boats are also available at about $20 an hour. PO Box 172, 1899 Deep Creek Drive, McHenry, MD 21541, ☎ 301-387-6977.

In order to rent a motorized boat in the State of Maryland, anyone born after July 1, 1972 is required to comply with the Maryland Boating Safety Certificate Law. You must also be at least 21 years of age. See page 10 for information on compliance with that law as it relates to non-residents.

Watersports

For **water-skiing** and **wakeboarding**, contact **High Mountain Sports**, the premier operation on the lake for most watersports. Their lessons are especially designed for people who are less than confident in the water, turning them into avid water-skiers. Reservations are essential, since most of their students are repeat customers who continue to build their skill levels. Route 219, Deep Creek Lake, ☎ 301-387-4199, a half-mile south of the Route 219 bridge, on the right side of the road. Open Sunday-Thursday, 10-6, Friday-Saturday 10-8.

Canoe & Kayaking

In various parts of **Savage River State Forest** there are several paddling opportunities, including **New Germany State Park**'s 13-acre lake. The boat rental and boat launch area is on the east side of the lake. See *Parks* above. Also in the park is the 360-acre **Savage River Reservoir**, which is accessed from Big Run State Park. Most of reservoir's shoreline is untouched by development. It sits in a basin surrounded by tall mountains, pristine, even though it is man-made. Put in at Big Run, Dry Run (an unpromising name for a place to paddle) or at the Weather Station. Primitive camping is available at this park. The Savage River below the dam is Class 5 whitewater or higher and depends upon releases; this is the river used for Olympic tryouts, not a place for intermediate paddlers.

*Serious whitewater enthusiasts don't have to be told about the **Youghiogheny River**. It's a legend. Most Sunday kayakers wouldn't try it even if they could pronounce it without coaching (it's yock-a-GAIN-y, but locally and in whitewater-speak, it's just The Yock). Dam releases on Saturday and Monday assure Class 5 water, but you need to verify these before you plan a trip.*

Friendsville, where I-68 crosses the river, is the headquarters for rafting, which gives the town a completely different culture than the rest of the county. Locals refer to it as a "granola town," although not scornfully. They enjoy their wild river as much as those who travel to get here.

More gentle is the **middle Youghiogheny**, which has a four- to five-mile stretch of Class 2 rapids. It is still advisable to have a guide through here, as there are places where you must carry. Put in behind the Wisp Golf Course and take out *before* the bridge at the whitewater put-in at Hoyes Landing. When you see the blue bridge ahead, look for the take out on the right. Beyond that is one of the most challenging and dangerous sections of the river.

> *The variety of license plates on the cars in the parking area – from Colorado, Alaska, California – should tell you that this is the put-in for a world class rapids.*

Herrington Manor State Park has a 53-acre lake for paddling. The lake has paddleboat, canoe and boat rentals at boat launch or you can bring your own.

For a family trip, join **Tagalong Adventures** (☎ 301-245-4084) on a paddle into beaver ponds, where you will see lodges, and perhaps their inhabitants. Check at the Garrett County Tourist Office for a schedule.

Broadford Lake, east of Oakland off Route 135, has an undeveloped shoreline that makes it attractive to paddlers. Admission is $3 per car, 9 am to sundown, daily from April 15 to October 15.

Jennings Randolph Lake, a reservoir created by damming the North Branch of the Potomac, is vast and has a boat ramp on the Maryland side but, unless the water level is high, it is a most unaesthetic place to paddle. Except during really high water, the banks are lined by a wide strip of ugly yellow riprap, and any sign of nature is well above vision level. The boat ramp is at the end of Mt. Zion Rd., off Route 135, west of Oakland. Most of the other facilities of the lake are on the opposite side, in West Virginia (it was a pet project of a West Virginia Senator, after all). These include the Howell Run Picnic Area, the Robert Craig Campground and the Howell Boat Launch. For that side, take Route 38 from 135 to Route 46 north on the West Virginia side of the river. The ramp fee is $2 a day.

Deep Creek Lake State Park offers a big lake with lots of long arms for exploring. Paddlers should be aware that this is a full-fledged summer sports lake with water-skiing and powerboats, so wakes are a fact of life. On the other hand, the man-made lake is big and there is a lot to explore along the shore. See *Parks* above for more information.

CANOE RENTALS

Deep Creek Outfitters, 1899 Deep Creek Drive, McHenry, MD, ☎ 301-387-6977, has a large selection of rental canoes at a reasonable $5 an hour or $15 a day.

In the Big Run area, rent canoes at **BJ's Store**, a half-mile from Big Run Rd. on Savage River Rd.; ☎ 301-777-0001. Rates are $25 a day, $46 for two days, four hours for $16. They provide paddles, life jackets and maps of the reservoir. They will also provide shuttles, but only if you are renting two or three canoes.

Whitewater Rafting

Rafting guides on the upper Youghiogheny must be licensed by the state Department of Natural Resources in order to work the river. They must not only know the river, but take safety emergency training. It is a very wild section, deep, steep and narrow. For six miles the river drops 600 feet with no place to regroup – just straight through-the-middle rafting. It is important to make reservations, since these world-class rapids are well-known and the two or three trips a day depend on the water level. For information on the water release schedule in the fast water areas, call the power company at ☎ 814-533-8911.

WHITEWATER OUTFITTERS

Precision Rafting runs trips on the Upper Youghiogheny, which drops an average of 115 feet per mile in this section. After a short flatwater it's one rapid after the other, 20 rapids in five miles. Their trips are Monday-Friday and the first Saturday of the month. Trips include lunch, with no more than three guests and one guide per raft. Rates for weekdays are $100 per person; Fridays, $105; weekends and holidays, $115. In addition to the whitewater, they have float trips on the upper Yough of about one to two hours duration with rates beginning at $20. They also do the Cheat/Big Sandy in Albright, West Virginia and for six weeks every fall they do the Gauley River in Summersville, West Virginia during the annual dam release. Contact them at PO Box 185, Friendsville 21531, ☎ 800-477-3723, www.precisionrafting. com, e-mail precisionrafting@gcnet.net.

Mountain Streams operates from Ohiopyle, PA, but they run trips on the Upper Youghiogheny as well on the other sections in Pennsylvania. Check with them for availability of the Upper Yough trips. They require that you have rafting experience because of this section of the river is so difficult. They put in at Sang Run and take out at Friendsville. Rates are $139 on Saturday;

$129 on Sunday; $119 on weekdays. PO Box 106, Ohiopyle, PA 15470, ☎ 800-723-8669, fax 724-329-4730, www.mtstreams.com.

Another operator from Ohiopyle is **Laurel Highlands River Tours**. They run the Upper Yough, as well as the sections in Pennsylvania. Monday-Thursday rates are $110; Friday, $120; Saturday, $136. In addition to the whitewater ventures, they have kayak and canoe instruction, guided fishing tours on the Yough, guided rock climbing and guided mountain biking. Write to them at PO Box 107, Ohiopyle, PA 15470, ☎ 800-472-3846, www.riversearch.com, e-mail 4raftin@laurelhighlands.com.

A third company in Ohiopyle is **Wilderness Voyageurs**. They run the Upper Yough in four-person rafts and require prior experience. Their minimum age is 18 and the season is March-November. Sunday-Thursday, $109; Friday $119; Saturday $139. PO Box 97, Ohiopyle, PA 15470, ☎ 800-272-4141.

WORD TO THE WISE

Precision Rafting, a Maryland company, seemed to be the unanimous choice of everyone active in the outdoor sports field. This is dangerous stuff, so we urge that you do it with professionals.

Lake Cruises

Take to the water in a more leisurely fashion on board *The Evening Star* for a guided afternoon cruise of Deep Creek Lake. The boat is a 42-foot catamaran type, very stable and fully enclosed with large, openable glass windows. The rates are low, at $6 adult, $4 child under 12. At 6 pm on Saturday they have an evening cocktail cruise for $7.50, plus drinks. They run cruises only if there are 10 or more passengers, so check with them before setting out and be sure to make reservations. Monday-Friday the cruises are at 4 pm, Saturday-Sunday at 2 pm. Deep Creek Outfitters, Marsh Run Cove, 1899 Deep Creek Drive, McHenry, MD, ☎ 301-387-6977.

AUTHOR TIP

*Garrett County is home to **Flying Scott Sailboats**. They make a sweet-sailing 19-footer in Deer Creek, just east of Oakland. Their boatyard is open for visitors during normal weekday business hours or you can call for weekend visits. They are at 157 Cemetery Street, Deer Park 21550, ☎ 301-334-4848, fax 334-8324, just off Route 135, six miles from Oakland.*

Fishing

Fly-fishing in the **Savage River** and **North Branch** of the Potomac in the spring is some of the nation's finest. Wild brook and brown trout will test the skills of expert anglers in these rivers.

The park area surrounding the Savage has 105 square miles of watershed for native brook trout. Savage River is stocked with rainbows above the dam, and is open to all kinds of bait and tackle. **Savage River Reservoir** has wall-eye, brown and rainbow trout, perch, crappie and both large- and small-mouth bass. For stream fishing, try the **Casselman River** south from I-68. Bear Hill Rd. parallels it on its west side.

Other streams to fish are **Back Lick Run**, **Poplar Lick Run**, **Bear Pen Run**, **Big Run**, **Monroe Run** and **Middle Fork**, all streams that flow from New Germany Rd. into Savage River. Get to them from Savage River Rd. and fish upstream. BJ's store, on Savage River Rd., about a half-mile from Big Run Rd., handles sporting goods, including everything you need for fishing. They can also tell you how all of these local streams are doing at the time.

RECOMMENDED READING: *A Fisherman's Guide to Maryland's Piers and Boat Ramps* *contains a series of small locator maps showing every ramp in the state and is an invaluable tool. It's hard to find but you can order it from Maryland Department of Natural Resources, Fisheries Office, Tawes State Office Building, Annapolis, MD 21401,* ☎ *800-688-FINS.*

Below the dam, the whitewater from the top to the second suspension bridge (the Allegheny Bridge) is for fly-fishing only. Those fishing there may have no other bait or tackle in their possession. From the Allegheny Bridge to the Potomac River is artificial lure water only, with no live bait allowed.

The **Casselman River** offers prime fishing and the **Youghiogheny** has good moving water for fly-fishing from Swallow Falls to Sang Run. Different sections of this river have different fishing designations, so always check with a local sporting outfitter before heading to the stream. Some are Catch-and-Return, others Put-and-Take and others Native Trout Waters. Releases of cool water from the dam keep trout thriving. The Casselman, from I-68 north, has been designated a Delayed Harvest Area. See "Caution" below.

Broadford Lake, east of Oakland off Route 135, is one of the best fishing lakes in the area. Admission is $3 per car from April 15 to October 15, but the park access is open for fishing only beginning March 1 and extending until November 30. No night fishing or ice fishing is allowed.

Although **Deep Creek Lake** is a man-made lake, fishing is good. Species found here are walleye, bass, stocked trout and yellow perch. Ice fishing is allowed on Deep Creek Lake and the Savage River Reservoir, where you might catch walleye or yellow perch or, more rarely, trout, pickerel or bass. You cannot take a vehicle onto the ice at Deep Creek Lake.

AUTHOR TIP

*At Deep Creek Lake, **Johnny's Bait House** on US 219 is the place for bait, tackle, information and advice. Owner John Marple is a fishing expert.*

FISHING LICENSES

You can buy fishing licenses at most general stores in the area, at park headquarters, and at the liquor store at I-68 Exit 24. With your license, get a copy of the state *Sportfishing Guide*, which lists special regulation areas as well as stocked streams. Maryland has three free fishing days each year, for freshwater areas only. One is always July 4, the others in early June.

Herrington Manor State Park has a 53-acre lake that the state keeps stocked with trout. The boat launch is convenient and they have boat rentals. In **Potomac and Garrett State Forests** are 21 miles of streams for fishing. Herrington Creek and Muddy Creek are in the State Parks that are surrounded by Garrett State Forest along the west border of the county. These streams are put-and-take areas, meaning that they are regularly stocked with trout. They are closed to fishing for a period after stocking so inquire as to whether they are open when you are there.

Designated **trout streams** are **Lostland Run** (accessed from Potomac Camp Rd.), **Laurel Run** (from White Church Rd.), and **Crabtree Creek**, accessed from Spring Lick Rd. These streams are not stocked and contain native species. Special rules apply to Designated Trout Streams, so check for regulations when buying a license. The North Branch of the Potomac, accessed via the Potomac Camp and White Church Roads, from the boundary of Potomac State Forest at Lostland Run to the boundary at Wallman is a **Delayed Harvest Area**.

CAUTION

In a Delayed Harvest Area, special conditions apply to fishing. From June 16 through September, you can possess two trout from this river and there are no bait, lure or tackle restrictions. From October 1 to June 15, you may not keep in these areas and can fish only with artificial lures and flies and streamers. You can't even possess any natural bait, scents or devices for catching fish.

FISHING OUTFITTERS

Area outfitters can arrange your fishing trip. **Spring Creek Out-fitters**, 578 Deep Creek Drive, PO Box 159, McHenry, MD 21541, ☎ 301-387-2034, www.springcreekoutfitter.com, has a large variety of options available for every skill level. They love to teach. On float trips along the North Branch of the Potomac you can catch four kinds of trout, including the Potomac Cutthroat. They also fish the Youghiogheny. Rental equipment is available for $35 a day. Float trips are $175 a day, $275 for two. Wading trips are $150. Half-day bass trips on Deep Creek Lake start at $125.

At **Streams and Dreams**, Don and Karen Hersfeld offer a complete immersion experience. They love the sport and they love teaching it. He is an aquatic ecologist and she is a fisheries science graduate. Their place is in a dappled, shady area within a stone's throw of the famed Youghiogheny. Some say they teach fly-fishing like it was a religion. They fish the Youghiogheny, Casselman River, Savage River and the North Branch of the Potomac. They welcome families to their three-room B&B and Brookside Cottage, suitable for up to five. Their learning programs especially emphasize fly-fishing as a family activity. 8214 Oakland-Sang Rd., Oakland, MD 21550, ☎ 301-387-6881, www.streams-and-dreams.net, e-mail Fishing4U2@Juno.com.

Reel Bass Adventures can also arrange trips in Garrett County, with guides to show you the where and how on Savage River and on Morgan Run. Their office is at 10100 Old Franklin Avenue, Seabrook, MD 20706, ☎ 301-839-2858.

In the northwest corner at Friendship, **Around the Bend Trout-fitters** offers float trips, wading trips and tackle and boat rentals. Their instruction program is Orvis-endorsed, and the fly-fishing school includes lunch and equipment. They will also take beginners out on a stream for live instruction. Their basic hourly rate is $25; all-day float trips are $250 for one or two people; half-day trips are $125. They fish the Yough, Savage, North and South Branches of the Potomac and the Casselman. Write A.T.B. Trout-fitters, PO Box 185, Friendsville, MD 21531, ☎ 301-746-5290, 800-477-3723.

Don Ringer is a professional fishing and hunting guide who knows the lakes and streams of Garrett County intimately. He operates **Outdoor Adventures Unlimited** and conducts guided fishing trips on the Potomac, Savage, Casselman and Youghiogheny Rivers and in the Lostland area. He also teaches fly-fishing on Deep Creek Lake. 414 Maple Avenue, Oakland, MD 21550, ☎ 301-334-7932.

AUTHOR TIP

Even if you don't fish, go to the fishing piers at Deep Creek Lake State Park in the spring, where you can see goslings and duck chicks in the water.

See the lead paragraph of *On Water*, above, for information on boat ramp and fishing pier access.

■ On Snow

 Those who live or travel in eastern Maryland, where the Chesapeake Bay's influence warms the weather, may be surprised to learn of the amount of snow that sometimes falls and accumulates in the western mountains. Note we said "sometimes." Snow cover is not reliable (which could also be said for places farther north in "snow country" during the past few winters). Although the ski area at Wisp can make snow in cold weather, sports such as cross-country skiing, snowshoeing and snowmobiling depend on natural snowfall. So if you plan a winter sports vacation here, be prepared for the uncertainties. As might be expected, January and February are the most promising months. The positive side of this, of course, is that the hiking season here is almost year-round.

Downhill Skiing

Wisp Ski Area is a full-service mountain with a vertical drop of 610 feet, averaging 96" of snowfall annually. A computerized snowmaking system services 90% of the trails and takes advantage of all possible snowmaking moments. They open in early to mid-November and expect to operate through March. Wisp has 23 slopes with approximately 14 miles of trails; 20% are rated beginner, 50% are ranked intermediate, and the balance are advanced. Long beginner trails on the north side of the hill are Possum-Chipmunk and Wisp Trail, although access to the latter is over a short section of intermediate called Longview. Night skiing helps take advantage of every skiable day. Early and late season, Wisp is open Tuesday-Saturday, 8:30 am-9 pm; Sunday-Monday, 8:30-4:30. Mid-December through mid-March they are open Tuesday-Saturday, 8:30 am-10 pm; Sunday-Monday, 8:30-4:30, with somewhat different hours on holidays. Ski-Wee and Mini-rider programs are available. Lift rates are much lower when purchased as part of a package that includes lodging and other services.

To get to Wisp from I-68, take Exit 14 and go south on Route 219 to Deep Creek. Just before the Visitor Center you will see the signs. Marsh Hill Rd., Deep Creek, PO Box 629, McHenry, MD 21541, ☎ 301-387-4911, www.gcnet.net/wisp.

Cross-Country Skiing

More than 12 miles of trails in **Savage River State Forest** and its adjacent parks are open to cross-country skiers. The **Green Trail** is the "turnpike" of these, wide and level as it runs alongside a brook, although parts can be difficult. It is the most crowded trail, but beautiful, lined with hemlock and rhododendron. Nine miles of trails in the state forest are groomed and tracked, and a warming hut provides a headquarters for skiers. The park opens at 8 am, closes at 4 or 4:30 pm, depending on the length of the days. The warming hut is in the Recreation Hall. The Margroff Plantation, Negro Mountain and Poplar Lick trails are also used for cross-country skiing, but are multi-use, so watch for snowmobiles.

The biggest disadvantage of trails in Savage River State Forest is that they are multi-purpose, so skiers share them with snowmobilers. There is conflicting opinion over who has the right-of-way, but it is prudent for skiers to get off the trail quickly when they hear a machine approaching, as snowmobilers expect you to do. In fairness, skiers should realize that a lot of the grooming and trail maintenance is done by local snowmobilers.

In the **Potomac/Garrett State Forest**, the Potomac River Trail and Backbone Mountain Trail are also used for cross-country. This is not the Backbone Mountain Trail leading to the state's highest point, which is not in this park.

Another really nice area is the **Potomac River/Wallman Rd. Loop**; see *On Foot*, above, for details. This is a wide trail of mostly gradual grade, with significant sections along a dirt road parallelling the North Branch of the Potomac. Remember that these are rough, mountainous trails and are shared with snowmobiles. Let them have the right of way.

*Although the **Monroe Run Trail** is sometimes suggested for cross-country skiing, we don't advise it. It is very steep and rocky in the lower section. In addition, unless the weather has been well below freezing for at least a week, you could find yourself wading across some of the 17 creek crossings.*

At **Herrington Manor State Park**, the snowmobile trails are also used by cross-country skiers. Begin near the lake house at Harrington and ski about 5.5 miles of gently rolling terrain to Swallow Falls Park, ending near the group camping area. This is a good trip to shuttle with two cars; there is a warming hut with a concession, fireplaces and restrooms at Harrington Manor State Park. Altogether there are 10 miles of cross-country trails available at Herrington. There are red-, green- and blue-blazed trails on the south side of the lake that extend out into the surrounding forests. Pick them up near the concession stand at the parking lot. Herrington has rentals from 8:30-4 daily except Christmas and New Year's Day, but you can't take them off the grounds. For conditions, e-mail PARK-HERRINGTON-MANOR@dnr.state.md.us.

Deep Creek Lake State Park at Deep Creek uses its hiking trails for cross-country skiing in the winter. Again, these are also used for snowmobiling; the wise skier moves off the track when the sound approaches. The park is on the east side of Deep Creek Lake off Route 22. From Route 219 about 2½ miles south of the Deep Creek Bridge, take Route 22 at Thayerville. It leads over the Glendale Bridge; State Park Rd. is about a mile farther on the left.

SKI EQUIPMENT RENTALS

For ski rentals in this area, call **Cross Country Ski Rentals** ☎ 301-689-8515. If they are not open, their recording will give you the day's snow conditions, as well as a number to call to reserve skis.

High Mountain Sports sells and rents downhill and Nordic skis and snowshoes on Route 219, Deep Creek Lake, ☎ 301-387-4199, a half-mile south of the Route 219 Bridge. They are open daily, 9-5. Downhill ski rentals are available from High Mountain's roadside facility, opposite the Visitor's Center on Route 219. The equipment here is better than you can rent at the Wisp ski slope.

Deep Creek Outfitters, 1899 Deep Creek Drive, McHenry, MD 21541, ☎ 301-387-6977, rents cross-country equipment with all-day rates of about $10 for traditional equipment and $12 for Revolution equipment.

Snowmobiling

Savage River State Forest and its adjacent parks offer miles of trails, about 12 miles of which are also used by cross-country skiers. The access trail is behind the park headquarters at New Germany State Park. **Margroff Plantation**, **Negro Mountain** and **Poplar Lick** are also suggested for snowmobiling. Snowmobiling is also permitted on the trails of Deep Creek State Park, Potomac River Trail and Backbone Mountain Trail (not to be confused with the highest point trail) in Potomac/Garrett State Forest.

You must have a Maryland snowmobile registration, which costs $15 per calendar year, but gives you access to all mapped trails. These are available at any place that sells fishing licenses, which includes most general stores in the area, park headquarters, and the liquor store off I-68 at Exit 24. Out-of-state visitors can get a seven-day permit for $7.

AUTHOR TIP *At Maryland State Park offices you can get, for a mere 50¢, a map of off-road multi-use trails in Garrett County. These are drawn against topo map sections and show allowed uses. The map also contains the addresses of all the state park headquarters and their phone numbers.*

Sledding & Sleigh Rides

Herrington Manor State Park offers horsedrawn sleigh or hayrides during January as special events. They start about 1 pm and run hourly until 5 or 6 pm. If there's no snow, they have hayrides. Call ☎ 301-334-9180 or 334-8464 for information, dates and reservations. **Deep Creek State Park** also offers sleigh/hayrides from the Discovery Center on a schedule during the winter. Call them at ☎ 301-387-7067 for specific dates, times and reservations, or check their Web site, www.dnr.state.md.us/publiclands/western/deepcreeklake.html. See *Parks*, page 20, for more information.

You might also call the stables listed below under *On Horseback* for hayrides and sleigh rides. Broken Bar Stables and Small Oaks Riding Stables both have these activities by prior arrangement.

■ On Horseback

 Broken Bar Stables (☎ 301-334-3114) is located nine miles east of Oakland off Route 135, about a mile west of Deer Park. They have horseback riding by the hour or by the half-day. In addition, they arrange hayrides by appointment on Saturday nights, ending with a hot dog roast. In the past, Herrington State Park and Deep Creek Lake Discovery Center have used them for hayrides in October.

Another option is **Small Oaks Riding Stables**, operated by Dick and Sue Smith, who offer horseback riding by the half-day and by the hour. They are open all year, weather permitting. Buggy rides and hayrides can be arranged by appointment. Reservations are important for either stable. Small Oaks is off Broadford Rd. in Oakland; look for the sign at Smith Drive. ☎ 301-334-4991.

Cultural & Eco-Travel Experiences

■ Natural Resources

Children will especially enjoy the **Deep Creek Lake Discovery Center** in Deep Creek Lake State Park. The 6,000-square-foot facility has lots of hands-on activities and an extensive schedule of programs for both kids and adults, including field trips into surrounding woods and streams. This center integrates the study of the area's terrain, flora and fauna with the current and historic uses of the land. An aquarium has fish that are native to the streams and lake, and other exhibits teach about the extraction of coal from local mines and the use of rivers by loggers. A schedule of events is on their Web site. The center is at 898 State Park Rd., Swanton, ☎ 301-387-7067, www.dnr.md.state.us/public-lands/western/discovery.html. See *Parks*, above, for more information.

■ Crafts & Culture

Penn Alps and Spruce Forest Artisan Village are easy to spot by the side of US 40-Alt just east of Grantsville, and also easy to find on the map, since they are between two marked historic sites, Stanton's Mill and Casselman River Bridge. The four are so close, you can visit them all in one stop. **Spruce Forest Artisan Village** is a fascinating combination of historic preservation, commercial endeavor and cultural center, well worth seeing. Historic log homes and cottages that would have fallen into ruin have been rescued and assembled here in a shady pine grove, like a little village. Each now houses a crafts studio and shop. You can watch the craftspeople work, learn about the craft, or shop. Nowhere will you find a more relaxed, low-pressure group of people; they are friendly, upbeat and genuinely happy to talk to visitors.

Workshops include a teddy-bear maker, bird carver, potter, blacksmith, basket maker, spinner and weaver, forged iron worker, herbalist and others. The basket maker and potter are especially skillful at blending old techniques with creative, fresh designs.

The oldest building, from 1775, is two stories tall, with a slate painter and bird carver in residence. Most of the buildings have placards telling their origins, and two are of particular interest. The first is the writing cabin of the writer Alta Schrock, and the second is her family homestead. If you are lucky, you will find her sitting by its ample fireplace, where she will invite you to sit down while she spins you a story or two about the fascinating family who lived here. Do allow time enough for this thoroughly enjoyable and relaxing interlude. Be sure to notice the very unusual photograph of her Amish grandfather, taken before the religion banned photography.

The village is open Monday through Saturday and is on Route 40 just east of Grantsville. From I-68, get off at Exit 22, go north to Route 40, turn left and continue for about a mile. Their **Summer Festival and Quilt Show** invites other craftsmen to sell and show at the village. There is no charge for entry and the crafts done and exhibited here are of first quality. Contact them at 117 Casselman Rd., Grantsville, MD 21536, ☎ 301-895-3332, fax 895-4665, www.spruceforest.org; e-mail tmorgan@spruceforest.org.

Penn Alps was a stagecoach stop on the National Road, and continues that tradition with a full-service restaurant specializing in local dishes. Adjoining the restaurant is a shop selling local products. The food section ranges from farmstead jams and jellies to dried corn and homemade cookies, while the craft section serves as a sales point for the work of local families. Along with quilts, wooden ware, baskets and knit goods they have an excellent selection of books on the Mennonites, Appalachian culture and western Maryland folklore. We suggest you see the work at the artisan village before you buy here, to get a full picture of the variety available in these twin craft centers. The baskets, for example, are of far better design at the artisan village, and at comparable prices. ☎ 301-895-5985; open same hours as Spuce Forest Village.

In Grantsville, **Shady Grove Market and Fabrics** sells fabrics especially chosen for quilters. It's on Route 669 north, just before the Pennsylvania border, 1493 Springs Rd., Grantsville, MD, ☎ 301-895-5660.

A relatively new project in Oakland, known as the **Mountain Arts Co-operative**, has a showing on weekends, but locations may vary. When we last shopped there, craftsmen were demonstrating and selling their wares in a former storefront opposite the Railway Station on Second St., but that was not a permanent home. Ask in Oakland to see where the group, which includes several hard-to-find traditional mountain crafts, is showing, or check on-line at www.oaklandmd.com.

About five miles south of downtown Oakland, **Grace's Craft Room**, 372 Joni-Miller Rd., ☎ 301-334-1010, features fabric crafts, especially quilts made by the women of the active local Amish community. The shop also has handmade woven rugs, sometimes called rag rugs because they are frequently made from scraps of leftover fabric. Each rug is different. Grace's is open Monday-Saturday, 8-8. From Route 219 south of Oakland, take Mason School Rd. on the left for about a mile, then turn left onto Pleasant Valley Rd. Make another left onto Joni Miller Rd. – watch for the sign.

There are a few other Amish/Mennonite family-operated crafts shops in the area. **Swiss Valley Crafts** specializes in patio furniture, gliders, rocking chairs, wooden toys and dollhouses. They are at 174 Landons Dam Rd., Oakland, MD 21550, ☎ 301-334-2980. For hand-forged metals, visit Randy Crabtree's **Starfire Studio** (by appointment) at 72 Crabtree Hill, Oakland, MD 21550, ☎ 301-387-5482, e-mail rcrabtree1@mindspring.com. **The Loft Shop**, 9415 Rock Ledge Rd., in Bittinger (near Accident), ☎ 301-

245-4528 or 895-3820, carries a variety of crafts by local artisans, including wood crafts, paintings, pottery, rag rugs and jewelry. They open Thursday-Sunday, 10-5 from Memorial Day through Labor Day; same hours weekends only through foliage season.

Walnut Ridge B&B in Grantsville offers quilting weekends that feature lessons at Four Seasons Quilt Shop, coupons for meals at local restaurants and a three-day/two-night stay. See *Where to Stay*, below, for details.

■ Local Foods

Throughout this western area are many Mennonite and Amish farms, some with bakeries and/or dairies where they make cheese. (In general, you will find more Mennonites in the north, Amish in the south.) As you travel US 219 south of Oakland, you will see the cautionary signs for buggies in the road, and will see black buggies parked in the yards.

Sugar & Spice Bakery is at one of these Amish farms, south of Oakland on US 219. They specialize in cheese, and along with the more common varieties, you will find unusual cheeses, including a tangy horseradish flavor with a kick. Baked goods are excellent, too, especially the apple dumplings. They are open Monday through Saturday, 7-5:30 pm; closed Sunday. ☎ 301-334-1559.

It's hard to decide whether **Yoder Country Market** should be listed under food, shopping or cultural experiences; it's a bit of all three. This family-run emporium sells meats, bulk foods, jams and jellies, fresh bread and gifts. Look here for books about the area, too. To reach Yoder's from US 40-Alt, turn north on Sprint St. (Route 669) in the center of Grantsville; ☎ 301-895-5148 or 800-321-5148, www.yodermarket.com.

Garrett County also has its own vineyards, **Deep Creek Winery**, Frazee Ridge Rd., Friendsville, MD, ☎ 301-746-4349. Using California grapes in Rhone blends, they don't pretend to be esoteric, offering simple "low-tech, unfiltered, full flavored blends" at an affordable $6-7 a bottle. They have Chardonnay, Cabernet and American Cythiana as well as limited bottlings of wines such as elderberry. After visiting the winery, have a picnic on their hilltop. Open Fridays, 3-8 pm; Saturday, 11-7, or by appointment. From December through April, call for hours. From I-68, take Exit 4 at Friendsville and go north six miles on Route 42. Go right on Frazee Ridge Rd.; it's on the left.

Farmers' Markets

A farmers' market is held every Tuesday at Exit 39 off I-68, at the intersection of Route 40-Alt., near La Vale. This is a good place to buy picnic components or stock your camping larder with fresh vegetables, honey, baked goods and other products of the local farms. In **Oakland**, the farmers' market is near the grand old railway station, a block downhill from the main street (US 219). It is open Wednesday through Saturday, 10 am-1 pm, with fresh produce, baked goods and some crafts.

■ The Arts

In search of the fine arts, call for the schedule of **Garrett Lakes Arts Festival**, held in various venues in the county. Performances generally start in late April and extend to Labor Day weekend. The schedule is particularly active from late June through August. Past shows have included the National Players, Elizabethan Roots of Appalachian Music, River City Brass Band and The Symphony at Deep Creek. For information and reservations, ☎ 301-387-3082, www.artsandentertainment.org, e-mail glaf@gcnet.net.

■ Walking Tours

One of the most unusual cultural and historical tours in Maryland is certainly the **Mayor's Tour of Oakland**. If you call ahead, and his schedule allows, Mayor Asa McCain (☎ 301-334-2691) will escort you on a walk through downtown Oakland that takes you behind the scenes of a small city and gives you fascinating insights on its history, architecture, culture and plans for its future. You'll hear how the town was cut off financially for 10 years when the state imposed a construction ban after a former city government refused to comply with environmental regulations. You'll hear Civil War stories, see beautifully restored Victorian homes and uniquely recycled downtown buildings. And because you're with the one man in town that everybody knows, you'll meet a lot of local people as you tour. Put on your walking shoes – this man's a mover. And he often carries the keys to the beautiful old railway station, which is under restoration, so you might get an inside look. For other local sights the mayor may point out, see *Museums & Historic Sites*, below.

One of the unique things you'll see on the tour is the outdoor stage which the local newspaper, *The Republican*, created from its loading platform. "We use it only part of the time," the publisher told us, "so we tried to find a way to make the platform and parking area useful and attractive." With the help of other local businesses, they created a stage with sound system and lights suitable for concerts and other programs. In fact, they invite local musicians to practice there, for the enjoyment of locals and visitors. *The Republican* has published every week since 1877, and takes its role in the community seriously.

■ Antiques

Reminiscence Antiques Mall, on Garrett Highway (US 219) south of Accident (☎ 301-746-6280), carries a wide range of antiques and collectibles, including glassware, books, tools, furniture, quilts and baskets. The mall is open Monday through Thursday, 9-5; Friday and Saturday, 9-7; Sunday, 11-4. About three miles north of the mall, **Crabapple Cottage** (no phone) carries collectibles and crafts.

Six miles south of Deep Creek Lake, near Oakland, you will find the **Western Maryland Antique Market and Country Store** (no phone). It's on Route 219 and is open Friday-Sunday, 9-5. Also south of Deep Creek off Route 219 is **Mt. Panax Antiques** (☎ 301-334-9249), featuring furniture, fine glassware, tools and a variety of other collectibles. From Route 219, two miles south of Oakland, go left on Jasper Riley Rd. for a bit over a mile; the store is the left. Open Monday-Saturday, 10-5.

Events

JULY: On the second weekend of July, craftsmen gather for a show at **Penn Alps**, Thursday through Sunday. This is a good opportunity to see the work of those cottage craftsmen who do not have shops of studios open to the public. ☎ 301-895-3332, fax 895-4665, www.spruceforest.org, e-mail tmorgan@spruceforest.org.

MID-OCTOBER: Autumn Glory Festival, in Oakland, includes music, parades and crafts, as well as the state's banjo and fiddle championships; ☎ 301-387-4386, www.garrettchamber.org.

Sightseeing

■ Museums & Historic Sites

Stanton's Mill and **Casselman River Bridge State Park**, east of Grantsville on US 40-Alt, lie on either side of the Penn Alps and Spruce Forest Artisan Village complex. Stanton's Mill dates from 1797, one of the area's oldest grist mills. Casselman River Stone Bridge was built over the Casselman River in 1813 as a part of the National Road project. At the time of its building, it was the largest single span arch bridge of its kind (80 feet), built bigger and higher than it needed to be, it is said, in hopes that the anticipated C&O Canal might use the Casselman River. It was in regular use until 1933 and is now preserved in a State Park with a picnic area.

The **Drane House** is a 1797 log farmhouse, the oldest building in the town of **Accident**, about five miles north of Deep Creek Lake. It sits amid smooth green fields of a farming valley, one of the area's few remaining original plantation houses. Even if it's not open the day you visit, you can look into the large windows to see the downstairs. One end of the house is dominated by a stone fireplace chimney. Just after the well-marked turn-off from US 219 is a picnic site by a pond. To arrange a free visit, call the town hall, ☎ 301-746-6346 on Monday, Wednesday or Friday.

Oakland is the commercial center of the southern part of the county, as well as its county seat. All that's left of Oakland's once grand hotel, a resort popular with presidents and other luminaries, is its gazebo, which was recently restored and stands beside the **Garrett County Historical Museum**, 107 South Second St. (☎ 301-334-3226). We are especially fond of this sort of community attic (which we will prudently resist calling the Garrett garret), where there are so many clues to the history and character of a place. This museum is much larger than it looks, one room leading to the next as you move through the county's history. You'll find old photographs, remembrances and artifacts of the Civil and later wars (including material on the battleship USS *Garrett County*), Native American artifacts dating from the Archaic period, folk art portraits, china dolls, coal mine tools, the wall of an Amish barn with Civil War inscriptions, and a variety of interesting household equipment and furnishings. Admission is free (although, like any museum, they welcome your contribution) and hours are Monday through Saturday, 1-4 pm.

So many presidents visited the area's resorts that **St. Matthew's Church** was nicknamed "The Church of Presidents." The 1884 stone church stands opposite the Victorian brick **B&O Railroad Station**, opened to serve those arriving at the area resorts via the main line of the B&O Railroad. This elegant building is under restoration, and its original lights and domed ceiling were discovered intact behind a later drop ceiling.

Oakland's historic railroad station.

OAKLAND'S HISTORIC TRAILS

Oakland's location as the transportation center of the region dates to prehistoric times, when three major Native American trails crossed there, at its springs. The **Seneca Trail** ran north-south, along the route followed today by US 219. A trail from the west, known as the **Glades Path**, ended in Oakland, where it intersected with the other two. From the southeast came the **Warrior Path**, which European settlers followed and made the main access to the area, known as the **McCullough Pack Horse Path**. George Washington followed it in 1748.

The town of **Deer Park** was once a thriving summer resort for the rich and famous, with grand summer homes clustered around the **Deer Park Hotel**. Follow Deer Park Hotel Rd. south from Route 135 to the site of the exclusive hotel, built in 1783 by the B&O Railroad. In the streets around it still stand the Victorian "cottages" including the **Cleveland Cottage**, where President Grover Cleveland honeymooned in July of 1886.

Farther east, Route 135 winds and climbs through scenic countryside, passing the unique **Our Father's House Log Church**, on the left. One of the country's last remaining log churches still in use, it is a mission, where Episcopal services are held regularly in the summer.

Where to Stay

ACCOMMODATIONS PRICE KEY
Rates are per room, per night, double occupancy.
$ . . . . Under $50
$$ . . . . $50 to $100
$$$ . . . . $101 to $175
$$$$ . . . . $176 and up

■ In the North

 Walnut Ridge B&B is a charming and comfortable B&B right off I-68 at Grantsville and convenient to Caselman State Park and Spruce Forest Artisan Village. Guests can relax in the wood-fired hot tub and stroll in the theme gardens. Walnut Ridge also offers special quilting weekends that include lodging, dining and quilting lessons. 92 Main Street, Grantsville, MD 21536, ☎ 301-895-4248, 888-419-2568, www.bbonline.com/md/walnutridge, e-mail walnutridge@usa.net. $$-$$$

Elliott House Victorian Inn, at Penn Alps, on US 40-Alt, is a beautifully restored Victorian home. Each guest room has a large private bath with tub or shower, telephone, TV and VCR, both hidden away out of sight. Details such as handmade quilts by the Yoder family, locally crafted and original antique furniture, lace shower curtains and a stocked refrigerator for guests' use set it apart from the ordinary B&B. Which it is not, since they do not serve breakfast. Breakfast is available directly across the street at Penn Alps, where three meals are served daily at very reasonable prices. Three cottages, each sleeping up to six persons, overlook the Casselman River across a garden. Cottages have both tea and coffee pots. 146 Casselman Rd., Grantsville, MD 21536, ☎ 301-895-4250, 800-272-4090, www.elliotthouse.com. $$-$$$ (most rooms $$)

Streams and Dreams is a B&B at Hoyes Landing that specializes in fishing; the owners are fanatic fishermen and good guides and teachers as well. Inn guests can book the whole package of lodging and guided fishing trip with instruction, with fishing in their private pond as a bonus. They are at 8214 Oakland-Sang Rd., Oakland, MD 21550, ☎ 301-387-6881, 301-3-TROUT-1, www.streams-and-dreams.net, e-mail Fishing4U2@Juno.com. $$

Hidden in the middle of the Savage River State Forest on 42 private acres, **Savage River Lodge** is a real mountain get-away. Eighteen brand new luxury log cabins and an expansive log lodge bring you close to nature. If TV is important, don't come. There are none here. But if proximity to nature, quiet and time to recover your sense of perspective are important, this is your haven. Cabins are furnished with comfortable queen-sized beds and sitting rooms with overstuffed furniture and gas fireplaces. Breakfast is included in the rates and they have a fine dining restaurant in the lodge. The wraparound deck with big porch furniture is a good place to enjoy the woods or watch deer. It's off I-68 at the Finzell exit (#29), near the Pennsylvania line, west of Frostburg. Go right on Beall School Rd. for one mile to a T intersection, then turn right onto Old Frostburg Rd. In just .1 mile at a Y intersection, bear to the left onto Frostburg Rd., and proceed 2.6 miles to a farm lane. Turn right onto a gravel road that leads to the lodge, which is about a mile. PO Box 655, Grantsville, MD 21536, ☎ 301-689-3200, www.savageriverlodge.com. $$$$

■ Near Deep Creek Lake

Most people come to stay for a week or two in the many rental condos and cottages around the lake. Cabins are fully booked on weekends, even in the winter and you must book by the week in summer, when rates are $2,000 to $5,000 a week. Rentals are from Saturday to Saturday, but things are a lot more flexible after Labor Day, when the weather is still warm. During mid-week, with all the kids back in school, lake traffic is minimal. Railey has several hundred homes of varying sizes to rent, ☎ 800-846-7368, www.deepcreek.com.

Carmel Cove sits above a deep cove – the largest no-wake cove on the lake – reached by a 200-yard access path. At the shore are canoes and a paddle-boat for guest use. Fishing equipment, flotation vests and mountain bikes are also available for guests. The large and comfortably furnished common room has magazines, games and complimentary wine and cheese while guests browse the menu collection from local restaurants. The inn was built in 1945 as a retreat for Carmelite brothers and has been nicely converted into a comfortable upscale lodging. Rooms are individually decorated, with queen-size beds, phones, private baths and individually controlled heat. Three premier rooms have whirlpool tubs and either a fireplace or a big deck. The hearty breakfasts are another reason to stay. Rates are $100 weekdays; $120 Friday-Sunday and holidays for the standard rooms; $20 and $40 higher respectively for the deluxe and premier rooms. From Route 219, take Glendale Rd. (Route 22) east. After crossing the Glendale Bridge keep to the right and go one mile to Carmel Cove (the name of the residential community) on the left. Turn into the road and bear left. PO Box 644, Oakland, MD 21550, ☎ 301-387-0067.

Point View Inn has motel-style rooms at $75 on week nights, $85 on weekends, plus two efficiency suites. All rooms include dock space. The inn sits overlooking the lake and has its own restaurant and lounge, The Boardwalk, with lake views. Deep Creek Drive, McHenry, MD 21541, ☎ 301-387-5555.

Oak & Apple B&B has a total of four rooms; the two third-floor rooms share a bath, but the second floor rooms have private baths. The congenial innkeeper prepares an upscale continental breakfast that includes fresh homemade breads, muffins and fresh fruit. The building is a large, comfortable 1915 family home on an elegant tree-shaded street of fine homes. Guests share the porches, enclosed sunporch, and parlor with fireplace. It's only one block from Third Street (US 219, and Oakland's main street); take East Crook Street north a block to find 208 North Second Street, Oakland, MD 21550, ☎ 301-334-9265, www.oakandapple.com, e-mail oakapplebbil2.genet.net. $$-$$$ (most rooms $$)

Deer Park Inn is a fine B&B in the Pennington Cottage of the former Grand Deer Park Hotel, long since destroyed. The cottage has intimate Victorian elegance and the three guest rooms have fireplaces and share the wrap-around porches and hot tub. They serve a full breakfast and there is a fine restaurant on premises. Bicycles are available for use by guests. 65 Hotel Rd., Deer Park, MD 21550, ☎ 301-334-2308, www.geocities.com/Area51/Keep/1118. $$$

■ Camping

New Germany State Park has camping in an "improved area" where 39 sites have level pads at $12 a night, with showers and other facilities. Sites are reservable from Memorial Day to Labor Day at an added fee of $8 per day (for a total of $20); ☎ 888-432-2267.

Unimproved sites at **Big Run** are not reservable, available on a first-come basis at a nightly fee of $8. Facilities for the 30 sites include outhouses and water from hydrants. One of the three campsite loops is on the water, past the day-use area.

Scattered through **Savage River State Forest** are primitive sites where you can have campfires (except in high hazard drought conditions, which the ranger will tell you of when you register). Register for these sites at the park headquarters, Big Run or BJ's store, on Savage River Rd., a half-mile from Big Run. The fee is $5 a night; sites are located along Big Run Rd., Western Port Rd., with some off-road backpacker sites. A number of these sites are along New Germany Rd., between the park headquarters and Savage River Rd., all but one (#40) set well back from the road. Site #40 has a shelter over its table, #41 is beside a brook, and all are in deeply shaded woods.

AUTHOR TIP

*Campers will appreciate the all-state **park reservations system**, which is available 24 hours a day at ☎ 888-432-2267.*

Herrington Manor State Park has a campground and log cabins complete with fireplaces and wood piles. But don't believe the sign at the park entrance that says "Hospitality Begins Here"; we finally gave up after a long wait for the receptionist to acknowledge our presence as she chatted on the phone. The cabins are pleasant, clean rooms with good mattresses (linen and blankets are provided). In this park they have a fully equipped kitchen, dining/living area and a porch. They heat with electric units and have woodburning fireplace inserts. The park has boating, swimming and fishing, but no camping. Rates for cabins are $75 a night for two persons ($375 per week) plus $10 a night for each two additional people. Route 5, Box 122, Oakland, MD 21550, ☎ 301-334-9180, reservations ☎ 888-432-2267.

Swallow Falls State Park adjoins Herrington, with camping in 65 attractive wooded sites that are moderately well spaced. On weekends unserviced sites are $15 a night, electric-serviced sites are $20 and fully equipped sites cost $30. There are three of these and they include tent, lantern, stove and instructions on how to camp if you need it. During the week all sites are $4 lower, except full-service sites. Weekday rates are half-price for seniors. Reservations are taken and camping is open April through mid-December. Contact information is the same as for Herrington Manor, above. Route 5, Box 122, Oakland, MD 21550, ☎ 301-334-9180.

Deep Creek State Park has 112 campsites at Meadow Mountain Campground and there are two mini-cabins. Several of the sites have electric hookups. Activities include swimming, boating, fishing, ball fields, hiking and a playground. Pets are allowed in designated spaces. The park is at 898 State Park Rd., Swanton, MD 21561, ☎ 301-387-5563, fax 301-387-4462, www.dnr.state.md.us/publiclands/western/deepcreeklake.html.

Garrett County

AUTHOR TIP *Throughout the state parks and forests there is one phone number to alert authorities of suspicious activity or crime. If you see something that's not right, call ☎ 800-825-7275.*

FORGET SOMETHING?

Deep Creek Outfitters at 1899 Deep Creek Drive in McHenry, ☎ 301-387-6977, has camping gear for sale in case you forgot that vital piece. They are on the shore of the lake at Marsh Run Cove on the northernmost arm of the lake. It runs parallel to Route 219.

Where to Eat

DINING PRICE KEY
The price key indicates the cost of *most* dinner entrées on a restaurant's regular and daily special menu.

$	Most under $10
$$	$10 to $20
$$$	Over $30

■ In the North

Penn Alps Restaurant, started life as an "Ordinary," a stop on the stage coach run in the days when this was the Western frontier and westward-bound settlers poured through here. Today it is an attractive restaurant serving good family fare at reasonable prices. Using local produce and locally made sausages and meats, they are known for their high quality. The Penn Alps Special is a Yoder smoked sausage served with dried corn and Dutch fries, but they also have honey-fried chicken, roast pork with sauerkraut and baked boneless cod, all priced under $10. Sandwiches and a light-option menu of six attractive offerings are less expensive. On Friday and Saturday evenings there is prime rib and a steamed shrimp buffet; brunch is served on Saturday and Sunday. Penn Alps is on US 40-Alt, a half-mile east of Grantsville, next to Spruce Forest Artisan Village. ☎ 301-895-5985. Memorial Day through October, hours are Monday-Saturday, 7 am-8 pm; Sunday, 7-3. From November-May, they open Monday-Thursday, 7-7; Friday & Saturday, 7-8; Sunday, 7-3. Closed Christmas and New Year's Day.

Grantsville Market, at 168 Main St. in Grantsville (☎ 301-895-5574) has a deli counter and tiny café overlooking the National Road and the old buildings of the historic little farming community. Enter this bright, clean little lunch-stop through the store, and choose from homemade soups, chili, sandwiches or the daily special, which may be hot turkey with mashed potatoes and coleslaw for $4.95.

Also in Grantsville, be sure to stop in at **Yoder Country Market**, which, among other things, features the products of the Mennonite Yoder family, including their wonderful meat products like garlic bologna, sausages, canned and processed meats, smoked hams and scrapple. They also have fresh baked breads, jellies and all sorts of other things. They're on Route 669, Grantsville, MD 21536, ☎ 301-321-5148 or 895-5148. Open Monday-Saturday, 8-6.

■ Near Deep Creek Lake

McClives, on Deep Creek Drive (Route 219) at the lake, is open for dinner daily, lunch Friday and Saturday. They serve a varied menu of pasta dishes and specials, such as scallops and shrimp on a bed of spinach, chicken Marsala, and chicken breast with rosemary. Look for their "double dinner deal," Sunday-Tuesday. They also have wine-tasting dinners. ☎ 301-387-6172.

The Point View Inn is on US 219, with an informal air but a sophisticated menu of well-prepared choices. Look for Deep Creek wines at $15 a bottle for an Artisan Red. Most entrées are $12 to $16. The salmon is perfectly cooked after being marinated in pineapple and soy sauce. Chicken is served with a delicately flavored crabmeat filling. Presentation details are nice: a vegetable medley arrives in half a baby summer squash. The inn serves three meals daily, except in winter when breakfast is served on weekends only. Deep Creek Drive, McHenry, ☎ 301-387-5555.

Carmel Cove, see *Where to Stay* above, will serve breakfast to non-guests if reservations are made the previous evening.

Deer Park Inn, off Route 135 in Deer Park, east of Oakland, serves innovative New American cuisine, with dishes such as saffron linguine with sautéed scallops and roasted peppers, risotto with porcini and forest mushrooms or peppered filet of beef with green peppercorn sauce. Most entrées are in the $17 range. Reservations are a must. 65 Hotel Rd., Deer Park 21550, ☎ 301-334-2308, www.geocities.com/Area51/Keep/1118.

AUTHOR TIP

Most lakeside pubs and restaurants in this area have their own dock, so patrons can also arrive by boat.

Canoe on the Run Café, on Route 219 next to the Visitors Center, is a coffee house serving soups, sandwiches and salads, all made there. Salads range from a chicken or portobello Caesar to baby spinach with strawberries, walnuts and blue cheese ($5-$6). Special sandwiches include portobello mushroom with roasted red peppers, havarti and spring greens and roast beef with baby Swiss cheese, red onion, romaine and horseradish (most under $5). Mini sandwiches, served on a French roll with your choice of meat and cheese, are about $2 and three-bean chili is $3.25. Canoe also serves a limited breakfast menu with scrambled eggs and bakery goods. On Route 219 on the north end of the lake, ☎ 301-387-5933, it's open every day for breakfast, lunch and dinner.

Arrowhead Deli is open 24 hours (note that the doors open backwards, so if you're not careful, you'll get whapped by someone leaving as you enter). The deli counter has a good variety of hot and cold foods for picnics, trail lunches or a whole dinner to serve in your condo or campsite. Prices are modest: $2.99 for a sandwich enclosing a giant slab of fish, 50¢ for a fat cookie. It's on Route 219 on the other side of the street from the Visitor Center at the north end of the lake near Wisp.

Deep Creek Brewing Company, opposite Arrowhead, is a good place for casual dining. Among their brews are Deep Creek Gold and Youghiogheny Red ales, or you can taste several in the six-brew sampler. They serve good sandwiches ($6-$7) and dinners (entrées $11-$17) – steak, fresh catch special daily – and they are known for their onion soup. On Sunday, when beer cannot be served in the county, the brewery is open for food only. Indoor and outdoor seating is available. Open Monday-Thursday, 11:30-10; Friday-Saturday, 11:30-11; Sunday, 11:30-9. The Brewery is located just behind the Deep Creek Visitor Center on Route 219 near Sang Rd. and Wisp Ski Area on the north end of the lake; ☎ 301-387-2182, www.deepcreekbrewing.com.

Just a short way outside of Oakland, the **Cornish Manor Restaurant** is one of the county's finest dining places. Founded more than 40 years ago in an old mansion dating from 1868, it has new owners – Christiane and Fred Bergheim – who have breathed new life into the world of local dining. Some of the offerings are grilled tuna in citrus beurre blanc, chicken Chesapeake (stuffed with crab), escalope de veau Romanichel (stuffed with prosciutto, spinach, and Swiss and goat cheeses) and black angus filet mignon served in three styles, one with crabmeat. Prices range from $12.50 to $24.50, with most $17-20. Good food, colorful and eclectic decor and friendly and charming hosts make it a complete experience. The Bergheims also operate a small French bakery, which supplies the restaurant with its breads and pastries. If you order in advance (by 1 pm Friday for Saturday delivery, or by 1 pm Saturday for Sunday orders), you can have **French Bakery By Boat** deliver fresh breads, croissants, muffins, quiches, and right to your dock on weekends. Just give them your dock and phone numbers. From Route 219 in Oakland (Third Street), take Memorial Drive (first traffic light). The restaurant is about a half-mile on the left, sitting back from the road; ☎ 301-334-6499, fax 334-7848.

Western Canal Country

The Chesapeake and Ohio Canal borders the Potomac River through central Maryland, providing a corridor for recreation as well as a historic link that ties the region together. Two interesting cities with rich histories provide the area with focal points at either end. Cumberland, to the west, is filled with elegant homes of the late Victorian era, when the town boomed with rail and mining commerce. Stately Hagerstown will surprise you with its abundance of arts and culture, which far outweigh its modest size.

This is agricultural land, dotted with farms, their houses and barns sitting alone among the fields, approached by lanes through grand allées.

Geography & History

The Potomac River swings northward at Cumberland, narrowing the state of Maryland to only a few miles, and even farther north at Hancock, where the state is a mere 1.6 land-miles wide (two miles if you count the river, which belongs to Maryland). West of this

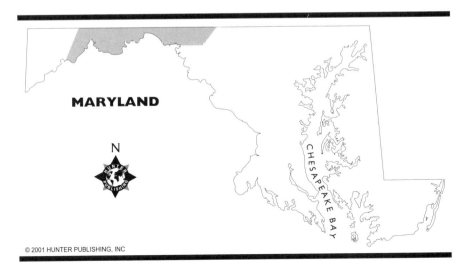

MARYLAND

N

CHESAPEAKE BAY

waistline in its hour-glass figure is a land many eastern Marylanders have never visited. Its flavor is as different from the area around the Chesapeake as its topography, which leaves the flat coastal plains behind. Roads climb steeply from the gouges made by fast-flowing rivers, swollen in the spring with melting snow from the state's western mountains.

Two great early thoroughfares, both dreams of George Washington, pass through this narrow waistline of Maryland: the **C&O Canal** and the **National Road**. Both of these, together with the railroad, fed settlers west into the Ohio Valley and the product of the settler's labor east to the markets of the growing country.

■ The National Road

More than any other state through which it passes, Maryland can lay claim to the National Road, for it began here, in Cumberland, in 1808, moving east and west simultaneously. The National Road was the first federally funded highway, and its Mile One marker is in the pavement in front of the newly restored railway station. Much of its route parallels old US Route 40 and the interstate.

The road east of Cumberland was not part of the original National Road legislation, but was patched together into the system by connecting and upgrading several older roads leading from the settlement to Baltimore. The five-arch Wilson Bridge (1819) was renovated with money originally earmarked for its demolition.

RECOMMENDED READING: *Look for* **A Guide to the National Road**, *edited by Karl Raitz, Johns Hopkins University Press, Baltimore, 1996.*

■ The C&O Canal

George Washington became aide-de-camp to General Braddock in Cumberland on May 10, 1755, and in 1758 he was back. Fort Cumberland was Washington's first military command, and from the first, he was a strong advocate of building a canal to connect it with the seacoast ports. The entire C&O Canal, from Washington to Cumberland, was built between 1828 and 1850, at a cost of $11 million. In all, there were eight dams along the Potomac, which the canal borders, to water the canal. These provided the water reserve necessary to keep the locks filled.

A surprising percentage of the canal's structural elements are still intact, including 10 of its 11 aqueducts, over which the canal crossed tributary rivers as they joined the Potomac. These, along with its locks and tunnels, make it the country's most intact example from the great canal era. It was in use until two major floods in 1924 destroyed segments of it. In 1971, its

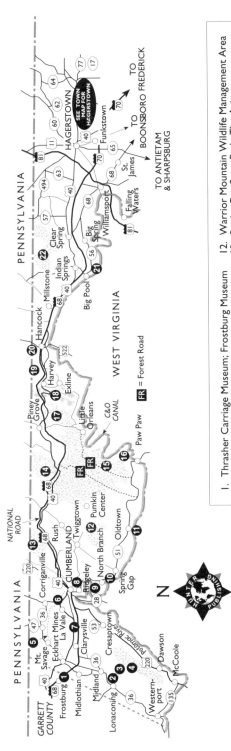

Western Canal Country

1. Thrasher Carriage Museum; Frostburg Museum
2. Lonaconing Iron Furnace
3. Dans Mountain State Park
4. Dan's Mountain Wildlife Management Area
5. Western Maryland Scenic Train Ride
6. Cumberland Narrows
7. Tollgate House
8. History House
9. Evitts Creek Aqueduct
10. 1850 Lock House; C&O Canal Boat
11. Thomas Cresap House Museum
12. Warrior Mountain Wildlife Management Area
13. Rocky Gap State Park; The Aviary
14. Bill Meyer Wildlife Management Area
15. C&O Canal National Historical Park
16. The Paw Paw Tunnel
17. Belle Grove Wildlife Management Area
18. Sideling Hill Wildlife Management Area
19. Sideling Cut Exhibit Center
20. Hancock Historical Museum
21. Fort Frederick State Park / Fort Frederick
22. Indian Springs Wildlife Management Area

Western Canal Country

entire 184½-mile length was designated a National Park. This secured its future as a historic and recreational corridor between urban Washington and the mountains of Western Maryland.

AUTHOR TIP

The best map of the canal and towpath is inside the free brochure given out by the National Park Service. It shows locks, aqueducts, camping areas and boat launches. You can find these at any park headquarters on the canal and in most visitor centers near the canal.

The race between the C&O Canal and the B&O Railroad makes some of the area's most colorful history. Both began in 1828, but the rail line reached Cumberland eight years earlier, and had continued over the mountains to Chicago before the canal reached the city. By then the canal was already obsolete, and the final years of its construction were costly beyond its investor's wildest nightmares. The 3,118-foot Paw Paw tunnel alone took 12 years to complete.

The canal's major cargo was fine anthracite coal from the George's Creek Mine, nine miles from Cumberland. It was brought by a short line railroad to Cumberland, where it was dumped into boats from the rail bridge. The high-grade anthracite was bound for ships in Baltimore, and subsequently to fire the mills of the Industrial Revolution in New England. Grain, farm produce, lumber and building stone were all carried on the boats; the Seneca Sandstone for the towers of the Smithsonian building were quarried within sight of the canal and carried to Washington on its waters. For historic sites by the canal, see *Along the C&O Canal*, page 89.

■ The Civil War

The Civil War was literally fought in the streets of Hagerstown, along the National Road, which is now Washington St. (Remember that Antietam Battlefield is only 10 miles away.) But like Frederick, Hagerstown was spared the torching that destroyed many other towns, because it was able to raise the ransom money demanded by Jubal Early in his 1864 advance toward Washington.

This being border country, the Civil War was a very sensitive issue, with neighbors supporting opposite sides. So sensitive it was, in fact, that not a single mention of it is made in Hagerstown's city minutes – only one reference to sending a doctor "to our boys in the wilderness." Farther west, the town of Hancock (named for a ferryman – not the patriot) was placed under siege by Stonewall Jackson and 8,500 Confederates on January 5, 1862, undergoing bombardment and heavy destruction from the hills across the river in West Virginia.

Today the region is known as the crossroads of the Civil War, 45 minutes or less from many of the major battlefields, including Gettysburg and Antietam. Throughout the area you will see historic markers describing events in the Civil War.

It was a chaotic time for the canal, which both sides recognized as a vital transportation link to prevent Washington DC from being cut off from the rest of the Union. Throughout the war, the Union struggled to keep the canal open, while Confederate parties tried equally hard to close it by blowing up the aqueducts. But the granite structures were well-built, and the raiding parties never succeeded in destroying one. But Mosby's Raiders damaged one, and in 1862 they did succeed in blowing up Lock 28.

WILSON BRIDGE

About 9½ miles west of Hagerstown on US 40, look for a narrow lane that leaves the road to the right, just before crossing a bridge. Beside the new bridge is one of the area's several old stone arched bridges, Wilson Bridge. There is room to park by the river below the new bridge.

Getting Here & Getting Around

The area is easy to reach from east or west, since interstate highways run through its entire length. Approaching from the east, **I-70** goes to Hancock, from which **I-68** continues west. Old **US 40**, the **National Road**, parallels in a meandering sort of way, weaving back and forth under the highway. Unnumbered local roads, some of them unpaved forest roads through the large Green Ridge State Forest, connect this corridor to the canal and the Potomac. The river makes a long series of sweeping bends that make the state boundary with West Virginia look as though it had been drawn around someone's outstretched fingers.

*Note that the interstate highway traversing Maryland changes number in Hancock. Here, **I-70** leaves Maryland and heads north into Pennsylvania. **I-68** joins it at Maryland's Exit 1, and continues west to the West Virginia border; the I-68 exit number at Hancock is **82**, and the numbers descend as they move west.*

In the east, just southwest of Hagerstown, I-70 crosses **I-81**, which passes through this narrow strip of Maryland on its way between Pennsylvania and West Virginia. At no point in this entire region are you very far from either state.

In addition to its highway access, Hagerstown is served by US Airways Express at the **Hagerstown Regional Airport**, 18434 Showalter Rd.; reservations, ☎ 800-428-4322.

Hagerstown is neatly laid out with quadrant designations, so you can tell at least which side of town an address is on. You can often tell which quadrant you are in by reading the street signs.

Information Sources

 A **Tourist Information Center** is located on I-70 as you enter Hagerstown; another is on the main square. It is the Washington County-Hagerstown Convention and Visitors Center, 16 Public Square, Hagerstown, MD 21740, ☎ 301-791-3246, www.marylandmemories.org. This center is well stocked with material on the whole area, and it's close to a nice café, 'Round the Square (see *Where to Eat*).

The **C&O Canal National Park** has a Visitors Center in Williamsport's Cushwa Warehouse, overlooking the rewatered canal basin. It is open daily, or Wednesday through Sunday in winter; ☎ 301-223-6447. The National Park's Hancock Visitors Center, at 326 East Main St. in Hancock, has canal information, a good selection of books, and some additional tourist information. It is open daily June through August, Friday through Tuesday in the spring and fall; ☎ 301-678-5463.

On **I-68**, tourist information centers are at Exit 50, near Rocky Gap, and at the visitor center for the Sideling Cut, which we feel is well worth the stop if only to see the cut through thousands of years of earth history. The **Sideling Cut Center** is open daily from 8:30-6; admission to the center and grounds is free.

FOR READERS: *The Book Center, at 15 North Center St. in downtown Cumberland, has a good selection of local and regional books, especially ones pertaining to the railroad;* ☎ *301-722-8226.*

For Allegany County information, contact the **Allegany County Visitor's and Convention Bureau**, Western Maryland Station, Mechanic and Harrison Streets, Cumberland, MD 21502, ☎ 301-777-5138, 800-508-4748, www.mdmountainside.com. They share quarters with the National

Park Service on the ground floor of the historic rail station at 13 Canal Street.

Adventures

■ Parks

The **Chesapeake and Ohio Canal National Historic Park** is a rare linear park, protecting and preserving the canal route, its towpath and adjacent structures. Park facilities include visitors centers at Williamsport, Hancock and Cumberland, the restored or stabilized locks and gatehouses, and the well-maintained towpath itself. Some of the most interesting features of the C&O Canal are in this region, where the Potomac – and with it, usually, the canal – loops back and forth in wide bends. Canal access points are well marked on the free national park map, along with campsites, Potomac boat launches, picnic sites and points of interest.

Ranger programs cover the history and natural environment of the corridor. Although it has no formal campgrounds, all along the river are small groups of campsites for those who hike or bike the towpath or canoe the river. The **Visitors Center** in **Williamsport** is at Cushwa Warehouse; ☎ 301-223-6447. The **Hancock Visitors Center** is at 326 East Main Street; ☎ 301-678-5463.

RECOMMENDED READING: *Before touring the C&O Canal sites, you will certainly want to read* **Towns Along the Towpath** *by Kate Mulligan, an engaging travel / history book with details on events, activities, places to stay and sights along the canal. It is available from Wakefield Press, PO Box 23392, Washington, DC 20036, $15 postpaid. If you don't get one before your trip, look for it in the shops at the canal visitors centers.*

Fort Frederick State Park packs a lot of interest into one place. Named for the impressive French and Indian War fort, which has been reclaimed from long years of neglect, the park also provides access to the C&O canal and its towpath, and to the Potomac River. The park charges the standard day admission fee daily in the summer, but only on weekends off-season. To reach the park from US 40, turn south on Route 56, about 4½ miles west of Clear Spring; the turn is signposted to the park. Fort Frederick Park, ☎ 301-842-2155, www.dnr.state.md.us/publiclands/wmrt.html.

Western Canal Country

Rocky Gap State Park is different from many others: highly developed, well manicured, with a luxury hotel and Jack Nicklaus golf course, as well as the expected camping area. Not everyone agrees that the state park system should be in the resort business, but everyone does agree that this is a nice resort. The park has a number of trails as well as a lake with rental boating available. The park visitor center schedules a variety of sports and other activities for guests, using local outfitters and operators, or they will provide information on the operators so you can make your own arrangements directly. The park is at 12500 Pleasant Valley Rd., Flintstone 21530, ☎ 301-777-2139.

AUTHOR TIP *Those interested in **spelunking** should ask directions to a small cave near the park, with tunnels and caverns. It is at Exit 50 off I-68 east of Cumberland.*

Green Ridge State Forest has everything to recommend it. Most of its superlatives stem from its huge tracts of wild land and its designation as a state forest, not a state park. This frees it from the obligatory mowed lawns and developed campgrounds and leaves it for those who prefer to camp in the quiet of the woods. Its excellent schedule of activities is designed for those who enjoy active sports: canoeing, hiking, cycling, and its rangers are well-versed in the nature and history of the area. Most of the area originally belonged to Richard Caton and William Carroll, son-in-law of Charles Carroll of Carrollton (whom you will hear more of in Baltimore and Annapolis). They ran an unsuccessful iron processing operation and timber business. Later the land became the "largest apple orchard in the universe" at the beginning of the 20th century before it, too, failed. From its original 14,000 acres it has now grown to over 40,000 acres. What more can an adventure traveler ask? Perhaps for fishing tips? Check with Mike, one of the rangers at the headquarters, an avid fisherman. Green Ridge State Forest, 28700 Headquarters Drive, NE, Flintstone, MD 21530-9525, ☎ 301-478-3124, TTY 974-3863; or check the DNR's Web site at www.dnr. state.md.us/publiclands/western/greenridge.html.

AUTHOR TIP *Western Maryland is brilliant in the fall, with shades of red, orange and yellow. The display is the equal of any we've seen, even in New England. Although the exact peak may vary from year to year, you can count on the best colors beginning the second week in October.*

Dan's Mountain State Park is a 467-acre park on Dan's Mountain, a 16-mile-long range south of Frostburg. The Park should not be confused with the Dan's Mountain Wildlife Management Area. The Park is a day-use area, with picnic areas, a fishing pond and an Olympic-size pool with lane swimming, diving, wading pool and handicapped-access ramp. These facilities are open Memorial Day to Labor Day from daylight to dusk. From US 40, take Route 36 or 936 south to Lonaconing, then Water Station Run east to the park. PO Box 100, Water Station Run, Lonaconing, ☎ 800-825-PARK (7275).

■ On Foot

Walking & Hiking

 One of the nicest flat walks in the entire Middle Atlantic region is the **towpath** of the **C&O Canal**, discussed in several chapters of this book. Cumberland was its terminus, but it makes a good starting point for walkers, who should expect to spend at least a week walking its full 184½ miles. Both AMTRAK and Greyhound Bus Lines provide return transportation. You can leave a car at either Cumberland or Great Falls, although in either case, you should tell the park ranger. Hancock, west of midway, also has ample parking and a park headquarters to inform.

CAUTION

Along one stretch of the canal, between mileposts 84 and 89 near its midpoint at Williamsport, the towpath has been washed away where it runs along a steep cliff. The detour is well marked, but adds nearly five miles to the towpath's 184½ miles. Occasional other closures are always bypassed by well-marked detours.

The National Park Service conducts lively **Paw Paw Tunnel Tours** on Friday, Saturday and Sunday in July and August, Saturday and Sunday only in spring and fall. You can make a circle hike through the tunnel, returning over the top via a two-mile trail that leaves the canal to the right beyond the upper (western) end. It's steep climbing, but the view from the top is worth it.

The 40,000-acre **Green Ridge State Forest** provides some of the best hiking in the area. This is the second largest of Maryland's state forests, and it essentially runs from the Pennsylvania border to the C&O Canal, about 24 miles. On the north, the **Pine Lick Blue Trail** links up with the Buchanan State Forest Trail in Bedford County Pennsylvania and descends six miles through Pine Lick Hollow to the Park headquarters near 15 Mile Creek Rd. From the headquarters, **The Long Pond Red Trail** wanders east, crossing Dug Hill Rd. twice prior to turning south. After its curve, it crosses Oldtown Orleans Rd. before intersecting with the C&O Canal Towpath close to Lock 58, west of Little Orleans.

From the headquarters, another trail that has been divided into two parts to create shorter hikes. At the headquarters, pick up the **Deep Run/Big Run Green Trail**, a seven-mile segment that runs parallel to and east of Green Ridge Rd. It ends at Kirk Rd. From that end point, **Log Roll Orange Trail** begins. This four-mile segment follows Kirk Rd. west and crosses Green Ridge Rd. before turning south, crossing Ackhorse Rd. It then crosses Green Ridge Rd. again, turns south and crosses Route 51 just west of Dailey Rd., ending at the C&O Canal Towpath at Lock 67.

RECOMMENDED READING: *The Green Ridge is a virtually unknown historical element. For the inside story of the people, the land and the development, take a look at* **The Land of the Living**, *by John Marsh, published by Allegany County Historical Society, 218 Washington Street, Cumberland, MD 21502,* ☎ *301-777-8678. At $49.95, the book is one you might prefer to consult in the Cumberland Library.*

As you must have figured out by this point, these Green Ridge Trails are linear, so you will have to arrange shuttles or double back. Another option is to combine these trails with the towpath trail to create a circular path. From the State Forest Headquarters to the C&O via the Deep Run and Log Roll Trails is about 11 miles. The Canal Towpath (which passes through the Paw Paw Tunnel) is about 18 miles from Lock 67 to Lock 58 and the Long Pond Trail back to the headquarters is seven miles, so plan accordingly. There are approximately 100 primitive campsites in the State Forest and a plan of them is available at the headquarters.

Aside from the towpath portion, these trails pass through oak and hickory forests over terrain that is mountainous and at times rocky and rough. They follow hilltop ridges and stream valleys. There are 59 species of trees in the forest, including five species of maples, nine coniferous species, seven types of oaks, as well as elm, walnut, poplar, aspen, sycamore, persimmon, ash, black cherry and yellow birch. Trails require fording of streams and hikers should be prepared with additional dry foot gear.

Tree-lovers will appreciate the short (about a quarter-mile) **Arboretum Trail** from the Green Ridge State Forest headquarters office, near the Route 40/I-68 intersection, to a scenic overlook. Trees are labeled to help you identify those you will see throughout the state forest.

AUTHOR TIP

*A rough map of the trails is available in a color-coded version at the headquarters, but they also have topo maps for sale, a good buy for safety. The trails in the park are blazed **white**, but they are marked periodically with **yellow** milepost markers. The posts have two numbers on them, the top one showing the number of miles already traveled and the bottom the number of miles to the end of that trail. The numbers are painted in a color that corresponds to the trail color. Thus, a post with green marker number with a five on top and three on bottom means that you are on the Deep Run / Big Run Trail and have traveled five miles with three to go.*

To get to the State Forest headquarters, take Exit 64 from I-68. It is about eight miles east of Flintstone. Green Ridge State Forest, 28700 Headquarters Drive, NE, Flintstone, MD 21530-9525, ☎ 301-478-3124, TTY 974-3863, www.gacc.com/dnr. For information on the C&O Canal and camping opportunities in this section, contact C&O Canal National Historical Park, PO Box 4, Sharpsburg, MD 21782, ☎ 301-739-4200. For the Pennsylvania end of the trail: Buchanan State Forest, Bureau of Forestry, RR 2, Box 3, McConnellsburg, PA 17233, ☎ 717-485-3148. (See *Camping* below for more information).

Close to Green Ridge, so close in fact that they seem almost to be part of it are **Bill Meyer** and **Belle Grove wildlife management areas**, wild areas without the amenities of parks but with trails and old roads for access. These date from the 1920s and '30s, when they were purchased to serve as a breeding place for wild birds, particularly wild turkey. While that function has long since ceased, they still abound with wildlife, especially, as you might you guess, wild turkey. Other bird varieties include grouse, woodcock and a number of songbirds. Mammals range from squirrel and rabbit to white-tailed deer. The is a Wildlife Management Area and not a groomed hiking area so it is best to contact the office for specifics on trails, which cover 1,100 acres of hilly terrain. To go to the Bill Meyer tract office, leave I-68 at Exit 68 and go north to US 40, then west over a mountain. Watch for Mountain Rd. on the left and take it a short distance to the headquarters. Go there also to get information on the Belle Grove area. To go to Belle Grove at Exit 68 off I-68, go south on Orleans Rd. and watch for Watson Rd. on the left (east), which leads to the tract. The Bill Meyer Office can be reached at ☎ 301-478-2525. It is the information center for Bill Meyer WMA, Belle Grove WMA, Dan's Mountain WMA and Warrior Mountain WMA.

Western Canal Country

IF ONLY I'D SAID THAT

"Trees are like people, they reach a certain height when they are young, then they get bigger around as they get older." – F.O. Zumbrun, Forester, DNR, State of Maryland.

Rocky Gap State Park's large lake is surrounded by a five-mile hiker-biker path. You can pick it up near the shore at any point, but be sure to check its condition with the activities office before you take it full-circle. The last time we were there, a section had been closed, but rain had washed away the ink on the paper signs, leaving us to walk the last mile along the lake shore, crawling over and under fallen trees and cutting across the golf course to return. The terrain is fairly level, but the land-scape is surprisingly varied and always scenic as the trail rounds each cove. At the western end of the lake is a side trail, the Canyon Overlook Trail, to an overlook above a deep gorge, an easy walk of about a quarter-mile. More ambitious hikers could follow the **Evitt's Homestead Trail** down into the gorge itself, a steep climb out again, but a lovely, cool place even in the heat of summer. Beyond, **Evitt's Mountain Trail** is a 2½-mile hike, each way, into the canyon and then up to what is believed to be the homesite of the settler that gave his family name to the mountain on the backside of the lake. It's a bit more difficult but does provide a nice experience in these western Maryland woods.

Another short walk is **Touch of Nature Trail**, which provides access to a fishing dock on Lake Habeeb. Evitt's, Canyon Overlook and Touch of Nature are open for hiking in the winter.

AUTHOR TIP

*If you need gear while in the Cumberland area, **Allegany Expeditions** rents backpacks, tents, sleeping bags and most other gear. They also conduct guided wilderness backpacking, canoeing, caving, and rock climbing adventures. On their guided trips they provide all of the equipment needed and tell you what personal things to bring. They are at 10310 Columbus Avenue, NE, Cumberland, ☎ 301-722-5170, 800-819-5170.*

Dan's Mountain Wildlife Recreation Area is not to be confused with Dan's Mountain State Park, just west of it on Water Station Run Rd. in Lonaconing. Both have their own charm, but this one is 9,200 acres of raw wilderness. Named for Colonial hero Daniel Cresap, the mountain range runs generally north-south, parallel to the Allegany County border and Route 220. It is an area known for wild turkey, white-tailed deer and forest songbirds like the scarlet tanager, ovenbird and yellow-throated vireo.

Timber rattlesnakes can be encountered on the trails, especially at Dan's Mountain. Bobcats, black bear and coyotes are occasionally seen. If you see them, stay back and let them walk away.

Most access is from Route 220, which you pick up from Route 40 on the west side of Cumberland. There are access points to the WMA from Rawlings and via Middle Ridge Rd.; look for the signs. On the west side of the WMA, access it from Buskirk Hollow Rd. off Route 36. Information is available from the **Bill Meyer Wildlife Office**, ☎ 301-478-2525.

East of Cumberland is another wildlife management area that is virtually unknown and undeveloped. **Warrior Mountain WMA**, with 4,400 acres of preserved wilderness, is not a place of manicured trails. There are miles of back roads and rough trails to wander. Woods songbirds predominate here with a healthy population of wild turkey and mammalian inhabitants as well. This, like all of the WMA areas, is a hunting ground during the season. At the peak of the mountain there is a cleared power line that permits views over a wide part of the surrounding area. From Exit 62 of I-68 go right onto 15 Mile Creek Rd. and immediately left onto Route 144. Go six miles and turn left onto Town Creek Rd. for 13 miles, taking Oliver Beltz Rd. to a 4-way intersection, where you turn left to the WMA office. For more information call Bill Meyer WMA Office ☎ 301-478-2525.

Walking Tours

Hagerstown has a nice series of brochures linked to their **Hagerstown Downtown Walking Tours**. The **"Little Heiskell"** Downtown Walking Tour features 19 churches, commercial and public buildings and homes in the central district. The county courthouse, which is on the tour, was built in 1873 on the site of an earlier courthouse designed by Benjamin Latrobe in 1816. All of the sites are within three blocks of Public Square.

LITTLE HEISKELL

All around Hagerstown you will see a symbol of a silhouetted figure or the title "Little Heiskell." The figure originated in 1769, when town father Jonathan Hager had a German tinsmith by the name of Heiskell make a weathervane for the new town hall. The result was a figure that represents a Pioneer Ranger, a role that Hager himself played during the French and Indian War. Despite being shot at during the Civil War, Little Heiskell stayed on top of City Hall until he was put in the Hager House Museum in 1935. His replacement is still on City Hall.

Western Canal Country

Downtown Hagerstown

N

TO GETTYSBURG

CHARLES ST

WAYSIDE AVE

N PROSPECT ST

BROADWAY

NORTH ST

BURHANS BLVD

BETHEL ST

N POTOMAC ST

NORTH AVE

MULBERRY ST

CHURCH ST

MCPHERSON ST

PROSPECT ST

JONATHAN ST

RANDOLPH AVE

TO
CLEAR SPRING
& HANCOCK

W FRANKLIN ST

EAST AVE

TO SMITHSBURG

W WASHINGTON ST

E FRANKLIN ST

4

E ANTIETAM ST

3
9

E WASHINGTON ST

S POTOMAC ST

TO
6

WALNUT ST

W BALTIMORE ST

E ANTIETAM ST

CANNON AVE

2

LOCUST ST

TO
7

KEY ST

W LEE ST

E BALTIMORE ST

8

FREDERICK ST

1

SYCAMORE ST

SURREY AVE

RAY ST

MILL ST

VIRGINIA AVE

REYNOLDS AVE

S POTOMAC ST

MEMORIAL BLVD

TO WILLIAMSPORT

5

TO **10**

TO SHARPSBURG

TO BOONSBORO
& HARPERS FERRY

1. City Park; Engine 202 train display	5. Rose Hill Cemetery
2. Hager House	6. Round House Museum
3. Maryland Symphony Orchestra; Maryland Theatre; Washington County Arts Council	7. The Train Room & Museum
4. Miller House	8. Washington County Museum of Fine Arts
	9. Washington County Arts Council Gallery
	10. Washington County Planetarium

The popular **Civil War In Hagerstown** walking tour includes 25 sites of importance during the Civil War. The town was touched by the war as a staging area or target each year from 1861 through 1864. On July 12, 1863 General George Armstrong Custer drove the Confederates out, and Hagerstown was held for a ransom of $20,000 by Confederate General John McCausland, no small threat since he burned Chambersburg, Pennsylvania. The tour starts in Wheaton Park where the Robert Moxley Band played in the 1850s and '60s, travels down North Potomac Street and west on Washington Street, with a few side trips along the way.

THE ROBERT MOXLEY BAND

In the years immediately before the Civil War a band of slaves were formed into the Robert Moxley Band, who gave very popular concerts in Wheaton Park in the northwest corner of Hagerstown. Their military-style music stood them in good stead. When the Federal government began recruiting for the United States Colored Troops in 1863, the slaves were given their freedom in exchange for signing up. For the duration of the war they, and their music, were used as recruiters in the Chesapeake Bay region.

Also interesting is the **Historic Church Walking Tour** of 18 downtown churches. The 1795 **St. John's Evangelical Lutheran Church** is the oldest, while a number date from the 19th century and the early 20th century. Styles include Gothic Revival and Romanesque and various permutations thereof, many reflecting the heavily German backgrounds of their congregants. The small **Asbury United Methodist Church** at 155 Jonathan Street is the oldest black congregation in the city. The present building was built in 1879 and rebuilt after a 1973 fire. Brochures with maps and descriptions of all of the buildings and sites are available at the Visitors Center. Several of these tours overlap, the most notable being the churches. We suggest that if time allows you have all three brochures and integrate them as you go along.

Cumberland is a fascinating place to walk and to examine the architectural heritage of a city whose high point was achieved during the late 19th and early 20th centuries. Most of downtown Cumberland and Washington Street are part of the **Cumberland Historic District** and contain significant architectural examples of the young republic. At the Cumberland Station Visitors Center, pick up the brochure *Looking Through a Window of Time*, one of the finest architectural reviews of any city. In its pages, 30 of the city's finest buildings are described and their architectural importance noted. It's also a good walk because of the hills in town. Other brochures available at the center describe various tours or historical events in the town. *Walking Tour of Historic Downtown Cumberland* concentrates on commercial architecture, particularly along Baltimore Street, Liberty Street and Centre Street. *Cumberland's Victorian Historic District - Wash-*

ington Street describes, building by building, the style and history of every home and public building in the town's finest residential district. Styles range from Greek Revival, Queen Anne and French Second Empire to Colonial Revival and later styles. *Railfans Guide to the Cumberland Area* provides a visual overlook of the impact of railroads on the community and the area. Cumberland Station Visitors Center is at Canal Place, where the railroads, canals and industry all come together in a celebration of the people who made the town.

Little **Frostburg** has a walking tour, fairly short but good exercise because, like your father's fabled walk to school every morning, it is uphill in both directions. This small town was very wealthy for a short time and hasn't destroyed its architectural heritage. The tour takes you past 20 fascinating buildings dating from the mid-19th century to the early 20th. Get the *Historic Frostburg* brochure at the Visitor Information Center in the old Palace Theater at 33 East Main Street, ☎ 301-689-6000.

Mt. Savage, a small town on Route 36 northwest of Cumberland, also has a walking tour. Mt. Savage was once a thriving mining and steel town, the place where the very first railroad rails were made in the United States, in 1844. Iron was mined locally, as was the coal to fire the smelters. There was also a successful brick kiln. From all that success, a number of fine mid-19th-century buildings were created that lie along the tour. Pick up a brochure of the walk at the Cumberland Station Visitor Center or contact **Mt. Savage Historical Society**, ☎ 301-264-3229.

Rock Climbing & Caving

Adventure Sports in Frostburg is an outfitter that conducts rock climbing, rappelling and caving trips in the area. Sites that they use include Rocky Gap State Park, the Narrows and Cooper's Rock State Park. They are at the top of the hill in Frostburg at 113 East Main Street, ☎ 301-689-0345.

■ On Wheels

Bicycling

 The towpath of the **C&O Canal**, discussed in several chapters of this book, is a favorite for cyclists, who usually prefer to follow it downhill from Cumberland to Great Falls, a three-day trip straight through without much side-touring in the towns along the way. Both AMTRAK and Greyhound Bus Lines provide return transportation, but AMTRAK will not carry your bicycle.

Leave a car at either **Cumberland** or **Great Falls**, and tell the park ranger. Hancock also has parking and access a block behind Main Street.

Campsites are spaced along the towpath, marked on the free National Park Service Map. Some B&Bs along the way will meet bikers at points along the canal and return them there the next morning. To plan a B&B trip, begin by calling **The Inn at Walnut Bottom** in Cumberland (☎ 301-777-0003, e-mail iwb@iwbinfo.com; see *Where to Stay*, below). The inn has bicycles for use in the area and can arrange for rental bikes and an outfitter to handle shuttles for towpath trips, so you can begin in Cumberland and bike the entire route without having to return by bicycle or pack it for bus travel. The towpath is a five-minute walk from the inn. **Catoctin Bike Tours** in Thurmont (☎ 800-TOUR-CNO) will provide shuttle service as well.

Hancock is a good place to bike a segment of the towpath trail, and **Pathfinders Canoe and Bicycle Livery** is close by, along the canal at 8 Pennsylvania Avenue, ☎ 301-678-6870, www.corphome.com/pathfinders. Sites readily available from their location are the abandoned remains of a cement factory and a pair of locks in the canal. They also rent some camping equipment and canoes.

Hancock is also on the **Rails to Trails path** that is planned to provide a 315-mile hiker/biker trail from Washington to Pittsburgh. The **Pittsburgh to Cumberland Trail** plans to create a trail link from Pittsburgh Pennsylvania through Frostburg to link up with the C&O Towpath trail at Cumberland and on the Washington. Its other name is the **Allegheny Highlands Trail** and it has branches in both states. Along most of the way it will follow the old B&O Railroad right-of-way; the Maryland section is 22 miles long. For current information on the status of the trail, or to volunteer, contact **Allegheny Highlands Trail Association**, PO Box 28, Cumberland 21501-0028 (no phone).

Just outside Cumberland is **Allegany Bike Works** at 14419 National Highway, LaVale 21502, ☎ 301-729-9708. They not only rent bikes, but also operate bike tours along the C&O Canal towpath and repair bikes, too. If you are interested in a biking/camping trip, contact **Adventure Sports** at the top of the hill in Frostburg, 113 East Main Street, ☎ 301-689-0345, although it's a long way from the towpath. They also do caving and rock climbing and their trips are outfitted and guided.

The **Western Maryland Rail Trail** has its southern terminus at Big Pool Junction, with parking and road access to the trail. From US 40, 4½ miles west of Clear Spring (the spring is down a side street to the south of the main road), go south on Route 56, signposted to Fort Frederick. The trail junction is about two miles on the right. Park across the street from the Post Office. From the other direction, it is about a mile past the entrance to Fort Frederick State Park. The trail, currently about 10 miles of paved route, uses the abandoned Western Maryland railroad right-of-way along the C&O Canal as far as Hancock. This is the only practical way for bicyclists to get through this narrow section of the state because the interstate overlies the bed of old Route 40, the only east-west route through this area. Plans call for an additional 15 miles to be added to the rail trail. Information is available from Fort Frederick Park, ☎ 301-842-2155; their Web site, www.dnr.state.md.us/publiclands/wmrt.html, has an eight-point description of historic highlights along the route.

Fort Frederick State Park provides access to the C&O Canal towpath, but parking is closer and admission is free at the nearby access at the end of McCoy's Ferry Rd., two miles east of the park entrance off Big Pool Rd. (Route 56). Start at Mile 109 at Four Locks and take the trail south to Two Locks. From Two Locks take Dam No. 5 Rd., which swings away from the canal and intersects with Route 56. Take Route 56 north through Big Spring to Four Locks Rd., going right. The whole trip is about nine miles. You can extend this to about 11 miles by staying on the towpath to Gift Rd., a bit over a half-mile from Milepost 104. Take Gift Rd. to Dam No. 5 Rd. and turn right, following the remainder of the directions above. This trip includes part of the secluded towpath and narrow country roads.

Green Ridge State Forest has 11½ miles of mountain bike trails, some on old roads, some woodland trails. They have a map showing these routes at the headquarters near the Route 40/I-68 intersection. To get to the parking area, take Exit 62 from I-68 onto 15 Mile Creek Rd. At the top of the ramp turn right and then left onto Route 144. Go 1.6 miles and turn left onto Williams Rd. for 2½ miles on the blacktop, then left onto Black Sulfur Rd. and right onto Wallizer Rd. Parking is on the left. A map is available, but the following is a rough guide to the trail.

Go to the right for .8 mile to Gordon Rd., which leads left for one mile to a single track on the right. Take the single track across Mertens Avenue in just under a mile, continuing on to Jacobs Rd. Cross Jacobs Rd. and continue 1.4 miles to Troutman Rd., following it 1.4 miles to a single track on the right. Follow it 1.6 miles to Williams Rd., crossing it and continuing on the single track to Black Sulphur Rd., about 1.4 miles. Turn right and follow Black Sulphur Rd. a short way, then left onto a single track that leads back to the beginning. The whole trail is about 11½ miles. A trail map is available at the headquarters.

See *On Foot*, above, for information on **Rocky Gap State Park's Hiker/ Biker Trail**.

AUTHOR TIP

Those traveling with bicycles should consider taking any of the city walking tours noted in On Foot, *above. Armed with those brochures, you can bike the routes instead of walking.*

Driving Tours

Western Maryland has some of the best autumn color in the mid-Atlantic regions and Green Ridge State Forest has outlined a route to help you see it. They have chosen a short **Fall Color Tour** that takes you through some of the best of the region if your time doesn't allow for more exploration. The route takes you from Park headquarters along back roads past some of the best scenic overlooks and through the heart of the State Forest. Follow Maple Leaf signs with their directional arrows. The packet of materials, done by the staff of the State Forest, is a wonderful combination of drawings of the trees and shrubs and written descriptions of the importance of what you see. It's a great example of the interest these rangers and the forest staff have for the lands they protect. Contact them at **Green Ridge State Forest**, 28700 Headquarters Drive NE, Flintstone 21530-9525, ☎ 301-478-3124. Ask for the Green Ridge State Forest Fall Color Tour.

By Train

That Cumberland was an important rail center is clear from the size and prominence of its newly restored railway station. Today it serves as the terminus of a scenic train ride to Frostburg, and on its third track are two restored cabooses. It is the center for the **Railfest**, held each October, when special trains run from Cumberland to Oakland, in Garrett County. The event is held on the weekend closest to the middle of October, starting with special events on Thursday and continuing through the weekend. There are steam excursions to Frostburg, special food events, art exhibits, railroad events and exhibits, foliage excursions to Oakland on Saturday and Sunday, diesel and caboose rides, music and a general rousing good time. Reservations are required for many of the events, especially for the train excursions, so call as early as possible. Excursion fares are $5 adults, $4 under 12. For information and reservations, ☎ 301-759-4400, 800-872-4650 (800-TRAIN-50), www.wmsr.com.

The **Western Maryland Scenic Railroad** excursion from Cumberland to Frostburg begins with a ride through The Narrows, a mile-long gorge, 900 feet deep, between Mount Wills on the right and Mt. Haystack on the left. The track used – that of the Western Maryland Railroad – parallels the National Road and an earlier rail line built in 1844. Along with lovely views across the valley farms, the trip is highlighted by a quick glimpse of the mouth of a cave in which 46 different species of fossils have been found, including some tropical animals. The Homesteaders Curve is a complete horseshoe, just before the track enters the Brush Tunnel though Piney Mountain.

The 1,300-foot difference in altitude between Frostburg and Cumberland makes the route quite steep – a 2.8% grade over the course of the trip. The layover in Frostburg allows time enough to visit the excellent Thrasher Carriage Museum, only $1 when you show your train ticket (see *Historic Sites & Museums*, below). Thursday through Monday, the train is pulled by a steam engine, a 1916 Baldwin locomotive called *Mountain Thunder*; other days by diesel. In addition to their regular runs, they also have Dinner Trains (departing at 6 pm, $47.95) and Mystery Trains (also at 6 pm, $44.95). For the steam train, rates are $16.50 for adults, May-September; $18.50 October-December. For the diesel, $14 and $16 respectively. Rates are lower for seniors (60+) and children (two-12). From May-September, departures are at 11:30 am, steam on Tuesday and Wednesday, diesel

Western Canal Country

Thursday-Sunday. In October, the steam train runs Thursday-Sunday at 11 am and diesel Monday-Wednesday at 11. In November-December, only the steam train runs, and then only on Saturday and Sunday at 11:30 am. Tickets are available at the Cumberland Station; reservations are recommended, and are required for special trips. ☎ 800-TRAIN-50 (800-872-4650), www.wmsr.com.

AUTHOR TIP *Try to get a seat on the right side of the train as you head west out of Cumberland. It has the best views, although you will need to find a seat on the left to see the cave. The guide on the train will give you plenty of warning so you can be close to a left-side window as you pass.*

In autumn the hardwoods forests of western Maryland turn into a blazing canvas of color that is truly spectacular, and one of the best ways to enjoy it is on the train. **Autumn Leaves Specials** run from Hagerstown to Cumberland and from Hagerstown to Thurmont. This is usually on the second weekend of October. The Thurmont trip leaves Hagerstown at 8 am and returns at 6:30 while the Sunday trip to Cumberland leaves at 11:30 am, returning at 6:30 pm. On the Thurmont trip there are side shuttle options to Union Bridge and Highfield (near Penmar). At Cumberland you can extend the trip to Frostburg by buying tickets on the Western Maryland Scenic Railway. Hagerstown-Thurmont fares are $35 adult, $20 child (side trips $10 and $5 respectively); for Hagerstown-Cumberland, $39 adult, $20 child. ☎ 800-TRAIN-50 (800-872-4650), www.wmsr.com.

■ On Water

Canoeing & Kayaking

A pleasant section of the Potomac passes **Fort Frederick State Park**, with a miserable put-in to the west of the park on Licking Creek, just above the point where the creek joins the Potomac. From US 40, *immediately* west of the bridge over Licking Creek, make a left onto Licking Creek Rd. (Ignore the other end of the same road, which leaves US 40 to the north on the east side of the bridge; the two sections don't connect.) You will at once pass under the two bridges carrying lanes of I-70 (this whole area is a bridge-builder's dream). Just before the road crosses the Western Maryland Rail Trail – you can see the sign for it ahead – is an overgrown lane leading down to the left. You can park on the side of the road, carrying kayaks or canoes down this track to a steep riverbank put-in, just to the left of yet another bridge. Plan to use a rope to slide your craft down the bank; this is no place to fall while carrying something awkward. Just be glad you're not taking out here.

After paddling under the rail bridge you will come to the **Licking Creek Aqueduct**, then to the Potomac. A long island cuts off the main river, to your left. About halfway on this six-mile route to the McCoy's Ferry boat ramp, is Fort Frederick State Park. You will see a set of steps up the steep bank. The fort itself is a bit of an uphill hike. McCoy's Ferry is easy to spot, since it has a concrete ramp. Although it's of no help to kayakers, canoeists without two cars for the usual river shuttle (which we call the river shuffle) can carry a bicycle in the canoe and return to pick up the car via the towpath, making the trip into a sort of biathlon. To reach the downstream take-out by car, follow Big Pool Rd. (Route 56) to McCoy's Ferry Rd., two miles east of the Fort Frederick entrance.

There is access to the Potomac at **Hancock**, off Pennsylvania Ave. and, although the river is easy paddling all the way to McCoy's Ferry, it is too close to I-70 for our taste. We'd opt for the shorter trip, even with the slippery put-in at Licking Creek.

KID-FRIENDLY

There are kayaks for rent at Little Tonoloway, at the C&O Canal access on Pennsylvania Ave. in Hancock. A section of the canal is flooded here, providing one of the few places you can paddle in the canal itself. This is a good place for kids to try out kayaking, made even more attractive by the proximity of Barnard's Ice Cream Parlor on the corner.

Western Canal Country

Licking Creek Aqueduct, near Fort Frederick.

Another access to the river is available at **Four Locks** (see *Sightseeing* below and *On Foot* above). The Potomac is dammed from Dam 5, below Two Locks, so the water here is less turbulent than elsewhere, but there are some strong currents. You can canoe or kayak down to Two Locks, about two miles, but plan on paddling back as well unless you have arranged a shuttle.

While paddling the Potomac in this area, be sure to avoid getting close to Dam 5. You don't want to be swept over as happened to one canal boat.

Little Orleans is so little and its few buildings so spread out, that you might not notice it was a town at all. A general store, **Bills's Bar, Beer, Bait and Boats** (☎ 301-478-2701) stands above the Fifteen-Mile Creek access to the Potomac River and the C&O Canal towpath. The store, locally called just "Bill's Place," is a piece of local history, originally sitting on the canal 100 yards away, where it served as a store and warehouse. Today the store is mostly the bar, with a small deli counter and a couple of tables. This is one of the few places close to the canal where you can buy cold drinks and reprovision for a long-distance river trip.

You can also rent canoes, get fishing gear and bait and meet people who live here. Canoe rentals are $20 per day and shuttle service is $10 extra to Paw Paw or Bond's Landing, but be precise about when and where they are to meet you. Bill's is at the canal, Little Orleans, ☎ 301-478-2701. From I-68, take Exit 68 and go south on Orleans Rd. to Little Orleans, then follow the road to the canal.

There are picnic tables between the path and the river here, where Fifteen Mile Creek enters the Potomac. The canal passes over the creek on Milepost 140 Aqueduct. The access is a gentle one for canoes, and has vehicle access for larger boats.

A CEILING COVERED IN MONEY?

You may wonder why the ceiling of the general store in Little Orleans – which most people there call "Bill's Place" – is papered in $1 bills. It's quite simple. If you fear that you might be back sometime and thirsty, but without the dollar for a beer, you can sign your name on a dollar bill and tack it to the ceiling at Bill's. That way, you'll always have a beer waiting for you, even if you're broke. You could call it bar insurance.

Canoes are also available here from **Apple Mountain Canoe Rentals**, which you can contact directly at ☎ 301-478-3421 or through the camp store at Little Orleans Campground (☎ 301-478-2325). To get to Apple Mountain from Exit 68 off I-68, go south on Route 26 for about six miles, passing the left that takes you to the general store and river access and going right at the T. Apple Mountain Canoe rental is just past the campground entrance, as the road begins to climb into Green Ridge State Forest.

Green Ridge State Forest will offer guided overnight canoe trips through reliable local outfitters. Call them at ☎ 301-478-3124 for information about guided canoe trips on the Potomac.

Not all outfitters are created equal. Some ignore a few of the basics, like insurance, and taking good care of their equipment. Always ask what liability insurance an outfitter carries to protect you in case of injury or accident with their equipment. Many will say something like "We're too small an operation to be able to afford liability insurance." On the water, it's better to go with the more professional operators who understand the necessity of protecting their clients.

The section of the Potomac between Oldtown and the point where Town Creek enters the river is very pleasant paddling. The river is wide and placid, with a few sections of riffles, but nothing more challenging, except in the spring when the water is high. July through October is the best season for canoeing on the Potomac. Although the rail line parallels the river along the bank above, unless your schedule coincides with the Chicago-bound AMTRAK, you would not know it. Tall trees line the bank, and great blue herons are a common sight.

WATCHABLE WILDLIFE

In addition to the plentiful blue herons, you may see great horned owls, wood ducks, killdeer and kingfishers during a canoe trip along the Potomac. Black bear are sometimes seen, and one evening at dusk we watched a family of deer drinking from the river. Beaver lodges and slides are common along the bank.

Put in right below the toll gate (they will let you drive through to unload, and you can park at the canal lock above) and take out at Town Creek, between the Potomac and the aqueduct. The riverbank is very shaley, so hauling canoes or kayaks up the hill to the towpath takes some work. To get to the Town Creek Aqueduct by car, follow signs from Route 51.

This is the only section we know of along the canal where you can make a round-trip loop by water. By portaging your canoe or kayak from the river to the canal at Town Creek, you can return along the watered section of the canal, taking out at Oldtown, where you parked your car.

Although nearly everyone in Oldtown will tell you that the bridge over the Potomac there is the only remaining private toll bridge connecting two states, it is not. The bridge across the Connecticut River, between Charlestown, NH and Springfield, Vermont is also a toll bridge and also privately owned. The one at Oldtown is a "low water bridge," meaning that it is only passable when the water in the river is low. Before the bridge was built, Greenspring Rd. had been a ford across the Potomac.

CANOE & KAYAK OUTFITTERS

■ **Allegany Expeditions**, at 10310 Columbus Avenue NE, Cumberland, ☎ 301-722-5170, rents kayaks, canoes, backpacks, and most camping gear, and they also provide guided canoe trips on the river.

■ In Hancock you can rent canoes and boats for use on the Potomac. **Pathfinders Canoe and Bicycle Livery** can provide the equipment for day or multi-day camping trips. They offer six segments that travel from Spring Gap just south of Cumberland to Fort Frederick, about halfway between Hancock and Frederick. Segment lengths vary from eight miles to 15 and cover some of the nicest water on the river. Some of these areas (for example, the two sections from Paw Paw to Stickpile Hill and Stickpile to Little Orleans, about 23 miles) cover an area where the river is virtually wild as it swings to and fro in huge arching switchbacks through the mountains. Rentals include two PFDs, paddles and a rope; tents and other camping equipment are also available for rent. They are close to the canal and trail at 8 South Pennsylvania Avenue, Hancock, ☎ 301-678-6870, www.corphome.com/pathfinders.

■ To explore the Potomac River from a base in Hagerstown, contact **Tom's Run Outfitters**, 16210 Fairview Rd., Hagerstown 21740, ☎ 301-733-0058, www.worldwideimage.com/hancock-outfitters. They have a number of packages available, from four hours to three days, which include canoe, PFDs, paddles and shuttle service. The shortest, from Cohill Station to Hancock, is seven miles and takes about four hours, for a cost of $35. The trip from Little Orleans, 17 miles, takes between six and nine hours, for $45. A two-day version of the latter is $65. Their trips are available April 15 through mid-October.

■ Another outfitter option is **Adventure Sports**, at 113 East Main Street, Frostburg, ☎ 301-689-0345. They conduct guided float trips that include all equipment.

For gentle paddling, the lake at **Rocky Gap State Park** offers rental canoes and kayaks (the sit-on-top-of variety), as well as rowboats and paddleboats. Rental rates are $5.25 per hour for a canoe or per half-hour for a kayak. These are at the docks just below the hotel and are available daily in the summer, weekends only in spring and fall. The park is off I-68 at Exit 50. The lake at Rocky Gap State Park has numerous coves and a varying shoreline, with lots of birdlife and beaver lodges. Canada geese are thick during spring and fall migrations and, if you hit the right three days in April, you may see as many as 200 loons on the lake. Mergansers, grebes, bald eagles and bears are transients.

Fishing

The canal is flooded for quite a distance west of Lock 70, at Oldtown. A handicapped-accessible fishing platform borders the water almost opposite the restored gate house. The canal is stocked with trout, and with catfish for the **Children's Fishing Rodeo**, the fourth Saturday in June. To fish in the canal, you need a Maryland fishing license.

Some of the best fishing in the Potomac is in the section from Spring Gap to Hancock. Up in this section of the river there is little intrusion of man onto the water because of the steep banks along the sides. Fishermen in this section are likely to encounter smallmouth bass, crappie and muskie. This area is long but can be broken up into smaller sections, such as the great meandering curves of the river from Paw Paw to Little Orleans.

The Potomac downstream from Oldtown offers fishing for smallmouth bass but, although the quantity is good, the quality is not generally good.

AUTHOR TIP *Actually, it's a tip from Green Ridge State Forest Ranger Mike Deckelbaum, who advises using pearl zoom fluke lures, a tiny torpedo or any type of grub for fishing this part of the Potomac.*

Lake Habeeb at **Rocky Gap State Park** is quite deep, so it's cold enough for good rainbow and brown trout fishing, as well as smallmouth and largemouth bass and bluegill. You can also catch catfish here, which are raised in the golf course pond. Those who wish to observe the fish underwater will soon be able to follow an underwater trail through fish habitat structures created by park volunteers. Scuba diving equipment is provided by Adventure Sports, in Frostburg. A Maryland license is needed for anyone 16 or older, but short-term licenses can be bought at the park. Equipment is available for rent.

Albert Powell Trout Hatchery produces about 150,000 fish for release in local streams every year. The hatchery is open to visitors 9-4 Monday-Saturday, ☎ 301-791-4736. It is on Route 66 north of I-70 at Exit 35, about six miles east of Hagerstown; no fishing allowed.

Western Canal Country

■ On Snow

Skiing

 The golf course at **Rocky Gap State Park** is open for cross-country skiing when there is sufficient snow. The terrain is rolling hillsides and it overlooks Lake Habeeb and Evitt's Mountain beyond. The trails at the park are also open in the winter for hiking.

Sledding & Sleigh Rides

At **Rocky Gap State Park** there is tubing available on the hills of their golf course. You can either bring your own or rent one at the park. To keep you warm they have campfires by the lake.

In Cumberland there is an opportunity to tour the town in a horse-drawn wagon. **Heritage Koaches**, PO Box 26, Cumberland, ☎ 301-777-0714, 800-336-7963, www.wstmr.com, conducts these tours daily year-round, by reservation only, so it is important to call for availability and times.

■ On Horseback

 Curly M Stables, 11200 Mexico Farms Rd. NE, near Cumberland, ☎ 301-724-1868, conducts a trail ride along the towpath; there is a 240-pound maximum weight and a minimum age of 10 years for riders. The rate is about $20 per hour. They can't go after heavy rain or when the towpath is muddy, so as to protect the path surface from damage. The trip passes a 300-year-old swamp white oak, the oldest and largest in Maryland, and an old farm site with Confederate soldiers buried in the family plot. Curly M is one of only two stables on the canal, and horses are only allowed on 1½ miles of the towpath.

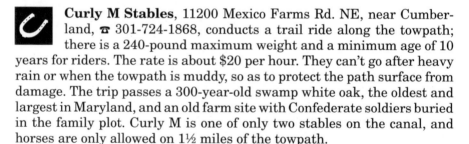

ACCESSIBILITY: *Curly M Stables welcomes visually impaired riders and has considerable experience teaching horsemanship to the blind.*

TENNESSEE WALKING HORSES

Curly M's Tennessee walking horses have a steady four-beat gait. This means that the back hooves hit the ground at different times, instead of together. This causes less bounce in the saddle, making a very smooth gait, even with some speed. The Tennessee walking horse, which includes some Morgan stock, was bred for use on plantations. The stable's good training complements the breed's natural smooth gait.

Cultural & Eco-Travel Experiences

■ Natural Areas

Sideling Cut, off I-68 where it passes just north of Harvey and west of Hancock, is a man-made natural attraction. In cutting an 800-foot notch through the mountain in 1984 to replace a long winding climb over it, highway builders removed 4½ million cubic yards of rock and soil, exposing a slice of geologic history visible nowhere else. You see this cut on the horizon, like a big bite taken out of the ridge, from many miles away, but only up close can you see the brightly colored stripes of the many swirling strata that make up the mountain. The dark gray marine rocks at the far end of the north slope are approximately 360 million years old; the white sandstone at the top about 340 million years old. Rivers, seas, and marshes all left layers, which folded, uplifted and eroded to form the designs on the cut face. The **Sideling Hill Exhibit Center** explains the forces that created the mountain, and a footbridge across the highway for travelers heading east gives good views. A trail leads onto the rock itself for up-close inspection. Microscopes in the center encourage visitors to examine these more closely, and core samplings explain each layer of formation. The Exhibit Center is open daily 8:30 to 6 and is free.

The **Aviary** at **Rocky Gap State Park**, northeast of Cumberland, has four species of raptors – a screech owl, barn owl, horned owl and red-tailed hawk. All are unreleasable due to their history – they were either hand-raised or born in captivity and unable to survive in the wild. The aviary is open Tuesday through Friday, 11 am-1 pm and 5-7 pm. On weekends it's open 10 am-2 pm. A nature center near the park's amphitheater is open sporadically for nature programs. Rocky Gap State Park offers free campfire programs on nature subjects every day in the summer. These are open to the public and feature park naturalists or guest speakers. The park staff also provides guided hikes with a naturalist on the various trails of the parks. Check with the staff for the schedule of guided nature hikes.

KID-FRIENDLY

Rocky Gap State Park has a Junior Rangers program for campers on weekends throughout the summer. Activities include nature crafts and hikes based on a theme, such as beavers, birds or history.

■ The Arts

The performing arts are alive and well in Washington County and in the capable hands of the Washington County Arts Council. The Council has an ongoing and ambitious schedule of events, from gallery shows to theater, concerts and ballet throughout the year. The dates and places vary from month to month and year to year, so pick up their schedule at the Visitors Center or call them for details of current offerings. There's something going on all the time. The primary venues for these events are the **Maryland Theater**, 21 South Potomac Street, Hagerstown (☎ 301-790-2000), the **Washington County Arts Council Gallery**, 41 South Potomac Street (☎ 301-791-3132), and the **Washington County Museum of Fine Arts** in City Park (☎ 301-739-5727). Recent offerings included concerts by the Maryland Symphony, Beau Soleil, Roger Whittaker, Hagerstown Choral Arts, and the Appalachian Wind Quintet. Gallery and art exhibits include the work of current artists as well as retrospectives. The Council presents a very active arts schedule that larger cities would envy. The Arts Council is at 41 South Potomac Street, ☎ 301-791-3132, www.washcoartscouncil.org.

Hagerstown's Washington County Museum of Fine Arts is an astonishing place, filled with riches far beyond the scope of many big city art museums, and housed in a well-designed building begun in the 1930s. Works by the Old Masters – Titian, Tintoretto, Veronese – hang in a large formal gallery, off which a rotunda features sculpture, set around a fine Diana by Anna Vaughn Hyatt. The Lalique collection fills a gallery of its own, and part of another, which it shares with art glass from Tiffany and Steuben, as well as several of Whistler's graphics. Other special collections include Bohemian porcelain birds, and bronzes by Malvina Hoffman, Rodin, Henry Moore and Daumier. Historical collections comprise not just the large group of early portraits – many by the remarkable Peale family – but silver, Pennsylvania German calligraphic marriage certificates, silk embroidered clothing, and fine furniture.

So vast are the collections of this museum that at least six of its galleries change every six weeks, and priceless paintings decorate the walls of its offices, instead of being placed in storage. Only a small fraction of its collections are on display here at any time, with the rest in traveling exhibits or storage. At least one gallery is always devoted to showing and selling the works of local artists. An active and ongoing schedule of special events and lectures adds even more richness to this gem of a museum.

A small shop has well-chosen gifts and books related to the collections and to art themes. The museum is free, but most visitors give a donation of at least $1 in the box by the door on the way in. Many leave another as they exit, in appreciation. The Museum is in City Park at the intersection of Virginia Avenue, Key Street and Memorial Boulevard in the southwest part of the city. From the west end of any of the east-west streets take Prospect Street south. PO Box 423, City Park, Hagerstown, MD, ☎ 301-739-5727, fax 301-745-3741, TDD 301-739-5764, www.washcomuseum.org.

Washington County has an active **music in the parks** program that is sponsored by the Department of Recreation and Parks. In Hagerstown the **Municipal Band** presents concerts of light favorites on Sunday evenings from June through August. The concerts are in City Park and begin at 8 pm. The Park is at the corner of Key Street and Virginia Avenue. At **Pen Mar Park**, northeast of the city on the Pennsylvania border, a regular concert series is held every Sunday afternoon from 2-5, featuring a different group each week. Concerts run from early June through September.

At their headquarters, the Washington County Arts Council Gallery showcases the works of regional artists in several disciplines. The visual arts include works on oil, water color, acrylic and other media, in both representational and more contemporary formats. The gallery also exhibits fine hand-crafted pottery, tiles, and handmade paper works. The gallery is open Tuesday-Friday, 10-5; Saturday, 10-2. 41 South Potomac Street, Hagerstown, MD, ☎ 301-791-3132, www.washcoartscouncil.org, e-mail wcarts@intrepid.net.

Cumberland has a very active theater company. **Cumberland Theater** has been producing professional live plays and musicals for more than 12 years. Productions start in mid-June and continue on, almost unabated, through October. A recent series had six offerings that included *Dames at Sea*, *The King and I* and the *Taming of the Shrew*. This is an Equity house. Individual ticket prices vary with the performance but run in the $12-$16 range. 101-103 North Johnson Street, Cumberland, MD 21502, ☎ 301-759-4990.

■ Crafts

In downtown Cumberland, close to Riverside Park and Washington's Headquarters is a small place called **The Gallery**, which shows the works of its owner-artist as well as the works of other local artists and craftsmen in a variety of media. It does make a nice stop. 8 Greene Street, Cumberland, ☎ 301-724-7936.

■ Antiques

There are a number of attractive shops in Hagerstown and the surrounding area, many of them right on US 40. On the east side of town, take Exit 32A and Route 40 east. **Antique Crossroads** is at 20150 National Pike (US 40), ☎ 301-301-739-0858. **Beaver Creek Antique Market**, 20202 National Pike (☎ 301-301-739-8075), is a group setting with 150 dealers, open 9-5, Thursday-Tuesday. Both of these are on the westbound side of Route 40.

The **Cooper Shed** specializes in vintage textiles from quilts to doilies, napkins to tablecloths. They also have other collectibles such as antique sewing aids, buttons and baskets. It is open Friday and Saturday, 10-5, and Sunday, noon to 5, or by appointment, at 20512 Beaver Creek Rd., Hagerstown, ☎ 301-797-6974, e-mail maryperini@msn.com. Beaver Creek Rd. parallels US 40, to which it is connected by Route 66. In town, US 40 is called Franklin Street, and on it are **Back Door Antiques and Collectibles** (☎ 301-739-1406), at the rear of 49 East Franklin, and **Ravenswood Antique Center** at 216 West Franklin Street, ☎ 301-739-0145.

In Hancock, the **Hancock Antique Mall is** at 266 North Pennsylvania Avenue; ☎ 301-678-5959. This is a multi-dealer shop with about 48,000 square feet of display space, open 9-5, Thursday-Tuesday.

In Cumberland is the **Historic Cumberland Antique Mall** (55-57 Baltimore Street; ☎ 301-777-2979), a multi-dealer shop that encompasses three downtown buildings with five floors of goods. There is plenty of parking nearby on Pershing Street next to the Holiday Inn. In addition to fine china, glassware, stoneware, brass and copper, the shops also have furniture, particularly Victorian and oak from the early 20th century. It is open Monday-Saturday, 10-5; Sunday, noon-5; closed on major holidays. Close by are two other individual shops, **Yesteryear Antiques and Collectibles**, 62-64 Baltimore Street, ☎ 301-722-7531, and **Charles W. Garber** at 74 Baltimore Street, ☎ 301-729-3999.

Events

 APRIL: The last weekend of April turns Fort Frederick into an **18th-century market**, when 100 traders and top craftsmen set up here, with an encampment of 1,300 people. ☎ 301-842-2155.

MAY: **Fort Frederick Muster** takes place the last weekend in May, when re-enactors of the French and Indian War gather. ☎ 301-842-2155.

JUNE: Hagerstown is host to the **Western Maryland Blues Fest** in early June, a Friday, Saturday and Sunday event that fills the city with some of the best current Blues artists. Venues are at various places throughout the city, including Miller House, the Maryland Theater, Public Square and City Park. Tickets for inside venues can be bought from the Washington County Arts Council, ☎ 301-797-8782. Outside venues have both paid and free admissions. The Sunday "Blues Picnic" is free admission. The event is held annually on the first weekend following the Federal Memorial Day observance. For more information contact Public Information Officer, City Hall, 1 East Franklin Street Room 100, Hagerstown, MD 21740, ☎ 301-739-8577 ext 116. www.blues-fest.com.

JULY: **Military Field Days** are held mid-month at Fort Frederick; ☎ 301-842-2155. On the Fourth of July, the **Maryland Symphony** plays at the Antietam National Battlefield starting at 7:30; admission is free, and it's followed by fireworks. This is a "bring a chair and a picnic lunch" event of more than 15 years duration that attracts a big crowd. The site itself makes it a meaningful experience and the setting is wonderful. Contact the Maryland Symphony Orchestra, ☎ 301-797-4000, or the Washington County Arts Council, 41 South Potomac Street, ☎ 301-791-3132, www.washcoartscouncil.org.

AUGUST: Maryland Symphony and the Washington County Arts Council **Augustoberfest**, Hagerstown, celebrates the city's German heritage with German food, beer, dancing and music. $15 for the Friday concert, $10 for Saturday events or $20 for both days, kids under 12 free. Tickets from MSO, 13 South Potomac Street, Hagerstown, ☎ 301-797-4000, fax 301-797-2314.

Sightseeing

■ Historic Sites & Museums

Frostburg

 The **Thrasher Carriage Museum**, in Frostburg, is among the finest in the United States, and well worth a trip to the interesting town of Frostburg, even if you don't take the train excursion from Cumberland. If you do, the train stops right at the museum's door. Although the museum is filled with more than 40 beautifully restored and maintained carriages, the highlight (to us) is President Theodore Roosevelt's inaugural carriage, built in 1890 in Rochester, New York.

Guides are on hand to tell you the stories, such as how the Park Drag Coach became a portable grandstand for parades in Central Park, or was used to give a better view of the race track at Saratoga. These were the venue of the original tailgate parties, as families moved from carriage to carriage visiting friends and sampling the food and drink. You'll see all the classics – a three-seated surrey with a fringed top, a jaunting cart, a milk wagon, a vis-à-vis sleigh owned by the Vanderbilts, a ladies' wicker Phaeton (the front was built very high to spare ladies a view of the horse's rear), a yellow piano-box buggy, even a hearse.

DID YOU KNOW?

So famous was the Thrasher collection that many of the carriages were used in movies – always with Mr. Thrasher as driver; it was in his contract.

The astonishing thing about the museum – which displays only 44 carriages from a much larger collection – is that it represents the work of one man. Mr. Thrasher collected these between the early 1950s and the 1980s, restoring many of them himself. Some are in original condition, such as the 1850 Germantown Rockaway with roll-down leather curtains. 19 Depot Street, Frostburg, MD, ☎ 800-508-4748 (800-50-VISIT), 301-689-3380, www.cumberland.com/thrasher, e-mail thrasher@hereintown.net. May-September the museum is open Tuesday-Sunday, 11 to 3; in October, every day; in November and December, Saturday-Sunday, 11-3. From January through April it is open by appointment only.

Western Canal Country

At the Depot in Frostburg, the old **Tunnel Hotel** has been transformed into a series of small shops and boutiques selling everything from Amish furniture, quilts and linens and jewelry to soap and candles. You can also get ice cream, sandwiches and drinks here while you wait for the return trip.

Above, in the town, **Frostburg Museum** tells the tale of the town, its mines, transportation and schools. It's not exactly high-tech, but it is the kind of volunteer effort to nail down the story of a community that we enjoy. At The Hill Street School Building, it opens Tuesday-Friday at 1 pm, Saturday-Sunday at 2 pm, and closes at 4 pm.

Although it's not really a museum, you'll want to stop in at the venerable **Gunther Hotel** on Frostburg's main street, almost directly above the rail station. Follow the stairs to the rear of its grand lobby down to the lower corridors to see the quirky collections of everything from turn-of-the-century costumes to kitchen utensils. At the foot of the stairs, look for the old jail (it looks like you're entering a men's room) where prisoners being transported were kept while their guards slept upstairs in the hotel.

The only remaining **Toll Gate House** on the National Road sits beside busy US Route 40, between Clarysville and La Vale, just west of I-68 at Exit 39. This unusual seven-sided building dates from 1836. You can visit inside the kitchen and family quarters, all tucked into this tiny building where the road toll was collected. A picnic area is beside it. The Toll Gate House is open Saturday and Sunday, 1:30-4:30 pm, May-October. ☎ 302-729-3047.

Lonaconing

Lonaconing is a small town stretched along Route 36, which runs south from I-68 from Frostburg to the West Virginia line. Apart from being the hometown of baseball star Lefty Grove, its historical interest lies in the huge stone **Lonaconing Iron Furnace**, set in an attractive park on the main street, Route 36. Lonaconing is about eight miles south of I-68. Be sure to stop if you are headed to Dan's Mountain State Park (see *Parks*, page 62).

Cumberland

History House, in Cumberland, was built in the height of the city's glory days, in 1867, for the President of the C&O Canal, Josiah Hance Gordon. The tour is filled with stories of life in well-to-do Cumberland. One upstairs bedroom is devoted to historic wedding dresses, dating from the mid-1800s to 1960. On the ground floor are the kitchens and laundry room, complete with early versions of the washing machine. Behind the house is a Victorian Garden with vintage plantings. History House is open June through October, Tuesday-Sunday, 11 am-4 pm; November through May, Tuesday-Saturday, 11 am-4 pm. Tours are given on the hour. Admission is $3; children over 12, $1; under 12, free. The Victorian Gift Shop features toys, ornaments and handcrafts, and they have special open house candle-light tours in December.

Be sure to walk along this section of **Washington Street** to admire the fine old homes in a variety of Victorian architectural styles. You will see stucco, turreted brick, patterned slate and shingle and a fine parade of "painted ladies." Fort Cumberland sat at the crest of this street, where the imposing brick courthouse and Emanuel Episcopal church stand today. Between these two buildings, at the corner of Prospect Square, is a plan of the fort, and the points of its outer walls are marked by special paving stones in the street. The fort was part of the plan to take Fort Duquesne (now Pittsburgh) from the French. General Braddock lost his life in the effort but his young aide and Commander of Fort Cumberland, George Washington, survived.

Ask at History House for the brochure **A Self-Guided Walk into History,** *which covers Washington Street and other parts of the historic downtown of Cumberland.*

Emanuel Church is at 16 Washington Street, Cumberland, on the hill-side overlooking the railroad tracks and sits directly over the site of the French and Indian War at Fort Cumberland. The stone church dates from 1848 and is one of the earliest Gothic Revival churches. Early in the 20th century the interior was redesigned by Louis Comfort Tiffany himself (not just by his studio) and in the attic were found Tiffany's original drawings for the crucifixes and candelabra. Three of its windows are by Tiffany: the Adoration of the Shepherds above the altar, the Second Coming of Christ in Art Nouveau style, and the Art Deco Rizpah over the west door. Beneath the church, the original tunnels of Fort Cumberland form catacombs. Tours of these are infrequent, but worth inquiring about, call the parish office at ☎ 301-777-3364.

The only remaining part of the fort is the tiny log building (1755) used as **George Washington's Headquarters** when he served here as an aide to British General Edward Braddock in the 1750s. It was moved from its original site and is now in Riverside Park on Greene Street at the foot of the hill. A brochure called *Fort Cumberland Walking Tour* is available at the Cumberland Visitor Center. The tour includes 28 stops and plaques; an audio unit is available.

AUTHOR TIP

Those doing genealogical research in Cumberland should know that the Appalachian Room at Allegany Community College has research material and genealogy records reaching back farther than those at the county courthouse.

Geroge Washington's Headquarters in Cumberland.

The **Transportation and Industrial Museum** is under construction in Cumberland, at the corner of Mechanic and Harrison Streets. The city is a fitting site for such a museum, since it was a significant center for three transport routes: the C&O Canal, the National Road and two major rail lines. Although the canal closed long ago, AMTRAK still passes through here on its Washington-Pittsburgh-Chicago line and maintains a major repair yard in Cumberland.

Canal exhibits will be in the **restored railway station**, where the National Park Service Visitors Center is located. A full canal lock and exhibits on the coal industry and boat building will be there, and the orientation center will be accessed through a miniature version of the Paw Paw Tunnel. The museum's opening coincides with the 150th anniversary of the opening of the C&O Canal in Cumberland, on October 10, 1850. Eventually, the former boat basin will be the harbor for rides in replica barges on the re-watered canal. Work on all these projects continues as we write.

The Cumberland Rail Station is also home to a museum of rail memorabilia operated by the Western Maryland Chapter of the National Railway Historical Society. They publish the *Railfans Guide to the Cumberland Area*, a comprehensive walking guide to rail operations in Cumberland. The brochure is available at the Visitor Information Center in the Rail Station.

Along the Canal - Cumberland to Hancock

The C&O Canal accounts for a number of interesting historic sites in this part of Maryland. Many of them can be reached by road; others require a walk or bike ride along the towpath.

*Although **Route 51** does not always run right alongside the canal, it roughly parallels its course and adjoins it in several places between Cumberland and the Paw Paw Tunnel, near where it crosses into West Virginia to become Route 9. It provides road access (in west-to-east order) to the Evitts Creek Aqueduct, the three locks between North Branch and Irons Mountain, the locks and gatehouse at Oldtown, Town Creek Aqueduct, and the towpath to the Paw Paw Tunnel.*

Evitts Creek Aqueduct, at Milepost 180, less than five miles from Cumberland, is the smallest of the 11 that carried the canal over creeks entering the Potomac. Now in very poor condition, it sits near a stone quarry that supplied the building material for it and the nearby locks at North Branch, before it was worked out. This is the westernmost of the aqueducts on the canal.

At **North Branch**, on dry land alongside the canal is a replica **canal boat**, which is open for inside inspection daily in the summer, staffed by the C&O Canal Society of Cumberland (☎ 301-729-3136). This is the only place where you can see the original layout of the boats, since those built for canal tours have been fitted with open-sided seating areas for passengers. None of the original boats used on the canal exists today.

THE CANAL BOATS

At least seven boat builders worked in Cumberland, constructing boats of oak and Georgia pine, timbers that gave the boats a life span of about 25 years. The base of the boat, which held the cargo, was 14½ feet wide by 92 or 95 feet long, only six inches narrower and five to seven feet shorter than the locks it had to pass through. In the front was the mule stable, where teams rested between their six-hour shifts pulling the boat. In the center was the hay house, used to store feed, and the third structure rising above the deck was the captain's 12x12-foot cabin, where the crew and captain's family ate and slept. The deck between these two was the combination of front porch and back yard, where chores were done and children played, tethered by ropes until they were old enough to be competent swimmers.

Across the canal lock is an 1850 **Lock House**, one of the few log lock houses where you can still see the log exterior – most others were later covered with clapboards. It's a far cry from the earlier more commodious ones closer to Washington. A locktender, hired by the canal company, lived here with his family, on call 24 hours a day, seven days a week, except in winter. There are guided tours of the boat, afternoons, June-August. The boat and lock house are at North Branch off Route 51 five miles southeast of Cumberland. ☎ 301-722-8226.

 Route 51 is designated as a Maryland Scenic Route, marked with a symbol of the state flower, the black-eyed Susan.

Two single locks – **number 72**, between Irons Mountain and Spring Gap, and **number 67**, near Town Creek – are located close to Route 51, and are both shown on the C&O Canal National Historic Park's canal map.

Another lock house, also small, is beside the locks at **Oldtown**. It was rebuilt after a fire destroyed the original one. Inside are displays on the canal and the history of the local Native Americans, tracing them from the Ice Age. The canal is filled with water from Oldtown to Lock 68, halfway between Oldtown and Town Creek, a stretch of about two miles. This makes the towpath here particularly scenic, with trees meeting overhead and reflecting in the placid surface of the water to form a leafy tunnel.

 As you leave Route 51 at the sign for Lock 70, you will come to an immediate T with no directional sign. Go right, then left onto Greenspring Rd., at the Cresap House, to reach the canal.

HOW A CANAL LOCK WORKS

Approaching boatmen signaled with their horns so the lock-keeper could set the lock for their approach. Westbound boats, which moved upward, had to enter an empty lock, eastbound a full one. Butterfly valves with wicket paddles allowed water in or out of the 15-by-100-foot lock, then the tender opened the gate to allow a boat to enter. Then water was allowed to flow in (to raise) or out (to lower) the level inside the lock and when it was even with the canal in the direction the boat was traveling, the other gate was opened and the boat moved on. It took 10 minutes for a boat to get through a lock. With more than 500 boats operating on the canal in the 1870s, the lock-keeper was kept busy.

The **Thomas Cresap House Museum** is hard to miss, right at the turn to the canal locks and gate house in Oldtown. It's the oldest surviving building, built in 1764, and young George Washington stayed here while working as a surveyor. The house is open the first weekend of each month from June-September or by appointment, ☎ 301-478-5154. The grounds are open all the time. The road directly in front of the house leads to the canal and Potomac, where there was a well-used ford across it to West Virginia. A Confederate group, McNeil's Rangers, used the ford after the skirmish at Chambersburg in 1864.

Of all the canal architecture, the most impressive is the 3,118-foot **Paw Paw Tunnel**. It was also difficult, time-consuming and expensive to build. Rather than build the six miles of canal around the long mitten shape of Paw Paw Bends, the C&C engineers decided to tunnel through the solid rock ridge that goes to the river's edge. Twelve years and 5,800,000 bricks later, the tunnel opened, but not until after it had bankrupted the contractor and claimed dozens of lives. In retrospect, it would have been cheaper to build around the bends. To reach the tunnel, follow Route 51 to the parking area just before it crosses the bridge into West Virginia.From there, it's is a 10- or 15-minute walk along the towpath to the right. The tunnel is closed in the winter, but a door gives access to the walkway year-round. Inside, look for the tow-rope burns on the railing. The National Park Service offers Tunnel Tours on Friday, Saturday and Sunday in July and August; Saturday and Sunday only in spring and fall. ☎ 301-739-4200.

TUNNEL VISION

The Paw Paw Tunnel is too narrow for two boats to pass, as is the long cut above it. But it is too long to see if another boat has already entered. In the early years, before a semaphore was installed to signal that the tunnel was in use, the mule driver would run through the tunnel and put a lantern at the other end to signal that his boat was coming through.

AUTHOR TIP *Be sure to carry a flashlight and wear a rain hat with a brim while inside the Paw Paw Tunnel (unless you enjoy having ice water drip down the back of your neck). The walk through it is spooky, even with a flashlight. At the center you can barely see a dot of light from either end. Hardly anyone can resist making loud noises, which echo in the brick cavern. A ghostly rising and falling woo-woo-woo is particularly effective.*

Hancock

The National Park's **Visitors Center** at 326 East Main St. in Hancock (☎ 301-678-5463) shows a film that is fascinating on two counts. First, it gives a very good history of the canal and life in the days when it was operating. But the film itself is also of great historic importance, a 1917 film made by the Edison Company. In it you will see boats passing through locks, gate keepers, boatmen, mules and their drivers, and scenes passing as the boats moved along the canal. The film is also shown at the Williamsport visitors center.

The **Hancock Historical Museum** is a block above Main Street at the corner of Pennsylvania Avenue and the appropriately named High Street. The museum collections relate heavily to the role of transportation in the history of the town. The presence of the C&O Canal, B&O Railroad and the National Pike, all passing through the less-than-two-miles-wide section of Maryland were bound to be critical to its people. It's a community memory bank, including the "largest postcard collection of Hancock anywhere." High Street and Pennsylvania Avenue, Hancock, MD. Open April-October, first and third Sundays, 2-4 pm.

CANAL HISTORY

Flooding of the Potomac River was one of the reasons for the building of the canal, but flooding bedeviled it for most of its useful life and caused the end of it. The first flood was in 1829, only a year after the canal was formed. Between that date and 1996 there were 17 major floods, including the 1924 flood that ultimately led to the closing of the canal for business. In the park Visitors Centers look for a small brochure, *Flooding of the Potomac*, which describes the effect of flooding.

Fort Frederick

Fort Frederick, inside the state park named for it, was built by the British during the French and Indian Wars, and later used as a POW camp during the Revolution. After nearly falling down – many of its stones were borrowed by nearby farmers to build homes and foundations – the four-foot-thick Vauban-design defensive walls were rebuilt. Although replaced in the original style, the line between the two-thirds that remained and the one-third that was replaced has been clearly marked.

What makes the fort especially interesting is that it is built of stone; stone forts were usually built by the French, and this is the only example of one built by the Colonists. The barracks and officers quarters, now housing interpretive displays about the fort and the area's history, were reconstructed from archaeological and historical records. Ongoing archaeological digs are open for public viewing and we had a fascinating talk with one of the archaeologists on a misty fall morning. Standard state park admission fees are charged daily in the summer, but only on weekends off-season; admission to the fort only is $2 adult and $1 child. Special programs are held; for example, in early August they offer a Children's Weekend, where kids ages six-12 can experience 18th-century military life. Later in the month there is an encampment of Revolutionary-era American, British, French and German troops. Call for their program listing. To reach the park from US 40, turn south on Route 56, about 4½ miles west of Clear Spring; it's about three miles to the park entrance and the fort is on the road to the left just after entering the gate.

At **Four Locks**, east of Fort Frederick, is the only remaining mule stable, used to house the animals that pulled the boats. The four locks, within a quarter-mile distance, are numbered 47 through 50. At this point, the canal cuts inland, rather than following the river, to cut off a long bend. Unlike Paw Paw, this bend was not blocked by a solid wall of stone, but it required four locks to lift the canal the 32-foot difference. Downstream from lock 47 about a half-mile is a 75-foot cliff of the same type of limestone that these locks were made from.

DID YOU KNOW?

As you stand by the canal and try to picture how it looked in the 1870s with 500-plus active boats, you may wonder how two boats passed with both tethered to mule teams on the same towpath. Here's how: The boat traveling downstream (which always had the right-of-way) stayed near the towpath, with its team close to the water. The upstream boat dropped its rope to the bottom of the ditch and stopped. The downstream boat floated over it and its team stepped over it as the boat passed.

In this part of the trail also stands the large **Lockhouse 49**, which is not open to visitors. A particularly interesting stretch of towpath begins here, and in the next two miles downstream (east) are the ruins of Charles Mill, a stone mill. Downstream from this point is another area called **Two Locks**, once a thriving community itself. Dam 5 here watered the canal downstream 23.3 miles and boats could lock into the river for a section of their trip, or continue down on the canal. Dam 5 was attacked and breached twice in December 1861 by Confederate raids under the command of Stonewall Jackson, but was soon restored. The canal was crucial to the defence and viability of Washington during the war. From the northernmost point, the Mule Barn, to Dam 5 is a distance of about 2¼ miles. To get to Four Locks, exit from I-70 west of Hagerstown at Big Pool and go south on Route 56 four miles to Hassett Rd. Go right on it a quarter-mile, then right again on Four Locks Rd. There is parking, a boat ramp and picnic facility at the site. Handicapped access is limited. There is also a parking area on Dam 5 Rd. south of Two Locks.

Hagerstown

Miller House, 135 West Washington Street, in downtown Hagerstown, has an interesting architectural history of its own, which is explained during a tour. It began in 1818 as a small house built by a potter in back of his shop, which faced on the new National Road. Seven years later, he sold it to a man who built a stylish new home facing onto the street where the shop had been, using the old house, attached, as the kitchen. The third of only three families to live here, added a doctor's office beside it, the rooms of which now house many of the collections. The central staircase is seemingly unsupported, cantilevered on metal rods and the grand parlor is elegantly furnished in period antiques. There are more than 260 19th-century European dolls and a collection of more than 200 clocks, including tall case clocks. The home of the Washington County Historical Society, it is a treasure house of local and Maryland history.

AUTHOR TIP *William Price, the second owner of the Miller House, was the grandfather of Emily Post. Please be on your best behavior and remember to say thank you when you leave.*

The house is a combination of furnished rooms and display galleries, the repository of several very good collections that have been donated to the museum. These include clocks, a particularly good collection of early dolls, Schonhutt circus toys, over 200 Currier and Ives prints, local pottery

The Miller House in Hagerstown has an extensive doll collection.

(some of which was made by Peter Bell, the potter who built the original house), and rooms dedicated to the C&O Canal and to the Civil War.

One of the most unusual and rare pieces in the house is a life-sized iron target shaped like a man, used for training in the Revolution. When the shot aimed true at either of the two strategically placed holes, a bell rang. It is dimpled with the dents of many misses.

Admission to Miller House is $3 for adults, $2 for seniors; school children are free. It is open April through December, Wednesday through Saturday, from 1 to 4 pm. During the holiday season, when it is specially decorated, it is also open on Sunday and Tuesday afternoons. ☎ 301-797-8782.

ESPECIALLY FOR RAILROAD BUFFS

Hagerstown has a really nice model train and railroad museum, **The Train Room**, with more than 5,000 items on display. The model collection is centered around Lionel trains, with items from that maker dating back to 1900. The main attraction is the two-level, four-track model railroad layout. They also have a large collection of rail memorabilia and they sell model railroad equipment. It's at 360 Burhans Boulevard, Hagerstown, ☎ 301-745-6681. Hours are 1-6 pm, except Wednesday, but they suggest a call to make sure.

The **Hagerstown Roundhouse Museum** also focuses on train history. Its goal is to preserve and restore antique railway equipment, from engines to rolling stock, and to promote the use of railroads as a viable part of the transportation system. In addition to a wide range of equipment and memorabilia there is a model railroad, photographic displays and a research library. 300 South Burhans Boulevard, Hagerstown, ☎ 301-739-1998 or 739-4665.

Another special treat awaits rail buffs in Hagerstown – the **Engine 202 Steam Locomotive and Caboose Display**. The engine was built in 1912 and worked the Baltimore to Hagerstown line with passengers and freight until 1953. The last of its type, it is displayed with eight cabooses in City Park, opposite Mansion House Arts Center, in Hagerstown. It's open Tuesday-Saturday, 10-4, and Sunday, 1-5, May-September. ☎ 301-739-8393.

Western Canal Country

AUTHOR TIP

*For a change of pace in the evening, the **Washington County Planetarium and Space Science Center** has public programs on Tuesday evenings from 30 minutes to an hour in length. It was renovated to a state-of-the-art facility in 1998. Popular with school groups, it is also the base of operations for the Tristate Astronomers, who meet the third Wednesday of the month from September through May at 7:30 pm. Commonwealth Avenue, off Frederick Street, Hagerstown, ☎ 301-766-2898.*

Located in the same park as the Washington County Museum of Fine Arts (see page 82), **Hager House** was built by the young Jonathan Hager in 1739-40. Hager, who immigrated from Germany in 1736 became a prosperous member of this frontier community, serving as a Captain of Scouts during the French and Indian War. The early stone house is furnished to its period and has thick stone walls and a cool cellar with a natural spring contained within it. Nearby, a smaller building houses a museum of hundreds of artifacts uncovered during excavations on the property, particularly under the stone porch as well as the original "Little Heiskell." On Sunday afternoons there are free crafts events and from the first Tuesday of December to the end of the month there is a German Christmas Celebration. Other programs are held through the season. City Park, 110 Key Street, Hagerstown, MD, ☎ 301-739-8393. Tuesday-Saturday, 10 to 4; Sunday, 2-5 pm. It is closed January through March and from the last week of November into December. Nominal admission fee.

ROSE HILL CEMETERY

Rose Hill Cemetery, in Hagerstown, is one of those grand park cemeteries popular in the 19th century, dating from 1866. The date is not insignificant. In the section known as Washington Cemetery, more than 2,000 Confederate soldiers were buried after the nearby battles of South Mountain and Antietam about 10 miles away. Only 346 of the dead were identified. It is at 600 South Potomac Street south of town toward Antietam. The tall stone tower on the hill served as the water tower on the farm of Dr John Wroe, the first inhabitant. In his day, the area was called **Wroe's Hill**.

Where to Stay

ACCOMMODATIONS PRICE KEY	
Rates are per room, per night, double occupancy.	
$	Under $50
$$	$50 to $100
$$$	$101 to $175
$$$$	$176 and up

■ Cumberland & Rocky Gap

The Inn at Walnut Bottom is an attractive, hospitable pair of townhouses built in 1820 and 1890, an easy walk from all Cumberland's attractions. Eight of the 12 guestrooms have private bath and all have in-room TV and telephone. The comfortable guest parlor has teas and juice available at all times, and a well-stocked library of books on the local area. The inn has its own unofficial adventure center, with bicycles and arrangements with an outfitter to handle shuttles for towpath trips. Children staying here get extra attention. It is at 120 Greene Street, Cumberland 21502, ☎ 301-777-0003, e-mail iwb@iwbinfo.com. $$-$$$

INSIDE ADVICE

Sometimes it pays to whine a little, especially when you are in a place as accommodating as the Inn at Walnut Bottom. Arriving at the inn the evening before they had arranged for me to begin bicycling the towpath, I complained of a very stiff knee. Innkeeper Kirsten suggested to our group that I would be a good model for her to demonstrate her specialty: a Swedish massage technique called *Ausbenning*, or "unbuckling." The therapy works with the specific muscles and ligaments, but combines it with teaching. Kirsten explained why my knee was stiff and gave me exercises to continue as I traveled. I descended the stairs to breakfast almost nimbly the next morning and biked 13 miles of towpath before lunch. So if you have a charley-horse from your day's hiking or biking, ask Kirsten about a massage session.

Rocky Gap Lodge and Golf Resort, a 220-room lodge, overlooks beautiful Lake Habeeb and the impressive Jack Nicklaus-designed golf course. In the late 1800s corporate moguls built themselves remote executive rustic getaways. This is a modern version with all of the comforts the rich and

Western Canal Country

famous Victorians didn't have. Spacious rooms, a fine dining room, an accommodating staff and a program of activities covering everything from caving and rock climbing to fishing and cultural affairs. They link you with all of the outfitters and check the credentials and safety features before they will list them. Rooms are large, very comfortable, in a rustic country style. You can see the hotel and lake from I-68; 16701 Lakeview Rd. NE, Flintstone, MD 21530, ☎ 301-784-8400, 800-724-0828, fax 301-784-8408, www. rockygapresort.com. $$-$$$

Braddock Motor Inn is a family-run Best Western affiliate outside of Cumberland in LaVale. It has 108 comfortable and attractive rooms and suites, an indoor swimming pool, fitness facility, dining room and lounge. 1268 National Highway, LaVale, MD, ☎ 301-729-3300, 800-296-6006, fax 301-729-3300. $$-$$$

The Oak Tree Inn is another new hotel facility in the LaVale section west of Cumberland. It has rooms that are equipped with microwave, refrigerator and modem ports. It also has an exercise room with Nautilus equipment and cardiovascular machines. Most of the rooms, which are priced around $70, are taken up by people here for training with CFX Transportation so advance reservations are suggested. 12310 Winchester Rd., LaVale, MD 21502, ☎ 301-729-6700.

■ Hancock

Hancock Motel, on the heights south of town, just before the Potomac Bridge, stands near the point from which Stonewall Jackson bombarded the town in the Civil War. Its clean and comfortable rooms are not fancy, but it is a reliable, friendly place to stay. The address is 2 South Blue Hill Rd. (Route 522); ☎ 301-678-6108 or 800-329-6108. Rates are between $50 and $60 a night.

■ Hagerstown

Sundays Bed & Breakfast is in a 14-room Queen Anne mansion dating from the 1890s. Comfortable rooms and breakfasts featuring waffles or quiche and other specialties of the house are only the beginning. In addition to the mid-afternoon tea there is early evening wine and cheese. Ask about special seasonal rates. Sundays is at 39 Broadway, Hagerstown 21740, ☎ 301-797-4331, 800-221-4828. Entering Hagerstown from the east on US 40 take Locust Street right, then go left onto Broadway. $

Winnie Price's Wilgrove Manor is a grand mansion elevated above the street on its knoll. Behind a porch supported by Doric columns, it can best be described as grand late Queen Anne with touches of Gatsby. Inside, the rooms are graciously decorated and all have private baths. A continental breakfast is served in the dining room or, during good weather, on the porch. 635 Oak Hill Avenue, Hagerstown 21740, ☎ 301-733-6328, 797-7769. $-$$

East of Hagerstown in Beaver Creek in the **Beaver Creek House B&B**, a charming Queen Anne-style with expansive porches and five air-conditioned guest rooms. They serve a full breakfast and afternoon refreshments. This inn is close to the Appalachian Trail, at 20432 Beaver Creek Rd., Hagerstown, MD 21740, ☎ 301-797-4764, www.bbonline.com/md/beavercreek. From Exit 35 on Route 70, go left (south) on Route 66 less than a mile to a right onto Beaver Creek Rd. $-$$

For a farm stay, contact **Lewrene Farm**, a 125-acre property operated by Lewis and Irene Lehman. In addition to comfortable rooms you will get a full country breakfast. The farm is at 9738 Downsville Pike, Hagerstown, MD 21740, ☎ 301-582-1735, www.inns.com.midatl/mdhagers.htm. From I-70 at Hagerstown, take Exit 29 (Route 65) toward town, then take West Oak Ridge to Downsville Pike. $

■ Camping

Green Ridge State Forest has an administrative office near the intersection of I-68 and Route 40 where you can register for campsites in the park. If it's closed, register at the self-service kiosk. Campsites are located along the woods roads throughout the park; the office can give you a map showing the locations. These campsites are different from those in state parks, undeveloped, and without water supply. For a fee of $6 a night up to six people are allowed in one site; more will cost an extra $1 per night per person. Group sites are available by prior reservation. All the camping in Green Ridge is dispersed, except for the sites at Bond's Landing, on the river. Open campfires are allowed only by specific permit obtained at the headquarters. These are primitive sites with no facilities other than great natural experiences. Contact Green Ridge State Forest, 28700 Headquarters Drive NE, Flintstone, MD 21530-9525, ☎ 301-478-3124, emergency ☎ 800-825-7275.

Close to Green Ridge, Belle Grove and Bill Meyer WMA's and to the Potomac and C&O Canal, the **Little Orleans Campground** is on 22 acres of woodland only six miles south of I-68. Fire rings are at all sites and there are showers, camp store, dumping station and a raft of recreation facilities including horse shoes, rifle range, basketball, nature trails, etc. They rent canoes for use in the nearby Potomac. Tenting section rates are $15 for a family of four, $2 extra per additional child. Ask about RV site availability. The campground store sells fishing supplies and equipment. 31661 Green Forest Drive, SE, Little Orleans, MD 21766, ☎ 301-478-2325. From Exit 68 of I-68 take Orleans Rd. south for about six miles.

West of Hagerstown, the privately operated **Indian Springs Campground** has tents-only sites without hookups for $10 a night or hook-up sites for $15. Prices are for two persons in the party; extra persons are $2-3 additional depending on their age. Facilities include showers, fishing, basketball and a camp store and dumping station. Indian Springs is at 10809 Big Pool Rd., Big Pool; ☎ 301-842-3336. From Route 40 west of Hagerstown, take Route 56 south; from I-70, Exit 12, take Route 56 north 0.6 mile.

For RV travelers who like the urban feel of KOA facilities, **Hagerstown Snug Harbor** has all of the amenities and entertainment that are expected in these campgrounds, including movies, karaoke, bands and magic shows. They also have canoe rentals. 11759 Snug Harbor Lane, Williamsport 21795; information ☎ 301-223-7571, reservations 800-562-7607, www.gocampingamerica.com/hagerstownkoa, e-mail snugharbor@gocampingamerica.com. From Exit 24 on I-70, take Route 63 south and immediately turn right onto Kemps Mill Rd.

Another socially oriented campground is **Yogi Bear's Jellystone Park**, but with more trees here in spite of the kitsch. Sites, even for big RVs have trees around them. They also have attractive and comfortable log cabins for rent on their 50 acres, which also has hiking and biking trails, a pool, playgrounds, 18-hole mini golf and enough activities that you don't have to contemplate nature if you don't want to. Look for Yogi at 16519 Lappans Rd., Williamsport 21795; ☎ 301-223-7117, 800-421-7116. Tent sites with no services are $23 on weekends in high season; full hook-up sites are $30, and the rustic cabin is $42; weekdays are $2-4 lower.

On the canal at Williamsport is **McMahon's Restaurant & Recreation Area**, at Milepost 88. In addition to their campground, they have a dining room with carry-out service. It's convenient to canoeing on the river, hiking the towpath and fishing, and Antietam is only a short distance away. They are on Avis Mill Rd., in the Downsville section of Williamsport; ☎ 301-223-8778 or 223-9314.

Rocky Gap Sate Park, with more than 3,000 acres, has a campground on the far side of the lake from the manicured lawns of the hotel and golf course. Shady sites – 278 of them – mix tents and RVs, but one loop is reserved for tent campers only. One loop offers electric hook-ups and two allow pets. Mini-cabins without kitchens, where you bring your own bedding and other camping gear, are adjacent to the campground. Reservations are essential on summer weekends, and a good idea spring and fall weekends, too. The park is open for camping year-round, but without services from November through April. From Sunday to Thursday, campsites are $16 a night, $5 more for electricity; on Friday and Saturday they are $20, $5 more for electricity. Mini-cabins are $35-$40. The park is visible from I-68 at Exit 50, 12500 Pleasant Valley Rd., Flintstone 21530; ☎ 301-777-2139; for reservations, ☎ 301-888-432-CAMP (2267).

Several campsites at Rocky Gap State Park are accessible to handicapped campers or those with limited mobility.

Fort Frederick State Park has 30 primitive campsites along the river, for tents or RVs. Two of the sites are handicapped-accessible; all have metal fire rings. No reservations are accepted. For access directions, see section on state parks at the beginning of *Adventures*, above. Fort Frederick Park, ☎ 301-842-2155, www.dnr.state.md.us/publiclands/wmrt.html.

Where to Eat

DINING PRICE KEY
The price key indicates the cost of *most* dinner entrées on a restaurant's regular and daily special menu.
$. . . . . Most under $10
$$. $10 to $20
$$$. Over $30

■ Frostburg

If you take the excursion train to Frostburg, you arrive at the railroad station, but there is much more to the town, which sits up on the hill behind the Thrasher Carriage Museum. While the Depot Restaurant in the train station is popular with tourists, it is generally jammed with tour groups. The following restaurants are downtown, which is reached via a free trolley.

For down-to-earth dining try **Princess Restaurant**, where three generations of the Pappas family have been feeding their neighbors since 1939. This is good, solid and dependable food at remarkable prices. They serve three meals a day, Monday-Saturday. Roast or grilled chicken, meatloaf, roast beef, pepper steak, grilled pork chops – you get the idea. Meals come as platters (about $5), with two veggies and rolls, or as dinners, with juice or soup, salad, two veggies, a dessert and beverage (all for under $10). In addition to regular sandwiches, most of which are under $2, they offer specialty sandwiches. Children's meals are available at about $3. At the soda fountain you can treat yourself to a shake, malt, float or banana split. 12 West Main Street; ☎ 301-689-1680.

For excellent whole-food dishes, locals turn to **Gandalf's**, whose very funky dining room is entered through the pub. Many of the offerings are Mexican or at least Hispanic-inspired, such as Budin Azteca or Enchiladas Mole. Picadillo combines roasted tomato, potato, peppers and corn with your choice of chicken, steak, or their vegetarian sausage, soyrizo. Asian stir-fry, African and Mediterranean dishes further expand options. This is one of the area's best options for vegetarians, with many well-conceived choices; $. Dinner is served Monday-Saturday, 5-10 pm. 16 West Main Street; ☎ 301-689-2010.

■ Cumberland

When Pigs Fly is a casual place for hearty and well-prepared dishes. A full rack of baby back ribs ($14) is tender, very lean and with a tasty sauce. Soup might be sausage chili, black bean chili with chicken, vegetable crab soup or chili with corn and chunks of fresh tomato. Scallops are dusted with cajun spices and broiled to a moist perfection. A carafe of wine is $10. Decor plays on the pig theme with an assortment of often amusing pig art. Desserts are the old-fashioned gooey kind updated: chocolate cake, Reese's peanut butter pie, cappuccino torte. Open Monday-Saturday, 11-10; Sunday, 4-10; longer hours in the summer. The restaurant is at 18 Valley Street in Cumberland; ☎ 301-722-7447; www.whenpigsfly.com.

The Bourbon Street Café has a Cajun influence, but it doesn't dominate the whole menu; pasta dishes are good, too. Pasta primavera New Orleans-style, chicken in Creole sauce over pasta, shrimp and ham in a seafood cream sauce, jambalaya, red beans and rice with andouille sausage, herb-crusted salmon, or panéed alligator tail with shrimp étouffée might be on the menu. Most dishes are well under $15. It's open Monday-Saturday, 11 am-9 pm, at 82 Broadway in downtown Cumberland; ☎ 301-722-1116.

If you are into local traditions – or just long for a good hot dog – stop at **Coney Island and Curtis' Famous Wieners - Since 1918**. That's the way they bill themselves and the same family, the Giatras, have been doing it the whole time. Originally only one location, there are now two, within doors of each other. In addition to wieners (hot dogs to the rest of us), they have burgers and sandwiches, but that should be some kind of sin in such a historic hot dog joint. 35 and 15 North Liberty Street, Cumberland, ☎ 301-759-9707 or 777-0380. They are open 365 days, 7 am-10 pm.

One mile east of Cumberland, off I-68 at Exit 46, is a group of restaurants owned by the Mason family. **Mason's Barn** (☎ 301-722-6155) began in the 1950s, selling hot dogs and homemade doughnuts. It's now a family-style restaurant, serving steaks and good soups. **JB's Steak Cellar** (☎ 301-722-6060) has an open kitchen and serves a slightly more upscale menu – Maine lobster and oysters – but in a casually elegant atmosphere with elements of stained glass and brass. The casual up-tempo **1819 Brew House** has booths and fireplaces, serving beer-related entrées such as strip steak with a stout demi-glace and mussels steamed in Scottish ale, all at under $15 (☎ 301-777-7005). A selection of their own brews are on tap here, and at **Uncle Tucker's** (☎ 301-777-7232), which serves excellent pizza and other entrées. Baby back ribs with roasted red potatoes are good, and the Santa Fe pizza isn't for wimps. Tuesday is two-for-one pizza night and Monday is all-you-can-eat pasta night, with your choice of topping. In the summer, Thursday evenings feature all the crabs you can eat for about

$20. Also in the summer, the deck is open, with entertainment on Friday and Saturday evenings. All these dining venues are open for lunch and dinner, and the price range is $-$$. Visit the Masons' Web site at www.ed-masons.com.

■ LaVale

Gehauf's Restaurant is a favorite locally and has served the area for a long time. It has a California-style menu, a change from the homestyle popular at most places. They serve breakfast, lunch and dinner and are open Monday-Thursday, 7 am-9 pm; until 10 pm on Friday-Saturday; Sunday, 8-8. Their more casual **Henny's Lounge** is a good family restaurant with freshly roasted turkey every day. Open Monday-Saturday, at 4:30, closing at midnight during the week and 1 am on Saturday, closed Sunday. Gehauf's is at 1268 National Highway, LaVale; ☎ 301-729-1746. $-$$

Penny's Diner, in front of Oak Tree Motor Inn, isn't really the old-time diner it appears to be, but it's carefully designed to seem real in a newly built Starlite case. The illusion is carried out in the menu, too, with skillet breakfasts and a big Sunday dinner. The specials, of course, are served on blue plates: macaroni and cheese with stewed tomatoes on Friday and sausage and gravy over biscuits on Saturday. Even if it isn't an original, the food is good and plentiful, the staff friendly and the diner is open every day, even holidays, serving the whole menu 24 hours around the clock. Its hearty specials and regular menu entrées are in the $6 range. Penny's is at 12310 Winchester Rd., SW, LaVale; ☎ 301-729-6700.

FARMERS' MARKETS

■ The **Hagerstown City Farmers' Market** opens at 5 am all year. You can get a cooked breakfast, buy baked goods or pick up picnic makings. In addition to foods they have a good selection of crafts by local artisans. 25 West Church Street, Hagerstown; ☎ 301-739-8577. Periodically throughout the year they present special craft shows and events.

■ In downtown **Cumberland**, a farmers' market sets up on pedestrianized Broadway Thursday at 9 am, but for some reason we've yet to make any sense of they won't sell you anything until 10 am. So if you would like to get an earlier start, stop at the farmers' market at Exit 39 of I-68, where it crosses Route 40 Alt, to stock up on produce from the local Mennonite farms.

■ At **LaVale** you'll find a farmers' market at the Country Club Mall on Tuesday, 10-2, and in Frostburg on Fridays from June until fall, 10-1:30. For information, ☎ 301-724-3320.

■ Hagerstown

Schmankerl Stube Bavarian Restaurant. The *gemuchlichtkeit* is easy and natural, and the menu represents the best of fine German cuisine, not usually found on this side of the Atlantic – in short it's the real thing with added flair. For example, you may find jalapeño spaetzle on the menu. Look for the old favorite *kassler ripperl* (smoked porkloin with sauerkraut or spaetzle) or a *schmankerl topf* (beef and pork medallions over spaetzle with hunter sauce) among the 19 authentic offerings on the menu. House wine, served in lovely iron *weinhalters*, is pricier than some bottled varieties on the list, but of very good quality. The Stube has, in addition to its comfortable dining room, a terrace beer garden with beautifully espaliered hedge and lights strung overhead; it could be in downtown Munich. Beer lovers will be pleased to find rare German draft beers such as Hacker Pschorr and Weissbier in genuine steins. At 58 South Potomac Street, Hagerstown (☎ 301-797-3354), it's open for lunch Tuesday-Friday, 11:30-2, and dinner Tuesday-Sunday, 11:30-10 (until 9 on Sunday). From the end of October through the end of April there is a Sunday Brunch, 11:30-2:30. $$

> *On the east side of Hagerstown, US 40 is a divided highway called Dual Highway, edged on both sides by malls, fast food restaurants and hotels. It feeds directly into town. From I-70 pick up US 40 at Exit 32, south of town, or from I-81 on the west at Exit 6. You can also get to the center of town by taking Exit 29 from I-70 (also marked for Sharpsburg-Antietam) and following Route 65 (South Potomac Street) north.*

Roccoco, sophisticated and casual, commanded our attention immediately with its well-informed waitstaff. Presentations are elegant, on fine tableware, and several good wines are available by the glass. But the bottom line is the chef's skills: nightly specials might include Veal Porcini, a scallopine encrusted with pignoli nuts and served with sautéed porcini mushrooms, or rabbit galatine on a bed of lentils. If you thought you didn't like lentils, try these. We wanted another serving for dessert – until we saw the pignoli-nut chocolate torte. For lunch they have soups, creative wood oven pizzas and a selection of sandwiches, such as the woodburned rib-eye wrap or roasted portobello with goat cheese and roasted red pepper. It's close to Public Square at 20 West Washington Street; ☎ 301-790-3331, serving lunch and dinner from Monday through Saturday. $$

If you cannot find a parking space when dining out in downtown Hagerstown in the evening, you can park behind the library, one block past Public Square. There is also a large parking garage just off East Washington Street that charges a maximum of $3 per day, free on weekends, and there is metered lot parking just north of Public Square on North Potomac Street.

The Plum, 6 Rochester Place, on an alley off West Washington Street, (☎ 301-791-1717), is open for breakfast and lunch, 7:30-2:30, building about 35 varieties of gourmet sandwiches to order. Place your order at the counter and admire the collection of quilts that decorate the walls, while you wait for your lunch to be delivered to your table – it won't take long. Sandwiches are thick with filling. If you will be hiking, stock up on the huge granola bars (Trail Mix Bars are $1.50) in the jar on the counter; they keep well and could easily replace an entire meal. $

Another option for breakfast, lunch or dinner is **'Round the Square** next to the Visitor Information Center at 12 Public Square in Hagerstown (☎ 301-745-6252). From the tin ceiling down, the café's decor recaptures the flavor of an earlier era. We like Mary Ann's Rondolais, roast beef on a baguette with rondolais cheese, onion and tomato. The turkey in their sandwiches is real, not pressed or mechanically formed. You can get a real fountain Coke, birch beer or sarsaparilla, or an ice cream soda. They also have live entertainment from time to time in the section known as Harry's House of Blues. $

■ Williamsport

For hearty, home-style food at low prices, go to the **American Legion Hall**. It's for members only, but they will sign you in as a guest if they have room. The roast beef is good, as are club sandwiches. Be prepared for smoke in the air, but a friendly atmosphere. Even if you don't eat here, ask to step inside to see the C&O Canal mural that runs around the dining room wall. To get here, look for the red, white and blue street sign on the south side of Route 68 East, just out of downtown. Call ☎ 301-223-7087 to find out when they are holding their next all-you-can-eat event, which may be the best bargain in the state for those with big appetites, $.

■ Hancock

Weavers, on Main St, is a tradition with area families. The casual restaurant is best known for its large salad bar, juicy ham steak ($8.95), pork chops, and the liver and onions special. Whether you eat at the tables or counter, end your meal with a wedge of pie (usually a choice of peach, apple, cherry, raspberry, blueberry or lemon) or one of their huge slabs of cake. Lunch sandwiches are priced from $3 to $6. The bakery in the front of the restaurant sells cookies, rolls, bread, pies and doughnuts, with a nine-inch pan of sticky buns laden with pecans costing only $4. A big cinnamon coffee cake (they call it small), a foot in diameter, is $2.39. Day-old goods are priced even lower.

Park N Dine, on 189 East Main St., serves good old fashioned breakfasts and the solid home-style cooking that has become Hancock's specialty. Look for pot roast and their special ham pot pie or roast turkey. Prices are under $10 for entrées.

AUTHOR TIP

SWEET TREATS: *For ice cream, the top place in Hancock is **Barnard's Ice Cream Parlor** at 125 West Main Street, ☎ 301-678-5676. They have 32 flavors of hand-dipped hard ice cream and soft-serve in chocolate and vanilla. Milkshakes, malts, fudge brownie supreme and floats are available, too. From Tuesday through Friday they serve soups; deli sandwiches are available every day.*

North-Central Maryland

Far enough away from the cities to let travelers forget they are still in the busy coastal corridor, this area is still within easy reach of day-trippers out of Baltimore. But it's not heavily touristed, despite its lush green mountainsides and lovely pastoral landscapes. Just across the Potomac in West Virginia, Harper's Ferry is tied historically and geographically to this part of Maryland, and you will certainly want to see it while you are here.

Geography & History

The central lands share some of the characteristics of the flat shorelands to their east and of the mountains to their west, a very pleasing blend. Carroll County, including the shiretown of Westminster, is an area of rolling farmlands, much of it open and actively worked. As you move westward there is a gradual change, hard to detect at first, as the hills become a bit steeper and taller, a change that becomes more pronounced west of Frederick as you move toward the Appalachians.

MARYLAND

N

CHESAPEAKE BAY

North-Central Maryland

These mountains form a spine along which the Appalachian Trail moves from West Virginia to Pennsylvania, marked by a string of small parks that protect much of the route. The steep slopes and foothills of Catoctin Mountain form a beautiful set of parklands north of Frederick.

The meandering Potomac, rising near Cumberland and winding down through steep mountain valleys until it broadens out in the more gentle lands closer to Washington, forms Maryland's southern border with West Virginia here.

■ Settlement

Settlement came late to what was once the western part of the colony of Maryland. While a few lived in isolated pockets on the edges of the westwardly expanding frontier, towns did not come until later. Originally settled in 1733, Frederick Town, now Frederick, became a town in 1748. To its east, in Carroll County, the city of Westminster was originally formed in 1764 as the town of Winchester, after its founder William Winchester. In 1837 it became the shire town of the new Carroll County, carved from Baltimore and Frederick counties, and prospered as a rail center at the end of the 19th century.

Both started as agricultural communities with growing small industrial bases. One of the earliest acts of rebellion in the British colonies came in Frederick in November, 1765, when 12 justices of the court refused to enforce the Stamp Act. Although small and remote, Frederick sent troops to Boston and more than 1,700 men to Washington's camp at Valley Forge, Pennsylvania, during the Revolution.

Even though it's in West Virginia, Harper's Ferry was historically crucial to this part of western Maryland. Here the Shenandoah and Potomac Rivers merge at the feet of tall mountains and cliffs that rise on all sides. As the British colonies pressed westward, these rivers became important highways of travel and commerce. In 1733 the first inhabitant of the area was Peter Stephens, who established a ferry service, which he sold to Robert Harper in 1747. Harper, a millwright from Philadelphia, not only improved the ferry service but he started a gristmill, harnessing the power of the Shenandoah. Other water-powered mills followed and a town slowly began to form.

DID YOU KNOW?

In 1783, before there was a town at Harpers Ferry, Thomas Jefferson, while on his way to the Continental Congress, stopped at the confluence of the Shenandoah and the Potomac with his daughter Patsy. He declared the view "... perhaps one of the most stupendous scenes in nature... " and observed that it was worth a trip across the Atlantic.

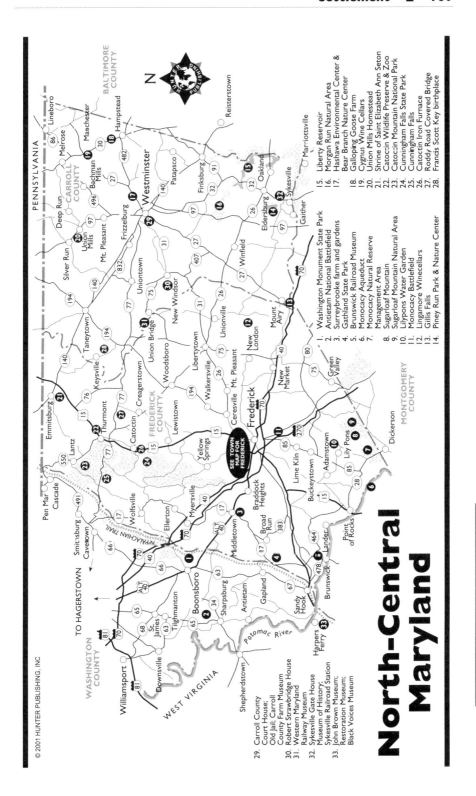

North-Central Maryland

1. Washington Monument State Park
2. Antietam National Battlefield
3. Surreybrooke farm and gardens
4. Gathland State Park
5. Brunswick Railroad Museum
6. Monocacy Aqueduct
7. Monocacy Natural Reserve Management Area
8. Sugarloaf Mountain
9. Sugarloaf Mountain Natural Area
10. Lilypons Water Garden
11. Monocacy Battlefield
12. Lingamore Winecellars
13. Gillis Falls
14. Piney Run Park & Nature Center
15. Liberty Reservoir
16. Morgan Run Natural Area
17. Hashawa Environmental Center & Bear Branch Nature Center
18. Galloping Goose Farm
19. Cygnus Wine Cellars
20. Union Mills Homestead
21. Shrine of Saint Elizabeth Ann Seton
22. Catoctin Wildlife Preserve & Zoo
23. Catoctin Mountain National Park
24. Cunningham Falls State Park
25. Cunningham Falls
26. Catoctin Iron Furnace
27. Roddy Road Covered Bridge
28. Francis Scott Key birthplace
29. Carroll County Court House; Old Jail; Carroll County Farm Museum
30. Robert Strawbridge House
31. Western Maryland Railway Museum
32. Sykesville Gate House Museum of History; Sykesville Railroad Station
33. John Brown Museum; Restoration Museum; Black Voices Museum

© 2001 HUNTER PUBLISHING, INC

North-Central Maryland

George Washington also knew this area from his early years as a surveyor and from his service as General Braddock's aide. After the Revolution, recognizing the need for firearms for the young nation, he chose Harpers Ferry as the site for a new Federal Armory, establishing it in 1796. The fame of the armory was sufficient by 1803 that Meriwether Lewis bought much of his equipment and firearms here for his explorations with William Clark. He also planned his trip while staying at the Hessian Barracks in Frederick. More than a half-century later the issue of slavery and the strategic position of Frederick and Carroll Counties would bring war to the area.

■ The Civil War

When, during the great national debate over slavery, a line designated as the Mason-Dixon Line was drawn across the continent to delineate slave and non-slave states, the Maryland-Pennsylvania boundary was selected and Maryland remained a slave state. While slavery was employed in this western part of the state, the numbers were small. For example, in the Harpers Ferry of 1860 there were about 150 slaves in a total population of 2,600 persons. People here tended to be individualistic, small farmers, mill owners and business people, as opposed to the bigger slave-owning plantations in the southern part of the state.

It was the armory at Harpers Ferry, with its musket factory, rifle factory and two arsenals that attracted John Brown, a violent abolitionist and maker of "Bloody Kansas." Gathering 21 fellow believers (including two of his sons and five blacks) at a remote farmhouse nearby across the Potomac in Maryland, on October 16, 1859, he crossed the rail bridge over the Potomac and captured the armory, holding it for two days. Attacked by local militia, and ultimately by a small contingent of federal troops, he was wounded, captured, tried for treason (among other crimes) in the courthouse at Harpers Ferry and hanged. His raid was a preamble to the Civil War.

DID YOU KNOW?

John Brown's raid was ended by US troops under the command of Robert E. Lee, then a Lieutenant Colonel. One of his aides, Lieutenant J.E.B. Stuart, tried to negotiate the release of 60 hostages held by Brown but failed to obtain Brown's surrender.

In 1860 Harpers Ferry was part of the state of Virginia, and when that state seceded from the United States the Federal armory and its arsenal again drew violence to the town. The armory was seized in April 1861 by Stonewall Jackson, its machinery dismantled and shipped deeper into Southern territory.

The Civil War made this part of the state a corridor of war, the place where General Lee sought to demoralized the Union and threaten its capital at Washington by surrounding it. Both Frederick and Westminster were important crossroads and served as important storage centers for Union supplies.

In 1862 Jackson again besieged Harpers Ferry, forcing its surrender and that of the whole federal garrison in the town as General Lee made his first move into the north. A raging battle across the Potomac along the Antietam Creek near Sharpsburg, Maryland, ended that attempt but was not the end of the war for Maryland.

In June and July of 1863, Confederate and Federal troops again passed through Frederick and Carroll counties. When General Lee invaded the north that year, initial federal plans called for defense in Maryland near Westminster, but Lee's forces moved toward the important junction town of Gettysburg, just a few miles north of Emmitsburg across the border in Pennsylvania. Troop movements before the battle literally clogged the northbound roads from Frederick and Westminster, and both towns were occupied and retaken. A year later, in June 1864, Federal and Confederate troops clashed once again, this time in farmlands just southeast of Frederick along the Monocacy River. Union troops lost the battle but delayed the Confederate army long enough to permit the reinforcement of Washington DC.

■ The Canal & The Railroad

Before the Civil War, the C&O Canal had been constructed along the Potomac, which was not navigable due to falls and shallows. From the start, competition was fierce between the railroad and the canal to see who would get West first. The first confrontation in the race between the C&O Canal and the B&O Railroad was over the limited right-of-way space at the small town of Point of Rocks, where the Potomac cuts through the long spine of Catoctin Mountain. There was room for one or the other, but not both in the narrow strip of ground between the rocks and river. The dispute held up canal construction there for four years, as Point of Rocks became a point of contention. (The Brunswick Rail Museum, nearby, focuses on this competition between the railroad and the canal; see *Museums & Historic Sites*, page 139.)

Getting Here & Getting Around

From Baltimore, the quickest route to Westminster is to take **I-695** to **I-795** as far as Reisterstown, then follow Route 140. To get to Westminster from Washington DC, take **I-270** from **I-495** (the Beltway) and, at Exit 16, a few miles northwest of Gaithersburg, take **Route 27**. Travelers from the Northeastern US should take **I-95** toward Baltimore, turning onto I-695 north of the city, then following the directions from Baltimore.

The fastest route to Frederick from Baltimore is on I-70 and the fastest from Washington is via I-270, both of which meet at Frederick, along with US 340 from Harpers Ferry and US 15, which leads to Pennsylvania. A number of smaller state roads add spokes to this wagon wheel design of routes converging in Frederick. Westminster, east of Frederick, looks much the same, but without the interstate highways. Whatever route you choose to reach either city will take you through beautiful rolling farmlands.

Information Sources

Tourism Council of Frederick County, 19 East Church Street, Frederick; ☎ 301-228-2888, 800-999-3613, www.visitfrederick.org, 9:30-4:30 daily, closed major holidays.

Carroll County Visitors Center, 210 East Main Street, Westminster; ☎ 410-848-1388 or 800-272-1933; www.carr.org/tourism. Guided tours are also available by reservation. Open Monday-Saturday, 9-5; Sunday and holidays, 10-2.

In Frederick, be careful of the parking lot next door to the Visitors Center on East Church Street. The entrance is on the left and exit on the right – very confusing unless you are a British driver.

Adventures

■ Parks

 North of Frederick are **Catoctin Mountain Park** (☎ 301-663-9330), a National Park Service property, and almost across the road **Cunningham Falls State Park** (☎ 301-271-7574). The latter is divided into the William Houck and Manor Areas, connected by a narrow corridor. To get there take US 15 north from Frederick to Thurmont, then Route 77 west. A 43-acre lake has a swimming beach and canoe rentals and the park offers orienteering, wildflower and other outdoor programs, as well as picnic areas and playgrounds. Day-use fees at the state park are $2 per car or, on weekends, $1 per person. Catoctin Mountain is free.

Farther west, at about the midpoint of Maryland's share of the Appalachian Trail, is **Greenbrier State Park**. The Appalachian Trail passes through the park and there is a small lake with canoes and paddleboats. Access is off US 40 just west of the I-70 overpass. There is a $2 per car day-use rate. South Mountain Recreation Area, 21843 National Pike, Boonsboro 21713; ☎ 301-791-4767.

 Most of the facilities at Greenbrier State Park are handicapped-accessible and there are aquatic wheelchairs for rent at the lake.

■ On Foot

Hiking

 North of Frederick, the twin parks, **Catoctin Mountain National Park** and **Cunningham Falls State Park**, reached by US 15 and Route 77, cover wild mountainous landscapes. Each is covered by networks of hiking trails.

Here in the Blue Ridge part of the Appalachians, moonshine was a popular product during Prohibition. In fact, at Catoctin Mountain National Park there is a nice half-mile walk through the woods to the restored remains of the **Blue Blazes Whiskey Still**, which was destroyed by the "revenuers" in the thirties. Start in the Visitor Center parking lot and take the trail from its edge. The trail gains about 60 feet in altitude as it runs along the side of a small brook, crosses a road and continues to the still.

For another family hike, try **Hog Rock Nature Trail**, about 1.3 miles north on the main park road. This trail is mostly level, but the terrain can be a bit rough in places. There are interpretive signs along this trail.

*Although they are rarely encountered, it is good to know that this area has two native **poisonous snakes**, the northern copperhead and timber rattler. Wise hikers watch where they step, especially in rocky areas.*

Cat Rock, a trail with an overlook as its goal, can be reached via a nine-mile hike from the Manor area of the state park or by a three-mile hike from the parking lot across from the Park headquarters on Route 77. Both of these are hard climbs, the former gaining 1,120 feet and the latter 720 feet. The **Chimney Rock** climb, 2.2 miles and 520 feet of elevation, is also rewarded by nice views from rock formations and is accessed from the Park headquarters on Route 77. Ask at the ranger station for maps and the trail list.

On Catoctin Hollow Rd., look for signs to the William Houck area and the beach parking area. In summer this is a fee facility. It is named for **Cunningham Falls**, one of the tallest in the state at 78 feet. This is a cascading falls, rather than one single drop and the effect is quite beautiful. The walk to the falls from the parking lot is about 1.5 miles and takes a bit more than half an hour over a good trail, but with a lot of uphill sections. This is a popular place for school groups, so it may be busy on weekdays. If you have the option, try to go the first sunny day after a rainy period to see the falls at their best. The park access and the trail to the falls are well marked.

A special accessible parking area and wide, level trail is provided on Route 77, close to Cunningham Falls. To park there, contact the State Park Headquarters at ☎ 301-271-7574.

There are also several other trails in Cunningham Falls State Park. The terrain here is hilly, occasionally quite steep and covered with a mixed growth of hardwoods. Trails are generally wide enough and well maintained, although some areas show erosion.

One of the most famous hiking trails in the country is the **Appalachian Trail**, and about 40 of its 2,000 miles are in Maryland. The trail roughly follows along the western boundary of Frederick County, from the town of Pen-Mar on the Pennsylvania border to the Potomac River east of Harper's Ferry. The trail generally follows along the ridge of the mountains, so the elevation changes are not extreme, except when it drops down to cross the valleys where the main roads are located. Because the trail runs roughly north and south across this part of Maryland, it crosses highways and roads fairly frequently and a number of trailheads allow for access at several points, allowing sections of the trail to be used for day hiking.

RECOMMENDED READING: *While there are several books that mention the Appalachian Trail, the most thorough treatment is the* **Appalachian Trail Guide to Maryland and Northern Virginia**, *published by The Potomac Appalachian Trail Club, $7. They also publish another excellent guide to hiking in this area,* **Hikes in Western Maryland**, *which has over 20 trails in the western part of the state, $6. These can be bought in many bookstores, information centers and sporting outlets or from the Potomac AMC at 118 Park Street, SE, Vienna, VA 22180;* ☎ *703-242-0315.*

A detailed description of the entire trail is beyond the scope of this book, but we suggest three segments that give good trail experiences with a goal as a reward. The first takes you to **Washington Monument State Park**, the first monument to Washington, predating both the one in Baltimore and the one on the Mall in Washington, DC. The jug-shaped monument is about 30 feet tall and is made of indigenous stone. It was dedicated in 1827 and rebuilt in the 1930s. The monument is situated along the top of a ridge, making nice views from the top. You can drive to the state park and take the short, steep trail up to the monument (about 20 minutes round-trip) or start at the parking lot at US 40 near the intersection with I-70 (about 10 miles east of Hagerstown) for a 3.5-mile hike over hillsides. Be

The Washington Monument, in Boonsboro.

North-Central Maryland

sure to wear good hiking boots because the trail can be rocky. For detailed instructions, see page 78 of the *Appalachian Trail Guide to Maryland and Northern Virginia*. You can double back to your car, or leave a second vehicle in the parking lot of the Monument before beginning the walk. To get directly to the park, take Alt-40 East from Boonsboro, then take Washington Monument Rd. 1½ miles to the parking area. The trails are behind the Visitor Center.

Another enjoyable walk is from **Gathland State Park** at Crampton Gap. In the park you will pass the unusual stone-arched **War Correspondents Monument** commemorating newsmen of the Civil War, erected by George A. Townsend. He was a 19th-century journalist who built an estate here. This was one of the sites of the series of battles in 1862 that were the prelude to the Battle of Antietam, called the Battle of South Mountain. The trail rises and falls several times and can be rocky and rough underfoot. It passes a white quartzite cliff with views and after about six miles it passes near Fox Gap, another site of heavy fighting in the Battle of South Mountain. In another 1.2 miles the trail ends at Turners Gap, site of more fighting, and the location of the South Mountain Inn, now a restaurant, which was Confederate headquarters during the battle. See page 84, *Appalachian Trail Guide to Maryland and Northern Virginia*. Again, this is a linear trail and it's good to have a shuttle back to the starting point.

One of the most popular segments of the trail is the one that leads to the **Annapolis Rocks** and **Black Rock Cliffs**, with beautiful views from both. The starting point is the same parking lot as for the Washington Monument hike, but instead of crossing I-70, head in the opposite direction by going under the US 40 overpass of I-70 and then following the trail into the woods. It is about two miles to the side trail for the Annapolis Rocks and about another mile from there to Black Rock Cliffs. It's a good idea to have a detailed guide; this hike is on page 75 of the *Appalachian Trail Guide to Maryland and Northern Virginia*.

AUTHOR TIP

One of the best outdoor sport shops in the area is **The Trail House***, 17 South Market St., Frederick;* ☎ *301-694-8448. They specialize in hiking, backpacking, camping, rock climbing and cross-country ski gear, clothing, maps and books. The shop is open Monday through Saturday 9:30-7; Monday-Thursday and Friday 9:30-8; Saturday 9:30-5:30; Sunday noon-4.*

Sugarloaf Mountain, close to the Monocacy Aqueduct in Dickerson, is privately owned, but the trails are open to the public. Pick up a trail map in the box just as you pass between the carriage sheds at the entrance. Trails wind up and over the small mountain, which is surprisingly steep for its modest 1,281-foot altitude. For a less strenuous exploration of its rocky summit, and a look at the views from its various look-offs, begin at the parking area marked West View, where there is a stone tower. Follow the Northern Peaks Trail to Bill Lambert Overlook, returning by the steeper, more heavily used Thomas Trail. Or, our preference, continue on the blue-blazed trail around the other side of the summit on a longer, less-used trail to East View and return to your car by the paved auto road. To get there from Route 28 in Dickerson, follow Sugarloaf Rd., just north of the railway underpass. On the Maryland state map, the entrance crossroads is labeled Stronghold.

There are a number of hiking and walking trails in Carroll County, including those south of Westminster in the **Morgan Run Natural Environment Area**. Take Bartholow Rd. from Route 97, then Ben Rose Lane. The trails are open daily, year-round, from 7 am to sunset. Maps are available at the Patapsco Valley State Park; ☎ 410-461-5005.

More trails are at **Gillis Falls** on the Grimville Rd. in Mt. Airy. You can get maps at the Visitor Information Center (☎ 410-848-1388, 800-272-1933) or the Carroll County Department of Recreation (☎ 410-386-2103). The trails here are open March through August, sunup to sundown. From September 1 through February they are open Tuesday, Thursday and Sunday, and closed the other days of the week. They also close for two weeks each year, beginning the Saturday following Thanksgiving, for hunting.

In the southeast part of Carroll County there are three places for hiking. North of Sykesville, at **Piney Run Park** in Eldersburg, the trails are open daily from sunup to sunset. Access the park from Route 26 via White Rock Rd. and Martz Rd. Trail maps are available from the park (☎ 410-795-3274) or the Carroll County Visitor Information Center and the Carroll County Department of Recreation (see phone numbers above).

Near Marriottsville is a part of the Patapsco Valley State Park called the **McKeldin Area**, at 3000 Marriottsville Rd. south of Route 26. Several miles of trails are open daily from 8 am to sunset and there is a fee of $2 per person from March through October. Nearby are the trails of the **Liberty Reservoir**, maintained by the Baltimore Public Works Department because this is the Baltimore water supply. The trails here are the woods roads used by the Department. Hunting is also allowed here; check with them at ☎ 410-795-6150 for trail and hunting information.

Walking Tours

The **Tourism Council of Frederick County**, 19 East Church Street, Frederick (☎ 301-663-8687, 800-999-3613), has printed a very good walking tour of the historic sites of the city, available at their office and at racks around town. The route passes most of the historically significant buildings of the city and the brochure has historic photos and short descriptions. A marked map allows you to decide how long a walk you want. The Council also has 1½-hour **guided walking tours** on Saturdays, Sundays and most holiday Mondays. Tours begin at the Council office at 1:30 pm,

April through December. The cost is adults $4.50, seniors $3.50, children under 12 free.

A pleasant 1.15-mile stroll runs along **Carroll Creek Linear Park**, which extends between East (and West) Patrick Street and All Saints Street. Start at the Delaplaine Visual Arts Center on South Carroll Street and walk westward crossing Bentz Street to the 44-acre Baker Park, with outdoor recreational facilities and summer concerts. The carillon tower in the park has concerts every Sunday afternoon.

Westminster has excellent walking tours of the city, too. The guide and map, called *A Walking Tour of Carroll County – Westward Expansion*, passes 31 historic properties in town, covering the period from 1800 through 1915. The estimated walking time is 1½ hours. It is available at the Tourist Information Center, 210 East Main Street. Another wonderful tour is the **Ghost Walk**, which will take you past eight sites that are said to be haunted by ghosts of everyone from Legh Master (see page 147) to a Confederate cavalryman with a penchant for taking pictures off the wall. Get the self-guided tour brochure at the Visitor Information Center. Another fascinating self-guided tour brochure available there is *Corbit's Charge*, a tour of the in-town battlefield where Captain Charles Corbit and a small troop of Union soldiers held off the cavalrymen of JEB Stuart long enough to delay their arrival at Gettysburg.

A **walking tour of Courthouse Square** takes you past buildings dating from 1800 through 1900, most erected by 1840. These were the days of great growth in Westminster, when it became a shire town and its citizens began to prosper. A thorough brochure, available at the Visitor Information Center, fully describes each of the buildings. Combine the Courthouse Square walk with the **Westward Expansion walking tour** for sights that exemplify the growth as the Baltimore Pike and the railroad brought prosperity to town.

Although these self-guided tours are very well described in the brochures, if you have a chance, sign on for one of the free tours led by historians, leaving the Westminster Tourist Office on Sunday at 2 pm. You should arrive 10 minutes before the hour. You will not only see things you would miss on your own, but will hear delightful stories that encompass every subject from architecture to ghosts (Westminster has more than its share of specters).

Just a few miles west of Westminster there is a nice **walking tour of Uniontown**; pick up the brochure in Westminster. Eighteen buildings are described in the tour, many dating from the early 19th century and others later in that century and into the early 20th century.

WESTMINSTER HISTORY

Westminster was founded by William Winchester, a high-class (meaning literate) indentured servant, who heard that the Baltimore-Pittsburgh Turnpike was slated to go through the area. He bought a tract of land and named it Winchester, but there was so much confusion between it and Winchester, Virginia, that he changed it to Westminster. It was exactly a day's trip from Baltimore for grain wagons, so it became a stopover point. In 1812, people became nervous about having money in Baltimore, threatened as it was by the war with Britain, so banks opened and thrived in Westminster. In 1837, when the new county was established, prosperous Westminster was the obvious site for a county seat.

AUTHOR TIP

Westminster has an active Volksmarch group (an international walking organization) that conducts a daily 10-km Volksmarch. The event begins at the Westminster Inn, 5 South Center Street, and the starting hours are 7 am to three hours prior to dusk, any day of the year. Call Carl Frock, ☎ 410-876-1108, or Steve Duex, ☎ 410-848-4469 for route information.

The **Hashawa Environmental Center** at 300 John Owings Rd., Westminster, has three walking trails. The Wilderness Trail, 2.2 miles, has several loops through wooded areas that allow you to vary the length of the walk. The Stream Trail roughly follows Bear Branch Creek for part of its 1.8-mile length. It is the link to the Wilderness Trail and is not a loop. Parking is available on the left at the foot of the hill before you reach the Nature Center. A small pond and wetlands boardwalk are adjacent. A loop can be made from the end of the Stream Trail by taking the Vista Trail through woods and between plowed fields. The Vista Trail is 1.2 miles and is also accessible from the parking lot at the **Bear Branch Nature Center**. A trail map is available at the Nature Center. Pets must be on leashes. The trails are open from sunrise to sunset daily from March 1 through August 31, and from September 1 through February on Tuesday, Thursday, Saturday and Sunday. They are closed Monday, Wednesday, Friday and the two weeks after Thanksgiving for hunting. From Westminster, take Route 97 north; three miles from the Route 140 crossing, turn right onto John Owings Rd. at the sport facilities. Follow it for 1.5 miles and turn left onto Hashawa Rd., following signs to the Center.

North-Central Maryland

RECOMMENDED READING: *Serious hikers and those with an interest in the history of the canal should get* **184 Miles of Adventure, Hikers Guide to the C&O Canal,** *which tells the story of the canal and area practically step by step. It also identifies camping, picnic and boat access points along the canal. Look for it in bookstores in towns near the canal or write Mason-Dixon Council, Boy Scouts of America, 18600 Crestwood Drive, PO Box 2133, Hagerstown, MD 21742.*

Opportunities for walking abound along the **C&O Canal,** which marks the western boundary of the state here. Access the canal trail system at the Monocacy Aqueduct, Point of Rocks, Brunswick, Harpers Ferry or at Antietam Creek. The trail is along the old towpath, a multi-purpose trail shared by hikers and bicyclists – and in places with horses. This is a linear trail so for long hikes without backtracking, arrange for transportation at the far end. By the very nature of the canal, this is flat walking and is a good place for a family outing with kids. There are picnic facilities at most of the major access points.

One of the pleasures of the towpath is its flat, smooth surface, which makes it ideal for wheelchairs or for those who have difficulty with rough, uneven trails. Access points have parking and easy approaches to the path.

■ On Wheels

Bicycling

The **C&O Canal** offers some of the best family bicycling anywhere. As one would expect, this is essentially flat-ground pedaling, but it offers wonderful views as it traverses the towpath of the historic canal. In the area covered by this chapter the canal runs from the Montgomery County line (near Dickerson) along the shores of the Potomac, through Harpers Ferry and to Williamsport, just south of Hagerstown. The towpaths were wide shoulders along the edge of the canal where mules and horses once labored drawing barges up and down the canal. Today the paths are used by bicyclists and hikers and, of course, they are linear and not loops.

For the most part, the towpath passes through the overhang of tall green trees growing along the path. At times the path is directly adjacent to the Potomac River and at other times the river can't be seen, even though it is always close. Along the route there are a number of access points. On the south (or east) end of this section access is available at **Point of Rocks**, where Catoctin Mountain literally drops into the Potomac River. This is at US 15 and Route 28. For years the canal company and the railroad fought each other over who was to have the right to use the narrow shelf of land here between the river and the mountain. There is some parking at the railroad station, but they don't like park-goers to use it during the week. To get to the towpath, follow Route 28 to Commerce Street.

Six miles upstream there is another access at **Brunswick**, once an important railroad town. Go through the parking lot at the train station just off Route 17, to the 55-mile marker of the canal. As in Point of Rocks, they don't like towpath users to clutter up the commuter parking lot during the week. They ought to re-think this attitude.

Continuing west along the river, there are two access points near Sharpsburg, one of them at the **Antietam Creek Ranger Station**, 13 miles from Brunswick. Follow Route 34 from Sharpsburg and take the Harpers Ferry Rd. south to Antietam. Canal Rd. and the park entrance will be on the right, with parking, camping and picnic facilities. Four miles upstream at a broad bend in the river is another access at the C&O Canal Park Headquarters. Take Route 34 south to the area near the bridge for West Virginia. The towpath access is on the left side of Canal Rd., across from the entrance to Park Headquarters.

At **Snyders Landing**, just outside of Sharpsburg (follow West Champline Rd., which becomes Snyders Landing Rd. at the sharp curve) is a boat launch and nearby is Barrons Hiker Biker Store, with provisions.

On the west end of this section (actually it's north here, but the overall canal direction is west) is **Williamsport**, a small town in 1790 when it vied for selection as the new capital of the new United States. It lost, becoming a canal town in 1830 and a railroad town in 1873. There is a small canal museum in the park as well as parking. Access to the park is off US 11, before the bridge over the river, west of the Route 11 intersection with Route 68. One of the highlights of the trail here is the triple-arched Conococheague Aqueduct that carried the canal over Conococheague Creek.

For practiced bicyclists, the terrain in Carroll County provides several good options for rides. The land varies from rolling hills to very hilly and the views along the roads are mostly pastoral. You ride here along the very roads used by Civil War soldiers.

For a nice route that begins at **New Windsor**, park at the New Windsor Carnival Grounds on Atlee Avenue, just off Route 75 on the north side of town. Cycle back along Atlee Avenue to Route 75; go right, then almost immediately left onto College Avenue toward the New Windsor Service Center. After a short distance, go right onto Blue Ridge Avenue, then left onto Route 31. Follow it to Springdale Avenue to the left, taking Springdale just under a mile to a right turn onto Rowe Avenue. Follow Rowe about 0.5 mile and go left onto Old New Windsor Pike, also called Wakefield Church Rd. At about 1.3 miles, turn right onto Wakefield Valley Rd., crossing Route 31

North-Central Maryland

and continuing on to Wilt Rd., where you turn left. From Wilt take a right onto Strawbridge Lane to visit the Robert Strawbridge home and memorial, a good resting point. Pedal back to Wilt Rd., go left a short distance and turn left, following Wakefield Valley Rd. to Route 31, about a mile. Take Route 31 to the right approximately 0.9 mile and go right on Main Street, then left onto Route 75 back to Atlee Avenue. The trip is about eight miles over rolling hills.

BIKE RENTALS & OUTFITTERS

C&O Canal Bicycling has rental bicycles available for use on the canal trail from Brunswick to Shepardstown. The best part is that you don't need a carrier. They will deliver the bike and equipment to you and will provide one-way shuttle service so you don't have to double-back on the trail. Their Standard Trek (four to eight hours) costs $30; one-four hours is $25. Two day rentals are available for $40. Riders must be 12 or older. Call ahead to reserve at ☎ 301-834-5180, e-mail Canalbikes@aol.com.

Mountain bike rental is available in Harpers Ferry from **Blue Ridge Outfitters**. In addition to regular rentals, they offer trips along the C&O Canal that include bike, helmet, maps, shuttle and water bottle. Rates are $20 per day. Ask about special packages or about specially planned trips; PO Box 750 Harpers Ferry, WV 25425, ☎ 304-725-3444, www.brocraft.com, e-mail brocraft@aol.com or brocraft@intrepid.net.

Also in Harpers Ferry, bike rentals are available at **The Outfitter at Harpers Ferry** in the lower town; ☎ 304 535-2087. At the Maryland end of the footbridge from Harpers Ferry to the C&O Canal are rental bicycles.

For bike rental or repair, see **Reels and Wheels** at 17328 Taylor's Landing Rd., Sharpsburg, across from the boat ramp at Mile Marker 81 of the canal; ☎ 301-432-7281. They are open Tuesday through Friday, 9-7, and Saturday and Sunday, 7:30-7.

While there is a lot of pleasant biking to be done in this area, much of it is over paved highways that are fairly narrow, curvy and hilly. Watch traffic carefully, pedal defensively and, above all, wear protective headgear – mandatory for age 16 and under, prudent at any age. In Sykesville, helmet use is required for all ages.

Another interesting tour over slightly more hilly terrain takes you around Westminster, out to **Union Mills** and back over rural country roads. This is also a longer trip, about 29 miles, but is off the more heavily traveled routes for the most part. Start at the Westminster Elementary School on Uniontown Rd., on the west side of town. Follow Uniontown Rd. left about three miles to Frizzellburg Rd. Take it to the right about 1.6 miles to Route 832, following it left 0.3 mile to a right onto Richardson Rd. Follow that road for about 3.2 miles, then go left onto Pleasant Valley Rd. for 0.2 mile. Go left onto Hughes Shop Rd. for 1.2 miles to Stone Rd. Go right a short distance, then take a left onto Murkle Rd. In just over two miles you will come to Route 97 in Union Mills. Go right 0.5 mile to Old Hanover Rd., where you turn left. The historic **Union Mills Homestead** is close to this intersection, a good place for a break. After going 0.2 mile up Hanover, turn right onto Deep Run Rd., following it 4.2 miles to a right onto Backwoods Rd. for 2.4 miles, to a left onto Bixler's Church Rd. Within less than a mile you will come to New Bachman Valley Rd., where you take a right. In 0.7 mile take a left onto Old Bachman Valley Rd., keeping to the right at its intersection with Fridinger and Beggs Roads, and following it to Lemmon Rd., where you turn left. Continue to Sullivan Rd. and turn right, crossing Route 140 to Sullivan Avenue, where you turn right. From Sullivan Avenue, turn left onto Pennsylvania Avenue, taking it 0.4 mile to a right onto Union Avenue and another right onto West Main Street after 0.2 mile. Follow West Main a half-mile to a left turn onto Route 31, and take an almost immediate right onto Uniontown Rd. and head back to the school.

AUTHOR TIP

The Volks group in Westminster has an active Volksbike (an international cycling organization) that operates year-round. They run a 27-km Volksbike route that begins at the Westminster Inn, 5 South Center Street. Hours are 7 am to three hours prior to dusk, any day of the year. Call Carl Frock, ☎ 410-876-1108, or Steve Duex, ☎ 410-848-4469, for route information.

One of the best ways to see **Antietam National Battlefield** is by bicycle. The terrain is rolling with a few hills to traverse but is generally easy to handle. The course of the self-guided tour is about eight miles and is studded with monuments on both sides. The battle took place with the Union coming from the east and Lee's Confederates from the west. Pick up the tour guide at the visitor center on Route 65, near Sharpsburg.

In the southwest part of the county there is an 11-mile run from **Mt. Airy** over moderately hilly territory. Start at Firemen's Park at the intersection of Route 27 and Twin Arch Rd. Go left on Twin Arch Rd. (the street name changes immediately to Park Avenue) until it merges with Main South Street, continuing to a left onto Buffalo Rd. Buffalo Rd. was used by the Union VI Corps on July 29, 1863, while on their way to Gettysburg. You fol-

North-Central Maryland

low it only as far as Harrisville Rd., which you take to the right 1.3 miles to the intersection with Ridge Rd., making a jog by going right and then immediately left onto Gillis Falls Road. Follow this 1.3 miles then turn right onto Watersville Road. After about 1.6 miles, keep to the right on Watersville Road when it intersects with another road at the Mennonite Church. In just under two miles you will come to Route 27, where you turn left and go 0.8 mile to Twin Arch Road and your starting point.

AUTHOR TIP

*The **Carroll County Office of Tourism** (☎ 301-848-1388) has a good free brochure for bicyclists. The kit includes maps and detailed directions for 10 routes in all parts of the county, including the one mentioned above. These road routes, for the most part, avoid the busiest highways, except where necessary to complete the loop.*

The **Hashawa Environmental Center** at 300 John Owings Rd., Westminster, has trails that are available for use by bicyclists. These are also walking trails, so extreme caution should be used if you bike them. Walkers have the right of way. Trail maps are available at the center. (See *On Foot*, above, for directions.)

Driving Tours

During the prelude to the battle of Gettysburg tens of thousands of men and their equipment, from both armies, passed through this part of Maryland. Tracing their route is a fascinating **driving tour of the Civil War.** Even though more than 130 years have passed, much of the terrain remains the same – rolling hillsides covered with farms and woods. You can follow the routes taken by both sides, on scenic driving tours that explore the countryside and its small villages.

J.E.B. Stuart came from the southeast with 6,000 men, entering through Sykesville on what is now Route 32 and the Old Washington Rd., west of town. From Sykesville take Route 32 north, turning left onto Liberty Rd. Turn right onto Linton Rd., then left onto Bartholow Rd., right onto Klees Mill Rd. and almost immediately left again to the Old Washington Rd., where Stuart met the other part of his troops.

In Westminster, Stuart fought a small battle, causing him a fatal delay in getting to Gettysburg (see Corbit's Charge, page 118). From Westminster, follow Route 97 north to Union Mills and then take Old Hanover Rd. toward Hanover, in Pennsylvania. As you drive Route 97, try to picture it then, so jammed with wagons on their way to Gettysburg that the foot soldiers cut across the fields to get around them. The III and XII Corp of Union troops entered the area from the west and southwest. From Bruceville follow the route along Route 194, the Francis Scott Key Highway. Other Federal troops came through Bridgeport, through Taneytown and along the Taneytown Pike (Route 140) into Westminster, then along Route 97 through Union Mills and on to Littlestown and Gettysburg.

The Union VI Corp came on through Ridgeville and up Ridge Road (Route 27) and Buffalo Road on through New Windsor and into Westminster with more than 18,000 men. In many instances Union and Confederate troops passed over the very same roads on their way to Gettysburg, meeting for only three minor engagements before the ultimate battle.

Stop at the Westminster visitor center for a copy of the map and brochure called **Roads to Gettysburg Driving Tour.** *Although you can drive the routes without it, the brochure will add historical detail and color.*

■ On Water

Canoeing & Kayaking

The **Monocacy River** is a favorite for paddlers. A boat access is located off Cris Ford Road, near a point marked Lily Pons on the map. There is parking for a few cars atop an old mill foundation, and the water access is just under it. Overflow parking for about three more cars is along the access road. The current of the river is fairly fast-moving here. For a shorter run along the river, continue on Cris Ford Road to Park Mills Road, turning left and continuing to the bridge, where there is another put-in.

Another, the last take-out before the river joins the Potomac, is just upstream from the Monocacy Aqueduct, reached by a road that branches right from the aqueduct approach road.

You can kayak **Antietam Creek** from Devil's Backbone Park to the take-out where the creek meets the Potomac near the old Iron Furnace in the town of Antietam, almost due south of Sharpsburg. One small rapids on the way is Class I or II. To reach the put-in, go north from Sharpsburg on Route 65 and right onto Route 68 to the crossing with Antietam Creek. The take-out on Antietam Creek, close to the aqueduct, has a steep path, but it's short and manageable.

From Brunswick to Point of Rocks, the **Potomac** is shallow with enough riffles and submerged ledges to make paddling good sport, but not enough to discourage moderate paddlers. Except in spring high water, of course, when only experts should be anywhere on the river. This stretch of wide river, only 30 miles from Washington DC, has almost no sign of encroaching civilization except one power line.

North-Central Maryland

SMELLY SKUNNERS

The only town visible from the Potomac River between Brunswick and Point of Rocks is **Lander**, a collection of four homes whose principal notoriety once came from the occupation of its residents, who were "skunners." They trapped skunks for their fur (which was dyed to simulate more expensive pelts), and as a result were easily recognized – even from quite a distance.

The Potomac is especially shallow in October, when we canoed it, and in several places we had trouble finding a route through the rocks and ledges just below the surface. Sometimes we were almost poling instead of paddling. Just north of Point of Rocks is a long island, and we suggest you choose the more interesting – although shallow – route along its south side, through the "Rock Garden."

WATCHABLE WILDLIFE

Strewn with outcrops, some of which are visible only after the canoe bottom catches and hangs there, the stretch north of Point of Rocks is even wilder than most, and you may, as we did, come upon eight white-tailed deer drinking from the river. We lost count of the Canada geese in the water, the great blue herons that flushed from the banks and flew just over our heads, and the kingfishers and swallows, out to feast on river insects.

At **Cunningham Falls State Park**, Hunting Creek Lake is popular for canoeing and kayaking. Fishing is reported to be good and canoe rentals are available here later in the fall than at most others – into October.

AUTHOR TIP

*Finding canoe and kayak rentals can be very difficult in many areas, but there is another option. Contact **Piney Run Park**, **Bear Branch Nature Center** and **Hashawa Environmental Center**, which run several canoe and kayak excursions in summer and fall that include all equipment. Those at Hashawa are priced at $20-$35 for a day trip, about $70 ($120 for two) for an overnight. Contact the Piney Run Recreation & Conservation Council, 30 Martz Rd., Sykesville 21784, (☎ 410-795-6043), or Bear Branch Nature Center, 300 John Owings Rd., Westminster 21158 (☎ 410-848-2517, 876-9234, fax 410-848-2567) for program dates and locations.*

CANOE & KAYAK RENTALS/OUTFITTERS

Canoe trips from Brunswick to Point of Rocks are offered by **Team Link** (☎ 301-698-2500), who provide, along with the canoes and PFDs, expert guides who know the river well and can instruct beginners or help advanced paddlers polish their skills.

Outdoor Excursions offers canoe, kayak and other water-related trips in Maryland and elsewhere. On the Potomac River they offer everything from tubing and rafting to kayaking lessons and whitewater. A number of options are available, such as Whitewater Kayak Sampler with lessons and a whitewater experience, single lessons, and a whitewater kayak weekend package. PO Box 24, Boonsboro, MD 21713, ☎ 800-77-kayak (775-2925), www.outdoorexcursions.com, e-mail oeikayak@aol.com.

River and Trail Outfitters in Knoxville, opposite Harpers Ferry, has rafting trips on the Shenandoah and canoe and kayak trips on both the Potomac and the Shenandoah. Tubing is done on the historic Antietam Creek, and they also offer whitewater trips on the Catoctin River and on Antietam Creek in the spring, as well as introductory canoe trips of varying length on the Potomac. Canoe rentals are $50 per day ($90 weekends) for a canoe and two paddles, vests and shuttle within 25 miles of their site. River and Trail will also provide shuttle service for your own canoe. They are off US 340 at 604 Valley Rd. in Knoxville, MD 21758, ☎ 301-695-5177, www.rivertrail.com.

In Harpers Ferry, **River Riders** offers whitewater rafting, whitewater and quiet-water canoeing and kayaking, tubing and instruction. Their whitewater rafting trips depart at 9 and 1:30 daily and travel over class I through III rapids. Self-guided tours by canoe, raft or tube are also available and include the watercraft, life jackets, paddles, maps and shuttle service. Whitewater rafting is about $39 weekdays, $5 more on Saturday. Guided whitewater tubing is $24 daily, tubing on your own is $15. Guided whitewater kayaking is $49 per person. Reservations and advance payment are required, preferably more than seven days before the trip. Route 5, Box 1260, Harpers Ferry, WV 25425; ☎ 304-535-2663, 800-326-7238, www.riverriders.com, e-mail trips@riverriders.com.

Blue Ridge Outfitters is another choice for whitewater rafting, canoeing, kayaking and more quiet water adventures. For $48 there is a three- to four-hour six-mile trip on the class II and III rapids of the Shenandoah from April through October. For $65 this trip can be extended to include a steak barbecue. Rafting departures are at 9:30 am and 2:15 pm. Reservations and payment in advance are required. Blue Ridge also offers self-guided half-day, full-day and two-day canoe float trips on the Shenandoah (two per canoe) for $55, $80, and $100 respectively. Guides can be arranged for an extra fee. Other offerings are a swiftwater canoe trip ($100) and tubing ($22), both on the Potomac.

Part of the same operation, **Blue Ridge Ducks** offers inflatable sit-on-top kayak-type rafts for whitewater trips. Their trip is about five miles and costs $40.50 for adults, $35.50 for kids. They have age restrictions (minimum 10 years, maximum 55); it will be interesting to see if the owners obediently pack up their kayaks and retire to dry land when they turn 55 themselves, as they evidently expect the rest of us to do. If you meet their criteria, contact them at PO Box 750, Harpers Ferry, WV 25425, ☎ 304-725-3444, www.brocraft.com, e-mail brocraft@aol.com or brocraft@intrepid. net.

Fishing

One of the best places for fishing in Frederick County is **Big Hunting Creek**, which runs alongside narrow and winding Route 77. You will find this road in Thurmont. Follow it west toward Catoctin National Park and Cunningham Falls State Park. In neighboring **Cunningham Falls State Park**, lake fishing is available at Hunting Creek Lake and you can rent canoes at the 43-acre multipurpose lake. A short way from Catoctin Park, take Catoctin Falls Rd. south to Cunningham State Park.

For river fishing try the **Monocacy River**, which flows from the Pennsylvania border, passing west of Taneytown through Union Bridge, finally reaching the Potomac near the village of Dickerson, south of Frederick. The boat launch is just upstream from the Monocacy Aqueduct. Fish here for bass (catch-and-return only) and tiger muskie (36-inch minimum).

Another option is the **South Branch of the Patapsco River** along the southern boundary of the county. From Route 32 at Sykesville to the confluence with the North Branch, east of Marriottsville, it is a designated put-and-take trout area. For lake and pond fishing try **North Carroll Community Pond**, on the east side of Route 30, south of Manchester, and **Bennett Cerf Pond**, off Route 27 in the Random House Industrial Park (both of these are one-acre ponds).

In the Westminster area is the **Landon Burns/Farm Museum Pond** (on the west side of Route 32 near Center Street south of town), **Westminster Community Pond** (on the east side of Route 140 north of town) and **Lake Hashawa** (on Route 140 off John Owings Rd.), a small one-acre pond, a catch-and-release area limited to artificial lures. **Liberty Reservoir**, along the southeast border of Carroll County, is a long sinuous body of water that is popular for fishing. It is the confined North Branch of the Patapsco River and is the water supply for the city of Baltimore.

Other designated trout waters and fishing areas are the **Beaver Run Watershed** east of Route 91 just south of Finksburg, **Piney Run Reservoir** in Piney Run Park south of Route 26 and the main stream of **Piney Run** from Arrington Rd. west of Marriottsville. In the **Morgan Run Natural Area**, on the east side of Route 97, Old Washington Rd., there is a special trout management area with year-round trout fishing. You must have a license with a trout stamp and may use artificial lures only. Catch and release is the rule and possession of bait or trout on the reserve is prohibited.

There are two fishing areas with access for the mobility-impaired. One is at Morgan Run on the Klees Mill Rd., which runs between Route 32 (Sykesville FAS Rd.) and Route 26. The other is at Piney Run Park.

If you just want to practice fishing, you might try **Cool's Fishing Ponds and Tent Sites**. The fishing ponds are stocked with trout and catfish, and the fishing rate is only $5 per day plus $5 for any fish kept. It is open sunup to sundown every day. Tent sites are available and include fishing. Cool's is close to the Pennsylvania border. From Route 418 cross the border and go right onto Pen-Mar Rd., then right into Maryland on Upper Edgemont Rd. 14425 Edgemont Rd., Smithburg 21783, ☎ 301-824-6353.

FISHING OUTFITTERS

Highly personalized fly-fishing and fly-fishing instruction is the forte of **Mark Kovach**. Mark operates a fishing service that does a trip from dam #3 above Harpers Ferry to Brunswick, Maryland, in waters that vary from Class III to deep pools. The boat is a 15.5-foot inflatable raft with an aluminum frame, and the trip includes a full selection of flies and lures, instruction on reading the water, selection of lures and flies and casting techniques. He also does trips on the Susquehanna and the Shenandoah. The cost of the Potomac trip is $350 for two anglers. Basic and intermediate fly-fishing classes are available in classes that are limited to 10 people for $125; advanced classes are $150. If you don't have gear, they will rent rods, reels and an outfitted vest for an unbelievable $5. Mark E. Kovach, 406 Pershing Drive, Silver Springs, MD 20910-4253; ☎ 301-588-8742.

Fishing trips on the Shenandoah and Potomac Rivers are available from **River Riders** in Harpers Ferry. You can spin or fly-fish for smallmouth bass from their guided specially outfitted raft. These are all day trips for one or two people and start at 7 am. You can bring your own gear or rent theirs. The rate is $285 and reservations and advance payment are required. Route 5, Box 1260, Harpers Ferry WV 25425, ☎ 304 535-2663, 800-326-7238, www.riverriders.com, e-mail trips@riverriders.com.

Swimming

Cunningham Falls State Park, north of Frederick, has swimming in Hunting Creek Lake, a 43-acre body of water that is also good for boating. It's on the south side of Route 77 (Catoctin Hollow Rd.) west of Thurmont, in the William Houck area. There is a fee in summer.

■ On Snow

Skiing

 While this part of Maryland is not thought of as ski country, **River and Trail Outfitters** has guided tours for beginners and more advanced skiers. Trips are to trails in the Catoctin and Appalachian Mountains and vary from single to multi-day and include equipment, instruction, guide service and meals and lodging as appropriate. Contact them at 604 Knoxville Rd., Knoxville 21758; ☎ 301-695-5177.

■ On Horseback

Well, not exactly on horseback, but you can tour Frederick by horse-drawn carriage with the **Frederick Carriage Company**. The price depends on the size of the vehicle, but for a family of four (or up to six if most are small children) you can have a vis-à-vis carriage for $40 (30-minute ride) or $65 (60-minute ride). Reservations are required, through the Tourist Office or ☎ 301-694-7433.

Southwest of Westminster, at New Windsor, the **J-Mar-B Corporation** at Smith Hill Farm also has covered wagon rides over surrounding back country roads. In winter, when there is more than four inches of snow, they also do sleigh rides. This is also a good chance to see their teams of registered Percherons, a breed of work horse seldom seen today. You can also see their collection of antique carriages and wagons used for special events. They teach the art of driving horse-drawn vehicles. For reservations, contact Smith Hill Farm, 343 Springdale Rd., New Windsor; ☎ 410-848-9015.

Equestrian trails are available at **Hashawa Environmental Center** at 300 John Owings Rd., Westminster, MD, ☎ 410-848-2517, 876-9234, fax 410-848-2567. Unfortunately, we can find no place to rent horses so you have to bring your own. Ask at the Bear Branch Nature Center for the equestrian trail map.

The **Carroll County Equestrian Council**, in conjunction with the Carroll County Department of Recreation, Parks and Facilities, has a number of trails. Horse rental is not available, but if you have your own there are some excellent trails. Near Mt. Airy are the **Gillis Falls Equestrian Trails**, off Grimville Rd. at the Carroll County Equestrian Center.

The wooded and grass trails are marked with yellow-and-black-striped ribbons. North of Sykesville, off Route 26 on Martz Rd., are the **Piney Run Equestrian Trails**. These, too, are over moderately hilly terrain through woods and open fields and along the shore of a lake. In Union Mills, off Route 97, the **Union Mills Equestrian Trails** form an extensive network over this rolling landscape. An excellent packet of trail maps is available from Carroll County Department of Recreation, Parks and Facilities, 225 North Center Street, Room 100, Westminster, MD 21157, ☎ 410-386-2103, 888-302-8978, fax 410-876-8284. Call for further information on the equestrian program.

Cultural & Eco-Travel Experiences

■ Natural Areas

The **Catoctin Wildlife Preserve and Zoo**, 13019 Catoctin Furnace Rd., Thurmont (☎ 301-271-3180, www.CWPZoo.com) makes a good family outing. Covering 26 acres, there are not only exotic animals such as a golden tiger, a rare black jaguar, monkeys, grizzly bear, alligator, and a huge Seychelles giant tortoise, but a petting area where kids can pat and get close to goats, rabbits, ducks, geese and other animals. And although you'd hardly expect it in the mountains of Maryland, you can take a camel ride here. Visitors are encouraged to learn about the animals, not just walk past them, by programs such as the 2 pm daily talk with the grizzly bear's keeper. Signs encourage further interaction when it's appropriate, telling, for example, that the 575-pound tortoise enjoys having his head scratched. The staff has a good rapport with both the animals and those who come to visit them, and the animals are very well cared for. Admission for adults is $9.95, children $6.75, seniors (over 60) $7. Open March and November weekends, 10-4; April and October daily, 10-5; May through September daily, 9-6. From June through August and in October there are special evening events.

Just outside of the city of Westminster, the **Bear Branch Nature Center** and **Hashawa Environmental Center** have a nice variety of activities for both adults and children. The Center has a bird observation room, a planetarium, aquarium, a discovery room and an exhibit hall illustrating the animals and habitat of the area, including deer and smaller mammals. The Discovery Room has kid-appealing exhibits on Native Americans, insects, turtles and water pollution. At the Environmental Center are three trails (see *On Foot*). During much of the year the Nature Center has an active schedule of programs for children and families, many of them free; call for details and schedules. The resource room has nature books and magazines, and a shop sells environmentally friendly gifts, toys and nature books; the wildlife art decorating the walls is for sale, as well. Gardens of native plants surround the center. It's open 10-5, Wednesday through Saturday; noon-5 on Sunday. Trails are open dawn to dusk daily. To get here from Westminster, take Route 97 north; three miles from the Route 140 crossing, turn right onto John Owings Road at the sport facilities. Follow it for 1.5 miles and turn left onto Hashawa Road. 300 John Owings Road, Westminster; ☎ 410-848-2517, 876-9234, fax 410-848-2567.

KID-FRIENDLY

*Rain or shine, the **Bear Branch Nature Center** and **Hashawa Environmental Center** in Westminster will fascinate kids. A clever Bear Path leads through the landscaping of native plants and, inside, a well-equipped Discovery Room, nature library and program schedule allow kids to learn and have fun. Programs include pioneer and Native American skills, canoeing, puppet theater and crafts.*

On the south end of Carroll County, near Sykesville, is **Piney Run Park and Nature Center**, with the same kind of programs available as at Bear Branch; programs are held on different days at each site. The nature center is open April 1 through October, Tuesday through Friday, 10-5; weekends, 1-5. From November 1 through March, it's open 10-4, Tuesdays through Fridays. There are fees for programs in addition to the park admission fee. Take Route 26 (Liberty Rd.) west of Eldersburg, then follow White Rock Rd. to the Park and Nature Center. For information, contact Piney Run Recreation & Conservation Council, 30 Martz Rd., Sykesville 21784; ☎ 410-795-6043.

AUTHOR TIP

The Hashawa and Bear Branch Nature Center and Piney Run Park and Nature Center are separately operated, but membership in one offers benefits at the other. Family program rates are $10 per child or participant for members, slightly higher for non-members. Contact them for Nature Center programs offered during the period when you expect to be in the area. The seasonally issued guide outlines all of the available programs by location, dates and cost.

The drive up **Sugarloaf Mountain** is an appropriate side trip from the nearby Monocacy Aqueduct, since it was from here that its building stone was quarried. The mountain is privately owned, but the road is open to the public without charge. The road winds up the mountain, with several parking places for those who wish to picnic, look at the views, or explore the rock formations such as Devil's Kitchen. To get there from Route 28, follow Sugarloaf Rd., left just before the railway underpass.

What can you do to turn a plain concrete bridge into an attraction, and a point of community pride and unity? In Frederick they made the **Community Bridge**, a large-scale trompe l'oeil mural creating the illusion of an ivy-covered stone bridge. Designed and executed by artist William M. Cochran and a team of local artists, the work incorporates almost a thousand images that citizens submitted as representing the theme of community. The bridge crosses the Carroll Creek Park on Carroll Street near the Delaplaine Visual Arts Center. Visit the Web site at www.sharedvision.org.

■ The Arts

The **Delaplaine Visual Arts Center** is part of Frederick's renovation plan, and it works. In a rehabilitated old factory building along Carroll Creek Park, the exhibit space features changing shows of quality art, mostly contemporary and by local artists. The Frederick County Art Association is headquartered here and has an expansive list of art-related programs. 40 South Carroll Street, Frederick; ☎ 301-698-0656, www.delaplaine.org.

The **Baltimore Symphony Orchestra in Frederick** season includes concerts in October, December, February and May at the Governor Thomas Johnson High School, featuring rising guest conductors and soloists with programs of varied classical works. Adult tickets are about $25 and students under $10. Contact The BSO in Frederick, PO Box 453, Frederick 21705; Sound Source at ☎ 301-695-2633, code 6358, or 301-620-1798 for information.

Emmitsburg is the site of the work and shrine of the first American Roman Catholic saint, Saint Elizabeth Ann Seton. In 1809 she founded the Sisters of Charity of Saint Joseph and performed many good works during her lifetime. The basilica of the **National Shrine of Saint Elizabeth Ann Seton** was built in 1965 in anticipation of her canonization and designated a minor basilica in 1991 by Pope John Paul II. It's at 333 South Seton Avenue, Emmittsburg, MD, ☎ 301-447-6606, www.setonshrine.org; e-mail setonshrine@fwp.net.

■ Gardens & Farms

Lily Pons may be the only "town" named for an opera singer. At this site on the banks of the Monocacy River, an avid opera fan began a water lily garden business, creating a series of shallow ponds where he grew exotic lilies and sold the plants by mail. So great was his volume of business that in a few years he convinced the post office to open a substation in his shop. He was asked to name it, so he seized upon the word-play between his favorite flowers and favorite singer. And on June 22, 1935, Miss Pons herself came to the dedication.

Although it is no longer a post office, the location name stuck and the gardens continue to flourish, their beds dotted with lilies in shades from white through yellows, pinks and brilliant reds. A display garden, landscaped with pools and stone paths around a gazebo, shows settings for water plants, and you can wander past the raising ponds, where all the varieties are labeled. Along with lilies, **Lilypons Water Gardens** sells bright carp for backyard ponds, from tanks behind the shop, which has a good selection of books on water plants and decorative fish. The shop is open October through February, Monday-Saturday, 9:30-4:30, and the rest of the year Monday through Saturday, 9:30-5:30, and Sunday 11-5:30. 6800 Lilypons Rd., off Route 85, Buckeystown, ☎ 301-874-5133.

WATCHABLE WILDLIFE

Along with the plants and fish, the center sells beautiful blue-burnished bronze garden statuary, including a life-sized great blue heron. As we were walking along the edge of a cultivation pond, we noticed one of these statues on the opposite bank. A moment later, it spread its wings and flew off. We discovered that the ponds are a favorite spot for the real thing, and we saw several more before we left.

An unusual garden center, **Surreybrooke**, is set on the grounds of a historic old farm and offers extensive gardens that you can tour on your own or see on a guided tour, by appointment. A log cabin is now used as a garden house and the old summer kitchen is a candle making room. Surreybrooke is in Middletown, west of Frederick, at 8537 Hollow Rd; ☎ 301-371-7466, www.surreybrooke.com.

Just south of Manchester on Route 30 is Hampstead, where the **Galloping Goose Farm** is a refreshing place to go on weekends from the end of April until July. Herb gardens and greenhouses are open and special herb workshops are held. There is a $5 per person fee for herb programs. From Route 30 south of Manchester turn onto Maple Grove Rd.; the farm is 2.5 miles from the turn, at 4226 Maple Grove Rd., Hampstead 21074; ☎ 410-374-6596.

Northwest of Westminster at the intersection of Routes 30 and 27 is the little town of Manchester, home to **Cygnus Wine Cellars**. In operation only since the mid-1990s, they produce reds, whites and sparkling wines. They are open to the public on Saturdays and Sundays, noon-5; other times by appointment. 3130 Long Lane, Manchester; ☎ 410-374-6395.

In Frederick County, take Glissan's Mill Rd. from Route 75 near New Market and follow the signs to **Linganore Winecellars**. A family-operated farm, they started producing wines in 1976. In addition to those from grapes, Linganore has a selection of berry and fruit wines. Tastings and tours of the winery are available and they hold outdoor festivals the first weekend of June and the third weekends of July, August and September. There are picnic tables and grills available near their pond so this is a good place for a picnic. 13601 Glissan's Mill Rd., Mt. Airy; ☎ 410-795-6432. They are open 10-5 on weekdays; 10-6, Saturday; noon-6, Sundays. Closed major holidays.

Southwest of Thurmont, **Pryor's Orchard** has a wide selection of fresh fruit from late June through October. Their season includes 13 kinds of apples, five kinds of pears, 10 varieties of peaches as well as cherries, plums, nectarines. apricots and fresh vegetables. Take Pryor Rd. off Route 77 west of Thurmont; ☎ 301-271-2693.

North of Thurmont is **Catoctin Mountain Orchard**. They have raspberries, cherries and blueberries starting at the end of June, followed by apricots, strawberries, plums, peaches apples and grapes through the balance of the season. Ten varieties of peaches and nine of apples provide a lot of choice. They are on Route 15 at North Franklinville Rd., Thurmont, ☎ 301-271-2737. Open June to late October, 9 am to 5 pm daily, and until 6 pm on weekends; from late October to the end of the year, 9 am to 5 pm; weekends only from January to the end of March.

In and around Westminster there are five active farmers' markets. In town, the **Carroll County Farmers' Market** is held Saturday from 8 to 1, mid-June to Labor Day. During November and December they also operate a Christmas market on Saturday, 8-2. This market is at the Agricultural Center at Smith Avenue. There is also a **Downtown Farmers' Market** Saturdays from 5 am to noon from the beginning of June through October at the Sherwood Square parking lot on Railroad Avenue. The **Mt. Airy Farmers' Market** is held Tuesday, 4:30-8 pm, from mid-June through Labor Day at the F&M bank parking lot on Main Street. **South Carroll Farmers' Market** is on Fridays from July through October at Eldersburg, Hemlock Drive and Liberty Rd., adjacent to the Carrolltown Mall. The hours are 3-7 pm. **Sykesville Farmers' Market** is at Baldwin Station on Main Street on Wednesdays, 3-6 pm, from the beginning of June through November.

■ Crafts

Annually, on the first weekend in October, a show and sale of the work of professional Maryland artists and craftsmen is held eight miles north of Frederick. On the grounds of Lynfield Farm, the **Maryland Mountain Festival** has juried exhibitors with fine quality crafts and traditional and contemporary works of art. Free parking with admission of $5. Contact Frances Lynch, PO Box 187, Walkersville 21793; ☎ 301-898-5466. Open Saturday, 10-6; Sunday, 10-5.

On the second weekend of October, Carroll Carvers hold their annual **Festival of Carving**. Carvings are exhibited and sold on Saturday, 10-5, and Sunday, 10-4, at the Carroll County Agricultural Center, Agricultural Center Drive (next to the Farm Museum) in Westminster.

Also on the second weekend of October, one of the largest art and craft shows is held in Thurmont. The **Catoctin Colorfest** has been going since 1993 and now includes more than 350 juried artists and craftspeople exhibiting in three venues throughout the town. The crafts include just about every imaginable type from ceramics to furniture, afghans to jewelry, children's clothing to wooden toys and Christmas ornaments. And the arts are well represented with oil paintings, watercolors, prints, photography, pen and ink drawings, sculpture and wood carving. A shuttle bus carries people between the three show areas and the designated parking. The whole area joins into the spirit with other events that are not sponsored by the Colorfest folks. The Colorfest is held annually on the second weekend of October at Thurmont Community Park, the Guardian Hose Company Activities Grounds and the Thurmont Middle School. Admission is free. Parking for the shuttle rides is at Catoctin High School off Route 550, Thurmont Elementary School on Route 77, and at Thurmont Shoe Company and NVR on Apples Church Rd. off Route 77 (East Main Street). Catoctin Colorfest, Inc., PO Box 33, Thurmont 21788 (no phone contact).

The **Annual Frederick Craft Fair**, operated by National Crafts, Ltd., is held Monday-Wednesday during the third full week of May at Frederick Fairgrounds; ☎ 717-369-4810.

In Jefferson, Susan Hanson runs a pottery studio from a handsome old mill. Her art includes lamps, tableware and ceramic art pieces that are contemporary in form and appearance and colorfully glazed. From Route 340 south of Frederick, get off at Jefferson, Exit 8, then take Route 180 west a half-mile. Take Old Middletown Rd. a half-mile, then go left onto Poffenberger Rd. to find **Catoctin Pottery**, Lewis Mill, Poffenberger Rd., Jefferson; ☎ 301-371-4274. Open 10-5, Monday through Saturday.

■ Antiques

Frederick county is one of the best areas of the state for **antiques shopping**. In Frederick there are more than 20 shops along East Patrick Street, on Carroll Street and around the intersection of 2nd Street and East Street. Antique Station, at 194 Johnson Drive, has 200 dealers in 35,000 square feet of showroom. The shops in Frederick have everything from furniture to china, pottery, glass and art. In New Market, off I-70 east of Frederick, there are more than 16 shops arrayed along Main Street and a number just off it and there are more in Mt Airy, Libertytown, Mt Pleasant, Brunswick and Braddock Heights.

Part of the renovation of downtown Frederick led to the rejuvenation of a number of 19th-century buildings and their conversion into more than 30 shops, collectively known as **Everedy Square and Shab Row**. Shops sell Irish goods, stuffed animals, gifts, antiques (including British antique furniture), pottery (at a shop where you can paint your own), home and garden accessories, jewelry, fudge and candy and more. There are several eateries as well. The **Shab Row Farmers' Market** takes place Thursdays from June to October, 3-6 pm; the **West Frederick Farmers' Market** meets in the same area on Baughman's Lane in the parking lot behind the Blue Cross building on Saturdays from 10-1, May through October. The center is at East Church Street and East Street. Call ☎ 301-662-4140 for information.

AUTHOR TIP

Parking in downtown Westminster is available for free on weekends and after 3 pm weekdays.

Events

The **Carroll County Visitor Center** (☎ 410-848-1388 or 800-272-1933) publishes a handy **annual calendar of events** that lists events in the county. If you are spending more than a day or so in the area it's well worth having. Included among the listings are church and volunteer firemen's suppers, craft fairs, dances, herb festivals, art festivals, musical performances and holiday-related events.

Frederick has a full schedule of festivals, concerts and other events from April through October, with as many as a dozen events a month. Call ☎ 301-694-2489 or 800 999-3613, www.cityoffrederick.com.

FEBRUARY: During the last weekend of the month, **Linganore Winecellars**, 13601 Glissans Mill Rd., Mt Airy, ☎ 301-831-5889, www.linganore-wine.com, lets you use their vines to make wreaths.

JUNE: Frederick Festival of the Arts takes place on the first weekend of the month in Carroll Creek Linear Park, with art exhibits, hands on programs, and watersports for kids. ☎ 301-663-8687 or 800-999-3613.

OCTOBER: The first weekend of the month brings **In The Street Festival**, which features a big parade and activities that fill several blocks of downtown Frederick with people. Street-corner concerts, kayaking for kids, games and other events include a dance ($5) on the top floor of the parking deck. ☎ 301-663-8687 or 800-999-3613.

NOVEMBER: The **Maryland Christmas Show** is held the last weekend of the month at the Maryland Fairgrounds in Frederick. It's also open the first weekend of December, Friday and Saturday, 10-6; Sunday until 5; ☎ 301-898-5466. Also taking place over the last weekend is **Christkindelsmarkt** (Christmas market) at the Schifferstadt Architectural Museum, Friday and Saturday, 10-4; Sunday, noon-4. Decorations, tree or-

North-Central Maryland

naments, gifts, and food are offered for sale. 1110 Rosemont Avenue, Frederick, ☎ 301-663-3885.

The annual **Dickens Open House** is held at Elk Run Vineyards during the last weekend of the month at 15713 Liberty Rd., Mt Airy; ☎ 301-834-2513, www.elkrun.com. They have a tour of a 1750s home, Dickens programs in the parlor, and music.

Sightseeing

■ Museums & Historic Sites

Along the C&O Canal

 The C&O Canal runs along the entire western side of the area covered by this chapter. This was one of the primary routes for westward migration and where the railroads and canal raced to control commerce from the new settlements in the west.

Near **Dickerson**, the seven-arched **Monocacy Aqueduct**, built between 1828-33, is 536 feet long and one of the icons, not just of the canal, but of transportation history. The red quartzite used to construct it was quarried in nearby Sugarloaf Mountain and carried to the canal by a specially built tramway and by boat down the Monocacy River. You can see Sugarloaf Mountain from the historic marker in the center of the aqueduct. No wood or metal was used in the aqueduct's construction.

Though the Confederacy tried unsuccessfully several times to destroy it, they never could make a large enough hole in its masonry to accommodate a charge of dynamite. But time has almost succeeded where the Confederate raiders failed. The aqueduct is now trussed up in a harness that looks like an orthodontic brace, and the C&O Canal Association, which has taken up the task of restoring it, was thrilled to get a repair estimate of $5-$6 million rather than the $30 million they had expected.

Upstream is **Point of Rocks**, where the canal company and railroad fought each other over four years for control of the narrow strip of land around the base of Catoctin Mountain. A few miles farther west, near Lander, is the one remaining arch of the **Catoctin Aqueduct**, which carried the canal over Catoctin Creek. It was a weak design from the start and was destroyed in a flash flood, finally replaced by a bridge in 1980. Look for the arch beneath it. At **Harpers Ferry** a whole series of locks took the canal safely around treacherous rapids on the Potomac, and a short distance upstream is the beautiful **Antietam Creek Aqueduct**.

To reach these points along the canal, follow Route 28 from I-270 in Rockville, or take Route 85 from Frederick to Route 28 near Nolands Ferry and travel a short distance south. Signs for the Monocacy Aqueduct are on Route 28. To reach other canal sites, follow Route 28 west and look for signs. Harpers Ferry is connected directly to Frederick by US 340. These sites are all shown on the excellent free map of the C&O Canal distributed by the National Park Service.

Brunswick, southwest of Frederick off Route 340, was a rail center and also on the route of the C&O Canal. Its history is captured at the **Brunswick Railroad Museum**, where three floors of exhibits show not just the history of the railroad, but how it affected life in the town. Little details, such as a pair of baby shoes encrusted with soot from the passing trains, complete the picture. Brunswick was the site of a 33-mile-long classification yard, with a 16-bay roundhouse, and during World War II, a train passed through every five minutes. It was not uncommon for 10-12 engines to be pouring out soot at any one time. Old photographs, rail memorabilia (such as dining car menus and railway-inscribed china) combine with railway tools and hardware, such as spike removers and tie lifting tongs, showing how technology and style have changed since the heyday of railroad travel. The museum is in the center of town, at 40 West Potomac St, Brunswick, ☎ 301-834-7100, www.bhs.edu/rrmus.rrmns.html.

KID-FRIENDLY

In the Brunswick Railroad Museum, an HO gauge model railroad re-creates the B&O railroad from Brunswick all the way to Union Station in Washington, with landmarks as they appeared in the 1950s and 1960s. Kids can change switches, work lights and move trains in the authentically re-created landscape. Traffic lights change, whistles toot, cows in the pastures alongside the tracks moo, and the trackside merry-go-round turns. Steps boost children higher, so they can compete on more equal terms with the adults who will also be playing with the train.

Harpers Ferry

Harpers Ferry, just across the Potomac in West Virginia, played a major role in the Civil War (and earlier) history of the area, and is accessible by footbridge from the C&O Canal towpath. The lower part of town, at the confluence of the Potomac and Shenandoah Rivers, is entirely in the hands of the National Park Service. Unfortunately, they have not done as well by

North-Central Maryland

Harpers Ferry as they have by the C&O Canal. Unlike the canal, which lives and breathes history for its entire length and is well interpreted and accessible both in its visitors centers and its lonely ruins, Harpers Ferry – at least the heart of the lower town – seems peculiarly dead.

Not that it lacks for tourists trying to understand what happened there. They are efficiently bused from out-of-town parking lots directly onto the main street of the restored area. From there they flounder about trying to picture what this spic-and-span street looked like when it was alive. Inside each building is a static display – all very nicely done with large pictures and educational signboards. But artifacts are few and live interpretation scarce. Even the visitors center, which is staffed, is reluctant to tell visitors anything – when we were there they were unaware that bicycles could be rented five minutes away at the end of the foot bridge.

The armory, where John Brown and his party stood off the government for two tense days, is open – although moved and rebuilt several times. The other buildings that line the street so picturesquely contain exhibits – a general store, the ecology of the river, a chronology of John Brown's raid, most slanted toward making a hero of Brown. After all, he's their icon and claim to fame. But even Stephen Vincent Benet, in his epic poem "John Brown's Body" had a bit more balance and breathed life into him. The **John Brown Museum**, which chronicles the raid with a few artifacts seems unsure of the line between protest and civil insurrection.

Of the various displays, two stand out, and one would make Harpers Ferry worth the visit if nothing else were there. The **Restoration Museum** shows how archaeologists use the clues found in an old building to date and learn about its history. Most compelling is the **Black Voices Museum**, which, although small, brings to life the people who once lived here. Interactive displays use readings from letters, reminiscences and contemporary descriptions to chronicle the life of blacks – slave and free – in the Civil War era. Don't miss it.

Admission to the park sites is $5, which you pay at the Visitors Center outside of town. It covers the bus fare into town. Parking in Harpers Ferry is very limited, so this parking at the Visitors Center and bussing in is the only way to guarantee a parking place.

To see a live town, head uphill, where souvenir and what-not shops in the old buildings are actually a welcome sight after the sterility below. Washington St. is lined by nice cut stone, brick and wooden buildings, homes and shops. The ruins of a large stone **grist mill** are on the canal (not the C&O, but a smaller canal alongside the Shenandoah River) above the historic District; you will pass it on your way in if you take the bus into town.

Sharpsburg

The Civil War rolled through this area during the 1860s, and no place brings it home more than **Antietam National Battlefield**, where the bloodiest single-day battle of the Civil War took place, with deaths on both sides totaling upward of 22,000 men. The battlefield is along Antietam Creek south of Sharpsburg (the Confederacy called it the Battle of Sharpsburg).

The battlefield is still rolling open countryside, and plans call for restoration of the fields and forests to their 1862 appearance. Highlights are the old **Dunker Church**, where troops first clashed in the early hours, the **Sunken Rd.** where the next phase of battle occurred and famed **Burnside Bridge** where Union troops finally crossed and forced General Lee to withdraw to Sharpsburg. Standing on the heights overlooking the simple stone bridge over Antietam Creek, it is easy to imagine the slaughter as Union troops repeatedly tried to cross.

ANTIETAM

The significance of Antietam was two-fold. It stopped Lee's northward thrust for that year, and the loss discouraged the British from supporting the Confederacy, as they were about to do. But it was also one of Lincoln's greatest frustrations of the war, because General McClellan blew it. He had the chance to win the war right here, but he didn't press his advantage by following the retreating Confederate troops to Sharpsburg. The President had stern words for him following the battle, and not long afterward relieved the general of his command.

AUTHOR TIP

ONE AUTHOR'S TIP: *Those who find battlefields profoundly boring should prepare to be profoundly bored. If, however, you find tales of the endless back-and-forths of armies across fields fascinating, prepare to spend half a day here. If you are the former, married to the latter, bring a good book, tour by bicycle (it is a pleasant ride), or read the next three chapters of this book and plan the rest of your trip while the car is stopped in front of descriptive signs. Get out of the car at Burnside Bridge, however, the one spot where the battle takes on immediacy and makes geographical sense. That said, Antietam is a major Civil War site and a turning point in the war; it is well worth seeing, even if you don't stop to read every sign.*

A vivid film, orientation talk (at least three times a day, more in summer) and an eight-mile self-guided tour are available at the Visitors Center. A two-hour caravan tour led by a ranger is free with park entrance. Battlefield Walks cover subjects ranging from Civil War flags to artillery. Inside the Visitors Center is a small museum with uniforms, equipment, personal items and a searchable archive of those who fought here. Take Route 65 south from I 70 at Hagerstown. Box 158, Sharpsburg, MD 21782, ☎ 301-432-5124.

The road south from Sharpsburg to Harpers Ferry plays hide and seek with the river and canal, then winds up hill and down dale and finally through a ravine scattered with boulders. It goes through the tiny crossroads of Antietam, with an imposing **Iron Furnace** beside the road. Here, and again just before Harpers Ferry, it parallels the C&O Canal, where bridges lead from parking areas to the towpath and locks. In summer the route is a leafy tunnel in places, rising to hilltop farm clearings.

The road you are traveling here was the road of march and of retreat for the Confederate troops before and after the Battle of Antietam. Because the Union Army didn't follow them, which it could have easily done since General McClellan had 30,000 troops in reserve that he never used in the battle, the war lasted three more terrible years. As you travel, notice the number of old log houses; they were here as the armies marched past, and when John Brown and his band plotted their raid.

About five miles north of Harpers Ferry is the **Kennedy Farm**, where a rough sandstone monument records the fate of the members of the band that assembled here with John Brown in the summer of 1859. Here they planned the details of the event that many consider the real beginning of the Civil War. The farmhouse, like others nearby, is built of chinked logs above a first floor of stacked fieldstone.

To reach the Kennedy Farm from Sharpsburg, go south on Mechanic Street, which becomes Harpers Ferry Rd. within two blocks. From the Harpers Ferry end, follow the brown sign to Kennedy Farm from US 340, opposite the large sign for River and Trail Outfitters. Continue following these brown signs, turning right onto Keeping Tryst Rd., winding down past the International Youth Hostel and through the narrow village of Sandy Hook, a row of stone buildings lined up along the railroad track. You will pass the entrance to the railway tunnel and a ruined stone house before meeting the canal.

Boonsboro

The **Museum of Rural Life** will be located at the Washington County Agricultural Education Center, south of Hagerstown, three miles north of Antietam Battlefield entrance. The Rural Life Museum is county owned and, as we go to press, it is close to being opened. Its goal is to show farm life in the county from the early years through 1940. The exhibits will include a complete original post office and country store, a fascinating collection assembled by two local women. Along with the store counter and a wide variety of display cases and racks, the store is fully stocked with everything from kitchen utensils and farm supplies to beaded cushions, crocheted gloves and coffins. A petting zoo is also planned. Call for the current status and hours. The entrance is at 7313 Sharpsburg Pike (Route 65), Boonsboro, ☎ 301-791-3125, 432-8371, fax 301-791-3481.

Frederick Area

The depth and duration of the battles of the Civil War in this area make Frederick a natural site for the **National Museum of Civil War Medicine**. Emphasis here is on the role of medicine in the armies of the north and the south in this grisly conflict. It is a testament to the hard work of surgeons, doctors, nurses, hospitals and medical stewards. Special programs are held most Saturday and Sunday afternoons or evenings on such topics as the role of nurses, the Southern caregiver, the battlefield embalmer, camp life and a host of other topics. The Museum Shop has most unusual offerings. When the museum is in its usual home, re-enactors often stage live action in front, on West Patrick Street. The town's Civil War skirmish took place on this street and during the re-enactment that takes place here, the "wounded" are carried into the museum and "treated." The museum is presently in temporary quarters at 100 Adventist Drive, PO Box 470, Frederick 21705, just off I-70 near Exit 54. By publication time, they hope to have returned to their historic home at 48 East Patrick Street, Frederick. ☎ 301-695-1864, fax 301-695-6823, www.CivilWar-Med.org, e-mail museum@civilwarmed.org. The museum is open 10-5, Monday through Saturday; 11-5, Sunday.

Among the best known sites of Frederick is the **Barbara Fritchie House**, whose 90-plus year-old owner defied orders from Stonewall Jackson's troops to tear down the Union flag she had raised. It's one of the few Civil War stories that both sides could take equal pride in – the north for Barbara Fritchie's gritty courage and the south for Jackson's gentlemanly behavior. The attractive little brick house is at 154 West Patrick Street; ☎ 301-698-0630. It is open April through September, Monday, Thursday, Friday and Saturday, 10-4; Sunday, 1-4. The last tour is 3:30. $2 adults, $1.50 children and seniors.

The **Roger Brooke Taney House and Francis Scott Key Museum** is at 121 South Bentz Street (☎ 301-663-8687) and is open April through October by appointment. Taney was the Chief Justice of the US Supreme Court that wrote the Dred Scott decision. His brother-in-law, and law partner, was Francis Scott Key. There is an elaborate century-old **statue of Francis Scott Key** at Mount Olivet Cemetery, 515 South Market Street in Frederick, where he and Barbara Fritchie are buried.

The collections of **The Historical Society of Frederick County** are housed in an 1820s home decorated with fine furniture, paintings tapestries and pottery. You'll find it at 24 East Church Street in Frederick;

☎ 301-663-1188, www. fwp.net/hsfc. Open Monday through Saturday, 10-4; Sunday 1-4; closed first two weeks of January and major holidays.

On the grounds of the Maryland School for the Deaf, 101 Clarke Place, Frederick, is the **Hessian Barracks**, built in 1777 and used later to house Hessian and British soldiers captured at Bennington and Saratoga. In the Civil War it served as a hospital. It's a walk-by, and not generally open to the public. Also in town, **Rose Hill Manor** is a large 18th-century classic plantation house that was the home of Thomas Johnson, Maryland's first elected governor. The Farm Museum has exhibits of early agriculture with special events and showings, at 1611 North Market Street; ☎ 301-694-1646. It is open April through October (and weekends only in November) Monday through Saturday, 10-4; Sunday, 1-4.

KID-FRIENDLY

Rose Hill Manor has a children's museum with specialized programs where costumed docents guide and teach elementary school age children, and their families, about the manor house, and its dependency shops and buildings.

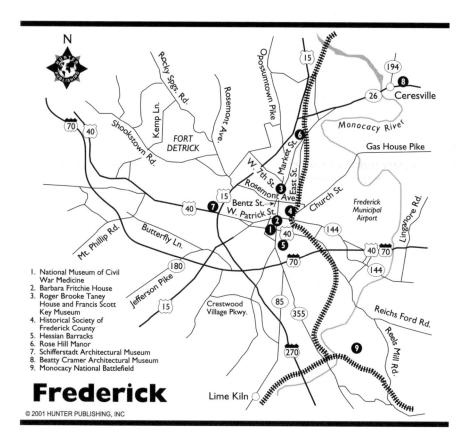

1. National Museum of Civil War Medicine
2. Barbara Fritchie House
3. Roger Brooke Taney House and Francis Scott Key Museum
4. Historical Society of Frederick County
5. Hessian Barracks
6. Rose Hill Manor
7. Schifferstadt Architectural Museum
8. Beatty Cramer Architectural Museum
9. Monocacy National Battlefield

Frederick

© 2001 HUNTER PUBLISHING, INC

In 1756 Joseph Brunner came from Mannheim Germany by way of Philadelphia and built a two-story sandstone home. It is a classic example of German Colonial architecture with thick stone walls, unusual eaves, a built-in German five-plate iron stove, wishbone chimneys and other unusual features. **Schifferstadt Architectural Museum**, 1110 Rosemont Avenue, Frederick (☎ 301-663-3885), is open for tours by donation, mid-April to mid-December, Tuesday-Saturday, 10-4. Another rare architectural treasure is the **Beatty Cramer Architectural Museum**, housed in the only building in the county that dates from its 1748 founding. The house has several unique attributes. There is also a well house and smokehouse on the property. It is on Route 26 east of Ceresville, on the left just past the bridge over Israel's Creek; ☎ 301-293-2215.

Just outside of Frederick is **Monocacy National Battlefield**. In 1864 General Jubal Early led 16,000 Confederates in a march on Washington after collecting a ransom for not burning Frederick. Just three miles outside of town they encountered 5,800 Union troops under the command of General Lew Wallace. While Wallace "lost" the battle, he stopped the drive on Washington DC. The Visitor Center has an orientation program and self-guided tour maps. The battlefield is on Route 355 southeast of Frederick off I-70; ☎ 301-662-3515. Open daily, April 1 through October 31, 8-4:30 (Memorial Day to Labor Day until 5:30 on weekends) and Wednesday through Sunday, November through March, 8-4:30.

DID YOU KNOW? *The well known novel **Ben Hur**, later made into an epic movie, was written by Lew Wallace, the same man who commanded Union troops at the Battle of Monocacy in July 1864.*

US 15 leads north from Frederick into rolling farmlands that border the wooded parklands of Catoctin Mountain. **Catoctin Iron Furnace** was built and put into operation in 1776; it provided cannonballs and other iron products for the revolution and for farmers and households thereafter until it closed in 1903. It provided 100 tons of shells used at Yorktown alone. The giant furnaces are in good repair; one, called "Isabella" by its workers, produced as much as 3,300 tons of pig iron annually. The unreconstructed but stabilized ruins of the rather grand ironmaster's house are fascinating, with brick and stone fireplaces intact. To the left of the sign, look into the woods to see a lintelled entrance, perhaps to a root cellar. Catoctin Furnace Rd. (Route 806) parallels US 15 south of Thurmont; ☎ 301-271-7574, www.dnr.state.md.us.

Cactoctin Iron Furnace has a separate handicapped-accessible parking lot and a level pathway to the ruins of the ironmaster's house.

North-Central Maryland

The Catoctin Iron Furnace, in Thurmont.

Three of Maryland's five covered bridges cluster north of Frederick, all close to US 15. The **Roddy Road Covered Bridge** is, not surprisingly, on Roddy Rd., which turns off US 15 about four miles north of the Catoctin Iron Furnace. The King Post Truss bridge crosses Owens Creek, less than half a mile from the main road. Follow Route 77 east from Thurmont to find another, its road marked by "Red Dot #19" sign. This one is easier to photograph, in a lovely setting with a picnic area and playground alongside the creek.

While here, and at the almost certain risk of getting lost, wander off to the north of Route 77 to see deeply rolling farmlands and the unusual ornate barn windows peculiar to this area and to northern Carroll County. You can't go too far without bumping into Route 194 on the east or Route 140 on the north, and you will enjoy a scenic ride through this peaceful rolling countryside. As you travel, look for signs to **Terra Rubra**, the birthplace of Francis Scott Key, outside of Keysville, north of Route 77.

Westminster Area

Westminster streets are lined with fine homes, mostly in the vernacular styles common to northern Maryland and eastern Pennsylvania. The earlier homes in the center of town have simple square lines; later ones show the influence of the Pennsylvania Germans, with rounded windows. The Flemish bond brickwork is typical of the Georgian style as interpreted in Pennsylvania. On East Main Street is **Cokey's Tavern**, from 1800, where the court met until the building of the court house and where Jeb Stuart's officers stayed. Like nearly every place in Westminster, it has a resident ghost.

The Episcopal **Church of the Ascension**, opposite the courthouse, built in 1854, was the first building in Westminster not built in vernacular style. The needlepoint kneelers were designed by the same artist as those of the National Cathedral in Washington, DC. Francis Scott Key contributed to the construction of the church, and taught America's first Sunday School for Blacks here. The church is open from dawn to dusk.

In its churchyard is a highlight of Westmister's ghost tours: the split stone tomb of Legh Master (see story below). Under a tree is the tomb of Lt. William Murray, who was killed in Jeb Stuart's raid.

THE STORY OF LEGH MASTER

In the mid-18th century an Englishman, Legh Master, abandoned his family and settled in Westminster. A man of wealth, greed and avarice, he had an iron furnace and an estate with 50 slaves. Master attempted to seduce a slave and when she refused he beat her. When her fellow slave and lover tried to protect her, Master had him thrown into the iron furnace, and, it was rumored, had the woman bricked into an old chimney of his mansion. After a fire in the house in the 1930s, a brick wall was opened, revealing the skeleton of a black female inside. Legh Master was buried on his plantation, but after his coffin repeatedly rose to the surface it was moved to the churchyard of Ascension Episcopal Church in Westminster. Within weeks of his re-burial the heavy tablet stone on his tomb split in half, further fanning the rumors of his ghostly escapades. His house, Avondale, is privately owned, but our local relatives tell us the family still has a difficult time getting baby sitters.

The **Carroll County Court House** is among the finest buildings in northern Maryland, a stately brick in the Georgian style. The American Bar Association has designated its Courtroom 1 as one of the 10 most beautiful courtrooms in America. Look at the original clerk's desk and the jurors' chairs, with their arms whittled by local farmers. The courtroom has its own ghost stories: litigants, attorneys and judges occasionally smell stew cooking from the almshouse that was in the courthouse basement many years ago. The courthouse is open Monday through Friday; ask the bailiff if you can see the courtroom. On weekends ask at the Tourist Office if guided tours are available.

A block behind the courthouse is the **Old Jail**, unmistakable among the finer residences that surround it. The Sheriff lived on the top floor, prisoners in the basement.

We have a weakness for farm museums, particularly ones that teach the techniques and technology of early agriculture. The **Carroll County Farm Museum** is one of these. It recycles the 19th-century county poor farm, opening the fine brick home and the splendid barns and outbuildings for visitors and filling them with the implements of rural life. Note the unusual treatment of windows on the barn, as you'll see throughout this area, but nowhere else in Maryland. The **Living History Center** is in the former almshouses (which replaced those in the basement of the courthouse). Working tin and blacksmith shops have demonstrations, and you can see the well-labeled tools used by generations of farmers. Upstairs in the barn (enter up the hill in the back) is a splendid collection of horse-drawn vehicles, including sleds used for ice harvesting, buggies, a florist wagon, hearse and an RFD exhibit with a mail wagon.

Docents demonstrate activities from baking and needlework to animal husbandry and planting. The green and tree-shaded grounds invite strolling, and from April to October there is at least one special program a month, several a month in June and July. Past events have been a blacksmith day, North Bay Deer Creek Fiddler's Contest, Civil War encampment, steam equipment show days and, of course a Fourth of July celebration. The museum is at 500 South Center Street in Westminster; ☎ 410-876-2667, 848-7775 or 800-654-4645, $. It is open noon-5 on Sunday, admission is $3 for adults, $2 for seniors and juniors; those under six are free.

At the **Robert Strawbridge House** in New Windsor, west of Westminster, is a collection of four structures closely associated with his ministry as an early founder of American Methodism. These include the Strawbridge house and farm, the John Evans House – home of the first American convert to Methodism, a replica of the log meetinghouse and the Asbury Smith Visitor Center. A map, available at the visitor center and in Westminster, shows the location of other related historic buildings and sites in the area. The curator is Rev. Charles Acker, 2650 Strawbridge Lane, New Windsor 21776; ☎ 410-635-2600.

The **Union Mills Homestead** is a fascinating repository of over 200 years of Maryland history. In 1797 Andrew and David Shriver set about building a home, a grist mill and a saw mill. In later years they added a tannery and other businesses and their original six-room house grew to 23 rooms. Occupied by the same family from 1797 until the 1960s, the place is a virtual compendium of American life for two centuries. The house and the mill are open for visitors. It's on Route 97, seven miles north of Westminster, at 3311 Littlestown Pike; ☎ 410-848-2288. Open June 1 to September 1, Tuesday to Friday, 10-4; Saturday and Sunday, noon-4. Admission is charged.

Uniontown, west of Westminster, has a lovely main street lined by buildings that span the entire 19th century. Architectural styles here include brick, wood, log, Dutch stepped gables and, out of town a bit, an interesting example of quoined architecture. The settlement of Frizzellburg, on Route 823, has a clutch of fine old homes and two antiques shops at its crossroads center.

The town of **Union Bridge**, on Route 75 west of Westminster, is lined with some fine old homes, too. In its center is the **Western Maryland Railway Museum**, operated by the Western Maryland Railway Historical Society. The museum is in the 1902 headquarters building of the railroad and has a wide collection of railroad memorabilia and artifacts, including an N scale model railroad showing parts of the Western Maryland route. Open Sundays, 1-4; ☎ 410-775-0150.

In **Sykesville**, the Historic District Commission has just recently restored the former gatehouse to the State Hospital as the **Sykesville Gate House Museum of History** with materials related to the history of the town. This includes a fine collection of historic photographs of the town and materials on the B&O Railroad, which came to town in 1831. It's at 7283 Cooper Drive; ☎ 410-549-5150, open Wednesday and Sunday, 1-6.

Of interest to rail aficionados is the Historic **Sykesville Railroad Station**, an 1884 Queen Anne-style brick station, now home to Baldwin's, a restaurant named for E.F. Baldwin, the structure's architect.

KID-FRIENDLY

Baldwin's Station, a restaurant in Sykesville, hosts a children's theater in the fall offering one show per month. In 1999 they did Aladdin, Cinderella, Peter Pan and Snow White. The shows are about 45 minutes long and start at 3 pm. Tickets are $6.95 for adults and children. 7618 Main Street, Sykesville, ☎ 410-795-1041.

Where to Stay

ACCOMMODATIONS PRICE KEY	
Rates are per room, per night, double occupancy.	
$	Under $50
$$	$50 to $100
$$$	$101 to $175
$$$$	$176 and up

■ Harpers Ferry & Sharpsburg

The **Jacob Rohrbach Inn** is a delightful old home, built in 1832, with wicker chairs overlooking Sharpsburg's Main Street from an ornamental-iron porch. It has been operated as an inn by the friendly and engaging Breitenbachs since 1986, and you will enjoy their stories of its (and the area's) history. The rooms are nicely furnished in period antiques and reproductions and guests have use of the porches, parlor and the hot tub in a detached cottage that was once the summer kitchen and still has an operating fireplace. Two of the rooms have private baths, the remaining two share one bath. The Breitenbachs serve a full breakfast to guests and will make box lunches for your excursion to the battlefield or C&O Canal, also close. Ask to see the canal boat pole; the former owner was the son of a captain. 138 West Main Street, Sharpsburg, MD 21782-0706, ☎ 877-839-4242, 301-432-5079. $$-$$$

JOHN BROWN IN SHARSPBURG

John Brown and his band picked up their pikes in Shepardstown (West Virginia) and came though Sharpsburg on their way to raid the arsenal at Harpers Ferry. When they mired down in the mud on Main Street, locals helped them through, not knowing who they were or what their mission.

■ Frederick

McCleary's Flat, 121 East Patrick St, Frederick, MD 21701, ☎ 301-620-2433, 800-774-7926, www.fwp.net/mcclearysflat. Wonderful hosts, a perfect location and beautiful rooms and public areas assure a great stay here. An 1876 Second Empire mansion, it's beautifully restored, in the heart of the antiques district and walking distance to just about everything. The Caroline McCleary Suite on the second floor is exquisite. Warm and cheerful hosts serve a wonderful breakfast in their dining room, or on the patio. Parking in a nearby public parking deck. No pets. $$-$$$, weekend rates higher.

Tyler Spite House, 112 West Church Street, Frederick, MD 21701, ☎ 301-831-4455, is a historic inn, dating from 1810, and also downtown in the historic district. A fine old antique-filled mansion, the "spite" refers to its erection to prevent the town from building a street. $$$-$$$$

■ Thurmont

Cozy Country Inn is near the Presidential Retreat of Camp David, in the Catoctin Mountains, and the Cozy is often used by journalists and government officials who don't have enough pull to get into Camp David. The Clinton cabinet stayed here before his first term. The rooms are themed to the administrations of the past eight Presidents and one is dedicated to Winston Churchill, who ate here during the 1940s. It is at 103 Frederick Rd. (Route 806), Thurmont, MD 21788, ☎ 301-271-4301, www.cozyvillage.com, e-mail cozyville@aol.com. $-$$$

■ Westminster

The oldest house in the county was the home of William Winchester, founder of Westminster, almost opposite the entrance to the Farm Museum. It is now the **Winchester Country Inn**, a B&B serving a full country breakfast. It is fully restored and is furnished with antiques of its

1760s period. An afternoon tea is available. 111 Stoner Avenue, Westminster, MD 21157, ☎ 410-848-9343, 800-887-3950, fax 410-848-7409. $$

Just a short distance out of Westminster on Route 75 between Union Bridge and Route 84 is Linwood and the charming **Wood's Gain Bed and Breakfast**. Our favorite room is the Summer Kitchen, a two-story separate building that forms a two-room suite, furnished in country antiques and with the feel of our own private home. (We like this little house so much that we don't tell local relatives we are in town, so we can stay here without hurting anyone's feelings.) Rooms in the main house are furnished in family antiques, each with a private bath. Breakfasts are splendid, served in the elegant family dining room. Be sure to ask the amiable hosts about the Civil War history of this house and the neighboring one. The B&B is at 421 McKinstry's Mill Rd., Linwood, MD 21791, ☎ 410-775-0308, www.woodsgainbnb.com. $-$$$

*The first-floor guest room at **Wood's Gain Bed and Breakfast** is fully handicapped-accessible, with a most thoughtfully arranged bathroom and totally barrier-free access through a private outside door. It's the nicest job we have seen of combining the decor and warm hospitality details of a B&B with full accessibility.*

Twelve miles west of Westminster (six miles west of Uniontown), in Middlebury, is **Bowling Brook Country Inn**, a quiet B&B in the countryside that serves a full country breakfast. They have six beautifully appointed guest rooms and a suite in a separate building; some have Jacuzzis. Rooms are named for race horses and race tracks because this farm was once the breeding and training ground of five Preakness winners (1878-82). Take the Middleburg Rd. from Route 84 in Uniontown or east from Route 194 south of Littlestown. Special package rates are available, some including dinner at the Restaurant 1899 in Westminster, owned and operated by the same owners. The inn is at 6000 Middleburg Rd., Middleburg, MD 21757; ☎ 410-876-2893, 857-4445. $$$

North-Central Maryland

■ Camping

Gambrill State Park, 21843 National Pike, Boonsboro, MD 21713 (☎ 301-791-3683, TTY 410-974-3683), has 35 sites with showers. Picnic shelters and hiking are available.

Cunningham State Park, 14039 Catoctin Hollow Rd., Route 77, Thurmont, MD 21788 (☎ 301-271-7574), has two campgrounds, a few cabins with electricity and RV serviced sites. One of these areas is open in winter as a primitive, unserviced, area. Basic sites are $13, cabins $35, higher on summer weekends and there is a reservation fee of $8. Each of the six camping loops has showers and flush toilets, and a camp store and a dumping station are in the park. Campsites are all level with gravel pads, and all in the woods. The Houck area (five loops) opens the first Friday in April and closes the Monday after October ends. The Manor area closes mid-December. For reservations, ☎ 888 432-CAMP (2267).

AUTHOR TIP *The Maryland State Parks system has a toll-free number for emergencies that is available 24 hours a day. In the event of an emergency or serious problems during your stay, call ☎ 800-825-PARK (7275).*

Nearby, there are two campgrounds at **Catoctin Mountain National Park**, also Route 77, Thurmont. The park entrances are within a short distance of one another. One of the areas has cabins. Park Rangers run special programs through the season.

In Gapland you get a chance to stay in the closest thing to a tree house, a cabin on stilts on a hillside in the woods. **Maple Tree Campground** offers the Tree Cottage, insulated and with table, benches and a wood stove for heat and cooking and available all year. It's $45 per night for four and $8 per person above. The Summer Tree House, seven feet in the air, has six bunks without mattresses and is $32 for four. There are also tent and field sites at $8. Reservations are suggested. Take Gapland Rd. from Route 67 north of Harpers Ferry then go left onto Townsend Rd. 20716 Townsend Rd., Gapland, MD 21779, ☎ 301-432-5585.

Greenbrier State Park, off Route 40 at the intersection with Route 34 west of Frederick, has 166 sites for tents and RV's. The Appalachian Trail passes through the park and there is a small lake with canoes and paddleboats. Access is via Route 40 just west of the I-70 overpass. On weekdays there is a $2 per car day-use rate; sites with electricity are $40 per day. South Mountain Recreation Area, 21843 National Pike, Boonsboro, MD 21713, ☎ 301-791-4767; for reservations, ☎ 888-432 CAMP (2267).

The city of Brunswick operates a camping area between the canal and the river. Tents and RVs are accommodated in separate areas and electricity is available at some sites. Volleyball, horseshoe and basketball facilities are on site and passes to the municipal swimming pool are available. Reservations are suggested, since space is limited. During the season, April through October, ☎ 301-834-8050 (campground); at other times, 301-834-7500 (City Hall), or write **Brunswick Family Campground**, 20 A Street, Brunswick, MD 21716. Rates are $8 per day or $12 with electricity, weekly rates are $48 ($65).

Where to Eat

DINING PRICE KEY
The price key indicates the cost of *most* dinner entrées on a restaurant's regular and daily special menu.
$. . . . . Most under $10
$$. . . . . $10 to $20
$$$. . . . . Over $30

■ Frederick

One of the liveliest places in town is **Frederick Brewing Company**, 124 North Market Street; ☎ 301-631-0089 (301-694-7899 for brewery tours). The restaurant is called **Brewer's Alley.** In the fall of 1993 the brewery brewed its first batch and now produces and sells a golden, amber and red ale as well as a porter and a wheat beer. They also make seasonal special beers and their own birch beer soda. The restaurant exceeds usual pub fare, with dishes like chipotle-garlic grilled strip steak, Louisiana boudin with jumbo shrimp or a pasta with Thai grilled chicken. Look for alligator on the menu – a delicious appetizer. It's usually busy, and noisy, with a youngish crowd on weekends. Entrées run $-$$.

The Province Restaurant, 129 North Market Street, ☎ 301-663-1441, is a very popular bistro-style restaurant focusing on imaginative American dishes. You'll find dishes such as seafood combo with herbed butter, veal piccata, veal Amontillado with almonds, pasta Parmesan with shiitake mushrooms or lamb chops with dill, Dijon mustard and garlic, all $16-20. The desserts are legendary. Tuesday through Thursday they offer prix-fixe dinners and on weekends they serve brunch. Open Tuesday-Sunday (except holidays) for lunch and dinner. **The Province Too**, 12 East Patrick Street, Frederick MD , ☎ 301-663-3315, is their other location, offering breakfast and lunch carry-out and a full bakery. Monday through Friday, 7-5; Saturday, 9-4; Sunday, 8-3.

Hana's Korean Kitchen, at 140-B West Patrick Street, ☎ 301-695-9150, serves Korean dishes – Jumm Pong, Bi Bim Bop and Kim Chee Chi Ge –

and traditional Chinese entrées, including sweet and sour pork and Kung Pao chicken. Next to Delphey Sport Shop, it's on the side alley, so you might not find it easily. Hana's serves lunch weekdays 11-3; dinner Sunday through Thursday, 5-9 pm, and Friday and Saturday, 5-10 pm. Lunch buffet $4.95 weekdays, dinner and weekends $6.95.

Di Francesco's, 26 North Market St. (☎ 301-695-5499), is upscale Italian, from its sidewalk café to its deep-toned dining room. The menu describes each dish in detail, and may feature lobster ravioli, rosemary-roasted pork loin with celeriac, lobster with grilled asparagus rissotto, ostrich steak with mushrooms, or fettuccine tossed with shrimp, scallop and crab, all in the $16-$20 range. We especially like the antipasto bar. Di Francesco's is open daily for lunch and dinner.

Beans & Bagels, 53 East Patrick St., opposite the Civil War Medicine Museum, is a popular coffee bar.

■ Westminster

Maggie's, on East Green St., ☎ 410-848-1441, serves American food with a French accent at this casual, cozy restaurant. You'll find everything from good burgers and light snacks to prime rib and chicken in Champagne sauce. The front has an English pub atmosphere, done all in dark woods with a brass bar, and there is a separate dining room is in the back. $-$$

A good place to pick up sandwiches for a picnic is at **Giulanova Groceria**, on the west end of Main Street in Westminster, near the Littlestown Pike (Route 97) intersection. Hoagies and salads are $4.50, soups $2.95 and they have lasagna, eggplant Parmigiana and pasta dishes for $4.95. They are open 9-4, Monday through Friday, 9-6 on Saturday, closed Sunday.

■ Thurmont

Mountain Gate Family Restaurant is right alongside Route 15. The food is very inexpensive and it's one of the most popular places in the area for turkey, ham, roast beef and roast pork dinners under $7 and sandwiches, from $1.75 for a hamburger. Breakfast, which you can order all day (from 5 am), includes many selections at equally friendly prices. Across the street, at their **Mountain Gate Convenience Store**, you can get meals to go, such as chicken dinners, two-four pieces for $4-$6, including two veggies and rolls. They also have sandwiches and can create your own designer sub, at 133 Frederick Road, Thurmont; ☎ 301-271-4373.

Cozy Country Inn, 103 Frederick Rd. (Route 806), ☎ 301-271-4301, www.cozyvillage.com, is too popular to be very cozy, probably because it serves large portions of traditional dishes and a Sunday buffet that would last you all week.

■ Boonsboro

At the site of the Battle of South Mountain is the **Old South Mountain Inn**, which served as Confederate headquarters for the battle. This historic property has an inviting and innovative menu, including American buffalo mignon with a green peppercorn brandy sauce, quail breasts stuffed with sausage, chicken saltimbocca and a good array of seafood dishes. It's popular, so reservations might be wise, especially on weekends. Sunday brunch is served 10:30 am-2 pm for $13.95. Open for dinner Tuesday through Friday; for lunch and dinner on weekends. US 40A, 6132 Old National Pike; ☎ 301-371-5400, 301-432-6155, fax 301-432-2211. $$-$$$

■ Sykesville

Baldwin's Station turns an old railroad station into dining rooms, with summer dining added on the old platform. The food is nicely done, although the service was a bit off at our last visit. Dinner begins with a good variety of breads and a tasty tapenade and progresses to entrées such as Louisiana-style fried chicken, rack of lamb, or grouper in an orange marmalade sauce, most priced $15-$25. End with a dessert that may include strawberry shortcake of fresh berries over an almond biscuit or a chocolate pâté with crème anglaise – or you can have it all, with a stunning dessert sampler plate for two. We suggest sampling the house wine before committing to $6 for half-glass servings; most bottled wines run in the $30 range. Baldwin's has live music performances several times a month featuring folk, traditional and contemporary blues. Reservations are a good idea, especially on weekends. It's easy to spot at 7618 Main Street, Sykesville; ☎ 410-795-1041.

North-Central Maryland

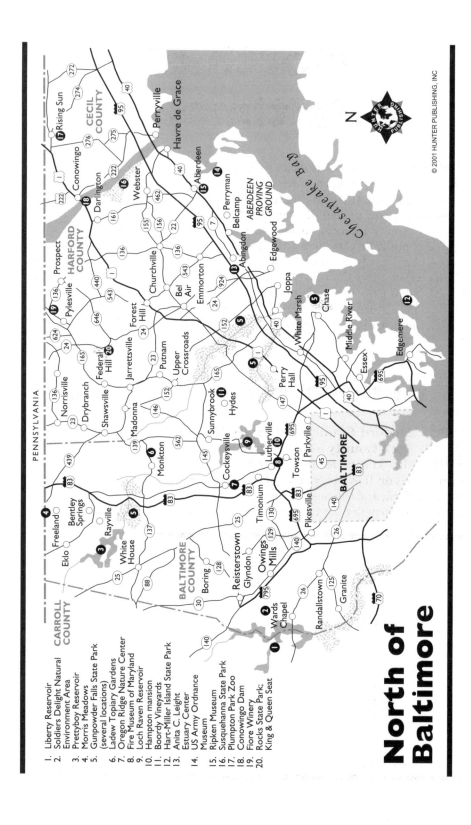

North of Baltimore

1. Liberty Reservoir
2. Soldiers Delight Natural Environment Area
3. Prettyboy Reservoir
4. Morris Meadows
5. Gunpowder Falls State Park (several locations)
6. Ladew Topiary Gardens
7. Oregon Ridge Nature Center
8. Fire Museum of Maryland
9. Loch Raven Reservoir
10. Hampton mansion
11. Boordy Vineyards
12. Hart-Miller Island State Park
13. Anita C. Leight Estuary Center
14. US Army Ordnance Museum
15. Ripken Museum
16. Susquehanna State Park
17. Plumpton Park Zoo
18. Conowingo Dam
19. Fiore Winery
20. Rocks State Park; King & Queen Seat

© 2001 HUNTER PUBLISHING, INC

North of Baltimore

The region north of Baltimore is largely bypassed by tourism. Its many parks with their rivers, trails, recreation areas and outstanding bird and wildflower habitats are enjoyed largely by local residents, who will probably not thank us for pointing them out.

In their backyards you'll find some of the state's best fly-fishing (the upper Gunpowder Falls), the finest wildflower display (the banks of the Susquehanna below Conowingo Dam), and the best landscape garden (Hampton Hall). The historic port of **Havre de Grace** adds to the superlative mix with a historic district of more than 300 buildings on the National Register.

Geography & History

Harford County, **Baltimore County** and the western part of **Cecil County** lie between Baltimore and the Mason-Dixon Line, also known as the Pennsylvania border. The broad **Susquehanna River** flows through the eastern corner, dividing Cecil County from Harford, and the meandering and often confusing incarnations of the various Gunpowder Rivers form a series of valleys that cut through the

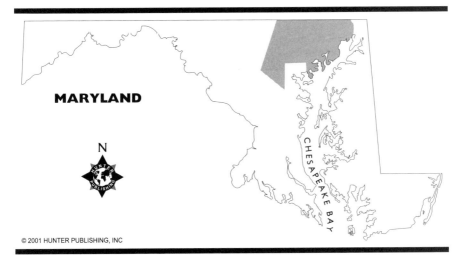

MARYLAND

N

CHESAPEAKE BAY

area directly north of the city. These form the nucleus of a state park complex that offers excellent hiking, cycling, paddling and fishing, as well as some beautiful river gorges and surprisingly rolling terrain. The eastern edge of the region is formed by the **Chesapeake Bay** and the **Susquehanna Flats**, which form the northern waters of the bay.

Before Baltimore achieved its prominence as a port, these bay towns to its north were larger and more important than Baltimore, significant ports from which the produce of fields, mines and mills of northern Maryland and Pennsylvania were carried to other Colonial and foreign ports. But river harbors silted in, and Baltimore continued to grow. By the middle 1800s, a canal system had facilitated shipping along the Susquehanna, by-passing the smaller ports. But rail transport made the canal obsolete in turn.

Apart from the destruction of Havre de Grace in the War of 1812, this part of Maryland has enjoyed a relatively peaceful history. Certainly more so than those areas directly in the path of the Civil War armies. But it was not idle in that war, with sympathizers on both sides moving either north or south to enlist. The Underground Railroad was busy along the eastern corridor, not an easy route in a state where slavery was not only legal, but the labor base of much of the agrarian economy.

THE UNDERGROUND RAILROAD

A Tours, in Havre de Grace, conducts Underground Railroad tours by appointment, Tuesday through Sunday, featuring sites and history of the pre-Civil War era. ☎ 410-939-1133.

Getting Here & Getting Around

Two interstate highways head from Baltimore into these northern counties: **I-95**, which follows the Chesapeake coast northeast toward Wilmington and Philadelphia, and **I-83**, which heads straight north. Old **US 1** runs between them, also headed northeast, but well inland of the newer interstate. Smaller roads leave Baltimore like wheel spokes, leading into every corner of this rolling landscape of farms and forests.

In general, these north-south roads are the most direct, with fewer routes cutting across. You may often find that your best route somewhere is to return to the larger north-south artery rather than head off as the crow flies. River valleys and uneven terrain, along with the historic needs that spawned roadbuilding, have contributed to this irregular road pattern.

Information Sources

Baltimore County Conference and Visitors Bureau, 435 York Rd., Towson Commons, Towson 21204; ☎ 410-583-7327 or 800-570-2836, fax 410-583-7327, www.visitbacomd.com.

Harford County Tourism Council, 121 N. Union Ave., Suite B, Havre de Grace 21078; ☎ 410-939-3336 or 800-597-2649, www.harfordmd.com.

Havre de Grace Chamber of Commerce, 220 North Washington St., Havre de Grace 21078; ☎ 410-939-3303 or 800-851-7756, www.hdgtourism.com.

Adventures

■ Parks

This section of Maryland is rich in state parks, the two most prominent of them protecting the landscapes and habitats of river corridors.

Gunpowder Falls State Park, which lies in several segments along the tributaries of the two Gunpowder Rivers, has its offices at 10815 Harford Rd., in Glen Arm; ☎ 410-592-2897. **Hart-Miller Island State Park**, accessible only by water, is administered through Gunpowder Falls. The two rivers join at Joppatowne, just in time to flow into the Chesapeake Bay. In early colonial times, before the rivers silted up, Joppatowne was a port of more importance than Baltimore.

Rocks State Park, at 3318 Rocks Chrome Hill Rd. (off Route 24) in Jarrettsville (☎ 410-557-7994, TTY 410-974-3683) is about eight miles northwest of Bel Air. Its main feature is the 190-foot rock outcrop with King and Queen Seat, reputed to have been a ceremonial assembly point of the Susquehannocks. The cliff, with views over the rolling countryside, is reached by a trail that winds up from the parking lot near the intersection of Route 24 and Rocks Chrome Rd. A separate section of the park, the Falling Branch area, is about five miles north of the main park, and has the second-highest free-falling waterfall in Maryland, at 17 feet.

The park has several picnic areas with playgrounds, and fishing in Deer Creek, which is bordered by giant rocks. Park entrance fee is $2. Campfire programs are held in the summer on Friday and Saturday evenings.

AUTHOR TIP *The two picnic area in Rocks State Park that are off the southern part of St. Clair Bridge Rd. (which leaves Route 24 just east of the bridge over Deer Creek) are wheelchair-accessible. The smaller one right by the bridge is not.*

Susquehanna State Park, bordering the river north of Havre de Grace, offers a wide variety of outdoor sports, as well as the 1794 Rock Run Grist Mill (with an overshot water wheel), a toll house and a mansion. These historic sites are open to tour June through August, 10-6; ☎ 410-557-7994.

WATCHABLE WILDLIFE *In the winter – especially cold ones when many open waters are iced over – one of the state's best places to see bald eagles is below the Conowingo Dam. The falling water and warming influence of the turbines creates ice-free patches in the river, which is already heavily populated with fish. It's a "candy store" for eagles!*

■ On Foot

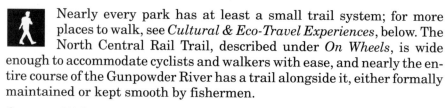

Nearly every park has at least a small trail system; for more places to walk, see *Cultural & Eco-Travel Experiences*, below. The North Central Rail Trail, described under *On Wheels*, is wide enough to accommodate cyclists and walkers with ease, and nearly the entire course of the Gunpowder River has a trail alongside it, either formally maintained or kept smooth by fishermen.

Oregon Ridge Nature Center, 13555 Beaver Dam Rd, Cockeysville (☎ 410-887-1815), although heavily used for its swimming area, has miles of trails over a rolling and interesting landscape. Rock outcrops, iron-ore pits, marble quarries, forests, meadows, swamps and streams, provide habitat for wildflowers and bird life you might not expect to see such a short distance from Baltimore. Pick up a trail map at the headquarters, where there are some interpretive displays; the trail system begins across the bridge which spans a ravine. One of the most appealing places on the trail system is Ivy Hill Pond, cool even in the summer and bordered by hemlock trees. Be prepared for short but steep climbs in a few places. The center is open Tuesday-Sunday, 9-5.

Scrambling over the rough, rocky terrain alongside the upper **Gunpowder River**, as it flows out of Prettyboy Reservoir, is the price you pay for one of the prettiest hikes in the region. A side hike of about .75 mile, round trip, can take you all the way to the looming face of Prettyboy Dam, but we find this the least appealing part of the trail and would skip it.

From Exit 27 off I-83 (the same exit for Monkton Station, but head the other way), follow Route 137 west to Evna Rd. Turn right and right again onto Falls Rd. Look for a small parking area under power lines atop a rise. Follow the trail from the parking area less than half a mile until it meets another trail at the river. Turn right. (You can go left to the dam and back at this point.) The trail follows the southern bank of Gunpowder River through a narrow gorge. The woods on its steep banks are broken with rocks, around which trees grab at what soil they can find; dogwood and laurel bloom in the spring, woodland wildflowers dot the forest floor occasionally. The trail is rough in places, as it finds its way around boulders and over roots, but the river below finds its path no easier, as it falls through chutes and rapids from pool to pool among the rocks. Shortly before you reach the bridge on Falls Rd., you must climb (scramble in places) up and over steep, sharp rock outcrops. At the bridge, walk to the right, uphill on Falls Rd. to your car.

Ladew Topiary Gardens has opened a 1.5-mile nature walk past a quarry pond and through fields, forest and marshlands. A boardwalk crosses a small stream. Habitats are discussed in interpretive signs and in a booklet. To access the trail, however, you must pay admission, so it is only practical if you combine it with a tour of the topiary gardens (see *Gardens*, page 169). Ladew Topiary Gardens, 3535 Jarretsville Pike in Monkton; ☎ 410-557-9466.

WATCHABLE WILDLIFE

*Along with the birds – Canada geese, wood ducks, mallards, woodpeckers, bluebirds, swallows, indigo buntings – seen at **Ladew Gardens**, you may also spot painted and snapping turtles, frogs, salamanders and several varieties of butterflies and moths along the nature walk.*

The climb to **King and Queen Seat**, the cliffs on the 190-foot rock knoll at Rocks State Park, off Route 24 in Jarrettsville (☎ 410-557-7994), rewards with views over rolling farm and woodlands. The best approach is by the trail from the parking lot near the intersection of Route 24 and Rocks Chrome Rd.

A flat three-mile trail borders the west river bank in **Susquehanna State Park**, below the Conowingo Dam; ☎ 410-557-7994. Birds are plentiful, especially near the dam, but the glory of this trail is its wildflowers. The area is a wildflower preserve, and in the spring the high river banks are literally covered in a carpet of spring bloom. The trail begins as a lane below the parking lot at Shures Landing, just off US 1, which crosses the dam. The trail runs between the river and a wetland area before entering a gorge nearly 100 feet deep, with sloping walls. As the land becomes level again, Deer Creek can be seen to the right, and the trail travels between the two until reaching the railway bridge, which connects it to the parking lot off Stafford Rd. in Susquehanna State Park. Although this is a good trail to walk with a car left at either end, it is short enough to be a good walk-and-return trip as well.

AUTHOR TIP *In few other places will you see as many trillium growing as along the Susquehanna Gorge – nowhere else in Maryland, certainly. Other April flowers you will see here in profusion are Dutchman's breeches, violets and Virginia bluebells. In May, the warblers and osprey return; waterfowl and kingfishers are common all season.*

■ On Wheels

 The former route of the Northern Central Railroad has become the **Northern Central Railroad Trail**, a wide multi-use rails-to-trails project that stretches more than 20 miles from the Pennsylvania state line south to Ashland, near Cockeysville. The trail follows the valley of the Gunpowder Falls River much of the way, crossing it several times. Access points are reached from Route 45, which runs parallel to I-83. Although several roads cross the trail, not all of them provide parking. The southern end of the trail is off Paper Mill Rd., alongside the Lock Haven Reservoir near Exit 20 of the interstate. About 3.5 miles north is another access with parking, on Sparks Rd.

To access the trail at the northern section of Gunpowder Falls State Park, take I-83 to Exit 27 and go east on Route 137. You'll quickly come to Route 45 in the village of Hereford. Go south (right) on Route 145, then almost immediately turn east (left) on Route 138. The trail crossing is at the nicely restored railway station, about three miles on the left. Before you see the station, you will see the tidy little ensemble of brick buildings that form the settlement of Monkton. The local historical museum is inside the station, along with information on the trail, open June-August, Wednesday-Saturday; weekends spring and fall. Contact **Monkton Bike Rental** (☎ 410-592-2897) for bicycle rentals in this area.

THE NORTH CENTRAL RAILROAD

The North Central Railroad was a major link from Baltimore to the northern Maryland farming communities and on to the north. During the Civil War, the Union Army used it to transport soldiers south. Lincoln rode it to Gettysburg to deliver his address. After his assassination, he was transported to Harrisburg on this line, en route to Illinois for burial.

About 11 miles north of its beginning, close to the halfway point, there is parking where the trail crosses White Hall Rd., off Weisburg Rd. just after its crossing with the river. Route 45 crosses the trail in Parkton, where there is also parking, and the northernmost parking area on the trail is where it crosses Freeland Rd. in Freeland.

To get there from I-83, take Exit 36, turning right at the T onto Route 439 and right again onto Route 45. In about 1.3 miles, turn left onto Freeland Rd. (Route 409); the trail crossing is about two miles from Route 45. You can get trail information from Gunpowder Falls State Park, ☎ 410-592-2897.

Chakra Cycles, at 1235 Paper Mill Rd. in Cockeysville (☎ 410-527-0593), is a one-stop center for cycling, with repairs, sales and rentals of road and mountain bikes, baby seats, children's carts and helmets. You can rent by the hour, half-day or full day.

■ On Water

The **skipjack**, a sturdy sailing vessel used for oyster dredging, still exists on the Chesapeake Bay (see *Martha Lewis*, below), and on the third Saturday of April you can see the fleet assembled for the annual races off Havre de Grace. If you love historic boats, you should be there.

Public **boat ramps** in Havre de Grace are at **Jean Roberts Park** on the northern end of town off Water St, near the railroad bridge, and at the far southern end in **Tydings Park**.

Sailing

The prime waters of the Chesapeake Bay are the ideal place to sail, and the protected Havre de Grace harbor is the ideal place to learn how. **BaySail**, at the Tidewater Marina at the foot of Bourbon St. (☎ 410-939-3779, www.baysail.net) offers courses at all skill levels, certified by the American Sailing Association. In addition to its sailing school, BaySail has recent-model Catalina and Hunter yachts, which you can charter on a bareboat, captained or instructional cruise basis.

For additional opportunities to sail on the Chesapeake from Havre de Grace, see *Boat Tours*, below.

Canoeing & Kayaking

The upper reaches of the **Gunpowder River**, which runs close to the Northern Central Trail (see *On Wheels*, above), are gentle enough for beginning paddlers, mostly flatwater with only minor riffles of whitewater to navigate. The biggest hazard is the occasional tangle of a fallen tree, creating strainers that can catch you up and plunge you into the icy water. Much of the river's route is through woodland protected by Gunpowder Falls State Park (☎ 410-592-2897). Although in high water seasons there is ample water for the river section upstream from Monkton, the seven miles of lower river from Monkton to Ashland is better in summer or fall when water levels are low.

Access to the lower river is in the northern section of Gunpowder Falls State Park. From I-83's Exit 27, go east on Route 137. You'll quickly come to Route 45 in the village of Hereford. Go south (right) on Route 145, then almost immediately turn east (left) on Route 138. In about 2.5 miles, you will come to the bridge. You can unload kayaks here, but must park farther along the road, at the crossing of the Northern Central Trail at the old rail station. **Monkton Bike Rental** (☎ 410-592-2897) has canoe rentals. If you don't have a second car for a shuttle, you might consider renting a bicycle, too, and returning for your car along the rail trail. The take-out for the trip is at a wooden fishing pier about 150 yards below the bridge on Phoenix Rd., which leaves Route 45 not far north of its connector with I-83 at Exit 20. A trail leads from the river to the rail trail here.

RECOMMENDED READING: *Experienced paddlers who look for more daring whitewater descents in this area will find them elsewhere on the Gunpowder Falls rivers, on Western Run and on Winters Run. The best information on these, with blow-by-blow accounts of the riverscape and hazards, is in the detailed book* **Maryland and Delaware Canoe Trails**, *by Edward Gertler, published by Seneca Press.*

Eden Mill Park, at 1617 Eden Mill Rd. in Pylesville, borders Deer Creek, as does nearby **Rocks State Park**. You can use either as a canoe put-in point for the creek.

The portion of Gunpowder Falls State Park that lies at the confluence of the two **Gunpowder Rivers**, just before they flow into the bay, is a broad marshy delta, ripe for paddlers. To explore the area, put in at Mariner Point Park, off Joppa Farm Rd. in Joppatowne, a pleasant park with picnic areas and other facilities, as well as boat launches. Powerboats make some of the main navigation lanes less than tranquil but, once past these, you can slip in and out of tiny coves and marshy channels that wouldn't interest those with motors. These areas are rich in bird life, with ducks, herons and eagles a common sight.

Since following any plan is difficult here (and even harder to describe), we suggest you get a topographical map of the area before wandering too far into this tangle of marsh-grass-lined channels, which begin to look very much alike. Although some of the tiny creeks are not on the map, at least you will have some notion of the lay of the water. Park offices are at 10815 Harford Rd., in Glen Arm; ☎ 410-592-2897.

RECOMMENDED READING: *For a good trip description beginning at Mariners Point Park, read Bryan MacKay's* **Hiking, Cycling and Canoeing in Maryland***, published by Johns Hopkins University Press, Baltimore. This excellent book is the work of a teaching biologist, and the information on the wildlife you will see on this and other trips described in the book is golden.*

The center for paddle sports in the Havre de Grace area is **Starrk Moon Kayaks**, 500 Warren St.; ☎ 410-939-9500 or 877-KAYAKS-1, www.starrkmoon.com. Along with lessons at all levels and a complete line of kayaks and equipment, they sponsor a number of events and special programs, including one on fall and winter kayaking and new product festivals. Small classes are strong on personal instruction, from beginning introductory classes to courses on whitewater paddling. They offer guided full- and half-day trips on the bay.

Canoe trips are among the nature programs offered by the **Anita C. Leight Estuary Center**, at 700 Otter Point Rd. in Abindon (☎ 410-612-1688), part of the National Estuarine Research Reserve on Otter Creek.

Amphibious Horizons, based at Quiet Waters Park in Annapolis (☎ 410-267-8742 or 888-I-LUV-SUN, www.amphibioushorizons.com), offers day-long Saturday trips through the Susquehanna Flats. An all-day excursion is $75, and includes lunch at a waterside restaurant.

Boat Tours

Operated by the Chesapeake Heritage Conservancy, the skipjack *Martha Lewis* is one of the few working oyster boats left that dredges under sail. The 50-foot, two-sailed skipjack offers discovery programs to schools and to the public, focusing on the environment, weather, celestial navigation, oysters, birds and marine life of the Susquehanna Flats and the Chesapeake Bay. Along with these programs, the skipjack provides a unique opportunity to sail as part of the regular oyster season (see *Fishing*, below). Schedules change often but, most recently, public trips were offered on weekends at noon, 1:30 and 3 pm and on Wednesday evenings at 6 pm. The 75-minute cruise is $10 for adults; $5 for children under 10. Since the boat goes to many festivals during the year, you should always call to be sure the Martha Lewis is available when planning your itinerary. The *Martha Lewis* is moored at the foot of Congress Ave. in Havre de Grace; ☎ 302-777-5488 or 800-406-0766.

A smaller version of the skipjack was also part of the history of Bay watermen, used for oysters, crabbing and fishing. One of the few remaining is *AppleGarth*, moored at Tydings Park in Havre de Grace. It was used in the Paramount movie *IQ* and afterward restored as a charter and tour boat. Customized day and evening cruises for up to six passengers run from May through October; call to discuss pricing. ☎ 410-879-6941.

Fishing

Rocks State Park, at 3318 Rocks Chrome Hill Rd. (off Route 24) in Jarrettsville (☎ 410-557-7994, TTY 410-974-3683), eight miles northwest of Bel Air, is on Deer Creek. Above and below the park area, where the creek parallels Route 24 and St. Clair Bridge Rds. respectively, there is good fishing. The area off Route 24 has parking; for the southern one, park at the lower picnic area.

Gunpowder Falls State Park, which follows the tributaries and main Gunpowder Falls rivers, includes four trout streams and tidal fishing waters at its mouth near Joppatowne. Its upper reaches, as icy waters flow out of the Prettyboy dam, have some of the best catch-and-release trout fishing in Maryland, with an astonishing trout-count. There is no parking on Prettyboy Dam Rd., but you can reach the river by a walk of less than half a mile along the Highland Trail, from Falls Rd. The reservoir area is accessed from Exit 31 of I-83, about five miles south of the Pennsylvania border.

Dundee Creek Marina, in the lower section of Gunpowder Falls State Park, has boat rentals, a bait-and-tackle shop and a launch ramp (fee $5). For current information on tides, weather and what's biting, call ☎ 410-335-9390. Park Headquarters are at 10815 Harford Rd., in Glen Arm; ☎ 410-592-2897. Hart-Miller Island State Park, on an island near the mouth of the Middle River and accessible only by boat, is administered through Gunpowder Falls.

Conowingo Dam, on US 1 in Darlington, blocks the progress of the Susquehanna River, creating a 14-mile impoundment that is popular for anglers year-round. The artificial environment created below the dam often teems with fish unable to pass the dam on spawning runs or attracted to the aerated waters when hot weather increases algae in the bay and depletes oxygen supplies. Even when the rest of the waters are ice-bound, water going through the turbines is warmed to create patches of open water. At the height of these seasons, don't expect solitude on the shore or along the catwalk; the area is hardly a secret.

To fish farther downstream, follow the gravel road south from the parking lot, past the wildflower reserve signs and look for trails to the adjacent river. A truck-lift project helps migrating species over the dam in the spring, but there will be plenty left. Parking is at Shures Landing below the dam, easily accessed from US 1, which crosses the dam.

Several public parks along the bay have fishing piers, one of the most attractive of which is **Mariner Point Park**, off Joppa Farm Rd. in Joppatowne; ☎ 410-612-1608. It also has a boat launching ramp.

The chance to take part in the work of a sailing **oyster dredger**, an endangered maritime species, is rare indeed. But the *Martha Lewis* will take a limited number of people on one- or two-night wind-driven trips during the oyster season (November through April – remember those months with "R" in them); moored at the foot of Congress Ave. in Havre de Grace; ☎ 302-777-5488 or 800-406-0766.

■ On Snow

Don't expect much in the way of snow sports this close to the warming influences of the Chesapeake Bay, but snow does indeed fall here, and sometimes stays on the ground long enough to enjoy.

Skiing

Oregon Ridge Nature Center, 13555 Beaver Dam Rd, Cockeysville (☎ 410-887-1815), has miles of trails over a rolling landscape, most of them old woods roads. Be prepared for short but steep climbs in a few places and be aware that what goes uphill must come down. If you are not comfortable with steep descents on Nordic skis, you might prefer a flatter trail system than Oregon Ridge's.

■ On Horseback

Although this part of Maryland is prime horse country, with its history of fox hunting, polo and steeplejacks and dozens of equestrian centers, finding a place to go trail riding if you don't have your own horse with you can be difficult. **Betty's Rest Riding Academy**, in Havre de Grace (☎ 410-272-5820) is the happy exception. Betty's offers guided trail rides by reservation, both western and English saddle, on the 300 acres of Mount Pleasant Orchard, overlooking the bay. Riding lessons and pony rides for toddlers, along with a saddlery where they do custom leather work (open Tuesday-Saturday, 10-6, and Tuesday, 3-6), makes Betty's an all-around center for things horsey.

Jousting, the official state sport of Maryland, has its home hero, with the Maryland Jousting Tournament Association (☎ 410-272-3086) and the American Jousting Club (☎ 410-592-8918).

Cultural & Eco-Travel Experiences

■ Natural Areas

Soldiers Delight Natural Environment Area, 5100 Deer Park Rd., near Wards Chapel, ☎ 410-922-3044, is one of the smallest and least known of the region's parks. On the far western edge of Baltimore County, Soldiers Delight is best known to botanists and geologists for the rare wildflowers that grow there, and the unique geology that nurtures them. The underlying rock is a metal-laden serpentine, rare in the eastern United States.

Most interesting of the trails shown on the map in the parking lot is the one marked with white blazes. It leads through a grassy landscape of low growth, over a stream where fringed gentians bloom on the banks in October, the only site where they grow in Maryland. In the uplands, the barrens grow even barer, with a few pine trees and lichen-dressed rocks.

At **Oregon Ridge Nature Center**, 13555 Beaver Dam Rd, Cockeysville (☎ 410-887-1815), you'll find the marble quarry that was the source of building stone for the two Washington monuments – one in Baltimore and the later one built on the Mall in Washington, DC. Rock outcrops, iron-ore pits, forests, meadows, swamps and streams, where you can see wildflowers and bird life, are other features of this attractive park just north of Baltimore. Open Tuesday-Sunday, 9-5.

The nature center building has displays and bird feeding stations, and is wheelchair-accessible. A 200-yard paved nature trail, beginning along the road from the center to the parking area, leads through the woods past iron and marble quarries.

Anita C. Leight Estuary Center, at 700 Otter Point Rd. in Abingdon (☎ 410-612-1688), is on Otter Creek, part of the National Estuarine Research Reserve. Along with its research function, the center has a number of programs for the public, which include hikes, canoe trips and children's events. Nature trails through the hilly forest leave from the Nature Center, which also has nature exhibits; open Saturday 10-5, Sunday noon-5, all year.

At **Plumpton Park Zoo**, at 1416 Telegraph Rd. in Rising Sun (☎ 410-658-6850), a giraffe may lean down to nibble on your hat. He's one of 250 well-tended animals in this family-friendly park, where you may also meet deer, zebra, camel, gibbon, monkeys or – not at close quarters – an alligator. Nature trails and a picnic area make this low-cost park good for a day's outing with children; Open daily, 10-5.

At the end of Union Ave. in Havre de Grace is the waterfront **Tydings Park**, with picnic tables, playground equipment and gazebos on a wide boardwalk promenade that skirts the shore, crosses a marsh and continues on to the historic Concord Lighthouse. A branch of the boardwalk connects it to the Decoy Museum (see *Museums & Historic Sites*, below). The park overlooks a marina.

**WATCHABLE
WILDLIFE**

The tall grasses of the marsh between the Decoy Museum and Concord Lighthouse, as well as the shore on either side, nearly always has several species of ducks. The boardwalk makes it possible to see them here in a marsh habitat, not easy to do elsewhere without a boat.

■ Gardens

Our pick for the loveliest garden landscape in the Chesapeake region is that of **Hampton**, the estate of the Ridgely family that surrounds the grand manor house built 1783-1790. The gardens grew throughout the early 1800s, when the great terrace in front of the Georgian house was planted with magnificent trees in a seemingly casual, but highly effective plan. Arbors hang with wisteria and garden ornaments popular in the Victorian era are used sparingly as accents.

But the gardens don't end there; instead, you emerge from the trees to find yourself overlooking a series of terraced parterre gardens, their geometric patterns outlined by boxwood, filled with colorful massed plantings of flowers and highlighted by white stone walks. They are the largest formal gardens in the state (and we know of none of this magnitude in Virginia, either), but their importance is in the beauty of their design and the delightful surprise of their location, not just in their size. The parterres are planted in different flowers – spring bulbs, roses, peonies – which accent the green borders throughout the season.

An herb garden shows the plants that would have been grown for household use as medicine, flavoring and fragrance. The greenhouses and orangerie (a reconstruction of the original one, which was destroyed by fire) housed delicate plants raised for food, bedding plants for the gardens and flowers that decorated the rooms.

Hampton is at 535 Hampton Lane in Towson (☎ 410-823-1309), just north of Beltway Exit 27-B (Dulaney Valley Rd.), where you should make an immediate right turn onto Hampton Lane. The grounds are open daily, 9-5, year-round. House tours are given regularly, but you can walk about the grounds on your own; there is no admission charge. For information on the house and its outbuildings, see *Historic Sites & Museums*, below.

Unusual topiary for which the gardens are known greet visitors almost immediately after they enter the gates of **Ladew Topiary Gardens**, at 3535 Jarretsville Pike in Monkton; ☎ 410-557-9570. A leafy fox hunt is underway, yew hounds bounding across the lawn following a fleeing green fox, the hunter caught in mid-jump over a white fence. This is a sample of the skillful and creative shrubbery sculpture in the garden beyond.

Hemlock hedges and figures of arbor vitae and yew are carved and trained into improbable shapes: swans swim along a waving hedge and sculptures range from fanciful birds and animals to a buddha. A Victorian garden, water lily garden, one for roses and several with single color schemes are among the themed gardens, where flowers bloom all summer and fall, but are their showiest in May. Some of the unique horticultural features here are the large climbing hydrangea behind the house, the wisteria on the portico and a berry garden for birds. Although the topiary is the best-known feature, each of the gardens is beautifully conceived and often marked by a touch of whimsy or surprise.

A 1½-mile nature walk with interpretive signs leads past the quarry pond and through forest and marsh habitats. The entire estate covers about 250 acres.

The house, while amusing in its decor and furnished with some fine pieces, is largely a paean to its socialite owner, Harvey Ladew, whose prime occupations beyond gardening seemed to be fox hunting and entertaining high-visibility friends like the Windsors. Even he found them boring, according to our guide, who pointed out the hidden door in the library, through which he escaped to his gardens. This elegant oval room was created especially to showcase a Chippendale partners' desk.

Open mid-April through October, Monday-Friday, 10-4; weekends 10-5. June-August the gardens are open until 8 pm on Thursdays. Flowers are at their height of bloom in May. Garden admission is $8 adults, seniors and students $7, children under 12 $2. Tours of the house with admission to the gardens are $12, seniors and students $11, children $4. From I-695, head north from Exit 27-B on Route 146. From I-95, follow Route 152 north from Exit 74 to Route 146.

■ Wineries

Boordy Vineyards, 12820 Long Green Pike, Hydes (☎ 410-592-5015), center around the restored fieldstone barn dating from the 1800s. This is Maryland's oldest vineyard, established in 1945. It is open year-round, Monday through Saturday, 10-5; Sunday, 1-5. Tours are given on the hour daily, 1-4. Admission is free. The winery lies between Routes 146 and 147, just west of Baldwin Falls State Park, and can be reached from either Exit 29 or 31 of I-695.

Fiore Winery, at 3026 Whiteford Rd. (Route 136) in Pylesville (☎ 410-836-7605), makes traditional Italian wines. The vineyard is open Wednesday through Sunday, noon-6, in the summer; noon-5 in the winter. In addition to taking tours and tasting the product, visitors are invited to picnic by the vineyards. Pylesville is in the northern part of Harford County, not far south of the Pennsylvania line.

■ Farmers' Markets

Spring Valley Farm, at 724 Conowingo Rd. in Conowingo (☎ 410-387-3280), has blueberries, grown free of sprays, which you can pick yourself or buy already picked. They also have sour cherries and other fruits, as well as a wildflower garden you are welcome to visit Monday-Friday, 8-8; Saturday, 8-4.

In Havre de Grace, a **farmers' market** operates May through October on Pennington Ave. between Washington and Union streets, Saturday, 9-noon; ☎ 410-939-3303.

In Bel Air a **market** is set up at the District Court House Parking lot, 2 South Bond St. April-October it runs on Tuesdays from 11 until 2 and Saturdays from 7 to 11. During November, it's held on Saturdays only. On Sundays, May through October, a market is held at the **Harford Mall** on Baltimore Pike; ☎ 410-836-6346.

■ Crafts

Anyone interested in early crafts or those of rural America in the 19th and early 20th centuries, should visit **Steppingstone Museum**, at 461 Quaker Bottom Rd., in Susquehanna State Park, Havre de Grace; ☎ 410-939-2299. Its theme and its mission is to preserve crafts and skills used between 1880 and 1920 and demonstrate them to later generations. Along with examples of the crafts and rural skills, its collections include the tools and implements of both domestic arts and skilled trades. It is a working museum in that it promotes traditional crafts and encourages visitors to learn these skills through workshops and special programs. For a description of the farm complex and its collections, see *Historic Sites*, below. It is open weekends, 1-5, May through September; admission is $2 for adults, children under 12 are free. Special events may have a modest additional charge.

Those who collect decoys can view and purchase examples of this really American art form at **Vincenti Decoys**, 303 West Lane, Churchville; ☎ 410-734-6238, www.vincentidecoys.com. Pat and Jeannie's decoys have been featured in the Smithsonian, and in several books about the craft. Prices begin at about $65.

For handmade chocolates, visit **Bomboy's** at 322 Market St. in Havre de Grace; ☎ 410-939-4970; www.bomboys-candy.com. Made fresh daily, the wide variety in their shop includes centers like peanut butter soufflé, lemon cream, Irish Cream truffle and marzipan, as well as nut combinations. The shop is open Tuesday through Saturday, 10-6; Sunday, noon-5. They also ship chocolates.

■ Antiques

Saint John St. in Havre de Grace is known as **Antiques Row**, and a number of other shops are on N. Washington St., Franklin St. and N. Union Ave., which run off Saint John. Pick up a map at any one of these, showing locations of the shops.

Events

 APRIL: The annual **Skipjack Invitational Races** are held mid-month at the Havre de Grace waterfront; ☎ 800-406-0766.

MAY: Early in the month, the annual **Decoy, Wildlife Art and Sportsman Festival** takes place in Havre de Grace; ☎ 410-939-3739, www.decoymuseum.com.

JULY: Independence Celebration Week in Havre de Grace brings fireworks, a parade, a carnival, and music, much of it centered in Tydings Park; ☎ 410-939-4362.

SEPTEMBER: The annual **Duck Fair** is held mid-month at the Decoy Museum in Havre de Grace; ☎ 410-939-3739, www.decoymuseum.com. Later in September, the **Fall Harvest Festival and Craft Show** takes place at the Steppingstone Museum in Havre de Grace. It includes scarecrows, apple butter making, pony rides, music, dance and craft booths; ☎ 410-939-2299.

DECEMBER: Mid-month **Candlelight Tours** in Havre de Grace open local homes, churches, museums and businesses festooned with holiday decorations, a chance to see the interiors of some fine buildings not usually open. A sale and carver celebration is held at the same time at the Decoy Museum, featuring working demonstrations and free museum admission; ☎ 410-939-3303.

Sightseeing

■ Historic Sites & Museums

Just Outside of Baltimore

 If you think shiny fire engines are of interest only to kids, firemen and dalmatians, a visit to the **Fire Museum of Maryland** may change your mind. We learned a lot of American history here, and admired some artistry as well, in the meticulous and often ornate painted decoration on hand-drawn firefighting equipment from the 1800s. We learned, in fact, that all equipment was pulled by the firefighters themselves until the time of the Civil War, when horses took over the job.

DID YOU KNOW?

 At the Fire Museum of Maryland, you'll see early fire hoses, which were made of leather and kept flexible by rubbing them with pig fat.

A Discovery Room for kids has a real live fire truck they can climb on and gear to try on; throughout the museum are old-fashioned red call boxes, where you can give in to that temptation to pull the lever and turn in a false alarm. If you do, hurry to the Fire Alarm Office to see how the city of Baltimore responded and kept track of which trucks were where. This is the original equipment used until the 1980s when 911 replaced the old technology. The museum is at 1301-York Rd., Lutherville; ☎ 410-321-7500, www.firemuseummd.org. To get there from the Baltimore Beltway (I-695), take Exit 26-B North, marked York Rd/Lutherville. The museum is behind the Heaver Plaza Office Building, a short distance from the highway interchange.

The 60 acres of National Historic Site property which surround **Hampton Hall** today are a bare remnant of the 24,000 acres once owned by the Ridgely family. But the graceful mansion and its outbuildings, as well as its outstanding gardens – between them the essence of the estate – remain and are beautifully maintained.

The pink tint to the house, which has been retained in restoration, was originally quite literally a reflection of the owner's wealth. It derives from the iron ore in the sand used to mix the stucco that covered it; iron mined and smelted on the property had made the Ridgeleys among the wealthiest families in the new United States. The mansion is classically Georgian, with a central section flanked by two wings, each connected by a hyphen. Above the center is a well-scaled cupola. It was among the largest country manors in the United States.

Fire bells at the Fire Museum of Maryland.

Because the Ridgely family continued to own and occupy the house until (and even after) it became a national site, much of the family furnishings remain. The John Findlay drawing room set, for example was done on commission for the house; other rooms are furnished with pieces and styles of later descendants. The house was clearly built for entertaining, and would hold 300 easily for parties. The dining room seated 50 comfortably.

AUTHOR TIP

Women should wear flat shoes when touring the interior of Hampton Hall, to protect the original floors from heel marks.

The house is not only an important architectural site, but the family that built it was highly influential in the history of Maryland. Realizing that the future of agriculture and commerce lay in grain, which did not wear out the soil as tobacco did, and which could be shipped to markets all over the world, the Ridgeleys turned their fields to wheat, corn and others, which they shipped from Baltimore on their own merchant fleet. Their commerce is credited with Baltimore's early emergence as a major port.

Another significant reason for seeing Hampton is the complete ensemble of outbuildings which remain – 27 in all – many of which date to the era of the original building. Outstanding are the orangerie, the smoke house, the ice house and the stables, where carriages are exhibited. Slave quarters, which can be seen in only a few Maryland plantations, sit beside the farmhouse that was the family's first home. These out-buildings sit on grounds filled with more than 200 species of trees, many imported by the family in the early 1800s. Below the winding pathway through the trees appears a stunning vista of terraced gardens; for a more complete description of these, see *Gardens*, above.

Hampton Hall is at 535 Hampton Lane in Towson (☎ 410-823-1309); heading north from Beltway Exit 27-B, which is Dulaney Valley Rd., make an immediate right onto Hampton Lane. The grounds are open daily, 9-5, year-round. Tours of the house, which you should certainly take, are given regularly; you can walk about the grounds on your own. The brochure produced by the National Park Service gives an excellent overview of the plantation's history and of life there for all its residents, from owners to slaves and indentured servants.

Near the Pennsylvania Border

An unusual museum, one of Maryland's several private museums based on the collections of a single family, is **Morris Meadows**, at 1523 Freeland Rd. in Freeland; ☎ 410-329-6636. Clyde Morris is the fifth generation of his family to live on the farm since his ancestors settled "Morris' Choice" in 1793. And to hear him tell it, none of the intervening generations ever threw anything away. This accumulation, plus his own avid collecting, has created a fascinating record of rural life and farming.

Along with the collections, which range from little everyday things to rare old farm equipment (such as a horse-powered merry-go-round-type thrashing machine), much of the museum's charm is in the personality of the family that created it, and in their unique vision. Clyde Morris himself will probably take you around, telling stories of how and where these things were used – and of where he found some of them – and encouraging you to add your own stories to his notebooks.

Arranged in alcove displays representing a schoolroom, his wife's father's general store, or a subject such as sewing and needlework, the furnishings and utensils of rural life are well displayed, although not always labeled. But the tour is part of the experience, so you can ask about anything that piques your curiosity.

Morris Meadows Museum is fully wheelchair-accessible, with special ramps for transferring from both buses and cars. Several wheelchairs are provided (sorry, but you can't try out the beautiful old woven wicker one on display), floors are smooth and level, and spaces wide. The entire building – even the phone booth – has been created with accessibility in mind. We give it a five-wheel rating.

Don't be surprised to see some of the collections at work – to find Virginia Morris at the player piano, to hear the clang of an original school bell or to be offered popcorn fresh from the old black popper on the woodstove. This is certainly not a mothball collection. The ingenuity of some of the machines, such as the meat chopper used during the Civil War, is impressive. Look for such things as the wagon that converts to a sled in the winter, and the unique show-and-tell case in the schoolroom.

A small collection of landmark newspaper headlines, photographs and memorabilia records the contribution of local people to defense efforts, from the time a Morris ancestor walked to Baltimore to enlist in 1812. Be sure to read some of the personal experiences recounted by visitors in the notebooks by the player piano – and add your own if you are a veteran.

A restaurant was under construction at our last visit, which will offer catfish fresh from a tank in the center of the room, and buffalo meat raised on the farm. The museum is open weekends, year-round, or by appointment (which you should not feel shy about making – the Morris family is genuinely pleased to share their farm and its treasures).

To get to the museum from I-83, take Exit 36, turning right at the T onto Route 439. It will almost immediately end at Route 45, where you turn right (north). In about 1.3 miles turn left on Freeland Rd. (Route 409); FreelandRd. winds through rolling meadows and hollows, passing a log cabin on the way. The museum is about 3.5 miles, on the left.

Aberdeen

The huge shaded area you see on the map between Route 40 and the Chesapeake Bay is the Aberdeen Proving Ground, the Army's center for developing and testing weapons. On the property is the **US Army Ordnance Museum**, whose collections provide an interesting insight into the history of firearms. As interesting as the weapons themselves – which include many rare examples of breechloaders, sharps and other early arms – is the story of how even the obsolete and outdated weapons here have proven useful in solving problems and designing new ones suited to modern defense.

DID YOU KNOW?

Research done on Russian weapons, which had been captured by the Germans during World War II and subsequently brought to Aberdeen along with captured German ordnance, proved invaluable in preparing US forces for the Korean War, where they faced an enemy armed with Russian equipment.

Along with the collections, which span from early rifles to firearms from all over the world, are homemade weapons encountered by US forces in Vietnam and an exhibit on spin-offs from Ordnance Corps research that have changed civilian life, such as miniaturization, the development of the proximity fuze (an explosive ignition device used in bombs, artillery shells, and mines), the jeep and the SUV. Outdoors, stretching across several fields, are row on row of tanks and heavy artillery, the **Mile of Tanks**. Admission to the museum is free, but the restoration and maintenance of the artifacts are paid for by private donation, which you are encouraged to support. Unlike many museums, you are welcome to photograph any of the collections. It is open daily, 10-4:45. From I-95, Exit 85, follow Route 22 east, crossing US-40, to the Proving Ground gate. The museum is well marked to the right; ☎ 410-278-3602, www.ordmusfound.org.

Baseball fans will want to visit the small, but very well done **Ripken Museum**, in the Aberdeen municipal building at 3 West Belair Ave. (Route 132); ☎ 410-273-2525. Hometown hero Cal Ripken, Jr. is not the only subject; this museum pays tribute to the entire family and the values and dedication that created this family heritage of baseball. When Cal, Jr. joined the Baltimore Orioles, his father – Cal Sr. – was its third base coach. When Cal's brother Billy joined the team as second baseman, Cal, Sr. became manager; the two brothers played five seasons together. Photographs, videos, interactive trivia games, and mementos of the family, the Orioles and baseball are combined in a bright and attractive setting. The museum is handicapped-accessible, and open daily June through August, Thursday-Monday in April and May and Friday-Monday the rest of the year; admission is $3 adult, $2 over age 62, $1 ages six-18. A small gift shop is a good place to find souvenirs for baseball fans back home. The museum is easy to spot; look for the bronze statue of Ripken at the corner of Routes 40 and 132 in the town center.

Havre de Grace

Havre de Grace (anglicized in its pronunciation) is an attractive town with quite an interesting history – it narrowly lost to Annapolis as the site of the state capital and was largely destroyed by the British during the War of 1812. General Lafayette, who was here several times during the Revolution, said that the port reminded him of the French seaport of Le Havre, hence the town's name (we can only imagine that Le Havre, France, must have been a good deal more charming then than it is today).

The streets of Havre de Grace, especially Union St., are lined with some fine Victorian mansions. Pick up a copy of the excellent street map and the **Self-Guided Tour** brochure at your inn or at the Chamber of Commerce at 220 North Washington St. The tour descriptions put all the fine examples of architecture here in their historical perspective.

Concord Point Lighthouse, the oldest continuously operating in the state, was built to last, of granite quarried up the river in Port Deposit. It was built in 1827, and Lt. John O'Neil, who had single-handedly tried to defend the town during the War of 1812, was named its first keeper. A cannon used in the War of 1812 is on the water-side of the lighthouse. Now electrified with a fifth-order Fresnel lens, its beacon was originally lighted by nine whale oil lamps. The stone house across the street was the keeper's house, now under restoration. The lighthouse is at Concord and Lafayette streets, at the end of the boardwalk from Tydings Park. It is free, and open weekends and holidays 1-5, April through October.

Not far from the lighthouse, and connected to it by a boardwalk along the shore, is the **Decoy Museum**, 215 Giles St. in Havre de Grace; ☎ 410-939-3739, www.decoymuseum.com. Displays show the history of decoy-making, materials used (which include wicker and reeds), poses, species and a panel of western decoys, which are sometimes made of tin or flat wood silhouettes. Havre de Grace was (and still is) a center for decoy carving, and a number of local artists are featured, along with the legendary Ward brothers and other carvers from different parts of the state. A shop has been replicated, and a tableau of realistic models of local artists is narrated in the voice of one of their best-known, Madison Mitchell. A gallery called "Gunning the Flats" shows skiffs, blinds, calls and weapons to illustrate the history of hunting on the bay in a setting surrounded by a mural of the marshes. The museum is handicapped-accessible, and a shop features art, gifts and books on a waterfowl theme. Special events include a Christmas show and sale and the annual Decoy and Wildlife Art Show in early May (see *Events*).

The museum is open 11-4 daily; admission is $4 for adults, $2 for seniors and ages eight-11. To get here from I-95, take Exit 89 east and continue to Juanita St. Turn right, then left on Revolution St. in a bit less than a mile.

Downtown Havre de Grace

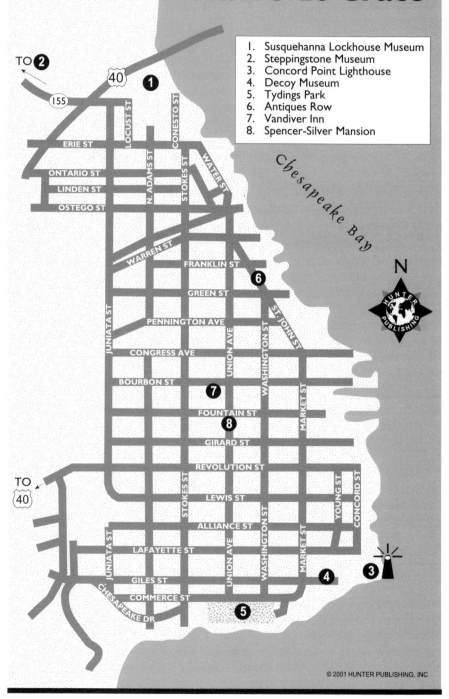

1. Susquehanna Lockhouse Museum
2. Steppingstone Museum
3. Concord Point Lighthouse
4. Decoy Museum
5. Tydings Park
6. Antiques Row
7. Vandiver Inn
8. Spencer-Silver Mansion

Chesapeake Bay

N

© 2001 HUNTER PUBLISHING, INC

Turn right on Union Ave. and follow it to the end, turning left into the museum's parking lot.

The three museums in this area, The Ripken, Army Ordnance and Decoy Museums, are all fully handicapped-accessible, as is the fine boardwalk along the shore in front off the Decoy Museum.

At the other end of town, along Susquehanna between the rail and highway bridges at Erie and Conesto streets, is the **Susquehanna Lockhouse Museum**; ☎ 410-939-5780. The Susquehanna and Tidewater Canal was opened in 1840, connecting Wrightsville, Pennsylvania with Havre de Grace, and to the Chesapeake Bay. By its connections with other canal systems, it opened all of Central Pennsylvania to trade with the ports of Baltimore and Philadelphia. Bordering the river, the canal's 29 locks lifted boats a total of 233 feet in 45 miles.

The 1840 brick lock house has doors at either end of its porch, one to the canal office where tolls were collected and the other to the keeper's quarters, which are furnished as they would have been in the mid 1800s. Upstairs a video on the canal is shown. The restored outlet lock, where boats entered the bay, and reconstructed pivot bridge are at the site, as well. Open weekends, May-October, 1-5; admission $2 adults, $1 seniors. A small gift shop carries books on local history and the canal, as well as crafts; a Christmas Boutique offers the work of local craftsmen during the holiday season.

Early crafts of the 19th and early 20th centuries are the focus of **Steppingstone Museum**, at 461 Quaker Bottom Rd., inside Susquehanna State Park in Havre de Grace; ☎ 410-939-2299. Located on a sprawling farm complex around a furnished brick farmhouse, its buildings include the shops and sheds common to working farms – a dairy, corn cribs and wood shed. Other buildings house shops showing rural trades, often demonstrated by working craftsmen: blacksmith, cooper, woodworking, wheelwright, and decoy shops, along with a weaving room and potter's shed. Carriage barns show carriages, wagons and sleighs, and a display barn recreates a general store and veterinarian shop. In each, the emphasis is on the process of making or doing, not simply on the artifacts.

In keeping with the working museum's mission to preserve and demonstrate these almost forgotten skills of rural living, frequent special events focus on particular aspects or seasons of rural life or on historic events of the valley. **Civil War Living History Day** in May brings an encampment of re-enactors to the farm, and in the fall a Harvest Festival features a craft show. It is open weekends, 1-5, May through September; admission is $2 for adults, children under 12 are free. Special events may have an additional charge.

Where to Stay

ACCOMMODATIONS PRICE KEY
Rates are per room, per night, double occupancy.
$ . . . . Under $50
$$ . . . . $50 to $100
$$$ . . . . $101 to $175
$$$$ . . . . $176 and up

■ Havre de Grace

Currier House Bed & Breakfast is one of most historic buildings in town, since its 1790s central section was among the few homes to survive the British attack in the War of 1812. The Currier family tree is on the dining room wall, and the house is decorated with a decoy collection, old photographs and memorabilia of a most interesting family. Staying here is a light-hearted romp through the highlights of town history. You may want to linger over the hearty waterman's breakfast while Jane (a Currier) spins a few tales of Havre de Grace's livery stable, thoroughbred track and hunt clubs that once covered the lands of the Aberdeen Proving Ground – all long gone.

Currier and Ives prints, along with the owner's original paintings, decorate several of the guest rooms, which are furnished in a mix of family antiques and newer pieces. Two rooms have a lighthouse view, one a small upstairs porch of is own. Each has a private bath and phone; rates are $85-$115. Currier House is close to the lighthouse, Tydings Park and the Decoy Museum, at 800 South Market St.; ☎ 410-939-7886 or 800-827-2889. www.currier-bb.com.

Vandiver Inn, at 301-S. Union Ave. (☎ 410-939-5200 or 800-245-1655, www.vandiverinn.com) is a three-story mansion built in 1886, listed on the National Historic Register. A wide front porch invites guests to stop and admire the tree-shaded streetscape of other fine Victorian homes. Guest and public rooms are elegantly decorated with fine Victorian furniture, some with stunning fireplace tiles and each with its own unique architectural details. The breakfast room has floor-to-ceiling step-out windows onto the front porch. We liked the Seneca Room, on the back of the first floor, which overlooks the large back yard. Rooms range from $80 to $115, suites from $125 to $140.

Spencer-Silver Mansion is an imposing and beautifully maintained stone Victorian with excellent painted medallions on the exterior and a two-storied wide front porch with a gazebo corner. Stained glass windows, a patterned slate roof and a third-floor cupola are among its other architectural features. Guest rooms in the main house and carriage shed are furnished in Victorian antiques; some have clawfoot tubs, others whirlpool baths. Breakfast is an event; rates range from $70 to $95 in the main house, $140 for the Carriage House, which sleeps four. Spencer Silver Mansion is at 200 Union St.; ☎ 410-939-1097 or 800-780-1485.

■ Camping

Camping at **Morris Meadows** (see *Museums*, page 174), is such an annual tradition to so many families that they have special reunion events each year to catch up with old friends. Transient and permanent trailer, and some tent sites spread across a hillside overlooking the rolling landscape just south of the Mason-Dixon Line, on Freeland Rd. in Freeland; ☎ 410-329-6636 or 800-643-7056. A busy schedule of daily activities is designed for children and adults and facilities include a swimming pool, driving range, miniature gold, game room and snack bar. Rates are $25-$35, depending on the size and location of the site, and four cabins (two of them handicapped-accessible) are available for two-night-minimum rental. The campground is less than two miles from an access point to the Northern Central Railroad Trail (see *On Wheels*).

To get to Morris Meadows from I-83, take Exit 36, turning right at the T onto Route 439 and right again (north) at the T onto Route 45. In about 1.3 miles turn left on Freeland Rd. (Route 409); the campground is about four miles, on the left.

Where to Eat

DINING PRICE KEY
The price key indicates the cost of *most* dinner entrées on a restaurant's regular and daily special menu.
$ . . . . Most under $10
$$ . . . . $10 to $20
$$$ . . . . Over $30

■ Just North of Baltimore

The **Avenue at White Marsh** is a shopping center built to re-create a Main Street feel, with facing rows of shops along a street of angle-parked cars. There's a square with outdoor tables belonging to the two flanking restaurants. It's a mall, but you have to give them points for their successful efforts at making it less generic and far more attractive than most.

Bayou Blues Café, on The Avenue, 8133 Honeygo Blvd, White Marsh I-95 at Exit 67-B, ☎ 410-931-2583. The last time we tried to eat here, early on a weeknight when the place was nearly empty, the noise level was beyond our tolerance. If you're immune to over-amplification or with someone who's a less-than-scintillating conversationalist, this could be a good place for dinner. The lively menu includes well-prepared jambalaya, étouffée, seafood Creole, pan-blackened fish and Cajun ribs, along with rack of lamb, trout stuffed with andouille sausage in a bourbon sauce, and several vegetarian choices. Most meat or seafood entrées are $15-$20, vegetarian $9-12. The upscale "main street" style shopping mall location has outdoor seating in the summer, live blues and jazz every night; open daily 11-11, midnight on weekends, bar open until 2 am.

Although the menu may not be quite as exotic, you can enjoy dinner table conversation at **Red Brick Station**, across the plaza, also on The Avenue at White Marsh; ☎ 410-931-7827. The atmosphere is lively, the setting a brew-pub; ales, bitters and stouts served are brewed here. Along with the British chef's traditional pub favorites – shepherd's pie, fish & chips, roast beef with Yorkshire pudding, bangers and mash – you'll find steaks, ribs, crab cakes, blackened chicken served with blue-cheese Alfredo sauce, several pasta combo dishes and a number of daily specials, which might include thick mahi-mahi served with Yukon Gold potatoes. Most entrées are $9-$15; the long sandwich menu is uniformly priced at $7-$8.

■ Havre de Grace

The Crazy Swede, 400 N. Union Ave. at the corner of Franklin St. (☎ 410-939-8020), offers the usual seafood dishes, but often with a different twist. Veal Havre de Grace, for example, pairs veal with jumbo shrimp and lump crabmeat in a creamy sherry sauce. The menu has more choices than most other local restaurants for those who don't want seafood: several chicken, pasta, beef and veal dishes. Most entrées are $14-$19. In season it's open Monday through Thursday, 11-10; Friday and Saturday, 11-11; Sunday, 10-10; shorter hours in the winter. The Crazy Swede Restaurant also has guest suites with one or two bedrooms; they offer a discount on meals in the restaurant to overnight guests and serve a complimentary continental breakfast.

Follow Frankin St. to the water to find **McGregor's**, at 31 Saint John St.; ☎ 410-939-3003 or 800-300-6319. The light menu offers quesadillas, sandwiches, calamari. Dinner might begin with fried oysters wrapped in bacon, crab fritters or scallops in puff pastry, before moving on to entrées like crab cakes, crab-stuffed flounder, baby back ribs, apricot-glazed salmon or veal scaloppine with asparagus and smoked portobellos (most entrées at $17-$20). The view of the bay is over a parking lot, but a water view nonetheless. Live music plays on weekends.

Tidewater Grille is just beyond, right on the bay with a water view from every table. As you might expect, seafood reigns, with fried or broiled crabcakes, shellfish and linguine Alfredo, or shrimp and scallops in shallot butter, although other dishes might include a mixed grill of chicken and fillet with andouille. Most are priced $16-$20. The lunch menu includes crabcakes, crab melt and a crab-and-ham croissant sandwich, along with burgers and salads. It's at 300 Franklin St.; ☎ 410-939-3313.

For a traditional crab house, go to **Price's Seafood**, unchanged since the 1940s. Along with mounds of hardshell crabs or succulent softies, you can get other seasonal seafoods. It's at 654 Water St., between the boat ramp and the Lock House Museum; ☎ 410-939-2782.

Baltimore

Baltimore is well defined by its distinctive skyline. From nearly any approach to the inner city, you will see a profile of domes, stceples, towers, monuments and tall chimneys, mixed with a few architectural giants that stand out above their fellow buildings.

From the first you will be struck by the variety of these sky-reaching features, which range from monumentally grand to very nearly absurd, from utilitarian to frivolous. In the latter department is the replica of a Florentine bell tower erected by the Bromo Seltzer company; the only hint of the great blue bottle that once stood at its top is the eerie blue light that enshrouds it at night.

Utilitarian doesn't have to mean ugly, as the fine brick work of Shot Tower reminds us; and on close inspection, you'll find equally impressive commercial and manufacturing buildings with façades of carved stone or elegantly patterned cast iron. Churches, an important feature of this predominantly Roman Catholic city, represent a history and geography of architectural styles: Georgian, American Gothic, neo-classical, baroque, Byzantine, even the gold onion domes of Eastern Orthodox. Public buildings and monuments are rightly impressive: George Washington and Lady Baltimore surmounting their respective pillars, and the ornate Second Empire-style City Hall with its lofty segmented dome. If architecture fascinates you, prepare to fall in love with Baltimore.

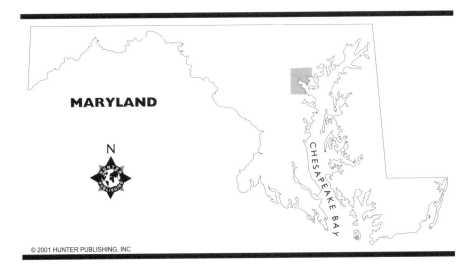

MARYLAND

N

CHESAPEAKE BAY

1. Cylburn Arboretum
2. Druid Hill Park; Baltimore Zoo
3. Johns Hopkins University;
   Evergreen House; Homewood House
4. Baltimore City Conservatory
5. Sherwood Gardens
6. Baltimore Museum of Art
7. Baltimore Streetcar Museum
8. Patterson Park
9. Fort McHenry National Monument
10. Mount Clare Museum House

Baltimore Area

© 2001 HUNTER PUBLISHING, INC

The skyline represents multi-faceted Baltimore in many other ways, revealing at first glance the influences of manufacturing, industry, commerce, religion and public pride, as well as the tough blue-collar grittiness that still clings to this modern and vibrant city. The only factor not evident from the high profile view is the harbor, always central to Baltimore's body and soul. This protected natural harbor on the Patapsco (not actually on Chesapeake Bay itself) gave Baltimore its early edge on commerce and shipbuilding and made it a natural transportation hub for the developing railroads.

Geography & History

Baltimore sits near the head of the Chesapeake Bay, on the Patapsco River, as it widens to join the Chesapeake. It is the westernmost port of any significance on the East Coast. About an hour northeast of Washington DC, the city is about the same distance north of Annapolis.

Although most of the city lies north of its **Inner Harbor**, several of its most attractive areas to visit curl around this harbor area, making water the fastest route between many points.

Encircling the city is the **Baltimore Beltway**, I-695, and major streets intersect it to converge on the center. Much of the central city is laid out in a grid street pattern, with streets running almost due north from the harbor, intersected by east-west streets.

The natural harbor on the Patapsco, and its easy access to Chesapeake Bay, made Baltimore a logical distribution port as early as the 1720s, when grain and tobacco growers brought their crops to load on ships bound for other eastern cities and for Europe. Mills to grind the grains into flour soon sprang up along the smaller rivers that converged here. Led by the Carroll family – of whom you will hear more – Baltimore officially became a town and customs port in 1729.

In the days before good roads and rails connected the eastern seaboard, nearly all transport was by ship, so the city grew quickly as a commercial hub. Merchants whose ships carried the flour and tobacco to far-flung corners of the British Empire built homes close to the harbour, followed by the more modest homes of ships' carpenters and others in the great network that built, outfitted and manned the ships.

The first threat to this booming maritime economy came with British attempts to regulate commerce in the emerging colonies, but the Revolution soon restored the thriving trade. Baltimore ships were quick to seize the opportunity to help their fledgling country – and themselves – by becoming privateers. The goods they seized from British ships not only failed to supply the British forces they were often intended for, but brought nice profits to the privateers.

This fine Baltimore tradition was not forgotten by the British, however, and the **War of 1812** brought military action right to the city. Bombarded from the water by the British fleet, Baltimore was successfully defended by the well-placed Fort McHenry, the city's prime historical attraction today. You won't be in Baltimore long without hearing the story of how the sight of Mary Pickersgill's giant American flag still flying over the fort inspired the writing of *The Star Spangled Banner*.

The end of the war in 1815 brought freedom of the seas to Baltimore captains, who quickly seized the lead in transporting flour and other goods, a thriving commerce that made Baltimore the new country's second-largest city. But however strong its sea commerce, Baltimore saw the need to complement this with land access to the western frontiers, and became a leader in building railroads. The B&O line reached the Chicago by the 1870s, providing a link that took goods both ways. The railroad and the C&O Canal also brought coal from the rich inland mines to the port of Baltimore, whence they traveled by ship to New England to power the mills of the Industrial Revolution.

The **Civil War**, which had sympathizers on both sides in Baltimore, gave rise to at least two industries there: ready-made clothing and canning. The sudden need for uniforms led to the modern idea of standard sizing, so clothing could be made in quantity. Baltimore soon had a thriving garment industry. The need to supply troops with safe food inspired the perfection of the canning process, which by the end of the war had not only become cost-effective but accepted for household use. Huge canneries rose along the wharves at Canton, supported by factories that made the cans and others that printed the labels, two other industries that were to thrive here. At one time, more than 100 canneries lined the waterfront.

TRANSPORTATION "FIRSTS" IN BALTIMORE

- 1784 – First hot air balloon ascent in the US
- 1827 – First electric carrier railway in the US
- 1830 – First passenger train in the US
- 1840 – First regular use of a steamboat to carry passengers
- 1893 – First elevated electric railway in the US
- 1895 – World's first electric railway locomotive
- 1897 – The US's first practical submarine, the *Argonaut*

During the great immigration boom of the 1800s, Baltimore was second to New York as a port of entry, a fact still evident today in the city's strong ethnic ties and thriving ethnic neighborhoods. The 20th century started well enough, but in 1904 the **Great Fire** ("What was so great about it?" wonders Fran Zeller of Harbor City Tours) destroyed a large part of the commercial district. But its rebuilding allowed for modernization, and Baltimore continued to prosper until the Depression in the 1930s.

Post-World War II prosperity worked against the city, instead of helping it recover from the depression, as its residents began to leave for more modern and spacious suburbs. Downtown businesses suffered and died until the 1960s seemed little different from the 1930s. But the factors that made Baltimore great in its previous centuries were still there, and under the leadership of a strong and far-sighted mayor and city government in the 1970s, Baltimore bounced back.

The city cleaned up its act, along with its harbor, renovating the deteriorated buildings and replacing decrepit wharves with a bright new waterfront, then stocking it with historic ships, lively museums and accessible arts venues. Fine buildings, unchanged in benign neglect, were restored and put to new uses, a process that still continues. Striking new ones were built.

With these visible improvements came the inner pride, the sometimes brash, but indomitable spirit born of gutsy people surmounting tough times. You can't help but like the Baltimore they've preserved and created.

"FIRST IN AMERICA"

And it happened in Baltimore...

- 1771 – First Post Office system
- 1817 – First street to be lighted with gas
- 1828 – First umbrella factory
- 1844 – First telegraph line (between Washington and Baltimore)
- 1851 – First commercial ice cream factory
- 1883 – First typesetting machine in the world was used
- 1892 – First bottle cap manufactured

Getting Here

■ By Car

 Baltimore is reached from the north or south by **I-95**, which passes through the city to the east of its center. **I-83** enters the city from the north, **I-97** from the south and **I-70** from the west. The **Baltimore Beltway** (I-695), surrounds the city, with access roads leading downtown like spokes on a wheel. Maryland's **Route 2** leads to Baltimore in an almost perfect straight line from Annapolis, and **Route 295**, the Baltimore-Washington Parkway, connects the Baltimore Beltway with Washington's **Capital Beltway**.

■ By Air

Between Baltimore and Washington DC, but much closer to Baltimore, is **Baltimore-Washington International Airport**, coded BWI (☎ 410-859-7100), only 10 miles south of the Inner Harbor. It is served by a number of major airlines and is a hub for Southwest Airlines' budget-friendly flights.

■ By Train or Bus

Both **Amtrak** (☎ 800-872-7245) and **Maryland Area Rail Commuter**, commonly called MARC (☎ 800-325-RAIL), connect the airport with Baltimore's **Penn Station**, a 20-minute ride that runs on weekdays. A free shuttle bus connects the main terminal and the airport rail station. Amtrak connects Baltimore and BWI Airport to both New York and Washington, DC, while MARC (☎ 800-325-RAIL) runs between Baltimore and Washington, a one-hour trip.

Mass Transit Administration (MTA) bus #17 (☎ 410-539-5000) also connects downtown Baltimore and the airport. More expensive, but also more convenient if you are carrying substantial luggage, **BWI Airport Shuttle** (☎ 800-258-3826) and **Baltimore Airport Shuttle** (☎ 410-821-5837) run between the Inner Harbor hotels and the airport.

Getting Around

■ The Neighborhoods

Baltimore's neighborhoods are among its several unique features, residential enclaves that grew to house groups with close economic or ethnic ties, and that to this day retain their distinct flavors. These residential neighborhoods have maintained their commercial cores, with shops and restaurants. Ethnic neighborhoods have maintained their churches – three Polish parishes are located in Canton, for example. These local meeting places help neighborhoods retain their sense of community and their individual character.

Little Italy

Closest to the Inner Harbor is Little Italy, whose commercial life is limited almost entirely to eating places, but whose culture is unmistakable in the homes and frequent religious festivals of its two parish churches. Its origins are from the era when the Port of Baltimore was second to Ellis Island in the number of immigrants it admitted. Many Italians came bound for the Gold Rush in California, but on arriving in Baltimore discovered just how far it was across the continent and stayed. To reach Little Italy, walk east on Pratt St., straight past the harbor. When you come to the wide President St. you'll see a painted brick wall welcoming you to Little Italy.

Fells Point

Fells Point is a rare maritime neighborhood of homes built close to the docks by the merchants, shipwrights, carpenters and others whose livelihood depended on the busy harbor. The modest row houses that line its streets have seen several waves of immigrants since the first of them was built in the 1700s.

Very few of these urban maritime neighborhoods remain in America, and this one nearly went the way of the rest before a preservation group intervened to save it. But they have not tidied it up into a museum village; Fells Point is very much alive, a weekend favorite of young people and students and a self-contained neighborhood with two of Baltimore's city markets on Broadway. Shops, antique stores, pubs and restaurants line waterfront Thames (usually pronounced phonetically, not Britishly) and other streets radiating from Broadway, its park-divided main street. Take the water taxi from Inner Harbor or walk south from Little Italy on Caroline St.

Mount Vernon

Mount Vernon was the center of high society for early Baltimore, and is still the prestigious in-town neighborhood. A thriving center for the arts and culture, it features fine shops, "**Restaurant Row**" and several museums. It centers around the gracious park-filled intersection of Charles Street and Mount Vernon Place, with the **Washington Monument** at its center. The neighborhood's name derives from the Monument.

Bolton Hill

Northwest of Mount Vernon are the quiet streets of Bolton Hill, lined with sedate brownstone and brick homes. Here stands the former home of **F. Scott and Zelda Fitzgerald**, and the Victorian cottage-style residence of Wallis Simpson's aunt. Few businesses other than the shops of **Antiques Row** invade the quietude, but two of the city's rare B&Bs are here, along with some restaurants and cafés favored by concert-goers at nearby **Myerhof Symphony Hall**.

Federal Hill

Federal Hill, a National Historic District across the Inner Harbor from the World Trade Center and Constellation Pier, includes streets of gentrified old row houses, along with antique shops and restaurants. **Cross Street Market**, at its center, is a boisterous melange of eateries and meat and produce stalls. At its northern edge, just before it drops suddenly to the harbor, is a park with a beautiful view of Baltimore's harbor and downtown skyline. It's also the place to catch a breeze on hot summer days.

Hampden

Hampden, north of Bolton Hill, is far enough from the center of the city to have its own beat – or to have retained the air of the Baltimore of two or three decades ago. It's just a little full of its own "image," and bills itself as home to the classic Baltimore "Hon" – big hair, chewing gum and all, but you could never accuse this free-wheeling neighborhood of taking itself too seriously. You must see the Christmas decorations that cover homes on 34th St. to fully understand Hampden, but you get a pretty good idea of it at **Café Hon** (see *Where to Eat*, page 230).

Canton

Beyond Fells Point to the east is Canton, once the estate of a merchant who named it for the Chinese port. Later it became the center for Baltimore's considerable oyster and vegetable canning industry, as boats brought Chesapeake shellfish and produce from the Eastern Shore farms straight to its canneries. Even the cans were made here. More recently, it has been home to the city's Polish immigrants, and has three Polish parish churches. Its main cannery has become a commercial center with Maryland's largest independent bookstore, **Bibelot**, complete with café. Canton is the easternmost stop for the Water Taxi.

■ City Transportation

Major attractions – the ships, the aquarium, science center, Port Discovery and the attractions of Charles Street – are within walking distance of the **Inner Harbor**. **Tourist trolley** or **MTA bus** and rail services (☎ 410-539-5000) reach other neighborhoods, but are designed for commuters, not tourists, so they may involve several transfers. The **Metro's** closest stations are about three blocks from the Inner Harbor.

MARC publishes an excellent map of bus and Metro lines, which includes a list of major attractions and hotels, with their best connections. It also includes some useful details on using the lines, including the fact that you must have exact change and that you push the yellow stripe on the wall to signal the next stop.

Baltimore's Inner Harbor and city skyline, as seen from Federal Hill.

AUTHOR TIP *If you plan to use the bus, Light Rail or Metro more than two rides in a day, or just to avoid having to fish for change, the $3 day pass is the best buy.*

The best and cheapest transport to many places, including Fells Point, is by boat. **Ed Kane's Water Taxi** (☎ 410-563-3901 or 800-658-8947), is a year-round service with 17 stops near major sights around the Inner and Outer Harbors. All-day passes are about $5 and include multiple re-boarding, plus trolley connections to Fort McHenry and discounts to attractions. They run daily, 11-6, November through March; 11-9, April, September and October (until midnight on Friday and Saturday); and 10-11, May through the first week in September (until midnight on Friday and Saturday). In the summer, boats arrive at each landing 15-20 minutes apart. In addition to being handy, the boats are staffed by the nicest people you'll find anywhere.

AUTHOR TIP *For the price of a Water Taxi ticket, you also get a Letter of Marque, which entitles you to discounts at a long list of restaurants, shops and attractions, including the science and maritime museums and the tall ship cruise.*

The **Seaport Taxi** connects the Inner Harbor, Fells Point and Canton, with free shuttles to Fort McHenry and Little Italy. Boats run year-round, although not as frequently in the winter; ☎ 410-675-2900.

■ Tours

While we think there's no better way to get the feel of a city than to hit its streets on foot, there's a lot to be said for getting the lay of the land (or water) first on a good tour. Unfortunately, the historical information included in most tour spiels is dubious at best. But visitors to Baltimore are in luck; **Harbor City Tours** is run by a woman with a keen interest in history, along with a good sense of humor and an eye for the bizarre. Fran Zeller's witty commentary includes a lot of stories about growing up here, so you'll get a healthy dose of the city's unique culture and character along with reliable facts. Tours ($10) leave from Harborplace four times daily and can include pick-ups at downtown hotels. They last about 90 minutes and include on-and-off reboarding, in case you want to stop for a while to explore on your own; reservations, ☎ 410-254-TOUR(8687).

AUTHOR TIP *For just $5 more, you can buy a combination ticket that entitles you to an additional one-hour narrated harbor cruise, along with your Harbor City Tours bus itinerary.*

Information Sources

Baltimore Area Visitors Center, on the Inner Harbor opposite Constellation Pier; ☎ 410-837-INFO(4636) or 800-282-6632, www. baltimore.org. This small office gets very crowded during the summer. The mailing address of the executive offices is 100 Light St., Baltimore, MD 21202.

AUTHOR TIP *A really good map of the harbor area is inside Ed Kane's Water Taxi Guide, free at the Visitors Center or on the boats.*

Maryland Office of Tourism Development, Department of Business and Economic Development, 217 E. Redwood St, Baltimore, MD 21201; ☎ 410-767-6270.

GOOD BOOKS ON BALTIMORE

Two books on Baltimore are especially worth having. *Wish You Were Here*, by Carolyn Males, Carol Barbier Rolnic and Pam Makowski Goresh, published by Woodholme House in Baltimore, is not only a really detailed guide to the city's neighborhoods, but it is fun to read, well-written and filled with quirky anecdotes and historical facts. The other is for those who, like us, love the line and texture of old buildings. *A Guide to Baltimore Architecture*, by John Dorsey and James D. Dilts (Tidewater Publishers), lists and shows in photographs all the significant buildings of the city, with interesting details on the architecture, history and the architects. From the 1750s Mount Clare mansion and the Art Deco former Kresge's store to the new aquarium and the pentagonal I.M. Pei World Trade Center, the book is golden. It's also well-written and has a good glossary of architectural terms. There's a lot of history written in the faces of Baltimore's buildings, and you'll find it here.

AUTHOR TIP

*Both of the books mentioned above are sold in the unique Hampden shop **Hometown Girl**, 1000 W. 36th St., ☎ 410-662-4438. Here you will find other books on Baltimore, as well as locally made crafts, local foods to take home, local cookbooks, even Maryland fortune cookies. Far from being a kitsch-filled souvenir shop, this is a tasteful and welcome collection of nice gifts and information. They are happy to ship your order, too. If you are not in Hampden, they have an affiliated shop on the second level of the Light Street Pavilion, 301 Light St., at the Inner Harbor.*

Adventures

■ On Foot

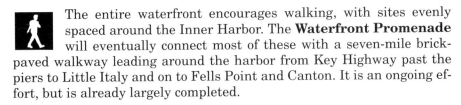

The entire waterfront encourages walking, with sites evenly spaced around the Inner Harbor. The **Waterfront Promenade** will eventually connect most of these with a seven-mile brick-paved walkway leading around the harbor from Key Highway past the piers to Little Italy and on to Fells Point and Canton. It is an ongoing effort, but is already largely completed.

Walking Tours

While several of Baltimore's distinctive old neighborhoods are perfect for exploration on foot, **Mount Vernon** has made it easy for visitors to see its highlights by showing and describing them in a handy free brochure that you can find at the Visitors Center or in many neighborhood shops. Most of the attractions listed are within three blocks of the gracious squares surrounding the Washington Monument. Along with the buildings and attractions, the map includes the numerous examples of public sculpture that decorate Mount Vernon's parks and streets. At the very least, stroll down Mount Vernon Place to see the fine row houses, especially the Engineering Club at numbers 7-11, a single mansion built from 1884 to 1904.

AUTHOR TIP

Remember that you must dial the area code for all numbers, even those within the same city, since area codes in Maryland are not always geographical.

The best – possibly the only – way to see the distinctive neighborhoods of Baltimore is on foot, and several good guided walking tours can help you do this. A company called **A Taste of Italy** (☎ 410-547-0479) introduces you to the Little Italy neighborhood, its history and its food. The theme of their two-hour Fells Point walking tour is on the various movies and TV shows filmed here, including *Sleepless in Seattle*, *Avalon*, and the NBC series *Homicide: Life on the Street* (lunch at the cast's favorite watering hole is part of the tour).

The romantic past of Mount Vernon is explored in a **one-hour walking tour** by a local historian that highlights the neighborhood's two best-known love stories: Jerome Bonaparte and Betsy Patterson and the Duke and Duchess of Windsor; ☎ 410-605-0462.

A TALE OF LOVE

Early in the 19th century the French Emperor Napoleon's brother Jerome happened to be traveling in Maryland, where he met Betsy Patterson and fell in love with her. Over the objection of Napoleon and Betsy's father, William, the two wed in 1803. Upon their arrival in France in 1805, Betsy was refused permission to leave the ship and had to turn back. Even though she bore a child by Jerome, she never saw him again. Napoleon annulled the marriage, married him to a princess and he became King of Westphalia.

Baltimore row houses.

■ On Wheels

 Bicycles are not an especially popular way to get around in Baltimore, partly because the streets are narrow and crowded with traffic and partly because so many of the north-south streets run uphill. But the lower areas around the **Inner Harbor** and as far as **Canton** and **Fort McHenry** are more suited to pedalers.

The neighborhoods of **Little Italy** and **Fells Point** are very pleasant to explore on bicycle, with less traffic and pleasant places to stop in parks and along the wharves.

■ On Water

Kayaking

 Sunrise Expeditions offers several three-hour harbor tours daily, and longer Chesapeake Bay tours, for experienced or first-time paddlers. Equipment and instruction are provided; harbor tours are $45, Chesapeake Bay tours are $55 and all leave from 800 Broadway in Fells Point; ☎ 410-534-9500.

Paddleboats can be hired from the **Paddle Boat Dock** at Harborplace; ☎ 410-563-3901.

Boat Tours

Clipper City (☎ 410-539-6277, www.sailingship.com) is a topsail schooner that operates two-hour and longer sailing tours from Harborplace. A unique experience, two-hour sails depart from the pier next to the Science Center, Monday through Saturday at noon and 3, Sunday at 3 and 6 – $12 for adults and $2 for children. Sunday brunch and weekend evening sails with live Caribbean music are $30 and $20 respectively.

Fells Point's tall ship, the schooner *Nighthawk* (☎ 410-276-7447), offers daytime cruises daily from the piers on Thames St.

Also boarding at Fells Point is *Harbor Belle*, a replica of the paddle wheeler steamboats that once plied Baltimore's harbor. Inexpensive after-work cruises on Friday are from 5:30 to 7:30; Saturday sunset cruises include a buffet dinner; they board at 7:15 (about $30). Sunday Champagne brunch cruises board at 10:45, all from Henderson's Wharf, at the end of Fell St.; ☎ 410-764-3928.

Harbor cruises on *Bay Lady* and *Lady Baltimore* include lunch, Monday through Saturday, noon-2, or dinner, Monday through Saturday, 7-10, Sunday 5-8. The costs are upwards of $25 and $35 respectively, with Monday's seafood dinner, Friday's crab feast and the Saturday buffet higher. Moonlight cruises without meals, on Friday and Saturday, 11:30 pm to 2 am are about $20. For the exact schedule, ☎ 410-347-5552; reservations,

☎ 410-727-3113. From June through August, you can cruise to Annapolis for the day, leaving at 8:30 and returning about 5.

Baltimore Harbor Tours, whose boats dock across from the visitors center at Inner Harbor, offers economical 60-minute narrated cruises in conjunction with Harbor City Tours two-hour bus tours, for a package price of $15. The tickets can be used on separate days; ☎ 410-783-4660.

■ On Ice

Ice Skating

 The **Inner Harbor Ice Rink**, at Rash Field, just past the Science Center, offers public skating and a busy schedule of special events. Before Christmas are lunch-hour concerts by local schools at the rink and a December 24 skating party. On New Year's Eve, fireworks entertain skaters and on Sundays all winter free skating performances are followed by public skating lessons ($5). Rink hours are 12-2, 4-6 and 7-9 on weekdays, with an added Friday night opening from 7 until 10. On Saturday the rink is open 10-6 and 7-10; on Sunday, noon-5 and 7-9. Admission is $4 for two hours skating on weekdays, $5 on weekends. The rink is open from late November through early March.

KID-FRIENDLY

Tykes on Ice takes place every Saturday morning, 10 to noon at the Inner Harbor Ice Rink. Kiddie music, visits by costumed mascots and discounted prices are featured during the entire skating season, from late November through early March.

Patterson Park, on Eastern Ave., also has ice skating, in a covered rink open October through April.

Northwest Ice Rink, at 5731 Cottonworth Ave. (☎ 410-732-4614), has well-groomed ice, a skate shop, skate sharpening, lessons and hockey instruction. Two hours of skating is $5.25; the rink is open every day and some evenings, although times vary greatly. It's wise to call first. Accessible by Light Rail.

Cultural & Eco-Travel Experiences

■ Science & Nature

 Without doubt, one of the premier aquarium complexes anywhere is the **National Aquarium in Baltimore**, at Pier 3, 561 E. Pratt St. (☎ 410-576-3800, www.aqua.org). Its exhibits and programs are aimed not just at displaying sea creatures, but at educating viewers on the conservation and environmental issues involving the sea. More than 10,000 creatures, representing upwards of 600 species of fish, birds, reptiles, amphibians and marine mammals share habitats close to those of their native homes, separated from visitors by viewing windows.

Although exhibits change and new ones are added to keep the museum fresh and interesting to local visitors, major exhibits are likely to be there for some time. Maryland habitats are featured in several of these, including ponds, rivers, tidal marshes, bay and the ocean.

"Surviving Through Adaptations" shows survival tactics developed in response to special environments, and includes a giant Pacific octopus, electric eels and seahorses. Elsewhere, a 335,000-gallon tank contains the most authentic Atlantic coral reef ever fabricated, filled with schools of bright tropical fish, while "Open Ocean" literally encircles visitors with several shark species, sand tigers and sawfish. The newest exhibit as we write explores a unique Amazon environment that is flooded for three months of each year, but dry the remaining nine. While a 16-foot anaconda may be the most dramatic resident of the ecosystem, our favorite is a large fish that adapts to the changing environment with the ability to eat hard-shelled nuts as they fall from trees in the flooded forest.

Atop all this grows a South American Rain Forest, where sloths hang limply from leafy branches far above and green parrots sit in front of a waterfall, not five feet from visitors. Other tropical birds, monkeys, frogs and fishes live in the pools and lush greenery.

In a separate building, connected by an elevated walkway, dolphins perform in the 1,300-seat Marine Mammal Pavilion at daily 25-minute shows. More interactivity is provided for children by a touch tank in the Children's Cove, with starfish, crabs and other small marine animals.

Near the aquarium entrance is an outdoor rock pool in which harbor and grey seals swim and the public can see them there without paying aquarium admission. Both buildings are accessible to wheelchairs, a few of which are provided. Strollers are prohibited, but the museum provides back-pack carriers. Hours vary with the season, usually 9-6 in the summer (later on weekends) and 10-5, September through June. It's always best to

Downtown Baltimore

1. National Aquarium
2. World Trade Center
3. Maryland Science Center
4. American Visionary Art Museum
5. Jewish Museum of Maryland
6. The Walters Art Gallery
7. Washington Monument
8. Enoch Pratt Free Library
9. Basilica of the National Shrine of the Blessed Virgin Mary
10. Edgar Allan Poe Grave
11. National Museum of Dentistry
12. B&O Railroad Museum
13. Babe Ruth Museum
14. Oriole Park at Camden Yards
15. Ravens Stadium
16. Great Blacks in Wax Museum
17. Baltimore Museum of Art
18. Maryland Historical Society
19. Antiques Row
20. Baltimore Area Visitors Information Center

N

© 2001 HUNTER PUBLISHING, INC

HUNTER PUBLISHING

.5 MILE

.3 KM

Federal St.

Oliver St.

Gay St.

Washington St

Johns Hopkins Hospital

Ann St

Broadway

Preston St

Biddle St

Chase St

Caroline Ave

Central Ave

Lombard St

Pratt St

Gough St

Bank St

Eastern Ave

Fleet St

Aliceanna Ave

Lancaster St

Fells Point

Northwest Branch

Hoffman St

Monument St

Madison St

Eager St

Fayette St

Exeter St

President St

Baltimore St

Inner Harbor

Key Hwy

40

83

Orleans St

Guilford Ave

Light St

St Paul St

Charles St

Cathedral St

Preston St

Mt Royal Ave

Park Ave

Conv Ctr

Conway St

395

Franklin St

Mulberry St

Lexington St

Howard St

Eutaw St

Laurette St

Dolphin St

Preston St

McCulloch St

Druid Hill Ave

Martin Luther King Jr. Blvd

Greene St

Paca St

Saratoga St

Fayette St

Lombard St

Pratt St

TO

Martin Luther King Jr. Blvd

call them for exact times. Admission is $14 for adults, $10.50 over age 60, $7.50 ages three-11.

AUTHOR TIP

Although the Aquarium has timed tickets to avoid overcrowding, the best hours to begin a visit are before 11 am and after 3 pm. You can expect that tickets will be sold out for midday admissions during the summer, on holidays and spring or fall weekends. One way to assure tickets is to go to the aquarium admission kiosk when you first arrive in Baltimore and buy advance tickets for the day of your choice. Expect to spend about two hours touring the two buildings.

The ecology of the Chesapeake Bay is further examined at the **Maryland Science Center**, 601 Light St. (☎ 410-685-2370), where you can also learn about space exploration at the national visitors center for the Hubble Space Telescope. Hands-on exhibits and live demonstrations fill three floors, and a demonstration stage explores electricity and other subjects hourly from 10:30 to 1:30 weekdays, 10:30-5:30 weekends. The IMAX Theater has a screen five stories high, and shows in the Davis Planetarium are – dare we say it? – stellar. Summer hours are Monday through Thursday, 9:30-6; Friday through Sunday, 9:30-8. Winter hours are 10-5, and until 6 on weekends. Admission is $9.50, $7 for seniors, military personnel and children ages four-17.

The **Baltimore Zoo**, in Druid Hill Park (☎ 410-366-5466), is home to more than 2,000 mammal, bird and reptile species in a 200-acre setting known for its wildlife habitats. The realistic African Watering Hole is a free-range area of six acres with rhinoceros, zebras and gazelles. Rare big cats include leopards from Africa and Siberian tigers. Open daily, 10-4, longer on summer weekends; admission is charged.

KID-FRIENDLY

The Baltimore Zoo also has a Children's Zoo; it's a special area with lots of hands-on activities for youngsters.

■ Uniquely Baltimore

Little Italy is more than a few streets lined with restaurants. It is a thriving Italian community, and few things show this better than the **Bocce Court**, on Stiles St. In case you think this is a dying sport for retired men, think again; you'll see kids intent on learning how to roll the ball just right. Tournaments during St. Anthony's Festival in mid-June and on Columbus Day in October bring out the pros.

Local pickles and preserves in a Baltimore city market.

■ Parks and Gardens

Baltimore City Conservatory, on Druid Lake Drive, between Gwynns Falls Parkway and McCulloh St. (☎ 410-396-0180), is an elegant Victorian "glass house" built in 1888. Filled all year with luxuriant tropical trees and plants, the Conservatory is highlighted seasonally with spring bulbs, fall chrysanthemums and poinsettias in the winter. Attached greenhouses show orchids, begonias and desert plants. An adjoining outdoor garden blooms with seasonal displays. The Conservatory is free and open Thursday through Sunday, 10-4.

Cylburn Arboretum surrounds the mansion of the same name, built in the Civil War era. Its extensive grounds, highlighted by oak trees, gardens and wandering paths, were designed by the Olmstead brothers. The park is now a nature preserve. The "Garden of the Senses" was designed for physically impaired visitors. Entrance to the gardens and grounds, which are open dawn to dusk, is free, and you can see the unrestored house interior, which serves as offices for the park. It also houses a small museum of birds, open Tuesday and Thursday, 10-3. Cylburn borders I-83 on the west, between exits 9 and 10, north of Druid Park; ☎ 410-367-2217.

The large square of **Patterson Park** forms the boundary of Canton, bordered by Eastern Avenue. It is the playground of Baltimoreans, with winter sliding hills, swimming pools, ball fields, jogging paths and an occasional folly – such as a multi-tiered Victorian observatory, which most Baltimoreans refer to as The Pagoda. For bike rentals, call ☎ 410-396-7012.

Sherwood Gardens is a small park with a big display of flowering spring bulbs. More than 80,000 tulips are the centerpiece, blooming in late April. The park is fully wheelchair-accessible. Located in the northern part of the city, in the neighborhood of Guilford, just west of Route 45 opposite 42nd St.

■ Crafts

Fells Point is a good place to find studios and shops featuring handwork. **Bay and Country Crafts**, at 1635 Lancaster St. (☎ 410-342-3317), specializes in crafts relating to the bay, such as waterfowl art and representations of local buildings and scenes.

Elzeard Pottery, at 602 South Ann St. (☎ 410-732-2928), shows functional and decorative pottery, jewelry and furniture, Thursday through Sunday. **.925 The Silver Store**, 1640 Thames St. (☎ 410-327-0036), has handmade sterling silver jewelry and a few other items, open until 7 pm daily. **Ten Thousand Villages**, at 1621 Thames St. (☎ 410-342-5568) has handmade items from around the world, especially from developing countries. Some of the Fells Point shops are closed on weekdays in the winter.

North Charles St., in Mount Vernon, has a number of art galleries and some fine craft displays as well. For homey-style handwork, such as knit mittens and baby gifts, stop by the **Women's Industrial Exchange**, at 333 N. Charles St. (☎ 410-685-4388). Founded more than 150 years ago to provide a respectable income for women who had fallen on bad times, the exchange is one of the few such shops left.

Paper-Rock-Scissors, at 1111 W. 36th St. in Hampden (☎ 410-235-4420), shows the work of dozens of local artists and craftsmen in several media, as the store's name would suggest. It's open Wednesday, 10-6; Tuesday through Saturday, 10-8; Sunday, noon-5.

A bit out of the usual sightseeing area, but if you're headed north to Gunpowder Falls State Park, on Route 147 (Harford Rd.), stop and visit **Moore's Candies**, at 3004 Pinewood Ave, just south of Northern Parkway in the Hamilton neighborhood; ☎ 410-426-2705. This family of chocolatiers has been in business more than 80 years, and many of their chocolates follow a Maryland theme. The shop is open 9-4:30 on weekdays, 10-4 on Saturday; tours of the candy making areas are given on Tuesday and Thursday at 10 and 1 ($2 adult, $1 children, who must be over nine years old).

■ Antiques

Antiques Row, along N. Howard and W. Reed Streets, is the place to look for silver, Victoriana and furniture in the higher price ranges. **The Antique Warehouse**, at 1300 Jackson St. (☎ 410-659-0662) in the Federal Hill area, has 30-plus dealers selling a wide range of antiques and collectibles Tuesday through Sunday.

Baltimore

Browse in **Fells Point's** cobbled streets for antiques and original art. The area is known for more affordable antiques than the pricier Antiques Row.

For mall shops, head for **Harborplace Pavilion** and **The Gallery**, connected by a skywalk, or shop in **Market Center**, bounded by Franklin, Liberty, Baltimore and Greene Streets.

■ Music & Performing Arts

Baltimore Opera Company, Lyric Opera House, 140 W. Mount Royal Ave (☎ 410-494-2712) is the city's resident company, with a full orchestra. Grand opera productions often star international artists; English translation is projected over the stage.

Baltimore Symphony Orchestra, Joseph Meyerhoff Symphony Hall, 12121 Cathedral St. (☎ 410-783-8000), presents an astonishing variety of well-known guest performers, both popular and classical. It is not uncommon to find musicians of the quality of Yo-Yo Ma, Pinchas Zukerman, Itzhak Perlman, the Canadian Brass Ensemble or the Vienna Boys Choir featured here. Conductor Yuri Temirkanov took the baton in January of 2000. A number of city music groups, including the Baltimore Choral Arts Society, use the Meyerhof as a performance venue.

The Peabody Conservatory of Music, 1 E. Mount Vernon Place (☎ 410-659-8124), presents a full schedule of recitals and performances by students of the nation's oldest music school, founded in 1857. These include programs by the school's own symphony orchestra, big band, Renaissance ensemble and chamber groups. Guest artists also perform here, in a range that includes opera, symphony and recitals.

Pier 6 Concert Pavilion hosts summer performances of rock, blues, country and jazz, with name performers and groups, such as B.B. King, Willie Nelson and the Gipsy Kings; ☎ 410-837-4636.

AUTHOR TIP *Harborplace Amphitheatre, at Pratt and Light Streets, is the site of free concerts starring local performers and groups, Friday through Sunday all summer;* ☎ *800-427-2671.*

Morris A. Mechanic Theatre, Hopkins Plaza, Baltimore and Charles streets (☎ 410-625-4230), presents popular shows and touring musicals, September-June.

AUTHOR TIP *Tickets for concerts and other events are sometimes discounted at the City Life Tickets kiosk, Inner Harbor Promenade, West Shore (between Harborplace and Maryland Science Center); ☎ 410-396-8342.*

Baltimore

The Vagabond Players, on the square at 806 S. Broadway, Fells Point (☎ 410-563-9135), has presented Broadway shows and plays at affordable prices for more than 80 years. Year-round performances are usually on Friday through Sunday, with both afternoon and evening Sunday shows.

Arena Players, Arena Playhouse, 801 McCullen St. (☎ 410-728-6500) is an African-American company that present classical and contemporary theater.

The Handel Choir of Baltimore (☎ 410-366-6544), with a choir of about 75 singers, performs choral works at various venues with full orchestra and guest soloists.

There are two movie houses of special interest to fans of classic films. **Orpheum Cinema**, 1724 Thames St. in Fells Point (☎ 410-732-4614), shows Hollywood and cartoon classics and foreign films, with weekend matinees in addition to its evening screenings. **The Senator Theatre**, at 5904 York Rd. (☎ 410-435-8338), is an Art Deco gem, on the National Register and considered one of America's best movie houses. Look here for art films and for premiers of Baltimore-filmed movies, including those of Barry Levinson and John Waters. The theater is fully handicapped-accessible. Be sure to admire the **Sidewalk of the Stars**, with film logos and star signatures in the concrete.

Events

JANUARY: In late January, the annual **Harborplace Ice Carving Competition** takes place at Harborplace Amphitheatre; ☎ 800-HARBOR-1.

APRIL: The **Baltimore Waterfront Festival**, featuring foods, boat rides, entertainment and activities around the Inner Harbor, is held at the end of the month; ☎ 888-BALTIMORE.

JULY: Several days of **Fourth of July events** and activities, including a huge fireworks display, kick off at the Inner Harbor.

SEPTEMBER: Star Spangled Banner Weekend is offered at Fort McHenry, culminating in Saturday night fireworks; ☎ 410-962-4290.

OCTOBER: Early in the month, **Fells Point Fun Festival** is a giant block party, with crafts, music stages and more food than you can imagine; ☎ 410-675-6756. Later in the month, the **Maryland Historical Society**

Antiques Show brings 33 selected antiques dealers together to sell their treasures, along with programs and lectures by well-known experts and a behind-the-scenes look at some of the museum's collections; ☎ 410-685-3750.

NOVEMBER: Baltimore hosts a **Thanksgiving Parade**, with equestrian unites, marching bands, colorful floats, clowns and Santa Claus; ☎ 410-837-4636.

DECEMBER: Early in the month brings **A Monumental Occasion**, the lighting of the Washington Monument, with street music and refreshments; ☎ 410-837-4636. Also at the beginning of December, **Christmas with Choral Arts**, a program of music and readings, is held at the Basilica of the Assumption; ☎ 410-523-7070. Mid-month offers **Merry Tuba Christmas**, with 200 tubas and euphoniums playing Christmas music at the Harborplace Amphitheater; ☎ 800-HARBOR-1, and the **Union Square Christmas Cookie Tour**, a neighborhood open house of two dozen decorated homes; ☎ 410-945-1497. During the entire month, Baltimore is filled with holiday celebrations and displays, including a **Lighted Boat Parade** (☎ 800-HARBOR-1), and a two-block stretch of **Preston Gardens** illuminated with animated figures and holiday symbols (☎ 410-332-9714). The Baltimore Zoo (☎ 410-837-4636) has special holiday illuminations, called **Zoo Lights**, and on one mid-December weekend local museums and attractions offer $1 admission with a "Baltimore On Ice" badge (☎ 410-837-4636). **Historic homes** are decorated for the season and host an open house with a single ticket and free shuttle (☎ 410-516-0341).

CELEBRATING ETHNIC BALTIMORE

For more information and exact dates, contact the Visitors Center, ☎ 410-837-4636; www.baltimore.org.

■ Early August - **AFRAM**, an African American expo at several venues.

■ Mid-August - **Hispanic Festival** at Market Place, off Pratt St.

■ Late August - **German Festival** at Carroll Park

■ Mid-September - **Caribbean Festival** at Park Circle

■ Mid-September - **Korean Festival** at Center Plaza

■ Mid-September - **Irish Festival** at Fifth Regiment Armory

■ Late September - **Ukrainian Festival** at Patterson Park

Sightseeing

For an overview of the city and a quick run-though of Baltimore's history, travel to the top of the world's tallest pentagonal building, I. M. Pei's 423-foot **World Trade Center**, at the Inner Harbor. Open Monday-Saturday, 10-5; Sunday, noon-5. Admission is $3, $2 for seniors and children.

AUTHOR TIP

Keep up with the local Baltimore weather conditions by calling ☎ 410-936-1212 for up-to-date forecasts.

Baltimore

Sports fans will want to tour **Oriole Park at Camden Yards**, 333 W. Camden St. (☎ 410-547-6234), the new 48,000-seat home field of the Baltimore Orioles. Daily tours include the dugout, scoreboard control room, press box and other facilities. Tour hours vary widely; admission $5 adults, $4 for those over 55 and under 12.

DID YOU KNOW?

The glove on the right hand of the young Babe Ruth's statue at the entrance to Oriole Park is not a mistake. He learned to play baseball here as a young boy, using equipment provided by the school, and all the gloves were right-handed.

■ Historic Sites

Inner Harbor & Little Italy

Fresh from its complete overhaul and restoration in 1999, the **USS *Constellation***, moored at Pier 1, Constellation Dock at 301 E. Pratt St. (☎ 410-539-1797, www.constellation.org), is once again open for tours. The restoration yielded new information on the ship's age and history, which includes the capture of three slave-trade ships off Africa, transporting precious American art works to the Paris Exposition of 1878 and a famine-relief mission to Ireland. Admission is $6 for adults, $4.75 for those over 60 and $3.50 for children six-14. The ship is open daily, 10-6 from May through mid-October, 10-4 in the off-season. In the height of summer it may be open evening hours, too.

Although the *Constellation* is the harbor's glamour-girl, three other historic ships moored close by are well worth touring. They are part of the **Baltimore Maritime Museum**, at Pier 3, E. Pratt St., on the Inner Harbor (☎ 410-396-3453).

The US Coastguard cutter ***Taney*** is the only surviving ship still afloat from the Japanese attack on Pearl Harbor in 1941, and saw later action in the Korean and Vietnam wars. The US submarine ***Torsk*** is a veteran of a record number of dives (11,884) and the sinking of two Japanese frigates in 1945 made it the last warship to sink an enemy vessel in World War II. *Torsk* saw further duty as part of the 1962 Cuban blocade. Lightship ***Chesapeake***, commissioned in 1939, served as a floating lighthouse in the Chesapeake Bay. All three are usually open daily, 10-6, but may have longer summer hours and be open only on weekends in the winter (the hours have changed several times lately). Admission is $5.50, $4.50 for seniors, $3 for ages five-12; buy tickets at the kiosk on Pier 3, by the Aquarium.

AUTHOR TIP

*The maritime attractions and others around the harbor have joined as **National Historic Seaport of Baltimore**, to offer a combined admission pass with water transportation. Included are the Maritime Museum ships, USS Constellation, Museum of Industry and Fort McHenry. Buy passes at the kiosk on Pier 3;* ☎ *410-396-3453.*

Although it is not an original clipper, ***Pride of Baltimore II*** (☎ 410-539-1151) is an authentic replica of the famous Baltimore Clipper, a topsail schooner built here between the Revolution and the mid 1800s. The ship is Maryland's goodwill ambassador, and when it is not under sail to other ports representing the state, it is berthed in Inner Harbor, where you can tour it.

Seven-Foot Knoll Lighthouse, almost hidden from view behind the Harbor Inn at Pier 5 Hotel, is Maryland's oldest screwpile lighthouse. You can get a good view of it from the end of the pier behind the Aquarium.

Flag House and 1812 Museum, 844 E. Pratt St., at Albemarle St. (☎ 410-837-1793, www.flaghouse.org), built in 1793, was the home of Mary Pickersgill, who made the 30-by-42-foot flag that flew over Fort McHenry during the British bombardment. The flag was so large that Francis Scott Key was able to see it in the early light of morning from a ship in the harbor, and knew Baltimore had not fallen. Open Tuesday through Saturday, 10-4; admission is charged. The house is easy to find – as you walk along Pratt Street past the piers, you will see a sign for Little Italy painted on a building straight ahead of you; the Flag House is the brick building across the street to its left.

Unfortunately, **Shot Tower**, at 801 E. Fayette St., was a victim of the closing of the City Museums, of which it was a part. The 1828 tower, 234 feet high, was built from more than a million wood-fired bricks and is one of the few remaining shot towers in the US. (Its cornerstone was laid by Charles Carroll of Carrollton, whose home is nearby at E. Lombard and Front streets.) It was once a major supplier of lead shot. Although it's no longer open, you can get a good view of its exterior, towering over neighboring St. Vincent de Paul Church's distinctive white steeple.

DID YOU KNOW? *Shot was produced by pouring molten lead from the top of the tower into the center of it. As the lead fell, it formed droplets, which solidified into spheres when they reached the water inside the base of the tower.*

FREE!

See entries below for more complete details on the following free sights:

■ **Basilica of the National Shrine of the Assumption of the Blessed Virgin Mary** (Cathedral and Mulberry streets)

■ **Enoch Pratt Free Library** (400 Cathedral St.)

■ **Westminster Hall Burying Ground** (Fayette and Greene streets)

■ **Baltimore City Hall** (100 N. Holliday St.)

■ **Baltimore Museum of Art** – on *Thursdays* only (N. Charles and 35th streets)

■ **Baltimore City Conservatory** (Druid Lake Drive)

St. Vincent de Paul Church is a historical landmark as Baltimore's oldest Catholic parish church; it's a fine example of Georgian architecture. Tours are available after any service, on request; services are Saturday at 7:15 pm, and Sunday morning at 9 and 11:45 (☎ 410-962-5078).

Mount Vernon

The prominent **Washington Monument**, N. Charles St. at Mount Vernon Place (☎ 410-837-4636), was the first architectural monument in America honoring George Washington (the one in the Appalachian Mountains, west of Frederick, was completed two years earlier in 1827, but is not an architectural design). The climb of 228 steps takes you above the surrounding rooftops of Mount Vernon for a bird's-eye view of the city ($1).

The **Basilica** of the **National Shrine of the Assumption of the Blessed Virgin Mary**, at Cathedral and Mulberry streets (☎ 410-727-3564), was the first Roman Catholic Cathedral in the United States, built from 1806 to 1821. Designed by Benjamin Latrobe, architect of the US Capitol, the basilica is considered one of the world's best examples of neo-classical architecture. It is open 7-5, Monday through Friday, 7-6:30 on Saturday and Sunday; tours are given after the 10:45 Sunday mass (about noon) or by appointment.

The elegant Second Empire-style **Baltimore City Hall**, at 100 N. Holliday St. (☎ 410-837-5424), will remind you of the Executive Office Building in Washington DC, except that it is topped by a 110-foot rotunda and a rare segmented dome. Inside are permanent exhibits on Baltimore history, and other changing exhibits. City Hall is open Monday-Friday, 10-4:30, and is free.

DID YOU KNOW? *The architect of Baltimore's City Hall, George Frederick, was not yet 20 years old when he submitted the designs that won him the contract for the building. You can tell he was inexperienced: the final tab came in $200,000 under budget.*

One of the nation's largest libraries, **Enoch Pratt Free Library**, at 400 Cathedral St. (☎ 410-396-5430), has collections on Edgar Allan Poe, H.L. Mencken and Maryland history. Open Monday-Wednesday, 10-8; Thursday-Saturday, 10-5; and from October through April, Sunday, 1-5; free.

Even when the grounds are not open, you can see Edgar Allan Poe's monument right in the corner of **Westminster Hall Burying Ground and Catacombs**, at Fayette and Greene streets. (☎ 410-706-2072). The 1852 Presbyterian Church, now inactive, has one of city's oldest burial grounds, with graves of many other prominent Marylanders. It's free, but reservations are needed for the scheduled tours of the cemetery and underground crypts, held first and third Friday and Saturday of each month, from April through November.

Edgar Allan Poe's gravestone is in Baltimore's Mount Vernon area.

EDGAR ALLAN POE

Edgar Allan Poe, although not a Baltimore native, lived and worked here, and won his first literary recognition in the city for the short story *MS. Found in a Bottle*. It was here he courted his 13-year-old cousin, and here he was found dead of unknown cause. Three sites are especially connected with Poe:

■ **Enoch Pratt Free Library**, at 400 Cathedral St. (☎ 410-396-5430), which has Edgar Allan Poe collections (seen by appointment only).

■ **Westminster Hall Burying Ground**, Fayette and Greene streets (☎ 410-706-2072, containing his grave.

■ The **Edgar Allan Poe House**, 203 Amity St. (☎ 410-396-7932), where he wrote the first of the gothic tales that were to spawn the genre.

Fells Point

Baltimore's oldest surviving urban home, the **Robert Long House**, at 812 S. Ann St. (☎ 410-675-6750), dates from 1765. Now the headquarters of Baltimore's Preservation Society, the home is restored and furnished with antiques of its period, as the home of an 18th-century merchant. Open for tours on Thursdays at 10, 1 and 3.

Elsewhere in Baltimore

Possibly Baltimore's best-known historic site is famous for inspiring the writing of *The Star Spangled Banner*. **Fort McHenry National Monument and Historic Shrine**, at the end of E. Fort Ave. (☎ 410-962-4290) is the 1790 star-shaped brick fort that withstood the British bombardment of Baltimore during the War of 1812.

THE STAR SPANGLED BANNER

Francis Scott Key, a Maryland attorney, was being held on board a British ship, where he was trying to secure the release of an American doctor, when the battle occurred. All night he heard the rockets exploding as Baltimore was attacked by British boats and, "by the dawn's early light," saw the huge American flag still flying over Fort McHenry and knew that Baltimore had not been taken. This inspired him to write the verse that later became the National Anthem, although it wasn't until many years later that the designation was made official.

After seeing a film at the visitors center, tour the fort to see officers' quarters, guardrooms, a restored powder magazine, cannons and earthworks. On summer weekends, interpreters in period uniform re-enact life in the garrison. The fort is open daily June-August, 8-8; September-May, 8-5. The grounds and visitors center are free, but admission is charged to enter the fort enclosure.

The Edgar Allan Poe House and Museum is at 203 N. Amity St. (☎ 410-396-7932), where Poe lived from 1832 to 1835, at the beginning of his writing career. The house contains Poe memorabilia and furniture of his era, which is further illuminated by a video presentation. Two factors make the museum a destination for serious Poe devotees only: its poor location in a sadly deteriorated neighborhood and its sometimes sporadic hours. It's best to call well in advance to be sure when it is open or to make an appointment; admission is charged.

Mount Clare Museum House, in Carroll Park, 1500 Washington Blvd. and Monroe St. (☎ 410-837-3262), is Baltimore's only mansion predating the Revolution. Completed in 1760 as the summer residence of Charles Carroll, Barrister, it is one of the nation's finest examples of Georgian architecture. The outstanding collection of 18th- and 19th-century furniture is original to Carroll and his wife, with additions by later generations of the family. Tours start Tuesday through Friday, every hour on the hour, 11-3, and on weekends at 1, 2 and 3. The house is closed in January. Admission is $3; for under age 12, 50¢.

THE ILLUSTRIOUS CARROLLS

Charles Carroll, Barrister, is so designated to avoid confusion with his famous relative, Charles Carroll of Carrollton. The former was a major figure of his time, but not as well known to history as Charles Carroll of Carrollton, the only Catholic signer of the Declaration of Independence (also the longest living signer), and the man who laid the cornerstone of the Baltimore and Ohio Railroad. In the same family was John Carroll, Bishop of Baltimore and the founder of the nation's first Roman Catholic Cathedral.

Across the Harbor from Fort McHenry, at Pier 1, 2000 S. Clinton St., is the *S.S. John W. Brown*, which, under the care of **Project Liberty Ship**, is a maritime museum and memorial to all those who built, sailed and defended Liberty Ships during World War II. Of the 2,500 Liberty Ships that survived the war, this is the only one left on the east coast. Liberty Ships were built from 1941 until the close of the war as transport ships, each capable of carrying 8500 long tons of cargo that supplied allied fighting forces all over the world. Built in Baltimore, the *John W. Brown* traveled back and forth across the Atlantic carrying war supplies and troops, and took part in the invasion of southern France. Plans call for the ship to have a regular schedule of day cruises in the Chesapeake, but for now it contains exhibits and is open for tours Wednesday and Saturday 10-2; ☎ 410-661-1550.

AFRICAN AMERICAN HERITAGE SITES

Baltimore has a number of sites important to African American history, and the city has recognized this in an attractive full-color booklet called *Baltimore's African-American Heritage*, available free from the tourism office (☎ 888-BALTIMORE). Along with the sites that are clearly related, the booklet features those collections or areas of general interest museums and attractions that feature black history or African subjects, such as the African habitats at the zoo and African art at area art museums. Historic churches, the tennis club where blacks were arrested for playing in defiance of segregation policies, and a newspaper founded by a former slave are among the listings. Also in the booklet are brief biographies of notable Baltimoreans, including Benjamin Banneker, Billie Holiday, Eubie Blake, Frederick Douglas and Thurgood Marshall.

■ A **Black Landmarks Tour** is hosted by the African-American Heritage Society; ☎ 410-367-2698.

■ An introduction to Baltimore's – and the nation's – black history is at **Great Blacks in Wax Museum**, at 1601 E. North Ave. (☎ 410-563-3404). America's only wax museum devoted to African-American history and culture, it displays life-sized figures in historical settings, with a replica slave ship commemorating the many who arrived in the Slave Trade. Open Tuesday through Saturday, 9-6; Sunday, noon-6. Admission $5.75 adults, $5.25 seniors and college students, $3.75 ages 12-17, $3.25 ages two-11.

■ Museums

Inner Harbor & Nearby

Jewish Museum of Maryland, at 15 Lloyd St. between Lombard and E. Baltimore streets (☎ 410-732-6400, www.jhsm.org), includes two restored historic synagogues. The Lloyd Street Synagogue was built in 1845, the B'nai Israel Synagogue in 1876. Along with these two National Register of Historic Places buildings, visitors can see extensive archives and collections on Jewish history, life and culture. The Golden Land is an interactive children's exploration of the turn-of-the-century immigrant experience, aimed at ages five-10. A research library is open by appointment. Open Tuesday through Thursday and Sunday, noon to 4, except National and Jewish holidays; guided tours are offered at 1 and 2:30. Admission is $4 adult, $2 children.

KID-FRIENDLY

One of the nation's largest children's activity and learning centers is not really a museum. **Port Discovery,** *at 35 Market Place (☎ 410-727-8120), is designed for ages five-13. It's interactive at its best, with unique and imaginative activities that include crawling into a giant kitchen sink or starring in a show in the TV studio. Open Tuesday through Sunday, 10-5:30. Admission is $10 adults, $7.50 for kids ages three-12.*

Visitors either find the **American Visionary Art Museum** very exciting or wonder why they went; no one comes away neutral. The works shown are by self-taught or untrained artists, unshaped by art schools or formal traditions of design and technique. Often highly original, sometimes bizarre and always unlike the collections of other art museums, the Visionary provides a new look at the creative process and is an evocative blend of the compelling and the whimsical. Shows have dealt with topics ranging from the unseen companions that move artists to produce (think angels, imaginary friends, tempting devils, chanelled "superior beings") to near-compulsive artistry as a means of dealing with adversity. Every artist's work is labeled with a short biography, which takes you into their world and helps you see their art the way they do. At first glance, the museum seems full of humor and whimsy, but reading more deeply into the works reveals the human mind and spirit within and its struggles with heartbreak, loneliness, imprisonment, and itself. Across the Inner Harbor from the Pratt Street piers, the museum is under Federal Hill at 800 Key Hwy. (☎ 410-244-1900, www.avam.org), open Tuesday-Sunday, 10-6; admission is $6 adult, $4 seniors and students. To join in the creation of an ongoing "work of art," be sure to add your admission sticker to the post in front of the museum when you leave.

If, like us, you find the Industrial Revolution right up there with the American Revolution, you'll like the **Baltimore Museum of Industry**, at 1415 Key Hwy. (☎ 410-727-4808). An 1870 oyster cannery, it still has some of the original equipment, including a belt-driven machine shop. But a pressure cooker that holds more than 100 cans at once is only the beginning. Baltimore's significant garment industry is represented with displays and actual cutting rooms, a print shop demonstrates the evolution from hand-set type to linotype machines, and kids can get some hands-on experience on an assembly line. Nicely designed panels recall some of Baltimore's industrial firsts and the companies that achieved them. Throughout, the museum is filled with actual artifacts, machinery and products, and docents are on hand to demonstrate or explain. Outside in the harbor, a 1906 steam tugboat is open for tours. Open Tuesday-Friday, noon-5; Saturday, 10-5; check for shorter winter hours. Admission is $5; seniors and children $3.

Mount Vernon

The outstanding collections of **The Walters Art Gallery**, at 600 N. Charles St. (☎ 410-547-9000, www.thewalters.org), cover more than 5,000 years of artistic excellence. Given to the city by Baltimore-born Henry Walters, the museum of 30,000 objects encompasses everything from ancient Egyptian to Art Nouveau; highlights are the Fabergé eggs, medieval armor, and Asian arts, which are shown separately at Hackerman House, at 1 Mt. Vernon Place, accessed through the museum's second floor. Although these Asian works of art merit attention, don't overlook the fine interior architectural detail of Hackerman House itself, especially the spiral staircase rising to a Tiffany skylight. Collections of European porcelains, the work of goldsmiths from the Renaissance to the early 20th century, classical antiquities, medieval illuminated manuscripts and the first Raphael madonna to reach an American collection are among the museum's other highlights. As we write this, the museum is undergoing major reconstruction to create better exhibition space, but portions of it will remain open during this process. Open Tuesday through Friday, 10-4; Saturday and Sunday, 11-5. Admission is free for one hour on Saturdays, from 11 until noon.

Already a treasure trove of regional arts and historically significant artifacts, **Maryland Historical Society Museum and Library**, at 201 W. Monument St. (☎ 410-685-3750) fell heir to many of the objects formerly in the Baltimore City Life Museums. The museum includes a Children's Gallery, the Enoch Pratt House and galleries on both the Civil War and War of 1812. You can see the original manuscript of Francis Scott Key's *The Star-Spangled Banner* here, and the American decorative arts are outstanding. The museum has the world's largest collection of paintings by Charles Wilson Peale and the nation's largest collection of American silver from the 19th century. Among the most interesting features of the museum is a sampling of the collections from the former City Life Museums, which are shown in a very well-designed exhibit that captures the heart of Baltimore. Historic photos and artifacts combine to paint a picture of the city's founding, its rich immigrant past and its often quirky and colorful traditions, from painted screens to parlor window displays.

Children get special attention at the museum with activities that introduce them to the exhibits. A line of soldiers is painted on the lobby wall, each "carrying" a haversack, which children are invited to take with them through the museum. Inside are activities, pencils, crayons and instruction sheets for simple crafts to do when they get home. The contents change with the museum's calendar of festivals and special exhibits. Open Tuesday through Friday, 10-5; Saturday, 9-5; Sunday, 11-5. Admission is $4; seniors and children $3.

Baltimore

AUTHOR TIP

FREE! *The three museums in Mount Vernon join neighborhood shops, cultural centers and restaurants for **First Thursdays**, held 5:30-7:30 on the first Thursday evening of each month. Free outdoor concerts, free museum admission, gallery receptions and special values in cafés, theaters and restaurants encourage Baltimoreans and visitors to sample this culture-rich neighborhood.*

Three blocks away, on the other side of the Washington Monument, is a historical museum of another sort, with a very specialized collection dedicated to a single subject: the incandescent light. But read on, because this is no ordinary collection. **The Mount Vernon Museum of Incandescent Lighting**, at 717 Washington Place (☎ 410-752-8586 or 410-323-2454) is the lifelong passion of a Baltimore dentist, Dr. Hugh Hicks. So knowledgeable an historian is Dr. Hicks (who will show you through the museum himself) that the Smithsonian comes to him for help. You will see only the tip of Dr. Hicks' incandescent iceberg, 8,000 of the 60,000-piece collection that includes the largest and smallest lightbulbs ever made, as well as the earliest. But you don't just see lightbulbs, you hear the story of their invention (and get an illuminating, but unflattering picture of Thomas Edison) and of their evolution, told by a charming gentleman with a keen sense of humor. Those interested in Christmas decorations will want to see the impressive collection of German and other figural Christmas tree lights, including comic characters Betty Boop and Dick Tracy. The museum is open Monday through Saturday, 9-5, but because Dr. Hicks is still a practicing dentist, you will need to call to be sure he's available to show you through, which is part of the museum's attraction.

Northern Baltimore

With the outstanding Walters Art Gallery, you might not expect to find a second world-class art museum in town. But the **Baltimore Museum of Art**, on Art Museum Drive, Charles St. at 31st St. (☎ 410-396-7100) has permanent collections of some 85,000 works. The Cone collection of 20th-century paintings by Matisse, Picasso and Cezanne would make the museum well worth visiting, but that's just the beginning. Ancient mosaics, old masters (eight galleries of them), folk arts from Africa and Oceania, and contemporary works share the spotlight. Gertrude's, several cuts above the usual museum café, is described under *Where to Eat*, below. Open Wednesday through Friday, 11-5; Saturday and Sunday, 11-6. Admission is $6 for adults, $4 for seniors and students; under age 18 are free; free admission on Thursday.

Two fine homes are preserved on the campus of Johns Hopkins University. **Evergreen House**, at 4545 N. Charles St. (☎ 410-516-0341), is a 48-room Italianate mansion. The house itself is well worth touring for its wealth of interior decorative detail. In the reception room, for example, the wall covering is a delicate lattice design of stucco applied with a stencil to create a three-dimensional pattern. Above is an elaborate ceiling molding. The intimate Reading Room and larger library are among the loveliest rooms we have seen. Here, visitors begin to know Ambassador John Garrett, who owned the house. Elsewhere, the flamboyant personality of his wife, Alice, is more evident, especially in the theater, where she performed for guests at their parties.

The art collections housed here would rank it as a significant museum – several Vuillards, an early Bonard, a Modigliani, a Picasso from his pink period, works by Derain and Degas, and a large collection by Dufy and the lesser-known Spanish artist, Zuloaga. Major collections of Japanese netsuke, Tiffany glass and Chinese porcelains join many other important pieces in the house. Well worth seeing, too, are the 26 acres of gardens, where contemporary sculpture is usually displayed. Open Monday through Friday, 10-4; weekends, 1-4; tours begin on the hour, with the last at 3. Admission is $6 for adults, $5 for seniors, $3 for ages six-18.

Homewood House is also on the campus of Johns Hopkins, at 3400 N. Charles St. (☎ 410-516-5589). Among the finest existing examples of Federal architecture, it was built in 1801 by another member of the prominent Carroll family, Charles Carroll, Jr. The craftsmanship of its interior architecture and ornamentation is outstanding, and it is furnished in original and period antiques. The design of the house is classic Georgian, based on symmetry with a main house and two wings attached by hyphens. In the central reception room was the first successful use of green as a color pigment of its own.

DID YOU KNOW?

Prior to the early 1800s, green paint was made by mixing yellow and blue paints, one of which would invariably fade faster than the other. Instead of just fading to a lighter shade of green, this changed the color drastically, making it into turquoise or chartreuse.

The floorcloths repeat the black and white squares of the marble portico, and the woodwork is painted in faux marble. The faux mahogany painting on the doors is original. In the master bedroom, be sure to notice the early flush mechanism in the convertible nightstand/commode. Open Tuesday through Saturday, 11-4; Sunday, noon-4 (last tour at 3:30).

The frustrating thing about most museums of early transport is that you can't even climb aboard, let alone ride in the artifacts. Not so at the **Baltimore Streetcar Museum**, 1901 Falls Rd. (☎ 410-547-0264), where you can ride historic streetcars all afternoon for one admission price. Exhibits, restored cars and a video tell about the history of Baltimore's streetcar system, but most people go to ride the cars, which are complete with clanging bells and costumed conductors. Open June through October, Saturday and

Sunday, noon-5; November through May, Sunday, noon-5. Admission is $5; for seniors and ages four-11, $2.50; families $20 maximum. It's a little out of the way (at the northwest of Penn Station), but MTA buses will take you to the corner of Maryland and Lafayette, two blocks away. Follow Lafayette west to Falls Rd. and turn right to find the museum.

While you are in the neighborhood, get a sampling of an old-time museum that you thought had gone forever. Maybe you never missed them, but the **Dime Museum**, at 1808 Maryland Ave., near North St. (☎ 410-230-0263, www.dimemuseum.com), represents the genre of curio collection that evolved into the traveling carnival sideshow. The owners, two historians with tongues firmly in cheek, have assembled a museum of the bizarre and often bogus artifacts that characterized these Barnum-esque collections. Many of the items were manufactured especially for dime museums, such as the devil-man and the Samoan Sea Wurm, a monkey's top joined with the body of a fish. The nine-foot mummified Amazon even comes with her original display case, as provided by her manufacturer. Some of the curiosities are just what they say they are, others are not, and the curators will tell you how some of them were made (the goat-turned-unicorn, for example). Downstairs exhibits illustrate the traveling sideshow form these collections later took. Hours are Wednesday through Friday, noon-3; weekends, 11-4; admission is $5, $3 for children. Good fun, and be sure to look for Abraham Lincoln's last... (but we'll let you discover this dubious bit of history for yourself).

West of the Inner Harbor

Okay, we didn't expect to like it, either, but the sparking new **National Museum of Dentistry**, at 31 S. Greene St. (☎ 410-706-0600, www.dental-museum.umaryland.edu) manages to make teeth, their care and their repair interesting and lively. Along with George Washington's dentures (not made of wood), Mrs. Tom Thumb's diminutive upper plate and the mother-of-pearl instruments kept solely for use in the royal mouth of Queen Victoria, you'll find a jukebox shaped like a giant Art Deco mouth that plays all the old toothpaste commercials. Odd facts abound – did you know that western novelist Zane Grey was a dentist? Open Wednesday through Saturday, 10-4; Sunday, 1-4. Admission is $4.50 for adults, $2.50 for those over 60, between seven and 18, and students with ID.

KID-FRIENDLY

Small people can don junior-sized lab coats and masks and play dentist in a pint-sized office with a low chair at the National Museum of Dentistry. Special event programs may include crafts or reading from children's books that tell tooth-related stories.

You are welcome to climb aboard many of the 120 beautifully restored rolling stock in the big bright roundhouse at the **B & O Railroad Museum**,

901 W. Pratt St, at Poppleton St. (☎ 410-752-2490, wwwborail.org). The roundhouse and museum are at the site of America's first passenger railway station, Mount Clare Station. The B&O (Baltimore and Ohio) dates from 1829, and is the nation's oldest railroad. Some of America's oldest steam and diesel locomotives, passenger cars and freight wagons are here and excursion trains run on weekends. These depart at 11:30, 12:30, 2:30 and 3:30 ($2). Along with the cars and engines, the museum has displays about the railroad and a collection of model trains. Open daily 10-5; admission is $6.50 for adults, $5.50 seniors, $4 for ages three-12.

Yet More Museums

There's almost no end to the subjects covered by museums in Baltimore, where you can see Bo Jangles' dancing shoes, George Washington's upper plate and a memento of Abraham Lincoln that you could probably live quite a happy life without knowing about.

Some of these museums are rich in interpretive displays but shy on artifacts, others are just the opposite, and others lie somewhere between. We have not visited some of those listed below; others we found fascinating, but they may appeal only to those with a consuming interest in the particular subject. Of course, the same could be said for a number of the ones we chose for longer descriptions above, too.

Baltimore Civil War Museum, 601 President St., between Inner Harbor and Fells Point (☎ 410-385-5188, www.civilwarinbaltimore.org) has historical exhibits in the old President Street Station, once a transfer point on the Underground Railroad. Open daily, 10-5; admission is $2, children $1.

Babe Ruth Birthplace Museum, at 216 Emory St. (☎ 410-396-6310), has memorabilia of the hometown kid who made history, and other Orioles; open May through October, daily, 10-5; November-March, 10-4. Admission $5, seniors $3, children $2.

Baltimore Public Works Museum and Streetscape, 751 Eastern Ave. on the eastern side of Inner Harbor (☎ 410-396-5565), concerns itself with the urban environment in exhibits on what lies under the streets and how trash and garbage are collected and disposed of. Open Tuesday through Sunday, 10-4; admission $2.50, seniors $2, children seven-12, $1.50.

Lacrosse Foundation and Hall of Fame Museum, 113 W. University Parkway (☎ 410-235-6882), follows 350 years of lacrosse history; open Monday through Friday, 9-5, and Saturday, 10-5, from March through May. Admission charge.

Museum of the American Urological Association, 1120 N. Charles St. (☎ 410-727-1100, www.amuro.org/museum), shows two centuries of specialized medical instruments and technical advances; free and open by appointment.

Fire Museum of the Baltimore Equitable Society, at 21 N. Eutaw St. (☎ 410-727-1794), was one of the early fire insurance companies that kept

Baltimore

their own fire brigade before the days of public fire departments. Their museum is not only filled with early fire fighting equipment, but allows you to try out some of it, including fire alarm devices and old firemen's helmets. It's free and open weekdays, 10-4.

World War II and military enthusiasts should seek out the Fifth Regiment Armory, and its **Maryland National Guard Museum**, in the Bolton Hill neighborhood at the intersection of 29th Division, Dolphin and Howard streets; ☎ 410-576-1441. The regiment's history predates the Revolution, and the collections, which you can see by appointment, cover all wars, but are strongest in the World War II era.

DID YOU KNOW?

The Maryland Fifth Regiment held the line against the British so that Washington and his troops could escape after the Battle of Long Island, earning the state the sobriquet "The Old Line State."

Where to Stay

Although Baltimore is well supplied with representatives of the major hotel chains, and a few independent ones as well, it is not replete with B&Bs and small inns, so rooms in these may be hard to find in busy seasons. Several of the larger chain hotels are close to Inner Harbor, including Renaissance, Omni, Hilton, Paramount, Days Inn, Marriott, Holiday Inn, Hyatt and Sheraton.

ACCOMMODATIONS PRICE KEY
Rates are per room, per night, double occupancy.
$ . . . . Under $50
$$. . . . . $50 to $100
$$$ . . . . $101 to $175
$$$$ . . . . $176 and up

■ Inner Harbor

Right on the harbor – balconies overlook the aquarium and water – is the modern **Pier 5 Hotel**, 711 Eastern Avenue (☎ 410-539-2000). We consider it one of the artistic landmarks of the I7nner Harbor and suggest you step into the atrium lobby just to see the sleek Art Deco interior. Above the sweeping lines of the velour lobby furniture, a mural encircles the atrium. Created by artist Sam Robinson, it depicts the harbor and city views in each direction. Room furnishings carry out the Art Deco design, and comforting details include bathrobes, in-room safes, coffee makers, irons and ironing boards. The biggest drawback of the hotel is the atrium design, which sometimes makes noisy groups returning to their rooms at night clearly audible in other rooms. Packages include breakfast, free accommodations for children and passes to nearby museums. $$$

AUTHOR TIP *If lodgings are short, you can enlist the help of* **Amanda's Bed and Breakfast Reservations Service**, *1428 Park Ave, Baltimore, MD 21217;* ☎ *410-225-0001.*

■ Fells Point

Our favorite inn in Baltimore is **The Admiral Fell Inn**, at 888 South Broadway in Fells Point, on the corner of Thames St., overlooking the harbor. An oasis of tranquility and gentility in a neighborhood that is sometimes neither of these, the Fell is a good choice for travelers looking for a lively evening of bar-hopping – or just sitting on the wharves watching the boats go by – before retiring to serenity and a healthy dose of pampering. Coffee and tea are available 24 hours, and in cool weather a fireplace warms the spacious lobby parlor. Guest rooms, too, are large and uncluttered, with individual heat control, hair dryers, ample reading lights, phones and televisions neatly enclosed in armoires. Dormers create cozy nooks in some, and furnishings often include antique wooden seamen's chests. The breakfast buffet is quite possibly the best in town, a bountiful display of fresh-cut fruit, premium cereals, a good selection of breads and pastries, European cheeses and steaming hot oatmeal in the winter. The staff is accommodating and friendly, the kind of people you may find yourself lingering over a second cup of coffee to talk to. Enjoy dinner in the cosseted elegance of Hamilton's at the inn, or in any of Fells Point's pubs and funky restaurants (see *Where to Eat*, below). $$$

A short water taxi ride from all the attractions of Inner Harbor is **The Inn at Henderson's Wharf**, 1000 Fell St. (☎ 410-522-7777 or 800-522-2088, fax 410-522-7087), a deluxe 38-room B&B on the water. The surroundings are elegant and club-like, with rooms and lobby overlooking a garden with brick terrace and café tables. The inn has its own marina, and both parking and breakfast are included in the room rates. $$$

There is also the small, quiet **Ann Street Bed & Breakfast**, 804 South Ann St. (☎ 410-342-5883), with fireplaces and a garden. $$$

■ Bolton Hill

Two B&Bs in the Bolton Hill area offer different atmospheres, even though they are under the same ownership. **Mr. Mole Bed & Breakfast**, at 1601

Bolton St. (☎ 410-728-1179, fax 410-728-3379, www.MrMoleBB.com), will knock your socks off from the minute you enter. What seems at first like visual overload of interior decor quickly seems just the right thing for rooms of soaring ceilings and extraordinary original architectural detail. Fine antiques and collections highlight it, but the unusually stunning color and fabric treatments make each room a work of art. The cheeky Australian innkeeper keeps you from taking the decor too seriously. Two of the suites accommodate three guests, good for families traveling with children over age 10; rates range from just over $100 to $175 for a suite.

More restrained in tone and style, but with elegantly decorated rooms, is the sister property, **Abacrombie Badger Bed & Breakfast**, at 58 West Biddle St. (☎ 410-244-7227, 888-9BADGER, fax 410-244-8415, www.badger-inn.com). Accommodations vary in size from cozy singles to large rooms with sitting areas and four-poster beds. Reading lights are everywhere, even places where one would be unlikely to curl up with a book, and some rooms have writing desks complete with thoughtfully filled pen caddies. Although the inn is on a corner with traffic passing on two sides, the location is unparalleled for music lovers, directly across the street from Meyerhoff Symphony Hall. Rates for single rooms are under $100, doubles range from $115 to $155. In the same building, beneath the B&B, is La Tesso Tana Restaurant (see *Where to Eat*, below), and you can depend on Paul's (the innkeeper) intelligent and discerning dining suggestions.

Both B&Bs serve a "Dutch-style" breakfast with fresh fruit, fresh-baked breads, cheese and coldcuts, along with a sweet, which may be shoofly pie from an Amish farmers' market. Both have off-street parking. Neither has a resident innkeeper (they live about four blocks away), and check-in times are 4-6 pm. Those arriving later will be given access instructions. If you are traveling alone, and are uncomfortable arriving at an empty house at night, this might not be the choice for you, but otherwise these are attractive, inviting and interesting places to stay.

■ Federal Hill

A historic neighborhood within an easy walk of the Inner Harbor sights, Federal Hill is filled with restaurants, shops, even its own market, and **Scarborough Fair Bed & Breakfast** is in the midst of it all. Six guest rooms have an assortment of amenities, some with fireplaces, some whirlpool baths, all with a tasteful blend of antiques and period reproductions. All rooms have private baths, but not all are en-suite. The beautifully restored brick building is one of the oldest on Federal Hill, dating from 1801. Rates range from $120 to $150. The inn is at One East Montgomery St., ☎ 410-837-0010, fax 410-783-4635, www.scarborough-fair.com.

Where to Eat

Baltimore restaurants tend to cluster into neighborhoods, with dozens around the waterfront alone. Nearby, Little Italy has most of the Italian restaurants (although certainly not all of them) and Charles Street, which bisects Mount Vernon, is often called Restaurant Row. Another clutch, possibly the most diverse collection of all, gather in Fells Point. There are, of course, notable exceptions to this cluster rule. If you have a particular place in mind, it is good to call for a dinner reservation on weekends, during festivals or in the busy summer season.

CITY MARKETS

A good choice for a casual lunch or to get picnic makings is any one of the city's several public markets. This market system is such a part of Baltimore culture that you'll find them crowded with neighborhood shoppers every morning, the activity rising to a crescendo at noon, when they are a favorite lunch-hour choice. More than a place to buy food, the markets are a way of life here, much as they are in European cities.

You are rarely far from one: Federal Hill has **Cross St. Market**, Fells Point has two on **Broadway** near the waterfront. Downtown's **Lexington Market**, on West Lexington St., founded in 1782, is packed with 140 food merchants selling ingredients for dinner or ready-made foods of every nationality from Caribbean to Greek.

DINING PRICE KEY
The price key indicates the cost of *most* dinner entrées on a restaurant's regular and daily special menu.
$ . . . . Most under $10
$$ . . . . $10 to $20
$$$ . . . . Over $30

■ Inner Harbor

Look here for the trendier places, the hotel restaurants, and the fast-turn-over eateries. This is not to say you should look elsewhere for fine dining, but in the staggering number of establishments here, you will find all kinds. Ed Kane's Water Taxi will take you to within a few steps of most of these – just tell the skipper what restaurant you're going to and the boat will stop at the nearest dock. Of all the Inner Harbor restaurants we've tried, these three rise well above the rest.

Joy America Café, 800 Key Highway, in the American Visionary Art Museum; ☎ 410-244-6500. With the Americas – especially Central American cuisine – as its inspiration, this bright, upbeat and slightly quirky café serves local seafood in ways you won't find in the city's other restaurants. Tangy ceviche and fish tacos give the fresh catch an altogether different taste. Presentation is artful (it is in an art museum, after all) and preparation is skilled; seared salmon comes to the table still creamy-textured in the center. The customized table-side guacamole is perfect for those who wish they could hold the onions or pour on the lime juice. The menu starts with a wide selection of first courses – tamales, REAL chalupas, calamari (the chef knows exactly how to cook these at their tender best), softshell crab with green papaya. They encourage patrons to order several of these and share as a meal, much like Spanish tapas. Their margaritas are impeccable. Open for lunch and dinner Tuesday through Saturday, and for Sunday brunch. $$.

Pisces, overlooking the harbor from the Hyatt Regency's roof, 300 Light St. (☎ 410-605-2835), is stylish in both decor and menu. Trust the fish to be perfectly cooked, the tuna blushing in the center, the scallops with a touch of translucence (sometimes served with portobellos and sweet pepper cream). To begin, sample the appetizers, which may include clams casino, tender calamari, shrimp tempura and always oysters. Known for their oysters, Pisces offers a choice, which may be Chincoteague, Malapeque or other prime source. Eat them from the raw bar selection or indulge in a sampler trio baked with such combinations as crab and spinach or leek and fennel. The pairing of flavors and textures is close to inspired, and the chef defies convention skillfully (his polenta takes on Santa Fe nuances with earthy white cornmeal) without overstepping. The pairing of baby spinach and Asian pear with toasted pecans and gorgonzola in a salad is brilliant. If you are lucky, you will be guided deftly through dinner by Seamus, a good-humored waiter with a rich (and genuine) brogue and a keen taste for which wine will complement each course. The wide choice of wines by the glass is designed for this flexibility. Not that you are likely to notice the smashing view once your first course arrives, but if you plan to be in Baltimore during the full moon, you will have the city's best view of the moonrise from a window table here. We were lucky on our last dinner there, to have both the full moon *and* Seamus. The raw bar opens at 5; the dining room serves 6-10:30. Dancing, Thursday-Saturday, after 10:30; $$-$$$.

At the eastern end of the Inner Harbor, on the way along the new Waterfront Promenade toward Fell's Point, is **Charleston**, 1000 Lancaster St.; ☎ 410-332-7373. Here down-home Southern meets haute cuisine, and the result is New American with an ever-so-slight and very well-bred Southern drawl. Salmon is encrusted with sesame seeds, venison is paired with andouille and grits with a red wine sauce, pepper-rubbed pork loin joins spoonbread over a tomato-cumin coulis. Tangy green tomato slices are fried crisp on the outside and used to "sandwich" lumps of delicately flavored crabmeat and lobster. While veal is not a meat that normally melts under your tongue, chef/owner Cindy Wolf chooses the finest quality and prepares it so lovingly that it's almost buttery in texture. One of the few restaurants in the region to offer a cheese course, Charleston takes it a step further by serving boutique cheeses from small farms in France and Italy. While each course is sparkling, Charleston doesn't stop there. The wine list, the setting, the hospitality and the service are equal to the kitchen. A highly professional waitstaff assures that this is a class act dining experience from start to finish. Most entrées range from $18 to $25.

■ Mount Vernon

The Helmand, at 806 N. Charles St. (☎ 410-752-0311), has long since outgrown its place as the latest curiosity. It's put Afghan cuisine on the map of Baltimore, using local ingredients like sea bass in ways no Chesapeake waterman ever imagined. Begin with the baby pumpkin appetizers – or you can also order some of the main dishes in appetizer portions to sample them. The surroundings are as appealing as the food, with sparkling white linen napery against a rosy setting. Prices are astonishingly low for the neighborhood and the consistent quality of the food.

Women's Industrial Exchange Tea Room, at 333 N. Charles St. (☎ 410-685-4388), offers inexpensive comfort foods in a comfortable lunchroom setting, served by cheerful staff that may include gracefully aging grandmothers who began working here as many as 50 years ago. The menu – with specialties like chicken salad, deviled eggs and tomato aspic – hasn't changed either. Open for breakfast and lunch only, Monday-Friday, 7-2, no credit cards.

Louie's Café, at 518 N. Charles St. (☎ 410-230-2998), makes the most of its stunning interior architecture and acoustics by devoting the entire window area of its two-story front section to a stage. Live jazz accompanies weekend brunch and evening meals, so if the menu and preparation does fall just a tad short of the decor, consider it the cover charge. Grilled venison, horseradish-crusted salmon, stuffed porkchop or mahi mahi baked in coconut milk are served with either couscous or garlic mashed potatoes. Appetizers include Japanese Okonomi Yaki, rare on US menus, and brunch features omelets, Belgian waffles and eggs with spicy deep-fried catfish. Most dinner entrées are $12 to $21, brunch dishes $8.

Kawasaki, at 413 N. Charles St. (☎ 410-659-7600), was the city's first Japanese restaurant, and has kept its sterling reputation for excellent sushi and an array of classics at moderate prices. The setting is authentic, too, with cushioned tatami mats and deft service in a subdued setting. They serve lunch and dinner Monday through Saturday.

WHERE TO FIND THE BEST CRAB CAKES

You'll find these Chesapeake delicacies whether you look for them or not, but we've collected a few places that are well known for them, adding our own favorites.

- **Faidley's**, in Lexington Market, ☎ 410-727-4898.

- **Nick's Inner Harbor Seafood**, Cross St. Market on Federal Hill, ☎ 410-685-2020, a lunch-hour and Saturday morning favorite.

- **Pierpoint**, Aliceanna St. in Fells Point, for an updated smoked version (see page 228).

- **Obrycki's**, a few blocks from Fell's Point, for regular and deviled (see page 229).

- **Café Hon**, on W. 36th St. in Hampden (see page 230), for the old-fashioned kind but more deftly seasoned.

- **Gertrude's**, in the Baltimore Museum of Art (see page 229), for some ethnic takes that lift the humble crab cake to immortality.

■ Little Italy

Perhaps we should note, for the benefit of visitors coming from Boston or other cities whose Italian quarter has embraced a wider variety of regional cuisines than the standard Sicilian menu of yore, that this is not usually the case in Baltimore. You are more likely to find the old standby dishes – veal marsala, shrimp diavola and spaghetti – than dishes from the Veneto or Tuscany. Your grandmother would recognize the menu in most – but not all. Several restaurants in this neighborhood will provide van transportation to and from your downtown hotel on nights when they are not busy.

Aldo's, at 306 South High St. (☎ 410-727-0700) is the most elegant of Little Italy's restaurants. Don't expect meatballs on this stylishly updated menu, but don't be surprised to see other traditional favorites. The chef-owner rightly believes that the comfort dishes of Italian cuisine are just too good to ignore, and he has taken them back to their roots, using the freshest local ingredients and lightening the preparations to let their natural flavors shine through. Although it is a rich beginning, we suggest at least sharing the outstanding escargot with shiitake mushrooms appetizer, following it with a salad of arugula and shaved Parmesan as a refreshing counterpoint. Entrées may include osso bucco, rarely found on a restaurant menu, served with porcini and wild mushroom risotto. Gnocchi are tender, served with lamb ragout, and agnoli are topped with truffle oil and shaved truffles. A good selection of wines is available by the glass, and the wine list represents a working cellar of about 3,500 bottles, many from small vineyards. Desserts are elegantly presented – a panna cotta (flan) is surrounded with a sunburst of sliced strawberries alternating with rays of mango syrup. The setting matches the menu – two narrow townhouses have been transformed into a small columned atrium and an adjoining dining room, while upstairs dining rooms have a clubby belle epoch air. Dinner is served daily from 5 pm and reservations are a good idea, imperative for Saturday evenings, which you should reserve as much as a week ahead; $$-$$$.

Dalesio's, at 899 Eastern Ave. (☎ 410-539-1965), recognizes that not everyone can pack away unlimited pasta in rich sauces. Their northern Italian menu specifies several dishes that are low in calories but high in flavor: chicken with mushrooms and sundried tomatoes in a veal demiglace, mustard-marinated shrimp with couscous and steamed vegetables, asparagus and sundried tomatoes over penne. The rest of the menu is as good, including scallops with prosciutto and mushrooms, crabmeat in Alfredo sauce, shellfish in Marsala, duck-filled ravioli, chicken with artichoke hearts in Marsala cream and veal with cream and Calvados. Most entrée prices are $14-$20.

For a predictably traditional Italian menu in a special-occasion atmosphere with good service, try **Ciao Bella**, 236 S. High St. (☎ 410-685-7733). The veal marsala – still one of the finest dishes in the Italian repertoire – is outstanding here, thin, white, moist and tender. The chef has other ways with veal, including stuffing it with prosciutto and provolone or pairing it with crabmeat or shrimp, as well as traditional saltimbocca or cacciatore. And your espresso, bless them, arrives hot. Most entrées range between $13 and $17, signature dishes $20-$25. Open daily for lunch on weekdays, dinner nightly until 10 (11 on Friday and Saturday).

Amicci's, at 231 High St. (☎ 410-528-1096), is a comfortable, homey place, family-run and family friendly. Begin with a scooped-out round loaf of bread filled with a luscious mixture of shrimp and garlic in creamy sauce. Share it with several people or you won't have room for the main event. Amicci's serves lunch and dinner daily, at prices well below most of their neighbors.

We are sorry to report that the old favorite Little Italy café **Vaccaro's**, 222 Abermarle St. (☎ 410-685-4905), has seen better days. It's no longer open for an early morning wake-up of cappuccino, but that's just as well. The last one we had there was a mug of murky coffee and milk, covered with a right-out-of-the-can swirl of artificial whipped topping. Two of these with biscotti weighed in at over $12, but the surly service was free. They may still crank up the big machine for the real stuff in the evening, but we don't suggest it for other times. We mention it only because you are bound to hear it recommended, based on its old and honorable reputation.

■ Fells Point

Hamilton's, in the Admiral Fell Inn at 888 S. Broadway (☎ 410-552-2195), is, in a word, superb. Chef Jeffrey Crise has an artist's eye for presentation, but never lets it become the purpose of a dish. His instinct for the nuances of flavors is as unerring as it is creative, pairing frogs legs with an onion and tomato marmalade, or foie gras in a tiny "sandwich" with apple and caramelized shallots. Those are just for starters. The main course may bring pheasant stuffed with wheatberries served over bitter greens, or spice-cured pork chop with Asian pears and couscous. A good selection of wines are available by the glass. And if you can still find room for dessert, there might be a warm apple and dried cranberry tart with ice cream made of buttermilk and honey. Most entrées are between $12 and $20. The atmosphere matches the menu, a gracious formal, but intimate dining room set in crystal and linens.

You can watch chef Nancy Longo at work in the open kitchen at **Pierpoint**, at 1822 Aliceanna St. (☎ 410-675-2080). But your attention will soon be drawn to the food in front of you – Eastern shore rabbit sausage as an appetizer, smoked crab cakes, crispy fried oysters served over fried tomatoes, lamb chops with Moroccan preserved lemon and cinnamon. Presentations are an art form in the small, intimate, if expensive, restaurant. Lunch and dinner daily, Sunday brunch; $$.

Bertha's, at 734 S. Broadway (☎ 410-327-5795), is renowned for mussels, but serves up a varied menu of other seafood dishes and a few meat entrées, which includes a chicken liver sauté and chicken with kumquat sauce. Oysters and other shellfish are paired with Smithfield ham in a cream sauce and the paella brims over with chicken, shellfish and sausage. But its the mussels we tuck into, served with the choice of eight different sauces, from tarragon to anchovy, all priced at $9 for a large bowl, with fresh Italian bread. Most other dishes range from $12 to $18. Sunday brunch (11:30-2) brings Welsh rarebit with country sausage or creamed oysters, $8. Baltimore-brewed and British beers are on tap. Open daily 11:30-11, until midnight on Friday and Saturday. Bertha's also serves "Mrs. McKinnon's Scottish Afternoon Tea," Monday through Saturday, 3-5, by reservation, a platter of fresh-baked scones, sweets and savories, $8.75.

Lista's, 1637 Thames St., at Brown's Wharf (☎ 410-327-0040), serves Mexican and Southwestern food with a Chesapeake twist. The usual south-of-the-border favorites are joined by creations such as Margarita shrimp, salmon al ajo, pecan-crusted catfish, or Potato Landscape, a mountain of garlic-mashed potatoes in a sea of meatless red chili. Small dishes include green chile with pork, catfish sandwiches and jalepeño burgers. Entrée prices range from $12 to $15. The upbeat, informal atmosphere is enhanced by live jazz Friday evenings, and tables spread onto the wharf in the summer. Open weekdays 11-10, weekends 11-11.

Ze Mean Bean Café, 1739 Fleet St. (☎ 410-675-5999), serves up Eastern European small plates and entrées, in varieties you'll look a long time to find elsewhere. Look for pierogi, blinchika (a crêpe filled with ricotta and wild mushrooms), kielbasa, a Reuben of roast pork loin and red cabbage, and a plate of grilled sausages that includes wild boar, pheasant and venison. It's not all borscht and brown bread, however. Mediterranean-influenced dishes such as rosemary-grilled chicken with panceta and Fontina on a panini share the menu. The Slavic dinner entrées are priced as low as $7; other specialties such as sea bass with fennel and polenta or pecan-encrusted chicken run $13-$20. Live music adds to the experience in the evening.

Obrycki's, a few blocks inland from Fell's Point at 1727 E. Pratt St. (☎ 410-732-6399), is one of the first places you will hear mentioned in a list of the city's old favorite crab houses. When Martha Stewart was looking for a place to talk about eating Chesapeake crabs, she chose this one. A bit fancier than the typical shore hall atmosphere, it's still a place where you can roll up your sleeves and crack into a pile of steamed hardshell crabs. Their spices are more peppery than most. Although half the experience is donning the goofy bib and attacking the armored crustaceans with a knife and hammer, you can choose a more genteel way to consume them, such as in crab imperial, marinara, stuffed, or over linguine. Most entrées are $15 to $24; open Monday-Saturday, noon-11; Sunday, noon-9:30. Obrycki's closes in the winter.

BALTIMORE FOOD SPECIALTIES

■ **Sour beef** – Baltimore's name for sauerbraten, served with dumplings

■ **Pit Beef** – slow-grilled top round, sliced paper-thin and served with onion and horseradish on rye or a kaiser roll

■ **Coddies** – fried codfish cakes served in a sandwich

■ **Lady Baltimore Cake** –white cake layered with pecans, dried fruit and white frosting

---

■ Bolton Hill and North

La Tesso Tana, 58 West Biddle St. (☎ 410-837-3630), in the ground floor of Abercrombie Badger B&B opposite the Meyerhof Symphony Hall, has chosen a pleasant middle ground between the Italian classics – veal Marsala, chicken piccata and calamari marinara, even spaghetti with meatballs – and the chef's own creations. These might include linguine tossed with shrimp and crab in a lobster cream sauce, or veal scallops with artichoke hearts, sundried tomatoes, toasted walnuts, capers and vermouth. Entrées range from $12 to $17; open Tuesday-Sunday, 11:30-midnight.

Gertrude's, in the Baltimore Museum of Art at 10 Art Museum Drive, off Charles St. (☎ 410-889-3399), features updated Chesapeake cuisine in a stylish atmosphere. The owner is John Shields, host of a popular PBS show on regional foods. Sole is stuffed with crab imperial, crab fills the lunchtime quiche, and at least two styles of crab cakes are offered. Our favorites are the crabettes, miniature crab cakes of sweet claw meat laced with ginger, serrano peppers and cilantro. The more traditional style is accompanied by garlic potatoes, apple-fennel coleslaw (an inspired combination) and roasted red bell pepper coulis. A late lunch here is the best way we know to rest feet tired after wandering through the art museum. Dinner, well worth the cab ride from town, might feature rockfish paired with goat cheese and asparagus spears or a Vietnamese-inspired five spice chicken with soba noodles and grilled vegetables. On Sundays and Wednesdays you can order Maryland pan-fried chicken with fresh buttermilk biscuits – real comfort food for those who think New American should go away. Desserts are a fine art: bread pudding is laced with rum; $$-$$$.

TEA FOR TWO

While Baltimore is not a town that puts on undue airs – in fact it rather prides itself on its proletariat upbringing – there are places where gentility reigns. You can have a proper afternoon tea at Gertrude's, Wednesday through Sunday from 3 until 4:30 pm. Selections to accompany your pot of real brewed tea include scones, tea bread, Gertrude's own stylish version of Lady Baltimore cake, clotted cream and their own lemon curd. Or you can add tea sandwiches or fresh strawberries drizzled in Grand Marnier. Prices range from $12 to $20, depending on the selection of accompaniments.

Café Hon, at 1002 W. 36th St. in Hampden (☎ 410-243-1230), is a cafe-restaurant with a small-town retro feel and gently updated versions of homestyle favorites: lasagna, chicken Parmesan, heart-healthy pasta (with or without chicken), "Much Better than Mom's" meatloaf and very good crab cakes. Blue plate specials on weeknights include fried chicken on Tuesdays and fish & chips on Fridays; on Mondays they offer one of the few chances you'll have to sample sour beef (see *Baltimore Food Specialties*, above). Entrée prices run from $9 to $13 (fish & chips is higher) and nothing on the long sandwich menu or hearty salad list tops $8. The atmosphere is informal and clearly neighborhood; the restaurant sponsors the annual search for "Miss Hon," and you might meet one there, unmistakable in big hair, capri pants and cat-eye glasses. The waitresses, of course, call you "hon," whatever your age. Open 7 am-9 pm, Monday through Thursday; Friday, 7 am-10 pm; Saturday, 9 am-10 pm; Sunday, 9 am-8 pm. And don't pass up the pie.

Nearby at 908 W. 36th St. in Hampden is **Holy Frijoles** (☎ 410-235-2326), where servings of black bean burritos and chicken chimichangas are huge and prices small. So is the place, and you may have to wait for a table.

North of Washington DC

Washington DC, although tightly bounded within its Federal District, sometimes seems to run right through the middle of suburban towns, so it's often hard to tell when you have left the District and entered Maryland. Maryland was once was heavily agricultural, but the growth of Washington, the Federal government, military operations and business have made

large tracts of suburban Maryland farmland into housing, apartment developments, and shopping centers. This doesn't mean that there are no adventures and no open space to be found, however. Federal, state and local governments have created parks and greenways that preserve many of the best wild places, especially along streams. In Montgomery County alone there are 27,000 acres of parkland.

Geography & History

This area is one of low rolling hills immediately east and north of the nation's Capital. Of the three counties in this area, **Prince George's** is the oldest, formed in 1695. **Montgomery County**

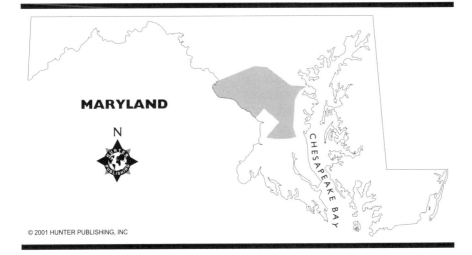

MARYLAND

N

CHESAPEAKE BAY

was not established until the eve of the **American Revolution**, in 1776. Only 15 years later it ceded 36 square miles of its territory to the United States as part of the new Capital. While the crops originally grown on this rich farmland were tobacco, during the revolution wheat growing began here and the area became known as the breadbasket of the Revolution.

In August of 1814, British army and naval troops sailed up the Chesapeake Bay and into the Patuxent River, disembarking and continuing northwest through Prince George's and Montgomery counties toward Washington. Federal troops opposing them were not only inadequate in number but they were poorly equipped and led. On August 24, 1814 Federal troops engaged the British in battle at Bladensburg and quickly abandoned the field. They left so rapidly that the battle became known as the Bladensburg Races. The British then entered the city and took revenge before heading off to Baltimore. But they failed to capture Baltimore, and their forces soon withdrew.

DID YOU KNOW?

President Madison's decision to go to war with Britain in 1812 was not universally popular. The Federal Republican, a Baltimore paper whose editor was Alexander Hanson, opposed the war in print. Hanson's editorial caused a riot, and a second riot when he repeated his attack. During that second one, Hanson and his supporters were put into the local jail for their protection, but rioters broke in and severely beat them, killing several of his followers. Hanson barely escaped with his life, and he subsequently retired to Montgomery County, which elected him to the US Congress.

The area continued to be an agricultural success. In 1828 the **Chesapeake and Ohio Canal Company** was formed and soon began the excavation of a canal along the banks of the Potomac River in Montgomery County. To the east of the city the population remained fairly stable, with slavery slightly more prevalent in this tobacco part of the state than in the north and west. During the **Civil War** the citizens vacillated between Union and Confederacy, many from these towns going to Virginia to join the Confederate army. Montgomery County had three battles on its soil, Harrison's Island in 1861, Point of Rocks in 1862 and Rockville in 1863. When John Wilkes Booth fled Washington in 1865 after shooting the President, he headed into Prince George's County, stopping to have his broken leg set and to get supplies at the Surrat Tavern.

After the Civil War, life resumed much as before, but this changed with the growth of the federal government during World War I. Close to the nation's capital, the influence of the city was felt in the countryside as federal agencies and the military expanded and housing expanded to keep pace.

The military was interested in the flight of the **Wright brothers**, and in 1909 the Army established the first flight school at College Park, where Wilbur Wright taught two soldiers the art of flying. This was the birth of the US Air Force. Lt. Henry "Hap" Arnold taught flight here in 1911 and in 1918 the first air mail flights took off from here.

World War II and the years that followed brought the most changes to this area, however, as the economic recovery and war effort brought increasingly large numbers of people into the Washington area. Some of the earliest work on space flight and rocketry was done at the **Goddard Space Flight Center**. Today people from the area work not only in Washington, but in the many federal agencies with offices and facilities throughout Montgomery and Prince George's counties.

Getting Here & Getting Around

The lands included in this chapter form a great semi-circle around the city of Washington DC and extend almost to the city of Baltimore. Included are **Montgomery** and **Howard** counties and the northern part of **Prince George's County**. Just a few miles out of Washington the infamous **"Beltway"** forms a circle around the City starting at the Potomac River in Bethesda and circling east and south through Silver Spring, College Park, Seat Pleasant/Largo, past Suitland and Andrews Air Force Base and on through Oxon Hill to the south of the city, before it passes over the Potomac into Alexandria, Virginia.

The Beltway is **I-495**, which is joined by **I-95** for its entire eastern and southern sections, as that North-South highway bypasses Washington. I-95 connects the city to Baltimore, joining the Beltway at College Park. The **Baltimore-Washington Parkway** (MD Route 295) parallels I-95 between the two cities. **US-50/301** leads east to Annapolis and **Route 4** connects the Capital to the mid-section of the Chesapeake Bay.

Montgomery and Prince George's County can be reached from Washington on the **Metro**, the city's public transportation system. The **Red Line** starts at Shady Grove and heads into the city via Rockville, Bethesda and Friendship Heights. The **Green Line** leads from Washington to College Park and the station is close enough so you could walk to Lake Artemisia, the hiker/biker trail and the Air Museum. The opposite is true, too, and many travelers prefer to stay well outside the city and take the commuter line into the city for sightseeing without having to stay there.

North of Washington DC

North of Washington

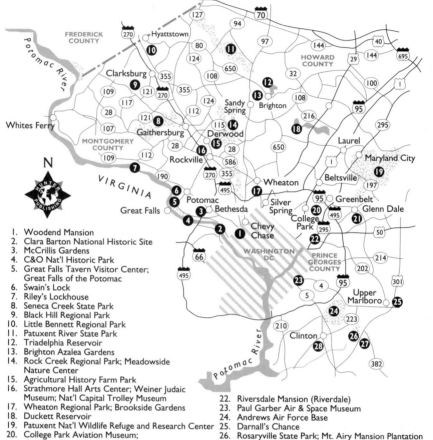

1. Woodend Mansion
2. Clara Barton National Historic Site
3. McCrillis Gardens
4. C&O Nat'l Historic Park
5. Great Falls Tavern Visitor Center;
   Great Falls of the Potomac
6. Swain's Lock
7. Riley's Lockhouse
8. Seneca Creek State Park
9. Black Hill Regional Park
10. Little Bennett Regional Park
11. Patuxent River State Park
12. Triadelphia Reservoir
13. Brighton Azalea Gardens
14. Rock Creek Regional Park; Meadowside
    Nature Center
15. Agricultural History Farm Park
16. Strathmore Hall Arts Center; Weiner Judaic
    Museum; Nat'l Capital Trolley Museum
17. Wheaton Regional Park; Brookside Gardens
18. Duckett Reservoir
19. Patuxent Nat'l Wildlife Refuge and Research Center
20. College Park Aviation Museum;
    Goddard Space Center
21. Marietta (Glenn Dale)

22. Riversdale Mansion (Riverdale)
23. Paul Garber Air & Space Museum
24. Andrews Air Force Base
25. Darnall's Chance
26. Rosaryville State Park; Mt. Airy Mansion Plantation
27. Merkle Wildlife Sanctuary
28. His Lordship's Kindness; Surrat House & Tavern

Information Sources

? **Conference and Visitors Bureau of Montgomery County**, 12900 Middlebrook Rd., Suite 1400, Germantown, MD 20874, ☎ 800-925-0880, www.cvbmontc21o.com.

Howard County Tourism Council, PO Box 9, 8267 Main St., Ellicott City, MD 21041-0009; ☎ 800-288-8747, www.howardcountymdtour.com.

Prince George's County Conference & Visitors Bureau, 9200 Basil Ct., Suite 101, Largo, MD 20774; ☎ 301-925-8300 or 888-925-8300.

Adventures

■ Parks & Natural Areas

 Seneca Creek State Park is one of many the state has created along the thread of a stream, in this case protecting Great Seneca Creek and providing a rural environment in an urban area. The 6,100-acre park has, in addition to the creek, 90-acre Clopper Lake. There are extensive hiking and bike trails in the park, rental shelters, fishing, canoeing and boating, including rentals, as well as picnic and playground facilities. From I-270, take Route 117 (Clopper Rd.) from Gaithersburg; the entrance is just beyond Long Draught Rd. on the left, at 11950 Clopper Rd., Gaithersburg 20878; ☎ 301-924-2127.

Merkle Wildlife Sanctuary is most exciting in the fall, when it becomes a feeding place for thousands of Canada geese. There are 1,670 acres of wild land to explore here along the trails that wind through the sanctuary. Even when the geese are not plentiful it is a good place for birding and hiking; the visitor center has trail and wildlife information. From US 301, south of Upper Marlboro, take Croom Rd. (Route 382) east and follow the signs. The Sanctuary is on Croom Rd.; ☎ 301-888-1410. Close by and a good place for a picnic is **Rosaryville State Park**, off US 301 south of Upper Marlboro. Rosaryville is the site of the **Mount Airy Mansion Plantation**; ☎ 301-888-1410.

Locally Operated Parks

The Montgomery County Department of Parks and the Prince George's County Department of Parks and Recreation operate numerous parks throughout the region. The following list includes the major ones. For information on any of the parks, contact the appropriate county office. In **Montgomery County**, ☎ 301-495-2525 for information and permits, TDD 301-495-2575, handicapped accessibility 301-650-2867, TDD 301-495-2576. In **Prince George's County**, information may be obtained from ☎ 301-699-2407, TDD 301-277-8456; sports 301-699-2400, TDD 301-699-2404; permits 301-699-2415.

In Montgomery County:

■ **Little Bennett Regional Park**, 23701 Frederick Rd., Clarksburg, ☎ 301-972-6581, is a large park on the northern border with Frederick County. It offers equestrian/hiker trails, a picnic area, playground and camping. Some of its facilities are handicapped-accessible.

■ **Black Hill Regional Park** is off Route 121 southwest of Clarksburg. The Visitors Center is open daily in the summer, but only on weekend afternoons in the spring and fall. The park maps, instead of being in an accessible box outside, as in most parks, are locked inside a glassed entry. You can see the stack of them there, but can't get to them when the center is closed (maybe it's a scheme to save paper); ☎ 301-916-0220.

AUTHOR TIP

The Black Hill Regional Park Visitors Center has brochures and check-lists for the dozens of dragonfly and damselfly varieties seen there.

Planned activities include hikes, seasonal bird programs and nature cruises on the pontoon boat. Ongoing activities are picnicking, fishing, boating (rentals and launches) bicycling, hiking, horseback riding (BYOH), exercise course and Nature Center. These are held on weekend afternoons, usually from May through September only, and cost $2 to $4. The park has a playground and picnic pavilions. 20930 Lake Ridge Drive, Boyds, ☎ 301-972-3476 (Visitor Center), 301-972-9396 (office).

Black Hill Regional Park has docks that are handicapped-accessible.

■ To reach **Rock Creek Regional Park**, follow Route 28 east of Rockville then take Avery Rd. The north section of the park has most of the activities, but the south entrance leads to fishing, a trail and the Nature Center. This is not the Rock Creek Park of Washington, DC, but does connect to it via a bike path. The park has two small lakes, Lakes Needwood (north part) and Bernard Frank (south part). Activities are picnicking, archery, fishing, boating, hiking, and bicycling, and there is a playground. The address is 6700 Needwood Rd., Rockville; ☎ 301-948-5053.

■ **Cabin John Regional Park**. Follow Seven Locks Rd. south from Rockville, then go left on Democracy Boulevard to the south entrance, or continue and take a left onto Westlake Rd. for access to the northern part. The picnic area is close to the miniature train ride and playground; the campground is on the north end as well. The south entrance from Democracy Boulevard leads to the hiking trails and to the Locust Grove Nature Center. There is also ice skating and tennis; 7400 Tuckerman Lane, Rockville, ☎ 301-299-4555.

■ **Wheaton Regional Park** can be reached from Georgia Avenue (Route 97) via Arcola Rd. (to Nairn Rd.), or from Shorefield Rd. in the town of Wheaton. Brookside Nature Center is located in the park and close by are the Brookside Gardens. Along with these two attractions, the park has a miniature train ride and carousel, playground, picnicking, ice skating, fishing and equestrian facilities with trails, at 2000 Shorefield Road, Wheaton; ☎ 301-946-7033.

In Northern Prince George's County

■ Near Langley Park, the northern part of **Adelphi Regional Park** is reached from Riggs Rd. An exercise course here is near the historic Adelphi Mill. Route 212, and University Boulevard (Route 193) leads to the archery, picnic area, swimming and other facilities. Part of the Northwest Branch hiker/biker trail is within the park, which is cut by the Northwest Branch of the Anacostia River. For information, call the Prince George's Regional Parks number above.

■ Close by you will find **College Park Regional Park**, with access from Berwyn Rd. and Calvert Rd. off Kenilworth (Route 201) in College Park, close to the airport and Aviation Museum (see page 250). This is a fairly large park along the Northeast Branch of the Anacostia River with many varied facilities. One of these is the College Park Airport, one of the oldest in the world and where the Wright Brothers taught the US Army airmen to fly. See *Historic Sites*, below, for the Air Museum. Elsewhere in the park are swimming, skating, tennis and a playground. The **Northeast Branch hiker/biker trail** passes through and along **Lake Artemisia Conservation Area**, which is popular for walks, fishing and boating. For information call the Prince George's Regional Parks number above.

■ **Watkins Regional Park** is a smaller park on Route 214 east of Largo (take Watkins Park Drive, Route 556, south to the entrance. This park offers a multitude of activities, including the second Denzel carousel from Chesapeake Beach (the first one burned), minus one kangaroo, which stayed at the Railway Museum in Chesapeake Beach. A miniature train, an animal farm and nature center, playground, golf and other sports round out the activities. There are also hiker/biker trails around the outer edges of the park. Information, ☎ 301-249-6900; for the carousel, miniature golf and train, ☎ 301-390-9224.

KID-FRIENDLY

The regional parks of Montgomery and Prince George's counties have some special treats for kids. Cabin John Regional Park, Wheaton Regional Park, National Capital Regional Park and Watkins Regional Park offer rides on miniature trains. National Capital is at 1313 Bonifant Rd. in Silver Spring (☎ 301-384-6088). At Wheaton Regional Park and Watkins Regional Park they can climb onto old-fashioned carousels.

■ On Foot

Hiking

 The **C&O Canal** towpath follows the historic canal from Washington along the banks of the Potomac all the way to Frederick County in the northwest corner of the area covered by this chapter. The terrain is level, passing through forested river banks. The most scenic attraction of the entire 184-mile towpath is in this section, as the Potomac plunges over **Great Falls** in a pounding froth of white water. **Great Falls Tavern Visitor Center**, **Riley's Lockhouse** and **Swain's Lock** are landmarks that make a hike along this section interesting. Swain's Lock can be reached from River Rd. (Route 190) in Potomac.

Black Hill Regional Park, near Clarksburg, has a number of trails, some of which follow the shore of **Little Seneca Lake**. The lake has three arms and, although the trails of the east side are accessible from the main park entrance, those on the west have a separate entrance. From Clarksburg Rd. north, turn east on West Old Baltimore Rd. for the main entrance, west for the west trails. The west trails and some of the east trails are hikers/equestrian and others are hiker/biker.

Nearby, north of Clarksburg, is **Little Bennett Regional Park** on Frederick Rd., where horseback riders share some of the 14 miles of trails. The park regularly schedules nature walks and night hikes. Hikers will be glad to learn that bicycles are prohibited on all of their trails.

Rock Creek Regional Park has a nice hikers-only trail that goes around Lake Bernard Frank and beyond. Access this from the southern park entrance. Along the way are the **Nature Center** and the **Pioneer Homestead**. This park also connects up to the Rock Creek Park hiker/biker trail that leads all the way into the city, following the banks of the creek. It's about 14 miles to the city limits.

Southwest of Rockville is **Cabin John Regional Park**, which also has a hiker-only trail, partially along a stream that flows through the park. Use the park entrance off Democracy Boulevard, where the Nature Center is.

In Chevy Chase, just over the northern DC border, is the headquarters of the Audubon Naturalist Society, **Woodend Mansion**, designed by architect John Russell Pope and built in 1928. The mansion sits on a 40-acre tract with self-guided trails, gardens and greenhouses. It is at 8940 Jones Mill Road, Chevy Chase, ☎ 301-652-8107; Audubon Society, 301-652-9188. Open Monday through Friday, 9-5.

Smaller **Wheaton Regional Park** has hiker/biker trails that can be accessed from the Shorefield Rd. or Nairn Rd. entrances. **Watkins Regional Park**, east of Largo, has a series of connected hiker/biker trails that connect its attractions, including the miniature train and carousel, making it a good choice for families with younger children.

The streams that drain this area all flow toward the Potomac and Anacostia Rivers, and along these rivers several **Stream Valley Parks** have been created. These run through narrow protected areas along the banks, often leading to parks and other recreational opportunities. Since these are hiker/biker trails, see *On Wheels* below for information on these interesting country trails in an urban environment.

More opportunities, close to the District, are in **Seneca Creek State Park**, just west of Gaithersburg. The park has a number of trails that follow Great Seneca Creek through lands that have been designated to protect the stream. There is also a trail around 90-acre Clopper Lake.

■ On Wheels

 The **Maryland State Bike Trail** passes through this area, along the runways of the historic College Park Airport, and a path connects it to the air museum there, and to the 94th Aero Squadron Restaurant (see *Where to Eat*, below). The trail continues along the shore of **Lake Artemisia**, through a park with fishing docks.

Each of the several **Stream Valley Parks** bears the name of the stream that it parallels, and these parks offer some enjoyable rides over trails shared with hikers. These trails do not loop and, once off them, you will usually be in heavy traffic so it's best to plan on an out-and-back trip. These trails are hard-surfaced, mostly asphalt and the terrain is not difficult.

The longest of these is **Rock Creek Stream Valley Park**, which is an extension of Rock Creek Park in the District of Columbia. It stretches about 14 miles from the DC border to Rock Creek Regional Park northeast of Rockville. The trail is essentially a country ride through the suburbs of Washington north of the city, with trees around you but city noises intruding. Enter it at the East West Highway, Route 410, east of Connecticut Avenue (Route 185) near Bethesda.

Another option is **Sligo Creek Stream Valley Park** off the northwest corner of the District in Silver Spring. You can access it in Tacoma Park. From East West Highway (Route 410) in Silver Spring, take Carroll Avenue east, the park is on the right. This hiker/biker winds along the banks of Sligo Creek through Silver Spring and on into Wheaton, ending at Wheaton Regional Park. The distance is about six miles.

Still in the same general area but in College Park is **Northwest Branch Stream Valley Park**, whose trail is about five miles long and runs through Adelphi Regional Park, then on to a point near the Beltway northeast of Silver Spring. It follows the Northwest Branch of the Anacostia River. Pick it up as it crosses the East West Highway, Route 410, south of Silver Spring.

One of the locks along the C&O Canal.

Farther on down Route 410, just south of Route 1 at College Park Regional Park, you can pick up the hiker/biker trail that follows the banks of the Northeast Branch of the Anacostia River through **Indian Creek Stream Valley Park** to Greenbelt Avenue. Along the way, it skirts historic College Park Airport and the eastern shore of Lake Artemisia. This trail is about three miles.

By far the longest bicycle and hiking trail around is the **C&O Canal**, which follows the towpath of the old historic canal from Washington along the banks of the Potomac all the way to Frederick County in the northwest corner of the area covered by this chapter. The terrain is level, as you would expect, and en route you pass **Great Falls**, which even at low water is a torrent of whitewater, the **Great Falls Tavern Visitor Center**, and **Riley's Lockhouse**. **Bicycle rentals** are available at Swain's Lock, off River Rd. (Route 190) in Potomac.

Almost equidistant from both Washington and Baltimore is the **Patuxent National Wildlife Refuge**, just off the parkway. The **North Tract** is off Route 198 and is the less developed of the two. There are about 20 miles of trails and roadways over what used to be an artillery test firing range. Today it offers miles of walking and hiking through a large forested area filled with wildlife. You must check in at the Visitor Contact Center and pick up your map and authorizations. There is also a **South Tract** with more walking and hiking available. This part of the park is the location of the **National Wildlife Visitor Center**. Walks here include wildlife viewing blinds and other focused opportunities to appreciate the inhabitants. (see *Cultural & Eco-Travel Experiences*, below).

■ On Water

Canoeing & Kayaking

The **C&O Canal** is filled with water along the entire lower stretch, from Georgetown to Violets Lock (Lock 23). Only one lock needs portage in the six miles between Swain's and Violets Locks, and the flatwater distance downstream from Swain's Lock reaches all the way to Great Falls, a distance of two miles without a lock.

On Thursday evenings at Swain's Lock (Lock 21), off River Rd. (Route 190) in Potomac, the **Canoe Cruisers** (☎ 301-299-3613) teach basic canoeing. This introductory lesson includes use of the canoes at Swain's Lock (☎ 301-299-3613), which are available for rent at other times as well.

AUTHOR TIP

*A number of the streams in this area can be run in canoes or kayaks. Each has its own conditions, water level variables and classifications. Some streams to investigate further are **Northwest Branch** through College Park, the **Anacostia River** from Bladensburg to the Potomac, portions of **Rock Creek** in Maryland and the District, **Great Seneca Creek**, **Little Seneca Creek**, and **Bennett Creek** near Clarksburg. Many of these must be run within a few days of heavy rainfall, some are whitewater, and others have obstacles, such as fences. For more information on these streams see pages 126-137 of* Maryland and Delaware Canoe Trails *by Edward Gertler, Seneca Press.*

Black Hill Regional Park (see page 235-236) offers one of the best flatwater opportunities in the area. A large part of Little Seneca Lake is within the park. The lake has three arms and thus quite a bit of differing scenery. It is open 6 am to sunset. The boat ramp is on Black Hill Rd (fee charged), off Lake Ridge Drive, the primary road servicing the park. Canoes, rowboats and paddleboats can be rented at the park docks behind the Visitor Center at the end of Lake Ridge Drive. From June through August, rentals are available Monday through Thursday from noon until 6 pm, and Friday through Sunday from 6:30 am to 6 pm. In May and September, rental hours are Friday through Sunday, 6:30 am to 6 pm. Rates are $5 an hour or $19 a day, cash only. Route 117 at Exit 10 off I-270 in Gaithersburg (Clopper Rd.) leads to Boyds, where you go right onto Route 121. As you cross the lake you'll see a non-trailer boat ramp on the right (fee charged); for the other boat launch inside the park, continue up the road and take a right turn onto Old Baltimore Rd.

Also on Clopper Rd. (Route 117) is **Seneca Creek State Park**, which has **Clopper Lake** as its centerpiece. You can bring your own craft or rent canoes, rowboats and paddleboats. Paddleboat tours run on a regular basis. Follow the directions for Black Hill Regional Park from the south. The park entrance is just north of Long Draught Rd. and south of the bridge over Seneca Creek. Boat rentals operate from May through September.

North of Washington DC

*If you are serious about canoeing or kayaking in the area, contact **Blue Ridge Voyageurs Canoe Cruisers Association**, PO Box 15747, Chevy Chase 20825, for information on area streams and programs offered.*

Along the Potomac north of the city you can take the last ferry across the river. The ferry holds 24 cars but, if you're taking yours, avoid the morning and evening rush hours. **White's Ferry** allows you to cross from Poolesville to Leesburg, Virginia on the *Jubal A. Early* any day of the week from 5 am to 11 pm. At White's you can also rent canoes and johnboats. They are at 24801 White's Ferry Rd., Dickerson, MD, ☎ 301-349-5200.

Fishing

Lake Artemisia is part of College Park Regional Park, just a few miles east of Washington. A path from the parking lot leads to its fishing dock, which is handicapped-accessible. You can reach Lake Artemisia via Berwyn Rd. and Calvert Rd. off Kenilworth Ave. (Route 201) in College Park close to the airport and Museum. Follow the brown signs to Branch Park Rd., which circles back under the highway, parallel to the rail tracks, and ends in the parking area for the park. This is a well-used green space surrounding a stocked pond. The area is also reachable via the Metro Green Line, College Park station.

Seneca Creek State Park provides good fishing. Off Route 117 west of Gaithersburg, you can land largemouth bass, crappie, catfish and bluegill. Rowboat rentals are available at the landing in the state park from May through September. (See *Parks & Wildlife Sanctuaries* above for directions.)

There are several fishing options at **Patuxent National Wildlife Refuge**, mid-way between Washington and Baltimore (see *Cultural & Eco-Travel Experiences* below). Valid State of Maryland fishing licenses are required for persons 16 or over. In the North Tract, fishing is allowed at New Marsh, Little Patuxent River, Cattail Pond, Bailey Bridge Marsh, Rieve's Pond and Lake Allen. Species you are likely to encounter are catfish, pickerel, smallmouth and largemouth bass, shad, bluegill, trout, striped bass and the scourge yellow perch. Get permits, passes, maps and other formalities out of the way at the Visitor Contact Center. In the South Tract of the Patuxent off Route 197, fishing is allowed with a special permit obtainable at the Visitor Center and there is a fishing pier. Here, too, you must hold a valid state of Maryland fishing license. For directions and hours, see *Cultural & Eco-Travel Experiences* below.

Boat Tours

The *Canal Clipper* is a replica canal boat with its cabin and deck structures replaced by seating for passengers. Beginning at Great Falls Tavern,

Swallow Falls, in Garrett County.

Above, left: *Drane House, in Accident.* Above, right: *Cart at Furnace Town Historic Site in Snow H*
Opposite: *The historic Episcopal Church in Westminster, built in 1854.*
Below: *Cypress trees along the Sassafras River, Maryland's Upper Eastern Shore.*

Above: *Canoes at Swain's Lock, along the C&O Canal near Great Falls, Maryland.*
Opposite: *Doorway of a private residence in Annapolis.*
Below: *A pristine tidal creek along Virginia's Eastern Shore.*

Above: *Swans at Hooper Island, along Maryland's Central Eastern Shore.*
Opposite: *The herb garden at Smallwood's Retreat, in Marbury.*
Below: *Watching eagles at Blackwater National Wildlife Refuge, Church Creek, Maryland.*

it rises through the canal lock, travels up and back along a watered section of the canal and descends through the lock again. The boat is pulled along the towpath by a team of mules, just as the original boats were in the glory days of the canal. Costumed lock keepers and boatmen work the boat and an entertaining guide spins tales and sings songs about the canal. The canal boat operates from mid-April through October; ☎ 301-299-3613.

LOCAL LORE

Guides on the canal boat sing a verse that makes it easy to remember the ancestry of the mule:

If your dad was a donkey
And your ma was a horse,
Then you'd be
A mule, of course.

■ On Horseback

While horses are everywhere in this area, it is difficult to ride unless you have your own. The following places might be worth checking with, however, since they would know of any new stables or riding programs. **Maryland Horse Center** 14309 Quince Orchard Rd., North Potomac (☎ 301-948-8585); **Meadowbrook Stables**, Meadowbrook Lane and East-West Highway, Chevy Chase (☎ 301-589-9026); **Wheaton Regional Park Stables**, 1101 Glenallen Avenue, Wheaton (☎ 301-622-3311); or the **Prince George's Equestrian Center**, 14955 Pennsylvania Avenue, Upper Marlboro (☎ 301-952-4740).

There is an equestrian center at Wheaton Regional Park (off Glenallen Rd.) and horse trails in the adjacent Northwest Branch Recreational Area. Black Hill Regional Park has a system of trails that are shared with hikers. **Little Bennett Regional Park**, 23701 Frederick Rd., Clarksburg, in the northern part of Montgomery County, also has an extensive equestrian/hiker trail system (☎ 301-972-6581).

If you are in the area and trailering a horse or two, you will want to reserve a beautiful room for yourself and another in the barn for your horses. You can do this by prior arrangement at **The Inn at Paternal Gift Farm**, 13555 Route 108, Highland 20777; ☎ 301-845-3353. For a complete description, see page 256.

North of Washington DC

Turkey Point Lighthouse in Elk Neck State Park.

Cultural & Eco-Travel Experiences

■ Natural Areas

 The outstanding natural wonder of this area is the **Great Falls of the Potomac**, great indeed, as it drops into a mass of jagged rocks, where it carves a gorge. Bald eagles nest in a sycamore tree on Olmstead Island, which can be reached by a pedestrian bridge from the Great Falls Tavern Visitors Center. Follow River Rd. (Route 190) to Potomac, then follow Falls Rd. to MacArthur Boulevard; ☎ 301-299-3613.

Agricultural History Farm Park, 18400 Muncaster Rd., Derwood (☎ 301-924-4141), has an activity center, a farmhouse and barns, where special weekend programs are held. These focus on different aspects of rural and farm history, and often include hands-on programs on tinsmithing, buttermaking, chestnut roasting and candle dipping. Most are free, but some which require materials, such as tinsmithing and candle dipping, carry a modest $1 fee.

> CAUTION
>
> *It's really easy to confuse Rock Creek Regional Park with the other Rock Creek Park – same creek, but different parks. Rock Creek Park is a National Park Service property in Washington DC. Rock Creek Regional Park is a park system in Montgomery County with a number of locations, including the Agricultural History Farm Park. On the state highway map, it is labeled simply as Rock Creek Park, compounding the confusion.*

Between College Park and Fort George Meade, on the east side of the Baltimore-Washington Parkway, lies the vast expanse – more than 12,750 acres – of the **Patuxent Wildlife Research Center**, the only national refuge that is also a wildlife research center. It is almost exactly mid-way between the two cities. Even though large parts of it was an artillery range until the early 1990s, it comprises one of the largest contiguous protected forests in the eastern flyway and a vital tool for the study of wildfowl, their habitats and environmental requirements. The **North Tract** is accessible via Route 198 from either the Baltimore-Washington Parkway (Route 198 is Fort Meade Rd., 1.4 miles) or I-95 (where it is Gorman Rd. before it becomes Fort Meade Rd.). Visitors must sign in and obtain a permit at the Visitor Contact Center.

The 8,100 acres of the North Tract have nearly 20 miles of roads and trails for hiking and biking and several ponds for anglers (see *Fishing* above). Guided bird and nature walks are conducted by staff members throughout the year. Note that there is also a hunting season in the refuge that is the same as the state season. The North Tract is open daily throughout the year at 8, closing at 4:30 November through February, 6 pm in March, 8 pm April through August, 7 pm in September, and at 6:30 in October.

In the South Tract of the Patuxent Refuge lies the **National Wildlife Center**, just off the Baltimore-Washington Parkway (Route 295) southeast of Laurel on Route 197. The Visitor Center is huge, with over 13,000 square feet of exhibit space showing thought-provoking interpretive exhibits on global concerns, habitats, endangered species and the life cycles of wild animals. On most weekends the center screens free wildlife films at 11. They also have viewing pods where you can use scopes and binoculars to watch wildlife. The guided tram tour allows visitors to learn about the surrounding lands and their role in the health of the environment. Tram tours start the last week of June and continue to September at 11:30 and 12:30, 1:30 and 2:30, with additional trams at 3:30 on weekends. In the fall the tours are on weekends only, but check for space on reserved group tours, which are often not quite full. Cost is $2 adults, $1 child and seniors.

The South Tract also has several miles of trails for walking, with wildlife viewing blinds. Fishing is available in **Cash Lake** from a pier and dock. The center is part of the Department of the Interior and serves as a research facility to help them manage refuges throughout the country containing more than 93 million acres. Most of the facilities at the Center are handicapped-accessible. 10901 Scarlet Tanager Loop, Laurel 20708; ☎ 301-497-5760, TDD 301-497-5779, fax 301-497-5765, www.fws.gov.

■ Gardens

Brighton Azalea Gardens is spectacular in the spring. There are more than 22,000 azalea bushes that break into a riot of bloom along with a number of other plants. It's a nice place to visit and picnic at anytime but especially when the azaleas are blooming. Brighton Dam Rd., Brookeville; ☎ 301-774-9124. It's east of Brighton near the Triadelphia Reservoir.

Brookside Gardens is a part of Wheaton Regional Park (see *Parks & Natural Areas* for park information) and is just over 20 years old. Wide, wheelchair-accessible paths wind through a landscape that varies between open woodlands, manicured lawns and carefully tended flower beds. The woodlands are filled with rare trees, many of them evergreen, which makes this a lovely place to walk even after the flowers have stopped blooming. The glass conservatory is especially appealing then, too, with its lush tropical plants and trees. In April and May the grounds are bright with azaleas, dogwood, flowering fruit trees and bulb displays. From then until early October the gardens are filled with a succession of perennials and annuals. In the fall, leaves of dogwood and Japanese maple add color, along with the bright berries of viburnum, barberry and holly.

A staff of 30 full-time gardeners and about 250 volunteers keep the gardens looking the way we'd like ours to look. Few visitors can resist patting the lemon balm or other sweet-smelling plants in the fragrance garden, before they enter the serene nine-acre Gude Garden. Surrounding a pond with bright orange carp swimming in it, this landscape has the feel of a Japanese garden, accented by an island and an open teahouse overlooking the water.

Workshops for adults cover everything from planting a wildflower garden to creating hanging baskets, while children's events include Saturday morning storytime followed by garden-related crafts.

KID-FRIENDLY

At Brookside Gardens, Phil and Rhoda Dendron logo signs highlight frequent special children's exhibitions or programs in the gardens, which might center around themes such as outer space or the awakening of the gardens in the spring.

Also look for the viburnum garden, aquatic garden, rose garden and other specialty gardens on the grounds. From the District, take Georgia Avenue, or take Exit 31 on the Beltway north of the District onto Route 97 north (Georgia Ave.) Pass Wheaton and Arcola Avenue and the park will be on the right before Randolph Rd., at 1800 Glenallen Avenue, Wheaton; ☎ 301-949-8230 and 8231; www.mc-mncppc.org/parks/brookside/index.htm. Free; open sunup to sundown every day except Christmas. The glass conservatory is open 10-5, and the gift shop from 10-4.

Like the Brighton Azalea Gardens, **McCrillis Gardens** are best seem in the spring, although they are a cooling place to visit all summer. These gardens feature 750 varieties of azalea and a number of rhododendrons that also bloom in the spring. This cool shady spot covers about five acres and is open all year daily from 10 am to sunset. It is off Bradley Boulevard, just east of Route 190, at 6910 Greentree Rd., Bethesda; ☎ 301-365-5728.

Woodend Mansion, the Audubon Society quarters, has gardens and greenhouses that are open to visitors. It was designed by architect John Russell Pope and built in 1928 on a 40-acre tract at 8940 Jones Mill Rd., Chevy Chase; ☎ 301-652-8107; Audubon Society 301-652-9188. It's open Monday through Friday 9-5.

Meadowside Nature Center, in Rock Creek Regional Park, occupies about 500 acres. In addition to their raptor aviary, there is a butterfly garden, a hummingbird garden and miles of nature trails. They have an activity center and a house and barn. The Extension Service, 4-H and Soil Conservation Service have offices here; they, and friends of the center, sponsor weekend programs for people of all ages. It is in the east arm of the park near Lake Bernard Frank. From Route 115, Muncaster Mill Rd., take

Avery Rd. south past the entrance to Lake Needwood and look for the sign at 5100 Meadowside Lane, Rockville; ☎ 301-924-4141.

■ Crafts

Two promoters operate several major craft and art shows during the spring and fall, featuring artists and craftsmen from around the country. Dates are approximate, since they vary from year to year. **National Crafts, Ltd.** usually runs a show Monday through Wednesday during the third full week of October at the Montgomery County Fairgrounds in Gaithersburg, near I-270. This show has over 425 exhibitors; ☎ 717-369-4810. **Sugarloaf Art Fairs** has five shows, each Monday through Wednesday, except the November show, which starts on Sunday. Their season begins the second full week of April with a show at the Montgomery County Fairgrounds in Gaithersburg, and ends with two pre-Christmas shows, Thanksgiving week and the second full week of December. Discount tickets for these events are available at ☎ 800-210-9990. For information, ☎ 301-990-1400.

Events

JULY: Both Gaithersburg and Wheaton are known for their **Independence Day** celebrations. One is held at the Montgomery County Fairgrounds in Gaithersburg, 5 to 10 pm (☎ 301-258-6310) and the other at Wheaton Plaza, on University Blvd. beginning at 7:30 pm; ☎ 301-217-6798.

SEPTEMBER: Early in the month, the **Annual Washington Irish Folk Festival** combines song, dance, food drink and other traditions of Ireland and Celtic culture, at the Montgomery County Fairgrounds; ☎ 301-565-0654.

OCTOBER: Taste of Bethesda brings together most of the restaurants in town, usually on the first Saturday of the month. Cuisines range from Greek and Italian to Tex-Mex and Asian. Buskers and live bands perform throughout the Woodmont Triangle, an area bounded by Old Georgetown Rd., Rugby Avenue and Woodmont Avenue. From the District, take Wisconsin Avenue (Route 355) and go left at Old Georgetown Rd. (Route 187). While there is no admission charge, you need tickets in order to sample the food. They can be bought in advance at Bethesda Urban partnership, 7906 Woodmont Avenue, Bethesda or at booths set up in the festival area during the event. ☎ 301-215-6660, www.bethesda.org/events/tasteofbethesda.htm. Mid-month brings the **Germantown Oktoberfest**, which does not concentrate only on the traditional beer theme. Programs are designed for children, too, with games and activities to amuse them while parents shop from craftsmen and food vendors. Route 118 and Crystal Rock Drive, Germantown (in Montgomery County); ☎ 301-217-6798.

DECEMBER: Early in the month, the **Audubon Holiday Fair** brings fine arts and crafts with a nature theme together in a display that is considered one of the best art and craft exhibits in the region. It's held at the Audubon Naturalist Society in Chevy Chase; ☎ 301-652-9188.

Sightseeing

■ Historic Sites & Museums

Along the Potomac

 The **Chesapeake and Ohio Canal National Historic Park** follows the Potomac River northwest from Washington, a project promoted by George Washington to bypass the rough sections of the Potomac. The goal was easier navigation to serve the new interior frontier. In 1828 a new company began the work of building a canal that was to link up with the Ohio River. The canal never reached the Ohio, but it did get as far as Cumberland, Maryland in the mountainous western part of the state, 184 miles from the starting point.

AND THEY THOUGHT LINCOLN WAS BRIEF AT GETTYSBURG...

At the groundbreaking ceremonies for the C&O Canal, President John Quincy Adams was given the honor of turning the first spadeful of dirt. He hit stone on the first two tries, then took off his jacket and finally succeeded in turning a shovelfull. He put his jacket back on and delivered a brief but prophetic oration: "To perseverance," he said, and sat down.

The Great Falls of the Potomac was one of the major obstacles to river navigation and the **Great Falls Tavern Visitor Center** is a good place to learn about the canal and the people who used and manned it. The lock there is operable, and if you are there between mid-April and October, you will likely see it in use. The center is open 9 to 5 daily, year-round. If you walk the path a half-mile south of the Visitor Center, there is a good view of the falls from the Olmstead Bridges.

A canal boat, not quite an authentic replica, but of the same size and hull structure, carries passengers through the lock in front of the tavern and along a flooded segment of the canal. Along with being an entertaining and instructive ride, it is a good way to see how the locks work, on a principle designed by Leonardo da Vinci. See *Boat Tours*, above.

This part of the park is at 11710 MacArthur Boulevard near Falls Rd. (Route 189). From Wisconsin Avenue, take River Rd. (Route 190) to Potomac then left onto Falls Rd. to MacArthur Boulevard. ☎ 301-299-3613.

Swain's Lock (Lock 21), about two miles from Great Falls Tavern, was rebuilt by the Civilian Conservation Corps in the 1930s.The canal has been rewatered through this area, and the park is used by hikers, cyclists and paddlers. Campsites and picnic tables, along with canoe and bike rentals, are all at this restored lock, on Swain's Lock Rd., off River Rd. (Route 190) in Potomac.

A bit farther up the canal at Seneca in a different segment of the Park is **Riley's Lockhouse** (1833). When the canal was operating, a lock keeper was housed near each lock in order to let passing boats through. Riley's is the only remaining original lockmaster house that is open to the public. It's open Saturday and Sunday from March through November from 1 to 4.

The **Clara Barton National Historic Site** is the home of the heroic nurse who founded the American Red Cross. Her home is open every day with tours on the half-hour from 10:30 to 4:30. It is next to Glen Echo Park, 5801 Oxford Rd. at MacArthur Boulevard in Glen Echo, toward Washington from Great Falls; ☎ 301-492-6245.

North of Washington DC

Great Falls Tavern.

Rockville & Wheaton

Strathmore Hall Arts Center is a splendid setting for visual and performing arts, situated in a neo-classical mansion dating from the beginning of the 20th century. Exhibits by local artists are mounted monthly and live concerts are presented throughout the year. They also serve a proper tea at 1 pm on Tuesdays and Wednesdays. While the Hall is open Monday through Saturday from 10 to 3, it is best to call for specific gallery and concert information. The center is at 10701 Rockville Pike (Route 355, Wisconsin Avenue from the District), Rockville; ☎ 301-530-0540.

Collections at the **Weiner Judaic Museum** focus on Judaic history, with archaeological artifacts from historic Judea right up to contemporary manifestations of Judaic culture and art, a fascinating journey. Open Sunday through Thursday, 9 am to 10:30 pm; Friday, 9-5; closed all Jewish holidays. The museum is at 6125 Montrose Rd., just south of Rockville, west of the Rockville Pike (Route 355); ☎ 301-881-0100.

DID YOU KNOW?

F. Scott and Zelda Fitzgerald, those literary darlings of the '20s and '30s, are spending eternity together in Rockville. The two of them are buried at St. Mary's Church Cemetery at the corner of Viers Mill Rd. (Route 586) and Route 355 in Rockville; ☎ 301-762-0096.

Almost directly north of the northern point of the District of Colombia is the **National Capital Trolley Museum**, with working antique trolleys from the United States and Europe. There is no fee for looking but it's worth the fare for a ride on one of these as its bell clangs and wheels rumble. In addition to the trolleys themselves, there is an exhibit and program on their history. It is open from January through November on weekends only from noon to 5, and on Memorial Day, Independence Day and Labor Day. In July and August it opens on Wednesdays as well, from 11 to 3. During December they hold a "Holley Trolleyfest" on weekends from 5 to 9, at 1313 Bonifant Rd., Wheaton; ☎ 301-384-6088. From Route 97 (Georgia Avenue, Beltway Exit 31), take Route 182 (Layhill Rd.) north to Layhill, then go east on Bonifant Rd.

College Park & Greenbelt

The new **College Park Aviation Museum** is bright, beautifully designed and filled with arresting interpretive displays. Its setting couldn't be more appropriate, overlooking the runways of the College Park Airport, the world's oldest continuously used airport, birthplace of airmail and the Army Air Corps, where the Wright Brothers trained early pilots.

The origin of the term "dogfight" in air warfare came from the World War I era, when primitive aircraft had to cut their engines off to avoid turning into the torque, then restart them. From the ground, this repeated noise of engines restarting sounded like dogs barking.

In fact, as you enter the display area of the museum, you will walk through a reproduction of Wilbur Wright's airplane shop, where his animated mannequin will "tell" you about his first students. Beyond, in the bright main hall of the museum are several restored and reproduced planes, well-displayed with costumed figures and actual film footage of their flights. These include a 1918 airmail plane used in the first flights from College Park and a reproduction of the Wright 1911 "B" Flyer, a pusher type aircraft (one that has engine and propeller location reversed so that it is "pushed" through the air).

KID-FRIENDLY

The College Park Aviation Museum was named the best children's museum in the Washington area. Interactive stations bring early flight alive for children, who can "fly" using a simulator of an early mail plane, make their own airmail postcards, learn about aerodynamics by making a paper airplane, or have their picture taken in the cockpit of a vintage flying machine – complete with flight jacket, goggles and scarf (a fan makes the scarf fly realistically behind). Outside in an enclosed play area are wheeled and rocking wooden airplanes for preschoolers to ride.

Displays are filled with blown-up photos and artifacts focus on some of the personalities of air history, including the Air Force's first five-star general, Hap Arnold. Others explore the WASPS, blind flying, the effects of airflow on different shapes, air relief missions, and include a flight simulator where you can "fly" antique mail aircraft. A free airshow in mid-September features two days of hot air balloons, helicopter and biplane rides, a parade of aircraft, and other events. The museum shop sells models, kits, and books on flight history.

Goddard Space Flight Center, named for rocket pioneer Robert Goddard, is where much of this country's space history was planned, and the place from which the Hubble Space Telescope is operated. The Visitor Center has exhibits and material on space exploration and the other fields of science that Goddard is involved with, such as earth science and technology. Every month there is a program entitled "Discover Goddard" that provides an inside look at the operations of the space center, presented by the people actually doing the research. There is also an extensive schedule of programs available to the public, many designed for children, explaining the work of this space laboratory. The model rocket launching program invites you to bring your own. The Space Center is open daily 9-4, except Thanksgiving, Christmas and New Year's Day; they have a picnic area and gift shop. Reach the center from Route 295 (Baltimore-Washington Parkway) at Greenbelt, turning onto Route 193 east (Greenbelt Rd.) and then left to the Visitor Center, on Soil Conservation Rd., Greenbelt; ☎ 301-286-8981, TDD 301-286-8103, www.gsfc.nasa.gov.

Admission is $4 for adults, seniors $3 and children $2. To get there, take Paint Branch Parkway from Route 1, directly opposite the main gate of University of Maryland campus, and turn left onto Cpl. Frank Scott Drive and follow signs to the museum, which is at the airport, 1985 Cpl. Frank Scott Drive, College Park; ☎ 301-864-6029, TTY 301-864-4765.

AUTHOR TIP

For those who (like us) love vintage planes and air history, this area provides a busy day's play. Begin by touring the Paul Garber Air and Space Museum (see below under Just South of DC*), then zip north on the beltway (I-95 / I-495) to College Park, grabbing a quick sandwich on the way, and visit the College Park Aviation Museum. End with a leisurely dinner at the adjacent 94th Aero Squadron restaurant, overlooking the runway of historic College Park Airport. The atmosphere feigns a French farmhouse used as headquarters for Eddie Rickenbacker's famous aviators, and the small planes taking off and landing outside add to the illusion.*

Riverdale

Riversdale Mansion was built between 1801 and 1807 in a style that combined Flemish and American attributes. A painted two-story brick mansion with a pillared portico, its wings and hyphens remain intact. Built by Flemish refugee Henry Steir, it was later home to members of the Calvert family and Senators Hiram Johnson and Hattie Caraway, the first woman elected to the US Senate. Open Sundays only, noon-4, March through December. From Route 201 (Kenilworth Avenue), take Route 410 (East-West Highway) west about a half-mile, following signs to 4811 Riverdale Rd., Riverdale; ☎ 301-864-0420, www.smart.net/~parksrec/riversdale.

In Glenn Dale, only a few miles away, **Marietta** is another simpler mansion of the same era. A plain brick two-story home in a simplified Federal style, it was built about 1811 and expanded in the 1830s. The builder and long-time occupant was Gabriel Duvall, Associate Justice of the US Supreme Court, Congressman and Comptroller of the US Treasury. From the Beltway, take Route 410 east four miles and turn left onto Glen Dale Boulevard (Route 193) and left again to find 5626 Bell Station Rd., Glenn Dale; ☎ 301-464-5291. Like Riversdale, it is open Sundays, noon-4, from March through December, so you can combine both on one visit.

Just South of DC

Not for the casual museum-goer, but if old airplanes make your heart soar, reserve a space in the unique tour of **Paul Garber Air and Space Museum Warehouse and Restoration Facility**, at the edge of Andrews Air Force Base in Suitland. Wear your walking shoes and eat a hearty breakfast, since you may be here for as much as four hours, if your docent-guide is as enthusiastic and well-informed as Jack Walker, who escorted us through the several giant buildings. We stopped to look at almost every one of the 140 planes stored here, not to mention pieces and parts of countless others.

RESTORING SMITHSONIAN AIRCRAFT

The Garber facility defines restoration not as making it **look** like the original, but making it **be** like the original. They begin by preserving and stabilizing as much as possible. If parts are missing, they search for authentic replacements. (In one case, guns on a plane had been disabled by removing the entire breech block, and a museum volunteer had an identical one in his basement. In another, a rare bomb rack was needed and a skier reported having seen one on a mountainside in Norway, where a plane had crashed in World War II.) When a part is not available, and only then, they make new parts, in exact replicas, including wear marks. And each of these new parts, clearly labeled as new, is made with authentic materials, tools and techniques. The only exception to this is fiber and fabric.

Restorers carry this even further. If they are restoring a Japanese plane, they use old Japanese tools. The pains to which restorers here will go to accomplish these goals make some of the best stories on the tour. For example, the museum owns the only remaining example of the German A16-D, used in World War I. It was made of wood, and had begun to de-laminate. It had to be restored immediately or they would lose it. They went to the original Swedish manufacturer that supplied these to the Germans, where they were able to replace sections using original methods.

The charter of the Air and Space Museum is to preserve air and space technology as it pertains to the United States. This includes foreign aircraft that influenced US technology or were used in engagements with the United States. Planes move back and forth between the Mall and storage here, as exhibits continually change.

We admit it, we are old plane nuts (which is better than being just plain nuts), so we could spend pages rambling on about what is in storage. We'll restrain ourselves and mention only a few. As we write, the *Enola Gay* is under restoration here, as is the only remaining example of a Japanese Seiran. One of 28 built near the end of World War II, this top-secret plane folded into a tube on top of a mammoth submarine, and was designed to approach close to the East Coast underwater, surface and take off at night to bomb major US cities. Its biggest problem was that it had to be put together on top of a submarine, in the dark, and took eight hours to assemble, leaving it no taxi warm-up time. As you tour these working shops, restorers will stop to explain what they are doing and answer your questions about the aircraft.

DID YOU KNOW?

The antennae on Courier B, one of the first communications satellites, are steel tape measures. They had trouble getting the antennae to erect when they came out of the capsule, and someone thought of the simple design of a steel tape. They worked just fine; you might say they measured up well.

These aircraft are stored in giant hangars, sitting, standing and hanging several layers deep, and in various states of repair. Seeing them involves hours on your feet and a lot of walking between and around buildings. Once the tour begins, the docent cannot leave the group, nor can you without an escort, so be prepared to stick it out or tell the docent at the beginning if you must leave early, so he can arrange to have someone come and get you.

Be aware, too, that this facility is slated to move to a new home at Dulles Airport in Virginia, possibly in 2003. No definite date has been set, but you need an advance reservation for the tour anyway, so they can tell you if it has moved. Tours begin at 10 am daily, at 3904 Old Silver Hill Rd., Suitland; ☎ 202-357-1400. To get to the facility, follow Branch Rd. (Route 5) north from Beltway Exit 7.

In Clinton, south of the Beltway and Andrews Air Force Base, is another pair of old houses to tour. **His Lordship's Kindness**, built 1785-87, is a brick two-story manse with wings and connecting hyphens. It is noted for its unusual hipped roof and window treatments. The property also still has its smokehouse, wash house, privy and other structures on its carefully tended grounds. Take Pennsylvania Avenue from Washington, or Beltway (I-95) Exit 11, south to Woodyard Rd. (Route 223). Follow it about 2.5 miles past the intersection of Rosaryville Rd. to 7606 Woodyard Rd., Clinton; ☎ 301-856-0358. Open March through December, Fridays, 1:30-4:30; second and fourth Sundays, noon-4:30. Admission is $5.

The mid-19th-century **Surrat House and Tavern** was the home of Mary Surrat, the first woman ever executed by the federal government. She fell afoul of the Feds when she harbored John Wilkes Booth after the President's assassination in 1865. As with many hostelries of the period, it was home to a family who made extra spending money operating a post office, tavern and hostelry from their wooden farmhouse. During the Civil War the family's Southern sympathies made it a safe house for confederates and the family became involved in a plot to kidnap Lincoln. Programs highlight farmlife contemporary to its era and the intrigue of the Civil War period. One special tour is the John Wilkes Booth Escape Route Tour, tracing his route after the assassination; reservations are required. Follow Branch Avenue from Pennsylvania Avenue, or Exit 7 from the Beltway (I-95), south to Woodyard Rd. On the way you will pass Andrews Air Force Base. Take Woodyard Rd. west one mile to the second light and turn left onto Brandywine Rd.; the museum is immediately on the left on Brandywine Rd., Clinton; ☎ 301-868-1121, TTY 301-868-8177, www.smart.net/~parksrec.

Farther west, in Upper Marlboro, is the earliest of the houses, the small, elegant, early Georgian mansion of **Darnall's Chance**, built in 1704 by Colonel Henry Darnall. He was a wealthy relative of the ruling Calverts. His daughter married David Carroll and they sired two preeminent Americans, Daniel Carroll II, who signed the US Constitution, and John Carroll, who became the first bishop of the Roman Catholic Church in America. Take Pennsylvania Avenue (Route 4), or Beltway Exit 11 east. At Upper Marlboro exit onto Water Street (north), crossing Main Street onto Gov. Bowie Drive. The museum is on the left at 14800 Gov. Oden Bowie Drive, Upper Marlboro; ☎ 301-952-8010, TTY 301-779-5321. Tours are given noon-4 on Sunday, March through December.

Where to Stay

ACCOMMODATIONS PRICE KEY
Rates are per room, per night, double occupancy.
$ . . . . Under $50
$$ . . . . $50 to $100
$$$ . . . . $101 to $175
$$$$ . . . . $176 and up

North of Washington DC

■ Along the Eastern Beltway

 Route 1, between the University of Maryland campus and the beltway, is lined with representatives of most of the major highway hotel chains, including EconoLodge, Super 8 and Comfort Inn. It's an area of hotels, not of B&Bs.

Best Western Maryland Inn, Baltimore Ave. (Route 1), College Park 20740; ☎ 301-474-2800, is not far from Paint Branch Parkway and College Park Air Museum, and is reached from the Beltway at Exit 25. Standard hotel rooms are about $100, and the hotel has an indoor pool with sauna and whirlpool, as well as a putting green. It is within reach of the College Park Metro station.

Club Hotel by Doubletree, 9100 Basil Ct., Largo 20774 (☎ 301-773-0700, fax 301-722-2016), is a pretty predictable upscale property close to the Beltway. Except for breakfast, when the staff is quite pleasant, we suggest avoiding the lobby coffee shop, which is not run by the hotel itself.

■ Northern Beltway

Just about every major and minor chain has a property in Bethesda, but you might try for one of the two rooms at **Lucy's B&B**, 9203 Wadsworth Drive, Bethesda 20817; ☎ 301-530-7256.

The **Park Crest House**, 8101 Park Crest Drive, Silver Spring 20910; ☎ 301-588-2845, is a three-room B&B not far from the Trolley Museum. They welcome pets, as well as people.

Farther north, and just over the line into Howard County, is one of our favorite B&Bs in Maryland, ideally located for visitors to this area and a handy first- or last-night stop for those using BWI airport. **The Inn at Paternal Gift Farm** is in an 1850s farmhouse set in manicured grounds and surrounded by nothing but green meadows and woods – and peace and quiet. It's hard to believe you're less than 10 minutes from busy I-95. Innkeepers Barbara and Bob Allen have created an atmosphere that really does make visitors feel like they are visiting friends in the country. Those guests who prefer to head straight for their rooms in the evening can do so easily, but they would miss the chance to relax in the spacious parlor with the charming hosts, who have a flair for good conversation and genuine hospitality. Guest rooms are filled with antiques – we especially like the hunt-themed room, in rich green and burgundy with a magnificent chest-on-chest. A pair of plush foxes, nattily dressed for the hunt, sit on Windsor chairs. Another room has a pencil post bed with a hand-stitched quilt. A tour of the closet turns up comfy details like a lusciously soft bathrobe, padded hangers and a teddy bear in case you left yours at home. Rooms are priced from $85 to $135. 13555 Route 108, Highland 20777; ☎ 301-845-3353.

■ Camping

Some of the best of camping is at the regional parks. In the north of this area, **Little Bennett Regional Park**, 23701 Frederick Rd., Clarksburg, ☎ 301-972-6581, has 91 sites, of which 25 have electrical hookups. Sanitary facilities, including showers, are close to the sites and there is a coin laundry. Camping is also available at **Cabin John Regional Park**, 7400 Tuckerman Lane, Rockville, MD, ☎ 301-299-4555. The facilities are like those at Little Bennett. **Louise F. Cosca Regional Park**, Thrift Rd., Clinton, MD, ☎ 301-868-1397, is another. In addition to a playground, tennis and other outdoor sports, this park also has a miniature train.

Where to Eat

DINING PRICE KEY
The price key indicates the cost of *most* dinner entrées on a restaurant's regular and daily special menu.
$. . . . . Most under $10
$$. . . . . $10 to $20
$$$. . . . . Over $30

■ Along the Eastern Beltway

 94th Aero Squadron is an illusion. It's not really a shell-scarred French farmhouse. But the vintage aircraft in the yard are real, and the food reaches well above culinary cruising altitude. The 94th was Eddie Rickenbacker's flying squadron, and old air memorabilia decorates the dining room, warmed by a big stone fireplace. The atmosphere is enhanced by 1940s music and the steady hum of small planes you can watch taking off and landing on the runway outside the windows. But while all this theater is fun, it's the food you go for. The combo platter of appetizers is a good lunch for two, an elegant pedestaled plate of crab-filled mushrooms, calamari, mozzarella sticks and onion rings thinner than a shoestring, for $14.

Signature entrées include the seafood collage, with lobster, scallops and fish in lemon-thyme butter. Filet mignon is stuffed with hot sausage and blue cheese, presented on a bed of bordelaise sauce. Grilled pork chops are garnished with apples and pears sautéed in brandy. Veal dishes include a sumptuous Oscar, and Veal Francis with marsala and exotic mushrooms. Presentations are artful and the staff is well-informed about the menu. Special drinks are the "Tailspin" – a Margarita with Grand Marnier – and the "B-52."

The restaurant ($$-$$$) is open for lunch Monday through Saturday, 11-3, and for dinner Sunday through Thursday, 3-10; Friday and Saturday, 3-11. On Sunday it is open 10-3 for brunch. You can walk there via a trail from the College Park Air Museum, or find it at 5240 Paint Branch Parkway; ☎ 301-699-9400.

One of the more unusual dining venues is **Sound Stage Restaurant**, a music theme restaurant of the Black Entertainment Television (BET) network. Dining here involves you in the entertainment as remote control cameras range through the facility on suspended railings putting diners into the show. They have Sunday brunch ($15.95 for adults, $7.95 for kids); regular breakfast is $9.50. Lunches are in the $12.50 range; dinner items include Jamaican chicken, blackened catfish, barbecued ribs and other Southern-style American dishes, most about $24. From the Beltway (I-95), take Exit 17A east (Landover Rd.) and turn right at the second light to find them at 9640 Lottsford Court, Largo; ☎ 301-883-9500. They are open Monday through Thursday, 11:30 am-1:00 am; Friday and Saturday, 11:30 am-2:00 am; Sunday, 11 am-midnight.

■ Northwest of Washington

Old Anglers Inn is a landmark, close to Great Falls, at 10801 MacArthur Blvd. on the Potomac (☎ 301-365-2425, www.oldanglersinn.com). Even before the inn was built in 1860, the spot was a favorite stopping place. Algonquins had a trading post nearby, and Captain John Smith camped here on a canoe trip in 1608. During the Civil War, couriers and officers from both sides found lodgings and food here. Later, President Theodore Roosevelt stayed here while fishing. However historic the inn itself, the menu is right up to date, with appetizers of goat cheese with crispy potato or mesclun salad with shallot vinaigrette. Entrees might be Atlantic halibut with manzanillo black beans or a duck confit with tarbais beans. The service tends to be a bit uppity, for which there is no excuse, but the chef makes up for it. In nice weather you'll want to ask for a table on the terrace, which, although it overlooks the road, also overlooks a leafy ravine.

Annapolis & Anne Arundel County

❝ Go Navy, Beat Army" is the theme of the town, especially in the fall, when the entire football season seems like a warm-up for this classic gridiron clash. You'll see the slogan repeated on mugs and sweatshirts in the tourist shops, and on signs as the day approaches. No doubt about it, Annapolis is Navy country, with midshipmen, active duty and retired Navy personnel in residence.

It's also sailing country, and on any day with a breath of air, you'll see sailboats on the water that surrounds the town. The hub of Annapolis activity is the waterfront and the streets radiating from it. Two of these climb the hill to the elegant State House and another hub, Church Circle, with its radiating streets. Main Street, which heads up the hill from the docks, is filled with shops and restaurants.

Annapolis abounds with historic buildings. Anne Arundel County has more structures from the 18th century than any other area in the country, and some of the finest are open for tours.

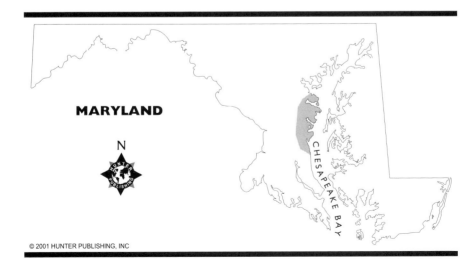

MARYLAND

N

HUNTER PUBLISHING

CHESAPEAKE BAY

Annapolis

Geography & History

Water defines both the geography and the history of Annapolis. The city lies on a point that juts into the Chesapeake, with the **Severn River** to its north and the **South River**, logically, to its south. But it's not that tidy. A variety of little creeks wander off from these rivers, poking wet fingers into every neighborhood. Weems Creek and College Creek cut parallel swathes from the Severn River on the north side of town, Spa Creek and Back Creek are south of the City Docks. Tiny coves make even more dents in the Annapolis shoreline.

Anne Arundel County stretches south along the shore and northward to the southeastern city limits of Baltimore. Its geography presents us with an interesting quandary. The enormous **Patuxent National Wildlife Refuge** lies almost entirely in the county, but the entrance to its Visitors Center, and the portion south of the river that you can explore is in Prince George's County. It makes more sense to discuss the refuge with the towns from which you will access it, so we have included it in the *North of Washington* chapter, with other sites in that area.

It was only natural that most of Annapolis history came to it from the water. In the first place, in the Colonial era, nearly everything came by water; not only were most of the colony's supplies from Europe, but the sea was the best route for trade with neighboring colonies as well. Any location with a good harbor, let alone one with so many protected moorings, was destined to find importance through its port.

Its first settlers were Puritans who left Virginia's tight Church of England controls at the invitation of the second Lord Baltimore. His offer of land grants in Providence, a newly settled addition to his colony of Maryland, was accompanied by a promise of religious freedom. In 1650, Anne Arundel County was formed, named for Lord Baltimore's wife, and 45 years later the settlement of Providence was renamed Annapolis, honoring Princess Anne, when it became the provincial capital.

DID YOU KNOW?

For nearly a year – November of 1783 until August of 1784 – Annapolis was the US capital, during which time the Treaty of Paris was ratified there, ending the Revolution.

Getting Here & Getting Around

 US-301/50, which cuts east-west across the north of Annapolis, connects it to Washington, DC and to the Eastern Shore via the **Bay Bridge**. **Route 2** and **I-97** connect it to the Baltimore Beltway. Route 2 approaches from the south.

The narrow old streets that make Annapolis so attractive also make it difficult to get around in, leading to traffic jams and limited parking spaces. Parking garages downtown handle most of the cars, well-marked by signs, and located off Main St., next to the visitor center and near Church Circle. The first hour is free and the daily maximum is $8 on weekdays, $4 on weekends. If you are shopping downtown, ask for validation to get discounted parking.

 While you may find a metered spot to park in Annapolis, you must move after the two-hour limit. Refilling an expired meter is a ticketable offense, and parking laws are enforced.

You can park all day at the **Navy-Marine Corps Stadium**, north of College Creek, and take the shuttle downtown, stopping at the visitor center, the Naval Academy and Main Street. Shuttles run daily from 6:30 am to 8 pm, May to mid-October; until 7 pm on weekdays only the rest of the year. This means that, if you plan to stay in town for dinner, you will have to eat early or pick up your car before dinner. Parking on weekends is $4 all day, and the shuttle is free. On weekdays the parking fee drops to $3, but you have to pay 75¢ for the shuttle.

AUTHOR TIP *RVs are not easy to drive through narrow Annapolis streets, and are impossible to park in downtown spaces or garages. You can leave them all day at the Navy-Marine Corps Stadium (see above) for $8 and ride the shuttles.*

Most attractions are downtown and best reached on foot. Other parts of Annapolis – especially the restaurants along Spa and Back Creeks – may be visited by **Jiffy Water Taxi**, Slip 20, City Dock; ☎ 410-263-0033. The taxi departs hourly from City Dock; from mid-May to early September, it runs Monday-Thursday, 9:30-midnight; Friday, 9:30-1 am; Saturday, 9-1 am; Sunday 9-midnight. From April through October it operates on a more limited schedule.

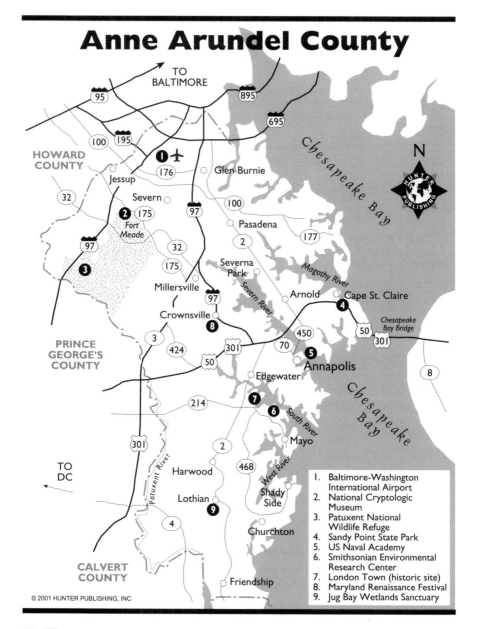

Anne Arundel County

TO BALTIMORE

95
895
695
100 195

HOWARD COUNTY

❶ ✈
176
Jessup
Glen Burnie

32
Severn
100

❷ 175
97
Fort Meade
Pasadena

97
32
2
177

❸
175
Severna Park

Millersville
97
Arnold
Cape St. Claire ❹

Crownsville ❽
Magothy River
Severn River

PRINCE GEORGE'S COUNTY
3
424
301
50
70
450
50
Chesapeake Bay Bridge
301

50
Annapolis ❺
8

Edgewater

214
❼ ❻
South River

TO DC
301
2
Mayo

Patuxent River
Harwood
468
West River

Lothian ❾
Shady Side

4
Churchton

CALVERT COUNTY
Friendship

Chesapeake Bay

N — HUNTER PUBLISHING

© 2001 HUNTER PUBLISHING, INC

1. Baltimore-Washington International Airport
2. National Cryptologic Museum
3. Patuxent National Wildlife Refuge
4. Sandy Point State Park
5. US Naval Academy
6. Smithsonian Environmental Research Center
7. London Town (historic site)
8. Maryland Renaissance Festival
9. Jug Bay Wetlands Sanctuary

■ Tours

Although nothing beats seeing Annapolis on foot (and the manageable size of its historic district makes this quite easy), a minibus tour is available daily, April-November, from the visitor center on West St. A one-hour tour is about $10 from **Discover Annapolis Tours**; ☎ 410-626-6000.

Rent-A-Wreck, the car rental people who understand that you probably don't drive a brand new car at home, so won't be offended by renting one with a few miles on it, have wheelchair-accessible vans among their fleet of rental vehicles. They offer free pick-up, too: ☎ *410-349-2199, www. rentawreck.com.*

Information Sources

Annapolis and Anne Arundel County Conference and Visitors Bureau, 26 West St, Annapolis 21401, ☎ 410-280-0445, is just off Church Circle. Parking (first hour free) is in the lot behind the building; open daily, 9 am-5 pm. An information booth is also on the City Dock.

Adventures

■ Parks

Sandy Point State Park lies just north of the Bay Bridge, on Cape St. Claire, where the Magothy River enters the bay. It has a range of day-use activities and facilities, including a beach with full changing facilities and food vendors, trails, boat ramps with rentals, and picnic areas. Access is from East College Parkway, signposted from US-301/50 immediately west of the Bay Bridge; ☎ 410-974-2149.

WATCHABLE
WILDLIFE

Located on the Atlantic Flyway, the waterfront Sandy Point State Park is a prime spot for bird viewing during spring and fall migrations.

Quiet Waters Park, on Hillsmere Drive off Bay Ridge Rd. (☎ 410-222-1777), sits along the scenic South River, with trails, formal gardens, picnic sites, rowboat rental, fishing piers and boat access. It has a variety of landscapes, open, wooded, marsh and ponds. This relatively new park has more facilities than most county parks, even to a café serving creative dishes made from local ingredients. Day-use fees for the park are $4 per vehicle.

But for its lack of parking, **Thomas Point Park** (3890 Thomas Point Rd., Annapolis, ☎ 410-222-1969) would be the perfect park, at the outskirts of Annapolis on a long wooded point surrounded by water, with a classic screw-pile lighthouse off its shore. But, unless you are as lucky as we are,

Annapolis

with a family home within walking distance, it's a very hard park to use – largely because its narrow venue doesn't leave room for parking. You must get a permit to use the park for fishing, cycling, walking or birding, but these are free. If you can't arrive by bicycle (it's a pleasant flat cycle route from Bay Ridge Rd.), call first to see if there are parking spaces available. The park is southeast of Annapolis, along the South River. The park office is open Wednesday-Sunday, 10-noon.

Truxtun Park, on Truxtun Rd., off Hilltop Lane (☎ 410-263-7958), is at the end of Spa Creek, with boat access and fishing as well as ball fields and playground. A fee is charged for boat launch and swimming (in a pool) only.

AUTHOR TIP

Nearly all parks of any size charge day-use fees, even those without swimming.

■ On Foot

A good way to tour Annapolis on your own, with stops to visit historic sites and museums as you choose, is to follow the map and listings in the free *Destinations* magazine-format guide to the city. The key describes 40 sites numbered on the accompanying map, each coded to show its historic period. The tour points out significant private buildings as well as those you can visit.

AUTHOR TIP

The entire center of Annapolis is a National Historic Landmark.

Guided Walking Tours

You can follow a guide in Colonial costume during two-hour tours of the Naval Academy or the historic district with **Three Centuries Tours of Annapolis**, 48 Maryland Ave; ☎ 410-263-5401. April through October, tours leave daily at 10:30 from the visitor center on West St. and at 1:30 from the information kiosk at City Dock. November through March, they are given on Saturday only, leaving from Gibson's Lodgings at 110 Prince George St. The cost is $8 for adults, $3 for children.

To cover the same places with an architectural historian, sign on with **Annapolis Walkabout**, 223 S. Cherry Grove Ave.; ☎ 410-263-8253. Tours leave at various times from the visitor center on West St. on Saturdays and Sundays, April through October.

Walter Cronkite narrates a recorded self-guided tour of the city, available as an audio-cassette from the **Historic Annapolis Foundation Museum Store and Welcome Center**, 77 Main St.; ☎ 410-268-5576. Open Monday-Saturday, 10-5; Sunday, noon-5. A second recorded tour leads to places significant in Annapolis's African-American history and heritage. Rental for either is $5.

For tours of the Naval Academy, see *Historic Sites & Museums.*

■ On Wheels

Annapolis has a number of designated bike routes, some on trails, others using city streets. Apart from the hill that rises from the docks in the center of town, the terrain is mostly level.

A new paved bicycle path of just under five miles loops around **Quiet Waters Park**, opening to views of South River. The park is well-kept, but has not lost the wild feel of the fields, woods and shoreline it covers. Surprisingly, even though the trail is close to the shore, it is not level, but has several short hills as it winds through the park, making it a lot more interesting and varied than the rail trail.

KID-FRIENDLY

Only twice does the trail in Quiet Waters encounter the park roadway, so this is a good place to bike with children and beginning two-wheelers, who have 10 feet of trail width as wobble space.

The landscape changes from open fields to cattail marshes filled with redwing nests to an open forest of tall tulip poplars to river overlooks. Colors and wildlife change with the season – white dogwood borders one section in the early spring, in the winter you may see loons in the river, and maples paint the trailside red in the fall. It's a thoroughly enjoyable route and, we think, well worth the modest park entrance fee. Quiet Waters Park is on Hillsmere Drive off Bay Ridge Rd., ☎ 410-222-1777. Bay Ridge Ave., a main artery from the Eastport section of Annapolis, meets Hillsmere Drive at its end, as it joins Bay Ridge Rd.

The **Baltimore and Annapolis Trail** goes through one of the most heavily settled parts of the state, yet for long stretches of its route you would hardly know it. Some parts travel past backyards, but much of it is wooded, so you can't see how close you are to civilization. For long stretches it runs through forests that obscure nearby housing developments; birds and wildflowers are not uncommon beside the trail.

The paved trail follows the old rail line for more than 13 miles from Glen Burnie to Route 301/50, in Annapolis. While you can do the entire route, we suggest picking out segments. Unless you have two vehicles available, you will be traveling the same route in reverse to get back to your car, so you might as well pick one you'll like twice. Our pick would be the first three miles or so from the Annapolis end, where development is sparse, woods border the trail, and a rolling terrain is created by small streams that have cut their way through the land. There are houses, to be sure, but for the most part the landscape in natural.

The other section we like is from the point where Route 2 crosses Route 100 at Marley Station south to Earleigh Heights Rd. in Pasadena, a stretch of about four miles. Again, much of the route is through woods in this stretch.

For the southern section, park at the beginning of the trail, just north of the interchange where US-301/50 crosses Route 2, immediately east of the Severn Bridge. For the northern section, park in the Marley Station Mall, on Route 2, south of the Baltimore Beltway, traveling south on the trail to the Earleigh Heights Ranger Station. The Trail Ranger Station (☎ 410-222-6244) itself is an interesting stop, in an 1889 building that was once a general store as well as the station for the rail line the trail has replaced. A bike shop is located just east of the trail, five miles north of the Annapolis end. **Pedal Pushers** (☎ 410-544-2323) can not only fix your ailing bike, but has rentals as well. The shop is right on the Baltimore-Annapolis Boulevard. A number of antiques shops in this area invite browsing.

■ On Water

 Surrounded by water, Annapolis is a center for all the usual water-related sports, from sailing and windsurfing to kayaking, swimming and fishing. Remember that Maryland law requires anyone born after July 1, 1972 to have a Certificate of Boating Safety Education in order to operate jet skis or other registered vessels in Maryland waters. Certification requires about eight hours of class instruction and successful completion of a test.

Sailing

Sailing is at the heart of Annapolis, and it's as good a place to learn as you'll find (it's where your authors learned as kids). Every Wednesday evening in the summer you can watch sailing races, or you can take to the water as a passenger, learning crew or in a rental sailboat.

KidShip Sailing School offers weekend or weekday courses for children or for entire families. Instructors are primed to make sailing a great adventure for kids aged five-15, while teaching parents at the same time. They are part of America's oldest sail-training program, **Annapolis Sailing School**, and they teach adults, too. If you have never sailed and just want to get the feel of it without committing yourself to a course or formal lesson, join them any morning at 10 for "Try-Sail." If you know how to sail, you can rent craft here, too. They are at 601 Sixth St.; ☎ 800-638-9192.

"BYO" MEANS BUILD YOUR OWN

If you live close by, or can spend some time here, you can build your own wooden boat, under the guidance of the skilled craftsmen at **The John Gardner School of Boat Building**, at 528 Second St.; ☎ 410-267-0418.

Both weekend and week-long sailing courses are tailored to individual skill levels, at **J World Annapolis** (☎ 410-280-2040 or 800-966-2038). Class sizes are limited and sailing craft are late model.

South River Boat Rentals has a fleet of Hobie Cats and other sailboats which they rent by the hour, day or week. They are at Pier 7 Marina, on Route 2 in Edgewater; ☎ 410-956-9729.

Quiet Waters Park, on Hillsmere Drive off Bay Ridge Rd. (☎ 410-222-1777), rents sailboats on weekends from its dock on a small cove on South River.

Windsurfing

Sandy Point State Park, just north of the Bay Bridge (☎ 410-974-2149) has excellent windsurfing off its long elbow-shaped beach.

Canoeing & Kayaking

Public boat access is found in the waterfront parks at Quiet Waters and Truxtun. While this watery town, where tidal creeks seem to abut everyone's backyard, offers plenty of places where you could easily pop a kayak or canoe into the water, finding a nearby place to park the car that carried it there may be more difficult. Sandy Point State Park has ramped access. Across South River, there are public launch sites at Londontown (at the historic site) and at the end of Route 255 in Galesville, with access onto the West River. Farther south in Deale, an access off Deale Rd. (Route 256) puts into Rockhold Creek.

At **Quiet Waters Park**, on Hillsmere Drive off Bay Ridge Rd. (☎ 410-222-1777), you can rent canoes and kayaks to explore the quiet waters of Harness Creek. Rentals are available Wednesday through Monday, June-August, Friday through Sunday in April, May, September and October. This service is operated by **Amphibious Horizons**; ☎ 410-267-8742 or 888-I-LUV-SUN, www.amphibioushorizons.com.

There is access to South River from the park, but the number of sailboats in the river on almost any day should give you the first clue that the open waters of the South River are very windy, so you need to stick close to the shore unless you are a very strong paddler.

Truxton Park accesses the farthest end of Spa Creek, where you are more protected from wind, but will find a lot of other boat traffic. It is attractive for paddling, however, with its marinas and boat docks, and a water view of the gardens of the Charles Carroll House.

Much quieter are the secluded fingers of **Rhode River**, which joins West River as it flows into the Chesapeake across South River, on the Edgewater side. Access this from Contees Wharf Rd., off Route 468, which parallels Route 2 for a short way, and can be reached from Route 214, which crosses both. (The spot you are looking for is marked on the Maryland state highway map with a red dot and the label "Camp Letts." The camp, in fact, owns some of the undeveloped shoreline you will be enjoying.)

You can explore this shoreline up into the reaches of **Muddy Creek**, following the shore to your right from the put-in. It varies from high wooded banks to low, marshy, grass-covered areas; Muddy Creek reaches nearly two miles into an environmental reserve operated by the Smithsonian. **The Smithsonian Center** has occasional canoe trips as part of their educational program; ☎ 410-269-1412.

GUIDED CANOE & KAYAK TOURS

Jug Bay Wetlands Sanctuary, at 1361 Wrighton Rd. in Lothian (☎ 410-741-9330), sponsors nature explorations by canoe on the Patuxent River. Canoes and handling instruction are provided and naturalists point out features of the wetlands ecosystem on these four-hour trips. Most trips are in the morning, but twilight trips are held during the full moon, a good time of day to see birds and beavers, who become active then. It is important to reserve a place on these trips ahead of time, since they fill quickly. The fee is $5 per person.

On alternate Friday evenings from May through September, **Amphibious Horizons** offers guided kayak tours of Harness Creek in Quiet Waters Park. Trips begin at the park at 6 pm, and the $35 fee includes boat, instruction and refreshments. Beginning and intermediate small-group lessons are offered on weekends; private lessons can be arranged as well. The company also offers evening and sunset paddles in Mataponi Creek and day-long Saturday trips through wild rice marshes in the Patuxent River Park. ☎ 410-267-8742 or 888-I-LUV-SUN, www.amphibioushorizons.com.

Boat Tours

One of the pleasures of viewing Annapolis from the water, in addition to its fine skyline view, is the chance to see some of the gracious old estates that overlook the creeks and rivers, but are hidden from road view. It also gives you a good sense of what life and commerce was like in the early days when nearly all transportation was by water. For our money, the best cruise experiences are under sail, but a number of options suit all tastes. For fishing boats, some of which also run excursion cruises, see *Fishing*, below.

Chesapeake Marine Tours, at Slip 20, City Dock (☎ 410-268-7600), cruises Annapolis Harbor, along the Severn River and into Chesapeake Bay. A 40-minute narrated cruise includes the Naval Academy and the Bay and Severn bridges or cruises the local creeks. In 90 minutes you can go to Thomas Point Lighthouse or explore the upper reaches of the Severn River. They also run day excursions across the bay to St. Michaels, on the Eastern Shore. Several different routes are offered daily from April through early October, $6-$12 (from $21.95 with lunch).

Schooner *Woodwind* (☎ 410-263-7837) is a 74-ft yacht offering two-hour cruises May-September, departing from the Annapolis Marriott Waterfront Hotel, next to City Dock. There are three sails daily (Tuesday-Sunday) in the summer; two per day during spring and fall. Sunset sails May-September have themes or entertainment; the Wednesday evening sail includes watching the weekly sailboat races. Fares $24-$27 adult, $2 discount for seniors, children half-price. See *Where to Stay*, below, for accommodations in its double-berth staterooms.

Beginagain (☎ 410-626-1422) is a 36-foot sailboat, sailing three times daily from City Dock. Cost for a three-hour trip aboard the 36-foot sloop is $55 per person.

Town dock, Annapolis.

Fishing

Sandy Point State Park is a popular fishing center, with boat rentals, a bait and tackle shop, and surf fishing from the beach and the jetty at the eastern end of the beach. There is a paved boat ramp here and at Truxtun Park, off Hilltop Lane in Annapolis, at the end of Spa Creek.

 AUTHOR TIP

*A Chesapeake Bay **sport fishing license** is required in order to fish from the shore if you are between the ages of 16 and 65. You can buy these at any bait and tackle shop.*

Chesapeake Bay Adventures leaves daily from Annapolis, for trolling and bottom fishing trips. Tackle is provided. They also do charter trips for groups.

Chesapeake Bay Fishing operates fishing and cruise excursions for groups of two-20; ☎ 410-974-4314, www.captclyde.com.

CAUTION

Although most fishing boats have all the proper certifications, it is your own responsibility to ask about this. No listing in a guidebook can possibly be up to date on the status of everyone's Coast Guard approvals.

Sea Venture Charters (☎ 4210-798-6459, www.baycaptains.com/sea-venture), takes up to six people trolling or bottom fishing from its dock in Edgewater. Half-day, $240; full day, $340; prices include all tackle, bait, permits and guide.

■ On Ice

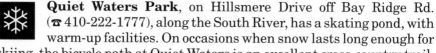 **Quiet Waters Park**, on Hillsmere Drive off Bay Ridge Rd. (☎ 410-222-1777), along the South River, has a skating pond, with warm-up facilities. On occasions when snow lasts long enough for skiing, the bicycle path at Quiet Waters is an excellent cross-country trail, with enough ups and downs to make it interesting.

Cultural & Eco-Travel Experiences

The Smithsonian Environmental Research Center (SERC) is on Route 468, which is accessed from Route 2 in Edgewater via Route 214; ☎ 410-269-1412. Occupying a large area of the peninsula between the Rhode and the West Rivers, its shore line and uplands support a tremendous variety of wildlife habitats. Forests of birch, oak, sycamore and poplar give way to extensive marshlands where beaver, bald eagles, osprey and dozens of warbler and waterfowl varieties live. Educational programs and canoe excursions are by reservation and the small education center is open to the public.

Jug Bay Wetlands Sanctuary, at 1361 Wrighton Rd. in Lothian (☎ 410-741-9330), is a 620-acre reserve on the Patuxent River. More than half of it is wetland, and it is among the most important migratory resting areas for waterfowl west of the Chesapeake Bay. It is also one of the largest freshwater tidal wetlands in the east, a significant birding area with blinds and observation platforms. Scheduled programs explore the natural environment, centering on wetland ecology and wildlife identification, with bird walks, nature walks for seniors and children, boardwalk tours and canoe trips. Most activities are on weekends. Jug Bay's offices are open March through November, Wednesday, Saturday and Sunday, 9-5; park fees are $2.50 for adults, $2 for those over 60, $1.50 for children under 18.

KID-FRIENDLY

*Jug Bay Sanctuary has a summer program of five-day **Summer Science Camps** for children in the third through eighth grades. These are divided into two-grade segments, so children are with others their own age. The fee is about $100 and sessions run 9:30 to 3:30, Monday-Friday. Hands-on activities and learning are emphasized. Most sessions include an all-day canoe trip and older groups have an overnight campout. Prior registration is required.*

Although it's not open year-round, the **Maryland Renaissance Festival** (☎ 410-266-7304 or 800-296-7304, www.renfest.com) is in residence on the fairgrounds in Crownsville on weekends from late August through October, too long-running and too big an occasion to be listed under *Events*. The grounds themselves are fascinating to explore, an entire town of permanent structures in Medieval and Renaissance style – or an approximation of it. Row upon row of fanciful buildings are set in acres of pine grove and around an open area that also includes an arena where a steady series of events, from jousting to human chess games, take place. Theaters, includ-

Annapolis

Actors at the Maryland Renaissance Festival.

ing a replica of London's Globe Theatre with regular Shakespeare productions, are scattered throughout the grounds, which take on the look and feel of an English market fair of 500 years ago. A constant schedule of top entertainers, each act appropriate to the era, fill the stages: a sword-swallower, juggler or fencing duel may be followed by a rollicking comedy-magic act by Tom Crowl and the Wench.

Shops and booths sell products that might or might not have been found in such places, ranging from meticulous handmade replicas of Medieval and Renaissance crafts, to pure silliness with some theme connecting it to the time and place. You can buy elegant feather-covered masks similar to those worn at Venice's carnival, crowns of dried flowers, beautiful swords made by a blacksmith who is also a student of early weaponry, pottery chalices and steins with dragons as handles, magicians' supplies, tapestry pillows, herbs, and period costumes. Around you will be modern people in shorts and T-shirts, as well as those magnificently attired in velvets and brocades of the era. A monk, looking just like Friar Tuck, may stroll arm-in-arm with a serving wench, a jester in pointed shoes and bell-studded cap may walk past munching a hot dog, a woman dressed like Queen Elizabeth I may be serenaded by a minstrel's madrigal as she stops for an ale. Food is at the merry heart of the fair, some of it authentic (the ales and meads certainly are), some of it not. Don't come here expecting strict authenticity; that's not the point. Expect a good time, good shopping, an eye-stopping setting, top entertainment in styles you won't find elsewhere, and a lively hands-on experience no theme park can match. It's anachronism at its very best; admission $14, ages 16-61; $12, over 62; $5, ages seven-15.

KID-FRIENDLY

The Chesapeake Children's Museum, at 2331D Forest Drive, at the corner of Riva Rd. (☎ 410-266-0677) has several interactive exhibits on general and local subjects, including the watermen. Admission is $3 and the museum is open Thursday through Tuesday 11-5 in the summer, 10-4 the rest of the year.

■ Gardens

The city's most outstanding gardens are those at **William Paca House and Gardens**, built between 1763 and 1765. They are at 186 Prince George St.; ☎ 410-263-5553. To look at these spacious terraces and the more rustic pool below, bounded by their brick walls, it is almost impossible to believe that 50 years ago this scene was largely covered by a hotel. Using old descriptions, a portrait of the owner that showed the gardens in the background, and what archaeology remained when the hotel was removed, garden historians and landscape architects have closely re-created the original garden.

Outstanding horticultural features of the gardens, which are further described below under *Historic Sites*, include a boxwood parterre with potted standards, five tall holly trees trimmed to cone shapes and a fruit "orchard" with espaliered trees. A rose garden features the types grown in Paca's day, which he most likely grew as well. An herb garden has medicinal plants. Below the terraces are a pond with a latticed bridge and watergardens, and a domed summer house. These elements, which cover an area of about two acres – quite a lot of space for an in-town garden – are connected by brick paths and steps. The Paca House Garden is open Monday through Saturday, 10-4; Sunday, noon-4; in January and February it's open Saturday and Sunday only. The garden is open until 5 pm, April through October. Entrance to the garden only is $4.

Other area historic homes with gardens are the **Hammond-Harwood House**, which has an herb harden (see page 278); the **Chase-Lloyd House**, with roses (page 280); and the **Charles Carroll House** (page 281), whose terraced gardens overlook Spa Creek. **Shiplap House** (page 277) has a front garden of narrow terraced beds.

The **Helen Avalynne Tawes Garden**, at the Tawes State Office Building on Taylor Ave. (☎ 410-267-8189), covers six acres, displaying plants and habitats native to Maryland. Here you can see plants from an Eastern Shore waterside habitat, Western Maryland forest and environemnets alongside streams typical of those found in northern Maryland. The gardens are free and open daylight hours. Taylor Ave. leaves West Street not far from Church Circle.

Across the South River in Edgewater, **London Town House and Garden** has created an idyllic woodland dell that drops to the river's edge in a wide curve from manicured lawns and nicely designed beds above a high bluff bank. Filled with azaleas in the spring, the dell is a showy blaze of pinks and reds. In April the grounds are covered in a stunning display of blooming daffodils. You can walk among them along a path or view them from a pavilion overhanging the brink of the ravine. Near the river is a pond with aquatic plants.

■ Crafts

Sign on as an apprentice to learn a skill of the 1700s, when the **Charles Carroll House** has its annual 18th Century Trades Fair. Visitors to the fair who are over eight years old can learn how to make wooden shingles, potpourri, brooms, at a $4 fee. In November, learn to make wreaths of boxwood; ☎ 410-269-1737.

At **Annapolis Pottery**, 40 State Circle (☎ 410-268-6153), you can watch stoneware pottery being thrown or hand formed. The pottery sells a wide variety of styles; open Monday-Saturday, 10-6; Sunday, 10-5.

The League of Maryland Craftsmen, at 54 Maryland Ave. (☎ 410-626-1277), showcases work in many media, including pottery, glass, wood, fiber and baskets. Open Monday and Wednesday-Saturday, 10-5; Sunday, noon-5.

Historic Annapolis Foundation Museum Store, at 77 Main St. (☎ 410-268-5576), sells fine crafts and reproductions reflecting Annapolis's social, cultural and maritime history. Look here for hand-blown glassware, pottery, jewelry, ship models and books; open Monday-Saturday, 10-5; Sunday, noon-5.

Save the Bay Shop, 188 Main St. (☎ 410-268-8832), features books, clothing, crafts and gifts, the profits from which support the Chesapeake Bay Foundation in its work to preserve the bay's environment. Open Monday-Saturday, 10-5; Sunday hours vary seasonally.

■ Farmers' Markets

In Annapolis the farmers gather on Saturday, 7-noon, at the corner of **Riva Rd. and Truman Parkway**, accessible from Exit 22 of US-301/50. In **Severna Park**, a market can be found at the same hours on Saturday at the Jones Statin Park & Ride.

At the **Pennsylvania Dutch Farmers' Market**, at Annapolis Harbour Center on Solomons Island Rd. (☎ 410-573-0770), stalls sell country cooking, baked goods, vegetables, cheese, meat and poultry. Open Thursday, 10-6; Friday, 9-6; Saturday, 9-3.

■ Antiques

State Circle and Maryland Ave., which runs from it to the Naval Academy gate, have a high concentration of antique and collectible shops. You may find anything hidden in their corners: ship models, books, 18th-century furniture, estate jewelry, dolls, china, rare prints, toy soldiers and things you never dreamed anyone collected.

Another concentration of shops is along Route 648, the Baltimore-Annapolis Boulevard, near its intersection with Riggs Ave. in Severna Park.

These shops are easily accessed from the Baltimore-Annapolis Bicycle Trail (although you probably wouldn't want to buy a brass bed if you're traveling by bike). One of the shops specializes in vintage fashions and estate jewelry, another is a group market.

Annapolis Antique Gallery, 2009 West St. (☎ 410-266-0635), shows the top of the line from 40 antique dealers: furniture, china, decoys and collectables. Open daily, 10-5.

Maryland's granddaddy of all multi-dealer antique malls is the **AAA Antiques Mall**, between Severn and Jessup at the intersection of Routes 175 and 295, just north of Fort Meade; ☎ 410-551-4101. It is open daily, 10-6, and has 58,000 square feet of space packed with collectibles and antiques.

Events

 APRIL: The **Annapolis Spring Boat Show** is the bay's largest, featuring sailboats and powerboats and everything connected with boating, such as fishing and water skiing; ☎ 410-268-8828, www.usboat.com.

MAY: The **Annapolis Waterfront Arts Festival** includes craftsmen in all media, with special emphasis on maritime arts; ☎ 410-268-8828, www.usboat.com.

JULY: On **Independence Day**, festivities include a parade, a concert by the Naval Academy band, and fireworks on the waterfront; ☎ 410-263-1183.

AUGUST: The world's largest **crab feast**, with heaping trays of steamed crabs, crab cakes, is held at Memorial Stadium; ☎ 410-841-2841.

SEPTEMBER (through November): Call 800-US4-NAVY for tickets to the **Naval Academy football games**.

OCTOBER: Annapolis is jammed to unmanageability on two consecutive weekends for the **United States Sailboat Show** and the **United States Powerboat Show**. It's a good time to be elsewhere unless you are there for the the shows themselves, in which case you should reserve lodging a year ahead and expect to pay handsomely for it. ☎ 410-268-8828, www.usboat.com.

NOVEMBER: **Christmas in Annapolis**, with decorated homes and historic sites, parade of lighted boats, house tours, concerts; ☎ 410-268-8828.

DECEMBER: The **Londontown and Gardens Holiday Tea and Greens Sale** is planned for the second Sunday; ☎ 410-222-1919. On New Year's Eve is **First Night**, featuring hundreds of performers, concerts, theater, and midnight fireworks. Children's activities begin late afternoon; ☎ 410-280-0700.

Annapolis

Performing Arts

 Theater and music take center stage in Annapolis, with a number of choices on any weekend evening. Major performances are at the **Maryland Hall for the Creative Arts**, at 801 Chase St.; ☎ 410-263-5544, www.mdhallarts.org.

Annapolis Opera, Inc. (☎ 410-267-8135, www.mdhallarts.org) has a year-round schedule of grand opera, operetta and Broadway musicals at Maryland Hall and other venues.

The Annapolis Chorale (☎ 410-263-1906) has a 150-voice full chorus, a chamber chorus and the Annapolis Chamber Orchestra which perform popular and classical works September-May in Maryland Hall for the Creative Arts.

Annapolis Summer Garden Theatre, at 143 Compromise St. (☎ 410-268-9212), presents Broadway musicals in a 200-seat theater under the stars, Thursday through Sunday, late May through Labor Day.

Annapolis Symphony Orchestra (☎ 410-269-1132) presents professional musicians in a classical repertoire, October through May at the Maryland Hall. Chamber concerts designed to attract family audiences are offered spring and fall.

Ballet Theatre of Annapolis (☎ 410-263-8289), a professional dance company, performs classical and modern ballet at Maryland Hall and occasionally at ot2her locations.

Chesapeake Music Hall, at Exit 29 off US-50, between the Severn and Bay Bridges (☎ 410-626-7515, www.toad.net/~musichall) presents musicals accompanied by buffet dinners, Thursday-Saturday evenings and Sunday at 1 pm.

Colonial Players, 108 East St. (☎ 410-268-7373) Five annual productions are performed in a theater-in-the-round setting.

Sightseeing

■ Historic Sites & Museums

The Historic District

 Begin your tour of the historic district of Annapolis at the docks, its historic heart. Among the boats you may see here are the *Stanley Norman*, a skipjack belonging to Save the Bay Federation. You may also see the sailing ship *Pride of Baltimore*, with its deeply raked masts, moored at Annapolis.

The historic homes and sites are arranged in a somewhat logical geographical order, beginning at the City Docks and continuing off the right-hand corner of Market Square, behind the market.

At the corner of Pinckney and Market Streets is a stone-ender, the **Tobacco Prise House**, a warehouse from the early 1800s. Exhibits illustrate the early tobacco trade, and include a press, which packed leaves into hogsheads. For admission, ask at the neighboring **Shiplap House**, at 18 Pinckney St., built about 1715, and one of the oldest houses surviving in the city. An early tavern, it has had many uses before becoming the offices of the Historic Annapolis Foundation. Inside are changing historical exhibits and outside is a garden, both free. Open Monday through Friday, 2-4, from March-October; ☎ 410-267-7619.

William Paca House and Gardens, at 186 Prince George St. (☎ 410-263-5553, is the restored home of William Paca, signer of the Declaration of Independence and former Governor of Maryland. Built between 1763 and 1765, the house is the earliest example of the five-part Georgian home in Annapolis. Thirteen of its 37 rooms are furnished in period pieces, which include a fine collection of antique silver and decorative arts, in addition to the furniture.

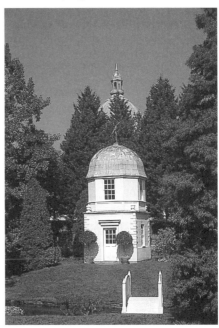

The garden of the William Paca House.

This house is a fascinating testament to the restorer's art, since it had been badly damaged by subsequent owners, one of which used it as the lobby of a hotel that completely covered its gardens. But painstaking research and archaeological evidence combined to recreate the showpiece it was when William Paca lived here.

The gardens are lovely, entered through a pergola overlooking a boxwood parterre with topiary centerpieces and potted standards, plus shaded benches to admire them from. Opposite are five tall holly trees, trimmed to cone shapes, and a fruit "orchard" bordered by a low fence of espaliered trees, including greengage plums. At the far end of the gardens, below the terraces and beyond a pool, a domed summer house provides a focal point.

Annapolis

A Visitors Center, almost hidden off to side, has changing exhibits examining crops or garden subjects of the period. These are not showy gardens, but true to their time, well-kept and very pleasant to stroll or sit in. The larger tree in front of the house is a mulberry.

The Paca House is open Monday through Saturday, 10-4; Sunday, noon-4. In January and February it's open Saturday and Sunday only. The garden is open until 5 pm, April through October. House tour (45 minutes) and garden together are $7 ($6 for visitors over age 65) and entrance to the garden only is $4.

Hammond-Harwood House, around the corner at 19 Maryland Ave. (☎ 410-269-1714), takes you back to 1774, when Annapolis was the cultural center of Maryland (there are those who claim it still is), and this house is the icon of the city's Golden Age. The final work of the 18th-century architect, William Buckland, the 1774 house is considered one of the most beautiful examples of late Colonial architecture in existence.

It is also significant because it is almost entirely original. The dining room is the signature room of the house, with its rococo carving on the overmantel, its fine detailed moldings, and the jib door, which pushes into the ceiling to open. Even the window shutters are carved.

THE CUT OF THEIR JIB

False windows, called "jib doors," are actually doors and are fairly common to Georgian homes here. Filling in lower panels creates the illusion of a window and retains the symmetry that is the cornerstone of Georgian architecture. From the outside, you can see that the back door is made to look like a window to match the others when seen from inside the dining room. Another jib door is in the gentlemen's study, and a further example of this Georgian preoccupation is in the front hall, where a false door opens onto a brick wall to balance the real one opposite it.

In the parlor, note the horizontal floor pegs, which would have been concealed originally, but are left visible here to show the construction. The quoined window under the cove ceiling of the stairway was inspired by the church of St. Martin-in-the-Fields in London.

The first floor is Rococo style, with a heavily carved over-mantel; on the second floor, decoration is more restrained. The salon was designed for formal entertaining, and is shown with silver service and piano. In the upstairs bedroom, note the Charles Wilson Peale portrait of a little girl with doll, and see the original doll below it. The house has several fine portraits by the Peales, including Rembrandt Peale's portrait of George Washington mounted, and two other portraits by his son Charles Wilson Peale.

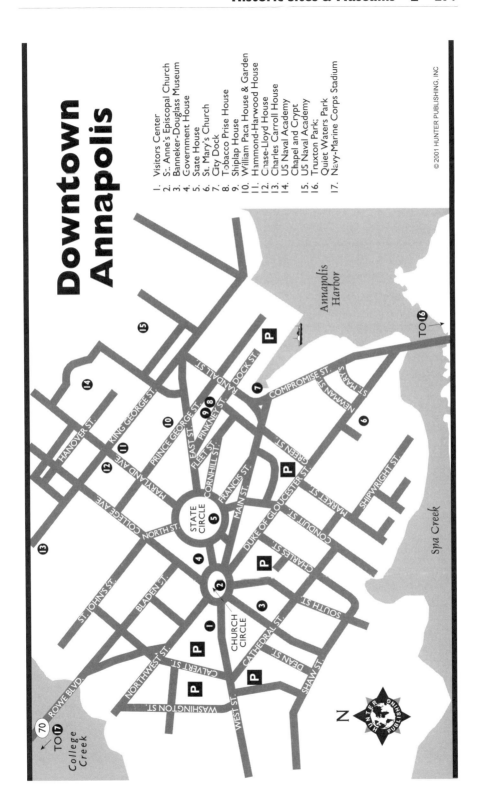

Downtown Annapolis

1. Visitors Center
2. St. Anne's Episcopal Church
3. Banneker-Douglass Museum
4. Government House
5. State House
6. St. Mary's Church
7. City Dock
8. Tobacco Prise House
9. Shiplap House
10. William Paca House & Garden
11. Hammond-Harwood House
12. Chase-Lloyd House
13. Charles Carroll House
14. US Naval Academy
15. Chapel and Crypt
16. US Naval Academy
17. Truxton Park;
     Quiet Waters Park
     Navy-Marine Corps Stadium

© 2001 HUNTER PUBLISHING, INC

Annapolis Harbor

Spa Creek

College Creek

Annapolis

Another outstanding collection is furniture by Charles Shaw, one of the finest cabinet makers in Colonial America. His linen press (in the upstairs hallway) and secretary are especially impressive. The house has interior shutters throughout, some fine examples of Chinese export porcelain, and a number of other good examples of Colonial cabinetmakers' work.

The kitchen is in one wing, with a huge fireplace; note the 18th-century six-pack for wines and the Pennsylvania spice cabinet.

Tours are on the hour, the only way to see the house. Guides are uneven, however: although ours asked in each room for questions, she always refused to answer them. We did learn that Matthias Hammond, who commissioned the house, never lived there; he lost the next election and did not return to Annapolis. Tours Monday-Saturday, 10-3:30; Sunday, noon-3:30; admission $5 adults, $3 children.

Across the street from the Hammond-Harwood House, at 22 Maryland Ave. (☎ 410-263-2723), is the **Chase-Lloyd House**, begun by another signer, Samuel Chase, in 1769. He sold the house before finishing it, and the next owner spared no expense in its completion. He hired William Buckland and the interior of the house is the result of Buckland's talent and Lloyd's money. The main stairway is cantilevered, among the finest stairways built in the colony. Ornate carvings and fixtures made of silver are among the extravagant decorations of its interior. In 1802, Lloyd's daughter married Frances Scott Key in this house. It is open Monday through Saturday, 2-4; $2 donation.

Maryland Avenue leads to another cluster of historic sites, at the center of which is the elegant brick **Maryland State House,** on State Circle; ☎ 410-974-3400. America's oldest state house in continuous use, the building was the US capitol for nearly a year, in 1783 and 1784 (the only state capitol to have this distinction). Here George Washington resigned the post of Commander-in-Chief of the Continental Army and here ended – officially – the American Revolution, with ratification of the Treaty of Paris. The dome, completed in 1788, is the largest wooden dome in the United States.

Displays inside include the intricately worked silver service that has been used aboard the cruiser, battleship and submarine bearing the name USS *Maryland*. The Old Senate Chamber, where the Continental Congress met when the building was the US Capitol, has original furniture by the Annapolis cabinetmaker John Shaw and portraits by Charles Wilson Peale. The building is open daily, 9-5, and 30-minute tours are offered daily at 11 and 3. Both tours and admission are free.

On the grounds are two often-overlooked historical features: the small brick treasury building from 1737, the oldest public building in Maryland, and a cannon that arrived with the first settlers aboard the *Dove*, in 1634.

Government House, at State Circle and School Streets (☎ 410-974-3531), is the Victorian-era official residence of the Governor of Maryland. Inside are collections of art and Maryland-made antiques, which you can see by appointment during regular visiting hours: 10-2, Tuesday through Thursday, except during January-March, when it's open only Tuesday *and* Thursday. Admission free.

St. Anne Episcopal Church sits aloof in the center of Church Circle, at the top of the hill where all the main streets converge in a wagon-wheel. Highlights of the interior are its Tiffany stained-glass window and the needlepoint kneelers. The silver communion service, still used, was a gift of King William is 1695, but that didn't stop three of its parishioners from signing their names to the Declaration of Independence. In fact, only one of the state's four signers was not a parishioner at St. Anne; he was the Catholic signer, Charles Carroll of Carrollton. The church is usually open in the daytime, and outside you can see the grave of the colony's last Colonial governor in the churchyard.

Banneker-Douglass Museum, at 84 Franklin St. (☎ 410-974-2893), occupies the former Mount Moriah African Methodist Episcopal Church. Named for two historically significant black Marylanders, Benjamin Banneker and Frederick Douglass, the museum is also the official state repository of African-American material. Changing exhibits display photographs and collections relating to Black heritage in Maryland and both African and African-American art. Open Tuesday-Friday, 10-3; Saturday, noon-4. Free admission.

The fourth of Maryland's signers of the Declaration of Independence, Charles Carroll of Carrollton, was born in the **Charles Carroll House**, at 107 Duke of Gloucester St., ☎ 410-269-1737. One of the most influential and wealthiest men in the colonies and the only Catholic signer, Carroll would also outlive all the other signers and be instrumental in founding the B&O Railroad. The house, which was his main urban residence until 1821, is in the process of restoration, and has 18th-century terraced gardens along the shore of Spa Creek. Open Friday, Sunday and holidays, noon-4; Saturday, 10-2; admission $5 for adults, $4 for seniors, $2 for students ages 12-17.

Next to the house, at 109 Duke of Gloucester St., ☎ 410-263-2396, is **St. Mary's Church**, a Gothic-style Victorian building with ribbed vaulting and a carved altar screen. Its cornerstone was laid by Saint John Neuman in 1858. The church is usually open during daylight hours.

Barge House Museum, on Bay Shore Dr. at the end of Second St. in Eastport (☎ 410-268-1802), houses collections and exhibits relating to the maritime and cultural history of the waterfront neighborhood and its boatbuilders and watermen. Admission is free, and the small museum is open Saturday, 11-4, or by appointment.

Fort Meade NSA Cryptologic Museum, on Colony 7 Rd., Fort Meade (☎ 410-688-5849), displays equipment used to make and break codes and tells stories of people involved in the work. The most famous code machine of all is here – Enigma, used by the Germans in World War II to encrypt the code they were sure could never be broken. The theoretical number of possible variations is so large that it takes 115 digits – beyond the vocabulary of "...illions" – to describe. (That's a trillion with another 34 sets of three digits tacked on.) Anyway, the allies did break it. But this is only one of the stories you'll hear in the guided tour, which you can request. Or you can wander through on your own, Monday through Friday, 9-3; Saturday, 10-2; free.

The Naval Academy

Just inside Gate 1, which is off King George St., is the **US Naval Academy Visitor Center**, ☎ 410-263-6933. Guided tours of the academy begin here, where you can also see a film about this 338-acre training center and college, where more than 4,000 students prepare for careers as officers in the Navy or Marine Corps. The center is open daily, March-December, 9-5; January and February, 9-4. The grounds are open to visitors without charge, but guided tours are $5.50 for adults, $4.50 seniors and $3.50 students.

The US Naval Academy is steeped in history and tradition, and a good place to begin is at the impressive **Chapel**, a rather grand building for such a modest name. You can spot it from some distance by its imposing dome. At the back, close to the entrance, is a brochure about the Chapel, its art and its history. The Chapel was designed by Ernest Flagg, and was intended to be the focal point of the Academy, a role it plays admirably with its soaring dome.

Inside, the stained-glass windows get the most attention. The Farragut window, on the right in the rotunda, depicts the Admiral in the rigging of his flagship, and the Archangel Michael guiding ships through the mine-studded Mobile Bay. To its right is a window by the Tiffany studio. The Sir Galahad window, on the opposite side of the rotunda, is an earlier Tiffany window of the Angel of Peace; Saints Peter and Andrew mend nets below. Sir Galahad, to the left, is the oldest Tiffany work here, intended for the earlier chapel.

Underneath is the small, dark and much more contemplative **St. Andrews Chapel**, reached by stairs to the left of the entrance, from either inside or outside. The baptismal font is made of wood from the USS *Constitution*.

John Paul Jones is a relative newcomer to the **Crypt** under the rotunda of the chapel. Flagg, the architect, greatly admired this naval hero, the whereabouts of whose grave was unknown when the chapel was built. But, in the hope that his remains would someday be located, Flagg designed a vaulted crypt under the rotunda worthy of this role model for midshipmen.

Entrance to the crypt is through an outside door under the central section of the Chapel, on the west side, nearest the Maryland Ave. entrance, Gate 3. Hours for the Chapel and the crypt are the same: Monday through Saturday, 9-4; Sunday, 1-4.

THE BODY OF JOHN PAUL JONES

General Horace Porter, who was Ambassador to France in 1899, was determined to find the grave of John Paul Jones (known to have died in France), and to return the body to the newly built crypt in Annapolis. Find it he did, and Jones was escorted to Maryland by a squadron of Navy ships. President Theodore Roosevelt delivered the memorial address.

Facing onto the same green lawn as the chapel is the **Academy Museum**, a fascinating trip through Naval history and through the traditions that bind today's midshipmen to their predecessors. Exhibits on Fleet Admiral Chester Nimitz, class of 1905, include the uniform he wore when he signed the Japanese surrender documents on board the battleship *Missouri* in Tokyo Bay, on September 2, 1945, as well as the pen he used and the table on which it was signed.

Downstairs is an entire room of ship models. The collection is highly unusual in that each ship model was made at the same time that the original ship was built. In many cases, these contemporaneous models, some several centuries old, are all we know of the details of the particular ships. Some of the models are incredibly detailed, with working parts hidden below the decks. The oldest of these models was made about 1650.

KID-FRIENDLY

The museum thoughtfully provides a guide for parents to help them make the model collections more meaningful to children. It points out details to look for, such as the decrease in decoration from older to newer ships, changes in rigging, the role of fire ships and even the location of toilets. Although this two-page flyer is intended as a resource in helping children enjoy the collection, we found it really interesting ourselves and suggest you pick up a copy.

Possibly the most fascinating, and certainly the most unusual collection here is the gallery of prisoner-of-war art, displaying beautiful ship models carved from bone by French sailors interned in British prison ships between 1756 and 1815. They saved the beef and mutton bones from their rations, softened them by immersion in wet clay and carved these detailed pieces from memory – their own and that of other seamen. The bone pieces are applied over wooden hulls and the rigging is of human or horse hair. Tools were fashioned from nails and from pieces of metal and glass.

This is one of the world's finest collections, with six complete ships about 12 inches long, one hull, and one unfinished ship showing its construction

Annapolis

over wood. Around the corner are three larger models, one more than three feet long.

The rest of the museum is an assortment reflecting life at the academy, naval art, mementos of the great naval explorers and survivors, great sea engagements, and exhibits on great naval figures – not always the most famous. Look for artifacts from Perry's expedition to Japan, and the watch that stopped at the moment its wearer, a naval gunner, escaped the *Utah* by plunging into the waters of Pearl Harbor. The museum is free, and open Monday-Saturday, 9-5; Sunday, 11-5.

In the same building is a must-stop for anyone interested in ships, the academy or naval history. The **US Naval Institute Bookstore** has, in addition to books on every possible subject relating to the sea and the US Navy, prints, nautical gifts and Naval Academy insignia items. The shop is open Monday-Saturday, 9-5; Sunday, 11-5; ☎ 410-295-1043, www.unsi.org.

London Town

London Town, south of Annapolis, overlooking the South River from a steep bank, is one of our favorite historical sites in Anne Arundel County – an area with a surfeit of them. We have watched it slowly emerge from near-obscurity over the past two decades and look forward to each visit to see what they have discovered since our last.

But first a little history: Londontown was located at the best crossing point over South River. Ships sailed here to load tobacco from plantations farther south, and a ferry carried travelers across the river to Annapolis. At its height it was home to 300 people in 40-50 houses, on 100 acres. It was the first county seat of Anne Arundel County, and from 1684-95 it rivaled Annapolis. But in 1747, the legislature passed a bill to promote the tobacco trade, called the Towns Act, which required all tobacco to go through one of 80 named inspection ports. Londontown was not among them, so planters could no longer ship from here. The town declined, and by 1800 was pretty much gone.

DID YOU KNOW? **LONDON TOWN OR LONDONTOWN?** *The original name of the town was London, and the peninsula (and hence the river crossing) was called Londontown (both with and without an "e" on the end). But the historic park, which was run by the county and is now in the hands of the London Town Foundation, is called London Town. It is on Londontown Road. When referring to the old settlement, either London (if it means just the group of houses that were there) or Londontown (if it means the geographical place) is correct. But the park – the attraction you visit today – is London Town.*

WASHINGTON SCHLEPPED HERE

Washington always crossed at Londontown, coming overland from Mt. Vernon instead of by boat, because he wanted to have his horse with him. Although he came ostensibly to visit his stepson at St. Johns College, he always went to the racetrack while he was in town.

Today you can watch archaeologists as they dig up that long-ago streetscape, still looking for some buildings they know must be there. These were post-in-ground houses, and by finding postholes they can tell the placement and dimensions of houses. Soil is mixed in the plow zone, but below that is clear evidence of post and fence holes. Archaeologists can also tell if the houses, which had a lifespan of 15-30 years, had wooden or brick chimneys.

Under the site of **Rumney's Tavern**, the cellar is a rich source of artifacts. It's a time capsule – or a series of them – as layer-by-layer the cellar silted up after it was flooded in each big storm. Between storms, they threw the tavern trash there, and each layer was preserved by the next flood. In a single layer they might find all the pieces to a broken pot, not just a few. They have found the entire tavern china service, a high quality Delft, lots of wine bottles, and bones and oyster shells that tell researchers what the tavern served. Over 1,800 pieces have been recovered at the 75% point. You can visit the dig, which is covered by a tent, and note the distinct layers as they uncover more. In 1780, the tavern added an ell; the cellar that was under it is still intact. Volunteers are welcome at the dig site on the third Saturday of each month, on Public Dig Days. Schoolchildren come with classes – the only place in the country where they work an actual dig, doing real, not simulated work.

To get from Annapolis to Londontown, cross the bridge to Edgewater on Route 2, south of Annapolis, and turn left on 253, less than a mile from the bridge. Go left again (there's a sign) at 0.8 mile on Londontown Rd., following it to the end; it's about two miles from Route 2.

Annapolis

Walk through gardens, which surround the visitors center, and into the dell that is filled with colorful rhododendrons in the spring. The 1720 log tobacco house is a rare surviving building, although not original to this site. The small shop in the visitors center has some very nice period gifts, and a good selection of books on the area, the age, and on heirloom gardening. Some of the artifacts recovered in the dig are displayed in cases in the visitors center. A $6 admission ($4 seniors, $3 children) admits visitors to the gardens and house tour; ☎ 410-222-1919. London Town is open year-round, Monday through Saturday, 10-4; Sunday noon to 4. In January and February, house tours are by appointment only.

THE WILLIAM BROWN HOUSE

Although all of London Town's wooden houses fell into the ground and were eventually plowed over by farmers, the large brick **William Brown House** stood firm. The house is a fine one, too fine for its owner, an only modestly prosperous man. An example of its grandeur is found in the brickwork, which is all in header bond brick, by far the most costly type because it uses many more bricks than other patterns. Anne Arundel County has America's thickest concentration of 18th-century houses, but none in Annapolis has all header bond brickwork.

The cost of the brick broke Brown. His family lived in an unfinished house, walls unplastered until later. There are other unusual things about the house. Although Georgian, it has no hyphens and no wings, and its position on the riverbank indicates that none were intended. The interior arrangement is not grand: for all its other grandeur, it is the house of a man without grand intentions, with a large family of six or seven children. The stairways are not grand, nor are they placed as they would have been by a man with pretensions of being a gentleman. The big mystery is why a middle-class carpenter would borrow so much money to build such a mansion.

The house was set at the ferry landing, on a major route from Charleston and the south to Philadelphia, and was evidently used as an inn for passing travelers. But it was built in 1760, 13 years after the 1747 list made the town obsolete as a port, when London Town was already becoming ramshackle. It's all quite odd. Brown went bankrupt in 1790, and lost the house. Different owners passed it around from the 1830s to 1960s, when it was in use as an almshouse.

The restored house is interesting today for its architecture, its story, and for the unique collection of handmade and painstakingly authentic household linens made by its volunteers. Colonial Williamsburg tried to buy the diapers of handwoven linen. Look all through the house for examples, from bed hangings to baby clothing and flame-work accessories on the dressing table.

Under the first floor is the kitchen, spinning room and unrestored rooms where visitors are welcome to touch things. The giant fireplace has its original strapwork.

Where to Stay

ACCOMMODATIONS PRICE KEY
Rates are per room, per night, double occupancy.
$ . . . . Under $50
$$ . . . . $50 to $100
$$$ . . . . $101 to $175
$$$$ . . . . $176 and up

■ Central Annapolis

Historic Inns of Annapolis, 16 Church Circle; ☎ 410-263-2641 is a group of four 18th- and early 19th-century buildings: the **Maryland Inn**, **Governor Calvert House**, **Robert Johnson House** and **State House Inn**. All surround State Circle, with check-in for all 137 rooms at the Governor Calvert House, 58 State Circle; ☎ 410-269-0990. Bell service and valet parking for all locations centers here, a not-altogether-smooth system that may leave you waiting as much as 45 minutes to retrieve your car if they are busy with an event. Rates are around $100, although they can rise to more than $185 during the boat show or other big events. Of these, our choice is the Robert Johnson House, newly renovated and quieter than the others, furnished in antiques and reproductions.

Gibson's Lodgings, 110 Prince George St. (410-268-5555), is just off the City Dock in three historic district houses, with 21 rooms and parking. Rooms are beautifully decorated with period antiques and the included continental breakfast is served in the garden in nice weather; $$-$$$

Flagg House Inn, 26 Randall St. (☎ 410-280-2721 or 800-437-4825) is set in a gracious mansard-roofed home with an inviting front porch. Off-street parking in the historic district conveniently located between the City Dock and the academy. $$$

William Page Inn, at 8 Martin St. (☎ 410-626-1506 or 800-364-4160, www.williampageinn.com), is furnished in antiques and reproductions. They offer a full breakfast and off-street parking. The third-floor suite is worth the climb, with a sleigh bed, window seats and whirlpool tub; $$$-$$$$.

Harborview Boat and Breakfast (☎ 800-877-9330, www.harborview-bnb.com) has a fleet of several classic yachts offering staterooms with breakfast and an evening cruise; $$$.

Annapolis

Schooner *Woodwind* (☎ 410-263-7837, www.schooner-woodwind.com, Marriott dock) is a 74-ft schooner accommodating eight guests in four double-berth staterooms with air conditioning. Lodging is available weekends only, and includes a two-hour cruise (which is also open to the public); rates are about $200 (single $160).

LODGING SERVICES

For help in securing lodgings, contact any of the following services.

Amanda's Bed and Breakfast Regional Reservation Service, 1428 Park Ave, Baltimore 21217; ☎ 410-225-0001.

Annapolis Accommodations, 66 Maryland Ave, Annapolis 21401; ☎ 410-280-0900 or 800-715-1000.

B&B of Maryland, PO Box 2277, Annapolis 21204; ☎ 410-269-6232 or 800-736-4667.

■ On the Outskirts

Country Inn and Suites, 2600 Housley Rd., Annapolis (☎ 410-571-6700 or 800-456-4000, www.countryinns.com), has spacious two-room suites with thoughtful amenities, including in-room irons and ironing boards. The location is convenient to downtown and to the Renaissance Fairegrounds, with van shuttles to the historic district. Indoor pool and continental breakfast. It's close to the intersection of Route 2, US-301/50 and I-97, just east of the city.

Lodgings across the Bay Bridge are within easy reach; see Kent Manor Inn in the *Upper Eastern Shore* chapter.

Where to Eat

DINING PRICE KEY

The price key indicates the cost of *most* dinner entrées on a restaurant's regular and daily special menu.

$	Most under $10
$$	$10 to $20
$$$	Over $30

■ Market Square & Main Street

For breakfast or lunch in a casual market atmosphere, mingle with the locals in **The Market House**, on the City Dock. Along with the ingredients to carry home, you'll find a bakery, deli, raw bar, pizza and sandwich stands, plus ice cream.

Aromi d'Italia Café serves gelato in countless mouthwatering flavors, including Grand Marnier and nocciola, a rich hazelnut confection. Along with ice cream and light dishes such as panini sandwiches, salads and pizza, Aromi offers full meal specials each day from 11:30 to 3, for $7, somewhat higher at dinner hours. Open Monday-Thursday, 10-10; Friday, 10-midnight; Saturday, 8 am to midnight; Sunday, 8 am to 10 pm. It is located along the docks, right behind the information center at 8 Dock St.; ☎ 410-263-1300.

City Dock Café, 18 Market Space (☎ 410-269-0969), is a casual coffee house with fresh-baked pastries and lunch menu, open Sunday-Thursday, 7 am-8 pm; Friday-Saturday, 7 am-midnight.

Middleton Tavern Oyster Bar and Restaurant, Dock St. (☎ 410-263-3323) serves up traditional Maryland fare in a 1750 building overlooking the dock. Specials may include flounder stuffed with crabmeat, mahi-mahi or soft crabs, priced at $20-$24. The bar is outside on the porch, and there is live entertainment. Open Monday-Friday, 11:30 am-2 am, Saturday-Sunday, 10am-midnight.

Maria's, 12 Market Space (☎ 410-268-2112), is firmly based in the family's Sicilian roots, which they adapt smoothly to the local seafoods. Rockfish sautéed in white wine and capers is served with asparagus, red snapper is served in a caper marinara sauce with clams and veal medallions are wrapped around jumbo shrimp before being sautéed in lemon butter. Five sidewalk tables and the downstairs area are casual, the upstairs dining room overlooking the docks is more formal upstairs. Most entrées are between $12 and $20; lunch, $8-$12.

Buddy's Crabs and Ribs, at 100 Main St. (☎ 410-626-1100), is best known for – surprise! – ribs and crabs. But that's not to suggest the yellow-fin tuna isn't just as good. Crab cakes are thick, crisp on the

Sidewalk café near City Dock in Annapolis.

Annapolis

outside and filled with chunk crabmeat, no fillers, and just a hint of pi-quant seasoning. Fried foods are not overcooked, oysters on the half-shell are redolent of the sea they just left. We like our softies sautéed, but if you like them deep-fried don't worry: Buddy's won't overcook them, as (sad to report) other places often do. It's not the spot for an intimate sotto-voce dinner, with its high tin ceilings, wide-open spaces and youngish crowd. From a perch here, high above City Dock, you can watch skateboarders practice, Midshipmen stroll with their dates, and boats moor and unload in the harbor. Entrées are $10-$18. All-you-can-eat buffet, served 11-2 weekdays, is $9; Sunday breakfast buffet is served 8:30-1:30, with om-elets, Belgian waffles, fresh fish, pickled herring and corned beef hash at $8. Don't be put off by the café/entry way – the restaurant is upstairs.

Yin Yankee Café, at 105 Main St. (☎ 410-268-8703), has a split personal-ity, with traditional Maryland seafood and Japanese dishes: fish & chips, steamed shrimp, sushi ($5.50-$8), half rack of ribs, vegetables with udon, udon noodles with chicken or shrimp, most priced at $9-$12.

Governor's Grill, on Main St. at Conduit St. (☎ 410-263-6555), offers an upscale, but casual environment of booths and tables, set in a mahogany-paneled room. The menu includes Norwegian salmon, tuna steak, seafood-stuffed shrimp and lamb chops with rosemary, most around $25. Open 11:30-3 daily for lunch, Sunday-Thursday, 5-9; Friday-Saturday, 5-10. Complimentary valet parking on Friday and Saturday evenings.

Piccola Roma, 200 Main St., has a way with Italian ingredients that may not be just like mama used to make, but who cares? Look for fettuccine al pesti (shrimp, scallops and crab in lemon-thyme cream sauce), penne al salmone (smoked salmon in basil, tomato and cream sauce), filetto ripieno (filet mignon stuffed with spinach, prosciutto and goat cheese in a grilled leek demi-glace, or duck with brandy and wild mushrooms on puff pastry, priced between $16 and $19. Open Monday-Friday 11:30-2:30, Sunday-Thursday, 5:30-10; Friday-Saturday, 5:30-11.

■ West Street

Ram's Head Tavern, 33 West St. (☎ 410-268-4545), is home of the Fordham Brewing Co, the only micro-brewery in town (and the first in three centuries). Clusters of seating overlook the two giant copper vats and a gleaming bar lines one wall of the brick interior. There is additional patio seating, and a nice little tea room with six tables overlooking the pa-tio. The original pub is cozy in dark wood and a separate entertainment area, with a bright music-mural covering one wall, keeps sound levels down in the restaurant. An interesting sandwich menu is served all day. The dinner menu stars shepherd's pie, crab cakes, London broil, jam-balaya, shellfish pie with prosciutto and baked chicken breast stuffed with crab imperial, at prices from $11 to $17. Open Monday-Saturday, 11 am-2 am; Sunday, 10 am (for brunch) until 2 am. Their Web site has the cur-rent schedule of performers: www.ramsheadtavern.com.

Ciao!, at 51 West St. (☎ 410-267-7912) creates an exciting fusion menu in a smart bistro setting, borrowing adroitly from French, Italian, Iberian and eastern Mediterranean styles. Begin with a hummus enlivened by roasted red peppers and garlic or a risotto of barley, artichoke and wild mushrooms. The fragrance of cinnamon lingers over the Spanish chicken with almonds, and roast duck breast tops a potato galette with a brandied fruit demi-glace. Dishes rarely found on restaurant menus, such as paella Valencia, cassoulet and bouillabaisse enrich an already full menu. Most entrées are $16 to $23. Open for dinner only, Tuesday through Sunday from 5:30.

49 West (☎ 410-626-9796) is a café and wine bar, a good place for breakfast with good scones, waffles, quiche and egg dishes. Soups, salads and sandwiches are served all day. Live classical music is featured on Tuesday evening; jazz from Wednesday through Friday.

■ Eastport

Carrol's Creek Restaurant, 410 Severn Ave., just over the Eastport Bridge (☎ 410-263-8102), overlooks the marina and a sweeping harbor view of Annapolis (and of the sunset). Fresh fish at its very best; the nightly special might be sushi-quality tuna on a risotto cake or rockfish simply baked and served with garlic mashed potatoes. Crab cakes are served on crispy polenta, shrimp and scallops are broiled to a perfect state, served on an orange coulis, with rice and finely slivered onion and pepper sauté. The four-course Bay Dinner ($25) includes their cream of crab soup. Non-seafood-lovers can have a mixed grill of quail, lamb and venison. The dessert cart may include coeur à la crème with mascarpone, a tart with fresh berries or espresso crème brûlée. Most entrées are $14-$20. Open Monday-Saturday, 11:30-4 and 5-8; Sunday brunch, 10-2.

■ Edgewater

Old Stein Inn, at 1143 Central Ave. (☎ 410-798-6807), is a traditional German restaurant and bierstube, just the right place after you've worked up an appetite paddling around Rhode and West Rivers. Look for tender smoked porkchops, juicy weisswurst and chewy rich spaetzle, served in a Bavarian atmosphere with good beers; $$. They are open Wednesday, Thursday and Sunday, 4-9; Friday and Saturday, 4-10. In October, they have special Oktoberfest events.

Annapolis

Washington DC

L ike capital cities everywhere, Washington is a mecca for tourists. Particularly in the spring, it is the destination for school groups, and on any April day you might find hundreds of buses filled with class trips. It's a worthy destination, not only for its historic and governmental importance, but because it has a

great many sights. Monuments, museums and places of historic or cultural significance are everywhere.

We have not even tried to list them, and in this way have diverged from the pattern we have set in the rest of the book. So many good guidebooks already exist that to repeat the information in them is pointless. Nearly every guide series has a book on the capital, and we suggest that if you plan to spend much time "doing the sights" of the city that you use one of them.

What we have done in this chapter is to point out those activities that fit into the adventure themes of the book, and in that pursuit, have left out the section on sightseeing altogether. As you tour the "must see" places in the city, we hope you will take time to seek out some of the unexpected corners we've discovered and the adventures they offer.

Geography & History

The wide riverbank upon which the city of Washington lies is nearly flat. A few sections rise higher than others, notably Capitol Hill and St. Albans, but most of it is a plain. On the southwest, the city is bordered by the Potomac River, here a broad body of water that once served as a commercial highway for the city. The southeast corner is cut by the Anacostia River. The Potomac is tidal as far as Georgetown, a historic neighborhood that seems like a town of its own.

■ Planning the District

In the opening days of the new American Republic there was no set capital. Philadelphia had its stint and New York City had a share, serving as the inauguration site of the first President in 1789. In 1783, unpaid war veterans marched on the Congress in Philadelphia; this unrest started the movement toward building a new capital city. In 1790 Congress voted to do this, delegating to George Washington the task of selecting the site.

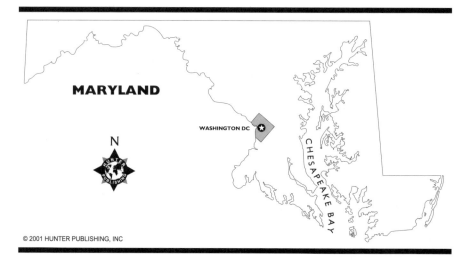

MARYLAND

N

WASHINGTON DC

CHESAPEAKE BAY

© 2001 HUNTER PUBLISHING, INC

He chose a piece of relative wilderness along the Potomac River and a square of land 10 miles on each side was ceded by the states of Virginia and Maryland. Washington chose this site because the river provided good navigation for ships. He also saw the river as the starting point for a great canal that could link the new capital with the Ohio River in the expanding interior.

As designer, Washington chose a young French engineering officer, Pierre-Charles L'Enfant, who had volunteered to fight for the Americans in the Revolution. Both men envisioned a grand city that would epitomize the ideals of the new democracy. To assure that grandeur, L'Enfant created a huge open area from the Capitol, on the city's high point, all the way to the river, calling it the National Mall. He also left open the land from the President's House to the mall and beyond to the Tidal Basin, creating the feeling of spaciousness that still characterizes the city.

George Washington died in 1798 and never got to see the city that he founded. It wasn't until 1800 that the second President, John Adams, moved into the newly finished President's House and the Congress began its first deliberations in the Senate wing of the still unfinished Capitol. The Capitol was not finished until well into the 19th century. The land of the new city was low and wet, hardly the place of grandeur we see today. Congressmen and visitors disliked the location and its lack of attractions and facilities. Pressure mounted to abandon this site before its basic buildings were completed.

Ironically, it was the British who sealed Washington as America's capital. In 1814, British troops under the command of Admiral Sir George Cockburn defeated American troops at Bladensburg, Maryland, and took possession of Washington, sending President Madison and the Congress fleeing. Before the British left, they had burned the Capitol, the President's House and the Naval Arsenal along the Anacostia River. The national sense of outrage at the burning of Washington quickly ended the movement to change the location of the capital.

The Virginia part of the city, which now contains the Arlington National Cemetery, the Pentagon and Reagan National Airport, was returned to Virginia in 1847. The coming of the Civil War in 1860 left the city in a precarious position. The Mason-Dixon line had established the boundary between slave and non-slave states between Maryland and Pennsylvania. Virginia, which abuts the city across the Potomac, was a leader of secession. The family home of its military leader, General Robert E. Lee, sat within view of the Washington.

East of the city, plantation owners of eastern Maryland, while remaining a part of the Union, had close personal and emotional ties with the South and many Confederate sympathizers. Between 1861 and 1864, General Lee's advances into northern Maryland at Antietam and Monocacy, and during the Gettysburg campaign, threatened to cut the city off from the rest of the nation. At the same time, the tremendous demands for men and material, and the need to have a government big enough to manage all this, gave a big boost to Washington's growth.

ROBERT E. LEE'S MANSION

In an act that has a strange twist of irony, the federal government seized the mansion of General Lee and his family, on a hillside overlooking the Potomac and the city, and made the grounds into a cemetery for Union war dead. This was done to prevent Lee from occupying his home again. But in the process of creating Arlington National Cemetery, the Lee property became a national shrine.

Washington's importance continued to grow after the war. The onset of World War I in 1917 gave it another push as wartime demands again expanded the government. Only 20 years later the city again grew as Franklin Roosevelt's administration prepared the nation for a war that was inevitable. The scope of World War II demanded huge numbers of people and temporary quarters sprang up all over the city, even on The Mall. Across the river in Arlington an enormous headquarters was built for the armed forces, the five-sided building called the Pentagon. The role of the Federal Government in social affairs increased, starting with the New Deal of the 1930s and continuing with the Great Society of the 1960s, and Washington's size and importance continued to grow until it spilled even further into neighboring states.

Washington DC

Getting Here

■ By Car

The City of Washington is at the southern end of the so-called East Coast Megalopolis that stretches south from Boston. The central artery of this northeast corridor is **I-95**, which begins in Maine, passing through Baltimore to Washington and continuing southward through the coastal states. In Maryland, I-95 intersects a large arcing highway that begins at the Potomac northeast of Washington and curves east, south and west around the city. This multi-lane free-for-all is Interstate **495**, known as the **Beltway**.

To reach the center of Washington from I-95, which joins the Beltway at College Park, follow it south a short way to the **Route 1** south (Baltimore Avenue) exit. This becomes Rhode Island Avenue before it enters the city limits. Or from Baltimore, take **Route 295**, crossing I-495 and exiting at **Route 50 west** to enter the city via New York Avenue. To enter via Pennsylvania Avenue, continue south on **Route 295** and follow **Route 4** northwest.

Also approaching Washington from the north is **I-83**, which passes through Pennsylvania to meet **I-695** (the Baltimore circumferential). Take I-695 west and south to I-95 or to the Baltimore-Washington Parkway to reach Washington.

From the west, **I-68** crosses West Virginia and western Maryland before ending at **I-70** (entering from western Pennsylvania) at the narrow point of Maryland in Hancock. Approaching from these highways, take **I-270** south at Frederick, which will quickly bring you to the I-495 east exit. The Connecticut Avenue exit (Route 185) will bring you into the downtown area.

From the southeast, follow I-95 and just south of Alexandria, Virginia take **I-395**, which takes you over the Potomac into the southwest part of Washington.

AUTHOR TIP

TOURIST TRAP: *The city of Washington has an unreasonable and unfriendly policy for people whose cars are towed. If your car (rental or otherwise) is towed anytime from Friday at 7 pm (best to read this liberally as late afternoon) through the weekend you will not be able to retrieve it until the following Monday after 9 am, regardless of your schedule. Note that you have to **retrieve** the impounded car before 7 pm. If you do get towed, call ☎ 202-727-9200 or 727-9201.*

■ By Plane

Washington is served by three airports, two international and one domestic. The closest to the city, with the shortest commute time is **Ronald Reagan National Airport** (DCA, ☎ 703-417-8000, along the Potomac in Alexandria. Landing here gives great overviews of the city. Try to time your arrival to avoid morning and evening rush hour. Thousands of Virginians flock to jobs in the morning and back home in the evening over the same few bridges that airport passengers have to use. Cab fare to the city should cost $12-$15.

Baltimore Washington International Airport (BWI, affectionately called Beewee, ☎ 800-I-FLY-BWI) lies south of Baltimore and is an easy ride into Washington. This is a major terminal for many international and domestic flights and, in spite of its size, is an amazingly easy airport to get in and out of. Access to the Baltimore-Washington Parkway is easy, with travel time about 45 minutes, longer during rush hours. Frequent trains run to Union Station in Washington, with additional ground transportation into the city hourly via bus and limousine. Many Washington hotels arrange transport. Taxi fare to DC should cost about $40; ask before you commit to a cab.

Washington Dulles International Airport (IAD, ☎ 703-572-2700) is a huge, modern airport west of Washington near Herndon, Virginia. Not as popular as BWI, it also serves a number of domestic and international carriers. A specially built highway, the Airport Access Rd., brings passengers to I-66 and then into the city. Bus service into the city is at 45-minute intervals via Washington Flyer Express (☎ 703-685-1400). Cab fare from the airport is about $40, but always check first.

AIRPORT SHUTTLE SERVICE

SuperShuttle provides shuttle service from Baltimore Washington International, Washington Dulles International, and Reagan National airports direct to downtown hotels or other locations. For information to/from Dulles and Reagan, ☎ 703-416-7873, 800-BLUE VAN, fax 703-416-0729; for Baltimore-Washington, ☎ 410-859-0800; or visit their Web site at www.supershuttle.com.

■ By Train & Bus

The northeast corridor is one of the nation's busiest train routes and it is served from Florida to Boston by **AMTRAK**. For access information and rates contact them at 400 North Capitol Street NW, #684, Washington DC 20001; ☎ 202-906-4971, fax 202-906-4974. Buy tickets at the Union Station AMTRAK Travel Center.

For information on train service from the many points in Maryland serviced by **MTA/MARC** transit service, ☎ 410-859-7422, fax 410-859-5713. They provide about 50 trains daily from BWI Airport to Union Station and from other Baltimore and Maryland sites.

Washington is served by the **Greyhound** and **Peter Pan** bus lines, from all over the Unites States. The terminal is at 1005 1st Street NE, close to Union Station. For information call ☎ 202-289-5154 or 800-343-9999.

Getting Around

■ Orientation

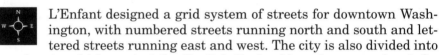

L'Enfant designed a grid system of streets for downtown Washington, with numbered streets running north and south and lettered streets running east and west. The city is also divided into quadrants, which meet at the Capitol. Each address has a quadrant, for example: 2nd Street NW or 23rd Street SE. Street numbers begin at the Capitol, so a low street number means an address is close to Capitol Hill. North, South and East Capitol Streets run from the Capitol as the dividing lines in those directions; The Mall divides the western quadrants. With this in mind, you can look at a street sign and locate yourself immediately, as well as determining how far you are from anyplace else in the city.

As with the numbered streets, lettered streets runs east and west, north and south of the mall. There are no J, X, Y or Z streets. Beyond W Street, lettered streets have two-syllable names in alphabetical order, such as Adams Street, and farther out they have three syllable names, such as Buchanan Street. Quadrant designations still apply to these.

AUTHOR TIP

A map to the city is extremely useful. Although many major attractions are clustered around The Mall, many more are outside the downtown area. One of the better maps is an advertising piece that you can find at the airports and visitor centers. Another good one is the AAA Washington DC Street and Visitor's Guide, *which also includes Annapolis, Alexandria, VA and Mount Vernon. A handy booklet of sectional and themed maps is called* Flashmaps: Washington. *It has maps dedicated to architecture, rush-hour traffic patterns, hotels, historic sites, bicycling routes, churches and even outdoor statuary, as well as maps of Rock Creek Park and the National Arboretum.*

Washington, DC

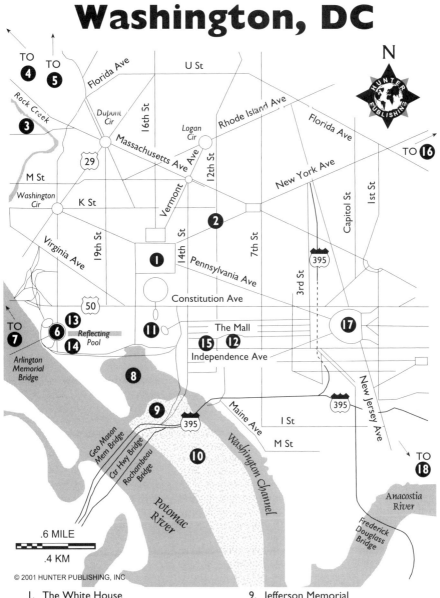

1. The White House
2. Washington Visitors & Convention Center
3. Rock Creek Park
4. Dumbarton Oaks; Washington National Cathedral
5. National Zoological Park
6. Lincoln Memorial
7. Theodore Roosevelt Island; Theodore Roosevelt Memorial
8. Tidal Basin
9. Jefferson Memorial
10. East Potomac Park
11. Washington Monument
12. Smithsonian Institution
13. Vietnam Veterans Memorial
14. Korean War Memorial
15. National Aquarium
16. Kenilworth Aquatic Gardens
17. US Capitol; US Botanic Garden & Conservatory
18. Anacostia Museum

© 2001 HUNTER PUBLISHING, INC

.6 MILE
.4 KM

Washington DC

Two grand avenues border either side of The Mall west of the Capitol, Independence Avenue on the south and Constitution Avenue on the north. On The Mall between them are the buildings of the Smithsonian Institution: National Museum of Natural History, National Museum of History and Technology and the National Gallery of Art.

L'Enfant foresaw the problem of having to zig-zag through the grid to get to opposing corners, so he overlaid the grid with a series of diagonal avenues, each named for the original states. At the intersection of these avenues are circle parks.

■ Public Transit

Washington is served by a splendid subway system, the **Metro**, and by buses that can take you to virtually any point in the city. Designed primarily for commuters and office workers, these are convenient for tourists as well. Stations are all well marked by brown pylons topped with a letter "M." The pylons have colored stripes indicating the lines accessed from that station. Trains run 5:30 am to midnight, Monday through Friday, and 8 am to midnight, Saturday and Sunday. The basic fare is $1.10, and "farecards" can be bought at any station turnstile. Bus transfers are also available at subway turnstiles. Subway lines are designated by color.

WASHINGTON DC METRO STATIONS

■ **Red** – from Shady Grove (northwest) into Union Station and then northeast to Silver Spring and Wheaton.

■ **Orange** – generally east-west, starting at New Carrollton and Landover, past the RFK Stadium, the Capitol area, then northwest past the State Department and under the river to Vienna, Virginia.

■ **Blue** – parallels the Orange line through the city, joining the Orange line at RFK Stadium and leaving it in Arlington at Rosslyn Station to go through Arlington National Cemetery to Reagan National Airport.

■ **Yellow** – runs generally north and south starting at U and 11th NW, going through the city then swinging west under the Potomac to the Pentagon and Reagan National Airport.

■ **Green** – follows the same route as Yellow line but diverges at the L'Enfant Plaza Station at 7th Street SE to head southeast past Waterfront station and the Washington Navy Yard to Anacostia.

Write in advance for a copy of the Metro Pocket Guide *or the more complete* A Metro Guide to the Nation's Capital, *which also has bus information. Get both from the* **Washington Metropolitan Area Transit Authority**, *600 5th Street NW, Washington DC 20001,* ☎ *202-637-7000, TDD 202-638-3780, www.wmata.com.*

■ Taxis

Cabs are available on the street; if you call a cab they charge an additional $1.50. There is also a $1 surcharge for rush-hour trips (4 to 6:30) and a $1.25 surcharge for each additional passenger in a group. Cabs are not metered, but operate on a zone system. The base fare for one zone is $3.70. A trip for one from Reagan National Airport in a DC cab should cost between $12 and $15. Note, however, that Reagan airport is in Virginia and Virginia cabs are metered (they can also bring you into the city). It's always best to get a price from the cab before your bags go into the car.

AUTHOR TIP

For cab-related problems, contact the **DC Taxicab Commission**, *2041 Martin Luther King Jr. Avenue SE, #204, Washington DC,* ☎ *202-767-8319, fax 202-889-3604.*

Information Sources

Downtown Washington Visitor Center, 1300 Pennsylvania Avenue NW, a block from the White House (☎ 202-638-3222, www.dcchamber.org), has a full range of brochures, maps and guides to sites, museums, attractions, hotels and restaurants. Open Monday through Saturday, 8-6; Sundays, noon to 5. They have narrated cultural and heritage tours of the city's neighborhoods.

DC Committee to Promote Washington, 1212 New York Avenue NW #200, Washington, DC 20005; ☎ 202-724-5644, fax 202-724-2445, www.washington.org. Contact them for information on transportation, special hotel rates, attractions and upcoming events and festivals.

White House Visitor Center has tours of the building and can provide a lot of additional information on it and the people who have lived there. It is in Baldrige Hall at the Commerce Department, 1450 Pennsylvania Avenue NW, at E Street between 14th and 15th Streets; ☎ 202-208-1631, open 7:30-4. Get there early or all of the free tickets will be gone.

Washington DC

Adventures

■ On Foot

Hiking & Jogging

Rock Creek Park lies along the valley of Rock Creek, a stream that enters the Potomac River at Thompson Boat Center on the north end of Virginia Avenue. It follows the Creek northward along its steep-sided and sinuous path past the National Zoo and on into Maryland. There are more than 1,750 acres within the boundaries of the park, interlaced with a network of trails. The facilities of the park are open from 8 am until dusk.

Blazed trails run along both sides of the Park. On the east side, a blue-blazed trail from the Maryland border is about 5.2 miles long. The green-blazed trail on the west side of the Creek is more difficult. About 15 miles of trails in the park span terrain ranging from flat and easy to hilly and difficult. Trail maps are strongly advised and are available at the Nature Center, located off Military Rd. and at the Visitor Information Center off Beach Drive. To get to Military Rd. from downtown, take 16th Street NW, or Connecticut Avenue north. Military Rd. runs between the two. You can also get to the park from 16th Street by taking Park Rd. NW. Running north-south in the park are Beach Drive and the Rock Creek and Potomac Parkways. Pick up Rock Creek Parkway at the north end of Virginia Avenue or at Porter Street and Klingle Rd. (off upper 16th Street). Beach Drive also begins at this point, following Rock Creek north. You can access it from Military Rd.

A 1½-mile jogging track in the woods south of the National Zoo has fitness stations and begins near the intersection of Rock Creek Parkway and Cathedral Avenue. For information contact Rock Creek Park, 3545 Williamsburg Lane NW, Washington DC 20008; ☎ 202-282-1063.

To experience a real wilderness within minutes of the bustle of downtown, follow Constitution Avenue west and when it crosses the Potomac on the Theodore Roosevelt Bridge, bear right (north) onto George Washington Memorial Parkway. On the right is a parking lot for **Theodore Roosevelt Island**, purchased by a group of his admirers in 1931 and given to the people of the United States. There is a fine memorial with a 23-foot statue of the outdoors-loving President, but the 2½ miles of trails are what bring most visitors. The 88 acres of park includes a wide range of ecological zones, from fresh water tidal marshes to upland woods. The forest is thick with hickory, oak, maple, elm, sycamore and dogwood and there is an abundance of small mammals such as rabbits, squirrels and woodchucks. Since it is completely surrounded by water and is completely unsettled, there is a healthy population of birds, including red-tailed hawks, great owls, kingfishers, pileated woodpeckers, wrens, red-winged blackbirds, and water fowl in season, especially wood ducks. The park is open every day from 8 am to dusk; look for maps and info in the container as you enter the island.

Walking Tours

A walk along **The Mall** takes you past some of Washington's outstanding sights, starting with the **Capitol** and ending two miles west at the **Lincoln Memorial**. One of the grandest two-mile city walks in the world, it passes offices, monuments and treasure houses in styles from the 19th and 20th centuries. This gigantic green swath, several blocks wide, leads past several museums of the **Smithsonian Institution** (including its distinctive red sandstone castle), the **Korean** and **Vietnam War Memorials**, and the **Washington Monument**. Visible to the north is the **Ellipse** and the **White House**.

To the south is the even bigger expanse of **Potomac Park West** and **Potomac Park East**, which enclose the famed **Tidal Basin** and the Washington Channel. The parks are open from 6 am to midnight daily. The east and west shores of the Tidal Basin in Potomac Park West are the site of the famed cherry trees that bloom in late March and early April, and two different facilities rent pedal boats in the Basin. In Potomac Park East you'll find the graceful **Jefferson Memorial**; at its southern end, Hains Point, is a huge bronze statue called *The Awakening*, as well as a golf course.

From the Mall you can fully appreciate L'Enfant's vision of a city with long, broad views. You can log a lot of miles walking in this exciting parkland area; for more information, ☎ 202-485-9880.

In southeast Washington, across the Anacostia River, the **Anacostia Museum** is dedicated to America's Black culture. The museum's George Washington Carver Nature Trail remembers his drive to experience and preserve nature, at 1901 Fort Place SE; ☎ 202-357-2700.

GUIDED WALKING TOURS

■ **Guided Walking Tours of Washington** runs a two-hour weekend tour of Georgetown on Sundays (and many Saturdays), beginning at the Georgetown Library entrance at R Street and Wisconsin Avenue NW; tour price is $9. Another specialty tour points out homes where US presidents lived before and after their stays in the White House. For other itineraries, contact them at

9009 Paddock Lane, Potomac, MD 20854; ☎ 301-294-9514, fax 301-309-0753, Mpitch@ix.netcom.com.

■ **Georgetown Walking Tours**, 1912 Glenn Ross Rd., Silver Spring, MD 20910 (☎ 301-587-5117, www.tourdc.com), gives a walking tour of old Georgetown and includes lots of tales about the people who once lived here.

■ On Wheels

 Bike the Sites, Inc. runs interesting three-hour guided bicycle tours on paths and trails, passing 55 city landmarks. They provide the bikes, helmets, water and snacks. Contact them at 3417 Quesada Street NW; ☎ 202-966-8662, fax 202-966-8662, www.bikethe-sites.com.

Rock Creek Park is a good place to bicycle. Start at the Nature Center, where you can get a copy of the park map. The trail is 8.4 miles long and ranges from easy in the south to moderately strenuous in the northern part. Using the trails and roadways in the park, you can bike from the Potomac at Thompson Boat Center through the District and well on into Maryland. Some of the interior roads are closed to car traffic on weekends. Contact Rock Creek Park, 3545 Williamsburg Lane NW; ☎ 202-282-1063.

BIKE RENTALS

■ **Thompson Boat Center**, on the Potomac at the mouth of Rock Creek Park, at the beginning of the above bike route, rents cruiser bikes. You will find them open 6 am to 8 pm daily, April through October at 2900 Virginia Avenue MW; ☎ 202-333-9543.

■ **Washington Sailing Marina**, 1 Marina Drive, Alexandria, VA (☎ 703-548-9027), has all-terrain and 15-speed bikes available for rent, 9-6 daily, April through October.

■ On Water

Canoeing & Kayaking

The shore of **Theodore Roosevelt Island** makes a good place for canoeing, completely unmarred by human presence. There are no rentals there so you will have to bring your own canoe or kayak. From Constitution Avenue, continue on over the TR Bridge (which passes over the south end of the island) and take the George Washington Parkway north a short way to the parking lot on the right. You can combine your paddle with a hike of the island's 2½-mile trail. Note that while the river is freshwater, it is also tidal here so the water level will vary during the day.

CANOE & KAYAK RENTALS AND TOURS

■ Across the Potomac River from Theodore Roosevelt Island, in northwest Washington, the **Thompson Boat Center** has canoes, kayaks and rowing shells for rent from April through October. This is a good place to rent for a trip around the island. Another option here would be to follow the shoreline of the river, past The Mall and Potomac Park West to the Tidal Basin. A paddle upstream from here will bring you to Georgetown and, eventually to the base of Great Falls. Thompson's is open from 6 am to 8 pm daily and they give lessons. 2900 Virginia Avenue NW; ☎ 202-333-9543, 800-654-6308, www.guestservices.com.

■ **Atlantic Canoe and Kayak** offers a number of guided tours of the waters around the city, from Georgetown to the Eastern Shore. These can be half-days or full days. Contact them at 1201 North Royal Street, Alexandria, VA; ☎ 703-838-9072.

■ **America Off-Road**, in addition to renting Jeeps and SUVs, also rents canoes, sea kayaks and boats. They are at 450 Jefferson Davis Highway, Arlington, VA; ☎ 703-418-0701 or 877-RENT-AOR, fax 703-457-0821, www.americaoffroad.com.

Pedal Boats

Cherry blossoms surround the Tidal Basin in April, but it is also pretty encircled by greenery throughout the summer and fall. Pedal boats are available for rent at **Tidal Basin Pedal Boats**, not far from the Jefferson Memorial, Ohio Drive and Tidal Basin NW; ☎ 202-484-0206. **West Potomac Park Paddle Boats** at 15th Street and Maine Avenue SW (☎ 202-479-2426), is another option for pedal boating in the Tidal Basin. They are open daily from March through September, 10-6.

Sailing & Windsurfing

Sailing craft, including windsurfers, Sunfish and day sailers, can be rented at **Washington Sailing Marina**, 1 Marina Drive, Alexandria, VA; ☎ 703-548-9027. They are open daily, April through October, 9-6; lessons are available.

Boat Tours

Like nearly any city on the water, Washington offers several options for boat tours. **Capitol River Cruises** has daily 50-minute Potomac cruises beginning each hour from Georgetown Harbor, on their boat *Nightingale II*. For reservations, contact their office at 14101 Parkdale Rd., Rockville, MD 20853; ☎ 301-460-7447.

Shore Shot Cruises has nightly and weekend cruises on the river for about $10 adults, kids 4-12 $5. They are at 31st Street and K Street NW, Washington DC 20007, ☎ 202-654-6500, www.shoreshot.com.

You can travel down the Potomac to Mount Vernon and back with **Spirit Cruises** aboard the *Potomac Spirit*. They also offer a dinner cruise with live entertainment, Tuesday through Sunday. The boat is handicapped-accessible and operates daily from Pier 4 at 6th and Waters Streets SW; ☎ 202-554-5100, fax 202-488-1330.

DC Ducks: The Boats on Wheels starts its 1½-hour tours from the National Theater on E Street NW near the White House and Pennsylvania Avenue. Traveling in a converted World War II amphibious assault vehicle, tours circle The Mall before swimming the Potomac. Tours operate 10-4 daily. 2640 Reed Street NE, Washington; ☎ 202-832-9800, fax 202-832-9040.

Potomac Riverboat Company operates a pair of boats from Alexandria, Virginia, that allow you to choose a 40- or 90-minute version. The *Admiral Tilp* does a 40-minute cruise around Alexandria and the highlights of waterfront Washington. *The Matthew Hayes* 90-minute cruise allows for a more leisurely viewing of Washington from the water. Their third boat, the *Miss Christin*, sails from Alexandria's Old Town down the Potomac River to Mount Vernon. Their boats are handicapped-accessible. Contact them at 205 The Strand, Alexandria; ☎ 703-684-0580, fax 703-548-9001.

Odyssey Cruises offers both a three-hour lunch cruise and a four-hour dinner cruise on the Potomac. The boat is handicapped-accessible. Gangplank Marina, 600 Water Street SW; ☎ 202-488-6000, fax 202-488-6011, www.odysseycruises.com.

The Dandy **Restaurant Cruise Ship** does slightly shorter lunch and dinner cruises, costing about $30 on weekends, a little less on weekdays for lunch cruises, which leave at 11:30 and return at 2. Dinner cruises, leaving at 7 pm and returning at 10, cost about $50 for a five-course dinner Sunday-Thursday, more on weekends. Contact Potomac Party Cruises, Inc, Zero Prince Street, Alexandria, VA 22314; ☎ 703-683-6076 (reservations) or 703-683-6090 (information).

The other famous bit of water in Washington is the C&O Canal, which enters the Potomac at Georgetown. Although the canal ceased operation in the 1920s, a section of it does have water. Travelers can enjoy **C&O Canal Barge Rides** on a mule-drawn replica of the original watercraft. From mid-April to mid-October, costumed docents from the National Park Service tell the stories of the canal and the people who used it. The tours aboard the *Georgetown* leave from Lock 3 and travel up the canal through another lift lock. This, and the other canal barge at Great Falls in Maryland, are the only opportunities to slip back a hundred years to another totally different way of life. Buy tickets for the Georgetown ride at the Foundry Mall at Lock 3 two hours before departure; ☎ 202-653-5844 (V/TDD) or 202-653-5190.

■ On Ice

Ice Skating

One of the joys of Washington is finding the ordinary in extraordinary places. In winter, you can find ice skating at the **National Sculpture Garden Ice Rink**, a large circular rink across the Mall from the National Gallery of Art at 7th Street and Constitution Avenue NW; ☎ 202-371-5340. Rental skates are available. Be prepared for long lines on weekends and holidays. When the weather and temperature cooperate there is also free skating on the **Reflecting Pool** in front of the Washington Monument and on the **C&O Canal** along the Potomac in the northwest part of the city. To see if these areas are open, call the National Park Service, ☎ 202-619-7222.

■ On Horseback

Believe it or not, you can go riding in the city. **Rock Creek Park Horse Center** offers rides along the 11 miles of gravel bridal trails through the park. Some of these are shared with hikers, so be cautious. Contact Rock Creek Park, 3545 Williamsburg Lane NW, ☎ 202-282-1063, or the stable at the Horse Center, ☎ 202-362-0117, for information on their programs.

Cultural & Eco-Travel Experiences

The **National Museum of Natural History** is one of the Smithsonian's 15 museums located throughout the city. Permanent and revolving exhibits delve into the natural sciences and the ethnography of the world's peoples. Recent exhibits examine the culture of Japan's Ainu peoples and another shows the complexity of prairies. A new permanent exhibit looks into the culture of African peoples and examines the influence they have had upon other cultures. Particularly popular are the outstanding Native American collections, the rocks and minerals (including a breathtaking gemstone display) and the dinosaurs. A 437-seat IMAX Theater (☎ 202-633-7400) has a steady program of shows. The museum is on The Mall between 12th and 14th Streets NW; ☎ 202-357-2700 or 202-357-1729 (TTY).

National Zoological Park is in the 3000 block of Connecticut Avenue, Washington. Over 3,000 species of rare and exotic animals live, and are bred here, in a park setting. Amazonia re-creates a tropical rain forest, with realistic habitats. Washington's zoo was one of the first to use settings without visible barriers. Over the years the old cage zoo has disappeared and new animal-friendly natural habitats have replaced them. Perhaps it's because this is the zoo we and our children grew up with, but it is one of our favorite zoos in the world; ☎ 202-673-4717, www.si.edu.

The **National Aquarium**, in the seemingly incongruous US Department of Commerce Building location, is the oldest aquarium in the country, with a large collection of fish and aquatic life. Sharks, piranha and alligators (is there a message here about politics in the city?) are only a part of the 270 species you can see here. US Department of Commerce, B-077, 14th Street and Constitution Avenue NW; ☎ 202-482-2826, fax 202-482-4946. It is open daily (except Christmas day) 9-5; a small admission fee is charged.

Kenilworth Aquatic Gardens showcases thousands of waterlilies, water hyacinths, lotuses and other water-loving plants in ponds along the Anacostia River in the northeast part of the city. It's a rare chance to see unusual and rare species in a naturalized setting. The gardens were founded by a disabled Civil War veteran who started with a few lilies brought from his former Maine home. He and his daughter added to their collection, bringing plants from around the world. Now there are more than 100,000 water plants and an additional 40 species of other plants that grow in or along water. The high season for bloom is from May through early fall. You can wander the paths around the series of ponds daily, 7-4; the visitor center is open 8-4. Admission is free. 1900 Anacostia Drive SE; ☎ 202-426-6905.

Rock Creek Park has a fine **Nature Center** just off Military Rd. in the northern corner of the District of Columbia. Naturalists present regular programs on the environment, nature and man's effect upon them. This is a nice stop in a day of hiking or biking in Rock Creek Park, the major recreational park of the city. The Nature Center is about a mile east of Connecticut Avenue or a half-mile west of 16th Street on Military Rd. in the northern corner of the city. Contact the Park Naturalist at Rock Creek Nature Center, 5200 Glover Rd. NW; ☎ 202-426-6832. It's close to the Friendship Heights metro stop.

■ Gardens

The king of gardens in the capital district is the **National Arboretum** on the eastern side of the city. Here, over 400 acres of carefully prepared grounds are filled with a huge selection of trees (including one of the few examples of the Franklin Tree) and flowering plants and shrubs. In the early spring their season begins with an exciting daffodil display. The Arboretum is noted for its exquisite bonsai collections, which include many masterworks of this Japanese art form, as well as 31 trees from the National Chinese Penjing Collection given by Hong Kong donors. Its extensive herb section includes 10 herb gardens – each of which is devoted to a specific use – a knot garden and a collection of antique roses. Bring a picnic lunch to enjoy on the grounds. 3501 New York Avenue NE; ☎ 202-245-

2726, fax 202-245-4575. It is open every day, 8-5 (except Christmas), and admission is free.

The **National Cherry Blossom Festival** is held annually at the end of March and the beginning of April. The centerpiece of the event are the hundreds of cherry trees that bloom along the shores of the Tidal Basin, a gift from the government of Japan to the United States at the beginning of the 20th century. For full details of any year's festivities, call the Festival Committee at ☎ 202-547-1500.

One of our favorite Washington secrets couldn't possibly be in plainer sight, but is seldom seen by visitors. The **US Botanic Garden and Conservatory** is directly at the foot of Capitol Hill under the west façade of the Capitol. The facility is actually in two parts, the charming pavilion at the foot of the hill and a set of greenhouses some miles away. The Capitol Hill setting has as its centerpiece a grand glass conservatory that was modeled after the Crystal Palace in London. In summer the conservatory is whitewashed to protect the plants from the strong Washington sun. In addition to halls and spaces for special exhibits (which take place at a number of times throughout the year), there are seven rooms dedicated to different purposes. It is a treasure house of rare and exotic plants of all varieties from around the world. Outside, there are a number of gardens with roses, perennials, annuals, and herbs, as well as a park with a bronze fountain designed by Frederic A. Bartholdi. The fountain, which features three caryatids, was originally made for the Philadelphia Centennial Exhibit of 1876. The garden is at 245 1st St. SW (1st Street and Maryland Avenue); ☎ 202-226-4082 or 225-7099. It is open daily all year, 9-5, except Christmas Day.

The magnificent Gothic **Washington National Cathedral** is the backdrop for a series of gardens that follow the design plans of Frederick Law Olmsted's firm. Go first to the Herb Cottage, to get the descriptive self-guided tour brochure. The gardens along the stone paths of the Cathedral's close are designed in the style of such gardens in the Gothic period and include a replica 9th-century herb garden, rose gardens, a Yew Walk and perennial gardens. Architectural features include an 800-year-old Norman arch, a Wayside Cross in the form of medieval French wayside crosses, a Carolingian baptismal font, a statue of the Prodigal Son and, at the foot of the Pilgrim Steps, a striking equestrian statue of George Washington. Massachusetts and Wisconsin Avenues NW, Washington DC; ☎ 202-537-6200; www.cathedral.org/cathedral.

AUTHOR TIP

*At the Washington National Cathedral, follow the path to St. Albans School for Boys and, near the Little Sanctuary, look for the **Glastonbury Thorn**, which blooms only at Christmas and whenever British Royalty is in town... really, we're not kidding. It's well documented.*

Dumbarton Oaks is the magnificent former residence of Ambassador Robert Wood Bliss and his wife Mildred, who, between 1921 and 1941, created a European-style garden featuring American native plants. One of the highlights is Forsythia Hill, a hillside covered in forsythia that becomes a torrent of yellow in late March. A few weeks later, Cherry Hill blossoms forth in an abundance of white and pink. The gardens are in varied form, rectangular or arabesque, fitting handsomely into the terrain and providing a series of vistas and garden rooms. Among the treasures are the Orangery, with a 19th-century climbing fig, and the Rose Garden, with more than a thousand plants set in geometric patterns. The 10-acre gardens were designed by Beatrix Jones Farrand, a noted landscape garden designer who worked with Mrs Bliss. From April through October, the garden is open daily (except major holidays), 2-6 pm; from November through March, it's open 2-5 pm. The museum in the house, which has splendid collections of medieval and Byzantine art, is open Tuesday-Sunday, 2-5 pm, all year. The entrance is around the corner from the garden. Take Wisconsin Avenue to Georgetown, then take R Street to the right. The entrance is on R Street, although the address is 1703 32nd Street NW; ☎ 202-339-6410, www.doaks.org.

SPECIAL EVENTS FOR GARDENERS

■ Several annual events in Washington center around gardens. The **White House Spring Garden and House Tour**, in mid-April, allows a rare opportunity to wander through the famed Rose Garden, the Jacqueline Kennedy Garden and the West Lawn Gardens. It's free and no passes are required. Enter the grounds at the southeast gate at E Street and East Executive Avenue. Fall garden tours are held in mid-October. ☎ 202-456-2200 for dates and details on either event.

■ The **Washington National Cathedral Flower Mart** is a free event that honors a different country every year, in mid-May. Flower booths, decorating demonstrations and entertainment take place at the Cathedral at Massachusetts and Wisconsin Avenues, NW; ☎ 202-537-6200.

■ The **Annual Georgetown Garden Tour**, also in mid-May, has been happening for about three-quarters of a century. A joint project of several local committees and sites, more than a dozen fine gardens are on view, including those of Dumbarton Oaks, Renwick Chapel and private homes. Bus rides and tea are included in the admission fee; ☎ 202-244-0381 or 301-656-2343.

Where to Stay & Eat

 There are a multitude of places to stay in the city in all price ranges, and dining choices abound. Chain hotels and motels line the streets and roads at nearly every Beltway exit, as well as major approach streets like New York Avenue. Downtown hotels include every major and most minor chains, as well as several independent hotels. Whatever guidebook you use will doubtless have suggestions aplenty for accommodations and dining. The lodging services below can help you find rooms for all tastes and budgets.

 RECOMMENDED READING: *One book you should take along on your tour of DC is the* **Blue Guide: Washington DC**, *by Candyce Stapen (W.W. Norton & Company, 2000). It's full of fascinating historical information.*

■ Lodging Services

Bed and Breakfast Accommodations, PO Box 12011, Washington DC 20005-12011; ☎ 202-328-3510, fax 202-332-3885, www.bnbaccom.com.

Bed & Breakfast League/Sweet Dreams & Toast, PO Box 9490, Washington DC 20016-9490; ☎ 202-363-7767, fax 202-363-8396. Accommodations in private homes and apartments.

Capitol Reservations, Inc., 1730 Rhode Island Avenue NW, #1210, Washington, DC 20036; ☎ 202-452-1270 or 800-847-4832, fax 202-452-0537, www.hotelsdc.com, a discount reservation service.

Washington, DC Accommodations, 2201 Wisconsin Avenue NW, #C-110, Washington, DC 20007; ☎ 202-289-2220 or 800-554-2220, fax 202-338-4517, www.dcaccommodations.com, a free reservation and booking service.

Arlington Convention & Visitors Service, 2100 Clarendon Boulevard, #318, Arlington, VA 22201; ☎ 703-228-3988 or 800-296-7996, fax 703-228-3667, www.co.arlington.va.us, finds lodgings on the Virginia side of the Potomac.

■ Camping & Hostels

Hostelling International, 1009 11th Street NW, Washington, DC 20001 (☎ 202-737-2333, fax 202-737-1508), has 250 beds in men's and women's dorm rooms close to The Mall and downtown.

Capitol KOA Campground, 738 Cecil Avenue, Millersville, MD 21108; ☎ 410-923-2771, 800-KOA0248, fax 410-923-3709, www.koakampgrounds.

com. Seventeen miles from the District, the campground is accessible to the city via public transport and open from the end of March through October.

Cherry Hill Park, 9800 Cherry Hill Rd., College Park, MD 20740-1210; ☎ 301-937-7116 or 800-801-6449, fax 301-595-7181, www.rvamerica.com/cherryhillpark.

Southern Maryland

Once outside of the immediate vicinity of Washington, southern Maryland quickly regains its rural character and the pace of life slows. There is still extensive farming here and small fleets of boats harvest oysters or crabs, maintaining traditions that are centuries old.

IN THIS CHAPTER
- **Calvert County**
- **St. Mary's County**
- **Charles County**

People tend to live well spaced out. There are no major cities in southern Maryland.

Geography & History

The lands south of Washington and west of Chesapeake Bay are generally low and flat, with a few gentle hills. Nowhere are you far from water, either the Potomac, the Chesapeake Bay, or one of the many creeks and rivers that flow into them. In fact, the area is almost completely surrounded by water. Only in the southern part of **Prince George's County** and the narrow north of **Calvert County** is there any land connection with the rest of the state. On the east, the Chesapeake Bay forms the borders of Calvert and **St. Mary's** counties, with the Patuxent River separating them and turning Calvert County into a long narrow peninsula. On their south and west, St. Mary's County and

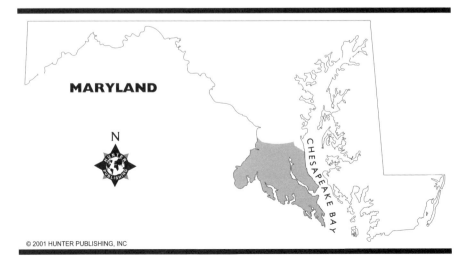

MARYLAND

N

CHESAPEAKE BAY

Charles County are bordered by the Potomac River, broad in its lower reaches and more like a bay itself. Along the shores of the Patuxent and Potomac, estuary rivers and bays indent the coast.

In the ancient past southern Maryland was the floor of an ocean. During the Miocene Epoch a shallow ocean extended almost to the present site of Washington DC. Over the millennia the sea receded, and the rivers cut new beds more deeply into the sediments of the former ocean, leaving a sedimentary cliff from Fairhaven to Drum Point.

Several different native tribes lived along the shores of the Bay for hundreds of years before the Europeans appeared, hunting, fishing and growing some crops. Several of their sites are now being explored, particularly in Jefferson Patterson Park.

■ The First Settlers

Maryland's first settlers put down their roots in this area, between 1634 and 1690. By 1776 the local economy had matured, with tobacco becoming the predominant crop and export. **Lord Baltimore** established his claim by setting up his capital at **St. Mary's City**, the first capital of Maryland and the capital of Catholic Maryland. When the Calvert family lost out to the Anglicans, the capital was moved to Annapolis, where it remains today. After centuries of abandonment, St. Mary's is now coming back to life. Excavations continue to reveal the life of these first settlers.

■ The 1800s

It was up the Patuxent River and past Sandy Island, later to be Solomon's Island, that the British fleet sailed in 1814 on their way to burn Washington DC. In the Battle of St. Leonard's Creek, June 26, 1814, Commodore Joshua Barney tried to stop the British, and near Leonard Town the remains of two of his gunboats have been found. During the War of 1812 farmers and settlers along the shores of the Patuxent were frequently harassed by British soldiers and sailors from the fleet that controlled the waters. Little Prince Frederick was burned by the British in 1814.

The **Civil War**, when Marylanders were on both sides of the fray, was particularly painful for the southern part of the state, which was primarily a plantation economy. Brothers and cousins fought on opposite sides. The Union Army established a prisoner of war camp in St. Mary's County at the end of the peninsula at Point Lookout. Remnants of it are still there.

Solomon's Island, the southern tip of Calvert County, was virtually unsettled until after the Civil War. In 1868, a Baltimore businessman named Isaac Solomon bought the island and established an oyster cannery. His cannery operated until the mid 1870s and was succeeded by others. The town became a busy fishing harbor, sometimes filled with as many as 400 oyster and fishing boats.

■ The 1900s

The tenor of life in south Maryland changed forever with the coming of **World War II** in the 1940s. Three major defense facilities opened in Calvert and St. Mary's Counties: the Patuxent Naval Air Station, the Naval Mine Warfare Test Station at Point Patience and the Naval Amphibious Training Station at Dowell Point. Within three years the population increased tenfold. Invasions of local shores by armed men became commonplace and fishermen and oystermen grumbled at the interruption of their lives and fishing grounds by naval vessels. Although the Patuxent Naval Air Station is the only of these facilities that remains active here, in Charles County the US Naval Ordnance Station sits at the entrance to Mattawoman Creek, where the dull thud of explosions can be heard periodically.

Getting Here & Getting Around

 To get to **Calvert County**, the eastern part of this section, leave the **Beltway** (I-495) at Exit 11, just north of Andrews Air Force Base, taking **Route 4** east. It crosses the head of the Patuxent River into Anne Arundel County and then drops south down the center of Calvert County, eventually crossing the Patuxent at Solomon's Island into the southern part of St. Mary's County.

Exit 7 of I-495 connects to **Route 5**, which goes south through Prince George's County into Charles County, then curves into St. Mary's County. From its intersection with Route 5, **Route 235** continues southeast to the end of the peninsula. **Route 301** leads south from Annapolis and the Bay Bridge, crossing the Potomac into Virginia on the only bridge over that river south of metropolitan Washington.

Information Sources

 Fairview Visitor Information Center, Route 4 (near Chaneyville Rd.), 8120 Southern Maryland Blvd, Owings 20736, ☎ 410-257-5381, 410-257-0801.

Calvert County Tourism, 175 Main Street, Prince Frederick 20678, ☎ 410-535-4583, 800-331-9771, TDD 410-535-6355, 301-855-1862.

Calvert County Parks and Recreation, Court House, Prince Frederick; ☎ 410-326-8383

St. Mary's County Division of Tourism, PO Box 653, Washington Street, Leonardtown 20688, ☎ 410-326-6027. You can also contact the St. Mary's County Chamber of Commerce Visitors Center, 6260 Waldorf-Leonardtown Rd., Mechanicsville 20659, ☎ 301-884-5555.

You'll see the **tourist information office** in **Solomons** as you enter town, opposite the Calvert Marine Museum, open 9-5 daily, later in the summer. It is close to the point where Route 4 crosses the Patuxent River on the Thomas Johnson Bridge. Watch for signs; it's easy to get confused here. If they are closed, you can get some good basic information from the open kiosk outside; ☎ 410-326-6027. **Public restrooms** in Solomons are just south of the charter boat dock.

Charles County Tourism Division, 8190 Port Tobacco Rd., Port Tobacco 20677; ☎ 301-934-9305, ext 195 or 800-766-3386, ext 146.

For those coming across the Potomac into southern Maryland over the Governor Nice Memorial Bridge, there is the **Crain Memorial Maryland Welcome Center** at 12480 Crain Highway (US 301), Newburg 20664; ☎ 301-259-2500.

 AREA CODE CONFUSION: *Calvert County has two area codes, and they are mixed throughout the county. Businesses that have more than one phone line may have numbers in each of the area codes, even though the lines are at the same address.*

Adventures

■ Parks

 Kings Landing Park has day-use areas that include picnic facilities, a fishing and crabbing pier, canoe and kayak access to the Patuxent River and walking trails. It is open daily, Memorial Day to Labor Day, 8:30-8; the rest of the year, hours are Monday-Friday, 8:30-4:30; Saturday-Sunday, 8:30-6. It is located 3½ miles from Route 2/4 on Kings Landing Rd. in Huntingtown; ☎ 410-535-2661.

Breezy Point Beach and Campground, on Breezy Point Rd., is south of Chesapeake Beach off Route 261, five miles south of the Route 260 intersection. In addition to picnic areas with grills, a bathhouse and a playground, they have a 300-foot fishing and crabbing pier and a half-mile of beach. The park is open for day-use Memorial Day through Labor Day from 6 am until dusk. (See *Camping* below.) Calvert County Parks and Recreation, Court House, Prince Frederick; ☎ 410-535-1600 or 301-855-1243, ext 225. From May-October you can call the park directly between 8 am and 9 pm daily at ☎ 410-535-0259. Entry fee is $4 for adults; for se-

Southern Maryland

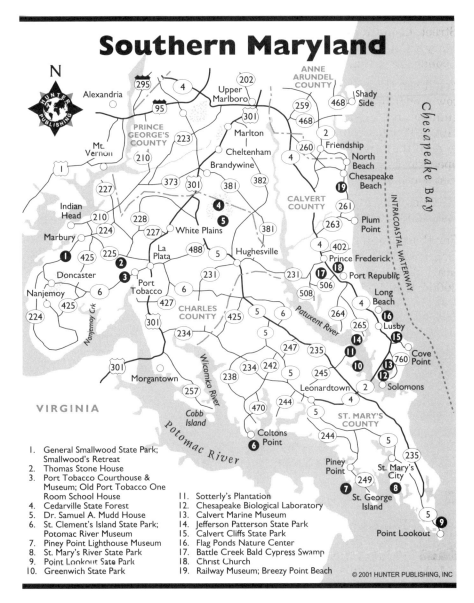

N

Alexandria
Mt. Vernon

PRINCE GEORGE'S COUNTY

Upper Marlboro
Marlton
Cheltenham
Brandywine

ANNE ARUNDEL COUNTY

Shady Side
Friendship
North Beach
Chesapeake Beach

CALVERT COUNTY

Plum Point
Prince Frederick
Port Republic
Long Beach
Lusby
Cove Point
Solomons

Indian Head
Marbury
Doncaster
Nanjemoy

White Plains
La Plata
Port Tobacco

Hughesville

CHARLES COUNTY

Morgantown

Cobb Island

Coltons Point

VIRGINIA

Leonardtown

ST. MARY'S COUNTY

Piney Point
St. Mary's City
St. George Island

Point Lookout

Chesapeake Bay

INTRACOASTAL WATERWAY

Patuxent River

Wicomico River

Nanjemoy Crk.

Potomac River

1. General Smallwood State Park; Smallwood's Retreat
2. Thomas Stone House
3. Port Tobacco Courthouse & Museum; Old Port Tobacco One Room School House
4. Cedarville State Forest
5. Dr. Samuel A. Mudd House
6. St. Clement's Island State Park; Potomac River Museum
7. Piney Point Lighthouse Museum
8. St. Mary's River State Park
9. Point Lookout Sate Park
10. Greenwich State Park
11. Sotterly's Plantation
12. Chesapeake Biological Laboratory
13. Calvert Marine Museum
14. Jefferson Patterson State Park
15. Calvert Cliffs State Park
16. Flag Ponds Nature Center
17. Battle Creek Bald Cypress Swamp
18. Christ Church
19. Railway Museum; Breezy Point Beach

© 2001 HUNTER PUBLISHING, INC

niors (55 and up) and children (three-11), $2. On Tuesdays and Thursdays there is a special rate of $10/vehicle for up to seven people.

Cedarville State Forest has facilities for freshwater fishing and for hiking. The state's only warm-water fish hatchery is located in the forest, whose more than 3,600 acres are split between Prince George's County and Charles County. From Route 301 take Cedarville Rd. and follow signs to 11704 Fenno Rd., Upper Marlboro; ☎ 301-888-1410.

The tabloid-style Calvert County Parks and Recreation Program Schedule *comes out seasonally and is filled with things to do. While many of them are continuing programs, some are day adventures, many of these especially for kids. Pick up a schedule at the Visitor Centers or contact Calvert County Parks and Recreation, 175 Main Street, Prince Frederick 20678;* ☎ *410-535-1600, 310-855-1243, Ext 225.*

General Smallwood State Park is named for Revolutionary War General William Smallwood, whose former home here is restored and open on a limited schedule. The park has a beach and boat launch with access to the Potomac through the end of Mattawoman Creek. The Creek, however, is the real gem, a bass fisherman's and paddler's heaven as the wide stream meanders inland in broad sweeps, with rich gatherings of lilypads. The park is off Route 1, Marbury; ☎ 301-743-7336.

Point Lookout State Park is at the tip of St. Mary's County, with Chesapeake Bay on one side and the broad point of the Potomac River on the other. Just follow Route 5 until it stops, and you are in the park. Once a Civil War POW camp for Confederate soldiers, the park is now popular for hiking, beaches, camping and fishing. PO Box 48, Scotland 20687; ☎ 301-872-5688.

St. Clement's Island State Park is the first point in Maryland where European settlers from the ships *Ark* and *Dove* landed in 1634. The 40-acre island is in the Potomac River off Colton's Point at the end of Route 242 and is accessible only by boat. It is under the supervision of Point Lookout State Park. Route 242, 38370 Point Breeze Rd., Colton's Point; ☎ 301-769-2222, fax 301-475-2225, TDD 301-475-4105.

St. Mary's River State Park contains a 250-acre lake created by a flood control project. The park's 2,176 acres are essentially undeveloped and the lake is a popular place for bass fishing. Access is from Camp Cosoma Rd., off Route 5. It is under the supervision of Point Lookout State Park.

■ On Foot

Parker's Creek, south of Prince Frederick, has the largest mixed fresh/salt water watershed on the Chesapeake Bay, part of it managed by the **American Chestnut Land Trust**, with 14 miles of good hiking trails through a surprisingly rolling woodland terrain over mixed highland with deep ravines. Old farm roads make trails six feet wide in most places. Pick up trail maps at the entrance, in a box on the little building, where you should also sign in. There are more than 10 miles of trails through these woods along the watersheds of Parker's Creek and

Governor's Run. The trailhead is on Scientist's Cliffs Rd. in Prince Frederick, ☎ 410-586-1570.

DIRECTIONS TO PARKERS CREEK: *Parkers Creek Rd. turns east (left if you are headed south) off Route 2/4 south of Prince Frederick, just south of the Farmers' Market. At 0.5 mile, turn right onto Scientist Cliffs Rd. In about a mile you'll see parking on the left and a small sign.*

Calvert Cliffs State Park has 13 miles of trails for walkers only (bikes are restricted to the service road). Gray's Branch Trail leads from the parking and picnic area down to the beach and the fossil cliffs (see *Fossil Collecting* under *Eco-Travel*, below). Captain John Smith recorded these cliffs in his log as he sailed by. The Thomas Branch Trail leaves Grays Branch close to the beach and leads back into the forest. Try to avoid coming here immediately after heavy rains, since the trails become very muddy and might be impassable. Admission $3 per vehicle and a trail map is on the board at the parking lot. We couldn't find a paper version anywhere, so suggest you take along paper to make a quick sketch of it. Open sunrise to sunset, use fee $3/car. Route 765, Lusby, ☎ 301-872-5688.

Flag Ponds Nature Center has several short hikes that explore miles of trails through forest, swamp, marshes and beaches (where you may find fossils). The park is especially noted for its wildflowers. A former fisherman's shanty now serves as a small museum depicting the fishing industry that once flourished here. There are two ponds with observation decks for birders. Flag Ponds is close to Route 2/4, four miles north of the Calvert Cliffs State Park entrance. The access road is very narrow, but only 0.6 mile. An entrance fee is charged, and the park is open Memorial Day to Labor Day, 9-6 daily, weekends only the rest of the year. ☎ 410-586-1477 or 535-5327, 800-331-9771, TDD 410-535-6355.

Greenwell State Park, on the Patuxent River, has several miles of hiking trails. From Hollywood, about four miles north of Leonardtown on Route 235, follow Route 245 east toward Sotterly Plantation and look for the park road on the right. It is open 8-sunset daily.

There are primitive unmarked trails at the 2,250-acre **St. Mary's River State Park** on Camp Cosoma Rd. in Leonardtown. This is wetland walking and hikers should be equipped for bushwhacking. The park is open 7-sunset daily, March through November.

Another opportunity for hikers in St. Mary's County is on **St. Clement's Island**, an uninhabited island off Colton's Point in the Potomac. The first settlement in the state was on this island where today there are hiking trails and a chance to view birdlife. Unless you have your own boat, you can reach the island only on Saturday or Sunday, when the public boat runs (see *Boat Tours*). To get there from Route 5, take Route 242 to its end at Colton's Point.

On the west side of Charles County there is a nice hiking trail at **Ruth B. Swann Memorial Park**, an active community park with sports facilities. The mile-long trail leads through a mature forest to the banks of the Potomac. The park is off Route 210, on Bryans Rd., just west of the Route 227 intersection. **Gilbert Run State Park** also has a Nature Center and Nature Trail. It is off Route 6 east of La Plata about eight miles.

■ On Wheels

Roads in Southern Maryland are relatively flat, the hills not too steep and the rises short. The down side is that the roads are fairly narrow and the shoulders not paved.

In Calvert County, cyclists should stay off Routes 2 and 4, high-speed divided highways where bikes are prohibited.

Try to get a copy of *Southern Maryland, Where the Times and Tides Meet - Bicycle Map*, which covers Calvert, Charles and St. Mary's counties. It shows a series of loop and in-and-out routes with highlights to look for along the way. Loop mileages range from 2.6 in Solomons to a Piney Point loop of 40½ miles, but there are a couple in the 15-mile range. It also has a handy list of cycle shops in the area. It was prepared by the Southern Maryland Tourism Council and Patuxent Area Cycle Enthusiasts (PACE) and is distributed at Visitor Information Centers. Another good place for biking is **Point Lookout State Park** where the roads pass through forests and along the Potomac River and Chesapeake Bay.

BIKE SHOPS

In Waldorf there are three bicycle shops. **Mike's Bikes of Waldorf** is at 3262 Leonardtown Rd. (☎ 301-870-6600, 301-645-6616); **The Bike Shop of Waldorf, Inc.** is nearby at 3265 Leonardtown Rd. (☎ 301-645-8666, 301-843-5356); and **Bike Doctor** is at 2957 Festival Way (☎ 301-932-9980).

Close to the Patuxent and Sotterly, in St. Mary's County, is **Signs and Cycles Bike Shop**, Old Three Notch Rd., Hollywood; ☎ 301-373-3789. South of the intersection of Route 235 with Route 4 as it crosses the river from Solomons is **Blue Wind**, 9001 Three Notch Rd., California; ☎ 301-737-2713, 800-442-5834. To the south is **Mike's Bikes**, 447C Great Mills Rd., in the Great Mills Shopping Center, Lexington Park; ☎ 301-863-7887.

In Calvert County there are two options, **Penn Auto**, 5 Church Street, Prince Frederick (☎ 301-855-1781, 410-535-2222) and **Sea Dive and Bicycle**, Routes 2-4, S&W Shopping Center, Solomons Island; ☎ 410-326-4386.

■ On Water

Mallows Bay, in the Potomac near Mattawoman Creek, is a watery graveyard for about 100 World War I transport barges, scuttled here long ago. Bits of their steel frames stick out of the water. Depending on wind and weather, you can go explore the site by kayak or on a local fishing boat – as you can imagine, it's a prime bass fishing target. However you explore these, be careful, since some of the jagged parts of these ships are barely submerged and could damage your watercraft.

Swimming

North Beach, just north of Chesapeake Beach, has a small public beach, but although there is free parking all along the half-mile boardwalk, it is hard to find a space if you don't arrive early in the morning.

Bay Front Park, known locally as **Brownie's Beach**, is south of Chesapeake City, near Tidewater Treasures B&B. It has no picnic tables, but you may find fossils there.

County-operated **Breezy Point Beach** has picnic tables, fishing piers and a beach, where you may also find sharks teeth. Day-use fees at Breezy Point Beach are $4 for adults, or $2 for seniors and ages three-11. It's open 6 am to 9 pm, but there are no lifeguards. It is 1.4 miles off Route 261, south of Chesapeake Beach.

Kings Landing Park is a free 260-acre park with grills and picnic tables, and a swimming pool. You must pay to use the pool: $3 for adults, $2 for children. The park is open Memorial Day to Labor Day 8:30 am to 8 pm, shorter hours in other months. It is 3½ miles from Route 2/4 on Kings landing Rd. in Huntingtown; ☎ 410-535-2661.

Canoeing & Kayaking

If you are adept at entering the water from a wharf, a paddle from Chesapeake Beach up **Fishing Creek** takes you away from the pier's bustle surprisingly soon. Paddle past several bends to the trestle, beyond which the creek winds through open meadowland, where the occasional house is hidden by summer foliage. When you come to a fork, left takes you to Dalrymple Rd., right takes you into wilderness. After the first big curve you are out of sight of everything. Fishing Creek Park will eventually be connected to the American Chestnut Land Trust properties.

WATCHABLE WILLIFE

Powerboats can go up Fishing Creek, but the waters are relatively quiet and you may see bald eagles, ospreys, herons, egrets, snakes, turtles and muskrats. From the wharves in Chesapeake Beach, you can see as many as 15 varieties of birds at one time during spring and fall migration seasons.

Also in northern Calvert County, public launch sites for canoes and kayaks are located at **North Beach Public Beach** (free) and **Breezy Point Beach**, ☎ 410-535-0259 (park admission charged); **Breezy Point Marina** charges an $8 ramp fee. **Kings Landing Park**, 3½ miles from Route 2/4 on Kings Landing Rd. in Huntingtown, has a launch site for canoes and kayaks. The free park, which also has picnic tales and grills, is open Memorial Day to Labor Day 8:30 am to 8 pm, shorter hours Labor Day through October, and weekdays only the rest of the year; ☎ 410-535-2661.

Hellowing Point Boat Ramp, Hellowing Point Rd. (Route 231), is in Prince Frederick, and **Warriors Rest**, at the American Chestnut Land Trust, is a free launch site that is handicapped-accessible.

Solomons Public Boat Ramp is at 14195 Solomons Island Rd. South. Under the bridge just as you enter Solomons Island is a put-in area for kayaks and canoes, and a full boat ramp; both charge a fee. Also in Solomons, there's a free put-in opposite the Victorian Inn, unmarked on a tiny street. It's not an official launch site, but it works. Solomons Harbor has a lot of fast-moving motor traffic and not much unbroken shoreline, so it's not ideal for paddlers, but still interesting.

In Charles County, the small **Gilbert Run State Park** surrounds a 60-acre lake impounded by a dam. Canoes and rowboats are for rent on weekends, April through October, 8-6. In July and August they may be rented the same hours, but daily. The park is on Route 6, eight miles east of La Plata, between Dentsville and Dubois.

Chapel Point State Park lies along the wide lower Port Tobacco River, near its junction with the Potomac. A small free boat landing, at the end of the right-hand fork just at the park signboard, is a good put-in for canoes and kayaks. The park is open during daylight hours.

General Smallwood State Park lies at the mouth of **Mattawoman Creek**, with boat ramps (fee charged). Straight ahead from the ramp lies the Potomac River, wide and windy, not good for kayaks on any but a calm day. But to the right lie miles of quiet protected waters in Mattawoman Creek. Because it is a wildlife sanctuary, powerboats are limited to six miles an hour, which makes kayaking pleasant. A Naval Ordnance Station occupies part of the land on one side (the occasional explosions will tell you where it is), but signs warn where you cannot go ashore. A tiny island of dunes with a stand of sycamores offers a sandy beach and place for a picnic, but be sure to pull kayaks or canoes well up onto its beach at any but high tide if you hope to find them there after lunch.

Along with a few fishermen, you'll find a lot of blue herons, brilliant wildflowers and tree-hung banks. Eagles perch in the snags over the water, and in the winter it is not unusual to see 20 or 30 of them in this one creek. Mallards will let you get quite close in a boat, but cormorants on the old dock pilings are more camera shy. In the spring, the waters seem alive with jumping carp. It's hard to believe that there are such wild places so close to Washington DC.

DID YOU KNOW?

Carp have no stomach muscles to expel eggs. They jump repeatedly to literally knock them loose.

Another access to this creek, at its upper end, is from **Stevens Ramp**, in the town of Indian Head. From Route 210, take the last left turn onto Mattingly Ave., which dead-ends at the landing. Parking is free in the public lot to the left if you are launching a canoe or kayak. But if you park to the right, you must pay a fee. Larger boats that require use of the ramp must pay a ramp fee.

One of the state's loveliest places to paddle is up the **Nanjemoy Creek**, reached from **Friendship Landing**. The boat ramp is free, as is fishing from the shore and the landing. Before descending the steep hill to the landing, however, stop briefly at the pullout on the left, where the road makes a sharp right. Walk across the street and up the driveway of the farm (it's park property) to look out over Nanjemoy Creek from the side yard. It's one of our favorite views, with the creek winding in long, lazy curves through golden marsh grass, between wooded shores. To the left, the creek opens out in a final sandbar-studded turn before joining the Potomac. You will run back to your car just to have a few more minutes to spend on this idyllic estuary.

To get to Friendship Landing from General Smallwood State Park, continue south about two miles and turn right onto Liverpool Point Rd. A little over four miles later, after passing a crossroads where the road becomes Baptist Church Rd., go left at the T, then at about 0.3 miles, go right on Friendship Landing Rd. to its end. These roads are not shown on the state highway map; the nearest point marked is Old Durham Church.

The **Wicomico River** in Charles County (there is another of the same name on the eastern shore) is a beautiful, big, flooded river valley that cuts well inland and forms part of the boundary between St. Mary's and Charles Counties. For access to the upper, inland, end there is a launch at Budds Creek, off Route 134 at **Wicomico Shores Ramp and Marina**. Take Coffee Hill Rd. west from Route 234. Farther south take Route 238 from Route 234 and turn west onto Chaptico Wharf Rd. to **Chaptico Wharf**. This one is mid-way on the Wicomico. The **Bushwood Wharf** is on Bushwood Rd., west of Route 238, near Bushwood. On the eastern side of the mouth of the Wicomico, at the Potomac, there is access from Route 520 on White's Neck Rd. This access is into White's Neck Creek, which flows immediately into the Potomac.

This southwest tip of St. Mary's County has three deep bays within close proximity, the Wicomico River, St. Clements and Bay Breton Bay which is separated from St. Clements Bay only by a narrow peninsula, over which Route 243 passes. All open onto the Potomac. Access to St. Clements is from Colton's Point (Route 242) and access to Breton Bay at Leonardtown. To reach the latter from the center of Leonardtown, at the intersection of Routes 245, 5 and Washington Street, take Washington Street (Route 326) southwest to the boat launch.

In Prince George's County there is a boat launch at **Patuxent State Park** on the west shore of the Patuxent, almost opposite King's Landing in Calvert County. To get there, take MacGruger's Ferry Rd. east from Route 382 (Croom Rd.) to the **Clyde E. Watson Boating Area**. On the west side of the county, just north of the Charles County border, is the **Fort Washington Marina** at Fort Washington National Park and Piscataway National Park. From Fort Washington Rd. off Route 210, take Warburton Drive and then King Charles Terrace to the boat launch. This launches into Piscataway Creek, a tributary of the Potomac.

CANOE/KAYAK RENTALS & GUIDED TOURS

Amphibious Horizons, based at Quiet Waters Park in Annapolis (☎ 410-267-8742 or 888-I-LUV-SUN, www.amphibioushorizons.com), offers evening and sunset paddles in Mataponi Creek and day-long Saturday trips through wild rice marshes in the Patuxent River Park. Cost of all day excursions is $75. A day-long excursion by kayak from Chesapeake Beach explores the beach and fossil cliffs of Calvert County. The trip includes stops for fossil hunting and lunch at a waterside restaurant. A weekend trip with Amphibious Horizons explores the Patuxent River Park and its freshwater tidal ecosystem in October, when foliage of the surrounding woodlands is at its peak. All equipment for kayaking and camping is included in the $200-$250 fee.

The **Calvert Marine Museum** has canoes, which are used for guided nature explorations of the shore. You can get a schedule of their trips from the museum (see contact information below).

Boat Tours

William B Tennyson, a historic Chesapeake Bay bugeye (ketch-rigged sailing vessel), takes passengers on one-hour cruises to learn about the natural and human history of the shore and bay, and about the boat itself, which was a sailing bugeye until 1907 when it was converted to engine power and used for carrying the oyster catch back to shore. Cruises run from May through October, Wednesday-Sunday at 2 pm (no cruise on the third Sunday of May), and July and August on weekends at 12:30, 2 and 4 pm. $5, Children (five-12) $3. Contact Calvert Marine Museum, PO Box 97, Solomons, MD 20688, ☎ 410-326-2042. Reservations are suggested because capacity is limited to 47 persons.

Solomons Water Taxi is a good way to get around and see the bay. Using the 46-passenger *Stars and Stripes* (☎ 410-535-7022 for pick up), you can travel between 24 stopping places, which include most waterside inns, restaurants, bars and marinas. It also stops at the Calvert Marine Museum. During the peak season it operates daily.

Jefferson Patterson Park Estuarine Center sponsors Friday tours for adults and children on its research boat. They bring back samples of marine life and examine them under microscopes. Reservations are necessary. The park is at 10515 Mackall Rd., St. Leonard, MD 20685, ☎ 410-586-8500, fax 410-586-0080.

Baileywick Company Sailboat Charters has a 35-foot Niagara (the *Segel*) and a Rainbow 24 (the *Pot of Gold*) on a timeshare arrangement, with a lease cost of about $2,200 for 14 days. Charter is $260 for weekdays and $340 for weekend days. Contact them at PO Box 710, Solomons, MD 20688, ☎ 410-326-3115, fax 326-3982, www.baileywick.org, e-mail bailey@baileywick.org.

You can get to **Smith Island** from this side of the bay without having to drive the length of the Eastern Shore. Smith's, settled in 1657 and named for Captain John Smith, who sighted it in 1608, is still heavily dependent upon the sea for its livelihood. From Point Lookout on the southern tip of St. Mary's County, the *Capt. Tyler* takes passengers on day-trips. Passage time is an hour and three quarters each way, a good chance to enjoy the waters of the Chesapeake. On the island you can visit their museum, take a bus tour of the island, dine or just walk the narrow streets. During the summer season, the boat leaves Lookout Point State Park Wednesday-Sunday at 10 am and returns at 4 pm. For reservations, contact Captain Alan Tyler, PO Box 41, Rhodes Point, MD 21824, ☎ 410-425-2771.

Skipjack Tours, Inc, cruises the Potomac and St. Mary's River as well as conducting natural history and environmental classes from it location on Piney Point Rd. (Route 249), St. George's Island, ☎ 301-994-2245, www.skipjacktours.com.

St. Clement's Island Boat Tours are operated by the St. Clement's Island Museum and leave from their pier Saturday and Sunday from May through October. They leave the museum at 12:30 on a 15-minute trip and return to the museum at 2:15 (leaving the island at 2 pm). A second trip begins at 2:30 and returns at 3:45. Bring a picnic lunch. Rates are $5 adults, $3 children 12 and under. The museum is at 38370 Point Breeze Rd., Colton's Point; ☎ 301-769-2222, fax 301-475-2225, TDD 301-475-4105.

Fishing – Chesapeake Bay

Chesapeake Beach is the fishing capital of the Chesapeake, with two fleets of headboats and charters, the largest concentration in the state. And for good reason. Within a short distance is some of best fishing in the bay, close enough for a six-hour trip to be productive. Rockfish (striped bass) is the quarry of choice, in season late April through the beginning of July and early September through mid-November.

The Maryland Department of Resources doesn't set season dates and limits until the very beginning of the season, so it's hard to make reservations early. But the usual rule allows two fish over 18 inches June through November. Trophy season usually allows one 28" minimum, but that may be changed each year. Bluefish are in season late May through mid-June and again from late July through the beginning of October. Black drum are reported to run from 40 to 80 pounds in this area; their season starts in May. From the end of July until the end of September, trout, flounder, croaker and spot are found in number. The Calvert County Department of Economic Development publishes a chart of the seasons for different species, ☎ 800 331-9771, www.co.cal.md.us.

AUTHOR TIP *Headboats catch bottom fish, including croaker, trout and flounder; smaller charters find these, plus bluefish and Spanish mackerel. Equipment is provided on charters, but live bait is extra.*

Chesapeake Beach Fishing Charters (☎ 301-855-4665) represents 15 boats. Rates are $400 for all-day (eight hours) or $300 for six hours. Night fishing is $300 for six hours, June through September. Some boats hold more than six people, some as few as four. For a good-humored captain with long experience fishing the Chesapeake, reserve the *Mary Lou II*, with Captain Russ Mogel; (☎ 301-855-0784, boat phone 301-758-5116). The charter headquarters is on Harbor Rd. (next to Abner's Crab House), PO Box 757, Chesapeake Beach 20732.

Fred Donovan, at the **Rod and Reel Tackle Shop**, is co-owner of a whole ensemble of fishing-related businesses. His tackle shop just behind Smokey Joe's is headquarters for 30 independently owned small charter boats and the two headboats, which hold 70 or 100 people. Each of the 30 smaller charters carries about six. Rod-N-Reel Charter Captains, PO Box 99, Chesapeake Beach 20732; ☎ 301-855-8450.

If you are trailering your own and want to put in at Chesapeake Beach, you can do so at **Fishing Creek Landing's Marina**. They have six ramps and charge a $10 fee. It opens an hour before sunrise and closes an hour after sunset.

At **Breezy Point Beach**, just south of Chesapeake Beach off Route 261, are fishing piers (one where alcohol is allowed); adult access is $4, ages three-11 $2, Seniors $2, open 6 am to 9 pm. The adjacent marina has three fishing charter boats headquartered there (☎ 410-535-0259) or contact Breezy Point Charter Association, 5230 Breezy Point Rd., Chesapeake Beach 20732, ☎ 410-760-8242.

Farther south on Solomons Island, **Bunky's Charter Boat Rentals** has ice, bait and tackle, plus a complete fishing shop with rods and reels. Their headboat, *Marchelle*, offers full-day, half-day and evening trips starting at about $30 per person, including a dozen bloodworms. Rods are an additional $5. Headboats leave at 7 am and 1 pm, returning at noon and 6 pm. Bunky's charter boats cost $390 for up to six persons for eight hours, and *Marchelle* is $480 for up to eight persons for eight hours. Rental boats are available at about $55 a day or $15 an hour. You can't miss them on the main street, at 14448 Solomons Rd. South; ☎ 410-326-3241, www.solomons-island.com/bunky.

Calvert Marina Charter Dock, Dowell Rd., PO Box 157, Solomons 20688 (☎ 410-326-4251) has charter services available, as does the **Solomons Charter Captains Association**, PO Box 831, Solomons 20688, ☎ 410-326-2670, www.cdslink.com/sca. **Solomons Boat Rental and Sales**, is at the north end of the boardwalk at Waterman's Memorial Park; ☎ 410-326-4060.

On the last weekend of June, the **Chesapeake Bay Pro/Am Fishing Tournament** is sponsored by the Solomons Charter Captains Association. Prizes total more than $88,000. Categories include: Heaviest overall rockfish, heaviest overall bluefish, heaviest overall trout and overall winner fly rod, reel and fly. On Friday there is a Beer and Bull Party with a fish tale contest; on Saturday, a Hawaiian luau; and on Sunday, an awards ceremony. Check-out time is 6 am, lines in the water after 7 am, and weigh-in 7 am-4 pm, but you must be in line by 4 pm to qualify; ☎ 410-326-2670, www.cdslink.com/scca.

For fly-fishing charters in this part of Southern Maryland, contact **Witch Charters**, 1410 Foxtail Lane, Prince Frederick 20678; ☎ 800-303-4950. The owner, Bob Toepfer, is a professional fishing guide.

AUTHOR TIP

CHARTER BOAT ETIQUETTE: *The Mate works for tips and doesn't get paid by the Captain. Tip about 15%, more if he cleans your catch for you. The catch belongs to the charter party so don't keep more than you'll use. You do not need a fishing license on a charter boat and all you need to bring is appropriate clothing and your own food. The boat supplies the gear.*

There is a public fishing and crabbing pier in Solomons right next to the Thomas Johnson Bridge that carries Route 4 over the Patuxent to St. Mary's County.

A pair of access points to the Patuxent River are off Route 235, north of its intersection with Route 4, just west of the bridge from Solomons. For **Clark's Landing**, take Clark's Landing Rd. from Route 235 to reach a collection of small coves, which are popular fishing places; the Patuxent River is straight ahead. A bit farther up Route 235, take Route 245 east and then turn right onto **Forest Landing** Rd. at Greenwell State Park. This launch goes into Forest Landing Cove and thence into the Patuxent.

Up the Patuxent in the southern part of Prince George's County there is a boat launch facility at **Patuxent State Park** on the west shore of the Patuxent, almost opposite King's Landing in Calvert County, across the river. From Route 382 (Croom Rd.), take MacGruger's Ferry Rd. east to the **Clyde E. Watson Boating Area**.

Point Lookout State Park has a fishing pier that extends out 710 feet into the Chesapeake Bay. The park, at the tip of St. Mary's County, is practically surrounded by the Bay and the end of the Potomac River. Fishing is also popular on the ponds in the park, from the shore and from boats launched at their boat ramp in Lake Conboy, which opens to the Potomac. PO Box 48, Scotland 20687; ☎ 301-872-5688.

Just north of Point Lookout at Ridge is **Scheible's Fishing Center**, a major outfitter for fishing in the Potomac and Chesapeake. They have 15 licensed boats and an 80-passenger headboat. On the grounds at their headquarters they have a 500-foot fishing and crabbing pier and a store with all the gear. Species in the areas where they fish include bluefish, flounder, sea trout, striped bass (called rockfish here), croaker and perch. From Route 5, take Wynne Rd. (Route 252) west two miles to the shore of Calvert Bay, to 48342 Wynne Rd., Ridge 20680; ☎ 301-872-5185 or 800-895-6132, fax 301-872-5915, www.webgraphic.com/scheibles.

Fishing – Along the Potomac

At the north end of St. George's Creek, west of St. Mary's Bay, **Tall Timbers Cove** has a fishing pier on the cove. The pier is just west of Route 249 (Piney Point Rd.) on Tall Timbers Rd. Another pier is on St. George's Island, at the end of Route 249 (Thompson Rd.). In St. Mary's there is a pier at **St. Mary's River State Park**, off Route 5. Farther south, follow Route 252 (Wynne Rd.) west to Fox Harbor Rd. and then County Wharf Rd., both on the right, to the fishing pier.

Reel Bass Adventures is an association of 16 Coast Guard certified charter captains and expert fly fishermen who provide guide services as a professional organization. They can guide anywhere in the northeastern and mid-Atlantic US and are very active in Maryland and the Chesapeake, where they seem to know every spot where a fish might hide. There are some wonderful creeks, rivers and bays along these shores, and each guide has a few favorite places, along with long experience about what will induce those fish to bite. They can provide guide service for stream fishing or boat fishing, and will teach beginners or coach the more experienced. They can help you find largemouth and smallmouth bass, striped bass (rockfish) and trout.

DID YOU KNOW? *In Mallows Bay are the remains of 100 transport craft, which were moth-balled there after World War I and left to disintegrate. Guide Andy Andrzejewski, with Reel Bass Adventures, is an expert on them.*

Reel Bass guides have fixed rates so you won't be surprised by add-ons at the end. Rates are $250 for up to two people for a full (eight-hour) day and $175 for a half-day. All you need bring is your appropriately clad self, a lunch, snacks and sodas. They will provide top-notch equipment and lures. If you want to fly-fish, however, you should have your own tackle. Reel Bass Adventures office is at 10100 Old Franklin Avenue, Seabrook 20706, ☎ 301-839-2858.

*The **Charles County Office of Tourism** has published a brochure called* Potomac Largemouth Bass *that tells you what sorts of places the fish are likely to be in at what time of year. The booklet also suggests what lures will work at those times, and gives a list of approved guides. Write PO Box B, La Plata, MD 20646; ☎ 800-766-3386, 301-645-0558, www.govt.co.charles.md.us; e-mail tourism@govt.co.charles.md.us.*

General Smallwood State Park, at the mouth of **Mattawoman Creek** in Charles County, is a good place to launch your own boat. You can head straight out into the Potomac, rated the number 1 tidewater river in the United States for largemouth bass. The estimated population is from 400,000 to 500,000. They gather especially among the rusting supports of the scuttled ships in **Mallows Bay**.

To the right from Smallwood State Park's boat launch, a wildlife sanctuary limits speed to six miles an hour, offering quiet waters with acres of lily pad fields and marshy banks, where several professional guides take clients to fish. Our favorite of these guides is Dale Knupp, of **Real Bass Adventures** (☎ 301-839-2858), who knows all the local hangouts for bass. A full day on the water in Dale's well-equipped boat is $250, a four-hour trip is $175. This includes rods and lures, as well as life jackets, but you should bring your own lunch and raingear.

The largest bass ever recorded in the Mattawoman was found among the lily pads in a quiet cove. Taken by a "shock boat," it was measured and returned to the water, where it still awaits the fisherman who can land it. This particular bass is one pound larger than the state's record catch. The best fishing is from April to the end of May.

INSIDE ADVICE

When fishing in the Mattawoman, Dale Knupp suggests the following tips for catching bass:

- Going into the far reaches of the creek, beyond the dunes.
- "Flipping pads," using line twice the length of the rod and making a silent entry into the water.
- Fishing the shallow waters filled with spatterdock, where bass hide among the roots or under the leaves.
- Going out at low tide, when receding waters pull bass out to the leeward end of plant-filled areas.
- Waiting at the end of a gut as the tide goes out and sweeps fish right to you.
- Fishing around downed trees or old boat remains.
- In the spring, fishing in the backs of coves.
- Thinking like a bass, which looks for places to take cover and ambush its dinner.

Friendship Pier is a county-owned facility is on Nanjemoy Creek, south of General Smallwood State Park, with easy access to the Potomac. There is a large boat launch there, open all year from dawn to dusk, as well as a fishing pier. It is on Route 425, called Durham Church Rd. from the north and Ironsides Rd. on the southern end. Baptist Church Rd. will also take you to Ironsides Rd. The landing is at the end of Friendship Rd.

AUTHOR TIP

*Friendship Pier at Nanjemoy Creek has been designated by the Department of Natural Resources as a **free fishing area**, which means that fishermen are not required to have a fishing license.*

At the south end of the County on the east side of the Wicomico River (don't mistake it for the river of the same name on the Eastern Shore) is a clump of three fishing piers close together. Follow Route 242 to Paul Ellis Rd., leading to **Paul Ellis Wharf**. If you continue on down Route 242 the road ends at Cloton Point, where another fishing pier is in Dukehart's Channel. Across the channel, on St. Clements Island, where the first settlers landed, there is a third fishing pier, but you must take the museum's boat to get there (see *Boat Tours*).

At the northern end of Charles County, **Marshall Hall Boat Launching Facility** is on the Potomac close to the Prince George's border. The facility is open from dawn to dusk and has parking for 25 boat trailers. The two boat launches and boarding pier are popular with fishermen. From Route 210, take Route 227 north to the end.

Cultural & Eco-Travel Experiences

■ Natural Areas

No matter how many times we have entered a cypress swamp, we always get the same shiver; few places are so mysterious – like a setting for a spooky movie. **Battle Creek Bald Cypress Swamp** is especially interesting because you can walk through it, instead of paddling through. A boardwalk meanders among the knobby cypress knees for closer looks without wet feet. Be sure to pick up a brochure at the Nature Center telling about the seasonal flora and fauna in the swamp. You will want to look at the displays here first, to learn more about the unique environment you are about to enter.

The Nature Center has an albino snapping turtle, a bee hive and a "tree house" – a trunk with little doors so kids can investigate who lives there: beetles, a salamander and a snake nest. An exhibit of disappearing wildlife in Maryland reports that the last black bear reported in southern Maryland was in 1634, so at least you don't have to worry about that. A pond next to the center is surrounded by plants that attract bees, butterflies and birds.

The cypress base is buttressed by exposed roots that drape in graceful folds like a well-tailored walking skirt. The knees, little independent mounds of root that surround the tree, help stabilize the tall trunks and provide air access. The knees do not become trees. The bald cypress has needles and cones, but is a deciduous tree, which lives almost 2,000 years, and can become 150 feet tall and 17 feet in diameter. The trees here are only kids, 75-100 years old. Although they once covered much of North America and Europe, they are now found only in the southeastern US.

The swamp is on Gray's Rd., Prince Frederick; ☎ 410-535-5327, TDD 800-735-2258. It is free and open from April through September, Tuesday-Saturday, 10-5; Sunday 1-5. From October through March it closes at 4:30.

To get to the Battle Creek Cypress Swamp: Travel south from Prince Frederick on Route 2/4, 2.1 miles from the intersection with Route 506, and turn west (right) on Route 505. Go left at 1.8 miles, onto Gray's Rd., where you will see a sign.

Jefferson Patterson Park is a large expanse of public land that was once an estate on the broad Patuxent River; everyone locally calls it "Jeff-Patt." Evidence of human history at this site dates back 12,000 years; it was known as King's Reach to early settlers. Wooden beams outline one of their early house sites, but even earlier Native American sites are not marked, to prevent vandalism.

Programs, trails and exhibits at the park show how the people have lived with and used the land over its history, and the best place to begin is in the Discovery Room, outstanding for all ages. Choose a topic and an object that interests you and take it outside to use. They provide backpacks, field guides, bows and arrows, woodland Indian hoes and digging sticks, archaic spears, Colonial grubbing hoes, Colonial and Native American games, which you are welcome to take outdoors.

Inside are other hands-on activities, one on how to distinguish artifacts from natural stones, another a chard puzzle. There are bone and stone tools to use, or you can learn flint knapping, hide tanning or knitting, piece puzzles, and use a pump drill. Children will enjoy trying on the old clothes in front of a mirror, and there is a reading room designed for both adults and children.

The more formal exhibits in the rest of the center focus on conservation of artifacts, on underwater archaeology, and on the Battle of Leonard's Creek. Look at the pictures and compare the size of the American "fleet" to the size and number of the British blockade, then wonder how the Americans ever won the War of 1812. One exhibit shows how land and water has changed, comparing the size of today's oysters with shells found from earlier times. This is what museums should do – bring visitors into the subject and use the artifacts to show something relevant and interesting.

SUNKEN HISTORY

A maritime archaeological site in the Patuxent River off Jefferson-Patterson Park marks the spot where two boats from the War of 1812 have been located. The British blockaded the Chesapeake during the war and, in June of 1814, the town of Leonard's Creek was wiped out by the British. This was one of the first times rockets were used in naval warfare.

Here we learn that studying wear on stone tools shows how they were used and what they cut – meat, wood, etc. We discover that incised pottery cooks faster, as does a round-bottomed pot. Each exhibit has an element called "unpuzzling the past," at kid level, some with hands-on feature, such as how to date a building by its brick pattern.

A few yards down the Woodland Trail is a replica of a Native American campsite with a meat-drying rack and a reed house.

The **Agricultural Center** is in the barn, where you can still see the stalls, now well fitted in displays of tools and techniques from the Native Americans to early bayshore farms and more modern farm equipment. A small shop carries books on nature and history.

Annual events, such as Earth Day, 1812 Days and Native American Technology Day, bring re-enactors and specialists in primitive skills, such as flint napping, basketry, archery, twine cording or hollowing out a grinding

Native American dwelling at Jefferson Patterson Park.

bowl. They share these crafts with the public by working at the campsite, where visitors can often take part in a hands-on experience.

The Jefferson Patterson Park and Museum, in conjunction with the Archeological Society of Maryland and the Department of Housing and Community Development runs **Calvert County Volunteer Archaeology**, a program that actually allows amateur volunteers to participate with trained archaeologists in the excavation of historic sites in the county. These expeditions are held on a regularly scheduled basis. Volunteers are also used throughout the year on weekdays and Saturdays for lab work. If interested, call Kirsti Uunila at ☎ 410-586-8555, e-mail uunila@dhcd. state.ms.us.

The park is free as we write, but admission may be charged in the future. The Visitors Center is open April 15-October 15, Wednesday-Sunday, 10 am-5 pm. The grounds are open year-round, and by 2002 the park hopes to have the center open year-round, too. 10515 Mackall Rd., St. Leonard 20685, ☎ 410-586-8500, fax 410-586-0080.

To get to Jefferson Patterson Park: Traveling south from Prince Frederick on Route 2/4, turn west (right) onto Route 264, about 3.6 miles south of the intersection of Route 506 to Battle Creek Cypress Swamp. Turn left onto Route 265 and drive until you're sure you're on the wrong road. The park entrance is just before Route 265 ends at the water. Traveling north on Route 2/4, Parran Rd. gives access from the south, and is also signposted for northbound travelers. Note that neither approach is signposted from the opposite lane.

The **Maryland Archaeological Conservation Collection and Laboratory** is on the grounds of Jefferson Patterson, a state-of-the-art facility that does conservation work not only for Maryland, but by contract for other states as well. The whole building is designed in conservation-friendly materials (wood, for example, gives off gases that are damaging to some artifacts), its floors and hallways are made for forklifts and to accommodate moving large and heavy objects. Interior windows into the lab area allow visitors to watch some of the delicate work of cleaning and restoring artifacts, with exhibits in the double-window area.

Southern Maryland has more than its fair share of very early Colonial sites, as display cases demonstrate. Displays show 1650s ceramics of English, Dutch and German manufacture, and demonstrate the efficacy of conservation, with two knife blades, one conserved, one not.

In the larger-object lab, you might see a cannon from the early 1800s in conservation. The equipment is as interesting as the objects they conserve there: a freeze-dryer to dry out underwater artifacts, isolation rooms, an X-ray for live ordnance suspects, even a rare paleo-environmental lab for pollen analysis.

The facility is open for tours on the first Friday of each month. The library is open to the public, but the books are for use there only. The non-lending collection has about 4,000 items on southern Maryland archaeology and history.

The Academy of Natural Sciences Estuarine Research Center (ANSERC) is also located on the grounds of the Jefferson Patterson at 10545 Mackall Rd., ☎ 410-586-9700, fax 410-586-9705, www.anserc.org. On first Fridays of the month (except January and July) they have an open house for the public with guided tours of their research labs and experimental facilities. Adults-only tours are 9-11 and tours when school kids are welcomed are 3-5 pm. Visitors must register in advance; ☎ 410-586-9700. This is a free program. The center has a number of other programs to which the public is invited throughout the year. They also invite volunteers to fill any number of positions, including participation in the scientific work of the Center. Call for program specifics.

The **Southern Maryland Audubon Society** has no building nor special exhibit hall but it doesn't need one. They have a series of field trips throughout the year that go into the most fascinating wild areas of the state in search of birds and nature. Contact them at PO Box 181, Bryans Road, MD 20616; www.audubon. org/chapter/md/smas. Remember also that southern Maryland is a birder's paradise, especially when it comes to sea birds. The Audubon Society owns the 50-acre **Nanjemoy Marsh Sanctuary** in Charles County.

The lighthouse at Calvert Marine Museum, Solomons.

Don't picture rows of dusty ship models at the **Calvert Marine Museum**. Well-designed exhibits are divided between the natural history of the Chesapeake and its human history. The former begins with the denizens of the Miocene Sea and the latter with the Triangle Trade and the Chesapeake in the War of 1812. Exhibits include an undersea exploration tank called an "aquascope," cutting-edge exploration technology in the 1950s. Other displays show the Navy presence on the Patuxent during World War II, tools and work of the watermen and the oyster packing industry, and a relief map of Solomons with lights to identify landmarks.

The area on the Miocene coastline explains why the fossils are so numerous here and shows how the fossils are removed. A skeleton reproduction (made in their shop, which you can also visit) shows a megatooth shark, whose single tooth can be six or seven inches long. Bald cypresses, such as those you see at Battle Creek, were here in the Miocene era, when crocodiles lurked about their knees (better theirs than mine).

Learn about the systematics of fossils here, and be sure to pull out the drawers to look at fascinating examples, including a fossilized leatherback turtle shell, like a jigsaw puzzle. This is a good place to go before you begin a fossil search on the beaches, since it helps you know what to look for. Some of the forms other than shark teeth would be easy to miss without seeing examples.

Fish in the aquarium come from various places, including an oyster reef and salt marsh; the beautiful flashes of iridescent blue are mummichogs. Visitors can look through a window to see backstage in the aquarium, where they grow microscopic sea life to feed each level of life here, hatching out baby sea horses, horseshoe crabs and eels.

A Discovery Room is geared toward youngsters, with a sandbox seeded with sharks' teeth for them to find and keep, and a board with sailors' knots to learn. The museum shop has a good selection of books on the area, covering nature, history, fossil hunting and ships. The library at Calvert Marine Museum has over 7,000 volumes, periodicals, plus archives of photos, ship logs and other research materials, much of which they hope eventually to have available on-line.

YOU REALLY OTTER SEE THESE: *Two river otters, raised in captivity, cavort in an indoor-outdoor pool at the Calvert Marine Museum. They seem to have as much fun people-watching as we do otter-watching, and are playful and interactive – they'll follow your hands along the glass. Doug Alves, the museum's director, laughs about their antics: "They're 60% otter, 40% ham." The otters are named Bubble and Squeek, because they bubble when they swim and squeek when they talk.*

On a self-guided marsh walk outside the museum, you can see fiddler crabs at low tide and watch herons come and go. Many more of the museum complex's attractions are outside its walls, too.

Drumpoint Lighthouse, a screwpile cottage style, was situated 120 yards offshore, where its pilings were hand screwed into the ocean floor. It took 33 days to build it in 1883, and it was used until 1962, brought here in 1975 and restored to its early 1900s appearance. It was one of two lighthouses that marked the entrance to the Patuxent River. Ascend stairs through a hole in the floor to the keeper's quarters, a tiny house with a potbellied heating stove and a wind-up Victrola in the living room. One keeper had seven children, and it's a puzzle where he put them all. A railed balcony goes around the outside – note the outhouse, not especially good in a hurricane. The boat hoist not only secured the keeper's boat in storms, but made off-loading easier than bringing supplies up through the hatch.

Weights in the closet operated the mechanism to strike the bell in foggy weather. When the keeper pulled on the chain, ratchets released, double-striking the bell every 15 seconds. It worked for two hours and could be heard two miles away. Like the lights, each fog bell had its own timing, so boats could tell where they were by the sound. The two kerosene lamps that were placed inside the lens were replaced by a 100-watt bulb. A film in the museum explains how the lens worked to magnify and focus the light, and how the lighthouse was moved to its present location. The lighthouse tour takes half an hour.

The *William B Tennyson*, a Chesapeake Bay bugeye, (see *Boat Tours*, above) was converted from sail to engine in 1907, then used as a buy boat for the oyster packing plant. It went out into the skipjack fleet to buy oysters for the plant, often returning with the deck heaped higher than the pilot house and its gunwales within inches of the water. It is docked at the museum and sails on scheduled cruises (see *On Water*, page 325).

Boat sheds on the grounds protect an extensive collection of water craft designed, built and used on these waters. The collection includes several examples of boats carved from logs, including one made from three logs carved to fit together as one boat. Other examples range from working boats to pleasure craft. Anyone who loves wooden boats will appreciate this collection and the effort being made to save these last examples of old craft.

On the main street of Solomon's Island, just over the bridge, you'll find the J.C. Lore and Sons Oyster House, a working 1888 oyster canning factory museum with all of its original equipment. A video with home movies tells the story of the island, the fishermen, and the packers. Although it is part of the Calvert Marine Museum, it is on the original site, a half-mile south of the museum on Solomons Island (an easy walk). It's open daily, June-August, 10-4:30, and on weekends and holidays in May and September.

The Calvert Marine Museum is on Routes 2 and 4 at Solomons, near the bridge over the Patuxent to St. Mary's County. Contact them at PO Box 97, Solomons 20688; ☎ 410-326-2042, or, in Maryland, 800-735-2258, fax 410-326-6691. The museum is open 10-5 daily and is closed only Christmas, New Year and Thanksgiving days.

Chesapeake Biological Laboratory's free Visitors Center, at the Solomon Marina on Charles St. (☎ 410-326-7282), is open 10-4, Tuesday-Sunday. Scientists here examine the environment of the bay and can contact buoys throughout the bay to monitor temperature, salinity and other variables. A video explains the lab's work and origins, and an aquarium shows local fish. Tours of the lab are offered and there are exhibits, displays and an aquarium with native species. From Route 2 in Solomons take Charles Street; it's at the end on the left.

THE TWELVE-MILE CHURCHES

This area is known for its "twelve-mile churches," each 12 miles from the last. An early cleric planned the churches this distance apart, saying that no one would have the excuse of being too far away to attend church, since it would be only a six-mile ride at the most in one direction or the other. Among these are St. Anne's, All Hallows, St. James, All Saints in Sunderland, Christ Church, and a final one which burned. St. James, in Lothian, has the state's second-oldest tombstones.

■ Fossil Hunting

One of the unique features of this side of the Chesapeake Bay and the lower Potomac River is its abundance of fossils from the Miocene era. The most commonly found (and by commonly, we mean a casual hunter might find several in half an hour's searching) are sharks' teeth, which range in size from tiny needles barely a quarter-inch long to several inches across.

DID YOU KNOW?

Unlike us, sharks lose their teeth on a continuing basis throughout their lives. Their jaws are like an assembly line, producing more teeth that move in succession to replace those that have become dull. (A shark with dull teeth is a skinny shark, and destined to grow skinnier.) A single shark might go through tens of thousands of teeth in a 50-year life span.

With X-number of sharks over the millions of years of the Miocene Sea, there could be trillions of these teeth at **Calvert Cliffs State Park**, maybe as many as 100 trillion. Not all would be fossilized, of course, but their hardness and number improve the chances for that.

Calvert Marine Museum, in Solomons, is a good place to go before beginning a fossil search on the beaches. Its exhibits and drawers of specimens help you know what to look for. There are several other types besides shark teeth. Look for the booklet *Fossils of Calvert Cliffs*, by Wallace Ashby, an excellent guide to the formation of the cliffs and to the fossils, with excellent drawings of fossils commonly found.

DID YOU KNOW? *CHESPAX is a program of the Calvert County Board of Education that focuses on teaching students from grammar school through high school about the environment and man's effect upon it. With offices at King's Landing Park, they use the many other parks in the county as their classrooms, including Battle Creek Cypress Swamp Sanctuary, Jeff-Patt and others. In summer special training programs are available for teachers.*

On the other side of southern Maryland, on the Potomac River, is an area rarely visited by collectors. At **Purse State Park**, 11 miles south of the entrance to General Smallwood State Park on Route 224, a short walk through the woods brings you to the ruin of a house at the top of sand bluffs. Below, on the narrow pebble beach, are several varieties of fossils. Easiest to find are tiny shark teeth. Look close to the bluffs and in their tide-worn surface for entire clamshell fossils. These look as if a pair of clam shells was used as a mold, which in fact it was.

The park is free, and you could easily overlook it. Watch for a parking pullout on the left as you head south, then walk back up the road a short distance to find the trail on its opposite side. A sign may be there, or it may be lying beside the road in the brush. When you return to your car, continue walking down the hill to see the turtles, which sun themselves on logs in the creek to the left.

■ Gardens

Annmarie Garden on St. John, a unique garden/public art space is laid out in a series of outdoor "rooms," each designed by a prominent artist or sculptor. The garden starts right at the entrance with a colorful and unique ceramic gateway by Florida artists Peter King and Marni Jaime. Inside, "Tribute to the Oyster Tonger" is an outstanding bronze of a Chesapeake Bay oyster tonger (called such because of the tool used), standing on his stone boat with water dripping from his tongs. The work is by Maryland native Antonio Mendez who has since been commissioned to do the Thurgood Marshall Memorial in Annapolis. The "Council Chamber" is used as an intimate stage and ballet venue by Vermont artists B. Amore and Woody Dorsey. "Surveyors Walk" is a succession of long wooden ramps leading into the woods, ending at treetop level. It is designed so that anyone, even those with limited mobility, can view the forest from the same vantage point of having climbed a tree. The most unusual work is "Generations Room," a curving walk with mosaic human figures and handprints, each becoming progressively larger. This is designed so each person who follows the path will make up his own story of what it means.

AUTHOR TIP **WATCHABLE WILDFLOWERS:** *The state of Maryland has undertaken to restore to the state's roadsides and gardens wildflowers that were prominent during the Colonial period. Some of the information for the project comes from collections sent to the Bishop of London by a young Welsh parson in 1696, collections now in the British Museum. Keep an eye out for patches of coneflower, chicory, phlox, yarrow, dames rocket, bidens, gaillardia, and especially* Rudbeckia hirta *– the black-eyed susan that is the state flower.*

This is a growing sculpture garden and plans call for new pieces to be commissioned with promising artists over the coming years. The link between the works and the natural beauty around them create an ever-changing experience as seasons. No bikes or pets are allowed in the gardens, to preserve its contemplative nature. Just north of Solomons, take Dowell Rd. east from Routes 2/4. It is well signposted and is just a short distance down Dowell Rd. Admission is free, open daily 10-4; ☎ 410-326-4640.

AUTHOR TIP *Be sure to see the restrooms at Annmarie Garden, which are decorated with tiles painted by people in the community.*

■ Farmers' Markets

Calvert County's Farmers' Market is held Saturday, 9-4; Sunday, 1-6; and Wednesday, 3-7. In addition to the freshest of fruits and vegetables, they have herbs, dried flowers and baked goods. There is a playground for the kids while you shop. It's just north of Parkers Creek Rd. on Route 2/4, next to Adams Ribs, two miles south of Prince Frederick. ☎ 410-535-4583 or 800-331-9771.

■ Crafts

Calvert Homestead, Sixes Rd., near the entrance to Battle Creek, is an old barn hung with dried herbs and flowers, most grown here. Many of the floral crafts designed here, including miniature braided wreaths, use tobacco leaves. Drying racks are made of tobacco sticks. During the holiday season, the barn is cozy with the heat from a potbellied stove, and the scents of simmering cinnamon sticks.

Cecil's Old Mill is an artisan's shop selling the art and crafts of Marylanders, who also demonstrate here throughout the year. Operated by the St. Mary's County Art Association, the shop displays ceramics, fabric arts and clothing, needle crafts, jewelry, scherenschnitte (hand-cut paper designs), dried flower arrangements and wreaths, woodworking, Christmas ornaments and art in several media. The mill is a historic structure located in Great Mills, on Route 5 about three miles west of Patuxent Naval Air Station. Open 10-5, Thursday through Sunday, from mid-March to November 1; daily from November 1 to December 23. Indian Bridge Rd., Great Mills; ☎ 301-994-1510.

■ Antiques

In Chesapeake Beach, **A-1 Antiques and Collectibles** is a multi-dealer shop, at 3736 Chesapeake Beach Rd.; ☎ 301-855-4500. They have 20 rooms of early bedroom, dining room and living room furniture, as well as coins. Open Thursday-Sunday, 11-5; in summer, open on Saturday and Sunday only.

There are five antiques shops in North Beach just a short distance up Bay Avenue from Chesapeake Beach. **Chesapeake Antique Center**, a multi-dealer shop, 4133 7th Street (☎ 410-257-3153), is open Friday-Sunday, 11-5, and handles collectibles, Victoriana and fishing items. **Nice & Fleazy Antique Center**, a multi-dealer shop at 7th and Bay Avenue (☎ 410-257-3044, 301-855-5066), is open longer hours: Tuesday-Sunday and holiday Mondays, 10-5. This shop has refinished oak and Victorian furniture, fine silver, nautical items, jewelry, advertising and antique slot machines. **Willetta's Antiques** at 7th and Bay Streets (☎ 301-855-3412) is open Thursday-Sunday and Monday holidays, 10-5, selling formal and period furniture, clocks, mirrors, porcelain and lighting. **Bay Avenue Antiques**, a multi-dealer shop, 9132-B Bay Avenue (☎ 301-257-5020) opens Thursday-Sunday and holiday Mondays, 10-5. In summer their hours are longer. Their merchandise includes china cupboards, fine glass and crystal, porcelain, country furniture, decoys, mirrors, paintings and prints and frames.

In Huntingtown, near Routes 2/4, are three dealers. The **Sunflower Shop** is in the Cherub's Closet at 3920 Old Town Rd. (☎ 410-535-6042), dealing in furniture and old lighting. They are open Tuesday, 4-8; Wednesday and Thursday, noon-8; Friday & Saturday, 10-6; and Sunday, noon-5. There are two multi-dealer shops. **Bowen's Garage Antique Center**, Old Town Rd. (☎ 410-257-3105), is a large shop with a wide range of goods from formal and country furniture to lighting, glassware, Flow Blue and Blue Willow, paintings, prints, depression glass, jewelry and more. The other is **Southern Maryland Antiques Center**, on Routes 2/4, 3176 Solomons Rd. (☎ 410-257-1677), open Thursday-Saturday and holiday Mondays, 10-5; Sundays, 11-5; daily in December. This is another very large shop with everything under the sun. They carry high-quality furniture, glass, lighting, dolls, mirrors, Civil War items, paintings, prints, tools, quilts, linens and myriad other items.

Architectural salvage is the specialty of **Calvert County Furniture** at 75 Armory Rd., Prince Frederick, ☎ 800-675-2389, 410-535-2389. They also have antique and used furniture and other collectibles, open Monday-

Saturday, 10-6. Down the road a short way look for **The JAD Center**, 4865 St. Leonard Rd., St. Leonard; ☎ 410-586-2740, 800-335-0105. They are open daily, 10-5, and carry furniture and collectibles. Also in St. Leonard, on Calvert Beach Rd., is **Chesapeake Antique Flea Market and Specialty Shops**, which has 70 dealers and is open Wednesday-Sunday, 10-5. On Wednesday and Friday they hold auctions at the shop. ☎ 410-586-3725, 800-655-1081; turn east onto Calvert Beach Rd. just before Routes 2 and 4 diverge.

Near Solomons, **Dodson's on Mill Creek** specializes in English and nautical antiques with a special emphasis on wardrobes. At 13690 Oliviet Rd., Lusby (☎ 410-326-1369), they are open Monday-Saturday, 9-7; Sunday, 11-5. **Grandmother's Store and Antiques Center** 13892 Dowell Rd. (☎ 410-326-3366) has nine rooms filled with mahogany and oak furniture, trunks, primitives, glass, books and more; open daily, 10-5. Turn at the Solomons Fire Department; they are close to Annmarie Garden. **Island Trader Antiques**, 225 Lore Rd., next to the Comfort Inn (☎ 410-326-3582), opens Thursday-Tuesday, 11-5, with country furniture, linens, trunks, advertising items and decorative arts. **Barb's Attic** is at the Lazy Moon Book and Antique Center on Main Street of the island (☎ 410-326-3720); open daily, 11-5, with collectibles. **Grandmother's Too**, on Main Street at Harmon House (☎ 410-326-6848), carries similar items, open daily, 10-5.

Events

APRIL: Usually held on the third Saturday, Jefferson Patterson Park and Museum hosts the **Southern Maryland Celtic Festival** (☎ 410-586-8500), celebrating the Scottish, Irish and English heritage of Maryland with traditional Celtic games such as caber and weight toss and traditional dance and bagpiping. The **Spring Gardenfest** (☎ 410-326-4640) at Annmarie Garden, Solomons, is a flower show, with local businesses and garden clubs landscaping portions of the park in containerized plantings.

MAY: The second Saturday of the month brings the **Lighthouse Festival** at Piney Point Lighthouse Museum and Park, 10-4, a day of fun and learning with lectures, guided tours, craft sales and food; ☎ 301-769-2222, fax 301-475-2225, TDD 301-475-4105. Late in the month, Historic St. Mary's City hosts **The Planting Season**, with tours of its gardens and fields; ☎ 301-800-SMC-1634.

JUNE: Mid-month is the **St. Mary's County Crab Festival** at Governmental Center in Leonardtown, with lots of steamed crabs, seafood and an antiques car show and craft sale; ☎ 301-475-8403. In late June there are **Blue and Gray Days** at Fort Lincoln, in Lookout Point State Park, featuring a re-enactment of the Point during the Civil War, Saturday, 11-5, and Sunday, 10-4; ☎ 301-872-5688.

JULY: The **War of 1812 Days** (☎ 410-586-8500), Jefferson Patterson Park, are usually held on the second weekend of the month, featuring a re-enactment of the period, including the Battle of St. Leonard Creek. Mid-month, the **Calvert County Farm Tour and Produce Sale** brings hayrides, music, food and tours of a number of local farms; ☎ 410-535-4583. In late July, amateurs get to do some archaeological excavation at the **Tidewater Archaeology Dig** at Historic St. Mary's City, part of their ongoing search for the secrets of the city. There is a fee for participation. Saturday and Sunday, 10-5; ☎ 301-862-0990, 800-SMC-1634.

AUGUST: Usually during the second weekend, Calvert Marine Museum sponsors **Solomons: The Cradle of Invasion** (☎ 410-326-2042), recreating the military life of Solomons during World War II, when it was the training ground for all US invasions around the world. The weapons and tactics of the period are used, as are several ships remaining from the period.

SEPTEMBER: **Working Hands**, held early in the month at Historic St. Mary's City, focuses on tobacco culture, period carpentry, shipboard life and domestic life; Saturday and Sunday, 10-5; ☎ 301-862-0990, 800-SMC-1634. **Artsfest** fills the sculpture gardens of Annmarie Garden with juried artists and craftsmen, especially jewelry makers; ☎ 410-326-4640.

County Fairs are very important parts of local culture in this predominantly agricultural area, a time to show off the best produce. **Prince George's County Fair** (☎ 301-952-7999) is held the second weekend of the month at the Fairgrounds in Upper Marlboro for four days; hours are Thursday, 4-10; Friday, 4-11; Saturday, 9am-11:30 pm; Sunday, 9-9. **Charles County** (☎ 301-932-1234) holds its fair at the County Fair Grounds off Route 301 south of La Plata the third weekend in the month, for four days; Thursday, 5-10 pm; Friday and Saturday 9 am-10 pm; Sunday, 10-6. The **St. Mary's fair** (☎ 301-475-2707) is at the fairgrounds in Leonardtown, on the third weekend in the month for four days; Thursday, 3-9; Friday and Saturday 9-9; Sunday, 9-6). And **Calvert County's** (☎ 410-535-0026) is at their fairgrounds on Route 231 in Barstow, just outside of Prince Frederick, over Labor Day weekend, lasting five days. Hours are Wednesday, 4-9; Thursday, 9-9; Friday and Saturday 9am-11pm; Sunday, 11-6.

OCTOBER: During the second weekend, the largest 17th-century military re-enactment in the country, **Grand Militia Muster** (☎ 301-862-0990), is held at Historic St. Mary's City; Saturday, 10-5. The third weekend brings the **St. Mary's County Oyster Festival**, at the County Fairgrounds in Leonardtown, with entertainment, food and kids' rides, and the National Oyster Shucking Championships and National Oyster Cook-off. Admission is $3 adults, under 14 free; ☎ 301-863-5015. **Halloween**

brings children to Annemarie Garden for a trick or treat party (☎ 410-326-4640).

DECEMBER: On the first weekend is the **Olde Fashioned Christmas Celebration**, at Sotterley Plantation in Hollywood; ☎ 301-373-2280. During the second weekend of the month, **Annmarie Garden** (☎ 410-326-4640) is bathed in thousands and thousands of twinkling lights throughout the month. You pay for your entrance with a contribution to their food baskets. During the same weekend is **Solomons Christmas Walk**, when streets are lit, carolers sing, lighted boats parade and wagons take people for rides. **Tudor Hall Open House** is held on the second weekend (☎ 301-475-9791), as is the **Holiday Home Tour** of several fine homes, also in Leonardtown; ☎ 301-475-6008. A series of Christmas events at Historic St. Mary's City include **Madrigals and Carols** at the Old Statehouse. Hours vary by the day, so call for dates, times and reservations; ☎ 301-862-0990, 800-SMC-1634.

Sightseeing

■ Historic Sites & Museums

Calvert County

 The **Chesapeake Beach Railway Museum** occupies the former terminus station of the Chesapeake Beach Railroad, which brought holiday-makers from Washington, DC to this seaside playground from 1900 to 1935. Inside you will see photographs of the town in its heyday, with its Great Derby roller coaster, boardwalk, and Denzel Carousel. You'll "meet" Otto and David Moffat, who built both the resort and the railroad to get there. The half-mile amusement park sat on a boardwalk running out over water. The station, in its original location at the end of the line, was built in 1897-8. The museum shows scenes and locomotives from the 32-mile excursion from Washington, through Seat Pleasant, in old photos and postcards. The 1914 Model-T Ford Depot Hack gleams in the baggage room and behind the museum is half of an 1889 railway car. Railway buffs should note that this is only one of the many sites connected to rail history within 100 miles of Baltimore.

Look for the sign to the museum on Main Street in Chesapeake Beach, just south of the bridge, 0.3 mile south of the intersection of 260 and 261. The museum is open May through September, 1-4 daily; from April and October, it's open on Saturday and Sunday only, 1-4. The museum is always open by request, and you shouldn't feel that you are bothering anyone, since they encourage and invite your interest. PO Box 783, Chesapeake Beach 20732; ☎ 410-257-3892.

While Chesapeake Beach was the hotel and amusement park area, neigh-boring **North Beach** shows the early resort cottages built by those who came to spend the summer. It still has the air of a summertime community, with its half-mile boardwalk, like a big front porch for the community. Kids skate and people cycle and walk past the cottages whose gardens look onto the boardwalk.

GOING DOWN THE TRACKS

If you look at a map, you will notice that Route 260 runs in a per-fectly straight line from Chaney, on Route 4, almost to Chesa-peake Beach. It is an old rail line, and old-timers still use the phrase "going down the tracks" to mean traveling on Route 260.

Christ Church (☎ 410-586-0565) in Port Republic has a biblical garden, and is the scene of the oldest known continuously held jousting tourna-ment, held for at least 350 years on the last Sunday in August. (Jousting is Maryland's state sport.) It's just off Routes 2/4 on Route 264 in Port Republic.

Patuxent River Naval Air Museum shows some of the work done here at the Naval Test Station, where four of the original astronauts – John Glenn, Wally Scherrer, Scott Carpenter and Gus Grissom – trained. The station is the Navy's test pilot school, and this is the only museum of naval air research and technology. Outside are 17 naval aircraft, including the F-18 Hornet, F-14 Tomcat, a Harrier and others, each with a sign describ-ing its mission; all were tested on this base.

While the displays and hardware inside will fire the interest of any avia-tion aficionado, it is also interesting to those whose knowledge of flight is limited to buying an airline ticket. Here you will see some of the cutting-edge prototypes tested at the base, along with some ideas that didn't quite work as planned. One of the latter was an F-82 twin Mustang, which could be flown by either pilot. One of the original G force test machines is here and another exhibit shows the development of the ejection seat for air-craft. A poignant alcove memorializes some of the men who lost their lives in test flights, including Major Rowland Stanley, who put his plane down to avoid the chance of hitting a school. Hanging over the central audito-rium is an unmanned remote control aircraft to which an entire Iraqi tank unit surrendered during the Gulf War. They weren't foolish, these un-manned aircraft brought down naval gunfire instantaneously upon any target they located.

Ask to see one of the films – the one on the Blue Angels is our favorite. Kids will like the chance to sit in a cockpit trainer. Tours of the base itself are of-fered on the first and third Thursdays of each month. The Museum is open Wednesday through Sunday, noon-5, all year, except on major holidays. Most of the docents here are former pilots who flew these machines and they know their stuff. Follow signs from Route 235 south of its intersection with Route 4 near the Patuxent River Bridge, in Lexington Park, ☎ 301-863-7418, fax 342-7947, e-mail paxmuseum@erols.com.

THE INFLATABLE AIRPLANE

In the Patuxent River Naval Air Museum is the last surviving inflatable airplane, which will not be there forever. The one at the Smithsonian has disintegrated, as this one will eventually, since, of necessity, its construction is of the lightest possible materials. It was designed to be dropped behind enemy lines to a downed pilot, who could then inflate it and fly to safety.

St. Mary's County

Sotterly Plantation (1710) is at once elegant and comfortable, an 18th-century tobacco planter's plantation house that has survived with many of its dependencies intact. Surrounded by fine old trees, its old out-buildings include the gatehouse, smokehouse, barns and an original slave quarters along the old road to the plantation wharf. Inside, the handsome rooms are considered to be among the best examples from their period. The main hallway has an exquisite Chippendale stair and adjacent to it is a Georgian room with two matched shell-motif alcoves. This is Maryland's only tidewater plantation house open to the public. The house is open May through October for guided tours ($5); the grounds are open all year, 10-4, Tuesday-Sunday. From Route 235 at Hollywood, head north on Sotterly Plantation Rd. (Route 245); ☎ 800-681-0850.

Those who look for the bright lights of St. Mary's City will be surprised. The city stood here in the 1600s, and is now in the process of being reconstructed, based on archaeological evidence and early records. Inhabitants of **Historic St. Mary's City** seem to have landed from another century, speaking to visitors in the accents of those freshly arrived settlers they portray, seemingly unaware of the century they have fallen into.

St. Mary's was the first capital of Maryland, a thriving community that grew from 140 residents in 1660 to a bustling 2,000 by the time they moved the capital to Annapolis. Because the buildings of St. Mary's City are being reconstructed on their original sites, instead of being gathered from elsewhere as many historic museum villages are, this is not a compact site to visit. The four main areas are connected by roads, so you can drive between them, but walking along the wide paths is the best way to get a sense of the land and the lives of these early settlers. The longest distance is one mile, from the Visitors Center to the capitol and dock area.

Wheelchairs and golf carts are available at the St. Mary's City Visitors Center for those with limited mobility.

Begin at the Visitors Center by learning about the Calvert family, whose colony this was. Here you will see two of the four lead coffins unearthed at the site, thought to be those of the Calverts.

A nearby hamlet of longhouses called "witcotts" represents the first year of the settlement, when colonists lived in bark- and thatch-covered shelters framed of bent saplings. They learned this building technique from the Native Americans. The buildings were well-designed, airtight at the top, so smoke from cooking fires below gathered above and kept bugs out of the food stored in the rafters. The longest of the present day witcotts took five years to build, using only stone and bone tools, as Native Americans would have used. In this area, workshops for visitors ages six and older teach skills such as basket making. Work continues on a variety of projects, including hollowing a log for a dugout canoe, tanning hides, and cultivating the gardens.

Set some distance away, across cultivated fields, is a substantial farmhouse. You may find its owner cultivating his garden or at work on a shaving horse, carefully handshaping wooden parts for a farm implement. Cattle grazing in the rail-fenced enclosures are breeds kept here in the 1660s, and tobacco is the main cash crop.

The busiest place in St. Mary's City is, as it was in the 1600s, the area close to the imposing brick capitol, a reconstruction of the second 1676 State House. Beside it is the Ordinary, owned by the sheriff, an early lodging serving meals of "whatever came out of the pot."

Below, at the foot of the bluff on the St. Mary's River, rise the masts of a merchant ship, *Maryland Dove*, a replica of one of the ships that carried the original settlers to these shores. Its captain or a seaman will explain that it carries 42 tons of goods under 2,000 square feet of canvas, at a top speed of eight knots.

You will get some idea of the magnitude of the project from the "ghost houses" you see along the roads. These timber-frame outlines mark the sites and dimensions of buildings identified by archaeologists. These will be reconstructed by costumed interpreters, using 17th-century building methods and materials, and visitors will be able to watch and discuss the construction with the builders. One of the first of these is Leonard Calvert's home, which will be rebuilt on Chapel Rd.

Special programs at the museum throughout the year might include "Storytelling around the Council Fire," "Woodland Indian Culture," a moonlight "Tavern Night" concert, madrigals in the State House, or "Giving Thanks: Hearth and Home in Colonial Maryland." The museum is open

April through November, Wednesday-Sunday, 10-5. It's at the southern tip of St. Mary's County off Route 5; ☎ 301-862-0990, www.smcm.edu/hsmc/.

Point Lookout State Park is home to a rare Civil War relic, **Fort Lincoln**, which served as a prisoner of war camp for Confederate soldiers. A pair of monuments honor the 3,364 of them who died and are buried here. The earth embankments of the old fort, along with reconstructed barracks, are open to the public. In the Visitor's Center there is a nice display on the Civil War and the role of the camp. The park is at the end of Route 5, in Scotland; ☎ 301-872-5688.

AUTHOR TIP

If you visit the old fort at Point Lookout State Park, be sure to use bug dope; the mosquitoes will try to carry you off.

The center of **Leonardtown** has several interesting old buildings, clustered close to the Courthouse, a brick and stone building on Court House Drive. **The Old Jail Museum** is the headquarters of the local historical society, with museum exhibits. Included is a "ladies" cell and a medical office used by doctors from 1918 until 1980. Open Monday-Friday, 10-4; ☎ 301-475-2467. The Old Jail Museum also operates **Tudor Hall**, at the end of Tudor Hall Street, a large building dating from 1742. It was once owned by the family of Francis Scott Key and is now used as a research library. Open Wednesday-Friday, noon-4; Saturday, 10-4.

If you follow Route 5 south of Leonardtown to Route 249, then follow it south you will come to **Piney Point Lighthouse Museum and Park** (☎ 301-994-1471). Built in 1836, this short white lighthouse was the first permanent lighthouse on the Potomac and it operated until it was retired in 1964. The museum has material on the lighthouse, and also contains artifacts from the U-1105, a World War II German submarine captured by the United States. Before it was scuttled off the coast of Piney Point, items from it were preserved and are exhibited here. The wreck itself is designated as a historic preserve for divers. The picnic area and boardwalk at the park offer nice views across the Potomac to Virginia. The museum is open weekends from noon to 4, April through October, but the park is open daily all year, sunrise to sunset. The museum gift shop opens weekends, noon-5 pm, May through October.

St. Clement's Island and Potomac River Museum is located at Colton's Point at the end of Route 242. The park sits on the end of the peninsula looking across the Potomac to St. Clement's Island, where the first permanent Maryland settlers landed in 1634. The main museum has materials and artifacts that depict the lives of the first settlers and of the other pioneers who settled along the Potomac River. An 1890s country store and 1821 schoolhouse add more interest to the story of this point. From the pier, those with their own boats can go to St. Clement's Island, where a cross commemorates the landing. The museum operates a cruise to the island on Saturdays and Sundays; see *Boat Tours* above. From October 1 to the end of March, museum hours are Wednesday through Sunday, noon to 4; from late March through September it's open weekdays, 9-5, and weekends, noon to 5. Route 242, 38370 Point Breeze Rd., Colton's Point; ☎ 301-769-2222, fax 301-475-2225, TDD 301-475-4105.

Charles County

Smallwood's Retreat is on the west side of Charles County overlooking the Potomac. The original house was built in 1760 and is surprisingly small for those of us who think of plantation houses as grand. The side of Smallwood's Retreat facing the river – in Smallwood's time the view was not blocked by trees – has no dormers, which was typical of the times.

DID YOU KNOW?

Back in Smallwood's time, tax assessors rarely visited homes, instead viewing them from the river to estimate their size. With no dormers to alert them, they would not notice rooms upstairs.

GENERAL WILLIAM SMALLWOOD

William Smallwood, born in 1732, was the son of a wealthy planter and was educated in England. Smallwood became involved in the American Revolution and was a friend of Washington, whose plantation was across the Potomac in Mt. Vernon. George Washington visited often and stayed here at least once; the two men were fellow members of the Order of the Cincinnati. He served in a number of engagements during the Revolution and was wounded three times. He mustered and commanded the Maryland Regiment. It was his battalion that successfully held the line at the Battle of Long Island so that Washington and his troops could retreat safely. He lost three-quarters of his men in protecting the Commander-in-Chief's retreat, earning for his regiment the title of "The Old Liners" and for Maryland, the nickname of "The Old Line State." Smallwood was the fourth governor of Maryland, first appointed by George Washington, then elected and re-elected, serving three terms in all.

The house is a reconstruction of the ruin; you can see the original brick wall remaining at one end. It is furnished in period antiques from the 1700s, based on the extensive records left by Smallwood, which catalog everything in the house. The mantel in the Great Room (actually quite small, like the house itself) is the original, taken from the house and stored in the barn of a local farmer when the roof caved in. The dining room has a pair of corner cupboards with shell alcoves at the top, and a chandelier that could be raised and lowered as needed. Every container is fitted with a lock to prevent servants from stealing the contents. The upstairs guest bedroom accommodated 15, sleeping crosswise propped against the wall with bolsters (sleeping prone was considered unhealthy).

DID YOU KNOW? *Corner chairs, such as the one in the Great Room of Smallwood's Retreat, were not designed to fit into corners, but were intended to allow room for a lady's large skirts or a gentleman's sword when they sat down. In Smallwood's day, a military uniform was a gentleman's formal wear and a sword a necessity.*

Smallwood's Retreat.

The tobacco barn near the parking area, built between 1801 and 1805, is all original; inside is a "tobacco prize" – a press to pack dried leaves into hogsheads for shipping. Also inside are exhibits on the house, which is handy, since the barn is open when the house is not. Smallwood had 59 slaves and indentured servants and the remains of his mill can be seen in the stream at the park entrance.

Smallwood's Retreat is open April through mid-October on Sunday afternoons from 1 to 5, and by appointment with a day's advance notice. Well-informed costumed docents lead tours. On the second Sunday in December the house is open the same hours, candlelit and decorated for the holidays. Refreshments are served (prepared using 18th-century recipes), along with hot mulled cider. Smallwood's Retreat sits inside General Smallwood State Park, off Route 1 in Marbury; ☎ 301-743-7336.

Port Tobacco, founded in 1634 and once the second largest seaport in the state, is now a tiny hamlet bypassed by the world. The first courthouse on the Public Square blew down in 1808 and a second was built. When it burned in 1892 there were about 60 houses, three hotels and twenty stores in town. A reproduction of the courthouse, built in 1965 as a museum, using the original north wing as its base. It is surrounded by a cluster of remaining early houses: Chimney House was built in 1765, Stag Hall in 1732 and the restored Burch House was erected about 1700; it is the one with the steeply pitched catslide roof. This square was once a prosperous county seat, but when the river silted up and ships could no longer reach its docks, the town withered. The county seat was moved to La Plata in 1895 and Christ Church was moved as well, stone by stone, to sit in the same position next to it, on Charles Street in that city. The **Port Tobacco Courthouse and Museum** are open Wednesday-Sunday, noon-4, with the last tour beginning at 3:30; ☎ 301-934-4313. A gift shop at the museum handles local crafts and books. Port Tobacco is off Route 6; follow the signs.

Close to Port Tobacco, at the intersection of Causeway Rd. and Chapel Point Rd., is the **Old Port Tobacco One Room School House**, an 1876 building that served whites until 1924 and black students from then until 1953. It was restored in the 1990s by the Retired Teachers Association and is now open Sunday, Wednesday and Saturday.

South of Port Tobacco, on Chapel Point Road overlooking Chapel Point , is **St. Ignatius Church**, founded in 1641 by Father Andrew White, the site of the first Catholic services (illegal at the time). His chapel was closer to the river. The present church dates from 1798. It is the oldest continuously active Roman Catholic parish in the United States. **St. Thomas Manor**, built 100 years later as a Jesuit residence, stands beside the church. Both the Manor House and the Church burned in 1866, but the walls of both survived and the structures were rebuilt using some of the original materials. Behind the cook's house, a small white building beyond the manor house, is an open bulkhead (pull it open if not) which enters a dry well. Off that is a tunnel leading out into the hillside, which may have been used to smuggle priests in and out, and was later used by the Underground Railroad.

 Chapel Point is not a town, but was a steamer stop and popular resort in the 1880s. Nothing is left of its amusement pavilions, but the area is a riverside state park with swimming, open sunrise to sunset.

The interior of the church is unusual, with Colonial-style pews, Victorian stained-glass windows and charming needlepoint kneelers depicting Biblical and historic themes. The balcony railings are original Colonial iron railings and the chandelier is from that period. A relic of the True Cross is the same brought here in 1641 by Father White, a gift of the Queen of England. Across the road are the Stations of the Cross, in a garden setting overlooking the river below. Masses are held on Saturday at 9 am and 5 pm; Sunday at 7:30, 9 and 11 am and 6 pm; weekdays at 8 am and noon. On the first Saturday of August, at 3:30 pm, a Blessing of the Fleet is held in conjunction with the Potomac River Festival. ☎ 301-934-8245.

If you are near Chapel Point late in the day, don't miss watching the sunset from the churchyard at St. Ignatius. The site is on a hilltop overlooking the Port Tobacco River close to where it joins the Potomac. The front of the church faces directly into the setting sun, which bathes its bricks in the deep warm tones of the reddened sky. Silhouetted against this sky are the ornamental iron fence and gate of the churchyard and its tall Celtic crosses and older stone markers.

North of Port Tobacco is the **Thomas Stone House**, a five-part Georgian home built about 1770, featuring a semi-circle of dependencies separated by hyphens typical of Georgian architecture. But unlike most, this house is not symmetrical. Thomas Stone, a lawyer and farmer, grew corn and wheat on his 2,000-acre plantation, Habre de Venture. Stone was a steady and reliable statesman, not flamboyant or outspoken, who went to the first Continental Congress in Philadelphia firmly convinced that reconciliation with Britain was possible. But when Britain refused to budge, he joined his fellow Maryland delegates as a signer of the Declaration of Independence and Articles of Confederation. Thomas Stone, his wife Margaret and other family members are in the cemetery on the grounds.

DID YOU KNOW? *Queen Elizabeth has the world's largest collection of autographs of the signers of the Declaration of Independence.*

The house was reconstructed following a disastrous fire in 1977. The two wholly replicated rooms are the centrally located bedroom, where Stone's invalid wife spent most of her time, and the splendidly paneled East Room, which was a combination of parlor and study. The overriding sense of this house and Stone's story, well told in a film in the visitors center and by the ranger during a tour, is of the stressful and tragic life this thoroughly decent man led amid these beautiful and prosperous surroundings. The home is between Route 225 on the north and Route 6 on the south, just a few miles west of La Plata, at 6655 Rose Hill Rd., Port Tobacco; ☎ 301-934-6027. It is open daily, 9-5, from Memorial Day to Labor Day, and Thursday-Monday the rest of the year.

It is entirely appropriate that the home of Stone's wife, who was badly crippled with arthritis from her mid-twenties, should today be wheelchair-accessible. A lift reaches the raised central rooms and a wide smooth path leads across the fields to the Stones' gravesites.

The aftermath of the act of assassination by John Wilkes Booth struck tragedy into the lives of many. (See *North of Washington*, page 255, for related material on Surrat House). The **Dr. Samuel A. Mudd House** tells the story of one of those tragedies. Dr. Mudd encountered two men on April 15, 1865, one of whom needed to have a broken leg set. The names given were Mr. Tyler and Mr. Tyson. After the doctor set the leg both rested for a while and left on horseback. Mudd did not even know of the assassination, but he, a civilian, was convicted by a military court and sentenced for life. After four years President Johnson pardoned him and he returned to his home here. Thirteen years later he died of yellow fever contracted because of his efforts to help fellow prisoners during his imprisonment. His was a tragedy of well-intentioned justice gone wrong in a sea of popular passion. To get here from Route 301 north of Waldorf, take Route 5 south when it divides from 301. This road is also called Mattawoman Beantown Rd. Turn left onto Route 205, and keep right at Poplar Hill Rd. Go four miles, then take a right onto Dr. Samuel Mudd Rd. and continue for about a half-mile. Open Saturdays and Sundays, noon-4, Wednesdays 11-3, April-late November; ☎ 301-645-6870.

Where to Stay

ACCOMMODATIONS PRICE KEY	
Rates are per room, per night, double occupancy.	
$	Under $50
$$	$50 to $100
$$$	$101 to $175
$$$$	$176 and up

■ Calvert County & St. Mary's County

Westlawn Inn Beach House is a cozy eight-room inn in a 1903 beach house from the heyday of the Chesapeake-North Beach area. On weekends they serve a full breakfast and during the week it's continental. The inn is open all year, at 9200 Chesapeake Avenue, PO Box 1199, North Beach 20714; ☎ 301-855-2607, www.westlawninn. com, e-mail innkeeper@westlawninn.com. Room rates begin at $65; most are under $100.

Tidewater Treasures B&B is in a modern home overlooking marsh and bay and Brownie's Beach (officially named Bay Front Park). It sits high above the shore, 0.7 mile south of the Chesapeake Beach bridge and Railroad Museum entrance. The four rooms all have water views and guests have easy access to the beach. Tidewater Treasures is at 7315 Bayside Rd., Chesapeake Beach 20732; ☎ 410-257-0785. $$$

Serenity Acres B&B, 4270 Hardesty Rd., Huntingtown 20639, ☎ 410-535-3744, fax 535-3835, www.bbonline.com/md/serenity/, e-mail lee@chesapeake.net, is among the most welcoming homes we have ever entered. Guests in the Calvert Room have a view of the garden through a Palladian window from their nicely decorated lodgings; the private bath is not en-suite, but terry robes are provided. The Huntington Room has a private bath en-suite. All rooms have handmade quilts. The Serenity Suite is a large room overlooking back gardens and pool and woods filled with flowers in spring. They welcome children of any age, and have rollaway beds.

Serenity Acres is well-named, set in beautifully kept gardens surrounded with walking trails through five acres of woods. Overlooking a lovely little vale is a hot tub in a screened house, complete with a double hammock, an airy but private little retreat. The adjacent swimming pool has an outside bath house in the garden, and an exercise room and bikes are available for guests. The owner, an avid and talented quilter, has a separate cottage devoted to her Quilt Room, which will turn any quilter or craftsman green with envy. She is considering hosting quilting weekends, so if you enjoy or would like to learn this art, check for the status of these plans. If you'd like to arrive by boat, the hosts will pick you up at the Chesapeake Beach Marina, 10 minutes away. From Routes 2/4 (about 2.2 miles south of where they join) go left onto Ponds Wood Rd., then left after 2.6 miles to Hardesty Rd. on the left. Take Hardesty for 0.4 mile to the small sign and driveway on the left. $$$

Solomons Victorian Inn, at Solomons Island, has, in addition to its main house, a newly built carriage house addition with antique architectural features. In the Harbor Sunset Room, for example, a grand chandelier is built into an octagonal ceiling alcove. A small balcony and a huge whirlpool tub are added features of this room, where windows in a curved bay form a round wall overlooking the town and water. Breakfast is served in the glass-enclosed porch overlooking the harbor and gardens, and begins with blueberry cake, a bowl of fresh berries, and a whole pot of tea (pampering tea-drinkers seldom get). French toast and sausages follow, and their presentation is lovely. All eight rooms and the suite have private baths, and rooms in the Carriage House have private entrances. Rates are $90-$105 for the main house; suite with whirlpool, $175; carriage house rooms, $135-$155. 125 Charles Street, PO Box 759, Solomons, MD 20688, ☎ 410-326-4811, www.chesapeake.net/solomonsvictorianinn.

By the Bay Bed and Breakfast, 14374 Calvert St., Solomons Island. Owners Joan and Tom Hogenson have restored their Victorian home, which sits in a yard with box hedges. A private dock in the backyard gives access to Back Creek; ☎ 410-326-3428. $$$

Back Creek Inn B&B, Calvert St. at Alexandra Lane, Solomons Island, is right at the entrance to the town marina. Their big back yard overlooks the water and they have a dock; ☎ 410-326-2022. $$$

■ Charles County

Chain hotels are easy to find along US 301, but this part of Maryland has few country inns and B&Bs. There is a **Holiday Inn** at 1 St. Patrick's Drive, Waldorf 20603; ☎ 301-645-8200, 800-645-8277. It's just off US 301.

La Plata Inn, 400 South Highway (US 301), La Plata 20646; ☎ 301-934-4900 or 800-528-1234. This modern and comfortable inn is a Best Western affiliate and is centrally located on the major route through the region. The 76 rooms and eight suites all have microwave and mini-fridge, cable TV with HBO, laundry and outdoor pool. Rates for rooms are $51-60, suites $60-75, two-bedroom suites under $100. Discounts are offered for families, seniors, military and corporate travelers.

■ Camping

Breezy Point Beach Campground, a county park, has RV sites on the water from Memorial Day to Oct 31, for $25 with hookup, $20 without. Call the main office in mid-January to reserve for summer weekends. Along with camping are a swimming beach, fishing piers and a marina with three fishing charter boats headquartered there. It is 1.4 miles off Route 261, south of Chesapeake Beach on Breezy Point Rd. Contact Calvert County Parks and Recreation, Court House, 175 Main Street, Prince Frederick, MD 20678; ☎ 410-535-1600 or 301-855-1243, ext 225. From May to October, call the park directly between 8 am and 9 pm daily, ☎ 410-535-0259.

General Smallwood State Park has a camping area overlooking the lagoon, with handy access to the marina via a footbridge. It is relatively free of mosquitoes. They have a boat launch, pump-out, and rental, a dumping station, snack bar, and fishing. There are also picnic areas for day-users. The campground has 16 sites, all with electricity. Route 1, Box 64, Marbury, MD 20658, ☎ 301-743-7613, Reservations: ☎ 800-784-5380, TTY 410-974-3683.

Where to Eat

DINING PRICE KEY
The price key indicates the cost of *most* dinner entrées on a restaurant's regular and daily special menu.

$	Most under $10
$$	$10 to $20
$$$	Over $30

■ Calvert County

 Rod and Reel Restaurant serves traditional seafood well pre-pared. They make their crab cakes with no binder but lots of crab. Who cares if they fall apart – they're tasty. Lunch will cost from $4.95-$11; dinners are $11.95 up to the low $20s. Fresh rockfish is $17.99; crab cakes are $19.99; a broiled seafood platter is $17.99; and New York strip is $17.99. It's in a new building across the parking lot from the Chesapeake Beach Railway Museum. Route 261 and Mears Avenue, Chesapeake Beach, ☎ 410-257-2735, 301-855-8351.

In Prince Frederick, the **Old Field Inn** is everyone's special occasion place. Their specialty is filet mignon sauced with cream and cognac, and the appetizer specialty is creamy crab dip, filled with crab and not too cheesy. Mussels served in the shell with spinach and cream are delicious, too. Veal Wellington is stuffed with a special cheese blend, pignolis (pine nuts), raisins and spices, wrapped in puff pastry to bake, and served with hunter's sauce. Cheesecake tops the dessert menu, with mango and raspberry or turtle (the caramel, chocolate and nuts variety, not the shelled kind). Entrées are $15-25, mostly in the high teens. About once a month, usually on the second Friday, they have a seven-course wine-tasting dinner with special boutique wines for $58.95 per person. The inn is at 485 Main Street, Prince Frederick; ☎ 410-535-1054, 301-855-1054, 800-698-1054. Open Monday-Thursday, 5-9 pm; Friday-Saturday, 5-10; Sunday, 5-8. From Routes 2-4 take Route 765 into Prince Frederick; the inn is just south of Route 231.

Stoney's Seafood House is known for seafood, and often on lists of the places that serve Maryland's best crab cakes. These are made from lots of lump crab and you can order the usual size or a half-pounder, one powerful lot of crab cake. A soft shell crab sandwich is about $9 and an oyster sandwich about $8. Crabs, crab cakes and snow crab legs are market price. From Routes 2/4, take Route 264 west to the end, Oyster House Rd., Broomes's Island; ☎ 410-586-1888.

Vera's White Sands Restaurant and Marina promises "romantic waterfront dining" and adds the attraction of a boat launch and marina. It's off Route 2/4 near Calvert Cliffs State Park. Route 4, Lusby; ☎ 410-586-1182.

The CD Café in Solomons serves espresso, pastries and creative cuisine based on fresh ingredients. Service is excellent, and since a pastry chef is co-owner, you can depend on good desserts or goodies to go with your espresso. Expect it to be crowded at dinnertime. 14350 Solomons Island Rd., Solomons, ☎ 410-326-3877.

Naughty Gull Restaurant at the Spring Cove Marina serves three meals a day, with the emphasis on steaks and seafood. They have a Sunday Brunch from 9-2. Spring Cove Marina, next to the Holiday Inn, Solomons, ☎ 410-326-4855.

The Lighthouse Restaurant overlooks Solomon's harbor, with a wrap-around deck and terraced interior for better views. The menu combines sophisticated options with the traditional local seafood dishes, something for everyone. Seafood is very nicely prepared.

Fire House Breakfasts are a Sunday morning tradition from late spring through September, 8-10 am. The price is right at $5, or $3 for children ages five-10. The menu includes scrambled eggs, hash browns, sausage, ham, bacon, pancakes, sausage biscuits and gravy, juice and a beverage. The fire station is on Routes 2/4 at Dowell Rd., just north of Solomon's.

■ St. Mary's County

Scheible's Crab Pot Restaurant is located at the dock of this family-owned fishing center, six miles from Point Lookout State Park. A complete crab cake entrée is about $18, fried clams or grilled chicken about $12. "basket-style" meals include fries only, with fish of the day about $5, six crabettes (bite-size crab cakes) $8 and a combo of crabettes, fish, shrimp and clams is about $9. Lunch and dinner weekday specials are real bargains. Scheible's is open Memorial Day to Labor Day, Monday-Sunday, from 6 am-9 pm; in spring and fall hours are Monday-Thursday, 6 am-2pm, Friday-Sunday, 6 am-9 pm. 48342 Wynne Rd., Ridge, ☎ 301-872-5185 or 800-895-6132. Wynne Rd. is 200 yards from the blinking light at the intersection of Routes 5 and 235 in Ridge.

■ Charles County

Everyone knows that in southern Maryland the place for a feast of steamed crabs is **Captain Billy's**, three miles off US 301 on Pope's Creek Rd., overlooking the Potomac. They have good crab cakes, fried oysters, scallops, catch of the day and fried chicken as complete dinners ($9-$20) or in baskets ($6-$10). Sandwiches ($6-$10) include rib-eye steak, crab melt, crab cake, chicken breast with crab and cheese on a croissant. But the real reason most people come here is to sit down to a great big pile of steamed crabs, the quintessential Maryland feast. This is a friendly, casual sometimes boisterous place with great views of the river. If you've had blue crabs before, you already know to wear something washable. If you have not, don't be bashful about asking your waitress for a demonstration; it's all in the strategy of attack. Market price for crabs varies. Pope's Creek Rd., Pope's Creek; ☎ 301-932-4323, fax 301-609-7978, e-mail captbilly@ olg.com. Pier 3, just past Captain Billy's is a bar, with volleyball on the beach.

Casey Jones Restaurant, at 417 East Charles St. in La Plata (☎ 301-932-6226), is really two separate eating places – fine dining on one side, a pub on other. In the restaurant ($$), look for oven-roasted rabbit with sundried tomatoes, seared tuna steak with wasabi, grilled duck with foie gras or veal with sage and goat cheese. The setting is warm and inviting, and while no one looks askance at casual wear, men will be comfortable here in jackets and ties. The adjoining pub ($) is best known for its unique pizzas, but has a menu of lighter dishes. Prime rib pizza, chicken Caesar pizza, crab sauté, portobello fries and fresh tuna steak melt are a few favorites you'll find, along with the usual quesadillas and nachos.

Laredo's serves up plentiful Mexican dishes, at its Route 301 location in White Plains (☎ 301-932-8667). Burritos, chimichangas, enchiladas, fajitas and other south-of-the-border standards fill the menu ($) and the atmosphere is bright and spacious, decorated with colorful folk art.

Topelino (☎ 301-870-1499), almost hidden in a mall at the corner of Route 228 and 301 (turn in by Circuit City) in Waldorf, is an unpretentious Italian restaurant with a brightly lit, upbeat air and booths. The country music is out of place (Neapolitan would better fit the mood), and you can expect your fish to be a bit overcooked even when you ask for it "rare," but the menu is varied and the food otherwise very good. All the southern Italian favorites are there: four veal dishes ($9.95-$10.85); six chicken dishes, from chicken Alfredo to chicken Romano ($7.75-$9.50); seafood, such as fresh mussels ($8.75) and stuffed flounder ($11.95); and steaks. Pasta dishes are even more reasonable. Wines are inexpensive, too.

Upper Eastern Shore

The upper portion of the Eastern Shore is less traveled than the central part, not on the way to anywhere, not as swish as St. Michaels, nor as brash and resort-laden as Ocean City. Which makes it just the right place for travelers who wish to avoid crowds. Chestertown and Chesapeake City are filled with history, and are pleasant towns to stroll through. The islands of Kent and Wye, close to Annapolis, are a pleasant blend of wild lands and the good life.

Geography & History

Like the rest of the Eastern Shore, this area is deeply cut by **tidal rivers** – the **Wye**, the **Chester**, the **Sassafras**, the **Elk** and the **North East**. Kent and Wye islands jut into the center of the Chesapeake, forming its narrowest central point, an opportunity for the only bridge to span the bay.

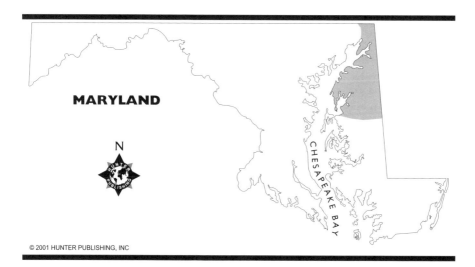

MARYLAND

N

CHESAPEAKE BAY

No big cities – not even any small ones – interrupt the rural and coastal charms of the countryside, which is more rolling than the rest of the Eastern Shore. North of the Sassafras River you will find real hills, and on the Elk Neck peninsula coastal bluffs.

Kent Island was the first English settlement in Maryland, when **William Claiborne** established a trading post in 1631. **Captain John Smith** had already traded here with the **Ozinies**, a branch of the Algonquin. Claiborne planned to annex this area for Virginia, but he didn't count on the tenacity of **Cecil Calvert**, the second Lord Baltimore, and after a few naval skirmishes, Virginia abandoned its claim.

The area continued as a trading center for **watermen** and for the **tobacco** grown on nearby plantations, and once had as many as a dozen packing companies that processed the catch of hundreds of boats. Queenstown, too, was an important port for shipping – so much so that it was the target of a British attack during the War of 1812.

In 1782 the county seat was moved to the geographical center of the county, to a new town called **Centreville**, and by the early 19th century, steamboats were navigating the tidal rivers deep into the interior, expanding markets for both seafood and the produce grown inland.

Chestertown, like the rest of the area, was a hotbed of patriots during the revolution, and had its own "Tea Party" in 1774, when local merchants revolted against the tea tax in sympathy with their Boston counterparts and dumped crates of tea into the Chester River from the brigantine *Geddes*. The event is still commemorated each Memorial Day weekend.

Georgetown, on the Sassafras River, was an important supply base for the colonists during the Revolution, which made it a target in the War of 1812, when the town was razed during Admiral Cockburn's Chesapeake attacks.

Getting Here & Getting Around

 From the rest of Maryland, there are only two ways to reach this area: across the **Bay Bridge** from Annapolis and through **Cecil County**, which surrounds the upper reaches of the bay. **I-95** brings traffic from nearby Wilmington and Newark, Delaware. **Route 8** connects the area with Dover, Delaware, crossing the north-south part of the Mason-Dixon Line into the northern tip of Caroline County. Leading from the southern parts of the Eastern Shore, **US 50** connects to **US 301** in Queenstown.

From the Bay Bridge, routes US 301 and US 50 split north and south respectively, and US 301 traverses the upper reaches of the Eastern Shore

Upper Eastern Shore

N

1. Fair Hill Natural Resource Management Area; Fair Hill Natural & Environmental Area; Tawes Drive Covered Bridge
2. Sinking Springs Farm
3. Upper Bay Museum
4. C&D Canal Museum
5. Elk Neck State Park
6. Mount Harmon Plantation
7. Watermen's Museum; Rock Hall Museum
8. Eastern Neck National Wildlife Refuge
9. Queen Anne's Museum of Eastern Shore Life; An Eastridge Garden
10. Tuckahoe State Park; Adkins Arboretum
11. Horsehead Wetlands Center
12. Wye Grist Mill; Wye Oak; Old Wye Church

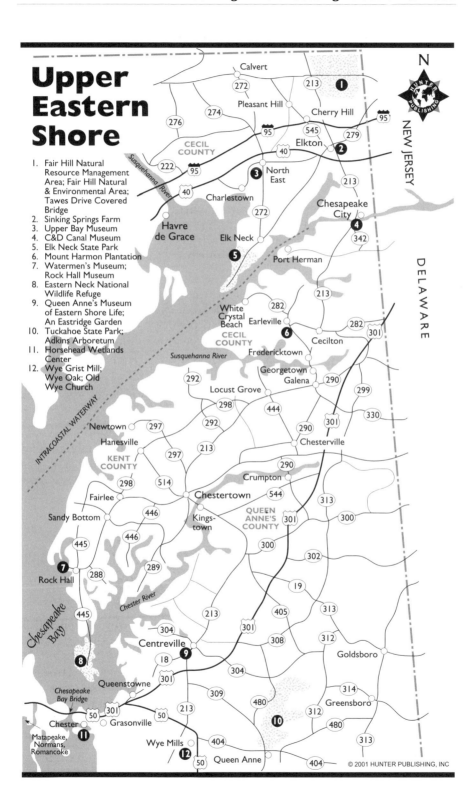

Upper Eastern Shore

© 2001 HUNTER PUBLISHING, INC

until it crosses the line into Delaware. **Route 213** heads north from US 301 through Elkton and into Pennsylvania. In this corner of the state of Maryland, you are never very far from someplace else.

Information Sources

 Cecil County Tourism, 129 East Main St., Elkton 21921; ☎ 410-996-5305 or 800-CECIL-95, fax 410-996-5305.

Kent County Chamber of Commerce, 400 S. Cross St., Chestertown 21620; ☎ 410-778-0416, www.kentcounty.com.

North East Chamber of Commerce, PO Box 198, North East 21901; ☎ 410-287-2658.

Adventures

■ Parks

 Elk Neck State Park, Route 272, nine miles south of North East (☎ 410-287-5333), is a high finger of land surrounded by water on both sides. The park and the State Forest adjoining it cover all but a small part of the peninsula separating the head of Chesapeake Bay (which is also the mouth of the Susquehanna River) from Elk River. The drive from North East to Elk Neck, along Route 272, is an adventure in itself as the road winds and rolls up and down over hills and through hollows, where you are almost certain to see deer. The landscape of the park is mostly wooded, with ak, poplar, beech, maple, locust and choke cherry. An understory of laurel blooms in June.

WATCHABLE WILDLIFE

REALISTIC LAWN STATUES: *So many deer wander about Elk Neck State Park that in the small residential enclave surrounded by the park we thought everyone had deer lawn ornaments in front of their houses – until a pair of them turned their heads to look at us.*

Fair Hill Natural Resource Management Area, which begins north of Elkton and runs for 5,613 acres to the Pennsylvania state line (☎ 410-398-1246), is best known for its thoroughbred racing center, and for fishing in Big Elk Creek. But its 75 miles of trails are not just for horses.

■ On Foot

Historic Walking Tours of the old streets of **Chestertown** begin at the fountain in the park on High St., at 11 am on Sundays, from March through November. Reservations are not needed, and the cost is $5; ☎ 410-778-2829. At other times, pick up a copy of the walking tour map, which has short histories of about 30 buildings identified by numbered bronze plaques. These numbers correspond to the map and descriptions.

Horsehead Wetlands Center (☎ 410-827-7029 or 800-CANVASBACK), at 600 Discovery Lane in Grasonville, is just south of US 301. Take Exit 43 to Main St., then Perry's Corner Rd. to the center, which has flat trails through a variety of beautiful bayside habitats. The map available at the Visitors Center shows various routes, some of which appear on the map to be trails, but are really just mowed areas. Not on the map is Piney Point Path, which is signposted to the left of the main exhibit gate, near the Woodland Pond. It passes through a forest and into a marsh of high reeds, with observation platforms.

The main exhibit trail, about one-third-mile long, circles a series of ponds featuring birds of the Pacific Flyway, the Central and Mississippi Flyway and the Atlantic Flyway, in addition to an enclosed aviary of songbirds and tree ducks indigenous to the region. Near the Visitors Center is a butterfly and hummingbird garden and a pond habitat for the largest flock in North America of dusky Canada geese, a rare sub-species.

A loop of about a mile goes to a boardwalk and observation tower overlooking a marsh, where you can often see migrating waterfowl. It continues around a pond (usually dry in the fall) with an osprey platform and two blinds. The Marshy Creek Trail, which returns to the parking lot, has an observation tower near the canoe landing, where you may see loons. The Horsehead Wetlands Center is open daily, 9-5; admission is $3 adult, $2 age 55 and over, $1 under age 18. For more on the center, see *Cultural & Eco-Travel Experiences*, below.

Tuckahoe State Park, just north of Hillsboro along the border of Caroline and Queen Anne's County (☎ 410-634-2810), is entered via Cherry Lane (which leaves Route 480 as Eveland Rd., just past the intersection with 404). The half-mile **Overcup Oak Trail** leads through a bottomland forest to a giant oak, now dead but still very impressive. The wildflowers are lovely here in mid-April. Also in the park, a trail leads along the eastern side of the old millpond, reached from Crouse Mill Rd. in the center of the park.

Also in the park is **Adkins Arboretum** (☎ 410-634-2847), reached from Eveland Rd., about two miles north of the intersection of Routes 404 and 480 just east of Hillsboro. Some of its five miles of trails through a variety of forest habitats are accessible to those with limited mobility, and provide level, even surfaces for easy walking. The **Piney Branch Trail** connects the **Lake Trail**, in the northern end of the park, with the two trail loops in the arboretum.

WATCHABLE WILDLIFE

The arboretum is a favorite nesting place for meadowlarks, grasshopper sparrows, red-tailed hawks, wild turkeys, several species of owls and bluebirds; bobolinks, snow geese, yellow warblers and killdeer can be found in spring and fall transit. The park is winter home to red-breasted nuthatches, Savannah sparrows, snow geese and golden-crowned kinglets. The arboretum publishes a list of birds seen there.

Tubby Cove Boardwalk, at **Eastern Neck National Wildlife Refuge**, at the end of Route 445 in Rock Hall (☎ 410-639-7056), leaves Route 445 on the right, a few hundred yards south of the bridge onto the island, and ends at an observation tower. The saltmarsh is a beautiful sight any time, with a succession of flowers in bloom from early spring through the fall asters.

MORE THAN SEVEN SWANS A-SWIMMING

By the middle of November, the shallow waters west of the bridge accessing the island at Eastern Neck Wildlife Refuge are filled with tundra swans and Canada geese. The refuge offers guided bird walks in May.

Other short trails in the refuge are about half a mile each, leading to the Chester River through old forest and marsh. The area is rich in birdlife at any time of year. Trailheads are marked by signs; to get to the river look for **Duck Inn** and **Boxes Point trails**, the latter to the left off Route 445, the former to the left of the road to Bogles Wharf landing. A loop wildlife trail is farther along Route 445, opposite the road to the Visitors Center, which is open weekdays, 7-4.

Fair Hill Nature and Environment Center, 376 Fair Hill Drive, Elkton, ☎ 410-398-1246, has miles of multi-use trails for cycling, walking or horseback riding, and they are well used by all three. The trail map shows paved and unpaved roads, single and double track trails. Loop routes are easy to plan from the map.

Elk Neck State Park, Route 272, nine miles south of North East (☎ 410-287-5333), has trails ranging from less than a mile to more than two miles. The shortest, **White Trail**, is a 0.75-mile nature trail through Thackery Swamp. Pick up a descriptive booklet at the park office. **Black Trail** connects the Susquehanna and Wye camping areas, traveling through a forest, along the edge of a marsh and along the Elk River. **Blue Trail** is an easy two-mile loop around the end of the peninsula where the Turkey Point Lighthouse stands.

■ On Wheels

 As you travel northward in this part of the Eastern Shore the land becomes rolling, dropping more abruptly to the water than the shore south of the Sassafras River. This makes cycling a bit more of a workout.

Although there is no alternate route back to make it into a loop, the road from **Rock Hall to Eastern Neck** is a good cycling route. Follow Route 445, crossing the bridge onto Eastern Neck to cycle the roads through the wildlife refuge.

Fair Hill Nature and Environment Center, 376 Fair Hill Drive, Elkton (☎ 410-398-1246), is criss-crossed by multi-use trails which cyclists share with walkers and horseback riders. A trail map distinguishes paved and unpaved roads, single and double track trails. Trails are plentiful enough to allow a lot of loop cycle routes.

BIKE RENTALS

■ To avoid the almost certain parking tickets of **Chesapeake City**, you can borrow a bike, free. Get a key to unlock one from Canal Lock Antiques, at 105 Bohemia Ave. Be prepared for some uphill pedaling.

■ See page 396 in the *Central Eastern Shore* chapter for information on a **VBT Bicycling Vacations** tour that combines the Chestertown and Rock Hill areas with Oxford and St. Michaels, farther south; ☎ 800-245-3868.

■ Rent bicycles from **Rob's Jet Ski and Outdoor Sports Rentals** at the jetty at Kent Narrows in Grasonville; ☎ 410-827-4436. Their rentals are hourly, half-day or daily, and the jetty is accessible from the bike path.

■ Guests staying at the **B&B at Pintail Point Farm** in Queenstown (☎ 410-827-7029) have free use of bicycles.

■ In Chestertown you can rent bicycles from **Bikeworks** on 208 S. Cross St. (☎ 410-778-6940).

■ In Rock Hall, rent bikes at **Rock Hall Landing Marina** on Hawthorne Ave. (☎ 410-639-2224), and at **Swan Haven Bed & Breakfast**, at 20950 Rock Hall Ave. (☎ 410-639-2527).

Upper Eastern Shore

■ On Water

 The upper bay and its wide river mouths have several good public beaches. Rock Hall's town beach, which locals call **Ferry Park**, is on Beach Rd., with picnic tables and fine views across the bay. **Betterton Beach** has lifeguards from Memorial Day to Labor Day, in its three-acre park by the mouth of the Sassafras River, at the end of Route 292. Picnic tables, bath houses, concession stand and fishing jetty all add to its appeal, as does free parking.

Elk Neck State Park has a nice beach on the Northeast River side of the park, quite shallow for some distance out, which makes it especially good for children. The fee for the beach is $2 per vehicle. There is no lifeguard.

Sailing

Both Chestertown and Rock Hall are sailing centers, although you will find boats and abundant marinas all along the shore and up the tidal rivers. **Sailing Emporium** in Rock Hall (☎ 410-778-1342) offers charters and sailing instruction, and the **Chester River Yacht Club** in Chestertown (☎ 410-778-1369) also offers sailing instruction.

Those who love sailing or boats will want to check on the construction of the schooner *Sultana*, a reproduction of a 1767 schooner, at the Sultana Shipyard, 346 Cannon St., in Chestertown; ☎ 410-778-6461, www.ChesterRiver.com/sultana. See page 373 for more information on the project.

Canoeing & Kayaking

Horsehead Wetlands Center, at 600 Discovery Lane in Grasonville (☎ 410-827-7029 or 800-CANVASBACK) has canoe rentals, reached from the Marshy Creek Trail. They are free to members of the Wildfowl Trust of America or the Wetlands Center; others pay $35 per person, $10 junior or $50 for a family. The Horsehead Wetlands Center is open daily, 9-5; admission is $3 adult, $2 age 55 and over, $1 under age 18. For more on the center, see pages 363 and 372.

Tuckahoe State Park, just north of Hillsboro along the border of Caroline and Queen Anne's County (☎ 410-820-1668), has a 20-acre lake accessible from a launch on Crouse Mill Rd., which cuts through its center. Once a mill pond, it is now open water and marsh, which is an outstanding habitat for bald eagles and ospreys as well as herons, beavers and otters. A channel leaves the northeast corner of the lake, allowing paddlers to explore about a mile into the lowland forest.

Below the lake, the Tuckahoe River meanders through swampy forest for about six miles to a take-out at Hillsboro Landing, about a mile downstream from the Route 401 bridge, off Route 303. The state park offers a number of guided canoe trips, as well as canoe rentals at the lake from spring through fall (weekends only early and late in the season). The rented canoes can only be used in the lake.

The Chester River has several tributary creeks that provide interesting waters to paddle. Close to Chestertown, **Morgan Creek** gives a good sampling of several watery ecosystems in its five-mile flow from a narrow bottomland creek to a channel through wide tidal marshes. A put-in is off Route 213, 3½ miles north of its intersection with Route 291, at the end of Riley's Mill Rd. Paddling upstream (to the left), you can go about 1½ miles and see the creek banks change from marsh grass to wooded bottomland, with dogwood and red maple adding arboreal decoration in the spring and fall respectively.

Downstream, you can canoe through the bird-laden marshes to the mouth of the creek, shortly below the Route 291 bridge, where there is a public boat landing. Or you can return to Riley's Mill Rd. It's about three miles one way. The marshes occasionally give way to higher banks where the creek has cut the soil out from under trees. In the spring look for mountain laurel under the tall oaks.

Southeast Creek also changes from wide marshes to tiny streams within a short distance of the Chester River, fed by several tributaries. The most interesting of these is Island Creek, where you will find an enormous variety of bird life. For a put-in, follow Southeast Creek Rd., just south of Church Hill on Route 213, to its end. About a half-mile west (paddle left) of the landing, Island Creek enters from the south (left again). Look for the remains of a house on a tiny island at its mouth. Forest and marsh provide an interesting habitat along this creek.

Eastern Neck National Wildlife Refuge, at the end of Route 445 in Rock Hall (☎ 410-639-7056), is a beautiful saltmarsh filled with birdlife (see *On Foot*, above) and a constant succession of flowers in bloom from early spring through the fall asters. The paddling here is some of the best on the bay, with deep coves and grass-enclosed channels to explore. This is the winter home for a large flock of tundra swans. A Visitors Center is open weekdays, 7-4. A put-in from Bogles Wharf Landing gives access to Durdin Creek and to the next one, Shipyard Creek. From the Ingleside Recreation area, where there are picnic sites, you can paddle to the right to explore Calfpasture Cove or Tubby Cove, both of which are prime bird habitats in the late fall.

On the Chester River, three miles south of Chestertown, you can rent canoes from **Knee Deep Water Sports**, at Rolf's Wharf Marina; ☎ 410-810-0514. Full-day rental is about $40; half-day, $25; hourly, $10, with a two-hour minimum. They are open daily (Wednesday only by prior reservation), 6-6, from May through August, and 7-4:30 in September and October, weather permitting. On weekends and holidays, it's wise to make a reservation.

Skipjack Cove Kayak Adventures, at the Skipjack Cove Marina, on the Sassafras River just north of the Route 213 bridge in Georgetown (☎ 410-275-2122 or 800-BOATSLIP), rents kayaks and offers guided trips from their docks. The cost of rental is about $10 per hour, $25 for half-day and $40 for full day. Guided trips are $30 per person. They are open Friday and Saturday, 8-7; Sunday through Thursday, 8-5, in the main season; 8-5 daily off season. Tours are by advance reservation only. Skipjack uses open-top kayaks, which are easy to paddle, but have no rudders.

The route upstream begins by a water tour of the boats in the marina, which might include an impressive replica of an old square-rigged sailing ship and restored oyster buy-boats, along with private yachts of all sizes. Once past the bridge, the riverbanks begin to look more as they did when this was the "Gold Coast" of wealthy British aristocracy, except that the plantations that once lined it are gone and the few homes you will see are far more modest. Banks are largely undeveloped, and birdlife thrives. The first creek to the right is Mill Creek, which you can explore for about a mile before encountering a dam. The next creek on the right past Mill is Swanton, or you can continue on the main river to Hen Island, a good picnic stop almost two hours from the marina. The end of the river, about nine miles from the marina, is another hour's paddling and a round-trip there would take about five hours.

Closer to the marina, you can explore the blue heron rookeries along Dyer Creek, almost opposite the landing, if the tide is high and will remain high enough for your return. (We mention this from experience, having been hung up in the sandflats here on our return.) Unlike many kayak rentals, Skipjack provides you with a brief descriptive brochure and a small map to point out the history and nature of the creeks, as well as advise on distances and landmarks.

THE UBIQUITOUS CAPTAIN SMITH

As you paddle in the Sassafras River, try to picture it as Captain John Smith saw it, when he sailed here from the colony at Jamestown in 1607. He named it, not after the medicinal shrub, but for the Tocwogh tribe that lived here. The name was changed later (maybe because nobody could spell Tocwogh).

Elk Neck State Park, at the end of Route 272, nine miles south of North East (☎ 410-287-5333), rents 14-foot open aluminum boats and 6hp outboard motors, but it is not a good place for canoes or kayaks. The park is surrounded by open water and the main shipping channel for the C&D Canal.

Amphibious Horizons, based at Quiet Waters Park in Annapolis (☎ 410-267-8742 or 888-I-LUV-SUN, www.amphibioushorizons.com), offers day-long Saturday trips in the Eastern Neck Wildlife Refuge, on an island near Rock Hall. This is a lovely place to paddle. Cost of all day excursions is $75, and includes lunch at a waterside restaurant.

A weekend trip by the same outfitters explores Wye Island, camping on the island at night and paddling around its shore during the day. Kayaks, tents, food, and intensive instruction are provided; suitable for beginners but still fun for those with advanced paddling skills. Trips run from Saturday morning to midday Sunday and cost about $200.

Boat Tours

Miss Clare, an authentic Chesapeake Bay "deadrise" working boat, does historic cruises from Chesapeake City. One-hour cruises on the Chesapeake Bay, two-hour cruises on the Bohemia River, 1½-hour twilight cruises and one-hour midnight cruises fill the summer schedule in July and August, with one-hour bay cruises spring and fall. Prices for an hour-long cruise are $10 for adults, $5 for children, Bohemia River cruises are $20. Bay cruises leave hourly, 1-4 pm; ☎ 410-885-5088.

Fishing

The **Matapeake Pier**, on Route 8, about three miles south of US 50 on Kent Island, has a 900-foot fishing pier and boat launch. The picnic area overlooks it from an open grove, with sunset views so beautiful they are sure to distract you from fishing. The fee is $3 per car; ☎ 410-974-2149. Farther down island, the road ends at **Romancoke Pier**, where you can fish or crab from May through October during daylight hours. The daily fee here is a bit steep: $3 per person for residents and $5 per person for out-of-staters.

For fishing lessons, both freshwater and saltwater, see **Pintail Point,** below, under *Shooting Sports*.

Island Queen is a headboat leaving daily at 7 am and 3 pm, April through December, from Captain Meridith Seafood Restaurant at Kent Narrows; ☎ 410-827-7737.

Rent fishing or crabbing gear and boats from **Island Boat Rentals**, at The Jetty Restaurant, off Exit 42 of US 50 at Kent Narrows in Grasonville; ☎ 410-827-4777. A 16-foot skiff is about $50 for a half-day or $90 daily, discounted for those in possession of a safe boating course certificate. For those without certification, a short instruction period and practice run are included.

Schnaitman's Boat Rental, at 12518 Wye Landing Lane in Wye Mills (☎ 410-827-7663), rents 16-foot wooden row boats for fishing or crabbing, or just enjoying the river scenery. Rentals are $20 per day, plus tax. You must have a personal flotation device, which they also rent if you don't have your own. They rent dip nets and sell other fishing and crabbing equipment and bait.

Freshwater fishing for pickerel, bass, channel catfish, and bluegills is good in the 20-acre lake at **Tuckahoe State Park**, and in the spring perch and herring can be found below the dam. There is a boat launch ramp, but gasoline engines are not allowed on the lake. Christian Park, on Red Bridges Rd. three miles north of Greensboro, is an excellent spring fishing spot.

Upper Eastern Shore

In Chestertown, you can rent boats for fishing or crabbing (or sightseeing) from **Chester River Marine Services**, at 7501 Church Hill Rd. on Route 213 at the Chester River Bridge; ☎ 410-778-2240.

At Eastern Neck, see **Eastern Neck Boat Rental**; ☎ 410-639-7100.

Fair Hill Natural Resource Management Area, which stretches to the Pennsylvania state line north of Elkton (☎ 410-398-1246), is cut by the good-sized Big Elk Creek where smallmouth bass fishing is quite good. It is also stocked with trout.

Elk Neck State Park, on Route 272 south of North East (☎ 410-287-5333), is ideally located for boat access, with water on both sides of the park. The boat launch has four docks ($5 launch fee) with a deep ramp. They rent 14-foot open aluminum boats and 6hp motors. Although the park is open all winter, the boating area closes December through February. A bass tournament is held here in the summer.

■ On Horseback

 Fair Hill Nature and Environment Center, 376 Fair Hill Drive, Elkton, ☎ 410-398-1246, is a major center for thoroughbred racing, with a track and about 400 horses stabled and trained there. More than 75 miles of trails are open to hikers and equestrians, and the area has one of the few places where you can rent horses for trail rides. Guided trail rides can be as short as two or as long as 26 miles, and include a lesson in basic horsemanship if you are not an experienced rider.

Route 273 bisects the property, a former DuPont estate, but bridges and tunnels provide connecting links between the trails on either side, so it is not necessary to ride along or across roads. The DuPonts have retained the right to hold fox hunts here, although they are more accurately fox chases, since no actual hunting is done.

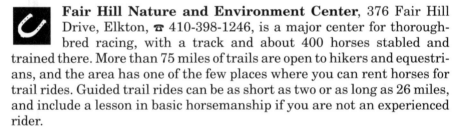

AUTHOR TIP

*The **Cecil County Fair**, held the last week in July and the first week in August at Fair Hill, is a traditional country fair with an internationally recognized three-star horse event. Enthusiasts gather here to see a real steeplechase.*

Tailwinds Farm, at 41 Tailwinds Lane (Route 272) in North East (☎ 410-658-8187), offers riding lessons and trail rides. **Crimson Stables**, at 27190 Morgnec Rd. (Route 291) north of Chestertown (☎ 410-778-7304), offers trail rides and riding instruction, with a newly built arena for sheltered riding.

■ Shooting Sports

 Pintail Point Farm, at 511 Pintail Point Lane in Queenstown (410-827-7029), is designed for those people who are not otherwise involved in shooting sports, but would like to learn proper handling of firearms and practice those skills on sporting clays (known elsewhere as clay pigeons) in a beautiful natural environment. The sporting clay route has 24 stations, combining electrical and hand-released targets, adjustable for skill level.

DID YOU KNOW? *How sporting clays differ from skeet shooting? Skeet follows a reliable pattern on each release, whereas sporting clays move irregularly, simulating animal activity. This can be geared to an individual's shooting skills.*

From shooting, it was a natural step to include fly-fishing, both fresh and saltwater, year-round, which they also teach in an Orvis-endorsed program. Four-hour private lessons are about $200 for the first person, $50 for each additional. Pond fishing in their stocked pond is $15 per person, with equipment rental available by advance reservation. Fly-tying classes and other related activities are offered, too.

ACCESSIBILITY: *Fishing and shooting at Pintail Point are both wheelchair-accessible, as is the clubhouse.*

A heavy focus here is on families, with a bright clubhouse, instruction aimed at all age groups and 50% reduction for children. Their hope is that people will be educated here about firearms. "If you don't like them, that's OK," is their message, "But it shouldn't be from lack of knowledge." Scout groups are welcome free of charge.

The property is beautifully maintained and landscaped with native plants, and continues operating the dairy farm it grew from (dairy tours are free by prior appointment). At their kennel they breed, board and train pointers, English setters and labs. An 18-hole Scottish links golf course has just opened on the property, under separate ownership, and is open to the public.

Upper Eastern Shore

Cultural & Eco-Travel Experiences

 Wildfowl Trust of North America runs the **Horsehead Wetlands Center**, 600 Discovery Lane, Grasonville; ☎ 410-827-7029 or 800-CANVASBACK. Here you can see native birds in aviaries and in the wild, in a wide variety of shore habitats. The Visitors Center has displays including a touch box with feathers, pinecones, snakeskins, turtle shells and other things found at the center. An observation room overlooks a pond, with binoculars and bird books available. A small shop sells birding aids, guides and books on the local area. For more information on the trails and the outdoor exhibit areas they connect, as well as the bird species seen there, see page 363. The Center is open daily, 9-5; admission is $3 adult, $2 age 55 and over, $1 under age 18.

Adkins Arboretum, in Tuckahoe State Park (☎ 410-634-2847), is located on Eveland Rd., about two miles north of the Intersection of Routes 404 and 480 just east of Hillsboro. Still under development, the 500-acre area will have examples of regional trees growing in their natural environments and showing the major types of forest found in the region.

> **ACCESSIBILITY:** *Some of the five miles of trails in the Adkins Arboretum are accessible to wheelchairs, and have level even surfaces for easy walking.*

■ Gardens

An Eastridge Garden, at 533 Dulin Clark Rd., in Centreville (☎ 410-758-3650) grows herbs and perennials, with several greenhouses filled with herbs, topiaries and herbal products. They are open Monday-Saturday, 9-6, and Sunday, 10-4, from March through December.

Sinking Springs Farm, 234 Blair Shore Rd., Elkton 21921 (☎ 410-398-5566), is one of the earliest farms in the area, with a record of occupancy on the land since 1717. Today it is an herb farm, where you can visit the gardens or take classes in herb growing and crafts such as indoor potting, herbal wreaths or cornhusk and cone Santas. Seasonal walks in the gardens and around the historic farm are guided by the enthusiastic owner, who points out the herbs and wild plants. The walk is about 2½ miles, but can be shortened. Heart-healthy herbal luncheons precede or follow the walks; the cost is $5 for the walk, $20 with lunch. The shop is a fragrant potpourri of books, dried herbs and flowers, plants and herbal crafts and condiments. At Christmas, house tours by candlelight bring to life the centuries of history that linger here. To spend a night at the cottage on the farm, see *Where to Stay*, page 384.

■ Crafts

Watch the construction of the **schooner *Sultana***, at the Sultana Shipyard, 346 Cannon St., in Chestertown; ☎ 410-778-6461, www.ChesterRiver.com/sultana. When finished, this reproduction of the original 1767 schooner will be a sailing classroom for bay history and aquatic sciences. The shipyard is open to the public year-round, and you are welcome to watch the work in progress. Bring a picnic and spend the afternoon seeing blacksmiths, sailmakers or ships joiners at work. Better yet, you can get involved yourself, through the shipbuilding school, sponsored by Chester River Art and Craft, where you can learn these skills or brush up on those you already have.

One of the most appealing craft classes we have encountered is another offered by **Chester River Craft and Art**, in Chestertown. On a weekend in January, you and up to two other people can sign up as a team to build your own canoe. In an intensive two-day workshop, you will build a simple functional 16-foot flat-bottomed wooden canoe, mastering the arts of lofting, marine carpentry and joining. The workshop fee is $250, and materials are $150. Family groups are encouraged, but all must be over age 10. The workshop is taught at the Sultana Shipyard, by their working shipwrights; ☎ 410-778-5954.

Sinking Springs Farm, 234 Blair Shore Rd., Elkton 21921 (☎ 410-398-5566), offers classes in herb crafts, including wreath making and cornhusk and cone crafts. See *Gardens*, above, for additional information about the farm.

Day Basket Factory, 714 Main St., North East (☎ 410-287-6100), makes white oak baskets entirely by hand. You can watch the whole process, from stripping the bark off the planks with a draw-knife to adding the final decorative touches to the finished basket, at the shop behind the show room. Even the dye process that turn splints red and green for Christmas baskets is done here. The attention to detail is meticulous, and you'll learn such niceties of basket weaving as why it is important that the splints not be cut across the wood grain. Unlike imports found in most stores, each Day basket is signed and dated by its maker, branded with the Day name, and carries a lifetime guarantee. And how many weavers make the 4,000 to 5,000 baskets Day produces each year? Two.

■ Antiques

Main Street in **Galena** (US 213) has several shops specializing in antiques, as does Cross St. in **Chestertown**, in the block between High and

Cannon streets. A group shop on High St., north of the park, displays the offerings of several dealers.

At Crumpton, near Chestertown, is **Dixon's Furniture, Inc.**, an area the size of three football fields filled with furniture – thousands of pieces – auctioned each Wednesday at prices that rarely exceed $70-$100. The goods are set up and the auctioneer goes around, disposing of them in a manner so rapid-fire that you really need to go once just to get hang of it first, before you even think about buying. It's cash only; the inspection begins at 6 am and the auction at 10, year-round. Dixon's is at Routes 290 and 544; ☎ 410-928-3006.

Several shops cluster at the corner of Bohemia Ave. and 3rd St. in **Chesapeake City**, featuring everything from furniture to vintage linens.

Fair Hill Antiques (☎ 410-398-8426) is opposite the Fair Hill Inn at the crossroads of Routes 213 and 273, north of Elkton. Each room of the rambling house is the "booth" of a different antique dealer, a very attractive way to set up a group shop. Hours are Thursday through Monday, 10-5. A flea market is held there the third Saturday of each month, April-October, 8-2.

Shoppes of Londonshire, on Main St. in North East, has a good selection of antiques, from ephemera to furniture.

For those looking for things more prosaic than crafts or antiques, **Prime Outlets** mega-mall is located 21 miles from Annapolis, on Route 50 just after it splits from Route 301, near Wye River.

Events

 SEASONAL: From mid-May to mid-October, one Saturday a month, houses and historic sites in Queen Anne's County are open; ☎ 410-604-2100.

MAY: During Memorial Day Weekend, the **Chestertown Tea Party** commemorates the revolt of local merchants against the tea tax and subsequent dumping of a shipload of tea into the Chester River, with boat rides, parades, re-enactments, crafts and food; ☎ 410-778-0416.

JUNE: Early in the month is the **Queen Anne's County Watermen's Festival**, with a crab soup cook-off, water skills contests and other activities, in Grasonville; ☎ 410-604-2100. **Chestertown Annual Garden Tour**, when the many beautiful backyard gardens, most of which are hidden by fences, are open to view at their height of bloom; ☎ 410-778-2829. Late June brings **Canal Day** in Chesapeake City, with crafts, food, music and entertainment; ☎ 410-885-3466.

JULY: Summer Music in the Park brings free concerts to Pell Gardens in Chesapeake City every Sunday evening, 6-8, during July and August;

☎ 410-392-5740. Mid-month, the **North East Water Festival** brings three days of music, food, crafts and a boat show to Town Park; ☎ 410-398-3569.

AUGUST: The **Susquehanna River Festival** in Port Deposit includes a crab feast ($25), parade music and more; ☎ 410-378-4223.

SEPTEMBER: Candlelight Walking Tours visit historic homes in Chesterton, sponsored by Kent County Historical Society; ☎ 410-778-3499. Later in the month, **Wetlands Fest** brings a day of celebrating the wildlife, waterfowl and other natural treasures of the Chesapeake marshlands, at Horsehead Wetlands Center in Grasonville; ☎ 410-827-6694.

OCTOBER: During the third weekend, a **Decoy Show** is held at the Upper Bay Museum, 219 Walnut St. in North East (☎ 410-287-2675).

Sightseeing

■ Historic Sites & Museums

Bay Bridge Area

 In Wye Mills, the **Wye Grist Mill** still grinds grain, as it has since it sold flour to the Continental army during the Revolution. You can watch it on the first and third Saturdays of each month from mid-March through mid-November. Water from the pond across the street operates the wheel and flour is carried on an elevator system invented in 1800. Look at the ceiling to see the evolution of the routes of old belts, elevators and chutes at different periods.

The lower level is a small museum with displays telling about the agricultural legacy of the area, which moved from the production of wheat and tobacco to fruit and later to chickens. Along with a model of an old village are agricultural tools. The ground floor is wheelchair-accessible. A **Fall Foliage Festival** and another event in the spring bring crafts, food, music and demonstrations to the mill, along with oxcart rides and re-enactors in Revolutionary period dress. The mill is open Monday through Friday, 10-1, and weekends, 10-4, from mid-March through mid-November, but operates only on alternate Saturdays. Entrance is free and picnickers are welcome to use the outdoor tables beside the stream. You can buy high-quality cornmeal, buckwheat and whole wheat flours at $2-$4 for two-pound bags.

Wye Oak, in Wye Mills, is the largest white oak in the United States, and is at least 450 years old. The little brick house beneath its branches is quite new – built about 1800, with Flemish bond brickwork. Picnic tables are also in the little park that surrounds it.

Old Wye Church is just down the road, built in 1721. It is an architectural gem, with box pews, a stunningly graceful pulpit in its center and a rare royal coat of arms, donated in 1770. Most such royal crests were destroyed during the Revolution, but this deep relief of the lion and unicorn is still very much intact. Notice the window cut beside the pulpit to let in light. If you are lucky enough to be there on the first Saturday of November for the **church bazaar**, you can have a delicious lunch of shepherd's pie and stock up on the kind of things church bazaars used to sell – hand-knit mittens, wild grape jelly, previously owned jewelry and an erudite collection of used books and music.

YOU CAN'T BEAT THESE BISCUITS

At the Wye Church bazaar you will also find the local specialty, Maryland beaten biscuits, which are made by the Orrell family, parishioners whose bakery is next door. These fat, round crackers are fine-textured and very hard, much loved by locals and barely known outside the area. Look for them in grocery stores; ☎ 410-820-8090.

The settlement here once had two churches and five blacksmith shops, one of which still stands and is in the process of restoration.

Centreville's shady streets are lined with homes spanning the Federal and Victorian eras, including a row of homes built by a local captain for families of the crews on his boats, which plied the bay. The Victorian homes frequently have wrap-around porches.

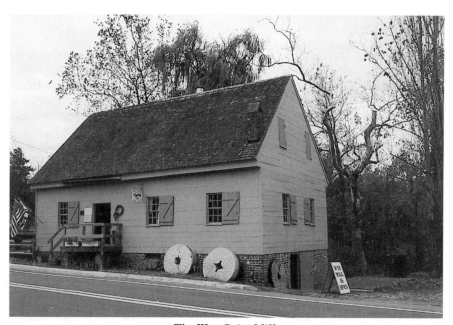

The Wye Grist Mill.

Wright's Chance, a plantation house built about 1744, and the 1792 **Tucker House** are both owned by the County Historical Society and furnished with their collections of furniture and china. They are open on request or during the monthly historical day when many such museum houses are open. Wright's Chance is at 119 S. Commerce St. and the Tucker House is at #124, Centreville; ☎ 410-604-2100.

Queen Anne's Museum of Eastern Shore Life, at 126 Dulin Clark Rd. (Route 18) in Centreville (☎ 410-758-0166), houses collections on several aspects of local life, including watermen's gear, agricultural tools and machines, household furnishings and implements, village trades and transportation. A complete blacksmith shop has been reconstructed here. The museum is open weekends, 1-4, April through October; admission is free.

RECOMMENDED READING: *The Historic Sites Consortium of Queen Anne's County publishes an excellent free folder with a timeline and area history from its aboriginal inhabitants through the 20th century, keyed to local sites that illustrate each era's history. Inside the folder are cards describing various historic places to visit. It is entitled* Explore Our History and Heritage. *Copies are available at local B&Bs and information racks, or from the Queen Anne's County Office of Tourism, 425 Piney Narrows Rd., Chester, MD 21619;* ☎ *410-604-2100 or 888-400-RSVP.*

Chestertown

If Chestertown weren't so alive with activity, its picture-perfect streets lined by historic homes might be mistaken for a historic recreation like Williamsburg. The active Kent County Historical Society has its headquarters in the restored 1780s Philadelphia-style town house, the **Geddes-Piper House**, at 101 Church Alley; ☎ 410-778-3499. It is open for tours on weekends, 1-4, May through October. For walking tours of the historic section, both guided and self-guided, see page 363. If you haven't time for a street-by-street tour, you might want to see at least a few of the more significant examples. **Widehall**, on the corner of Water and High Streets, next to the landing, is one of the most elaborate town homes, built about 1770 by the wealthiest merchant. It was at this landing that Chestertown's Tea Party took place; the building opposite was the Customs House. **Queen Street** is lined by 18th- and early 19th-century tradesmen's homes and a few owned by wealthy merchants, including the **Nicholson House** at #111. The **Palmer House**, at 532 High St. (north of Kent St.) is one of Chestertown's most unusual homes from the 1700s, built entirely of oddly shaped stones.

RECOMMENDED READING: *For a good selection of books on Chestertown history and the local area, stop at* **The Compleat Bookseller,** *opposite the park at 301 High Street;* ☎ *410-778-1480. You might also check their calendar of appearances by authors of books on Maryland and the Chesapeake Bay.*

Rock Hall

In Rock Hall, the **Watermen's Museum** (☎ 410-778-6697) is open weekends and holidays 10-5, or on weekdays, you can ask for the key at the Marina next door. Their exhibits include the tools and lore of the crabbing, fishing and oyster fleets that once made this a thriving port. The **Rock Hall Museum**, in the town hall on Main St. (☎ 410-778-1399) continues the story with model boats, shipping displays and equipment, as well as Native American artifacts. It is open Wednesday-Friday, 2-4:30.

Earleville

"World's End" was the original name for the property on which stands **Mount Harmon Plantation**, Grove Neck Rd., Earleville; ☎ 410-275-8819. Almost surrounded by tributary creeks of the Sassafras River, the name was well chosen. Brick gates lead to a long tree-framed lane that looks like low Gothic arches in a cloister passageway. The three-story Georgian manor house dates from 1730, and is furnished in American and British antiques, appropriate to its prime period of 1760-1810. It is open for tours on Tuesday and Thursday, 10-3, and Sunday, 1-4; admission is $5.

AUTHOR TIP

Even if the mansion is closed, it is worth going to Mount Harmon Plantation to see the winding lane through it, as well as the gardens, terraces of boxwood parterre, with wisteria vines twining along the ornamental iron railings and a serpentine brick wall. Magnolias overhang the garden and the walkway leading to it is flanked by a pair of English yews with trunks more than a yard in diameter. These terraces overlook the marshlands along the river bank, which are filled with birds.

Chesapeake City

Chesapeake City sits along the banks of the Chesapeake and Delaware Canal, known as the C&D. The canal's 14 miles cut off about 300 miles around the peninsula for shipping bound to the ports of Baltimore and others – about a day's travel. It claims to be the busiest canal in the world, with over 15,000 transits a year, and it's fun to watch the barges go by.

 DID YOU KNOW?

Because the C&D Canal provides a "shortcut" for thousands of ships each year, it helps save more than 40 million gallons of fuel annually.

The **C&D Canal Museum**, in Chesapeake City (☎ 410-885-5622), is small, but very well designed, showing how the canal works and the history of its construction in lively exhibits. The visuals are good, especially the model that shows how locks worked (the canal's two locks were removed in 1921). A television monitor allows visitors to track ships in the canal.

The museum is located beside the canal, in the original lift wheel pumping station that provided water for the locks. Its giant wheel, which moved 20,000 gallons of water a minute, and the original engine that ran it, adjoin the museum, and you can inspect these from catwalks and through windows. The museum is open Monday through Saturday, 8-4:15, Sundays, April-September, 10-6. Even when it is closed, you can see the wheel through windows on the canal side.

BAD COP, NO DOUGHNUT

Unfortunately, along with its historic charm, Chesapeake City is also famous for its not-so-charming police, who take particular pleasure in ticketing out-of-state drivers. You can get a parking ticket here while you set your luggage on the curb in front of your B&B – or while changing a flat tire. It makes for a lot of breakfast table can-you-top-this tales in B&Bs throughout the state, which always begin, "You'll never believe what happened to us in Chesapeake City... " Leave your car in the backyard of your lodging and walk.

Elkton & North East

The **Tawes Drive Covered Bridge** is in the northern section of Fair Hill Natural Resources Management Area, north of Elkton. In 1860, when the bridge was built, Tawes Rd. was the main route between Baltimore and Philadelphia. Nearby are the buildings of the former DuPont Hunting Lodge and the huge barns, which now store hay for the horses stabled in the park.

The **Upper Bay Museum**, at 219 Walnut St. in North East (☎ 410-287-2675), is a delightful accumulation of boats and reminders of the life and culture of the bay's past. One, a double sinkboat that rode with its deck at water level in the days of commercial duck hunting, is among very few in existence. All the displays, crafts and artifacts relate to this upper bay area of the Susquehanna Flats. They cover the history from Native American stone weapons to tools that are just barely obsolete. Boat lovers will find a lot to interest them, including a skiff based on a Viking design, with a flat keel for shallow water. A decoy shop and collection, a display on drag seining and numerous historic photographs fill the museum. It's open Memorial Day through Labor Day, Saturday, 10-3, and Sunday, 10-4.

RAILROAD LORE

In the winter of 1852, railroad tracks were laid across the frozen surface of the Susquehanna flats, from Havre de Grace. Entire trains laden with cargo crossed on top of the ice. In January and February, 10,000 tons of goods were carried across by rail each month.

Elk Neck State Park, Route 272, nine miles south of North East (☎ 410-287-5333), occupies the high point of land separating the Elk River from the mouth of the Northeast River, which along with the Susquehanna forms the upper reaches of the Chesapeake Bay. **Turkey Point Lighthouse** stands at its southernmost tip. The lighthouse is an active one, its steady light powered with solar panels. Follow the walkway to the edge to see the former pit for the foghorn that once sounded there. To the left is the main channel to the C&D Canal, which makes it a good place to watch ships and barges.

The cliffs at Turkey Point Lighthouse are undercut, and are dangerous to climb on.

Where to Stay

ACCOMMODATIONS PRICE KEY	
Rates are per room, per night, double occupancy.	
$	Under $50
$$	$50 to $100
$$$.	$101 to $175
$$$$.	$176 and up

■ Bay Bridge Area

Kent Manor Inn, 500 Kent Manor Drive (☎ 410-643-5757 or 800-820-4511), is just south of US 50 on Kent Island. We were among the first people to stay and dine in this inn when it was so new you could almost smell the varnish on the gleaming hardwood floors. The big, bright airy rooms were beautiful and dinner outstanding. We're happy to report that it hasn't changed; the rooms and the menu still sparkle, and the sunset view is every bit as good as when we first relaxed on the expansive veranda over a glass of wine. You can go home again. The inn is located on a 225-acre tidewater farm, with its own docks, walking trails and bicycles for guests' use. The building was constructed in stages, the earliest wing in 1820 and the center section just before the Civil War. $$$

The Queenstown Inn Bed & Breakfast, at 7109 Main St. in Queenstown 21658 (☎ 410-827-3396, www.queenstowninn.com), has seven guest rooms in the main house and two in a connected house. A mix of modern and antique furniture decorates large rooms with amply sized modern baths. The Seaside Room is fully handicapped-accessible, with a private entrance from the parking area. The guests' parlor is large and well stocked with books. As we checked in at our last visit, the air was filled with the fragrance of homemade bread, which was transformed the next morning into apple French toast. Although the B&B is in the center of the village, it is very quiet, with no traffic noises. The public boat landing, giving onto a cove, is a few blocks down the street, at Second Ave. $$-$$$

The Manor House and Irish House at **Pintail Point Farm**, 511 Pintail Point Lane in Queenstown (☎ 410-827-7029), are available for rental as a whole or on a room-by-room B&B basis; The smaller house sleeps six in three doubles with two shared baths, at $400 for the whole house. Bicycles are provided free of charge. $$$$; cottage $350.

■ Chestertown

The Parker House, 108 Spring Ave. (☎ 410-778-9041, fax 410-778-7318, www.chestertown.com/parker), is an easy walk from the center of the historic downtown. Victorian bedsteads and other antiques furnish the good-sized guest rooms, each with private bath. Public rooms are furnished in antiques and reproductions. Rooms range from $90 to $110, and credit cards are not accepted.

Great Oak Manor, at 10568 Cliff Rd. (☎/fax 410-778-5943 or 800-504-3098), is a stately brick plantation house overlooking the bay, near Great Oak Landing, where there is a golf course and tennis courts (guests have free access). Rooms are tastefully furnished, some with working fireplaces; all have private baths and telephones. Rooms and suites are $95-$145, including a continental-plus breakfast. A private beach is reserved for guests, who are also welcome to stroll in the 12 acres of gardens and lawns. The Inn is west of Melitota, about eight miles west of Chestertown.

White Swan Tavern, opposite the park at 231 High St. (☎ 410-778-2300, fax 410-778-4543), has four rooms and two suites, all with private baths. The building, which dates from about 1733, has been beautifully restored, and an archaeological dig of the property yielded a large deposit of 18th-century artifacts from its earlier days as a tavern. Today it is fully restored to its original interior and furnished in period antiques. Perhaps the most unusual guest room is in the original kitchen, with its huge walk-in fireplace, on the first floor overlooking the terrace. Continental breakfast and afternoon tea are included in the rates, $100-$150, discounted in the off-

The White Swan Tavern in Chestertown.

season. If you have a special interest in historic buildings, ask to see the booklets about the archaeology and restoration.

■ Georgetown

Kitty Knight House, on Route 213 in Georgetown (☎ 410-648-5777 or 800-404-8712, fax 410-648-5729) sits above the Sassafras River, about halfway between Chestertown and Chesapeake City. It has accommodated travelers since the days when that was a long journey by horse. Rooms vary greatly in size, but all have private baths; suites are available for families. Breakfast is included in the rates, which are $50-$100 for rooms, about $125 for suites.

KITTY KNIGHT

Kitty Knight was as courageous as she was pretty, and when the British came to torch the inn, she met them at the door and convinced them to spare not only the inn, but the home of an elderly man next door. Her original rocking chair is in one of the rooms, and if you rock in it, her ghost might come to sit in it during the night. Or so they tell.

■ Chesapeake City

The Blue Max, 300 South Bohemia Ave., Chesapeake City 21915 (☎ 410-885-2781, fax 410-885-2809), has large well-decorated rooms, each with a private bath and thoughtful touches. The third floor has a guest sitting room and the second has a refrigerator stocked with complimentary juices and soft drinks. In the elegant, but inviting front parlor, you can relax in the evening reading – what else – *The Blue Max*, a copy of which is prominent on the table beside a comfortable wing chair. Breakfast is served on the sun porch, where dappled light filters through the trees and you can look up the street through white porch columns to see a line of similarly colonnaded porches. We recommend the full breakfast (included with room) over the very light continental.

A LITERARY PAST

Chesapeake City has strong literary connections. The Blue Max was named by former owner Jack Hunter, author of the book of the same title, a bestseller that was made into a movie starring George Peppard. The James Adams Floating Theatre, a model of which is in the Canal Museum, was the inspiration for Edna Ferber's book and the subsequent Broadway show and movie, *Show Boat*.

Upper Eastern Shore

AUTHOR TIP

*The Garden Cottage **at Sinking Springs Farm**, although it has an Elkton address, is only a short distance over the bridge from Chesapeake City. See below for a description of the cottage.*

■ Elkton & North East

Garden Cottage at Sinking Springs Farm, 234 Blair Shore Rd., Elkton 21921 (☎ 410-398-5566), is only a short distance north of the bridge to Chesapeake City. Although the oldest sycamore tree in Maryland is in Westminster, the one at this farm is no spring chicken. It dates from Shakespeare's teenage years in the 1500s.

The 1740s farmhouse is young by comparison; its original two rooms were a log cabin and the original stone fireplace in the dining room was once the kitchen fireplace. At Christmas, the owners do house tours by candlelight, bringing to life the centuries of history that linger here. The cottage where guests can stay is a rustic cabin with antique linens and a cozy warm air, filled with good reading material. Breakfast is served in the dining room of the farmhouse, featuring herbal delicacies and a hearty dishes that provide a good start for the day. $$.

Crystal Inn, 1 Center Drive, North East, at Exit 100 from I-95, at the intersection with Route 272 (☎ 410-287-7100 or 800-631-3803, fax 410-287-7109), is a convenient, reliable lodging with an indoor pool, hot tub, 24-hour restaurant and complimentary buffet breakfast. Rooms have microwaves, refrigerators and hair dryers. Rates begin under $100.

■ Camping

Elk Neck State Park, at the end of Route 272, nine miles south of North East (☎ 410-287-5333), has more than 250 campsites in its wooded setting overlooking the water. The campground is open year-round. Every site is reservable, and reservations are essential on holiday weekends. One loop, sites 1-31, has full hook-ups with paved platforms and driveways; 27 sites have electricity only. The rest have no hook-ups and are used mostly by tents and pop-ups. Each site has a lantern post and fire ring and a 20-by-22-foot pad of stone dust; showers are free. A maximum of six campers may use each site. Rates are $15 a night without hookup, $20 with electricity, $23 with full (note that all state park rates are subject to yearly change). Mini cabins are $30 a night. 15 walk-in sites are open only on weekends.

Note that the deer population at Elk Neck State Park makes it a prime habitat for deer ticks. Be sure to check your clothing for ticks after walking in the woods.

Tuckahoe State Park, on Crouse Hill Rd. in Queen Anne (☎ 410-820-1668), has a campground with 71 sites for tents or trailers, open mid-April to mid-October. No hook-ups are available, although there is a dumping station. Reservations are not accepted.

Where to Eat

DINING PRICE KEY
The price key indicates the cost of *most* dinner entrées on a restaurant's regular and daily special menu.
$. . . . . Most under $10
$$. . . . . $10 to $20
$$$. . . . . Over $30

■ Bay Bridge Area

You will be besieged by seafood restaurants almost from the moment you leave the Bay Bridge, each with a sign larger, taller and more garish than the last. It would appear that people cross the bridge for no other purpose than to eat fried food. As you might imagine, not all these places are created equal. Rather than regale you with the many trials and errors – our own and those of our family and friends – we will simply tell you our good experiences, and hope the chefs haven't changed.

The one place where we can almost promise that the chef will always be tops is **Kent Manor Inn**, at 500 Kent Manor Drive (☎ 410-643-5757 or 800-820-4511), just south of US 50 on Kent Island. We've been sending our Annapolis friends here for special occasions for at least a decade, and they always thank us for the advice. The chef has winning ways with buffalo steak, roast duck and crab cakes... oh my, the crab cakes. Whatever you choose as an entrée, begin with a broiled crab cake. We measure everyone else's by these, and keep coming back to check our criteria. Dining rooms are in the antebellum central part of the manor house, small, with only a few tables each. Lunch and dinner are served daily, $$-$$$.

Hemingway's, at the foot of the Chesapeake Bay Bridge on Kent Island (☎ 410-643-CRAB) serves traditional seafood dishes, well prepared and with more flair than the run-of-the-mill seafood restaurants that line US 50 east of the bridge. For appetizers, mushroom caps are filled with escargot and crabmeat, crab and artichoke dip is served in a boule of sourdough bread, and shrimp are served Spanish-style, sautéed in olive oil and garlic. $$

Main dishes may include sesame-crusted rockfish, salmon and portobello mushrooms baked in phyllo, grilled catfish with Béarnaise or flounder stuffed with shrimp mousse. Most entrées are $15-$18, and the Chesapeake Sampler (crab cake, duck breast, clams and two styles of oysters) is $21. Hemingways is open year-round, daily from 11 am. Save your receipt from the Bay Bridge for a refund here. $$

Harris Crab House, at Kent Narrows in Grasonville (☎ 410-824-9500), is not a fancy dining room: it has all the savoir faire of a Munich beer hall, and about the same ambiance. Which is just the right atmosphere for consuming messy foods like crabs, what Harris's is best known for. Traditional brown paper covers the tables, and instead of napkins you are presented a roll of paper towels. But half a dozen impeccably fresh soft crabs with onion rings, coleslaw and a muffin are $15. Half a pound of boiled shrimp with two sides is $13; tea, coffee and soft drinks include unlimited refills. Upstairs is a small, very crowded bar. Expect a wait, which might be a long one on Saturday night. The word gets around. They open at 11 am daily. $$

■ Chestertown

Blue Heron Café, on Cannon St. just south of Cross St. (☎ 410-778-0188), serves an innovative New American menu featuring regional ingredients. It is open for lunch and dinner Tuesday through Sunday. $$-$$$

Play It Again Sam can be forgiven for misquoting Rick, if only because its sandwiches are so good and the staff so pleasant. Multiple layers of thick-sliced ham or creamy white-meat chicken salad are piled on a fresh croissant for $4. Pies and cakes, good coffees, ice cream and milkshakes are served to the sound of classical music in a café-cum-cultural center, where local art and used CDs are also sold. It's open Monday through Saturday, 7-5:30; Sunday, 9-4. 108 South Cross St.; ☎ 410-778-2688.

White Swan Tavern serves afternoon tea from 3 to 5 every day except Wednesday or when the inn is booked for a special event. If you are traveling some distance, it is wise to call ahead. In the winter they serve tea and hot cider, in summer hot or iced tea or lemonade with accompanying goodies for $4 (complimentary for inn guests). The White Swan is opposite the park at 231 High St.; ☎ 410-778-2300, fax 410-778-4543.

The Stam Drug Company, opposite the park on High St., has an old-fashioned soda fountain; ☎ 410-778-2940.

■ Rock Hall

Bay Wolf Restaurant, 21270 Rock Hall Ave. (Route 20 South), in Rock Hall (☎ 410-778-6855), is in an old church, and serves a good continental/ regional menu. On Monday evenings in the winter, the German-born chef recalls the favorite dishes of Bavaria in his specials, but some – Wiener schnitzel and roast pork with dumplings – stay on the menu from mid-September through April. Pastries here are excellent – as one would expect from a Salzburg-trained chef. $$ $$$

Durding's Store, on the corner of Main and Sharp Streets (☎ 410-778-7957), is an authentic 1930s ice cream parlor, still serving hand-dipped ice cream, sundaes and ice cream sodas.

■ Georgetown

The **Kitty Knight House**, on Route 213 in Georgetown (☎ 410-648-5777 or 800-404-8712, fax 410-648-5729), above the Sassafras River bridge, has a good dining room, serving dishes such as cashew-crusted chicken breast, tomato-basil crab crêpes, blackened tuna with shrimp, or a complete shore dinner. Most entrées are $15-$22. Dinner is served in small dining rooms or in the large one overlooking the river. For the story of Kitty Knight, see *Where to Stay*, above. $$-$$$

The Granary Restaurant, off US 213 on the north side of the Sassafras River bridge in Georgetown (☎ 410-275-1603), serves a traditional Eastern Shore menu, daily year-round. $$

■ Chesapeake City

Bayard House Restaurant, at 11 Bohemia Ave. (☎ 410-885-5040), over-looks the canal, where it is not unusual to see several large ships pass during dinner. Maryland crab soup doesn't get any better than Bayard's: a spicy (but not over-spiced) tomato base with chunks of crab, potato, onion, carrot, peppers and celery. Other appetizers include oysters baked with backfin crab cake and warm brie in puff pastry. Anaheim peppers may be on the entrée menu, stuffed with lobster, shrimp and crab. The monkfish is crusted in cashews and finished with mango chili; mesquite-smoked wahoo is filled with pineapple salsa. Most entrées are $20-$23. Lunch entrées are $10-$14. The dessert list tempts with such options as lemon mousse, chocolate torte, Key lime pie or a chocolate chip cookie pie with pecans. Well-informed professional service and the view across the water combine with the food for a thoroughly satisfying experience. $$-$$$

Chesapeake Inn Restaurant, at 605 Second St.(☎ 410-885-2040), also overlooks the canal. Informed, experienced waitstaff is genuinely helpful in steering you to wines and entrée choices, which may include seared tuna medallions topped with crab imperial, veal marsala with shiitake mushrooms, or a splendid veal Oscar, made with lightly sautéed veal, generous lump crab and a just-barely-tart hollandaise. Vegetables here have their own identity, treated as a dish worthy of attention, not an afterthought. And, bless them, they tell you the prices on the nightly specials when describing them. Desserts include tiramisu, crunchy chocolate torte, lemon chiffon cake, and sorbets of mandarin, lemon, peach or cantaloupe, served in fruit. Entrées are priced at $13-$22. Lunch entrées are $7.50-$12, and in the summer the deck menu offers sandwiches of soft crab or crab cake, pasta entrées and creative pizzas. On Friday and Saturday evenings there is piano or other live music. The ship models that decorate the dining room are for sale. $$

■ Elkton & North East

Fair Hill Inn (☎ 410-398-4187), at the intersection of Routes 213 and 272 by the entrance to Fair Hill Management Area, is an impressive stone building dating from the 1600s. Each of its dining rooms has a slightly different atmosphere: the Colonial Room is part of the original building and has a huge stone fireplace, the Hunt Room has a brick floor and fireplace, the Mitchell Room has two fireplaces and dates from the 1760s, the Victorian Room is the newest, part of an 1821 wooden addition. But the food is the reason for going there: veal saltimbocca, roast duck with orange, lamb chops with mint jelly. Most are priced at $18-$23. Lunch is served Tuesday-Friday, 11:30-2:30; dinner, Tuesday-Sunday, 4-9. $$

Sinking Springs Farm, 234 Blair Shore Rd., Elkton 21921 (☎ 410-398-5566), offers seasonal herbal luncheons, combined with a guided walk through the herb gardens and around the historic farm. The cost is $20, or $17 without the walk. Call the farm for the schedule, which is usually the second Thursday and Saturday of each month from May through December. $$

On Main St. in North East, look into Shoppes of Londonshire to find **Perry's Pastries Plus**, where you can eat ice cream in flavors like pumpkin cheesecake and cappuccino crunch, while listening to rock 'n roll on the free jukebox.

Woody's Crab House, at 29 Main St. in North East (☎ 410-287-3541), is a very popular traditional crab house. It's open March through December. $$

Central Eastern Shore

The entire eastern shore is a charming blend of the traditions of watermen, farmers and waterfowl hunters, who range from local boys to the moneyed gentry. In the rarified atmosphere of Easton and St. Michaels, the latter is more often seen than the former. Oxford's quiet streets of old homes seem less a showplace than St. Michaels, more comfortably authentic and without the rows of trendy boutiques. Outside that golden triangle are the more earthy pleasures of muskrat dinners and oyster shucking competitions. The landscapes are wild, open and flat, often bordered by blue waters of the Chesapeake and its many bays and estuaries.

The Central Eastern Shore offers a little bit of everything, from the foremost festival of waterfowl art to a history rich in maritime traditions. Watersports and waterfowl enthusiasts will like this region, as will those who enjoy the genteel lodgings and upscale menus of its small, but well-known destination towns: St. Michaels, Oxford and Easton. Our own preferences? We enjoy the quiet tidewater reaches around the Blackwater refuge and the sense of working history in Cambridge, but like to nip into Oxford for dinner at Le Zinc.

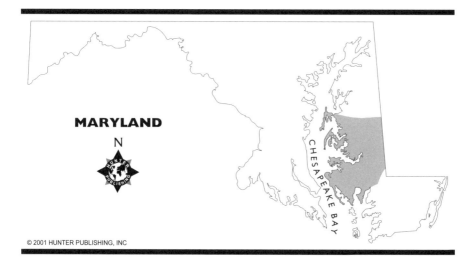

MARYLAND

N

CHESAPEAKE BAY

Geography & History

 The central part of the Eastern Shore includes the coastal **Talbot** and **Dorchester** counties, along with the southern part of landlocked **Caroline County**. **US 50** is the main artery through this region, dropping almost straight south to Cambridge before turning east toward Salisbury, in Wicomico County.

The entire area is rich in history and in historic sites and buildings, settled in the middle 1600s, with a number of active ports by the time of the Revolution.

DID YOU KNOW?

*Oxford was home to two men of particular significance in the Revolution. **Robert Morris** is known as the man who financed the war and **Tench Tilghman** was Washington's aide-decamp. Tilghman carried the news of Cornwallis's surrender to the Continental Congress, assembled in Philadelphia.*

While **Oxford** was a thriving trading port well before the Revolution, the old Quaker settlement of Easton made its mark in the 19th century as a steamboat port. Its Quaker Meeting House is among the country's oldest. St. Michaels is a Johnny-come-lately, founded in the late 1700s as a shipbuilding port.

Harriet Tubman, founder of the Underground Railroad, was born at Brodess Plantation, on Greenbriar Rd., south of Cambridge. The site is marked by a state historical sign, but is on private property.

*For books on local history, go to **Rowans Bookstore**, on Courthouse Square in Easton; ☎ 410-822-2095. For old and new books on nautical and maritime subjects, travel to Tilghman Island's **Book Bank,** open weekends, April through December, 10-6; ☎ 410-886-2230.*

Central Eastern Shore

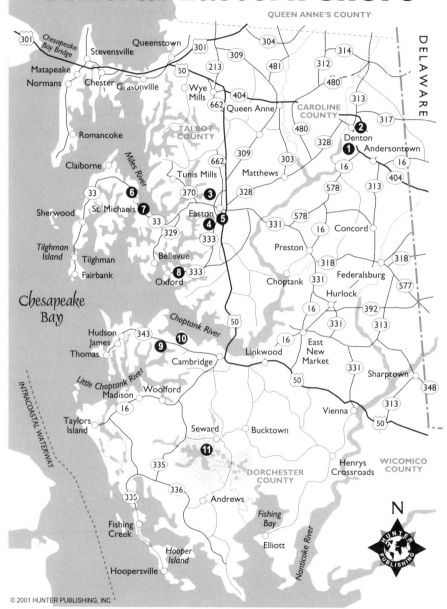

QUEEN ANNE'S COUNTY

DELAWARE

301 Chesapeake Bay Bridge
Stevensville
Queenstown
301
304
309
314
481
312
50
213
480
Matapeake
Normans
Chester
Grasonville
Wye Mills
404
313
662
Queen Anne
CAROLINE COUNTY
480
317
Romancoke
TALBOT COUNTY
480
328
Denton
Andersontown
2
1
16
Claiborne
Miles River
662
309
303
16
404
Tunis Mills
Matthews
313
33
6
370
3
328
578
St. Michaels
7
33
578
16
Concord
Sherwood
Easton
4
5
331
329
333
Tilghman Island
Tilghman
Bellevue
Preston
318
318
Fairbank
Oxford
8
333
Choptank
331
Federalsburg
577
Hurlock
Chesapeake Bay
Choptank River
50
16
392
Hudson
343
10
331
313
James
9
16
East New Market
Thomas
Cambridge
Linkwood
50
331
Sharptown
348
Little Choptank River
Woolford
Madison
50
16
Vienna
313
Taylors Island
Seward
Bucktown
50
INTRACOASTAL WATERWAY
11
Henrys Crossroads
WICOMICO COUNTY
335
DORCHESTER COUNTY
335
336
Andrews
Fishing Bay
Fishing Creek
Elliott
Nanticoke River
N
Hooper Island
Hoopersville

HUNTER PUBLISHING

© 2001 HUNTER PUBLISHING, INC

1. Martinak State Park
2. Museum of Rural Life
3. Pickering Cover Environmental Center
4. Third Haven Friends Museum
5. Historical Society of Talbot County
6. St. Mary's Square Museum
7. Chesapeake Bay Maritime Museum
8. Oxford Museum
9. Sopcot Windmill
10. Dorchester Heritage Museum; Dorchester County Historical Society
11. Blackwater National Wildlife Refuge

Getting Here & Getting Around

 US 50 peels off to the south shortly after crossing the Bay Bridge from Annapolis, leading straight through the heart of this beautiful agricultural countryside. Nearly any road to the right will end at the water. **Route 33** leads onto a sprawling arm, passing through Easton and St. Michaels on its way to Tilghman Island.

 It may seem odd that US 50, which heads south straighter than a flock of migrating geese, from Wye Mills to Cambridge, should be labeled "US 50 East." The answer is that the rest of its route does lead east-west, from Washington DC to Ocean City. (It continues westward from Washington, out of the range of this book.)

To get to St. Michaels from Annapolis by boat, take a day excursion with **Chesapeake Marine Tours**, at Slip 20, City Dock; ☎ 410-268-7600.

Information Sources

Talbot County Visitors Center is at Tred Avon Plaza, off US 50; ☎ 410-822-4606 or 888-BAY-STAY, www.talbotchamber.org. This also serves as ticket sales and information center for the Waterfowl Festival, during which time shuttle buses leave regularly from the parking lot.

Dorchester County Visitors Center, Sailwinds Park, Cambridge 21613; ☎ 410-228-1000 or 800-522-TOUR, www.tourdorchester.org. This Visitors Center has an interpretive display on the culture of the local area. Cambridge has an active heritage tourism group.

Caroline County Visitor Center, 16 North 2nd St., Denton; ☎ 410-479-2055. Open Friday and Saturday, 10-3; Sunday, noon-4.

Adventures

■ Parks

Martinak State Park, south of Denton on Deep Shore Rd., off Route 404 (☎ 301-479-1619), is a well-designed park along the wooded shore of the Choptank River. Picnic and campsites, a boat pier and ramp and an amphitheater with weekend evening ranger programs are among its facilities.

■ On Foot

Walking Tours

St. Michaels is a pleasant town to explore, and the **St. Mary's Square Museum** (☎ 410-745-9561) has made that easier with an excellent map that describes historic sites and buildings and arranges them into a **walking tour**. You can find these free maps in a number of other places if the museum is closed. Look for the brochure entitled *Explore St. Mary's Square Museum*. Among the interesting things you'll find with this map is a log house hidden beneath Victorian-era siding.

To explore St. Michaels on a guided walking tour, get the latest schedule from **Dockside Express**. Tours from mid-April through mid-November may be of a general historic nature or may highlight some feature, such as the fall Ghostly Tour; ☎ 410-886-2643.

Self-guided walking tour maps of **Easton** are available at their Historical Society, at 25 South Washington St.

By far the most complete and detailed walking tour map and guide takes you past many of the distinguished buildings of the **Cambridge** waterfront neighborhoods. A free 20-page booklet, ***Historic Walking Tour of Cambridge***, is well illustrated and explains not only the history, but the architectural niceties of the buildings it passes – and these are considerable. High Street is lined with outstanding examples of Federal, Queen Anne, Second Empire and high Victorian. Pick up a copy at the Dorchester County Visitors Center (see *Information Sources*, above).

Nature Hikes

The **Isaac Walton League** manages a nature area in Trappe, which is south of Easton on US 50. Trails total about 1.3 miles and you can pick up a map and nature guide brochure at the pavilion. An observation platform gives a good view over the marsh, and at the far end is a mid-19th-century cemetery plot. From the traffic light in Trappe, turn east onto Barber Rd., then go south on Chancellor Point Rd. In about two miles, you will come to

Money Make Rd. on the left; follow it 0.2 mile to the nature area entrance. If you come to the bridge, you've gone too far.

Although it is only one-third mile in length, the **Marsh Edge Trail** at Blackwater refuge takes you through a lovely stand of loblolly pines to a marsh boardwalk and overlook platform. A brochure describing the plants and habitats you will see is available at the park office. The **Woods Trail**, which is just slightly longer, makes a loop through a forested area.

The Marsh Edge Trail and the 80-foot board-walk and marsh overlook platform are wheel-chair-accessible.

■ On Wheels

Easton, Oxford & St. Michaels

One of the favorite bike routes on the Eastern Shore combines easy riding with charming towns, scenic shorelines and a ride on a historic ferry. Leave **Oxford** on North Morris Street to reach **Route 333**, following it to **Easton**. You can explore Easton before leaving via Bay Street to St. Michaels Rd. (Route 33). Follow it to a left onto Royal Oak Rd. (Route 329), turning left again on Bellevue Rd. This leads to the town of **Bellevue** (be sure to stop at the antique shop there) and to the ferry, which returns to Oxford.

To access this loop from St. Michaels, follow **South Talbot Street**, taking **Route 33** to a right turn just past Solitude Rd., leading to **Royal Oak**, where you follow Bellevue Rd. to **Bellevue** and the ferry, picking up the above route description after exploring Oxford's lovely streets.

To shorten the trip and cut out the part with the most traffic, you can ride between **Oxford** and **St. Michaels** and return by the same roads. We actually prefer this, and find the scenery different each way, since we are facing a different direction. This trip is about 20 miles, and whichever direction you take it, the halfway point will put you in a charming town with plenty of places to stop for refreshments and sightseeing.

Cambridge to Hooper Island

You can visit the **Blackwater National Wildlife Refuge** by bicycle from **Cambridge** on a 20-mile loop. Follow **Maple Dam Rd.** south from the high school for about eight miles, turning left onto **Key Wallace Drive**, which cuts through the northern end of the refuge. Stop here to see the displays in the headquarters, or to cycle the refuge roads, especially interesting to birders. At the end of Key Wallace Road, turn right onto Route 335, then right again onto Route 16 to return to Cambridge.

A somewhat longer loop includes **Key Wallace Rd.**, but circles south from the refuge on Route 335, turning left at **Gootee's Marine** (where you can get cold drinks) onto Route 336, then taking **Blackwater Rd.** left to the unpaved **Liners Rd.** to **Shorters Wharf Rd.** (turn left) through another portion of the refuge and back to Key Wallace.

A scenic short loop follows the refuge tour route, returning to your starting place by Key Wallace Rd. You can park at the trailhead for **Marsh Edge Trail**. See *Cultural & Eco-Travel Experiences*, page 402, for more information on the refuge.

WATCHABLE WILDLIFE

The best bird viewing here is along the pools, and the best eagle-spotting we've found is just after we pass the western access to Key Wallace Rd., where the road crosses an area of open water with a number of tree snags.

In the southern part of this area, miles of flat roads wind through the shore marshes and onto **Hooper Island** (the "oo" is pronounced as in *cook*). We like the route along the narrow spit of the island, even though it cannot be made into a loop. Water views are varied enough to make the trip interesting in both directions, and changing times of day provide a variety of colors and shadows. Begin at **Gootee's Marine** (or at the Blackwater refuge for a longer trip) and follow **Route 335** until it ends. Several watermen's breakfast and lunch spots are spaced along the way. It's about 15 miles out to the end of the island and back.

Hooper Island, Maryland.

BIKE RENTALS & GUIDED TOURS

Rent bicycles by the hour (about $4), day ($14) or week at the **Town Dock Marina**, 305 Mulberry St. in St. Michaels; ☎ 410-745-2400. These are single-speed bicycles. Rentals on Tilghman Island are at **Island Treasures** on Wharf Rd.; ☎ 410-886-2058. In Oxford, bike rentals (and just about everything else) are available at **The Oxford Mews**, at 105 S. Morris Street; ☎ 410-820-8222.

VBT Bicycling Vacations leads small groups (never more than 20) on bicycling trips along the Chesapeake shore, completing the part of the circuit between Oxford and Chestertown by working skipjack. The daily mileage varies with individual cyclists and the day's itinerary, but can range from 17 miles to 55 miles, along flat country roads or bike paths. The terrain is never more than gently rolling, and rarely even that. Accommodations are in two historic inns, and most meals are included in the price, which ranges from $1,050 to $1,250. Trips vary in length; most are about a week. They target, according to their publicist, "an older audience," which she continues to define as ages 25-45. Older than whom, we're not quite sure, but if you are past this age group, we suggest you ask pertinent questions. VBT Bicycling Vacations; ☎ 800-245-3868.

■ On Water

 This part of the Chesapeake is home to the last working fleet of **skipjacks** engaged in oyster dredging. Most are based out of Tilghman Island, and a good place to see these historic skipjacks is at **Dogwood Harbor**.

 To get to Dogwood Harbor, take Route 33 from St. Michaels until you cross the drawbridge onto Tilghman Island. In about half a mile, not far past the fire station, look for the entrance to Dogwood Harbor on the left.

To explore St. Michaels Harbor on your own, rent an **electric boat** with a shade canopy. These clean, quiet craft hold a family very comfortably, and are available by the hour, half-day or full day at the Town Dock Marina, 305 Mulberry St. in St. Michaels; ☎ 410-745-2400.

America's oldest privately owned ferry, established in 1683, crosses the Tred Avon River, saving many miles of driving between Oxford and St. Michaels, in the process making a nice loop for cyclists. The **Oxford-Bellevue Ferry** crosses every 20 minutes from June through August, weekdays, 7 am to 9 pm; weekends, 9-9. From Labor Day through November and from March through May, hours are 7 am to sunset on weekdays and 9 am to sunset on weekends. The ferry does not operate from December through February. One-way rates are $5 for car and driver, 50¢ for each passenger. Walk-on rates are $1, bicycles $2. The ferry can accommodate RVs and trailers, too; ☎ 410-745-9023.

Public boat ramps to the Nanticoke River are located on Race Street in Vienna, beside the US 50 bridge, and at Cherry Beach, between the bridges in Sharptown, on the eastern bank. Cambridge has six public access points for the Choptank, one off River Walk and three clustered around the mouth of Cambridge Creek, just west of the US 50 bridge. Several on Hooper Island and its approach roads are reached from Route 335. Nearly every creek has at least one access point, all of which are shown on the excellent map, *Fisherman's Guide to Maryland's Piers and Boat Ramps*.

Sailing

Sailing boats fill the waters on pleasant days – even on not-so-pleasant ones – and every Wednesday evening in the summer you can watch sailboat races in the Miles River.

Several sailing vessels offer charters from the St. Michaels area, among them the *H.M. Krentz* and the *Lady Patty* (see *Boat Tours*, below) and the bay's oldest (and one of its fastest) skipjacks, **Rebecca T. Ruark**. Built in 1886, this beautiful old craft is still a working oyster dredger in the winter, and you will sail with a third-generation waterman who has a thorough knowledge of the bay, its boats and its history. Two-hour sails are $30 per person. For our money, there's not a better sailing experience on the bay, and it's a chance to help preserve a museum-piece vessel. The boat is docked at Dogwood Harbor, about 0.6 mile south of the drawbridge on Tilghman Island; ☎ 410-886-2176.

Rent your own day-sailer with a motor from **Little Boat Rentals**, at 846 Port Street in Easton; ☎ 410-819-0881 or 800-221-1523. Boats are $75 for a full day, $50 half-day or $30 for two hours.

In Oxford, **Skylark Sailing Yachts**, at Campbell's Boat Yards on Myrtle St. (☎ 410-226-5654), also has day-sailers, along with sailing instruction.

Canoeing & Kayaking

Tiny **Kings Creek**, which contributes to the Choptank River east of Easton, is one of the prettiest paddling streams in the area. Follow Route 328 from Easton to the town of Matthews, then follow Kingston Landing Rd. south (right) until it ends at the river, where you can put in. Paddle down the Choptank (to your right) to the mouth of Kings Creek, which will enter from your right. Follow the creek past marshy wetlands and between its high banks, which are mostly wooded. Or, our preference, look for the unmarked road to your right, off Kingston Landing Rd., where you can put in at the bridge, about 1½ miles upstream from the mouth of the creek. You can paddle in either direction from here; the creek splits upstream and either branch is easier to explore at high tide.

Martinak State Park (☎ 301-479-1619) gives access to the Choptank River, where there is wreckage of a century-old sailing pungy (a two-masted sailing vessel).

WATCHABLE WILDLIFE

Look for ospreys and their untidy nests atop the channel markers in the Choptank River; they have adopted these handy perches as nest-sites. Early in the morning you may also see loons, and bald eagles are not uncommon in this area.

Blackwater National Wildlife Refuge and the miles of water around it offer excellent canoeing and kayaking. Where the Refuge lands occupy both banks, you can canoe only between April 1 and October 1, but elsewhere you can take to the water whenever the weather allows, which can be at any time of year. From the put-in at Coles Creek it's three hours of easy paddling to the refuge waters. You cannot put in canoes or kayaks anywhere in the refuge, but there is a public ramp at Shorters Wharf, on Shoters Wharf Rd., which runs through the refuge.

In late April, the **Nanticoke River Shad Festival** features a canoe and kayak race as part of its river festival to promote the restoration of shad to the river. In early May the **Blackwater Refuge Spring Fling** includes guided canoe trips through the sanctuary's wetlands and marshes.

CANOE & KAYAK RENTALS / GUIDED TOURS

Island Kayak, on Mission Rd., Tilghman Island (☎ 410-886-2083) rents kayaks and offers guided trips in the flats around the island to watch herons and egrets fish for their dinners. Mission is the third left past Knapp's Narrows, off Route 33.

Rent canoes from **Little Boat Rentals**, at 846 Port Street in Easton; ☎ 410-819-0881 or 800-221-1523. With the canoe comes a chart of the river and its entering creeks. Canoes are about $35 for a full day, $20 half-day or $6 per hour with a two-hour minimum.

Chesapeake Bay Kayak, at Molowes Wharf Marina on Route 33 in Sherwood (☎ 410-745-9744), guides kayakers on nature tours of the waters around Tilghman Island, and also rents kayaks.

Loblolly Lodge (see *Where to Stay*) has canoes and maps showing the best places to put in near the Blackwater National Wildlife Refuge. Rentals are $15 for a half-day, $30 for 24 hours, including tie-downs. Rentals are available to non-guests, as well as to those staying at the lodge; ☎ 410-397-3033.

Amphibious Horizons, based at Quiet Waters Park in Annapolis (☎ 410-267-8742 or 888-I-LUV-SUN, www.amphibioushorizons.com), offers a day-long Saturday trip in the Blackwater Wildlife Refuge in September. Migrating wildfowl cover the refuge's saltmarshes at this time of year, when the foliage color of bordering woodlands is at its height. Cost of all day excursions is $75.

Loblolly Lodge offers canoe guide service and accessibility for those with impaired mobility. They have backrests, transfer facilities via ATVs, and experience; they work regularly with groups from the Paralyzed Veterans of America. The bunkhouse and cottages are also wheelchair-accessible.

Boat Tours

A variety of boats offer cruises from St. Michaels and Tilghman Island, and you can choose from authentic working skipjacks, small cruisers or larger excursion boats to explore the bay, the Miles or the Choptank River. Individual captains share their personal interests with passengers, so no two trips are the same.

H.M. Krentz is a working skipjack, a member of the fleet that dredges for oysters in the "R months." During a two-hour tour ($30 for adults, $15 for ages 12 and under, discounts for groups), you will have a chance to help the crew sail this boat, under the command of a captain who has been a working waterman for 25 years. The *H.M. Krentz* is also available for charter; ☎ 410-745-6080, www.bluecrab.org/members/hmkrentz. The boat is docked at Dogwood Harbor, on the left, about half a mile south of the drawbridge on Tilghman Island.

The ***Lady Patty***, a 45-foot classic bay ketch, sails daily on two-hour trips on the Choptank River and the bay. Like others, this teakwood yacht is also available for charter. Two-hour scheduled sails are about $30 and leave from Knapps Narrows Marina, at 5907 Tilghman Narrows Rd. on Tilghman Island; ☎ 410-886-2215 or 800-690-5080.

St. Michaels Lady is a 42-foot Chesapeake workboat captained by a fourth-generation waterman whose cruises emphasize the work of these people as they harvest fish and shellfish. Cruises on the Miles River also offer plenty of chance to see ospreys, ducks, swans, herons, possibly even bald eagles. Each of the four daily one-hour cruises explores a different arm of the river, two of which are lined with opulent homes. Evening 90-minute cruises Friday-Sunday head down the river to watch the sunset over Tilghman Point. Day cruises are $9, evening $12. The boat is docked at the Town Dock Marina, 305 Mulberry Street in St. Michaels; ☎ 410-745-5776.

CHOPTANK ESTUARY TOURS

The docks at Cambridge are also a center for boats that take passengers on tours of the **Choptank estuary**, with two skipjacks and a classic motor yacht. Reservations are recommended, often essential, on any of the following.

The *Lady Katie* (☎ 410-228-1277, 1805 Hudson Rd., Cambridge), moored in Cambridge Creek behind Snappers Waterfront Café, is the only working skipjack out of Cambridge. Its captain, Scott Todd, is from several generations of skipjack captains, and his two-hour cruises include watermen's tales and a chance to see how oysters are harvested by these historic boats. To get to the boat, follow High Street from the center of town to Commerce Street, where you will see Snappers Restaurant.

Moored at the waterfront park at the end of Washington Street in Cambridge is the *Nathan of Dorchester*, a newly built ship launched here in 1993. Sunday afternoon cruises are $10 for a two-hour trip on the Choptank; they do not run every week, so it's a good idea to pick up a schedule or call for dates. Saturday evening sunset cruises are $15 (which includes a complimentary drink after the cruise at McGuigan's Pub). They leave at 7 or 7:30 on alternate Sundays; more often from late May through September. You can also sign on for the four skipjack races the boat enters, at $25. A number of special event cruises go to races or local festivals, even to Baltimore, and prices vary by length of trip. Follow High Street from the town center to its end at the park; the boat is on your right. ☎ 410-228-7141.

Cambridge Lady is a passenger boat built in the shape of a classic motor yacht, docked at the corner of Court and Gay Streets, off High Street; ☎ 410-221-0776, www.shorenet.net/cambridgelady. One-hour or 90-minute narrated cruises ($10) run Friday and Saturday June-August, Saturday only in May, September and October. Sunday afternoon cruises run May-October.

Express Royal, a new 49-passenger boat, departs St. Michaels every morning on a 90-minute nature cruise, and in the evening for a sunset cruise. Both are $20 for adults, $10 for children under 12. Reservations are required; ☎ 410-886-2643. The large tour boat *Patriot* leaves the Maritime Museum dock on four cruises daily, at 11, 12:30, 2:30 and 4, April through October, exploring the Miles River (about $9 adult, $5 children). Passengers can choose between the air-conditioned main deck or the shaded open upper deck, as they listen to a narration that includes local history as well as nature and wildlife information; ☎ 410-745-3100.

Captain Dan Vaughn, who operates Island Kayaks on Mission Rd., will take you on custom nature tours by boat from Tilghman Island; ☎ 410-886-2083.

PICTURE THIS: *As you stand on the dock over-looking Cambridge Creek, imagine it in the glory days of sail, when the creek was so filled with skipjacks that you could literally walk across it on their decks.*

Fishing & Crabbing

Fishing packages at **Harrison's Sportfishing Center**, Route 33 on Tilghman Island (☎ 410-886-2121, fax 410-886-2109), include dinner, overnight lodging, breakfast and box lunch, in addition to the fishing trip for $175 per person. Fishing only is $75 per person. Bait and tackle are included; fish cleaning and packing are not. Boat charters at Harrison's are $450-$600.

The ***Lady Katie***, moored in Cambridge Creek behind Snappers Waterfront Café (☎ 410-228-1277), is a working skipjack, dredging oysters during the winter, but available for fishing charters the rest of the year. Its captain, Scott Todd, is from several generations of skipjack captains, and he knows the bay and its fishing grounds well.

Six-hour crabbing trips on board the workboat ***Miss Kim*** cost $60 per person, which includes a bushel of crabs (or $30 if you don't keep the crabs). Fishing trips are $50. The boat is docked at Dogwood Harbor, about 0.6 mile south of the drawbridge on Tilghman Island; ☎ 410-886-2176.

You can rent a motorized crab skiff from **Little Boat Rentals**, at 846 Port Street in Easton; ☎ 410-819-0881 or 800-221-1523. You can also rent an additional equipment package for $15 that includes everything you'll need: hand lines, bait, traps, net, tongs and a basket. Skiffs are $75 for a full day, $50 half-day, or $30 for two hours.

You can fish from the dock at **Long Wharf Pier** in Cambridge, without a license.

Central Eastern Shore

■ In the Air

Vintage biplane rides are available at both the Easton and the Salisbury airports. At Easton you can ride in the open cockpit of a 300 hp 1942 Stearman biplane (☎ 410-820-5959), and at Salisbury you can ride in another WWII Stearman, also with an open cockpit; ☎ 410-770-3017.

Cultural & Eco-Travel Experiences

■ Natural Areas

The **Blackwater National Wildlife Refuge**, on Route 335 in Church Creek (☎ 410-228-2677), is a vast stretch of tidal marsh and water, where you can drive, walk, kayak or cycle to see birds in profusion. It is a beautiful place in the late afternoon, when the low sun catches the white heads of a pair of eagles against the deep blue sky. Bald eagles are a common sight on the tall snags that stick out of the water. Geese and ducks float in the water, looking like decoys against the gold marsh grasses. Roads passing the refuge are studies in blue and gold, with nothing except a few stands of pine to break the vista of grass and water.

Watching eagles at Blackwater Wildlife Refuge.

Between October and March the refuge is winter home to migrating waterfowl, including tundra swans, snow geese, and at least 20 species of ducks. Blackwater has the highest nesting density of bald eagles of any place in the east, north of Florida. The park map marks the most likely places to see these, but we've always had the best luck along the raised roadway that goes between the westernmost access to Key Wallace Rd. and the end of the park road where it meets Route 335. Tall snags of dead trees here make perfect perches, close enough to dry land that you can get a good view. The refuge is open dawn to dusk all year, and visitors are almost certain to see some resident or migrating birds whenever they come. The Visitors Center is open 8-4 on weekdays and 9-5 Saturday and Sunday. A daily permit is required; $3 per car, $1 walking or cycling. Golden Eagle, Golden Age, Golden Access or Duck Stamp holders can use the refuge free.

In addition to the eagles, geese, wild turkeys and other birdlife at Blackwater, you may see **sika deer**. This Asian elk was imported to Jane's Island, near Crisfield, at the turn of the 20th century and immediately began spreading throughout the area. They are half the size of a white-tailed deer. So plentiful that they must be hunted to keep the population from outstripping the food supply, sika number between 10,000 and 15,000 in the immediate area. The deer live in the marshes, spending most of their time in the water.

It's one of those immutable rules that the places where there are the most birds also have the most things for them to eat – like mosquitoes and other biting insects. Bring insect repellent if you plan to walk in Blackwater between April and September.

While it rightly belongs under "Events," the **Easton Waterfowl Festival** is of such major importance in the local area that it has become a part of its culture. Waterfowl are central to this part of Maryland. They are watched, admired, protected, hunted (and these two are not mutually exclusive) and imitated in a variety of forms that range from folk art to fine art. All this culminates in November, when this waterfowl culture simply takes over Easton and the towns for miles around it. Parking is at the Tred Avon Shopping Center, on Marlboro Ave. off the Easton Parkway (Route 322). There you can buy your ticket and board one of the regular stream of shuttle buses that make two circuits covering all the event sites – which is every place in town where five or more people can assemble: schools, churches, public buildings, empty stores, parks, the streets themselves. ☎ 410-822-0065, http://eastonmd.org.

AUTHOR TIP

Don't even think about going to Easton during the Waterfowl Festival for general sightseeing; there are no lodgings, and restaurants and roads are jammed. But if you are even mildly interested in waterfowl art, don't miss at least a look at the granddaddy of all shows.

And since we have mentioned this side of Eastern Shore life as a cultural experience, it's only fair to treat the annual **Outdoor Show** equally. Held in **Church Creek** every February for the past 50 years or so, the Outdoor Show celebrates the more practical arts. Although you may find decoy carvers here, you are unlikely to find the moneyed art collectors that frequent the Easton Festival. Local people gather in numbers, however, to watch competitions of lumberjack skills, duck and goose calling, muskrat skinning, oyster shucking and log sawing. Here, too, is the Muskrat Cook-off, where you can sample the latest creations of local chefs using the area's abundant meat resource in everything from muskrat jambalaya to muskrat pizza. For information, contact Dorchester County Tourism, ☎ 410-228-1000; www.tourdorchester.org.

Pickering Cove Environmental Center is northwest of Easton, over 400 acres of nature reserve that includes forests and wetlands. Trails traverse the property and you can rent canoes to explore its wetlands. 11450 Audubon Lane, Easton; ☎ 410-822-4903.

Horn Point Environmental Laboratories are located just west of Cambridge in a former Dupont estate on the Choptank River. Along with hiking its trails, you can visit the aquaculture hatchery and their observation labs; ☎ 410-228-9250.

Cutts & Case Shipyard, in Oxford, ☎ 410-226-5416, builds boats in the style and character of 100 years ago, preserving and nurturing those specialized trades that create and reproduce the cabinetry, hulls, engines and embellishments that made boats works of art. If you want a boat that's beautifully built, or if yours needs repair, this is the place. Several historic buildings are part of their shipyard, including a former house boat.

■ Performing Arts

The **Avalon Theatre**, at 40 East Dover Street in Easton, was built in 1921, in the height of the art deco era, and has recently been restored to its former grandeur as a performance venue. Events include symphonic concerts, children's theater, dance, and classic films. Most events are open to the public and admission usually ranges from free to $15; ☎ 410-822-0345.

The **Easton Choral Arts Society** is made up of singers from all over the Eastern Shore, and presents two concerts annually, in April and December. These are often accompanied by a full symphony orchestra, and are held in several venues in the area, including the Avalon Theatre in Easton. You can request a schedule by writing to them at PO Box 13, Easton 21601, or ask at the Visitor Center in Easton.

Thursday evening **Concerts in the Park** are held in St. Michaels, June through August, and weekend evening concerts are held in the summer at Long Wharf Pier in Cambridge. For information, contact the St. Michaels Business Association, ☎ 410-745-2916 or 800-660-9471.

IT'S IN THE STARS: *Stargazers and amateur astronomers always comment on the night sky in southern Dorchester County. Horizons are low and no city lights reflect into the sky, so every star, planet and other celestial feature shows clearly.*

■ Crafts

The **Cambridge Arts Center**, in a restored Victorian-era hotel on High Street, shows and sells the work of local artists and craftsmen; ☎ 410-228-7782. It's open Monday-Saturday, 10-2, and the fourth weekend in September they sponsor an arts festival along tree-shaded High Street. Art, crafts, music and food highlight the weekend.

Artiste Locale, 112 North Talbot Street in St. Michaels, ☎ 410-745-6580, is a showcase for local crafts in several media, including pottery, furniture, baskets, art prints and metal arts.

Captain Dan Vaughn carves **decoys**, which you can see at his shop on Mission Rd. in Tilghman Island; ☎ 410-886-2083.

Brooks Barrel Company is one of the last slack cooperages operating in the United States, creating sturdy barrels and buckets from local pine logs. You can watch these made or buy them at the factory, which is opposite the Cambridge Airport at 5228 Buckthorne Rd., south of US 50 on the eastern edge of Cambridge; ☎ 800-398 BROOKS (2766), fax 410-221-1693.

■ Antiques

Although shops in St. Michaels and Easton tend to be – like the towns themselves – pricey, you will find some fine pieces in their upscale displays. **Canton Row Antiques**, 216-C Talbot St. in St. Michaels, has more than a dozen dealers specializing in high quality pieces. At 300 North Talbot is **Consignment Treasures**, with vintage clothing, jewelry and a miscellany of collectibles.

North Harrison Street in Easton, opposite the Tidewater Inn, has several shops, with more on South Harrison, Washington and along US 50. Easton has a **Charity Antiques Show and Sale** at the Academy of the Arts in late June; ☎ 410-820-5170.

Events

MAY: The **Maritime Arts Festival** at the Chesapeake Bay Maritime Museum in St. Michaels features decoys, ship models, maritime music, crafts, food; ☎ 410-745-2916. Held mid-month. In late

Central Eastern Shore

May, the **Antique Aircraft Fly-in** is offered at the Dorchester Heritage Museum, 1904 Horn Point Rd., Cambridge (off Route 343), and includes aviation displays of antique and classic planes; ☎ 410-228-1899.

AUGUST: In mid-month, **Chesapeake Bay Log Canoe Races** are held on the Choptank River and feature traditional river craft. Check locally for flyers posted about this event.

SEPTEMBER: An annual race of traditional boats takes place mid-month on the Miles River, and includes bugeyes, skipjacks and schooners; ☎ 410-745-2916.

OCTOBER: Tilghman Island Day features waterman exhibits, skipjack races, music, food, maritime competitions; www.tilghmanisland.com.

NOVEMBER: The **Waterfowl Festival** is held in Easton, and is the premier wildlife art show in the United States (see page 403 for description); ☎ 410-822-0065, www.eastonmd.org. The **Fall Lecture Series** at the Chesapeake Bay Maritime Museum in St. Michaels explores the area's history and archaeology. These lectures are held on consecutive Wednesday mornings; ☎ 410-745-2916. The early November, **Oysterfest** takes place at the Chesapeake Bay Maritime Museum in St. Michaels, with cooking contests, kids' activities, boat rides and music; ☎ 410-745-2916.

DECEMBER: Christmas in St. Michaels brings mid-month house tours, decorations, a parade, boat tours, food, music and church bells; ☎ 888-465-5428.

Sightseeing

■ Museums & Historic Sites

Denton

 The Caroline County Visitor Center, 16 North 2nd St., in Denton (☎ 410-479-2055), has a **Museum of Rural Life** that includes the homes of families in four different social and economic levels, dating from 1790 to 1840. The complex is open Friday and Saturday, 10-3; Sunday, noon-4.

Easton

The **Historical Society of Talbot County**, at 25 S. Washington Street in Easton (☎ 410-822-0773), maintains three homes facing its Federal-style gardens. The James Neall House is a fine example of Federal architecture, a restored 1810 brick home of a Quaker cabinetmaker. Joseph's Cottage was built in 1795 and Ending of Controversie is a reconstruction of a 17th-century house. Tours are given regularly during open hours: April-November, Tuesday through Saturday, 10-4; Sunday, 10-3. Shorter hours in the winter. The gardens are open Monday-Saturday, 10-4.

Easton's **Third Haven Friends Meeting House**, built in 1682, is the earliest dated building in Maryland, and thought to be the oldest religious building still in use in the United States. Located at 405 South Washington St. (☎ 410-822-0293), it is significant in the history of the Society of Quakers in America.

The **Oxford Museum**, at Morris and Market Streets, is a collection of local artifacts, open Friday-Sunday afternoons (2-5) from mid-April to mid-October.

St. Michaels

The **Chesapeake Bay Maritime Museum** celebrates the history and the culture of the entire bay, from its beautiful wharf setting in the center of St. Michaels; ☎ 410-745-2916, www.cbmm.org. The centerpiece of the multi-building complex is the 1879 Hooper Straight screw-pile lighthouse, which has been restored and furnished as the keeper's cottage it once was. On a beautiful summer day, it's hard to imagine what it must have been like to be hovering above the water in one of these during a hurricane.

Dozens of historic boats, exhibits on decoys and their makers, fishing since the time of the Native Americans, shipbuilding and maintenance, steamboating and the skills of the watermen – all are explored here. Hands-on experiences encourage visitors to try crabbing or to examine a tank full of shedding soft-shell crabs up close. The museum is open daily, 9-6 in the summer, 9-5 in spring and fall, and 9-4 in the winter.

This outstanding maritime museum is a tough act to follow, but if you are in town on a weekend, you can learn about the town's land-based history in the **St. Mary's Square Museum**, ☎ 410-745-9561. It's open 10-4 on weekends from May through October, or by appointment.

READY, AIM, MISS

St. Michaels is known as the "Town that Fooled the British" for its clever method of diverting the aim of cannons from British ships during the War of 1812. Residents darkened the town and hung lanterns at the tops of ships masts and in treetops, which made the British aim too high and caused most of the cannon fire to fly right over the town.

Cambridge

The **Richardson Museum**, at 401 High Street in Cambridge (☎ 410-221-1871), celebrates and records the city's rich maritime heritage. A mural shows the waterfront on the wide Choptank River as it was in the harbor's glory days, and you can spot some landmarks that are still there today, such as Crockers.

The museum is named for Jim Richardson, a larger-than-life local skipjack builder known as the dean of the boatbuilding profession. He advised James Michener on the chapter of "Chesapeake" about shipyards, and the owner in the book was patterned on Richardson. He felt very strongly about preserving and passing down the unique skills of past generations of craftsmen.

Replicated in the museum is a waterman's boat shop, and all about are the tools of his trade, from basket-like eel pots and crabnets to oyster scrapers and clam rakes. A 75-year-old muskrat skiff, which went into the marsh to check traps, is interesting, too. Model boats include a freight transport ship built there in World War II, the *Pride of Baltimore* and a ¾-inch scale of the *Nathan of Dorchester*, launched here in 1993, whose building is also recorded in photographs, from the dedication of the keel to underway in full sail.

PRESIDENTIAL BRIDGEWORK

Franklin Roosevelt's yacht once moored in Cambridge, when the President came to dedicate the first Choptank Bridge, a 1930s WPA project.

The museum portrays the role of the watermen and of shipbuilding in Cambridge, and shows the evolution of boats from the simple crabbing boat to the skipjack and bugeye. The museum is open April through October, Wednesday, Saturday and Sunday, 1-4; admission is free, but you will see the donation box – a model boat.

The waterfront streets of Cambridge are lined with nice old homes. Head toward the water on Washington Street from its intersection with High St. near the Richardson Museum, to see several, then turn left at the docks onto Water St. It is aptly named, and closed during exceptionally high tides when it is quite literally a water street. Follow the green "Scenic Drive" signs to Glenburn Avenue, where you will see the Commodore's Cottages on the corner.

Behind the pergola in its beautiful gardens is the privately owned **Brannock Museum**, another maritime collection. This one features, in addition to its models and artifacts, an extensive historical research library of old ships' logs, shipping records and more than 7,000 photographs. Travelers from Maine, or those who have sailed its windjammer fleet will be interested to find records on the *Edwin and Maud*, built in the Chesapeake as a working ship and now sailing the Maine coast as the windjammer *Victory Chimes*. The Brannock Museum (☎ 410-228-6938) is open weekends, 1-4:30, or by appointment. Admission is free, but donations are welcome.

SKIPJACKS AND BUGEYES

The skipjack was the boat of choice in this area, single-masted with a tall, powerful sail and fairly flat V-shaped bottom to navigate the shallower waters of the rivers. About a dozen of these are left today, most on Tilghman Island. The other watermen's boat of local fame is the bugeye, a two-masted boat with a rounder bottom than a skipjack.

Dorchester Heritage Museum, on Horne Point Rd., off Route 343 west of Cambridge, is housed in the airplane hangar of a former Dupont estate. Founded by a group of high school students, the museum has displays on archaeology, shellfish harvesting, farming, and vintage toys and clothing. The museum is free and open mid-April through October on weekends, 1-4:30; ☎ 410-228-5530.

The **Dorchester County Historical Society** maintains a museum complex on LaGrange Avenue, off Crusader Rd.; ☎ 410-228-7953. The **Meredith House**, begun in 1760 and "modernized" in the 1850s, is furnished in fine antiques, and features a collection of antique dolls and toys. The **Neild Museum** is dedicated to preserving the rural and agricultural heritage of the region, with agricultural and household tools, equipment from the various maritime trades, and a collection of Native American artifacts. The **Goldsborough Stable** contains a collection of early vehicles and tools of those trades that created them: blacksmith, wheelwright and harnessmaker. An **Herb Garden** re-creates a typical Colonial garden to show the horticulture and uses of herbs. The museum buildings are open for tours Thursday through Saturday, 10-4, year-round.

Sopcot Windmill, about six miles west of Cambridge on Washington Street (Route 343), is a restoration of one on this site that was destroyed by a blizzard in 1888. Dorchester was one of the last counties on the east coast where windmills were used commercially to grind corn. The windmill operates on special occasions; ☎ 410-228-7090.

The entire town of **East New Market**, established in 1660, is listed on the National Register of Historic Places, and you can get a walking tour map there describing the residences of its founders and others of the 1700s. The town is at the intersection of Routes 14 and 16, just off Route 392; ☎ 410-943-8112.

Vienna, about 30 miles east of Cambridge, was once the maritime capital of the area, with a busy harbor well protected on the Nanticoke River. So important was it that it was attacked several times during the Revolution and War of 1812. Today you can still see the breastworks that were thrown up, using ships ballast, to help protect the town. These are along the shore, near the original 1768 Customs House, built into the banking.

Where to Stay

ACCOMMODATIONS PRICE KEY	
Rates are per room, per night, double occupancy.	
$	Under $50
$$.	$50 to $100
$$$	$101 to $175
$$$$	$176 and up

■ Easton

 Gentility pervades the **Tidewater Inn**, 101 East Dover St. in the center of Easton; ☎ 410-822-1300 or 800-237-8775, www.tidewaterinn.com. Even the lobby of this large hotel seems more like the sitting room of a country estate, and in season you are likely to find a pair of hunting dogs, which are welcomed at the inn, lying in front of the fireplace. Hunters are just as well-cared-for as the dogs that bring them – breakfast begins at 4:30 am on autumn mornings. Guest rooms and suites are warm and inviting, in reproduction Colonial furnishings. Rates begin slightly above $100.

We never said Easton was a low-budget town, and you can prepare to forget any budgetary concerns at **Ashby 1663 Bed & Breakfast**, 27448 Ashby Drive; ☎ 410-822-4235 or 800-458-3622, fax 410-822-9288, www.ashby1663.com. The nightly rate for the least expensive of its 12 suites begins at well over $200. But it's no ordinary place. Most of the suites have whirlpool tubs or fireplaces (one suite combines the two in a stunning marble bath), half have their own decks or patios. Guests relax in the pool, play on lighted tennis courts, use the exercise room and paddle about in the inn's canoe or paddleboat. The mansion overlooks its half-mile of riverbank through Palladian-style windows, fine antiques furnish the spacious public rooms and formal gardens adorn the grounds. The word gracious seems inadequate.

■ St. Michael's

Four guest rooms overlook the cove or garden of the mansard-roofed **Victoriana Inn**, 205 Cherry Street; ☎ 410-745-3368. Most share baths, except for the first floor room with a four-poster canopied bed and fireplace. Rates, which include a hearty breakfast, begin just under $100. The inn is close to the Maritime Museum.

The emphasis is on your individual preferences at **Dr. Dodson House Bed & Breakfast**, 200 Cherry Street; ☎ 410-745-3691. Explore the town on wheels with one of their bicycles, enjoy evening wine and snacks in the parlor, read the Sunday paper in bed, with a steaming cup of coffee – both delivered to your room. Choose breakfast entrées from a menu and tell them when you'd like to have it served; if there is a chill in the morning air, you can eat beside the warming fireplace. The two guest rooms, one in the 1700s part of the house, the other in the 1860 part, also have working fireplaces, along with antique furnishings and vintage quilts. Weekend rates begin at $115.

If one member of a couple is a ships-and-boats man and the other a Laura Ashley fan, we have the perfect place for them to stay. The **Inn at Perry Cabin**, 308 Watkins Lane (☎ 410-745-2200 or 800-722-2949, fax 410-745-2200, www.keswick.com/keswick.html), was built by Commodore Perry's aide-de-camp, who designed one of the mansion's wings after Perry's cabin on board the *Niagara*. Now owned by the husband of the late Laura Ashley, the inn is a showcase of her designs. Rooms are lushly feminine, but not oppressively so. The sizeable inn (41 guest rooms and suites) has an outstanding dining room ($$$), swimming pool, sauna, snooker room and both boats and bicycles available for guests. Rates begin at about $200, and include afternoon tea and breakfast.

Black Walnut Point Inn, on Tilghman Island (☎ 410-886-2452, fax 410-886-2053, www.tilghmanisland.com/blackwalnut), seems to be at the end of the earth, on its own private point surrounded by the Chesapeake Bay. You can contemplate this idyllic world from a hammock with an unobstructed view of the setting sun. Rates for bed and breakfast are about $120, except for the private riverside cottage with its own kitchen.

■ Oxford

This quiet town center's only B&B (as far as we know) is **The 1876 House**, at 110 N. Morris Street (☎ 410-226-5496), in a beautifully restored home furnished in Queen Anne style. This is a good place to stay if you are arriving without a car, since the owners also operate a limousine service and can pick you up at BWI airport quite reasonably.

The dining room of **The Robert Morris Inn**, on Morris Street (☎ 410-226-5111, fax 410-226-5744), is well known, but the inn's guest rooms are just as lovingly tended, some with high four-poster beds and the clean lines of Colonial decor. Room descriptions for this early 1700s inn are quite honest, classifying them as "very tiny," (which they are). Some have a view of the Tred Avon River. Rates begin just under $100 in the main house, rising to $220 for an efficiency in the nearby Sandaway Lodge, where rooms have private porches over the water. Discounts available for dinner and lodging packages.

■ Cambridge Area

Commodore's Cottages, at 215 Glenburn Ave. (☎ 410-228-6938 or 800-228-6938), has its own private maritime museum at the far end of its lovely gardens, and small nautical antiques decorate the two comfortable guest cottages reached by the same garden paths. "All sides of both our families were in the maritime trades as shipbuilders, ship carpenters, chandlers and oystermen," owner Shirley Bannock explained, when asked about their fondness for boats. "I crawled all over these dredge boats with my father." The brick cottage sleeps four, costing $85 for two and $15 for each additional person. The larger Carriage House ($95 base price) is larger, with a separate living room, bedroom and full kitchen. Cottages are stocked with breakfast makings, and fresh baked goods are brought each evening. Minimum stay is two nights on weekends, three on holiday weekends.

The gardens are difficult to leave: a marble Aphrodite enjoys the shade of a pergola beside huge trees that include pine, crape myrtle, magnolia, walnut, pecan, a giant willow oak and three other oak varieties. Guests often choose to have breakfast among the roses overlooking the fish pond, sharing crumbs with the 25 varieties of fish that watch hopefully.

At **Loblolly Landings and Lodge**, 2142 Liners Rd., south of Church Creek (☎ 410-397-3033), Marlene and Len Slavin have created a combination B&B and retreat for people who enjoy hunting and fishing. They are adding comfortable log cabins to the cozy king-bedded rooms in the main house. Downstairs a cathedral-ceilinged room welcomes guests with a blazing fireplace set in a giant fieldstone wall. Rooms are newly decorated in a tasteful blend of new and antique furnishings. Breakfast is designed to carry outdoors enthusiasts through the day; the crab quiche is delectable.

AUTHOR TIP

If you love wild blackberries, as we do, come to Loblolly in July to pick your fill. Marlene will gladly freeze them for you. At any time of year, you can enjoy them there in the homemade jams served at breakfast.

Set in miles of tidewater wildlands, the property also offers an archery course of 17 stations with moving targets. Be sure to get directions, since it is some distance from the town of Church Creek shown on the map, closer to the Blackwater refuge.

Sarke Plantation sits on the Choptank River, at 6033 Todd Point Rd., off Route 343 (Washington Street) about 10 miles west of Cambridge; ☎ 410-228-7020 or 800-814-7020. Its wide wrap-around porch invites lolling; prices are more than reasonable, at $50-$90, singles from $40. A continental breakfast is included.

Tideland Park, on Taylor's Island (☎ 410-397-3473 or 800-673-9052), has waterfront log cabins for rent by the night (about $70) or week ($350) on a tidal creek. You can rent boats or bicycles there to explore by land or sea.

■ Camping

Martinak State Park, south of Denton on Deep Shore Rd., off Route 404 (☎ 301-479-1619), has 60 campsites on the wooded shore of the Choptank River, with a boat pier and ramp and an amphitheater with weekend evening campfire programs.

Taylors Island Family Campground, on Bayshore Rd., Taylors Island (☎ 410-397-3275, fax 410-221-8191), is right on the bay, with boat ramp and slips, even its own bait and tackle shop. Rates are $12 a day and $65 a week for RVs, $9 a day for tents.

Tideland Park, on Taylors Island (☎ 410-397-3473 or 800-673-9052), offers campsites, primarily designed for RVs, on a tidal creek. You can rent boats or bicycles there, too.

Where to Eat

DINING PRICE KEY
The price key indicates the cost of *most* dinner entrées on a restaurant's regular and daily special menu.
$. . . . . Most under $10
$$. $10 to $20
$$$. Over $30

■ Easton

The dining room at the **Tidewater Inn**, at 101 East Dover Street in the center of town (☎ 410-822-1300 or 800-237-8775), is a legend, not without good reason. It has a warm and inviting atmosphere in which to enjoy outstanding shore specialties, and is on our short-list of favorite places to order crab cakes. Most entrées are over $15. On weekends they serve a bountiful buffet brunch.

Restaurant Columbia, at 28 South Washington Street in Easton (☎ 410-770-5172), serves elegant dishes, such as quail stuffed with wild rice and pecans, in a stylish setting. $$$

For breakfast, stop at the **Hangar Café** at the Easton Airport (☎ 410-820-6631), a diner with a view of planes landing and taking off. It is open daily, 6 am to 3 pm. Breakfast enough to keep you running all day is under $3. And if you're going for a plane ride in the World War II-era biplane, you get a 10% discount.

■ Oxford

Le Zinc, at 101 Mill Street (☎ 410-226-5776), is a stylish and casual small restaurant with a Euro feel and menu. The ever-changing menu may offer peppered mackerel with fresh horseradish cream, oysters with scallion-lime tartar sauce, grilled tuna poivre with citrus butter, usually about six entrées each day, priced at $10 to $20. Open Tuesday through Saturday from 6 pm; Wednesday and Thursday are pasta nights, with several innovative pasta entrées on the menu.

The Robert Morris Inn, on Morris Street (☎ 410-226-5111, fax 410-226-5744), serves outstanding crab cakes, as anyone on the Eastern Shore will tell you. But they also serve a variety of other dishes, depending heavily, but not wholly on local seafood. The dining room is gracious, with murals on the walls. From April through November, dinner is served daily, 6-9; lunch, noon-3. Winter hours vary. $$-$$$.

For breakfast, we meet local friends over the red-checked tablecloths at **Chatterbox**, on Mill Street, right next to Le Zinc. It's run by one of the theater directors of the Oxford Community Center, so it's a good place to get the skinny on local theatrical events.

Open only April through October is the **Pier Street**, located on West Pier Street; ☎ 410-745-3737. Picnic tables on the deck overlook the water, and the mounds of steamed crabs and the rockfish are fresh from the Tred Avon River. Sail right to the door and use one of their guest slips while you eat lunch or dinner.

The place to provision for picnics or a day's bicycling is the **Oxford Market and Deli**, at 203 South Morris Street. Assemble coldcuts to accompany fresh-baked breads, or choose one of their made-to-order subs. Eat the hand-dipped ice cream on the spot.

■ St. Michaels & Tilghman Island

Suddenly Last Summer, at 106 North Talbot Street (☎ 410-745-5882), is very small (fewer than a dozen tables) with a cozy, intimate air and excellent food. A local guitar player provides music on Friday and Saturday evenings; Sunday brunch is a specialty. A nice antidote to the steady round of traditional Eastern Shore seafood treatments, Suddenly brings a west-coast/European touch to St. Michaels, along with a well-chosen wine list. Expect to find dishes such as rabbit or breast of duck with peppercorns.

Harrison's, on Route 33 on Tilghman Island (☎ 410-886-2123), is the fish center of the island – and perhaps the bay itself, with the largest fishing fleet, sport fishing charters and a restaurant that has become a local (and by local we mean all over the bay) institution. The food isn't fancy, and accompanying dishes are served family-style, but the fish is wonderfully fresh. The traditional Eastern Shore dinner combines Maryland fried chicken with crab cakes at about $20, and they offer several other combination dinners – all under $20. And, of course, you can set to a tray of steamed crabs with a mallet on the deck. You can often find excursion boats coming here for dinner from Baltimore and as far away as Point Lookout in Southern Maryland.

■ Cambridge Area

Snappers Waterfront Café (112 Commerce St., ☎ 410-228-0112) is on the wharf, and you can eat inside or outside overlooking the deck of the *Lady Katie* while you enjoy their Mexican and Cajun-influenced dishes. Hours are Monday through Saturday, 11 am-10 pm; Sunday, 11-9.

McGuigan's Pub, at 411 Muse Street (☎ 410-228-7110), serves Scottish and traditional English pub food in a pub-like atmosphere.

Portside Seafood Restaurant, at the foot of Creek Bridge, 201 Trenton Street (☎ 410-228-9007), has a deck that is enclosed by curtains to extend its season, and boat slips for those who arrive by sea. It serves local seafood at lunch and dinner, Tuesday-Sunday.

Locally popular **Old Salty's**, on Hooper Island, south of the Blackwater refuge (☎ 410-397-3752), serves down-home dishes at low prices that range from a veal patty for $6 to a seafood platter at $12. Lunch specials include chicken-and-dumplings on Monday and ham with cabbage on Saturday. Closed Tuesday.

For a quick lunch, stop at the **Taylors Island Store**, on the right as you cross the bridge. The restaurant in the back of this old country store serves crab cakes.

Central Eastern Shore

Lower Eastern Shore

1. Fenwick Island State Park
2. Assawoman Wildlife Area
3. WWII watch tower
4. Discoveries From The Sea Museum
5. Cape Henlopen State Park
6. Ocean City Lifesaving Station Museum
7. Merry Sherwood Plantation; Globe Theatre; Taylor House Museum
8. Assateague Island Visitors Center
9. Verrazano Bridge
10. Nassawango Iron Furnace; Furnace Town Historic Site
11. Pocomoke State Forest
12. Julia A. Purnell Museum; Mt. Zion One-Room School
13. Shad Landing State Park
14. Nassawango Creek Cypress Swamp Preserve
15. Salisbury Zoo; Ward Museum of Wildfowl Art; Salisbury Pewter; Newtown; Poplar Hill Mansion
16. Pemberton Historic Park
17. Teackle Museum
18. Deal Island Wildlife Management Area
19. Janes Island State Park
20. Gov. J. Miller Tawes Historical Museum; Marion Station Railroad Museum

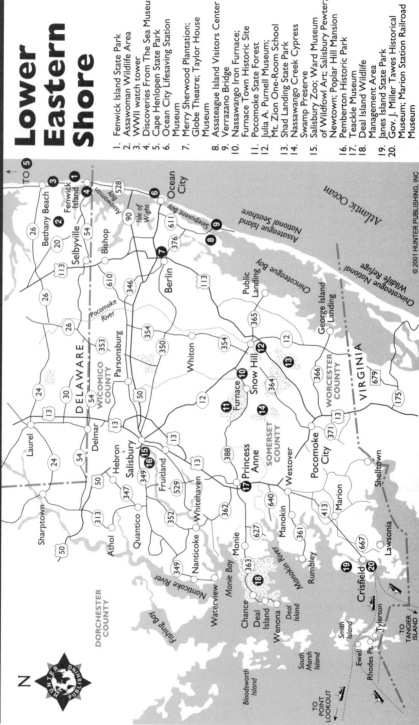

© 2001 HUNTER PUBLISHING, INC.

Lower Eastern Shore

Maryland's three lower counties are deep into watermen's country, where shell-fish rule. The landscapes are low and beautiful, stretching from the sandy sweep of the narrow barrier islands, across an inland cut with meandering creeks and mysterious cypress swamps to the irregular creek-cut and island-studded Chesapeake Bay shore.

If you look at a map, you will see both these shores colored almost solid green, showing how much of their coastline and its neighboring wetlands is protected by parks and public lands.

Two contrasting attractions lie side by side on the eastern coast: highly developed Ocean City and the wild dunes and beaches of Assateague Island. And not far from the sunswept barrier island are the deeply shaded watery recesses of the Nassawango cypress swamps. Scattered among these natural riches are small historic towns.

Geography & History

The area is bounded on the west by the Chesapeake Bay and on the east by the Atlantic Ocean. The entire coastline is protected by the long low barrier island of **Assateague**, known best for its wild horses. During a hurricane in 1933, the ocean cut an inlet between Ocean City and Assateague. Prior to that the barrier island was a solid land mass from Indian River Bay, north of Bethany Beach in Delaware, to Virginia.

Smith and **Tangier islands** lie offshore, in the Chesapeake and, although Tangier is part of Virginia, its mail and ferry connections are from Crisfield, in Maryland.

© 2001 HUNTER PUBLISHING, INC

DID YOU KNOW?

The Mason-Dixon Line, the dividing boundary between slave and free states before the Civil War, doesn't always run east-to-west. A long section of it runs due south – or we should more accurately say due north, since its first stone was laid at the southwest corner of Delaware, where it meets Wicomico County north of Salisbury.

Native American relics have been unearthed showing habitation here from 5,000 years ago, and these people were still living here when Captain John Smith, on an excursion out of Jamestown, described the shore and Tangier Island in 1608. It wasn't long before the area was inhabited by small groups of English settlers: both Snow Hill and Pocomoke City trace origins to the middle of the 17th century.

Pocomoke City became a center for shipyards in the 19th and early 20th centuries, at first building ocean-going schooners and later steamships. Snow Hill, which still has several pre-Revolutionary buildings, was an active trading port, with schooners plying the river until the steamboats replaced them. The products of the iron furnace on Nassawango Creek were brought by canal to the river, where they were transported by boat until trains, in turn, replaced these.

Crisfield was already a sailing port at the end of the 17th century, prospering on its fishing industry in virtual isolation from the mainland. When the railroad extended to its docks in 1867, Crisfield became a boom town, its oysters unloaded and shipped right from the docks. By 1910 it had the largest registry of sailing vessels of any port in the nation.

Princess Anne, a latecomer founded in 1733, has the appearance of an 18th-century town, expanded in the 19th century with gracious homes in Federal to Victorian styles.

Getting Here & Getting Around

 To reach this part of the Eastern Shore from Baltimore and Annapolis, follow **US 50** across the Bay Bridge and south through Talbot County to Cambridge. There it makes a sudden eastward turn and heads into Wicomico County, ending in Ocean City. Driving distance from Annapolis to Salisbury is about 90 miles. **US 13** leads from Salisbury to the southern counties, eventually crossing into Virginia, which borders this region to the south. **US 113** connects Ocean City and Berlin to the lower counties, meeting US 13 before entering Virginia.

Ocean City is a long, narrow strip of sand, a barrier island barely joined to Delaware at its northern point. **Route 528** becomes the **Coastal Highway** at 25th Street, in the northern part of Ocean City, eight lanes of traffic leading past high-rise hotels, motels, restaurants and the usual string of beach town amusements. By 90th St., a solid wall of these rise ahead on the ocean side, with strip malls on the bay side. By the 140s, these thin out a little, with a few empty lots and trees beginning to show as you approach the Delaware line and Fenwick Island.

To leave this barrier island via **Route 20/54** on Fenwick Island, look for the blue and white "Evacuation Route" signs. These mark roads that lead to the mainland; others dead-end at the bay.

AUTHOR TIP *Public parking in Ocean City is at the inlet, south from the terminal point of US 50. A public tram ($2) circles the main beach and business areas. RV parking is available at the 100th St. lot and at Boardwalk Beach Park at Wicomico St. and Philadelphia Ave.*

Two **ferries** cross the wide Wicomico River west of Salisbury, saving a lot of driving. One is between **Whitehaven** and **Mount Vernon**, connecting routes 352 and 362, the other closer to Salisbury at the town of Upper Ferry. These are free and continuous until late evening. Note that every few months, at the times of the highest tides, the ferry closes for an hour.

GEORGE WASHINGTON'S
GRANDMOTHER SLEPT HERE

George Washington's grandmother lived in Whitehaven, and her second husband started the ferry there.

Information Sources

Wicomico County Visitors Center is a modern building where local people who really know their area are always happy to tell you about it. Telephones have direct lines to area lodgings. You are welcome to use their picnic area (tables on the big porch have umbrellas) and enjoy the nature trails around the pond. The center, which is handicapped-accessible, is at 8480 Ocean Highway (US 13). It's open daily, 8-6 in the summer, 8:30-5 in the winter, except for major holidays. ☎ 410-548-4914 or 800-332-8687.

KID-FRIENDLY *Be sure to pick up the free coloring book and crayons for children, who will enjoy the playground at the Visitors Center in Salisbury. You'll also find diaper-changing facilities in their men's and women's restrooms.*

Ocean City Visitors Information Center is just south of the Convention Center, on Coastal Highway (Route 528) at 40th St. Winter hours are Monday through Friday, 8:30 am until 5 pm; Saturday, 9 am to 5 pm; and Sunday, 9:30 to 5 pm. The center often stays open later in the summer.

Assateague Island National Seashore Visitors Center, 7206 National Seashore Lane (Route 611), Berlin, can be reached from US 50 just before entering Ocean City, or from Berlin, via Route 376 (☎ 410-641-1441). Along with maps and other free information about the park, they have a good selection of books and publications on the nature and wildlife of the area, as well as exhibits, a hands-on aquarium and a video about the park. The center is open daily, 9 am-5 pm.

Worcester County Tourism, 105 Pearl St., Snow Hill 21863; ☎ 410-623-3617 or 800-852-0335.

Crisfield Visitors Center, Somers Cove Marina, Crisfield 21817 (☎ 410-968-2501) is open weekdays, 9-4:30, all year; from May through October it's open on weekends as well, 9-3.

Adventures

■ Parks

 It's very confusing, but **Assateague National Seashore** is a federally managed park with **Assateague Island State Park** in its midst. To fish or hunt in the state park you need only the Maryland license. On the southern part of the barrier island (called Assateague for its entire length) is **Chincoteague National Wildlife Refuge**, which is in Virginia and cannot be entered from the northern park except on foot along a 10-mile wild beach. Each state has its own visitors center for the barrier island. The one at Assateague, Maryland, is open from 9 to 5. You will need two passes, since each facility has a separate admission fee, but the Golden Eagle Pass is good at either.

WATCHABLE WILDLIFE

WHERE TO SEE MISTY*: For many visitors, the reason for going to Assateague is to catch sight of the wild horses. This is usually not too difficult; we have never been to the Maryland section (where they can roam freely) without seeing at least two or three groups of them. Usually, simply driving slowly along the park roads will turn up several. But remember that you should not stop on the road or shoulders to watch them; you must stop or park only in designated areas. On humid summer days, you are more likely to see the horses on the beach, where biting insects are fewer. They aren't stupid.*

Fenwick Island State Park, over the line into Delaware, north of Ocean City, charges $2.50 per vehicle for Delaware cars, $5 for out-of-state. The park is a beach only, with bathhouses. On the bay side are places offering lessons in windsurfing and kayaking. In a pretty stretch of scrubby trees and sea grasses are private homes and intermittent stretches of state park with beach access.

Pemberton Historic Park, off Route 349 just west of Salisbury (☎ 410-548-4870), occupies a variety of Eastern Shore ecosystems along the Wicomico River. Marsh, swamp, forest and meadow environments include both freshwater and saltwater ecosystems.

*An easy way to remember the difference between a **marsh** and a **swamp** is suggested in the Blue Trail Guide prepared by the Boy Scouts for Pemberton Historic Park: A swamp has trees, a marsh does not.*

Pocomoke State Forest and **Pocomoke River State Park**, with headquarters at 3461 Worcester Highway in Snow Hill (☎ 410-632-2566), lie in several parcels along and near the Pocomoke River. The park protects several habitats, including cypress swamps, marshlands and forests. **Shad Landing**, part of the state park, is on US 113, south of Snow Hill. It offers swimming, fishing, camping, hiking and boat rentals. Entrance to all parts of the park is free (as we write).

Janes Island State Park, near Crisfield (☎ 410-968-1565), really is an island, accessible only by water. You can rent boats to get there quite easily. Canoe trails lead through the tidal and intertidal marshes and walking trails explore the mature forests of loblolly pine. A mainland portion of the park has its offices, campground, and marina. To reach the park, head south toward Crisfield on Route 413 and turn west (right) just past the Highway Holiness Church.

AUTHOR TIP

OF INTEREST TO GOLFERS: *Within an hour of Salisbury and Ocean City are about 30 golf courses, many open to the public. The Whitehaven Yacht and Country Club in Whitehaven is open to the public by reservation, and their restaurant is open to those playing golf.*

■ On Foot

Hiking

Assateague has three short (half a mile each) nature trails, each of which gives a good view of a particular park ecosystem. **Life of the Dunes** trail is a good one to take early in the morning, when you might see fresh tracks from the nocturnal wildlife. In the daytime this desert-like environment doesn't encourage its residents to wander around. **Life of the Forest** trail passes through a stand of tall loblolly pines and thick tangled woods made impenetrable by greenbriar. It's just as well, since the woods are filled with ticks and poison ivy, neither of which you really want to encounter. In each of these environments it's wise to stay on the trail, for your own sake as well as for the fragile environment. **Life of the Marsh** explores the rim between forest and water, a habitat rich in songbirds, wading shorebirds and birds of prey.

IT'S AN ILL WIND... *The terrible northeaster in March of 1962 was the biggest factor in saving the barrier island of Assateague from the fate of its northern counterpart, which is now Ocean City. Work had already begun on reconstructing the land to drain it and control mosquito habitat so that resort developments could be built. Severe damage caused by the storm made its promoters re-think the wisdom of building here, giving conservationists the chance to push for its inclusion in the national park system.*

Pemberton Historic Park, off Route 349 just west of Salisbury (☎ 410-548-4870), has 4½ miles of walking trails through a variety of Eastern Shore ecosystems, along the Wicomico River. Six loops vary in length from one-third to nearly 1½ miles, with the outstanding historical sites labeled on the free park trail map. Observation platforms provide views of the marsh and river.

WATCHABLE WILDLIFE

The riverside meadows, marshes and woods of Pemberton Historic Park are filled with more than 150 species of nesting birds. The variety of habitats is unusual here, the only place on the eastern shore where tidal and freshwater wetlands, freshwater ponds, a river island, upland pine groves, hardwood forests and meadows exist so close together. Birds favoring each of these environments – including great horned, barn and screech owls and bald eagles – find a home here. So do deer and fox, whose dens can be found in the fields and meadows. You can get a free bird checklist at the park.

The trails lead through a holly forest and along a boardwalk through a tidal marsh. Those with a taste for wild raspberries and blackberries will find them beside the road near the beginning of the **Blue Trail**. This 1.3-mile trail has a very good nature guide prepared as an Eagle Scout project, which points out habitats and individual plants, trees and wildlife evidence as well as the history of the land. Guided hikes are held occasionally, focusing on a seasonal or other nature theme, most costing $2 or $5 for an entire family.

Most of the trails in Pemberton Historic Park are wheelchair-accessible. Trails are well mapped on a signboard near the Environmental Education Center.

Pocomoke State Forest and **Pocomoke River State Park** (☎ 410-632-2566) preserve a remarkable stand of loblolly pines and the cypress swamps that border the Pocomoke River. Trails lead through both these environments, and a Trail of Change in the Shad Landing area, off Route 113, tells about the nature and history of the area, which was once the hiding place of escaping slaves.

Pocomoke City has a four-mile nature and exercise trail in **Cypress Park** (☎ 410-957-1333), which circles a pond and has a boardwalk. It also has a 1½-mile loop for a shorter walk.

The Nature Conservancy's **Nassawango Creek Cypress Swamp Preserve** has a mile-long Nature Trail that loops through the cypress forest

with benches and boardwalks. The trailhead is accessed through the Furnace Town Historic Site, so you must pay admission to reach the trail (unless you are a Nature Conservancy member), but the fee is low and the historic village is as interesting as the nature trail. Also, a tour of the village will explain the old canal and several other things you'll see along the trail. When Furnace Town is closed, from November through March, you can walk right through it to the trail head.

Walking Tours

Salisbury's urban greenway connects the Ward Museum, the Riverwalk and the free Salisbury Zoo, an attractive wide path for walkers and cyclists. For a short leg-stretch, follow the one-third-mile nature

Iron furnace at Furnace Town in Snow Hill.

trail behind the Tourist Information Center in Leonard's Mill Park. A walking tour map with descriptions of the historic Newtown neighborhood is published by the Newtown Association; ☎ 410-543-2111. See *Historic Sites*, below.

The gracious streets of **Princess Anne** are lined with fine homes dating back three centuries, many with fine gardens which you can enjoy on a self-guided walking tour. A handy map with descriptions of the many historic buildings is free from the tourist office on US 13; ☎ 800-521-9189.

■ On Wheels

The entire Eastern Shore is prime cycling country, but these lower counties offer the best, we think. Being more out of the way, traffic on country roads is lighter, and the miles of open country provide peaceful and scenic routes. Hills are almost unknown – the slight rise in the town of **Snow Hill** is so remarkable that they named the town for it.

Landscapes are fields of green and golden farmland bordered by stands of trees and interspersed with low forest. Tidal estuaries and meandering creeks are either lined by waves of marsh grass or by cypress forests. Even in the winter, landscapes are colored with green and gold. **Salisbury** is a center for cycling, with an active bicycle club at Salisbury State University. Wicomico County Tourism publishes a handy map with routes outlined and briefly described; ☎ 410-548-4914 or 800-332-8687.

RECOMMENDED READING: *Serious cyclists will want to purchase the thick packet of cycling maps published by the **League of American Bicyclists**, 190 Ostend St., Suite 120, Baltimore 21230; ☎ 410-539-3399. Each route is shown on a single page which also shows and names every street and road along the way and suggests the best direction of travel. On the back of each is a description with mileages and notes on how to identify unmarked streets and roads. This is one of the best sets of cycling maps we have encountered, and we were very grateful to have it on several occasions. You might also be able to get copies at the Tourist Information Center at 8480 Ocean Highway (US 13) in Salisbury; ☎ 410-548-4914 or 800-332-8687.*

Assateague Island has three miles of bike paths along Bayberry Drive and the Oceanside campground. A new bicycle bridge parallels the access bridge to the park, solving a real safety hazard that used to plague both cyclists and pedestrians. Bikes can be rented at the end of Bayside Drive, near the picnic area. Bike racks are provided at the entrance to each of the nature trails. No ATVs or dune buggies are allowed on the beaches or trails except those designated an ORV zone. Even then, a limit on the number in the park at any time is strictly enforced.

Lower Eastern Shore

The three-mile boardwalk at **Ocean City** is off limits for bicycles except during limited hours in the summer, but in the off seasons it offers a nice ride along the beach.

BIKE RENTALS

Bike rentals are in several Ocean City locations, the handiest being **Bike World**'s three sites: their shop at 6 Caroline St., and beside the boardwalk at 15th St. and 17th St. They are open 6 am to 4 pm; ☎ 410-289-2587. Farther north is **Continental Cycle**, on the Coastal Highway at 73rd St.; ☎ 410-524-1313.

KID-FRIENDLY

A public playground is on the bayside of Ocean City, at the end of 4th St. A public skate-board ramp is at the same end of 3rd St.

Pemberton Historic Park, off Route 349 just west of Salisbury (☎ 410-548-4870), sponsors bike tours of lengths ranging from eight to 65 miles. On the first weekend of October, Salisbury is headquarters for the **Seagull Century**, one of the nation's biggest bicycle races. Racers can choose between the 100-mile or the 100-kilometer events. People come from all over the country for this event, and hotel rooms are booked far in advance. Another smaller race takes place in late May.

Salisbury's urban greenway provides bicycle and walking paths that connect the Ward Museum, the Riverwalk and the free Salisbury Zoo (but you must walk your bike through this part). A pleasant ride west from Salisbury passes Pemberton Historic Park, crosses the river on a ferry at Upper Ferry and returns to Salisbury along the southern bank.

Viewtrail 100 is a well-marked 100-mile cycling route from Berlin past Furnace Town and along country roads that wind through Worcester County. Well marked by signs, the route is also shown on a free map that describes sites along the way. **Pocomoke River Canoe Company**, on the bridge at 312 North Washington Street in Snow Hill (☎ 410-632-3971), rents bicycles in this area.

The entirety of **Tangier Island** is flat and has only three miles of roadway, few cars, and a 15-mph speed limit, all of which make it a great place to bicycle. The main street of its only town is so narrow that two cars cannot pass; you can take your bicycle on the ferry with you.

Waterloo Country Inn, at 28822 Mount Vernon Rd (☎ 410-651-0883, fax 410-651-0883), has four bicycles for guests to use on the level country roads that border the Wicomico River. The nearby car ferry makes it easy to cross to Whitehaven and many more miles of good cycling.

INN-TO-INN BIKE TOURS

Several area inns and Pocomoke River Canoe have combined to offer cycling packages, providing route maps, baggage transfers, shuttle and bike rentals for an inn-to-inn tour. For information, contact **River House Inn**, at 201 East Market St. (☎ 410-632-2722) in Snow Hill, **Waterloo Country Inn** at 28822 Mount Vernon Rd. in Princess Anne (☎ 410-651-0883, fax 410-651-0883), or check their Web site, www.inntours.com/top.asp.

■ On Water

We make no excuses for the fact that this area has a longer canoeing and kayaking section than any other in the book. That's because we spend a lot of time paddling here. *That's* because we love cypress swamps and the area has enough of them to keep us busy. Assateague, Janes Island, the upper Nanticoke and the bays behind the barrier islands add plenty of other habitats for variety.

If you look at a map, note the wide Wicomico River running from Salisbury to the Chesapeake Bay. You may wonder why you see no upper reaches or tributaries entering town to feed it. The answer is simple: there aren't any. Its headwaters are in the town itself, and the ponds and streams create the habitat for about 50 species of waterfowl that hang around the zoo looking for handouts. Locals and tourists enjoy these waters, too, in paddleboats and by fishing in them, especially for bass.

Swimming

Choose your style from busy, crowded and lively **Ocean City**, whose beautiful white sand beach is backed by a boardwalk, or **Assateague Island**'s state park beach, a long strip of white sand backed by nothing but dunes, open April through October. No ATVs or dune buggies are allowed on Assateague's beaches.

FOR SURFERS: *Ocean City is a prime surfing beach, used year-round. To find out where the surf is best, ask at Cloud Break Surf Shop, between 58th and 59th streets on the bay side of Coastal Highway.*

Canoeing & Kayaking

Perhaps the most pristine paddling waters in the northern part of this area is the **Nanticoke River** and its tributaries, whose headwaters are above Seaford, Delaware. The river forms the boundary between Wicomico and Dorchester counties, west of Salisbury. Ask at **Survival Products** (see below) in Salisbury for topographical maps to help you locate some of the more obscure tributary creeks. Broad Creek is the easiest to find if you are not familiar with the area, and is best reached from a park downstream from Laurel, Delaware, off Route 492, which is off Route 24. Take out at the public landing on the left bank, where Route 496 ends. Broad Creek flows through the Nanticoke Wildlife area.

The upper Nanticoke itself is best reached from the public boat ramp in Seaford, at the end of Porter Street, which runs from Route 536 (Harrington St.) You can take out at the Route 313 bridge in Sharptown, in Maryland, the first bridge you will see. About halfway is the ferry across the river in Woodland. This swamp-bordered tidal river is nearly wild in this section, and without obstructions.

RECOMMENDED READING: *Paddlers should look for a copy of* **Maryland and Delaware Canoe Trails**, *by Edward Gertler. The information is very detailed, right down to location of fences and barking dogs. You can buy it at area bookstores or write the publisher, Seneca Press, 530 Ashford Rd., Silver Spring, MD 20916.*

CANOE & KAYAK RENTALS & OUTFITTERS

Survival Products, at 1116 North Salisbury Blvd. (US 13 Business Route), Salisbury, ☎ 410-543-1244 or 543-1493, gives kayak and canoe lessons on the pond behind the Ward Museum in Salisbury, and rents both craft by the day (24 hours). Canoes are $40 a day, kayaks $35, which includes tie-down kits for your car. They have more than 400 boats in stock, including sailboats. If you are buying a kayak and are not sure about the attributes of each, they will give in-water demonstrations, which includes a lesson. In April, factory representatives assemble on the shore behind the Ward Museum with hundreds of demonstration craft.

Survival Products is this northern area's clearing house for all things of interest to paddlers – events, tours, lessons, races and shows. They can put you in touch with outfitters who will take you on guided overnight and weekend trips or provide shuttles. They are not outfitters themselves, and don't plan to be, but they work with the best and are very generous with their time and expertise. If you paddle, stop here before you try the local waters, since they have up-to-date information on the condition of waterways, as well as maps.

Pocomoke River Canoe Company, on the bridge at 312 North Washington St. in Snow Hill (☎ 410-632-3971), rents kayaks for about $5 an hour or $30 a day and canoes $7.50 an hour or $35 a day. An entire weekend rental is $40 for kayaks or $50 for canoes. Guided trips are $35, or from Whilton Crossing to Snow Hill, $50. Two-day trips are $75. Their skilled instructors also give lessons in canoe and kayak handling. All trips include gear and shuttle; they are open daily April through November.

Ocean City Kayak, Shantytown Village (☎ 410-213-2818), offers two daily trips through the waters of a nature preserve in open-top kayaks or one ocean surfing trip daily at Assateague. Each includes instruction, equipment and a two-hour guided tour, at about $40 for adults, $25 for children.

Dividing Creek Canoe Rentals, on Dividing Creek Rd. (☎ 410-957-0858), offers a number of guided trips along the Pocomoke and through the cypress swamps. You can also rent canoes at Shad Landing, 3461 Worcester Highway, Snow Hill; ☎ 410-632-2460.

You can rent kayaks from **Tangier Sound Outfitters**, 27582 Farm Market Rd., in Hopeville, about three miles north of Crisfield on Route 413; ☎ 410-968-1803. In addition to rentals, they give four-hour lesson-and-tour packages that are designed for people who have never paddled before. They also lead daily sunset paddles along the unique Janes Island Water Trail, sponsored by the state park.

Amphibious Horizons, based at Quiet Waters Park in Annapolis (☎ 410-267-8742 or 888-I-LUV-SUN, www.amphibioushorizons.com), offers kayaking trips in the waters of **Smith Island**, exploring the sloughs that indent the archipelago's shores. Lodging is at a B&B in Tylerton, where participants can learn about the unique culture of this insular community. Three-day trips are on holiday weekends: Memorial Day, July 4 and Labor Day, and cost about $400.

A boat launch on the pond at the Visitor's Center on US 13 north of Salisbury gives access to the river, but the **Wicomico** is not a very good place for paddlers. It is wide, straight, and windswept, and busy with powerboat and commercial traffic. The area to the north has a choice of much better places to paddle in peace and quiet through more natural settings.

DID YOU KNOW?

Salisbury is the second largest port on Maryland, with much of its oil and other supplies arriving by boat.

On the mainland north of Route 90 and east of US 113 is Martins Neck Rd., with boat ramps giving access to **Martin's Creek**. From here, you can begin to see the highrises of Ocean City across the bay, but nearer at hand is low woods and grassy marshes, and a causeway to the Isle of Wight National Wildlife Refuge.

Assateague has several good places to paddle along the western shore, in Chincoteague Bay. At Pope Bay are campsites that can only be reached by canoe or kayak or by backpacking in overland. The Assateague National Seashore and Assateague State Park nature programs include canoe trips, for which you must reserve at the park headquarters; ☎ 410-641-2120. Canoes may be rented in the park, at the Bayside picnic area, past the campground. **Rainy Day**, on Race Track Rd. in Berlin (☎ 410-641-5029), also rents canoes, open 7-4 daily.

The **Pocomoke River** and its tributaries wander winding routes through wild and watery cypress swamps, beautiful at any time of year. A canoe put-in on Porters Crossing Rd., off Route 354 north of Snow Hill, gives a six-mile trip

Canoeing in Pocomoke River Cypress Swamp.

down the Pocomoke River, a narrow meandering stream that draws great loops through cypress-lined banks, with only one bungalow visible on the entire route.

A longer trip along the Pocomoke is from Whiton Crossing, also close to Route 354, to **Snow Hill**. Birdlife is abundant, and the trip is especially beautiful in the fall, when cypresses turn flame-orange. The take-out for either is below the bridge, at the park on the left bank in Snow Hill. **Pocomoke River Canoe** will provide canoes and take you to either of these put-ins by van; in this case, the trip ends at their dock, by the bridge in Snow Hill – a few yards downstream from the River House Inn, which also has a boat landing for its guests.

For a longer trip, you can continue down the **Pocomoke**, still fairly narrow, to take out at Shad Landing State Park or go all the way to Pocomoke City, where canoe launch sites are all along the riverside nature trail and boat ramps at Laurel St. and at the end of Winter Quarters Drive. The Pocomoke in its lower reaches is much less attractive, and even above Pocomoke City you may meet powerboats.

A put-in on Red House Rd., just south of Old Furnace Rd., gives a shorter trip on **Nassawango Creek**, which opens out quickly to a wide creek before entering the main river about three miles later. Water levels can be too low for this trip during the lowest tides. Take out at the bridge on Nassawango Rd. or continue down the Pocomoke to Shad Landing State Park.

In **Janes Island State Park**, three marked trails for paddlers take you through the wetlands that surround the island, a habitat rich in bird life. Tangier Sound Outfitters (see page 429) leads daily sunset paddles along the unique Janes Island Water Trail, sponsored by the state park.

Waterloo Country Inn at 28822 Mount Vernon Rd. (☎ 410-651-0883, fax 410-651-0883) has three canoes for guests, and you can put in just across the road for a beautiful paddle along the tidal creek that winds through marsh grass banks and under giant trees. Muskrat lodges loom out of the grass, which is also home to a variety of birds.

INN-TO-INN CANOE TOURS

Several area inns and Pocomoke River Canoe have combined to create paddling packages, providing canoes, route maps, baggage transfers and canoe shuttles for an inn-to-inn tour. Imagine the fun of arriving at River House Inn's private landing on the Pocomoke River, with a welcoming room and dinner across the street in the Snow Hill Inn awaiting you. For information, contact **River House Inn** at 201 East Market St. (☎ 410-632-2722) in Snow Hill, **Waterloo Country Inn** in Princess Anne at 28822 Mount Vernon Rd. (☎ 410-651-0883, fax 410-651-0883) or check their Web site, www.inntours.com/top.asp. Prices for a five-day canoe adventure, with lodging in fine country inns, all meals and transportation is about $1,200 for two people. A three-day trip is about $600 for two.

Boat Tours & Ferries

A number of boats make tours from Ocean City, some of them operating in the off seasons as well as summer. *OC Princess*, for example, follows the whales and dolphins as they swim along the coast in the late fall; ☎ 410-213-0926 or 800-322-3065. **Discovery Nature Cruises** (☎ 410-289-2896) carries a naturalist on board its 90-minute trips May-September, which land on Assateague Island for some beachcombing and nature investigations. Five trips daily in the summer, three spring and fall leave from the pier at First Street; $12.50 adults, $10 seniors, $8 ages seven-12. *Assateague Explorer* (☎ 410-289-5887) runs several 90-minute cruises daily, mid-April-mid-October, also landing on Assateague Island. **Shantytown Nature Cruises** leave from the fishing center on Shantytown Rd. (☎ 410-213-0926) to look for dolphins, whales, sea turtles and sea birds.

The 38-foot sailing packet *Therapy* makes three-hour cruises from the Fishing Center, off Shantytown Rd., departing at 9, 1 and 5:30 daily for about $40 per person; ☎ 410-213-0018. *Secret Affair*, a 32-foot racing cruiser, sets sail from Old Town Marina, at the foot of Dorchester St. at the same times and rates; ☎ 410-289-2955.

Smith and Tangier Islands are reached by passenger ferries from Crisfield. Tangier also has a ferry from Virginia's Eastern Shore, and both can be reached from the other side of the bay, but access is closer from this side. The ferry ride makes a pleasant boat excursion, staying on the island long enough for a tour and lunch. See *Cultural & Eco-Travel*, page 434, for more information.

Smith Island Cruises (☎ 410-425-2771) operates from Memorial Day through October, leaving Somers Cove Marina at 12:30 daily. A package includes the boat ride, a family-style seafood lunch on the island and a narrated bus tour, and leaves the island at about 4 pm. *Island Belle* and *Island Princess* (☎ 410-968-3206) leave City Dock at 12:30 in the summer only, and your cruise can include family-style lunch at an island restaurant. The *Captain Jason* (☎ 410-425-5931) operates from City Dock year-round, leaving Crisfield at 12:30 and 5 daily. In the summer they run a later round-trip from the island on Sunday and Friday evenings. The island has no beaches and no boat rentals.

Tangier Island Cruises (☎ 410-968-2338, www.dmv.com/tangiercruises) leave the City Dock in Crisfield on the same schedule, at 12:30 daily, May 15-October, leaving the island at about 4. Lunches are available on the island, or you can bring a picnic to eat at the tables on board the boat.

Maryland Lady cruises the Wicomico River daily, from Salisbury Marina, just across the US 50 bridge from the downtown shopping district; ☎ 410-543-2466.

Fishing & Crabbing

Assateague Island State Park is inside Assateague National Seashore which is a federally managed park. To fish or hunt in the park you need only the Maryland license, not a federal permit, but you must check in with both offices, since they have different season dates and different rules. The National Park Service publishes a free brochure with the fishing rules and identification charts of common species, along with suggestions on the most effective baits. Surf fishing on the island is best in spring and fall. Park rangers offer demonstrations of surf fishing several times each week during the summer to give beginners an introduction.

AUTHOR TIP

CRABBING REGULATIONS: *No license is required to catch crabs for your own use, but you must obey the size regulations and return all egg-bearing females. The season is April through December, but the best crabbing is in late summer and early fall, in the morning or early evening.*

On Assateague Island, the best crabbing is at the old ferry landing, on the northern end of the park, which also offers good clamming. Turn off Route 611 to the right, just before the Visitors Center to get to South Point, where there is good crabbing by the boat launch. From Snow Hill, follow Route 365 to its end on Chincoteague Bay for crabbing waters.

In **Ocean City**, the public fishing pier is on the bay side, just south of 10th St. and on the ocean side opposite the end of Wicomico Street, south of the US 50 intersection with Philadelphia Avenue.

Near the Delaware border, you can fish from the public docks in Mardela Springs and between the bridges at Sharptown. At the bridge and at Byrd Park, both in **Snow Hill**, you can fish in the Pocomoke River without a sportfishing license, whether you are from Maryland or out of state.

On the **lower Nanticoke River**, fishing and crabbing are good from the docks at Bivalve and Tyaskin and at Nanticoke Park, off Route 349 (follow Spring Lane). In this lower part of the estuary you may catch striped bass, flounder, bluefish, perch, drum and croaker; crabs are caught May though October. (See *Camping*, page 450, for a campground facing these fishing waters.)

RECOMMENDED READING: *The Wicomico County Parks and Recreation Department publishes an excellent brochure with a map and chart of all county parks, describing facilities and showing at a glance where the fishing sites are. Several of these parks also have swimming beaches, a good combination for families where everyone is not enthusiastic about fishing. Look for the brochure at the Tourist Information Center or get it directly from the department; ☎ 410-548-4900.*

Fly-fishing is good at North Lake and Schumaker Parks in Salisbury, also on Leonard's Pond, near the Tourist Information Center on US 13. All the local lakes are stocked. The Salisbury Fly Shop is also well stocked, and in addition to equipment, they offer lessons when you buy a fly rod.

Ocean City has an extensive charter fleet that can take you fishing for tuna, shark, bluefish or marlin, as well as headboats that fish primarily for flounder. **Ocean City Fishing Center** offers full-day and half-day

Lower Eastern Shore

deep sea fishing trips with the largest charter fleet in town. Boats carry four-six persons and prices are for the group, beginning at about $350 for a half-day. Off-shore marlin or tuna trips begin at $675 and overnight trips start at $1,400. The marina is at US 50 and Shantytown Rd; ☎ 410-213-1121 or 800-322-3065, www.ocfishing.com.

Bahia Marina, on the bay side between 21st and 22nd Streets (☎ 410-289-7438), has a fleet of about a dozen charter boats that offer full- and half-day trips. Each boat takes four to six anglers, and prices for the group begin at $350 for a half-day or $450 for eight hours. Headboat rates for deep sea fishing are about $22 for a 4½-hour trip, bay fishing about $18. They also rent boats with motors for fishing.

Bass fishing on the Pocomoke, Wicomico, Nanticoke and Choptank Rivers doesn't have to be a budget-breaking experience. **Captain Bruce Wooten**, 6661 Snow Hill Rd. in Snow Hill (☎ 410-632-1431), takes one or two anglers for eight-hour trips for a per-trip cost of $150. No extra charges and as much instruction as you want or need is included.

KID-FRIENDLY

Captain Wooten welcomes children, and reports that parent-child teams are among his fastest growing clientele. He encourages fishing as a family activity.

You can rent fishing boats at **Shad Landing State Park**, south of Snow Hill.

Cultural & Eco-Travel Experiences

■ Natural Areas

Smith and **Tangier** Islands seem lost in time, with a culture all their own. Smith is actually three islands, one of which is a National Wildlife Refuge. The passenger ferry from Crisfield passes between Smith and a second island before landing in Ewell. Smith Island has about 600 residents, whose lives revolve around the seasons and the tides. A school teaches island children through the fourth grade – after that they take the "school-boat" to the mainland (no, it is not bright yellow – we checked).

FOOD FACTS

Smith Island Layer Cake is a rich stack of eight to 15 layers with frosting in between. It can be in any of several flavors, including chocolate, lemon, orange or coconut.

Trips to the island on the passenger ferry from Crisfield make a good day-excursion into what seems like another world. Islanders have arranged a short tour or you can rent bikes at the dock to explore the island. Be sure to stop and watch women deftly separate crabmeat from its shell at the **Crabpickers Co-operative**. Short programs of island music are often given at the Cultural Center (☎ 410-425-3351) in Ewell, where costumed guides play the parts of real characters from island history. It is open daily, April through October, noon-4.

Assateague Island National Seashore Visitors Center, 7206 National Seashore Lane (Route 611), east of Berlin, (☎ 410-641-1441), has a touch tank where kids (and adults, too) can play with sea creatures. Plenty of information is available on the famous wild horses, and there is an 18-minute film about them. Other nature films cover different aspects of park wildlife, and are slightly longer. The center is open 9-5, daily. Adjacent to the Visitors Center, is a state park with boat landing and picnic area.

The waterfront in Crisfield, Maryland.

While you will certainly want to see the island's famous wild horses (often called ponies), remember that these are wild animals, and you should neither touch nor feed them, which could be dangerous to both you and the animals. They can and do kick and bite, and their bites can carry rabies. Feeding teaches them to come near the roads, where many meet their death each year in car accidents. It's better for both you and the horses if you keep a polite distance.

The **Verrazano Bridge** (a bit smaller than the one crossing the narrows in New York) leads across the Sinepuxent Bay to the barrier island on which the Assateague Island National Seashore is located. A separate bridge parallels it for walkers and cyclists. The only parking is at the Visitors Center (from which you must walk or bike into the park) or in the state park at the beaches. There is not much road here, except for 4X4 vehicles.

RECOMMENDED READING: *The National Park Service publishes a series of outstanding brochures on the wildlife and ecosystems of Assateague, all of them available free at the Visitors Center. They include booklets on seashells, mammals, wild horses, and shellfishing.*

The Salisbury Zoo is one of our favorites, a small but outstanding community zoo that does a fine job of introducing both native and exotic wildlife. Because it is free, it is heavily visited by local families, whose children get to know the animals and see them at all times of year. More than 300 individuals of 90 species have spacious quarters in the 12.5-acre park. Native and migratory waterfowl come and go at will. The natural settings provide refuge for injured and orphaned wildlife as well as a nursery – six baby eagles hatched here were released into the wild in a recent year.

Seasonal programs prove that the zoo (and its energetic director) have a sense of humor, with the Critter Christmas and Halloween night walks as highlights. The zoo, on South Park Drive, (☎ 410-548-3188) is open 8-4:30 daily in the winter, and until 7:30 in the summer, free.

WATCHABLE WILDLIFE

Raised boardwalks at the zoo provide good vantage points for watching animals, which include buffalo, spider monkeys, a rare black jaguar, prairie dogs, spectacled bears (one of the most endangered of bears), guanaco (ancestor of the llama) and capybaras, the largest rodent. The best time to watch the otters is early in the morning and just before closing in the afternoon, and the sloth is most active (a bit of an oxymoron) in the morning as the zoo opens. Bright tropical birds, including Amazon parrots, inhabit a forest compound.

Pemberton Historic Park, off Route 349 just west of Salisbury (☎ 410-548-4870), interprets its wide variety of Eastern Shore ecosystems with regular nature programs, led by the park naturalist. These take place five days a week, year-round, exploring the changing seasons along the Wicomico River. Habitats in the park include tidal and freshwater wetlands, freshwater ponds, a river island, upland pine groves, hardwood forests and meadows, providing habitat for nearly 160 bird species. Adding in the migrating birds, a total of 200 species have been seen here.

The **Environmental Education Center** at Pemberton has regular programs on nature subjects, all open to the public, but some need prior reservation. The usual charge is $2 per person, $5 for a family. A full schedule of seasonal activities includes a "Haunted Trail" walk at Halloween, Earth Day observations in the spring, maple sugaring in January, full moon hikes, owl prowls and special programs for toddlers. The park is off Route 349 just west of Salisbury; ☎ 410-548-4870.

TENNIS HEAVEN: *All tennis courts in Salisbury are free and open to the public. The indoor courts at Salisbury State College require reservations (☎ 410-543-6248), but the college's outdoor courts, as well as all others in the city, are on a walk-in basis, and many are lighted at night. At one time the city had more tennis courts per capita than any other city in the nation.*

■ Museums

Salisbury's **Ward Museum of Wildfowl Art**, at 909 S. Schumaker Dr., in Salisbury (☎ 410-742-4988), features world-class collections of art ranging from decoys to sculpture and paintings, most of which have been winners of prestigious awards. The museum also traces the history of the art from the earliest known decoys, through early hunting weapons and craft, and includes replicas of the Ward brothers' original workshop in Crisfield. Lem and Steve Ward are credited with taking waterfowl art from hunting decoys to decorative art. According to the Ward Museum, there are only four original American art forms: scrimshaw, quilting, decoy making, and jazz.

DID YOU KNOW? *The first known use of decoys to lure waterfowl into the range of hunters was more than 2,000 years ago. Examples of ducks made of bound and shaped reeds were found in prehistoric caves in Nevada and are replicated at the Ward Museum.*

The stunning modern building was designed to house the museum, with galleries for changing exhibits that focus on the evolution of the art and on the craftsmanship involved. A large shop sells museum quality waterfowl art. Admission to the museum is $7 for adults, $5 seniors, $3 for children; this is an "adult" museum, where children are likely to get antsy very quickly.

■ Prime Birding Sites

The Atlantic is separated from the mainland shore almost solidly by a series of barrier islands that run from Cape Henlopen, in Delaware, to below the Virginia line. Most of the barrier is included in Fenwick, Assateague and Chincoteague islands. The long, narrow strip of sand is backed by lagoons and wetland marshes that are outstanding bird habitats. Other wetlands are common along the coastal area's low landscapes, as well as fields and forests, making this a particularly good area for birders. On the western side of the peninsula is another major birding area along the shore of the Chesapeake Bay.

RECOMMENDED READING: *Worcester County publishes two useful free brochures for birders, one "A Guide to Birdwatching" and the other a checklist of species seen there. These are in all the information centers or available from Worcester County Tourism, 105 Pearl St., Snow Hill 21863; ☎ 410-623-3617 or 800-852-0335.*

Cape Henlopen State Park, at the head of the barrier island in Delaware, is among the East Coast's finest birding locations, with a variety of habitats that include forests, beaches, marshes and a saltwater lagoon. A nature center there has information on the park's nature trails and on the current bird populations; ☎ 302-645-6852.

Assawoman Wildlife Area (☎ 302-739-5297), near Fenwick Island in Delaware, just north of Ocean City, also has a variety of bird-inviting habitats that include forests, marshes, creeks, ponds and bays. An observation tower and nature trails give good viewing perspectives.

In Berlin, a quarter-mile nature trail wanders through a waterfowl nesting habitat at the **Stephen Decatur Memorial Park**; ☎ 410-641-2770. Boardwalks give closer access to a man-made pond created as a nesting area.

Assateague Island is well known for its birdlife, best seen in the marshes of its western shore. Endangered piping plover nest in the sands of island beaches.

Pocomoke River State Park in Snow Hill (☎ 410-632-2566) is the best place to look for prothonotary warblers, bright yellow species that are easiest to observe in the spring, from the park's canoe trail. Look also for wild turkeys.

Deal Island Wildlife Management Area, on Route 363 west of Princess Anne (☎ 410-543-8223), supports the state's only breeding colony of black-necked stilts, and some of the largest concentrations of ibis, herons and egrets, along with geese, swans and ducks.

AUTHOR TIP

Delmarva Birding Weekend, in late April, brings birders from all over to witness the migration of warblers, waterfowl and shorebirds, as well as the nesting of resident birds of prey and other species. A number of special activities are planned, for which reservations are essential; ☎ *410-623-3617 or 800-852-0335.*

■ Gardens

Princess Anne's main street has a number of boxwood gardens, which you can admire over the fences as you stroll along the streets. The large boxwood garden at the Teackle Mansion is always open; walk around the left side of the house to enter.

Garden lovers should plan to stay at **Merry Sherwood Plantation**, in Berlin (see page 449). Its 18 acres of gardens surround an 1850s plantation house, and are studded with tall specimen trees. The gardens are not open to the public, but inn guests are invited to stroll there at will.

■ Crafts

An art colony is under development in the old wharfside buildings in **Crisfield**, with artists and craftsmen working in studios and exhibiting their work. The colony is a short walk from the docking point for ferries to Smith and Tangier islands; walk along the wharf, past the Captain's Galley restaurant.

Lower Eastern Shore

The **Globe Theatre** in Berlin has a crafts center on the second floor, with a good variety of media and artists represented, from fine art and photography to pottery, quilts and basketry.

Family-owned **Salisbury Pewter** creates beautiful jewelry, tableware, Christmas ornaments and presentation pieces at its workshops on Ocean Hwy. (US 13 in Salisbury); ☎ 410-546-1188 or 800-824-4708. Although they are the largest hollowware pewter manufacturer in the United States, the atmosphere is that of a studio, not a factory, and you can watch craftsmen at work through a large window area adjoining the salesroom. It is fascinating to see a flat disk of pewter "spun" into a cup by spinners who have perfected their techniques over a lifetime. These artists make their own tools and wooden chucks, just as their predecessors did in Colonial times. But the pewter they use is lead-free. Salisbury Pewter creates heirloom-quality gifts for the White House and embassies in Washington, as well as making all Tiffany's pewterware.

AUTHOR TIP

We tend to shun souvenirs, but we can't think of a better one than a pewter crab formed in a mold made from an actual Dorchester County crab. Showroom prices are at least 20%, sometimes as much as 50%, lower than in retail stores, and if you climb a few steps from the second showroom, you'll find a roomful of seconds at 50% to 80% discounts. Salisbury Pewter is open weekdays, 9-5; Saturday, 10-5. You'll see spinners at work on weekdays until 4:30, except during lunch hours.

The Local Artisan, at 212 Downtown Plaza in Salisbury (☎ 410-860-2895), features the work of more than 30 area potters, jewelers, woodcarvers, etchers, glass workers and others.

■ Antiques

Antique shops and group dealers are fairly common in the area, as are weekend auctions, where you can still get some real bargains. These are listed in the newspapers. In downtown **Salisbury**, look for **Parker Place Antiques Shop** and the **Market Street Antiques**; for a small, but tasteful selection of Asian and local antiques, look in at **Aesop's Table**.

Events

MAY: The Salisbury Festival (☎ 410-548-4914 or 800-332-8687) is held during the first week of the month. The entire town is abloom in dogwood and azalea. The average home in Salisbury has at least one dogwood and five azaleas, so you can imagine what a colorful display these create. Also in early May is the **American Indian Festival and Powwow** in Marion, which features crafts, foods, music and dancing; ☎ 410-623-8329.

JUNE: The **Delmarva Chicken Festival** is held at varying places and brings crowds of upwards of 35,000 to sample chicken in every way known; ☎ 410-548-4914 or 800-332-8687.

JULY: The **J. Tawes Crab and Clam Bake** is held mid-month in Crisfield, offering all you can eat for $25; ☎ 410-968-2500 or 800-782-3913. **Pony penning** takes place at Assateague on the last Wednesday and Thursday of the month, when the horses swim the channel to Chincoteague; ☎ 757-336-6161.

AUTHOR TIP

On Sunday afternoons during the summer, free concerts are held at the bandstand in the park in Salisbury.

SEPTEMBER: During Labor Day weekend the annual **Hard Crab Derby** and fair is held in Crisfield; ☎ 410-968-2500 or 800-782-3913.

OCTOBER: **Newtown Festival** in Salisbury brings a rare chance to tour private historic homes; ☎ 410-543-2111. The **Chesapeake Wildlife Showcase** is offered at the Ward Museum in Salisbury; ☎ 410-742-4988.

NOVEMBER: From mid-November into December, Ocean City's **Winterfest of Lights** fills Northside Park with animated lighted figures, viewed from a miniature train. Berlin, during the first weekend in November, hosts several **church bazaars**, with chicken-and-dumpling and oyster suppers and a variety of crafts, foods and jumble for sale; check locally for flyers or in the "events" sections of area newspapers.

DECEMBER: **Victorian Christmas Week** in Berlin takes place at the beginning of the month and includes caroling, a parade, carriage rides, concerts and more; ☎ 410-641-4775. Salisbury goes all out for the holidays, creating a **Winter Wonderland** of scenes outlined in tiny lights along the Riverwalk in the park. Concessions sell food and drinks and music fills the air on December evenings; the display remains in place from late November through mid-January.

In some years, Crisfield's town's fleet joins in a **parade of decorated boats** to celebrate the season in mid-December; check with the Chamber of Commerce there for dates, ☎ 410-968-2500, 800-782-3913. **Princess Anne** celebrates with an entire weekend of events, breakfast with Santa, a parade, street entertainers, candlelight tours of historic homes, church services and dinners; ☎ 410-651-2968 or 800-521-9189. On December 31, a **New Year's Eve Party** fills Salisbury's downtown streets, centering

Lower Eastern Shore

around Downtown Plaza with the countdown at the Old City Hall; ☎ 410-548-4914 or 800-332-8687.

Sightseeing

■ Touring

Berlin

 The little town of Berlin, west of Ocean City on US 113, has a number of historic buildings. The most interesting of these is the **Globe Theatre**, a 1910 garage, recycled in 1917 into the art deco Hollywood Theater. It thrived as such for 50 years, then, after a 20-year intermission, it was again recycled, this time as a venue for art. There is a café, a few shops and a smaller movie theater where classic films are shown. It's also the unofficial community center, and you may find on its bulletin board notices for the church bazaar or for clogging lessons. Upstairs is a gallery of handcrafts, downstairs a bookstore, gourmet food shop and café.

Berlin's **main street** looks very much as it has for the last century – so much so that the town is often chosen as a movie setting (*The Runaway Bride* was filmed there). The county Visitors Center in Salisbury can tell you if one is scheduled during your visit. It can, however, be confusing if you arrive just after a shoot, when business signs may not say what they mean. Local merchants are very friendly about letting props people rename their stores to fit the story.

KID-FRIENDLY

*In 1902, Daniel Trimper bought the 50-foot Herschell-Spillman carousel at **Trimper's Rides** in Ocean City. The only change since then has been converting it from steam to electric power – and raising the price of a ride on one of its 45 animals from a nickel to 90¢.*

Crisfield

Crisfield is at the end of the road; Route 413 literally stops at the ferry dock, where boats take passengers to the islands of Smith and Tangier. It is an old port, once the end of the railroad line, which ran through its center to the docks, taking on cargoes of seafood right from the boats. The town life centers around these wharves, home port to a fleet of **watermen** who bring in their catch, usually around noon, although some arrive as early as 10, or as late as 1 pm. Crisfield springs to life during this midday time, with the arrivals and departures of island ferries and their cargo of people, bikes, pets and mail.

Walk around the docks on the boardwalk, from the ferry landing to Somers Cove Marina. Crisfield has one of the largest marinas on the East Coast, with 450 slips. Cruise boats to the islands (not the ferries) leave from the marina. On the other side of the ferry pier are seafood processing plants, where you are welcome to watch crab pickers and oyster shuckers at work. During the summer, walking tours are sponsored nearly every day by the **Governor J. Millard Tawes Historical Museum** (see page 445), at Somers Cove Marina (☎ 410-968-2501).

DID YOU KNOW? *Talk About Crabby! Crisfield ships more than six million soft-shelled crabs each summer (about $5,000,000 worth), plus about a million pounds of processed crab meat and nine million hard crabs shipped live. If stretched claw to claw, it is estimated that these crabs would reach from New York to San Francisco and halfway back. Which is a really silly idea, since crabs are far too cantankerous to remain in a straight line, and would immediately begin fighting amongst themselves.*

Later in the day, the Crisfield docks have what many claim to be the best **sunset view** on the bay. Get an ice cream cone at the Ice Cream Gallery, or bring a take-out dinner and join locals on the docks to cheer as the sun drops splendidly into the bay.

CAUTION *Tidal flooding is a way of life in the tidewater areas around Crisfield, especially in the spring. When driving at night during these times, watch out for flooded roads and driveways.*

■ Museums & Historic Sites

Salisbury

The **Newtown** neighborhood of Salisbury was built following a fire that destroyed much of the town in 1886. It was new at the time, hence the name, which has stuck despite the fact that it is now the city's oldest section. It has been declared a Historic District for its abundance of significant architecture. If you are there in the spring, you will see it at its glory, since nearly every homeowner takes pride in the blooming shrubs and trees that have become a neighborhood tradition.

Newtown's architectural styles include Queen Anne, Second Empire, Eastlake, Colonial Revival and cottage, with accents and flourishes characteristic to these Victorian tastes. You'll see patterned shingles and slate-work, a variety of towers and turrets, columned porticos, verandas, gingerbread trim and windows in mullion and stained glass. A few older homes that escaped the fire are scattered among them, including the 1805 **Poplar Hill Mansion**, a museum house furnished in antiques and sometimes open to the public on Sunday afternoons; $2. It is located at 117 Elizabeth St.; ☎ 410-749-1776.

Pemberton Historic Park, off Route 349 just west of Salisbury (☎ 410-548-4870), is the site of Pemberton Manor, a small 1700s brick home. The adjacent Heritage Center is a museum of early local artifacts. An archaeological dig there has disclosed pre-Colonial artifacts, as well as the original docks on the river at Bell Creek Marsh Overlook, from which Pemberton Manor's plantation sent cotton and other crops to market. You can reach this dock area on the 0.3-mile History Trail. The park is open April-November. On the last Saturday in September a **Colonial Fair** brings the plantation to life, with Colonial re-enactors showing the evolution of life there with tools and authentic foods, including those of the Native and Black residents. Visitors can sample venison and roast goat, and oysters cooked as Native Americans would have prepared them.

The entire towns of **Whitehaven** and **Quantico** are on the National Register of Historic Places. Both are west of Salisbury: Quantico is one mile north of Route 349, Whitehaven is south of it, off Route 352. Before the Wicomico River was dredged to open the port of Salisbury, Whitehaven was the turn-around point for ships.

Princess Anne

The **Teackle Mansion**, in Princess Anne, is a grand five-part American Federal home built of Flemish-bond brick (alternating headers and stretchers) at the turn of the 1800s. The story of its various owners, as the original owner had to sell it to relatives three times, each time buying it back, threads through a tour of its rooms, now under restoration. The entryway is unusually large, more like a church vestibule, and here visitors get the first taste of Teackle's passion for symmetry – a passion he shared with Georgian architects and their Federal counterparts in the new United States. As you tour the house, look for false doors and windows that maintain this illusion of everything matching, reminiscent of the Harwood Harmon House in Annapolis.

Behind the house are gardens, with some of the boxwood thought to be original – the clump behind the south hyphen in particular – and an original smoke house. The Blacksmith Shop has a working smith demonstrating during Princess Anne Days in October. The gardens are open even when the house is not: go around the left-hand side of the house to find the gate. The mansion is at 11736 Mansion St. (you can see it from the main street); ☎ 410-651-2238. It's open April through mid-December, Wednesday, Saturday and Sunday, 1-3; January through March on Sunday, 1-3. Admission is $3. A gift shop is stocked with well-chosen reproductions and good pottery and baskets.

The original Teackle property stretched from Route 13 to the main street of Princess Anne, and the two houses across the street were originally the homes of the gatekeeper and estate manager.

Crisfield

The **Marion Station Railroad Museum**, on Route 413 north of Crisfield (☎ 410-623-2420), is a private museum that began when a couple bought the old station and began renovations. The treasures they found as they began to strip away later changes and poke into corners – signs, baggage tags, seals – led them to turn the building into a museum, instead of the offices they had planned. Locals joined in, donating their own collections and mementoes of the railroad, which once ran several hundred rail cars a day to this remote station. Admission to the station and its museum are free and a gift shop sells train-related books, games and model railroad supplies. It is open Thursday-Saturday 10-6, Sunday 10-3, April through December.

MARION RAIL HISTORY

Why did little Marion have such rail traffic? Marion was the strawberry capital of the world and, in season, ice-refrigerated cars waited for the wagonloads of berries brought each morning by local farmers. If you think hundreds of rail cars waiting to load filled the town, add the mile-long line of farm trucks and wagons waiting to unload.

The **Governor J. Millard Tawes Historical Museum**, at Somers Cove Marina in Crisfield (☎ 410-968-2501), concentrates on the history of the bay and of Crisfield, from its earliest Native American inhabitants to the still-flourishing seafood industry. Two guided walking tours begin here, one on the port and its activity, which includes a visit to a crab and oyster packing plant. The museum is open June through August, 9-4:30 on weekdays, 10-3 on weekends. November through May it is open 9-4:30 on weekdays only; admission is $2.50 for those over 12 years old.

Snow Hill

Nassawango Iron Furnace would be well worth seeing even if it were not part of a growing museum village, **Furnace Town Historic Site**. Thriving around the giant brick furnace from 1828 to 1850, the village was an iron manufacturing center, using bog iron from the nearby swamp, shells from the bay and charcoal made from local timber. These three components, all available locally, made the site ideal, and the product could be transported to market by a mile-long canal leading to the river.

But when the railroads came, there was no way to get the iron to the railhead, so the furnace and its company town of 300 families slowly died, finally becoming a ghost town. Costumed docents demonstrate home and village skills, including weaving and blacksmithing, and a museum in a little gothic cottage shows the entire process of iron-making. Although there are iron furnaces elsewhere, this is the only one we know of with such a clear picture of how it worked – and the only one where you can walk the charging ramp to the top of the giant structure and look in. The interpretation here is so good that you should allow about 1½ hours if you are at all interested in seeing how iron was made in the early 1800s.

A particularly interesting opportunity is to become a part of their monthly public archaeology digs held on Sunday afternoons. These and their Saturday afternoon workshops on skills ranging from blacksmithing to gardening require advance reservations.

Furnace Town Historic Site is open daily April through October, 11-5, and admission is $3, children $1.50. It is on Old Furnace Rd. in Snow Hill, and is signposted from Route 12, west of town; ☎ 410-632-2032.

AUTHOR TIP

Swamps being what they are, we suggest you bring insect repellent to the Nassawango Iron Furnace.

The **Julia A. Purnell Museum**, 208 West Market St. in Snow Hill (☎ 410-632-0515), is one of those charming repositories of local treasures that give travelers an insight into a town. The home of an accomplished folk-art needleworker, the museum has become a town project, displaying everything from cooking utensils and farm tools to a country store. It's open weekdays 10-4 and weekends 1-4 from April through October.

The tiny **Mt. Zion One-Room School**, on Ironshire St. in Snow Hill (☎ 410-632-0669), looks as though the children who studied there until 1931 would return after recess. You can inspect their McGuffy Readers from 1 to 4, Tuesday through Saturday, mid-June through early September; admission is $1, children 50¢.

Berlin

The **Taylor House Museum**, at the corner of Main and Baker Streets in Berlin (☎ 410-641-1019), is noted particularly for its decorative features, which include false graining and a fine doorway. It has both furnished rooms and local memorabilia on display. The house is open June through September on Wednesday, Friday and Saturday, 1-4.

Ocean City Area

Ocean City Lifesaving Station Museum, on the Boardwalk at the Inlet (☎ 410-289-4991), is in an 1891 Life-Saving Station, one of the town's oldest buildings. Inside are exhibits on the old beach resort, on lifesaving in the Delmarva Peninsula, and on the items recovered by wreck divers. Some of the most fascinating displays are photographs of damage done by past storms. The museum is open daily, June-September, 11-10; during May and October and on winter weekends, 11-4. Admission is $2 adults, $1 children under 12.

Shipwrecks off the Delmarva coast and the objects recovered from them are explored in the **Discoveries From the Sea Museum**, at 708 Ocean Hwy. in Fenwick Island, Delaware; ☎ 302-539-9366. Coins, weapons, pottery and gold and silver bars recovered from wrecks are in the expanding collections of an underwater archaeologist. Open daily, June-August, 9-9; September-October, 11-4; November-March, weekends, 11-4. The museum is on the second floor of Sea Shell City.

The Atlantic shore gives rise to two relics of coastal history on the barrier island, one north and one south of Ocean City. At the northern edge of the north section of Fenwick Island State Park, just south of Bethany Beach in Delaware, is a round **World War II coastal defense watch tower**. **Assateague National Seashore** has several historic sites with explanatory signs, one of which explains the remains of a vessel shipwrecked here.

AFRICAN-AMERICAN HISTORY: *The Worcester County Tourism Office publishes excellent brochures highlighting places that are associated with the area's **African-American heritage**.*

Where to Stay

ACCOMMODATIONS PRICE KEY
Rates are per room, per night, double occupancy.
$ . . . . Under $50
$$ . . . . $50 to $100
$$$ . . . . $101 to $175
$$$$ . . . . $176 and up

■ Near Salisbury

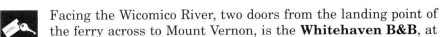

Facing the Wicomico River, two doors from the landing point of the ferry across to Mount Vernon, is the **Whitehaven B&B**, at 23844 River St. (☎ 410-873-3294). This comfortable home has rooms in two adjacent houses, with private and shared baths. A hearty breakfast is served in the morning and a refrigerator is available for guests' use. Front rooms overlook the river, and a derelict fishing boat moored on the shore. The innkeeper has the key to the little local museum.

Although it is close to David's at Waterloo, you cannot have dinner there because the Whitehaven Ferry stops running at 5:15 in the winter, 7:30 in the summer. But you can have dinner at the Green Hill Yacht and Country Club, where the Whitehaven B&B maintains a membership for their guests. They will take you there by boat, a 15-minute cruise on the Wicomico River, and pick you up after dinner. The chef at the yacht club is usually good. Rates January-March are $75; April-December, $80-$100.

■ Ocean City

Commander Hotel, a 1927 original that updated and opened a brand-new building in 1998, is a family-owned business with an eye to guests' comfort. Instead of facing the ocean squarely as most do, it sits at an angle, so rooms on two sides have direct ocean and boardwalk views. Its large rooms are all suites, with full-sized refrigerators, microwaves, in-room safes, two double beds and a convertible couch. Decorating the large, comfortable lobby and throughout the hotel are nicely framed enlargements of old postcards of Ocean City and the hotel. The full breakfast buffet, with ham, eggs, bacon, pancakes, sausage, cereal and muffins is $6.95. The hotel is at 1404 Baltimore Ave., ☎ 410-289-6166 or 888-289-6166. $$$$

The boardwalk at Ocean City is fully wheel-chair-accessible, as are rooms at the newly built Commander Hotel, right on the boardwalk. Handicapped access points on the boardwalk are well-marked from the main streets.

Inn on the Ocean, 1001 Atlantic Ave. (☎ 410-289-8894 or toll-free 877-466-6662), sits on the boardwalk, over which most rooms have ocean views. Each is in a different decor: one, in burgundy and green, has a Maryland hunt theme with golfing touches. Another room is in blue and white, one in gold and brocades. Luxury right on the beach begins at $115 off season. Adults only.

Another centrally located B&B – a bit of a rarity in this hotel-dominated town – is the **Atlantic House**, at 501 North Baltimore Ave.; ☎ 410-289-2333. Interior wood decor is softened by floral fabrics and decorated in quilts. On the porch is a hot tub. A full buffet breakfast is served in a beautifully decorated sunroom. Off-season rates are exceptionally low, beginning as low as $50. June-September begins under $100.

■ Berlin

The Atlantic Hotel, at 2 North Main St. in the middle of Berlin (☎ 410-641-3589 or 800-814-7672), welcomes guests to authentically restored Victorian hotel rooms, with matching suites of furniture, most marble-topped with oak-leaf cluster pulls, carved or brass beds, claw-foot tubs. We like Room 10 with its four-poster canopy bed and loveseat. Rooms 10, 11, 12 and 14 overlook the quiet main street. Rates are $75-$100 for standard rooms, $95-$150 for deluxe.

Merry Sherwood Plantation, on US 13 (Worcester Hwy.) south of Berlin (☎ 410-641-2112 or 800-660-0358, fax 410-641-9528) is a showstopper, appearing suddenly slightly set back in gracious tree-shaded grounds. Its dozen-plus acres of gardens are beautiful, with huge old maples, Irish yews, Japanese pines and topiary shrubs, but they don't prepare you for the lush interior. Rescued from near ruin and restored to its plantation-era opulence, the inn is furnished in Victorian antiques, many one of a kind. Marble fireplaces and showers, grand chandeliers and fine arts fill the inn, but it doesn't just rely on its eye-appeal. Thoughtful touches – a welcoming glass of iced tea in the summer, a full breakfast in the dining room, fireside stories about the house's history – make it a place to relax and enjoy. Rates are $100-$200; all but two rooms have private baths.

■ Snow Hill

River House Inn, in the center of town at 201 East Market St. (☎ 410-632-2722, fax 410-632-2866), has large and nicely decorated rooms, all with private baths. Each room is furnished in antiques. We especially like staying in the one with a full suite of matched serpentine-front furniture, but would have been equally happy in the one with the elegant metal canopy bed. Two parlors are reserved for guests, both very inviting and filled with books on the local area.

At the end of their lawn is the Pocomoke River, and a private canoe/kayak landing. The inn is only a few steps from Pocomoke River Canoe, where you can rent canoes and kayaks, and is affiliated with other inns for a canoe inn-to-inn trip. Congenial hosts, the Knudsons can give you good advice on Eastern Shore dining options, and a credenza in the entryway is filled with menus from area restaurants. One of the best of these is directly across the street. Bicycles are free for guests' use, and the innkeepers can take you on a guided nature tour of the Nassawango on their pontoon boat for a nominal charge. Rooms are $100 to $120, suites with whirlpool tubs and the private cottage in the carriage barn, $160-$175.

■ Princess Anne

Waterloo Country Inn, 28822 Mount Vernon Rd (☎ 410-651-0883, fax 410-651-0883), is an oasis of elegance set in the middle of rolling meadows cut by grass-lined tidal streams. The parlor of this stately plantation-style house is furnished in pale blue, with fine art from the owners' native Switzerland. Leading upstairs is a staircase with hand-carved balustrades, and landings are enlivened by small antiques. A two-room suite has a 200-year-old armoire and a working fireplace; the large honeymoon suite on

Lower Eastern Shore

the third floor has a Jacuzzi. Downstairs rooms have separate entrances and handicapped access. Room rates begin at $125 in high season, $105 in off-season.

Breakfast is served on Rosenthal china, with individual pots of tea and coffee and a fresh fruit cup with giant raspberries. Breakfast choices include a cheese plate with five cheeses – brie, Jarlsberg, Gruyere, blue and goat – with fresh croissants, muffins and German-style wheat rolls. In nice weather you can have breakfast outside on the terrace serenaded by bird song. Guests on August 1 can enjoy the annual Midsummer bonfire.

A small dependency building, once a doctor's office, is a charming gift shop filled with ethereal white cotton hand-embellished lingerie, Christmas ornaments, ceramics and floral art, most of it created by owner Therese Kraemer.

Three canoes and four bicycles are kept for the use of guests, and it's a difficult choice between the meandering country roads and the tidewater. You can canoe almost from the door, along a quiet winding tidal creek alive with birds as the late afternoon sun turns its marsh grasses to gold. The inn is almost equidistant to Salisbury, across the Wicomico River via Whitehaven Ferry (but you can't take that route to have dinner in Salisbury because the ferry closes too early).

■ Camping

In the town of Delmar, three blocks south of the Delaware border, is **Woodlawn Family Camping**, on Walnut St., off US 13; ☎ 410-896-2979. Tent and trailer sites are in an open wooded setting

Roaring Point Campground, in Nanticoke, on the lower end of the Nanticoke River (☎ 410-873-2553), spreads along a wooded shore that offers the best of both worlds: shaded campsites and good fishing. Unlike many campgrounds, this one is not an RV park that tolerates tents. Tent sites are in a large wooded area and 25 primitive sites are perfect for those who wish greater solitude. There's a sand beach and a 135-foot pier for crabbing and fishing – this is a prime fishing area – and you can rent boats or buy supplies at the bait and tackle shop. Sunfish sailboats are also available for rent.

Assateague Island has several campgrounds, administered separately by the National Park Service and the Maryland State Parks, with sites on both the bay and ocean side of the island. You can reserve National Park sites three months in advance (☎ 800-365-CAMP). The sites are open and unshaded, so a canopy is almost essential in the summer. Mosquitos are voracious, ticks rampant, wild ponies predictable only in that they will try to get at any unsealed food. All that said, the park is a prime place to camp, close to beaches, fishing, canoeing, biking and walking trails. There are no hook-ups. Sites are $10 in the off season, $14 during reservation season

(May 15-October 15); you must also have the park entrance pass, $5 for seven days.

Fees for the state park section are $20 a night per site, and reservations can be made by the week only (although this may change); ☎ 410-641-2918 for information.

Backcountry camping is allowed on Assateague, with sites available to both hikers and paddlers. All sites are on a first-come basis and you must obtain a permit from the park headquarters. Canoe rentals are available at the park June-August. Because of the wild and unstable nature of the island, as well as the strong tides around the island, expect hiking and paddling to be more difficult than they would be elsewhere. You will need to carry everything, including water, with you, and cannot depend on the availability of firewood. Before considering this type of trip, get a copy of the leaflet "Backcountry Camping" from the Visitors Center; ☎ 410-641-1441.

Pocomoke State Forest and **Pocomoke River State Park**, with headquarters at 3461 Worcester Hwy. in Snow Hill (☎ 410-632-2566), have campgrounds at both the Milburn Landing and Shad Landing segments, with rates of $10-$15, depending on the season. Shad Landing, on US 113, south of Snow Hill, has a swimming pool.

Janes Island State Park, near Crisfield (☎ 410-968-1565), has a campground in its mainland portion, where the marina and boat transport to the island are located. Camping is allowed April-October. Camper cabins are available in those months and four full-sized log cabins are rented year-round. To reach the park, head south toward Crisfield on Route 413 and turn west (right) just past the Highway Holiness Church.

Where to Eat

Look for church suppers in the spring and fall, and picnics in the summer, where parishioners put on feasts of local oysters, chicken-and-dumplings or other favorites. Every local organization seems to specialize in cooking something – oyster fritters to chicken and dumplings – and locals have their own definite preferences, which they share readily. Local firemen's musters and carnivals are advertised by signs, and nearly always serve some local specialty or include a pig roast.

CRAB FACTS

■ The best crabs are eaten when the moon is full; after that they break out of their shell and are less meaty.

■ Crab cakes should be made from the backfin meat only.

■ Blue crabs are a Chesapeake specialty.

■ Crabs hibernate in winter, sleeping in the mud. Crab season begins in March, and by April all the crab houses are up and running.

■ Saltwater hardens the crab's shell.

DINING PRICE KEY
The price key indicates the cost of *most* dinner entrées on a restaurant's regular and daily special menu.
$ . . . . Most under $10
$$ . . . . $10 to $20
$$$ . . . . Over $30

■ Salisbury

Traditional Eastern Shore seafood doesn't get much better than at **Watermen's Cove**, at 925 Snow Hill Rd. (☎ 410-546-1400), where the chef respects sea creatures and knows exactly when to take them off the stove. In short, here's a place where your food will not be overcooked unless you insist on it. Left on his own, the chef will provide you crunchy-juicy soft-shelled crabs, pure backfin crab cakes (and a heretical, but delicious variation that adds baked ham), succulent fried oysters... you get the idea. Most entrées are under $15, and shellfish combination plates are under $18. Non-seafood entrées include prime rib and several chicken dishes. The long menu of sandwiches at lunch are mostly under $6, lunch entrées $6-$8. Open daily for lunch and dinner.

Legends, on Downtown Plaza (☎ 410-749-7717), serves a New American menu with grilled tuna steak encrusted with lemon pepper, blackened pork chop in onion marmalade, and pasta dishes that may include shrimp ravioli with roasted corn and maple-cured bacon. Most entrées are $13-$19.

We haven't eaten there, but local friends who love good food also love **Cactus Taverna**, 2420 North Salisbury Blvd. (Business US 13); ☎ 410-548-1254. Specials may be New Zealand lamb chops with chipotle sauce or Shrimp Cancun, grilled in the shell and served in raspberry sauce. No atmosphere and noisy, with entertainment nightly. $-$$

Aesop's Table, 124 North Division St., just off Downtown Plaza (☎ 410-742-6600), is a café popular with local business people. Bagels, muffins and rolls start the day, and the lunch menu has sandwiches from $2.75, soups and desserts. The setting is an antique shop, wine and beer are served, and the coffee bar has espresso, latte and cappuccino (still somewhat rare along the Eastern Shore).

Stroll down Salisbury's **Downtown Plaza** (look up to see some of the nice upper-story architecture) to find places for lunch or to get picnic makings. The cast iron chairs and tables are for the public, not just for the restaurants.

English's Family Restaurant, on South Salisbury Blvd. (US 13 South), is in an O'Mahoney Diner, and specializes in traditional Eastern Shore dishes, serving breakfast, lunch and dinner. Stop there to sample sweet potato biscuits, a local specialty. For $3 you can buy a dozen of these tasty, moist biscuits to take with you. $

Near Whitehaven is the **Red Roost** (☎ 410-546-5443 or 800-953-5443), a local institution located in a former chicken coop, and known for crabs. Basic menu items, in addition to crabs, are ribs, chicken, hushpuppies and corn on the cob. Locals gather here on Wednesday evenings to sing along with the Backfin Banjo Band. The Red Roost is open daily in the summer, weekends only in the spring and fall. It is closed December through February. To get there from Whitehaven, go straight from the ferry landing and turn left onto Capitola Rd., and again onto Clara Rd., where you will see signs to the Red Roost. $

About 10 minutes north of Salisbury in the border town of Delmar ("The Town Too Big For One State") is **The Old Mill** (☎ 302-537-2240), a good crab house. It doesn't have as much down-home atmosphere as the Red Roost, but it's open year-round and serves up an all-you-can-eat feast of steamed crabs or shrimp Monday-Thursday, offering the regular menu on weekends. You don't have to eat seafood; the ribs are good, too. $-$$$; all-you-can-eat crabs, $22.95.

■ Ocean City

Phillips by the Sea, at the Beach Plaza Hotel, Boardwalk at 13th St. (☎ 410-289-9121), serves good Sunday morning breakfasts year-round, and a full dinner menu of fresh seafood. All the usuals – flounder stuffed with crabmeat, fried oysters, lump crab au gratin, crab cakes, grilled or blackened tuna – are nicely presented and priced at $14-$18. Phillips a local family, and although their restaurants are now found elsewhere, they are original to Ocean City and still a favorite with locals.

So is **Harrison's Harbor Watch**, on the Inlet (☎ 410-219-5121), a giant of a place serving traditional seafood dishes plus some original ones, such as hickory barbecued shrimp. An impressive list of fresh fish is offered simply, without embellishment, either broiled baked or grilled. Pasta dishes, a vegetarian plate and other entrées are mostly $12-$19. It is open year-round.

Reflections, in the Holiday Inn on Coastal Hwy. at 6th Street (☎ 410-524-5252), dances gracefully between New American and classic French cooking, with tableside flambé for entertainment. Grilled salmon is topped with artichoke hearts, shrimp and a delicate béarnaise, or pork tenderloin is served over fried leeks in a sauce of green peppercorns and shallots. It's a stylish menu, pricier than most, but a refreshing change; most entrées are over $20.

Windows on the Bay, on 61st St. overlooking the bay (☎ 410-723-3463), has an updated seafood menu, with dishes like flounder l'orange, sesame flounder and shrimp marsala. They also offer an equal number of non-seafood dishes, such as roast duckling with peaches and port wine, or Wiener schnitzel. In the off season, they have frequent specials, including two-for-the-price-of-one dinner and extended early-bird special hours. $$

Kitty Hawk Grill, Bayside at 46th St. (☎ 410-723-5966), makes people want to eat their vegetables, which are usually an integral part of the dish. marinated chicken breast is served with a mound of steamed vegetables and black bean salsa, shrimp is combined with artichokes over linguine, fresh vegetables are tossed with creamy roasted garlic over penne with Parmesan cheese. Asian and California cuisine meet the Chesapeake, and they get along fine; most entrées are $11-$16. Open all year.

DID YOU KNOW?

The Delmarva Peninsula raises more than 620 million chickens in a year. It's no wonder fried chicken is found on so many menus there. When you see "Maryland Style," expect it in a crunchy, crispy coating.

Delvecchio's Bakery, on Route 54, just west of Fenwick Island, Delaware, has good breads, pastries and doughnuts, with tea, coffee and juices to enjoy with them at its two café tables.

■ Berlin

The Atlantic Hotel's dining room serves an updated continental menu, in keeping with its fine old hotel atmosphere and elegant dining room. Dishes might include salmon bouillabaisse, veal medallions, or crab cakes, most $24-$31. It also has a good wine list. The less formal Drummer's Café serves lunch and dinner daily and is very popular for lunch on weekends. Entrées there are $14-$24. The hotel is at 2 North Main St. in the middle of Berlin; ☎ 410-641-3589 or 800-814-7672.

A good lunch stop is the café inside the **Globe Theatre**, in downtown Berlin. Generous sandwiches are named for classic film stars: the Mae West is chocked full of roast beef with dijonaise and Fatty Arbuckle is remembered with a delicious liverwurst and red onion on seven-grain bread. Prices are $3.25 to $5.50.

■ Snow Hill

Snow Hill Inn (☎ 410-632-2102), in the center of town opposite the River House Inn, has an excellent menu of entrées – petite filets topped with Maryland crab, chicken Marsala, crab imperial, scallops with mushrooms and wine – all priced under $17. It's the kind of place the local gentry from the surrounding area travel to, and for good reason.

LOCAL FOODS

Several dishes you will see frequently on local menus may puzzle you. *Seafood Delight* is crab, scallops and sometimes other shellfish broiled in a cheese sauce. *Chicken Catalina* is chicken in Catalina dressing. *Corn fritters* are usually prepared pancake-style, rather than deep-fried.

On Sunday night, when Snow Hill Inn is closed, **The Judge's Bench** is the only act in town, next to the fire station, a block off Market and Washington Streets. It serves plain home-style dishes at plain home-style prices. Liver and onions is $7.95; chicken and dumplings, $6.95; other entrées include fried chicken, steak, crab cakes, fried seafood. The salad bar is a good choice for vegetables. Although they do serve wine, we suggest you stick to the beer.

■ Princess Anne

The historic **Washington Hotel and Inn**, 11784 Somerset Ave. (☎ 410-651-2526), serves traditional Eastern Shore dishes, and has muskrat dinners on Friday evenings in late fall, served spicy, similar to Cajun-style. It's usually served elsewhere as a mild stew. $$-$$$

David's at Waterloo, 28822 Mount Vernon Rd., ☎ 410-651-4649, is the happy marriage of a good chef-owned restaurant and a fine inn, whose elegant dining rooms are an appropriate setting for a first-class meal. The changing menu features local ingredients, prepared in original ways. We were especially impressed with the flavorful filet served with crabmeat-stuffed shrimp. Vegetables get special attention. Wine tasting dinners are held once a month, and occasional other special events include a Swiss dinner. David's is open year-round, Thursday through Saturday evenings, 6-9; reservations are strongly advised. $$-$$$; with four-course complete dinners at $30.

AUTHOR TIP *Ask in Princess Anne for the date of the Holly Grove School's Winter Game Supper, where you can sample venison, muskrat, rabbit and game birds, or just pig out at the pig roast.*

■ Crisfield

The **Captain's Galley**, facing the ferry pier at 1021 Main St., offers fresh seafood from the docks where watermen unload their catch daily. Crab cakes are baked, broiled or fried, your choice, but we find all the seafood here overcooked for our taste. They have an outdoor crab deck in the summer; ☎ 410-968-1636 or 800-CRAB-MIX. $$; crab feasts, $$$

Virginia's Eastern Shore

By a quirk of early land grants, a small section at the very southern tip of the Eastern Shore is part of Virginia, although it has no land connection to the rest of the state except the up-again-down-again Chesapeake Bay Bridge Tunnel that links it to Newport News. The bridge-tunnel has been

responsible for a lot of travel to the Eastern Shore, diverting north-south traffic from the interstate highways, which saves 90 minutes. But it has not changed the rural quiet character of the Delmarva.

Not that the area has escaped tourism, for Chincoteague Island is a busy destination. The barrier island of Assateague that protects the entire Maryland shore extends south into Virginia, as well. Here live the most famous residents of Virginia's Eastern Shore: the wild "ponies" (really horses, but locals refer to them as ponies) immortalized in Marguerite Henry's book, *Misty of Chincoteague*.

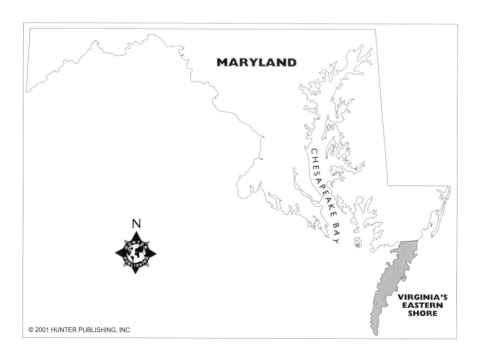

MARYLAND

CHESAPEAKE BAY

N

VIRGINIA'S EASTERN SHORE

© 2001 HUNTER PUBLISHING, INC

Geography & History

■ Orientation

 The Delmarva narrows to about half its width right at the Virginia-Maryland line, making the Virginia portion a long thin peninsula of its own. On this narrowest part of the Eastern Shore, flat landscapes are never far from water. On the west, the shore is deeply cut by creeks and to the east the peninsula is protected by a string of barrier islands, separated from the mainland by lagoon-like bays. Every road that leaves US 13 ends at the shore, often in a small waterside village. Their names – Oyster, Birdsnest, Willis Wharf, Silver Beach, Harborton – give clues to the character and nature of this narrow spit of land.

The best-known feature of the area is **Chincoteague**, although its name creates a lot of confusion. The long barrier island that borders the entire Maryland shore and extends into Virginia is **Assateague Island**, and is protected as a wildlife refuge. The smaller Chincoteague Island lies just west, and is a town with abundant resort facilities. So far so good, but the confusion comes with the fact that the Virginia part of Assateague Island is called the **Chincoteague National Wildlife Refuge**. So when we refer to Chincoteague, it will be to the town and its island. When we mean the part of Assateague Island, we will use its full name, identifying it as the Chincoteague National Wildlife Refuge.

Along Virginia's scenic Eastern Shore.

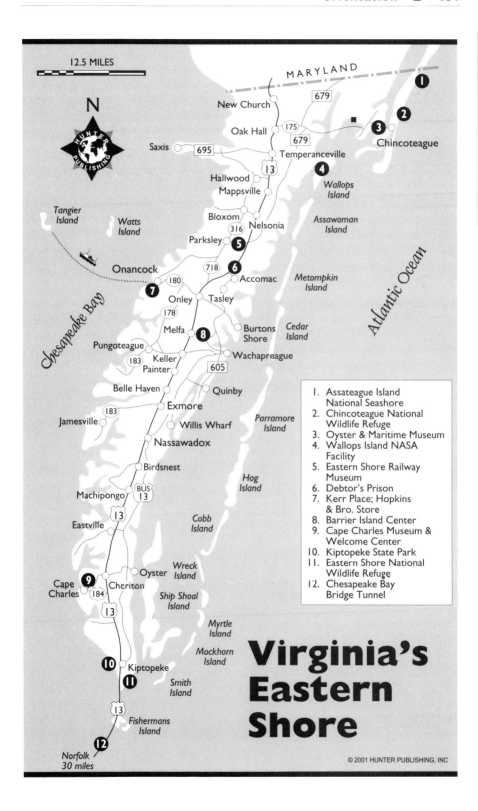

12.5 MILES

N

HUNTER PUBLISHING

MARYLAND

New Church

679

Oak Hall

175

679

Saxis

695

Temperanceville

❶

❷

❸

Chincoteague

13

❹

Hallwood
Mappsville

Wallops
Island

Tangier
Island

Watts
Island

Bloxom

316

Nelsonia

Assawoman
Island

Parksley

❺

Onancock

718

❻

Accomac

Metompkin
Island

180

❼

Onley

Tasley

178

Melfa

❽

Burtons
Shore

Cedar
Island

Pungoteague

183

Keller
Painter

Wachapreague

605

Belle Haven

Quinby

Jamesville

183

Exmore

Willis Wharf

Parramore
Island

Nassawadox

Birdsnest

Hog
Island

Machipongo

BUS
13

13

Eastville

Cobb
Island

Oyster

Wreck
Island

Cape
Charles

❾

Cheriton

184

Ship Shoal
Island

13

Myrtle
Island

Mockhorn
Island

❿

Kiptopeke

⓫

Smith
Island

13

Fishermans
Island

Norfolk
30 miles

⓬

Chesapeake Bay

Atlantic Ocean

1. Assateague Island
   National Seashore
2. Chincoteague National
   Wildlife Refuge
3. Oyster & Maritime Museum
4. Wallops Island NASA
   Facility
5. Eastern Shore Railway
   Museum
6. Debtor's Prison
7. Kerr Place; Hopkins
   & Bro. Store
8. Barrier Island Center
9. Cape Charles Museum &
   Welcome Center
10. Kiptopeke State Park
11. Eastern Shore National
    Wildlife Refuge
12. Chesapeake Bay
    Bridge Tunnel

Virginia's Eastern Shore

© 2001 HUNTER PUBLISHING, INC

South of Assateague Island are more barrier islands, all remaining in their natural state and most under the protection of the Nature Conservancy or the government. These barrier islands were once thriving villages or sportsmen's resort communities, but a succession of coastal storms took their toll and the islands became uninhabited before the 1940s. On the Chesapeake side is **Tangier Island**, settled in 1686, with a current population of several hundred.

■ Early Settlements

The very earliest recorded European encounter on Virginia's eastern shore came in 1603 when Thomas Canner wrote of an ambush by Indians while he searched for traces of the Roanoke colony of North Carolina that had been founded about 1588. Like most of the Eastern Shore, the area was first charted by John Smith in 1608, and it was settled by the Englishman Thomas Savage in 1614.

A Native American tribe under the leadership of Chief Debedeavon sent relief supplies by canoe across the Chesapeake in 1614 to save the struggling English colony at Jamestown. By 1632 this was a flourishing community that was already keeping permanent court records (which are still at the Clerk's Office in Eastville).

From early times, seafood and agriculture were the staples of the economy, with abundant oysters, clams, crabs and about 40 varieties of fin fish. The isolated Barrier Islands, which bear the brunt of all storms from the Atlantic, were settled and **Hog Island**, now deserted, once had a town with a population of 250.

The town of **Cape Charles** was founded in 1884 as the southern terminus of the railroad. From there, passengers and freight transferred to a steamship bound for Norfolk. Cape Charles became the headquarters for the Norfolk Division of the railroad, and in just a few years its streets were filled with late Victorian and turn-of-the-century buildings, perhaps the highest concentration from that period on the entire east coast.

■ The Area Today

Today, agriculture is the largest business in the area with 118,000 acres under production. **Potatoes** are the largest crop, with over 30,000 acres, followed by grains and vegetables. The production of **chickens** is also a growing business in Accomack County. The **seafood industry** provides employment for many local watermen and others who work in the packing plants. The largest packer of clams in the world is located in Chincoteague and oyster farming takes place on both Chesapeake Bay and the ocean sides of the peninsula. As with the rest of the bay, crabbing is big business here.

EASTERN SHORE STYLE

This part of the Eastern Shore has its own architectural style, called "big house, little house, colonnade and kitchen." You will recognize these homes with four different roof lines wherever you travel here.

Getting Here & Getting Around

From the south, the only access is over the fascinating Chesapeake Bay Bridge-Tunnel which starts just east of Norfolk. US 13 and Route 600 converge at the bridge, and run parallel nearly half the length of the peninsula. From the north, US 13 and the smaller Route 679 enter from Maryland. Although there are ferry connections seasonally to Tangier Island, in the center of the Chesapeake, it can also be accessed by ferry from Crisfield, in Maryland, and by seasonal cruises from Onancock, on the Eastern Shore, or Reedville, in Tidewater Virginia.

Information Sources

Eastern Shore Visitors Center, PO Drawer R, Melfa, VA 23410; ☎ 757-787-2460. The Welcome Center, a mile south of the state line on US 13 in New Church, is well-stocked with brochures for the whole state, and the staff is especially helpful in connecting travelers with local activities that interest them.

Chincoteague Chamber of Commerce Visitors Center, 6733 Maddox Blvd. (PO Box 258), Chincoteague 23336 (☎ 757-336-6161) is well sign-posted from the causeway on the way to the refuge.

Adventures

■ Parks

Chincoteague National Wildlife Refuge is the highlight of this area, much visited by those hoping to see the wild ponies that have made the barrier island famous. Wider than the part of Assateague island farther north, the Chincoteague refuge end has forests of mature pine and good-sized oaks and maples which have been able to develop in its interior (upper Assateague has no interior). On a drive through, you are likely to see wildlife along the roads, even the famous wild horses. Kids are sure to recognize Misty among them. More than 15,000 snow geese winter in the refuge on Assateague island. The National Park Service maintains a visitors center (open 9-5 daily) at Tom's Cove, where there is also a swimming beach. Pets are prohibited, even inside vehicles and no camping or beach fires are allowed.

A 14½-mile Wildlife Tour is available, which takes the group along private back trails examining the wildlife of the island. Make reservations at the Visitors Center (☎ 757-336-6155) or at Bayside Arts and Crafts (☎ 757-336-6798). In April, May and September there is one trip daily and from Memorial Day through Labor Day there are two trips daily. Private trips are available, too, but for any of these tours you should reserve early. For information on the Park call the Refuge Manager, Chincoteague, VA 23336, ☎ 757-336-6122.

When visiting Chincoteague on an outdoor adventure wear long, light-colored pants and a light but long sleeve shirt. Deer ticks live here and they can carry Lyme disease, which can be debilitating and deadly. Also, the refuge abounds in poison ivy and hungry mosquitos. Carry a repellent that is good for both mosquitos and ticks and when you finish your trek check your clothing and exposed skin for tiny black spots – deer ticks. They show up best on light-colored fabrics. These annoyances are good reasons to stay on the trails.

You will need another pass even if you already have one for the Maryland part of the park, since each segment has a separate admission. The Golden Eagle Pass is good in either state.

Kiptopeke State Park, at Cape Charles (☎ 757-336-6161), offers camping, swimming, fishing, boat access and abundant birdlife at the southern end of the peninsula. This is the only state park on the eastern shore of Virginia and has 375 acres, some of which is closed to all access. Among the assets of the park are a campground, swimming beach on the Chesapeake, fishing pier, walking trails and a bird banding station. The breakwater is made of nine surplus World War II concrete ships that were sunk here. The Baywoods Trail is 1½ miles long and there are six dune walks. Numerous interpretive programs run by the park's naturalists are offered during the season, Memorial Day to Labor Day. In September and October the hawk observatory and bird banding station are open. The address is 3540 Kiptopeke Drive, Cape Charles, VA 23310, ☎ 757-331-2267, www.state. va.us/-dcr/dcr_home.htm. For campground reservations, call ☎ 800-933-PARK.

■ On Foot

Walking & Hiking

 Fifteen miles of trails give access to several different areas of the **Chincoteague National Wildlife Refuge**. To avoid confusion, remember that the Wildlife Refuge is really on the south end of Assateague Island but, in Virginia, bears the name of Chincoteague, the island from which you gain access.

> **CAUTION** *Since this area is environmentally fragile, hikers must stay on marked trails. No matter how enticing, stay off the dunes. Visitors should also know that pets are prohibited, even inside a vehicle.*

The 3.2-mile **Wildlife Loop** is reserved until 3 pm daily for walkers and cyclists only. You can get to it by following Swan Cove Trail on the north end of the road near the Visitor Center. The Wildlife Loop circles Snow Goose Pool, a good place for waterfowl sightings. The **Marsh Trail** takes you from the Wildlife Trail out into a group of small islets, on the far side of which is a side trip on the **Boardwalk Trail**. Be sure to get the Wildlife Loop Trail brochure before heading out; it will enrich the experience. **Lighthouse Trail**, off the beach access road, is a quarter-mile long, with no bikes allowed. The **Woodland Trail** is a 1.6-mile loop leading along Tom's Cove and the Assateague Channel to an overlook where you can often see wild horses.

A short, self-guiding nature trail is near the Toms Cove building. The beach stretches 12 miles north from the Visitor Center, perfect for beach walking and limited to walkers. South of the Visitor Center is more beach, which may be used by off-road vehicles with a permit. This beach leads to a section called "the Hook," which is generally closed between March 15 and August 31 because it is a shorebird nesting area, particularly for piping plovers. In late November the refuge holds its annual **Waterfowl Week** when it opens its 7½-mile service road so visitors can view the tens of thousands of waterfowl that congregate here during migration. Vehicles have to be in line by 2:30 pm each day and off the service road by 3:30. Bird walks are also conducted during this period, by reservation. For more information on the events and dates of Waterfowl Week, ☎ 757-336-6122.

The last week of every July, a **round-up of the wild horses** (which are locally often called ponies) takes place in order to ensure that they do not overpopulate the island's sensitive environment. The horses are driven to a point on the Assateague Channel behind the District Office of the Wildlife Refuge, just north of the Woodland Trail. From there, the horses swim across the channel to Assateague, where they are corralled before being sent to new homes. The best place to see this is on the Chincoteague Island side. From Maddox Boulevard in Chincoteague, take Ridge Rd. south and follow the side road that runs along the channel.

■ On Wheels

You cannot ride a bike across the **Chesapeake Bay Bridge-Tunnel**. To get around this, either arrange for a ride or cross via the cruise boats that operate from Onancock, Virginia or Crisfield, Maryland to Tangier or Smith Island and from either of them to Reedsville or Sunnybank, Virginia. This lands you in Northumberland County, well north of, and a long pedal from, Williamsburg.

RECOMMENDED READING: *County maps can be ordered from the* **Virginia Department of Transportation**, *1401 East Broad Street, Richmond, VA 23219;* ☎ *804-786-2838. Ask for the map of Northampton and Accomack counties.* **Bicycling on Virginia Roads – Laws and Safety Tips** *is available from the State Bicycle Coordinator at the same address;* ☎ *804-786-2964 or 800-835-1203.*

BICYCLING REGULATIONS

■ In Virginia, bicycles must obey all of the traffic laws that apply to motor vehicles. Although they may be ridden on most highways, they are not permitted on interstates or other controlled-access highways.

■ Riding abreast is forbidden; single file only. You must ride with the flow of traffic and stay to the right of the road.

■ Bikes can use sidewalks where not prohibited, but must yield to pedestrians. Hand signals must be used for stops and turns. Earphones are prohibited.

■ Between sunset and sunrise, bikes must have a white light on the front that can be seen 500 feet away and a red reflector on the rear capable of being seen from 300 feet. A rear light, while not required, must be visible for 500 feet if used.

US 13 travels down the center of this long peninsula. It is a busy highway with speeding traffic and not a good place for bikes. The few side routes, however, such as **Route 600**, are very nice routes for bicyclist. In Virginia, any route numbered over 600 is a satisfactory one for bicycles.

A good trip of approximately 50 miles leads from **Accomac**, on the northern part of US 13, to **Kiptopeke**, at the southern tip near the bridge. From

Accomac take Route 605 south and east to Wachapreague on the waters protected by the barrier islands. Next, take it to Quimby and then go east toward Painter, cutting off and going south on Route 600. This road parallels Route 13 to its east, along Hog Island Bay, Cobb Island Bay and the inner waters of the barrier islands. Do take enough time to try the side roads toward the water. You will need to arrange a shuttle unless you want to double back, because there is no suitable northward leg that doesn't repeat the trip.

Two of the trails at **Chincoteague National Wildlife Refuge** are paved for bicycle travel. The 3.2-mile **Wildlife Loop** is reserved until 3 pm daily for walkers and cyclists only. The **Woodland Trail** is a 1.6-mile loop leading to an overlook where you can often see ponies. A bike path connects the town of Chincoteague to the refuge. On the short **Lighthouse Trail**, no bikes are allowed. The terrain here is flat and easy. The land is sand covered by a thin layer of delicate vegetation, so stay on the trails in order to protect the fragile environment. For more information, write the Refuge Manager, Chincoteague National Wildlife Refuge, Chincoteague, VA 23336, ☎ 757-336-6122.

Trails suitable for bikes are also available at **Assateague Island National Seashore**, the outer of the two islands. Here, too, the terrain is flat and over sandy scrub and dune areas. Get a map at the visitor center. Assateague Island National Seashore, PO Box 38, Chincoteague, VA 23336, ☎ 757-336-6577. Riding off-trail is prohibited and, even if dismounted, you should not climb or walk the dunes.

Tangier Island is a nice change of pace for bicyclists. While you can take the tour cruises over and back in the same day and have time to see the island, we suggest an overnight stay, preferably longer, so that you can get the true sense of the island and its lifestyle. The island is flat, only 2½ miles long and a mile and a half wide, so there aren't any places to get lost. This is a poke-about place with lots of character. See *Boat Tours*, page 468, and *Sightseeing*, page 474, for information on how to get there. You can bring your own bike or rent one from Wendy Marshall (☎ 757-891-2255) or Joan Parks (☎ 757-891-2452). Be sure to call in advance of your trip to make sure one is available.

At the end of October, Citizens for a Better Eastern Shore and the Eastern Shore of Virginia Bicycle Club team up for the annual **Between The Waters Bike Tour**. This program offers a choice of four routes that run from the bay side of the peninsula to the ocean side; ☎ 757-678-7157.

BICYCLE & EQUIPMENT RENTALS

The Bike Depot, 7058 Maddox Boulevard, Chincoteague Island, VA 23336, ☎ 757-336-5511, has a wide variety of bikes for rent and they are close to the refuge. In addition to mountain bikes and cruisers, they have tandems and three-wheelers. They also have additional gear such as baby seats, tag-alongs, baskets and carts. Helmets are available, but are not included in the rental fee and cost $1 extra. Cruisers without gears are $3 for the first hour, $2 for each additional hour, or $10 a day; geared ones run $4 for the first hour and each additional hour, or $22 a day. Mountain bikes cost $5 an hour or $25 a day.

In Onancock, you can rent bicycles at **Hopkins & Bro. Store**, on the wharf, at 2 Market Street; ☎ 757-787-3100.

■ On Water

 Kiptopeke State Park, at Cape Charles (☎ 757-336-6161), offers a swimming beach with lifeguards. The beach is reached by a handicapped-accessible wooden walkway. See page 462 above.

The town of **Onancock** has provided a boat launch facility at the town dock, three blocks from downtown. The launch is on Onancock Creek, which opens into the Chesapeake; ☎ 804-787-3363.

Boats are permitted to land in the Chincoteague National Wildlife Refuge at **Assateague Point** (off the Woodland Trail) all year and on the **Hook** from the beginning of September through March 14. Other areas are not open for landing. See more details below under *Canoeing & Kayaking*. Contact the Refuge Manager at ☎ 757-336-6122.

Canoeing & Kayaking

You can access the Chesapeake at **Kiptopeke State Park**, which is right off US 13, three miles north of the bridge-tunnel and the wildlife refuge. Additional access to the bay is available at Cape Charles. For access to the inviting waters on the Atlantic side, protected by the Barrier Islands, go to Route 600. The southerly access is at Oyster, opposite Mockhorn Island Wildlife Management Area, and farther north at Willis Wharf there is access to the part called Hog Island Bay. See page 462.

Canoeists and kayakers can land on **Assateague Point** at Chincoteague National Wildlife Refuge at any time of year. The Point is on the Assateague Channel inside the Hook of Assateague Island on the northwest side of Tom's Cove. You can also land on the Hook from September 1 through March 14, but not thereafter, because it is a sensitive shorebird nesting area. Refuge pools, such as Snow Goose Pool, are off-limits to all boats and flotation devices.

Tidewater Expeditions offers canoe and kayak trips all year along the wonderful and undeveloped coast of the Assateague Channel. Another part of their business is the Riversport School of Paddling, good for beginners or to pick up your technique. The Early Morning Excursion is just that, departing at 6:30 am and returning to base at 9 am. Cost is about $37 for a one-person kayak or $21 per person for a double. The evening excursion leaves at 6 pm and returns at dusk. Both trips explore Assateague from the channel side and include forays into Tom's Cove, visits to the oyster and clam beds, views of the horses and lots of beautiful marshlands. You need not have any previous experience and they provide all gear, other than personal items. If you don't need a guided tour, you can rent one of their kayaks (they have Aquaterra Chinooks, Gemini, Kahuma, and Scupper Sit-On-Tops) for about $40 a day. Look for them at 7729 East Side Drive, Chincoteague; ☎ 757-336-6811 or 757-336-3159.

Boat Rentals

On the causeway crossing to Chincoteague Island, you will see a number of signs advertising boat rentals, or you can reserve ahead with **Capt'n Bob's Marina**, which also has pontoon boats; ☎ 757-336-6654.

Boat Tours & Ferries

Around the coast off Chincoteague there are many islands and rich marshes. **Island Cruises** aboard the *Osprey* are professionally guided tours of these waters, from Memorial Day through October. Cruises are an hour and a half in length and they depart from the Town Dock, at the water end of Cropper Street in Chincoteague, just south of the Route 175 causeway. From Memorial Day to mid-June they sail on Tuesday, Thursday and Saturday at 6 pm; mid-June to the end of July they depart daily at 5 and 7 pm; in August daily at 4:30 and 6:30 pm; September daily at 6 pm; and in October on Tuesday, Thursday and Saturday at 5 pm. Buy tickets at the Refuge Motel, 7058 Maddox Boulevard, or Queen Sound at 4107 Main Street, both in Chincoteague; ☎ 757-336-5511. Fares are about $10 adult, $5 child.

Saltmarsh Tours explore the marshes for birding, photography or to go crabbing or clamming, using six-passenger open platform boats that can navigate in very shallow water. Ninety-minute trips are custom scheduled, and cost from $45 each for two people ($90) to $24 each for a group of six ($144). Captain Ken Marshall, along with being a naturalist with a lifetime of experience in the marshes, is a skilled carver who creates decoys in the traditional style of the barrier islands at his studio in Willis Wharf. To reserve a trip, contact him at ☎ 410-4442-4246, www.saltmarshtours.com; e-mail saltmarsh@accomack.com.

East Side Rentals and Marina also does boat tours from Memorial Day through Labor Day at 4, 5:30 and 7 pm. Before and after that season they run at 4 and 5 pm. These one-hour tours operate in the Assateague Channel; rates are $10. The address is 7462 East Side Avenue, Chincoteague; ☎ 757-336-3409, 800-889-1525.

Chincoteague View is a pontoon-style craft that operates from the Curtis Merritt Harbor of Refuge on the south end of Main Street in Chincoteague. They run inshore fishing charters, nature cruises and custom cruises. Fishing charters cost about $30 per person for from two to six people, including bait, tackle and instruction, if necessary. The nature cruises cost $10 per person for a one-hour cruise or $15 per person for a two-hour cruise. The shallow draft of the boat allows it to snuggle close in to shore for fishing and wildlife viewing. Reserve with Captain Mike or Gwynn Handforth, PO Box 35, Chincoteague, VA 23336, ☎ 757-336-6861. From the end of the Route 175 causeway, go right (south) to the end and look for the signs.

During the summer season, from mid-May through October, there are regularly scheduled cruises to **Tangier Island** in Chesapeake Bay. The ships take passengers only (you can take bikes with you) from Onancock, Virginia, on the eastern shore; ☎ 757-787-8220. Another boat, the **Capt. Eulice**, leaves Onancock at 10, arriving back in Onancock at 3 pm, giving you two hours on the island; ☎ 757-891-2240, fax 891-2586.

Fishing

Almost a year-round sport here, fishing is especially popular for the variety of fish. This variety is explained by the diversity of watery habitats the cape provides. The bay, the Atlantic, the barrier islands and ocean wrecks offer different fishing conditions, as well as different fish. In the summer, ocean trolling may yield dolphin, tuna, mackerel, marlin or blues. In the spring, the bay has blues and drum, joined by croaker, trout and flounder throughout the summer and fall.

FISHING LICENSES: *Virginia recognizes saltwater licenses issued by Maryland on the waters of the Chesapeake Bay and the saltwater portions of any tributaries that fall within its boundaries. Freshwater fishing licenses for nonresidents are $30 for an annual statewide permit and $6 for a five-day license. To fish in tidal waters of any stream, you mus also have a saltwater license, which is $5 for 10 consecutive days or $7.50 a year. Be sure to pick up a copy of the state* Freshwater and Saltwater Fishing Regulations, *which lists all the fish and their season, size and creel limits.*

FISHING TIPS

Seasons for fish vary, but peak periods are usually as follows:

■ **March-April** – mackerel on the Atlantic side (grill them within a few hours of catching)

■ **April-mid-June** – in the Bay red and black drum, Tautog and bluefish

■ **April-August** – flounder in the Barrier Islands, and ocean trolling in the open Atlantic for tuna, dolphin, marlin, bluefish and mackerel

■ **June-October** – in the bay for trout, flounder, croaker and spot

■ **Late August-October** – in the Bay and the Barrier Islands for red drum

■ **October-December** – Tautog, flounder and trout in the bay

At Chincoteague National Wildlife Refuge, fishing and crabbing are permitted on **Tom's Cove** (at the south end of Assateague Island) and at **Swan's Cove** adjacent to the Beach Rd. Other areas are open from time to time, so check at the Visitor Center.

Cultural & Eco-Travel Experiences

■ Natural Areas

Chincoteague National Wildlife Refuge occupies the southern tip of a unique and fragile barrier island that stretches south from the Delaware shore. It is a prime wildlife watching area, made famous by its wild horses. But they are certainly not the only wildlife you will see here, especially if you go in the late afternoon, when birds and animals are the most active.

> **CAUTION**
>
> *Be very careful driving in the refuge. The car in front of you may come to a halt at the sight of deer, snowy egrets or a pony. This is even more dangerous because you, too, will be scanning the roadsides as you drive. Foot and bicycle are much better ways to explore Chincoteague.*

On the route to the park entrance the **Refuge Waterfowl Museum** is a private collection with a resident decoy carver, decoys, waterfowl art and a gift shop. It is open 10-5 Wednesday through Monday in the summer, Friday through Monday spring and fall, closed January and February; ☎ 757-336-5800. Admission is $2.50, children $1.

The **Eastern Shore National Wildlife Refuge** (☎ 804-331-2760) has a visitor center just off US 13 and 600, close to the bridge-tunnel ramp, where exhibits relate to the wildlife seen nearby. Settled early in Colonial times, this piece of land served as Army Fort John Custis in World War II and had 16-inch guns in heavy bunkers, later serving as an Air Force radio and radar base until the base closed in 1981.

This is a major area for birds, including bald eagles, peregrine falcons, black ducks and blue herons. The refuge's marshes and grasslands are a staging ground for fall migrations, with large flocks of birds assembling and waiting for favorable wind and weather to cross the mouth of Chesapeake Bay. In spring look for ibis, egrets, willets, bobwhites, quail and osprey. Horned and screech owls, warblers, wrens and songbirds are common. In fall there are multitudes of waterfowl and other migrating species such as hawks, falcons and songbirds. Winter is the time to watch for hunting marsh hawks and kestrels.

Most of the 651 acres are visible from the half-mile interpretive trail that passes through woods to a raised area that once served as a military bunker, an environmental version of sword to plowshare. At the Visitor Center are exhibits and a video on the role of the refuge. The refuge is open during daylight hours, but picnicking is not allowed. Refuge Manager, Eastern Shore of Virginia National Wildlife Refuge, 5003 Hallett Circle, Cape Charles, VA 23310-9725; ☎ 804-331-2760, TDD 800-828-1140.

Waterfowl in one of the Eastern Shore's tidal creeks.

The Nature Conservancy has undergone a shift in thinking, recognizing that it cannot buy properties and seal them off from the public. They have instituted programs to bring people into these sensitive areas and allow them to appreciate the land while learning the importance of conservancy. It's a fine combination and supports their ultimate purpose. In the Eastern Shore they conduct birding and kayaking programs, called Virginia Coast Reserve Field Trips, throughout the year. These take place all over the peninsula in numerous locations, including Wachapreague, Willis Wharf, Nassawadox and Chincoteague. Trips usually include B&B accommodations. For reservations and information, contact the Nature Conservancy, Virginia Coast Reserve, PO Box 158, Nassawadox, VA 23413; ☎ 888-827-4673 (888-VA SHORE).

■ Crafts

Decoy art is highly prized on the Eastern Shore. **A Work of Art Decoys** is the shop of carver Jay Cherrix, descendant of one of the island's legendary carvers. A full range of decoys is available, from primitives to works of fine art, at 7721 East Side Drive, Chincoteague Island; ☎ 757-336-6811.

Eastern Shore Pottery is a shopping adventure – you never know what you will find here. They have clay pots and painted vases in all sizes, from traditional shapes to roosters, pigs, cats and foxes. They also have a good selection of Southwestern and Mexican patterns. Visit them on US 13 in Capeville; ☎ 757-331-4341.

On US 13 in Onley is **Turner Sculpture**, the studios and shop of William and David Turner, father and son sculptors. Theirs are some of the finest works in bronze being produced today. Examples are in the White House, the Chicago Botanic Gardens and the American Museum of Natural History. All of their work is realistic interpretation of wildlife found along the Eastern Shore of Virginia. You can also see their work at the Salisbury Zoo in Salisbury, Maryland. Contact them at PO Box 128, Onley, VA 23418; ☎ 757-787-2818, fax 757-787-7064, www.esva.net/~turner, e-mail turner@esva.net.

■ Antiques

Worcester House, on US 13 in New Church, handles 18th- and 19th-century furniture, china and accessories. They are open Monday-Saturday, 10-5; Sunday, noon-5; ☎ 757-824-3847. **Bluewater Trading Company**, also on US 13, tends toward 19th- and early 20th-century furnishings, art and maritime items. It's open all year, but closed on Tuesdays in the off season; ☎ 757-824-3124 or 824-3781.

In Chincoteague there are four places to visit, all of them on Main Street. At number 4076 is **Shotwell's General Merchandise**, with a line of antiques and collectibles, open Thursday-Saturday and Monday-Tuesday, 10-9; Sunday, 1-9; ☎ 757-335-6484. **Collectibles, Etc.** is at 4089 Main Street; ☎ 757-336-1177. They handle furniture, old tools and other collectible items and are open during the season daily, 10-8; in the off season, Friday-Monday, 10-8. **Salt River Company** carries antiques and early 20th-century items for collectors, focusing on the unusual. The shop is at 4169 Main Street; ☎ 757-336-1833. **Reflections on the Creek** goes a bit further, with architectural details and lighting as well as furniture, accessories and collectible antiques from the mid-19th century to 1930. Open all year, Monday-Tuesday and Thursday-Saturday, 10-6; Sunday, 1-5. ☎ 757-336-6018.

Just a bit down the road in Accomac is **Mary Scott Antiques**, with old decoys, glassware and furniture, as well as fine china and old silver. It is at 2339 Back Street (Route 1503), Accomac; ☎ 757-787-2882.

Shops in Onancock allow for a side-adventure while awaiting the boat to Tangier. **Deadrise Enterprises Ltd.** and **North Street Gallery** offer folk art, collectibles and oddities, at 3 and 5 North Street, Onancock; ☎ 757-787-2077. Each is open Wednesday-Saturday, 10-5:30. **Evergreen Antiques and Gallery** has architectural detail, glassware, jewelry, hand-painted furniture and folk art at 9 North Street, Onancock; ☎ 757-787-1905.

At 17 Main Street in Wachapreague, **Main Street Antiques** not only sells antiques, but has an on-premises restoration studio for art, porcelain and china; ☎ 757-787-8709.

Treasures of the Past, 12138 Bank Street, Exmore (☎ 757-442-4952), deals in glass, from fine pieces to collectible depression glass. They also handle small furniture, jewelry and the works of local artisans. The shop is open June-August, Tuesday and Thursday-Saturday, 10-5. September-May, they open Thursday-Saturday, 10-5. **Exmore's Antique & Craft Emporium** is a large shop with over 40 dealers, some of whom sell the arts and crafts of local artisans as well. Find them at 3304 Main Street, Exmore (☎ 757-414-0111). Open Thursday-Saturday and Monday, 10-5; Sunday 1-5.

Events

APRIL: Early in the month, the **Easter Decoy and Art Festival** takes place in Chincoteague; ☎ 757-336-6161. In mid-April, Wachapreague hosts the **Annual Wachapreague Spring Flounder Tournament**; ☎ 757-787-2105.

MAY: The Eastern Shore of Virginia Chamber holds its annual **Seafood Festival** at Chincoteague in early May; ☎ 757-787-2460. Mid-month brings the **Annual International Migratory Bird Celebration** at the Chincoteague National Wildlife Refuge, with guided walks and expert-guided workshops; ☎ 757-336-6122. Later in May, **Railroad Days** are held at the Exmore Railroad Museum in Exmore, ☎ 757-442-4374; and the Chincoteague town dock has **The Blessing of the Fleet**; ☎ 757-336-6861.

JULY: During the last weekend of the month, the Chincoteague Volunteer Fire Department holds its **Annual Pony Swim and Auction**, offering a chance to see the historic event that preserves the herd of wild horses by controlling their numbers; ☎ 757-336-3138.

AUGUST: Early in the month, Cape Charles hosts the **Eastern Shore of Virginia Music Festival and Chili Cookout**, with all types of music from blues, country and gospel to classical; e-mail esvamusicfestva.net, Web site www.esvamusicfest.esva.net.

OCTOBER: During the second weekend, the **Annual Chincoteague Oyster Festival** takes place at the Maddox Family Campground; ☎ 757-336-6161. Also mid-month is **National Wildlife Refuge Week**, with wildlife art shows and family wildlife-related activities all week; ☎ 757-336-6122.

NOVEMBER: Chincoteague National Wildlife Refuge sponsors the **Assateague Island Waterfowl Festival** and the **Annual Waterfowl Week** during the last week of the month, featuring programs throughout the refuge, including bird walks and interpretive hikes. Some areas of the park that are usually closed to the public are opened up for special tours during this avian migratory period. ☎ 757-336-6122.

Sightseeing

■ Touring

The **Wallops Island NASA** facility is on Route 175, and you pass it on the way to Chincoteague, about halfway between US 13 and the island. The **Visitors Center** exhibits, many of them interactive, follow the history of flight and of rockets. Along with moon photos, you can see a piece of the moon. Satellite weather tracking is carried out from the Wallops Island site, and photos taken from these show a hurricane from above. Outside is the original "Little Joe" used for the early monkey launches, the Scout rocket used to launch satellites, and several others. The Wallops Island facility uses rockets, balloons and aircraft to conduct inexpensive scientific research into weather and environmental problems. It is also one of the major facilities for tracking satellites and balloons as they perform their missions. A small gift shop specializes in flight- and rocket-connected items and books. The Visitors Center is free and open March-June, Thursday through Monday, 10 am to 4 pm; July 4 through Labor day, daily during the same hours; September through November, Thursday-Monday, 10-4. NASA Visitor Center, Wallops Island Flight Facility, Wallops Island, VA 23337, ☎ 757-824-1344, 757-824-2298.

KID-FRIENDLY

*On Saturdays and Sundays at 11 am, the **NASA Visitors Center** presents puppet shows, and at 1 pm on Sundays there is a space suit demonstration where kids can find out what astronauts wear in space and aboard the space shuttle. Kids' flight programs are held in November. If you want to explore NASA on the net, try these addresses: the main site is www.nasa.gov; for the space shuttle and international space station, spaceflight.nasa.gov; Mars exploration site, www.jpl.nasa.gov/mars; space science enterprise, spacescience.nasa.gov; earth science enterprise, earth.nasa.gov.*

Tangier Island lies like a low-slung ship at anchor in the vast space of Chesapeake Bay. Approximately 2½ miles long and 1½ miles wide, the island has a year-round population of about 650. You can get to Tangier Island year-round on the mailboat, which makes one round-trip a day between the island and the mainland; ☎ 757-891-2240. During winter it leaves Crisfield, Maryland at 12:30 pm, arriving in Tangier about 1:15. It returns to Crisfield from Tangier at 8 am, arriving at about 8:45, so you have to stay over, except on Sunday, when you can leave Tangier at 3 pm on a special run that returns at 4 pm. During the summer the mailboat leaves Tangier at 8 am and returns at 9. It is also serviced by cruise boats that operate from mid-May through October. The Crisfield boat leaves at 12:30 pm, arriving at about 1:15, and leaves Tangier for the return trip at 4 pm, allowing time on the island for a walk or biking trip, or to eat at one of the local restaurants; ☎ 410-968-2338.

Another boat leaves from **Onancock**, Virginia (on the eastern shore); ☎ 757-787-8220. From mainland Virginia, a ferry leaves from **Reedsville**; ☎ 757-333-4656. **Chesapeake Aviation** has a charter service; ☎ 757-787-2901.

The southern end of Virginia's Eastern Shore is connected to the rest of the state by one of the greatest engineering feats of the 20th century, the **Chesapeake Bay Bridge-Tunnel**, a 17-mile highway over and under the water. This fascinating piece of civil engineering crosses the bay alternately by bridge above it and by tunnels that travel below it. The fare for a passenger vehicle is $10. In the process of construction, two islands were built in the bay; you can stop on one of these as you cross.

■ Museums & Historic Sites

Accomac has a rare museum: a **Debtor's Prison** that dates from approximately 1784. It was originally built as the house of the jailor of the "gaol" that stood where the parking lot is now located. In 1824 the house was renovated to serve as a prison for debtors and served that purpose until jailing for debt was ended in 1873. One of the two rooms on the first floor is furnished as it would have been when used by the jailer (1784-1824), the other as the debtor jail (1824-1873). It's a look back at our less compassionate past.

About halfway between Chincoteague and Accomac, Route 176 leads west to Parksley and the **Eastern Shore Railway Museum**, which tells the story of the railroad that was built down the Delmarva peninsula in the late 1880s. The railroad opened up the peninsula and made it possible for city people to summer along the shore here. The railroad continued to carry passengers well into the 20th century. The museum is housed in a nicely preserved 1906 depot, with an 1890s maintenance shed full of period railroad tools, a crossing guard shanty and antique railcars lined up on the side rails. It's two miles from US 13. As you enter town, turn right on Dunne Avenue. The museum is on the left in Railroad Square, open Tuesday-Saturday, 10:30-4; Sundays, 1-4 pm; ☎ 757-665-4618.

The story of Chincoteague, its people and industry is found at the **Oyster and Maritime Museum** in Chincoteague, close to the entrance to the Wildlife Refuge. It houses island artifacts like the lens from the Assateague lighthouse that was used from 1869 to 1961, exhibits on oyster farming and harvesting and an aquarium with typical local species. It's on the left, just before the Assateague Island Bridge, at 7125 Maddox Boulevard, Chincoteague; ☎ 757-336-6117.

Kerr Place, in historic Onancock, was built in 1799 to be the home of John Shepherd Kerr, a well-to-do local merchant who spared no expense in the construction of his manse. Inside are fine detailed plasterwork and woodwork typical of the homes of the new Federal period. The first floor has been furnished and decorated to its period while the second floor rooms are used to interpret the history of the town and surrounding area. The property is the home of the Eastern Shore of Virginia Historical Society, at Kerr Place, Onancock; ☎ 757-787-8012. Admission is $3 and the museum is open Tuesday-Saturday, 10-4; closed January-February and holidays.

THE BARRIER ISLANDS

Along the outer edges of Virginia's Eastern Shore are a series of at least 19 sandy islands called the "Barrier Islands," strips of sand and grasses that protect the main part of the peninsula. From the time of the early settlers of the 1600s hardy people lived there and eked their lives from the sea. Many people shipwrecked on these shores were saved through the efforts of the local people who served in the U.S. Life Saving Service. On Hog Island was once a village of 250 people, but today all that is changed and many of the islands are owned by organizations dedicated to their preservation as natural areas.

The **Barrier Island Center** is an organization dedicated to the preservation of the memory of the Barrier Island people and their way of life. They actively solicit items and artifacts related to the lives and livelihoods of Barrier Island settlers and expect shortly to establish a museum telling the history and culture of the hardy people who once lived here. For more information on the society or the status of their museum, write or call The Barrier Island Center, PO Box R, Melfa, VA 23410; ☎ 804-787-2460.

Also in Onancock, **Hopkins & Bro. Store** is an 1842 general store on the wharf, at 2 Market Street; ☎ 757-787-3100. One of the oldest functioning stores on the East Coast, it has its original shelves, counters and display cases. Unique gifts, home-made foods and visitor information are all available here.

The town of **Eastville** is off US 13, about 15 miles north of the bridge. Established about 1715 as the county seat, Eastville has records of its court that run back to 1632, the oldest legal records in the country. The courthouse was built in 1731 and contains a museum with native and Colonial artifacts. The Debtors Prison was built in 1743, the Eastville Inn in 1780, Christ Church in 1828 and the Clerk's Office in 1830. Since it is in Virginia, during the Civil War Eastville was part of the Confederacy.

Cape Charles was founded in 1886 to serve as the southern terminus of a railroad. Its fine harbor made it a natural for shipping and for the ferries that brought goods and produce for shipment to markets via the railroad. The town quickly prospered and its situation on the Chesapeake made it an attractive place for wealthy city dwellers to build summer "cottages." It thrived until after the end of World War II. In 1950 the ferry terminal was moved out of town and, not long after, the railroad ceased to operate. While the downtown and harbor areas still need tender loving care, the residential sections have remained attractive with many Victorian and early 20th-century mansions and residences maintaining their grandeur. To get to Cape Charles, take Route 184 west from Route 13 about 10 miles north of the Bridge-Tunnel.

The **Cape Charles Museum and Welcome Center** shows how the New York, Philadelphia and Norfolk Railroad created the town and dominated it until the opening of the Chesapeake Bridge-Tunnel in 1964. The museum is in a building that served as an auxiliary power generating facility into the 1980s. In the rear of the building are two railroad cars under restoration and inside is a collection of historic photos and railroad-related memorabilia. But the railroad is not the whole story, and the museum also emphasizes the growth of the town and area. Like any good museum, it is an evolving showcase, and future exhibits will cover local boat artistry, archeological remains, oral histories, World War memorabilia, decoys and a collection of early films starring Nell Shipman, whose last major film, *The Story of Mr Hobbs*, was filmed in Cape Charles in 1947. From Route 13, take Route 184 west about 1.8 miles to the museum, PO Box 11, Cape Charles, VA 23310; ☎ 757-331-1008. It is open Saturdays, noon-5; Sundays, 2-5 pm.

Where to Stay

ACCOMMODATIONS PRICE KEY	
Rates are per room, per night, double occupancy.	
$	Under $50
$$	$50 to $100
$$$	$101 to $175
$$$$	$176 and up

■ Chincoteague

1848 Island Manor House B&B is an attractive 2½-story home offering six guest rooms with private baths and two that share a bath. Located on Main Street in Chincoteague, it's convenient to the refuge; they offer free use of a bike to guests. It's furnished with antiques and a brick courtyard and rose garden add more charm. They serve a full breakfast. The Island Manor is at 4160 Main Street, Chincoteague, VA 23336; ☎ 757-336-5436 or 800-852-1505, fax 757-336-1333, www.chincoteague.com/b-b/imh.html. $$-$$$

Miss Molly's Inn is also on Main Street. Five rooms have private bath, two share a bath. Built in 1886, this home was the mansion of a clam packing king. It was in this house that the plot for *Misty of Chincoteague* was conceived by Marguerite Henry. It is furnished with antiques and at tea time they serve fresh scones and trifle. A full breakfast is served each morning. Look for it at 4141 Main Street, Chincoteague, VA 23336; ☎ 757-336-6686 or 800-221-5620, fax 757-336-0600, Web site www.chincoteague.com.b-b/molly.html. $$-$$$

Refuge Motor Inn is on Maddox Boulevard very close to the Assateague Bridge, making it possible to walk to the refuge. The inn is a very attractive contemporary building with generous use of natural wood for accent. All rooms have either a patio or balcony. The rooms themselves are attractively furnished with king or queen beds and in-room refrigerators. In addition to an observation deck and sundeck, guests have the use of a sauna, hot tub, exercise room and an indoor/outdoor pool. Rooms are air conditioned. Guests are also welcome to use the picnic areas with charcoal grills and a playground. On the grounds is a corral where you can see and pat a genuine Chincoteague pony. PO Box 378, 7058 Maddox Boulevard, Chincoteague, VA 23336; ☎ 757-336-5511, 800-544-8469, extension 2. $$-$$$

Beach Road Motel is a modern single-level building with one and two bedroom units, a cottage, apartment and mobile home as alternatives. The motel units all have covered approaches and open onto the pool area.

Rooms are comfortably furnished and are clean and attractive. An outdoor picnic area and grills are free to guests and rooms have refrigerator, in-room coffee service, color cable TV and air conditioning. The motel is at 6151 Maddox Boulevard, Chincoteague, VA 23336; ☎ 757-336-6562 or 800-699-6562, e-mail beachrd@shore.intercom.net. $$

If you want a longer stay, check with **Vacation Cottages**, a company that represents owners of many cottages available for rent in the Chincoteague area. Cottages are divided into eight categories, based on the facilities that each offers. Prices range from $135 for a category 1 to $365 for a category 8 weekend, which is defined as Friday to Monday. Week prices for the same units would be $210 to $580, with a week defined as Monday to Monday or Friday to Friday. Some are detached units, others are units within condo developments or apartment-style units. A brochure that pictures each structure, describing the amenities of each, is available from Vacation Cottages, 6282 Maddox Boulevard, Chincoteague, VA 23336; ☎ 757-336-3720, 800-457-6643, fax 757-336-5227, www.chincoteague.com/cotts.html.

■ In the Northern Area

Garden and the Sea Inn is in a fine home built in 1802, with later Victorian ornamentation. It has twin bow fronts and a big front porch. Furnishings are fine antiques and oriental rugs. Each room is different in decor, but all six rooms have a private bath, some with Jacuzzi. Swag drapery over fine sheer curtains provide privacy while preserving light. The inn's dining room is one of the best in the area, and innkeepers all over the Eastern Shore suggest it to their guests. A hearty continental breakfast is served in the morning on the patio and light refreshments are available in the afternoon; they are participants in an inn-to-inn canoe package that includes fine inns in Snow Hill and Princess Anne, both in Maryland. Follow signs from US 13 to 4188 Nelson Rd., New Church, VA 23415; ☎ 757-824-0672 or 800-824-0672, fax 757-824-5605, e-mail baker@shore.intercom.net. $$-$$$

If you're planning to catch the ferry to Tangier it could be handy to stay in Onancock. **Colonial Manor** is a fine old home on two acres, and its accommodating innkeepers will pick up guests from the ferry and sell tickets to those heading there. The eight well-appointed rooms are air conditioned and have TV. Guests are welcome to use the bikes and have privileges at the local golf course. Colonial Manor is at 84 Market Street, Onancock, VA 23417; ☎ 757-787-3521, fax 757-787-2448. $$

■ Cape Charles

Wilson-Lee House B&B began in 1906, when the owner of a very successful department store contracted with architect James Lee to build a suitable home. James Wilson's resulting showplace was occupied by family until 1958. Today it is an elegant B&B furnished in antiques, with contemporary prints and accessories. The decorating is exceptional. Inn-keepers David Phillips and Leon Parham serve a full gourmet breakfast. From US 13, go west to Cape Charles, entering on Randolph Avenue. At Fig Street, turn right and go one block to Tazewell, then turn left. The B&B is on the right just beyond Plum Street at 403 Tazewell Avenue, Cape Charles, VA 23310-3217; ☎ 757-331-1954, fax 757-331-8133, www.wilsonleehouse.com. $$-$$$

■ Tangier Island

Accommodations on Tangier are limited, with only three places to stay. All are pleasant and comfortable, helping the traveler to experience the island way of life. **Sunset Inn** (☎ 757-891-2535, $$) and **Bay View Inn** (☎ 757-891-2396, $$) are both open all year. Bay View has five rooms sharing two baths. If you are planning an off-season or winter stay ask about dining options when you book, since choices tend to be limited then. **Hilda Crockett's Chesapeake House** is open from mid-April through October; ☎ 757-891-2331. Rates here are about $40 per person per night and include meals. Address any of these at Tangier, VA 23440.

■ Camping

In addition to camping, **Kiptopeke State Park** has a guarded swimming beach on the Chesapeake, a fishing pier and a boat launch. The park is off US 13, three miles north of the Chesapeake Bridge-Tunnel. The campground is in several loops on the north side of the access road. Bath houses with hot showers are available and boardwalks provide access to the swimming areas. The park is at 3540 Kiptopeke Drive, Cape Charles, VA 23310; ☎ 757-331-2267, www.state.va.us/-dcr/dcr_home.htm. For reservations, ☎ 800-933-PARK.

Little Acres Campground is a private campground in Bloxom, Virginia, west of US 13 near the Maryland border. Sites run from water, sewer and electric serviced ($15 a night) to no hook-up tent sites for two adults and two children at $11. The campground has a dumping station, a camp store which sells fishing gear and bait, laundry facilities and a game room with pool table. From US 13, take Route 187 west to Bloxom. Turn right after the railroad tracks, then left onto Route 684, about 1½ miles, to 25011 Guard Shore Rd., Bloxom, VA 23306-3317; ☎ 757-665-4788.

At Chincoteague there is no public camping in the refuge so you have to find space outside the refuge. **Maddox Family Campground** is a full-service campground with over 500 sites for everything from RVs to tents. They have a swimming pool, playground, store, recreation hall, bath houses with hot showers, dumping station, propane filling area and laundry facilities. The campground is on the main road to the Wildlife Refuge, only a half-mile from the bridge to Assateague. PO Box 82, Maddox Boulevard, Chincoteague, VA 23336; ☎ 757-336-3111 or 757-336-6648.

Another full-service option is **Tom's Cove Campground** which is on Chincoteague Island facing onto Tom's Cove and overlooking Assateague Island and the wildlife reserve. They, too, have a store, recreation hall, dumping station, bath houses with hot showers, but they also have piers and beach frontage on the cove. Tom's Cove Campground, Chincoteague, VA 23336; ☎ 757-336-6498, fax 757-336-6153.

At the south end of the peninsula, **Cherrystone Family Camping and RV Resort** has a location right on Chesapeake Bay and offers a full schedule of facilities and activities. Planned events and activities occur just about daily. There are more than 700 sites here, all lined up close together. They have a pool, pedalboat pond, fishing piers, crabbing and clamming area, wading and swimming area in the Bay, horseshoes, shuffleboard, fishing supplies store, camp store, etc. Base daily rates are about $17-$20, depending on the season, with small extra charges for additional services. They also offer camping cabins, trailer and rentals. The campground is off US 13, north of Cape Charles, PO Box 545, Cheriton, VA 23316; ☎ 757-331-3063.

Where to Eat

DINING PRICE KEY
The price key indicates the cost of *most* dinner entrées on a restaurant's regular and daily special menu.
$ . . . . Most under $10
$$ . . . . $10 to $20
$$$ . . . . Over $30

■ Chincoteague

 Steamers, at 6251 Maddox Rd. (☎ 757-336-5478) is a local favorite, specializing in steamed crab and shrimp, served in an informal setting. $-$$

At **Luna Seas Café** (☎ 757-336-2268), the name ought to tell you something. Their motto is, "We're all here cuz we're not all there." It's a good place for breakfast, with a menu offering everything from eggs to scrapple and chipped beef. In addition to the usual luncheon offerings, their menu has crab cakes, grilled portobellos, pasta dishes, pizzas and Jamaican jerk chicken. Dinner brings grilled shrimp or tuna, crab imperial or cakes, red snapper or New York strip. It's at 7077 Maddox Boulevard, Chincoteague Island. $-$$

Don's Seafood Restaurant, 4113 Main Street (☎ 757-336-5715), is a casual family sort of place just north of the Route 175 bridge. Breakfast dishes are mostly $3-$4, as are lunch sandwiches. A good range of dinner entrées are priced under $10 (ham, chicken, roast beef, clam strips), with others up to $16. From 9 pm until closing there is a raw bar and late fare served in the lounge, where there is dancing nightly.

Captain Fish's, on the wharf off Main Street, is known for its fresh seafood and for its equally fresh waitstaff. In clement weather, eat on the dock, but hold onto your napkin since it's often breezy. $$

■ In the North

The Garden and The Sea Inn, near the Chincoteague turn-off in New Church, is excellent, serving appetizers such as Chincoteague oysters in a four-pepper sauce or sautéed shrimp in bourbon cream sauce (each about $8) and entrées of lamb in currant-rosemary sauce, mountain trout filled with crab imperial or salmon with Béarnaise, priced from $15 to $22. Tom Baker is the owner. Check during the off season, as it may not be open year-round. 4188 Nelson Rd., New Church, VA 23415, ☎ 757-824-0672, 800-824-0672, fax 757-824-5605, e-mail baker@shore.intercom.net.

Eastern Shore Steamboat Co. Restaurant, on the wharf at 2 Market Street, Onancock, VA (☎ 757-787-3100, www.downtownonancock.com), has an upstairs dining room overlooking the harbor and an outdoor deck downstairs. One of their specialties is impeccably fresh oysters stuffed with crabmeat. Their warm, down-home staff will make your stay memorable, as will the good local beer. Open for lunch and dinner, the restaurant has its own boat slips for arrivals from the sea. $$

■ On Tangier Island

Fisherman's Corner Restaurant (☎ 757-891-2571) and **The Islander Restaurant** (☎ 757-891-2249) are open mid-May through October. Though seafood is prominent on the menu, other options are available. $-$$

Hilda Crockett's Chesapeake House, open from the end of April through October, serves a family-style seafood dinner for a fixed price under $15; ☎ 757-891-2331. It's at the inn of the same name.

AUTHOR TIP *In addition to these restaurants, there are ice cream and sandwich shops, but options for eating are few in winter. If you are staying in winter or otherwise off season, ask about dining options when you book your rooms.*

Index

Sugarloaf Mountain: hiking, 116-117; scenic drive, 132-133

Surfing, Ocean City, 427

Susquehanna and Tidewater Canal, 179

Susquehanna River, fishing, 166

Susquehanna State Park, 160; crafts, 171; walking, 161-162

Swallow Falls State Park, 20-22; camping, 51; hiking, 27-28

Swimming: Lower Eastern Shore, 427; North-Central Maryland, 130; Southern Maryland, 331; Upper Eastern Shore, 366; Virginia's Eastern Shore, 466

Sykesville, 149; dining, 155

T

Tangier Island, 432, 434; accommodations, 479; biking, 426, 465; boat tours to, 468; dining, 481; sightseeing, 474

Tennis, 437

Thurmont: accommodations, 150; dining, 154-155

Tilghman Island, 415

Trains: B&O, 111, 149, 218-219; Hagerstown, 95; railroad museums, 139, 344, 445, 475; Western Canal Country, 73-74

Trout hatchery, 79

Tuckahoe State Park: camping, 385; fishing, 369; paddling, 366; walking, 363

Turkey Point Lighthouse, 380

Twelve-mile churches, 338

Tydings Park, 168-169

U

Underground Railroad tours, 158

Union Bridge, sightseeing, 148

Union Mills: biking, 123; horseback, 131; sightseeing, 148

Uniontown: sightseeing, 148; walking tour, 118

Upper Eastern Shore, 359-388; accommodations, 381-385; adventures, 362-371; antiques, 373-374; camping, 384-385; crafts, 373; culture and eco-travel, 372-374; dining, 385-388; events, 374-375; on foot, 363-365; gardens, 372-373; geography and history, 359-360; getting here and getting around, 360-362; on horseback, 370; information sources, 362; map, 361; parks, 362; shooting sports, 371; sightseeing, 375-380; on water, 366-370; on wheels, 365

V

Vienna, sightseeing, 409

Viewtrail 100, biking, 426

Virginia's Eastern Shore, 457-481; accommodations, 477-480; adventures, 461-469; camping, 479-480; culture and eco-travel, 469-472; dining, 480-481; events, 472-473; geography and history, 458, 460; getting here and getting around, 461; information sources, 461; map, 459; sightseeing, 473-476

W

Wakeboarding, Garrett County, 31

Walking: Annapolis, 264-265; Baltimore, 195-196; Central Eastern Shore, 393-394; Chincoteague, 463-464; Garrett County, 28-29; Lower Eastern Shore, 424-425; North-Central Maryland, 117-120; North of Baltimore, 160-162; safety, 7-8; Upper Eastern Shore, 363-365; Washington DC, 302-304; Western Canal Country, 63-70

Wallops Island NASA facility, 473-474

www.hunterpublishing.com

Hunter's full range of travel guides to all corners of the globe is featured on our exciting Web site. You'll find guidebooks to suit every type of traveler, no matter what their budget, lifestyle, or idea of fun. Full descriptions are given for each book, along with reviewers' comments and a cover image. Books may be purchased on-line using a credit card via our secure transaction system. All online orders receive 20% discount.

Alive! guides are a refreshing change from the "same-old" guidebooks. They are written for the savvy traveler who is looking for quality and value in accommodations and dining, with a selection of activities to fill the days and nights.

Check out our *Adventure Guides*, a series aimed at the independent traveler who enjoys outdoor activities (rafting, hiking, biking, skiing, canoeing, etc.). All books in this signature series cover places to stay and eat, sightseeing, in-town attractions, transportation and more!

Hunter's *Romantic Weekends* series offers myriad things to do for couples of all ages and lifestyles. Quaint places to stay and restaurants where the ambiance will take your breath away are included, along with fun activities that you and your partner will remember forever.